Radwell parish

Mill

Bygrave parish

Nortonbury

St Nicholas church

River Ivel

Baldock

Way (Highway)

Willian parish

Members of the Historical Documents section of NCAG photographed at their 2013 Open Day at the close of the annual archaeological dig.

Hertfordshire Record Publications Volume 29

RECORDS OF THE MANOR OF NORTON IN THE LIBERTY OF ST ALBANS, 1244 - 1539

Translated by Peter Foden

Edited and with an Introduction by the
Norton Community Archaeology Group

Hertfordshire Record Society

Volume for the membership year 2013/14

Hertfordshire Record Society

The publication of this volume has
been assisted by generous grants from
The Letchworth Garden City Heritage Foundation
The Heritage Lottery Fund
North Hertfordshire District Council

© Hertfordshire Record Society and the
Norton Community Archaeology Group 2014

ISBN 978-0-9565111-2-6

Printed and bound in the UK by Stephen Austin Ltd,
Caxton Hill, Hertford, England

Contents

	Page
Norton Community Archaeology Group	v
Acknowledgements	viii
Illustrations	x
Introduction	
Norton before 1244 – the archaeological evidence	xii
Medieval Norton – the archaeological evidence	xvi
Norton's manorial records	xxi
The manorial court	xxviii
Management of the estate	xxxi
Agriculture	xxxvii
Villeins and villeinage	xl
Leyrwite	xlv
Population trends	xlviii
Proximity to Baldock	liv
Family names of medieval Norton	lvi
Place names	lviii
The Manor court and Norton post 1539	lxi
Editorial method	lxiii
Abbreviations	lxiv
Norton Manor Court Records (1244-1539)	
Court books Henry III (1244-1272)	1
Edward I (1273-1307)	19
Edward II (1307-1326)	51
Edward III (1327-1377)	89
Richard II (1377-1399)	187
Henry IV (1400-1412)	210
Henry V (1413-1416)	230
Henry VI (1423-1460)	235
Court rolls Edward IV (1464)	270
Richard III (1484)	272
Henry VIII (1511, 1531-1539)	273

Appendix 1 – View of accounts of rent collector, 1488-1489	301
Appendix 2 – Charter of Æthelred, 1007	304
Glossary	307
The Hertfordshire Record Society	318
Bibliography	321
Index of Persons	324
Index of Places	
Locations within the manor	350
Places outside the manor	353
Index of Subjects	355

Norton Community Archaeology Group

The village of Norton has an incredibly well preserved heritage. This has given the Norton Community Archaeology Group (NCAG) a rare opportunity to research over 6,000 years of continuous settlement in the area.

During a short early morning walk back along Norton Road from our local garden centre I reflected on just how I could outline what we do, why we research this historic village and the fascination it holds. In the 800 yards to my home I first passed Church Field, the site of a partially abandoned medieval village. Church Field is a special place for the group. Over many years we learnt together a range of skills that have held us in good stead ever since. Church Field was also particularly challenging with some unexpected outcomes. The medieval hollow way was in fact a modern drainage ditch, the metalled village road stopped abruptly and the medieval house platforms were elusive. Significant finds were made including a thirteenth century cob-built structure; it taught us to make no assumptions and that considerable tenacity is needed to make real discoveries.

However, our finds here include Victorian marbles, Tudor and medieval discoveries of every day implements such as a beautiful bone-handled knife, medieval buckles, pottery, broken quern stones and a Bronze Age linen rubber. The geophysical surveys by Pauline Gimson and her team have given us an understanding of the complex boundaries and other features of this area.

As our group grew we turned our interest to the documentary records of the village; perhaps the most tangible remaining evidence of our social heritage.

This publication is a translation and interpretation of our manorial court records from 1244 to 1539. The detailed, meticulous and sustained work over the last few years to produce this book has added to our understanding of the ancient customs of the manor and the day-to-day regulations affecting the life of tenants. We have learnt much of life in the manor such as the need for permission to marry, to travel, to receive an education and other everyday tasks. These records note the punishments for using the quern stones we excavated and grinding grain 'other than at the lord's mill'. We have learnt of the great fluctuations in population arising out of plague, economic changes and the relationship with other villages. The changes in the relationship between the lord of the manor and the tenants can be seen in the rights of ownership, inheritance, services owed to the lord and the various amercements levied on tenants for misdemeanours. We now know of the agricultural systems and the crops and livestock on which the village subsisted.

Opposite Church Field is Alan and Evelyn Goodwin's home. Alan is our meticulous treasurer and Evelyn is part of the team who organise and run our popular open days. These give so many people the chance to learn of our discoveries.

Past Church Field are Church Lane and the parish church dating from about 1100. Norton's first record of a priest appears in the Domesday Book of 1086. The manorial records have perhaps given us a different perception of vicars. They note their deeds and misdeeds, the part the church played in everyday medieval life and the decisions of the manor.

Church Lane leads down to the site of the Neolithic henge, further Bronze Age features, a Roman farmstead and medieval ridge and furrow ploughing which teams of up to 120 of us have surveyed and excavated over the last few summers. We discovered that the henge is of a particularly early form of this type of ritual meeting place. It is of national importance.

Next on Norton Road is the field called Fullers Well with its various earthworks (something for the future), the pub and the bowls club where we hold our various meetings. From the manorial records we have learnt that a pub was established in 1338 after a drunken brawl in the neighbouring town. In 1593, three men each forfeited 6s 8d for playing bowls on Sunday. The current pub was also the site of the first school.

Around the corner is a 'chocolate box' thatched cottage, home of one of the many neighbours who have agreed to have test-pits dug in their gardens. These test-pits have helped us to understand the extent and phasing of settlement of the manor. Just beyond this cottage is my home; a red brick, red-tiled, beech-hedged house typical of the early Letchworth Garden City style. One of our early digs here discovered a tile and pottery, dated to about 1000 AD which were far older and of a far higher status than we could have anticipated. Their origin remains a mystery.

How fortunate we are to have such well-preserved archaeology and contemporary records. With the support of the landlord, The Letchworth Garden City Heritage Foundation (LGCHF), and the coaching, patience and tenacity of Keith Fitzpatrick-Matthews, North Hertfordshire District Council's (NHDC) Archaeology Officer, we have developed our skills in planning, geophysics, excavation, recording and processing our finds on medieval, Romano-British and prehistoric sites.

Sue Flood, our County Archivist, and her team have conserved and made available Norton's records spanning over 700 years. Again, how fortunate we are to have the help of Peter Foden to interpret the Medieval Latin palaeography. And above all: what a huge effort has been made by so many people within the group in so many different ways and roles as is now evident with this publication; something that we in turn are adding to the heritage of this village. This must certainly be said of the sustained efforts of David, Ursula and their team of 20 who have created this book.

Over the last six years the group has grown to over 100 members. We have made many personal and collective discoveries about the past communities of our village from the 5,000-year-old ritual meeting place, through medieval manorial life to the more recent influence of 'The World's First Garden City'. Each of our archaeological and documentary discoveries has a special memory for the individual who has made the find. Each of our discoveries add to a certain sense of a rich heritage and place. This publication helps to record and so share these discoveries with a wider audience and for future research.

I do hope that this publication is of general interest, supports your understanding of medieval life and perhaps even helps you develop your research and learning in this area. I also hope that sharing my early morning thoughts in preparing this Foreword has helped to give a sense of what we have gained in discovering more about us then.

Chris Hobbs
Chairman: Norton Community Archaeology Group
2014

Scan this image for link to NCAG website: www.nortoncommarch.com

Acknowledgements

This book is the work of the Historical Documents section of NCAG whose aim is to provide an enduring record of the history of Norton drawing upon surviving written documents. The main project, for which we have received generous grant funding, is to provide a complete transcription and translation of Norton's manorial court records. The original documents are held at Hertfordshire Archives and Local Studies (HALS) and they run from 1244 to 1916, about 85 per cent complete.

Firstly, we must mention those who provided the inspiration for our members. Deborah Giles, author of the most thoroughly researched history of Norton to date, was a founder member of NCAG.[1] Her untimely death in 2008 robbed us of an irreplaceable wealth of knowledge. Indirectly, this led to the formation of the Historical Documents section.

Keith Fitzpatrick-Matthews, NHDC's Archaeology Officer, along with our Chairman, Chris Hobbs, developed the concept of how our documents section would work: photographing and transcribing documents, supported by grant-funded translations by a professional. It was Keith who, when we were approached by Hertfordshire Record Society (HRS) to publish a translation of the court books (1244-1460), provided encouragement and advice. At his suggestion we have also added the few court rolls which survive for the period after 1460, giving a complete collection of the existing records under Norton's ownership by St Albans Abbey prior to the Dissolution. Keith later provided archaeological maps and his translation of the 1007 Charter.

When our members visited HALS in August 2009, Sue Flood produced for us all Norton's surviving court records; a unique collection probably assembled in one room for the first time. We compiled a list of what needed to be translated, photographed samples, counted the number of folios in each batch and recorded measurements of different document sizes. We then set about the task of selecting a translator and getting a quotation for the work which would form the basis of a grant proposal. A month later we had selected Peter Foden to do the work and six months after that three organisations had agreed to provide funds for the project: the LGCHF, the Heritage Lottery Fund and NHDC. Chris keeps these organisations constantly informed of our progress and they have generously and efficiently supported us with all promised funding.

---

[1] D Giles, *Norton before the Garden City* (Baldock, 2003).

Peter Foden MA(Cantab) MArAd at work on one of Norton's documents.

Initially, Peter was working on the Tudor period, but we changed his work plan when HRS approached us to write this book. Our members had been relying on a 650 page handwritten translation of the court books (1244-1460), compiled between the 1950s and 1970s by an unknown hand, forming part of the papers of Welwyn local historian W Branch Johnson.[2] The translation however was not sufficiently accurate for publication purposes so Peter reviewed and modified it sufficiently to call it his own. Our grant providers have also given funding for our training and interpretation of the records, and we are indebted to Peter for many of the insights contained in the Introduction to this book.

Finally, we must record our thanks to Sue Flood, who provided her considerable expertise in editing all our work. In addition she translated the 1488-9 account and a series of wills which gave us invaluable additional information about Norton tenants in the later medieval period. Our thanks also go to Mark Bailey who gave advice on interpretation, translation and glossary issues and to Heather Falvey for her very helpful comments on the final draft. By kind permission we were allowed access to the records at HALS and to take photographs, some of which are reproduced in this book.

The content of this book, except the translation itself, has been researched by NCAG members, all of them amateur enthusiasts, and written up with invaluable guidance from Peter, Sue and Mark.

NCAG Historical Documents section members who have contributed to the publication of this book: Allan Coates, David Croft, Philip Dean, Pauline Gimson, Alan Goodwin, Jonathan and Julie Goodwyn, Nigel Harper-Scott, Chris Hobbs, Henry Marshall, Ann Pegrum, Graham Pointon, Sid Rowe, Ursula Scott, Jim Skipper, Michael Spencer, Christl Squires, Philip Thomas, Tim Vickers, Christine Vincent, Howard Webber and Karen Woolford.

---

[2] HALS: DE/Jn/Z33.

Illustrations

Frontispiece	Members of the Historical Documents section of NCAG photographed at their 2013 Open Day at the close of the annual archaeological dig.
Endpapers front	Sketch showing some key features of medieval Norton and its surrounding parishes. The trackways and buildings are drawn from Dury and Andrews, *A Topographical Map of Hartford-Shire, 1766*, (HRS 2004).
Endpapers back	Norton c.1700: the earliest detailed map of the parish (HALS: 19336) (compass points added).
Page ix	Peter Foden, MA(Cantab) MArAD at work on one of Norton's documents.
Page xii	Map of Norton's early archaeology. The inserted archaeological diagrams and key have been provided by Keith Fitzpatrick-Matthews. Reproduced from the 1959 (Provisional Edition) Ordnance Survey map, scale six inches: one mile (ref TL23SW).
Page xviii	Map of archaeological evidence of medieval habitation in Norton. The inserted archaeological diagrams and key have been provided by Keith Fitzpatrick-Matthews. © Crown Copyright 2013 Ordnance Survey 100054945.
Page xxiv	Hexton court book showing fragment of medieval oak board used to rebind the pages in the eighteenth century (HALS: DE/B2355/M1/1/1); and page for court held 23 April 1426 with Norton tag (HALS: 65529, f1v).
Opposite Page 1	The first folio of the Norton court books, beginning in 1244 (HALS: 65498, f1).
Page 17	The final folio of the courts held in the reign of Henry III (HALS: 65498, f6v).
Page 140	The first two courts in 1349, the year of the Black Death when 27 tenants died (HALS: 65514, f5).

Page 141	The end of the second court in 1349, the year of the Black Death (HALS: 65514, f5v).
Page 186	The first of a series of folios in a new hand bound in the Hexton court book (HALS: DE/B2355/M/1/1/1).
Page 230	The first of only a few folios of records in the time of Henry V (HALS: 65528, f1).
Page 277	Examples from a roll of Norton records which needed conservation before translation work could begin. The courts run from 1531 until 1541 (HALS: 65535).

Introduction

Norton before 1244 – the archaeological evidence

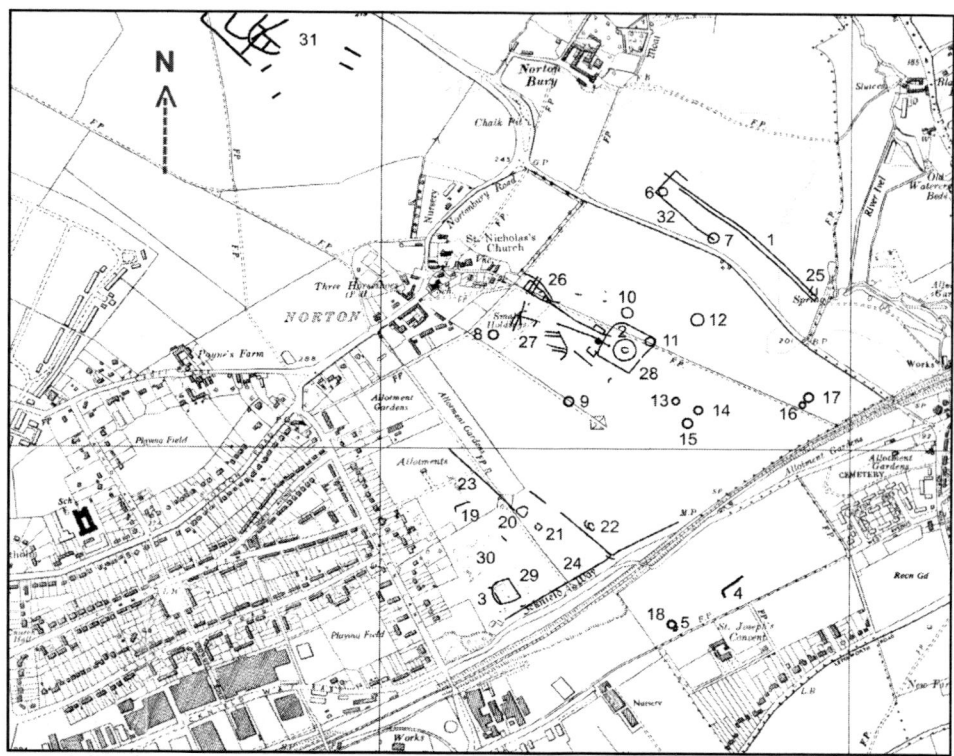

Map of Norton's early archaeology.

Neolithic: 1 Nortonbury cursus; 2 Stapleton's Field henge; 3 Blackhorse Road D-shaped enclosure and flint mines; 4 Works Road enclosure; 5 Works Road hengiform; **Bronze Age:** 6-18 ring ditches representing ploughed-out round barrows; **Iron Age:** 19 Kristiansand Way enclosure; 20-22 Blackhorse Road enclosures; 23 field boundary ditch and pit cluster; 24 Icknield Way and field boundary ditches; 25 Norton Road enclosure; **Roman:** 26 Stapleton's Field farmstead; 27 field boundary ditches; 28 Stapleton's Field industrial enclosure; **Early medieval:** 29 Blackhorse Road Pagan Saxon cemetery; 30 Kristiansand Way settlement (*Rodenhanger*); **Undated:** 31 settlement enclosures (Bronze Age or Iron Age?); 32 Norton Road linear enclosure (Neolithic?).

INTRODUCTION

The landscape of the historic parish of Norton, which to the south is bordered by the Icknield Way and to the east by the River Ivel, is archaeologically diverse, stretching from the Palaeolithic through to 'The World's First Garden City'.[3] Yet for most of its considerable history, Norton (Saxon 'North Tun': an enclosed farm north of something or somewhere else, although it is not known where)[4] sat in semi-isolation, bordered only by similarly small settlements such as Radwell and Rodenhanger, the latter probably to be identified with a settlement excavated in 1988 during the construction of Kristiansand Way, south of the village centre. Letchworth was still merely a minor grouping of dwellings at the time of the Norman conquest.

A significant year in the history of Norton is 1244 because it was from this time that written records have survived. Our knowledge of earlier occupation has to be derived from archaeological exploration, from sporadic records such as a mention of Norton in relation to a charter of 1007,[5] and a Domesday entry in 1086 stating Norton to be among land owned by the Abbot of St Albans, and from assumptions derived from known regional and national historic events.

There is only limited evidence of what was going on in the area in earlier prehistory before about 4000 BC. To the north of Norton Road a probable processional way ('cursus') comprising two parallel V-shaped ditches dates from before 3100 BC and is now being subjected to renewed archaeological investigation, initially via geophysical survey.

Neolithic remains have been uncovered at Wilbury and, closer to present-day Norton village, at Blackhorse Road. The most recent archaeological excavations have unearthed on the slope of Stapleton's Field overlooking Baldock, the ploughed-out remains of a 'formative' chalk henge, which began sometime before 3000 BC in the form of a large circular outer ditch around 55 metres in diameter enclosing a chalk bank with an east-facing entrance and a circular inner ditch. Excavations within the henge have revealed Neolithic pot sherds, worked flint blades and, in 2012, the remains of a cremation, deposited towards the end of the site's use, supporting the latest view of the site as a henge rather than a dedicated burial mound/complex. Pieces of Impressed Ware and Grooved Ware pottery have been unearthed, and, in 2013, a few small pieces of Beaker Ware. This suggests that the henge fell out of use around 2200 BC –

---

[3] Letchworth Garden City was founded by Ebenezer Howard in 1903.
[4] 'Norðtune' translated as 'north farm' in J E B Gover, *The Place-Names of Hertfordshire* (Cambridge, 1938, reprinted 1970), p114.
[5] A full translation of this charter can be found in Appendix 2.

INTRODUCTION

some time after a horseshoe-shaped inner ditch was cut into the chalk bank, possibly marking a transition from formative (circular) to the 'classic' (oval) henge pattern.

During excavations in 2013, our understanding of the henge site expanded considerably. A section of the outer ditch was excavated and revealed to be under a metre deep, having a flat base and near-vertical sides and containing Early and Middle Neolithic material including pottery and lithics. The entrance through the outer ditch and bank contained a line of three pits which had subsequently been back-filled, but which contained no man-made material and whose purpose is unclear. Over the entrance area, and through into the centre of the henge, had been laid a chalk platform, while at the centre of the henge a substantial cremation pit was uncovered, containing undifferentiated remains of a neonate, a child and an adult.

The remains of a low-lying inner chalk bank were also revealed, whose material appears to have been derived from the inner edge of the outer bank. Of the outer bank, only a very thin layer of chalk remained, and beneath it were discovered the remains of three pre-henge houses. One in particular shows a clear horseshoe-shaped foundation trench which is believed to have accommodated the vertical planks constituting the sides of the structure. Like the orientation of the henge's banks and ditches, this building's entrance is also east-facing. Finds of small pieces of daub, with wattle groove impressions, also supports the interpretation of these structures as having supported habitation.

From around 3100 BC, as the Neolithic transitioned to the Bronze Age, there was a significant change in the pattern of life – and death, as evidenced in the landscape with long barrows giving way to round burial mounds, constructed by heaping excavated spoil (probably chalk) from round ditches onto a central mound. Although subsequently flattened by ploughing, these are clearly visible in aerial photographs in the form of circular soil/crop patterns.[6] There are several in Stapleton's Field, including one within the eastern-most corner of the later Romano-British enclosure ditch surrounding the now-revealed henge. Two more lie towards opposite ends of a ditch paralleling, and seeming to form a partial enclosure of the parallel ditches of the Neolithic cursus in the adjacent field to the north of Baldock Road. A biconical cinerary (cremation) urn was excavated from one of the barrows beside Norton Road in 1961. Records of

---

[6] For instance, held by the Cambridge University Collection of Aerial Photography, The National Monuments Record (Swindon) or Hertfordshire County Council Historic Environment Record (HHER).

INTRODUCTION

these round barrows are also preserved in the 1007 charter which references the 'smooth mound' and the 'willow height', although we are as yet unable to assign these to particular patterns on the ground.

The first millennium BC saw a reoccupation of the area around the current Blackhorse Road, where an extensive Iron Age settlement has been excavated comprising four enclosures, not all of which are believed to have been occupied simultaneously. These were sites of farmsteads dating from the fifth or sixth centuries BC and within which the remains of Middle Iron Age round-houses and storage pits have been excavated. Several Middle to Late Iron Age pits were found, containing human remains. Also discovered were pottery, animal bones and other remnants of domestic occupation, including part of the collar and rim of a second or third century BC iron 'La Tène' cauldron.

In the Late Iron Age, from about 50 BC, Norton was overshadowed by, and had become effectively an outpost of, the developing Roman town (or *oppidum*) of Baldock. Roman pottery, glass and coins have been found at St Nicholas' school and in nearby Church Lane.

Excavations in 2012 have shown the Norton henge site to be surrounded by a Romano-British enclosure ditch containing substantial Roman tile fragments, coinage and ironstone deposits, suggesting an industrial complex (to serve nearby Roman Baldock) superimposed on the Neolithic site, and hinting at the presence of workshops, warehouses etc still to be located. These finds are entirely consistent with the picture of widespread Roman occupation in the area, revealed by earlier finds at Wilbury Hill, Blackhorse Road, Church Lane and other parts of Norton/Letchworth.

Following collapse of the empire and withdrawal of Roman troops from Britain in 410, the way was left open for a further series of occupation by Anglo-Saxons, supplanting the remaining British tribes. Norton, whose name is Saxon, fell within the kingdom of Mercia and may have been occupied by tribes such as the Gifle (whose Celtic name lingers in the Anglo-Saxon name of the River Ivel) and the Hicce, from whom nearby Hitchin derives its name. Saxon remains have been found in the area, with a small seventh century cemetery at Blackhorse Road and a settlement at Kristiansand Way, occupied from the tenth to twelfth centuries.

In 794 Mercia's King Offa, of Welsh border dyke fame, is alleged to have passed ownership of Norton to the Abbey of St Albans, founded only two years earlier. This proved relatively short-lived as Mercia was defeated by Viking invaders in 865 and Norton fell under the eastern area of England known as the

INTRODUCTION

Danelaw until reconquest by Edward the Elder at the start of the tenth century. But under the 1007 charter Norton was granted to St Albans, after having been bought earlier for the Abbey by the Archbishop of Canterbury.

Norton next appears in the Domesday survey commissioned in 1086 by William the Conqueror, in which the manor is reported to be held by the Abbot of St Albans.[7] Among the inventory, a reference to a priest in Norton implies the existence then of a church, and certainly the current church of St Nicholas was dedicated by Hervey, Bishop of Ely shortly after 1109.[8] Also included are two mills each valued at 16s and, intriguingly, 'a Frenchman' and 'a slave'.

Medieval Norton – the archaeological evidence
There had already been a great deal of archaeological work carried out on medieval sites around Norton prior to the first dig by NCAG in 2007. Six burials excavated at Blackhorse Road formed a small pagan Saxon cemetery of early seventh-century date.[9] One of these burials still had an early seventh century spearhead embedded in its upper chest, having evidently been attacked from behind. Further medieval evidence was uncovered during excavations in 1988 at Green Lane, where a series of cellared buildings was excavated, indicating a settlement.[10] This may be the 'lost' village of Rodenhanger adjoining Norton and mentioned in the Domesday Book of 1086.

Excavations and watching briefs by The Heritage Network on extensions to St Nicholas' JMI School in the 1990s recorded significant medieval activity, consisting of more cellared buildings and other domestic remains. From the fourteenth to the seventeenth centuries, there was little activity on the site.

On the 1 July in the dry summer of 1976 Gil Burleigh photographed Church Field from the air in the low evening sunlight with the setting sun showing up a

---

[7] J Morris (editor and translator), *Domesday Book 12: Hertfordshire* (Chichester, 1976).

[8] Hervey was enthroned at Ely in 1109 (E B Fryde, D E Greenway, S Porter, and I Roy, (eds), *Handbook of British Chronology* (Cambridge, 1996) p290). See also W Page (ed), *Victoria County History, Hertfordshire* (4 vols, 1902-1914) vol ii, p364 and H T Riley (ed), *Gesta Abbatum Monasterii S Albani* (3 vols, Rolls Series, 1867-9) vol i, p148.

[9] J Moss-Eccardt and others, 'Archaeological Excavations in the Letchworth area', *Proceedings of the Cambridge Antiquaries Society*, LXXVII (1988), p74.

[10] K J Matthews and G R Burleigh, 'A Saxon and early medieval settlement at Green Lane, Letchworth', *Hertfordshire's Past*, 26 (Spring 1989).

INTRODUCTION

number of interesting earthworks.[11] A survey of the earthworks in Church Field, situated directly to the north-east of the churchyard, was carried out in December 1985 by the North Hertfordshire Museum Service Field Archaeology Section directed by Gil. Two or three abandoned village streets and several probable building platforms were identified. A trackway was identified as leading in the direction of the former moated manor at Nortonbury. It is highly likely that some of the medieval manorial courts referred to in this book were held at the original Nortonbury manor.

Nortonbury Farm stands immediately west of the moated site and is likely to be its successor as a manorial centre. The farmhouse, which is not Listed, is a multiperiod house dating in part back to the early sixteenth century, but extensively renovated between about 1670 and 1840.[12] A view of the house today shows mainly the late Victorian yellowish-grey brick walls, very similar in style to the village school. The rectangular moat, c.45mx30m, lies to the east of Nortonbury which at its centre has a raised area forming a rectangular platform. Two test pits dug in the area of this platform in 2003 uncovered a tiled floor in mortar that sealed fifteenth century pottery, suggesting that the original building was abandoned around the time the current farm house was built.[13] The whole manorial complex may once have been more extensive, possibly enclosing the current house. In winter 2009 and spring 2010 NCAG undertook a field survey to record earthworks to the north of the manor house.

The parish church of St Nicholas, the oldest standing building, dates from the early twelfth century and there are several surviving timber-framed houses and farms that can be dated to the late medieval period. Of the two mills mentioned in Domesday Book, one was almost certainly on the site of the present Norton Mill on the River Ivel, at the Baldock end of Nortonbury Lane.

Much of the archaeological evidence for the medieval habitation of Norton where the characters in this book were born, worked and died, can still be seen today by way of well-preserved earthworks of ridge and furrow ploughing of their field system, building platforms and enclosures where they lived and the trackways that survive in Church Field.

---

[11] Photographs and surveys referred to in this section may be accessed through either the North Hertfordshire Archaeological Society or the NHDC's Museum Service.

[12] Hertfordshire County Council Historic Environment Record (HHER) no 1357, Building Norton Bury Farm.

[13] HHER no 1931, Moated site, Norton Bury.

INTRODUCTION

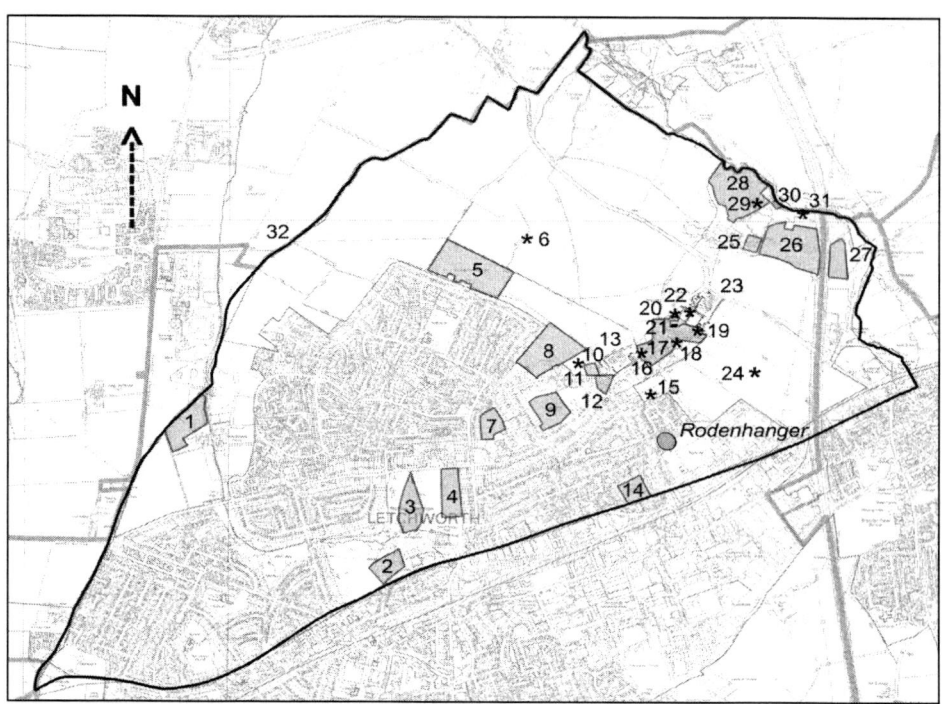

Map of archaeological evidence of medieval habitation in Norton
1 Ridge-and-furrow north-west of Standalone Farm (HHER 2859); **2, 3** and **4** Ridge-and-furrow on Norton Common (HHER 4531); **5** Ridge-and-furrow on The Grange Playing Field; **6** Silver penny of Edward III (HHER 1253); **7** Ridge-and-furrow between Eastern Way and Cashio Lane; **8** Ridge-and-furrow north of Croft Lane; **9** Ridge-and-furrow between Croft Lane and Norton Road; **10** Medieval pottery (HHER 16264); **11** Earthworks of probable farmstead (HHER 4226); **12** Village green (HHER 15829); **13** Ridge-and-furrow north of Norton Road; **14** Ridge-and-furrow between Glebe Road and Icknield Way; **15** Field ditches and plough furrows, Cade Close (HHER 18268); **16** Pottery, 90 Norton Road (HHER 15689); **17** Village core (HHER 2699); **18** Occupation at St Nicholas' School (HHER 7390); **19** Pottery, 15 Church Lane (HHER 15688); **20** Excavated features, Church Field 2007; **21** Church of St Nicholas (HHER 4326); **22** Excavated house, Church Field 2008-9; **23** Earthworks, Church Field (HHER 4203); **24** Pottery, Stapleton's Field; **25** Nortonbury moat (HHER 1931); **26** Ridge-and-furrow east of Nortonbury; **27** Ridge-and-furrow east of A1 motorway; **28** Earthworks including hollow way and probable windmill mound west of Norton Mill; **29** Gullies (HHER 12146); **30** Norton Mill (HHER 5800); **31** 11th century iron spoon auger (HHER 4890); **32** Hedgebank on county boundary, *Stodfaldes dic* in 1007 (HHER 13411).
Location of find is indicated by *.

INTRODUCTION

Lying to the north-east of St Nicholas' church, Church Field, with its trackways and potential building platforms, was an obvious archaeological target for some of the questions NCAG has set out to answer such as: 'What were the dates of habitation?' and 'Why was the site abandoned?'

Following the initial training excavation in Church Field in 2007 the Group undertook a more ambitious excavation in the centre of Church Field in 2008 and 2009 under Keith Fitzpatrick-Matthews' onsite direction. The target which we hoped would help answer our questions was a possible building platform on a cross roads and the track way crossing the field.

2008 saw limited progress due to extremely difficult digging conditions, only reaching late medieval deposits by the end of the excavation. However, while there was little evidence of a structure, we did find plenty of medieval pottery, tiles, building material, repairs to the road surface, coins, a quern stone, an iron knife with a lovely decorated bone handle and a copper alloy buckle. These are all signs of occupation and everyday items used by the medieval inhabitants of Norton.

In 2009, the Group completed the excavation across the possible building platform, identifying the corner of a pounded clay floor and the remains of demolished cob walls, potentially pushed over and left to weather when the building was demolished. This style of building was also found in the 1970s excavations by Guy Beresford at nearby Caldecote, where it was used for peasants' houses between about 900 and 1350.[14]

Although needing confirmation by a specialist, the finds associated with the demolition of the building all looked to be of high medieval rather than late medieval date. If this is the case, it makes it look as if desertion in this part of the village occurred by the first half of the fourteenth century. This would be contemporary with the evidence for desertion found at the nearby St Nicholas school in 1997. It was not clear if it could be directly related to the economic and demographic crises of the early fourteenth century or of a rearrangement of space within the village.[15]

Although the surface of the trackway was exposed, little headway was made in understanding the context of the various layers exposed by a modern ditch which had been dug through the medieval trackway. A small excavation in

---

[14] G Beresford, *Caldecote: The Development and Desertion of a Hertfordshire Village* (2009).
[15] These are questions explored further under the section on 'Population trends'.

INTRODUCTION

2010 showed that what was thought to be a crossroads, where Shefford Lane crossed the village high street, was in fact a T junction. The medieval high street did not continue to Nortonbury and some other track must have led there.

Alongside the major excavations in 2008/9 and subsequent smaller digs in 2010/11 in Church Field NCAG has opened approximately 30 test pits since 2008 across Norton. These test pits have given us valuable dating evidence and helped us to fill in some of the gaps in our knowledge of the timings and location of medieval habitation in Norton. The test pits have also given us some truly fantastic finds including a beautiful and high status eleventh century tile from a back garden on Norton Road, an area not known to have a high status building nearby.

In 2011, building on the photographic survey and excavation evidence, NCAG members led by Pauline Gimson also undertook a 14-day geophysical survey of the whole of Church Field, covering 2.84 hectares, in order to find any further evidence of medieval Norton. The survey was successful in that it highlighted a number of further interesting anomalies including a number of possible field boundaries and other areas that would benefit from further investigation.

Much of the medieval village of Norton as understood by the generations of inhabitants brought to life in this book is still recognisable today. The area around Nortonbury manor house, with its water mill, fish ponds and meadows remains largely undeveloped and retains much of its medieval landscape and feel. Even around the present core of Norton, with the Church at its centre and the surrounding fields still showing traces of the ridge and furrow where they worked, I'm sure our medieval predecessors recorded in this book would have no problem walking through Church Field and pointing out where they lived and recognising some of our finds.

INTRODUCTION

Norton's Manorial Records
The surviving manorial records for the manor of Norton translated for this volume form two distinct series: court books and court rolls.[16]

The Court Books, or more correctly, the now unbound pages which once formed part of several original volumes, are noted by Levett as being the most complete set of unbound quires remaining for any of the St Albans manors, and as such they provide evidence for some of the earliest manorial courts to survive in England.[17] They fall into four distinct parts:

A 27 numbered folios dating from 1244 to 1327 (28th year of Henry III to the end of the reign of Edward II) representing four quires (the last five pages are blank and not numbered). Each quire, representing eight numbered folios, is made up of four pieces of parchment folded down the middle, and placed inside each other ready for binding. Sometimes two pieces of parchment are sewn together to make a large piece of the required size so that it can be folded in the same way. Each numbered page measures 34 x 51 cm. On the last page of each quire the scribe has written a few words from the beginning of the next page, being the first in the next quire. This would have aided the binder and ensured that the correct sequence was maintained in the finished volume. At the bottom of the last page on which writing occurs is written 'the total number of folios in this book written for the Norton court is twenty and seven'.[18] The sewing holes used when binding can be seen clearly as well as original ruling lines used by the scribe. (HALS: 65498-65509)

B 24 numbered folios dating from 1327-1377 (reign of Edward III) representing three quires – the numbering beginning at one. They are of the same dimensions and make up as **A** and appear to have been written by the same hand. Again a scribe has counted the folios and made a similar note to that at the end of **A**. Page 24v is blank and very dirty suggesting that this page was once on the outside of the bundle (or the last page in a volume from which the binding had

---

[16] In addition the British Library holds a short account dated 1488/9 (BL: Add Roll 35509) a translation of which can be found in Appendix 1 and a custumal of *c.*1332 (BL: Cott Ms Tib E vi ff35-37).
[17] A E Levett, *Studies in Manorial History* (Oxford, 1938), p85. However she did not have sight of the Hexton or Tyttenhanger volumes discussed in more detail below. Apart from the odd year where nothing is copied the Hexton pages have short gaps only for the years 1241-47, 1253-55, 1270-73, 1325-26 and 1344-48. See also Z Razi and R Smith, *Medieval Society and the Manor Court*, (Oxford, 1996), p39.
[18] '*Summa foli in hoc libro cur' de Norton script' viginti et septem*'.

INTRODUCTION

disappeared). In addition this section has a parchment tag fixed to the edge of the first page on which is written the name 'Norton'. (HALS: 65510-65518)

C 21 numbered folios dating from 1385-1415 (8th year of Richard II to 3rd year of Henry V) representing the remains of three quires. At the bottom of the last page the title for a court to be held in the fourth year of Henry V is written suggesting that other pages followed which are now lost. The folio numbering begins at number four. Folios numbered one to three, not seen by Levett, and representing the earlier years of Richard II's reign, have recently been discovered bound in with the Hexton court book (HALS: DE/B2355/M/1/1/1). These pages are smaller than **A** and **B**, measuring 32 x 45 cm, and are written in a completely different hand. (HALS: 65519-65528)

D Eight numbered folios dating from 1422-1460, and probably representing the whole of the reign of Henry VI, make up just one quire. Again the numbering begins at one and on the last page the scribe has counted the folios as above. These pages are slightly larger in size (34 x 53 cm) and are written in yet another hand. The first page bears a Norton tag similar to that in **B**. (HALS: 65529-65534)

Levett notes a similar sequence of foliation, sizes of page and handwriting in the surviving records for the manors of Croxley, Codicote, Abbots Langley, Cashio, Park and Barnet, particularly the new sequences begun in the reigns of Richard II and Henry VI.[19] Records now at HALS for the manors of Bramfield, Hexton and Tyttenhanger, not seen by Levett, also exhibit the same sequence of parchment size and handwriting.[20] The Hexton volume is still bound and is the only set of folios to include part of a fourteenth century oak board clearly demonstrating how the original St Albans Abbey volumes were made up.[21] This volume now contains all the surviving Hexton quires dating from 1237 to 1460 of various sizes of parchment bound together in sequence, together with eight unnumbered loose folios (one quire) dated 1531-1537. Folio one for the reign of Henry VI has a tag labelled Hexton. The three Norton folios for the first years of Richard II are bound after the Hexton folio for 1422 (the end of the reign of Henry V) and are of the same size as those listed at **C** above. A detailed comparison of the visible sewing holes in the Hexton volume with those from

---

[19] Levett, *Studies in Manorial History*, pp83-87.
[20] Bramfield, 1236-1460 (HALS: 40702-40705); Hexton, 1237-1460 and 1531-1537 (HALS: DE/B2355/M/1/1/1); Tyttenhanger, 1238-1460 and 1531-1536 (HALS: DE/B2067B/M1 and M3).
[21] See photograph on front cover and overleaf.

INTRODUCTION

Norton suggest that all of the folios of a similar size for the two manors were once bound together. Labelling tags would have been unnecessary if one volume held only the records from one manor. The Bramfield folios covering the reign of Edward III also mirror the sewing holes of Norton and Hexton and folio one has a tag attached, so originally these folios for the three manors may have been bound all together.

Date	Court Rolls HALS ref:	Court Books HALS ref:	Provenance
1244-1377		65498-65518	Reginald Hine
1377-1384		DE/B2355/ M/1/1/1	Hexton court book – British Records Association
1385-1416		65519-65528	Reginald Hine
1423-1460		65529-65534	Reginald Hine
1348	10549		Capel archives, Cashiobury House
1380	47283		Hawkins solicitors
1425/6	10555		Capel archives, Cashiobury House
1426/7	10556		Capel archives, Cashiobury House
1430	47284		Hawkins solicitors
1432/3	10558		Capel archives, Cashiobury House
1433/4	10559		Capel archives, Cashiobury House
1438	47285		Hawkins solicitors
1446	47286		Hawkins solicitors
1457/8	10560		Capel archives, Cashiobury House
1464	**40706**		British Records Association
1484	**40709**		British Records Association
1511	**47296**		Hawkins solicitors
1531-1539	**65535**		Reginald Hine

Table of the surviving manorial court records for Norton, 1244-1539, available at Hertfordshire Archives and Local Studies (HALS). (Those which are included in this book are shown in bold).

INTRODUCTION

Hexton court book showing fragment of medieval oak board used to rebind the pages in the eighteenth century (HALS: DE/B2355/M/1/1/1).

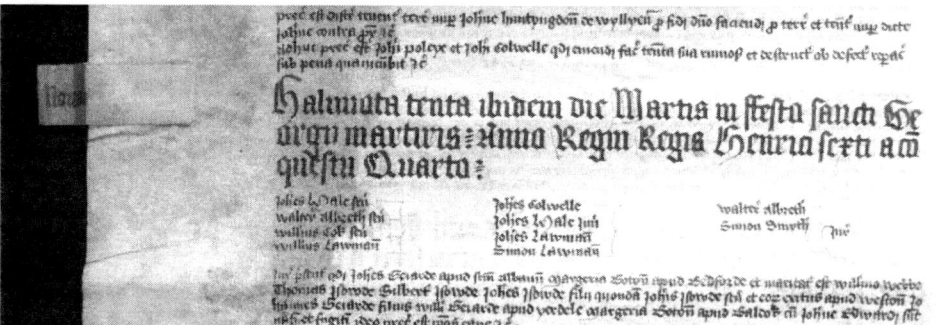

Page for court held 23 April 1426 with Norton tag (HALS: 65529, f1v).

The Hexton volume as now survives was probably made up in the seventeenth or eighteenth century using the remains of the original board. It has been re-drilled for the new leather thongs which are held in place by brass domed headed nails more likely to be of seventeenth or eighteenth century date.[22] In addition a handwritten date of 1746 is visible on the underside of paper used to cover the inside of the board, perhaps applied to minimise the stain of acid transfer from the board to the parchment. Clearly visible are the original

---

[22] The group is grateful for this technical information provided by Jeff Cargill, archive conservator at HALS.

xxiv

INTRODUCTION

binding holes in the oak in which survive the remains of leather thongs carefully and smoothly cut away. It is tempting to conjecture that these were cut after the Dissolution when the original volumes were broken up.

The Tyttenhanger folios for the reigns of Edward III, Richard II and Henry VI also follow the Norton and Hexton sequence in size and handwriting, those for Edward and Henry having a tag. However the sewing holes for these pages do not match Norton or Hexton suggesting that these folios were once in a different volume. Three folios for the Manor of Northaw for the first to fifth years of Richard II follow those for Tyttenhanger dated 3 Henry VI.

It is very difficult to estimate how many original volumes are now represented by the surviving loose folios. They were written at the Abbey, and probably bound there too. It would appear from the above analysis that new volumes were often begun at the beginning of new reigns – those for Richard II being written on smaller pieces of parchment, Henry VI slightly larger – and that the records for several different manors were bound together. All of the manors mentioned above were the property of the Abbey cellarer and Levett concludes that the work of extracting entries from the court rolls and collating them in centralised court books was begun after 1355 and before 1374, during the administration of cellarer John Mote.[23] The first volumes to be created would therefore have been bound during this period. The records of many of the St Albans courts discussed above, and listed by Levett, end in 1460, the later ones produced while William of Wallingford was cellarer in the mid fifteenth century.[24] The lack of pages for the later fifteenth century for so many manors seems to suggest that the practice of copying was halted rather than a dismal survival rate. However it would appear that copying was revived early in the sixteenth century - Barnet, Croxley, Hexton, Norton, Park and Tyttenhanger all have a few surviving pages dating from the 1530s.

Levett concludes that the books are full and accurate copies of the rolls but do not contain everything that would have been originally recorded. Occasionally the phrase 'nothing of note' is added to the margin so some selection was made.[25] However, undoubtedly, they do contain everything that was of any permanent value to the Abbey administration. A copy was made of all entries

---

[23] Levett, *Studies in Manorial History*, pp89-90.
[24] Levett, *Studies in Manorial History*, p92.
[25] Levett, *Studies in Manorial History*, p90 – *nichil in eo notabile* occurs as a marginal note in the Norton book between the courts of 32 Henry III (St Etheldreda) and 33 Henry III (St Peter ad Vincula), 1248/49.

INTRODUCTION

'which might conceivably be used as precedents', such as lists of jurors, property transactions, marriage payments and tenant deaths. There is also evidence that the books were later searched for information. There are many marginal notes including the word '*nativus*' which occurs alongside records of marriage payments, providing evidence for hereditary serfdom. Generally, though, 'they exclude nearly all the business normally grouped under the heading of View of Frankpledge'.[26] In the Norton books for the four years from 1409-1412, the scribe has unusually included these details showing that the business of the View of Frankpledge and the (halimote) court were dealt with separately, but on the same day of meeting.[27] A different list of jurors is given for the View from those at the court, and confirmation that the common fine had been levied, lists of those found outside the tithing, and details of assaults and other acts of nuisance are included. Also, for the same period appear wills of tenants totally omitted at other times.[28] Entries in the books are often long, suggesting that they were copied verbatim from the rolls. This is clearly demonstrated by comparing a surviving membrane from a Bramfield court of 7 July 1383 with the corresponding court book. The book is an exact copy of every transaction recorded in the roll for that day. In addition a scribe has written clearly at the bottom of the roll 'this is entered truwly into the great booke of court recordes'.[29]

The Court Rolls: the table on page xxiii lists the surviving court rolls for the manor of Norton, all now held at HALS. For the purposes of this volume only those rolls which date after 1460, the final date of the court books, have been translated. This represents four rolls out of an approximate total of eleven but even this must be only a tiny fraction of what had once existed. All of them are composite rolls containing not just Norton but several other St Albans manors too. The cellarer travelled in circuit to hold meetings, calling in at all his Hertfordshire manors in turn. For instance, in the earliest surviving roll for 1348, courts were held at Hexton on 20 October, Norton on 21 October and Bramfield on 22 October.[30] The records were written in chronological

---

[26] See later under 'The Manor Court' and Levett, *Studies in Manorial History*, p94.
[27] View of Frankpledge are included in the Hexton volume from 1408-1422.
[28] Levett, *Studies in Manorial History*, pp224-234 includes transcripts of wills found in the Park, Croxley, Barnet, Cashio, Winslow and Norton books. They also occur in Hexton, 1399-1421 (HALS: DE/B2355/M/1/1/1).
[29] HALS: 40698B and 40704 and see Levett, *Studies in Manorial History*, p96 for her comparison of a Cashio roll and book for 1433/4.
[30] HALS: 10549.

INTRODUCTION

sequence, so one roll might contain records from a dozen or more different places. As Levett notes, 'the task of searching such a record must have presented formidable difficulties. These composite rolls were, in short, large and confusing records'.[31] The drive for a leaner administrative organisation under cellarer John Mote during the third quarter of the fourteenth century may have prompted the copying of the rolls into the books described above. Volumes, with tags clearly identifying the records of individual manors, would make any required searches in them much easier and swifter. As a result, the original rolls may have seemed increasingly unnecessary and may have been lost or perhaps deliberately destroyed by monastic officials. However this may not explain completely why so few rolls for such miscellaneous dates have survived. The *Gesta Abbatum* relates that during the Peasants' Revolt the rebels 'in their fury' burnt many records belonging to the monastery.[32] They had been kept in the stable in the courtyard of the Abbey and by 1381 many of them would have already been copied into the books, so perhaps their loss during the revolt was not seen as a serious hindrance to the Abbey's administration. The rolls for 1348 (HALS: 10549), 1425/6 (HALS: 10555), and 1485 (HALS: 40709) have the appearance of being in their original format. They are made up from between four and six parchment membranes of varying sizes stitched together at the top, the year date on the outermost membrane, and contain the records for ten or more courts for that year. The remainder are generally in very poor condition. Surviving membranes appear to have been sewn together randomly, possibly centuries after they were originally compiled. The records for part of a court may be missing or not easy to identify as the entries do not always clearly state the place where the court was held.

The Norton records were transferred to HALS from four different sources but the greater majority came from Messrs Hawkins and Co solicitors of Hitchin in 1940 (Accession 13). Partners of this firm had acted as stewards of the manor from at least 1830 and would have acquired the records through this legal business. However at the period in which Ada Levett was conducting her research the earliest books were in the possession of local Hitchin historian Reginald Hine (a former partner in Hawkins) and were later transferred to HALS by him personally (Accession 109). The British Records Association rescued the remainder from London legal firms who had acted for lords of the manor in the past.

---

[31] Levett, *Studies in Manorial History*, p78.
[32] See Levett, *Studies in Manorial History*, p76; *Gesta Abbatum Monasterii S Albani*, vol iii, p370.

INTRODUCTION

The Manorial Court
The Abbey of St Albans was one of the wealthiest Benedictine monasteries in medieval England, and a significant landowner.[33] As well as holding a number of manors in the area around St Albans, there were other outlying manors in Hertfordshire, such as Codicote, Northaw, St Paul's Walden, Bramfield, Hexton, Norton and Newnham, and in Buckinghamshire Aston Abbots, Grandborough, Little Horwood and Winslow.[34] The Hertfordshire *Victoria County History* alone lists a total of 54 manors and sub manors, including Radwell not acquired by the monastery until 1438.[35] Further afield the abbey's sphere of influence included cells at Beaulieu (Hampshire), Belvoir (Lincolnshire), Tynemouth (Northumberland) and Wymondham (Norfolk) amongst others.

The territory, within which Norton lay, was named the Liberty of St Albans. The Liberty was co-terminous with the Hundred of Cashio, the largest in Hertfordshire, and covering some 89,661.5 acres.[36] The Abbey also enjoyed additional jurisdictional rights over this area, in which the operation of Leet and Hundred courts had been effectively privatised by the Crown and handed over to the Abbey to run, and to profit from. These included wide powers of civil jurisdiction over the Abbey's tenants such as the right to take the fines charged against wrongdoers as well as the market tolls in St Albans. A charter granted to the Abbey by King Henry II in 1162 confirmed the individual crimes which the Abbot could try in his court: cattle-stealing, breach of the peace, breaking and entering, possession of stolen goods, assault on the King's highway and harbouring a fugitive.[37] Considerable income was to be made from these powers but the right to them also allowed the Abbot to enforce his seigneurial

---

[33] St Albans Abbey 'was the tenth wealthiest monastic house in England in 1066; by the Dissolution it was the fourth', T Williamson, *The Origins of Hertfordshire* (Hatfield, 2010), p227.
[34] Records for the Manor of Winslow have been published by the Buckinghamshire Record Society: D Noy, (ed.) *Winslow Manor Court Books, 1327-1377, 1423-1460* (2011).
[35] Summarised in *VCH Hertfordshire*, vol ii, pp319-22; described in detail in ibid., pp323-515.
[36] The group are grateful to Anne Rowe for these area measurements from data collected in her work for *The Origins of Hertfordshire*. Norton itself is a relatively small parish of some 1,770.85 acres. The Hertfordshire Post Office Directory dated 1859 stated Norton had 1,780 acres. In 1876 a small part of the parish was annexed to Baldock (*VCH Hertfordshire*, vol iii, p65).
[37] HALS: VIIIB60. In this document the Anglo-Saxon words are used namely Team, Grithbrice, Hamsoche, Infangthief, Forsteal and Flemenefermthe.

INTRODUCTION

rights over both his free and unfree tenants. The Abbot held two types of court: the Court Baron (known as the Halimote or just the 'Court') and the Court Leet (known as the View of Frankpledge). The Court, or Halimote, was held for all the Abbot's tenants, both free and unfree, and primarily administered the customs of the manor with regard to tenure. It is here that changes in ownership of the manor's lands were reported and any disputes arising therefrom settled, customary payments made for the freedom to marry etc and the manor's officials, such as the reeve or bailiff were elected. The right to hold the Court Leet, or View of Frankpledge (*visus francplegii*), had been granted to the Abbot by the crown and he used it to enforce his judicial rights over his tenants.[38] In Norton we have detailed evidence for the holding of the View of Frankpledge court only from the court books during the period, 1409-1412.

The courts would have been held in customary places: in Norton this could have been the parish church or the manor house at Nortonbury. Deborah Giles suggests that a previous building called *Halleorchard* was located at Nortonbury and was the possible site where the manor court was held in the 1500s.[39] However sometimes Norton tenants were summoned to attend a court held under the ash tree (*sub fraxino*) in St Albans itself, the earliest reference being in 1248.[40] More than being 'simply a matter of convenience to the cellarer' if evidence was required from earlier records detailed consultation was undoubtedly easier in St Albans itself. The Halimote traditionally met every three weeks but no records survive of a court being held this frequently. Levett suggests that draft notes may have been kept from the three-weekly Court meetings perhaps held without the presence of the cellarer until a later court took place.[41] Often two courts were held annually, only very occasionally three, but in the majority of years only one court seemed to be necessary.[42] The View of Frankpledge was usually held only once a year.

Manor courts established proof of the cases brought before them in a number of

---

[38] A detailed discussion of the historical development of these courts can be found in M Bailey, *The English Manor c.1200-c.1500* (Manchester, 2002), pp167-189 and P D A Harvey, *Manorial Records* (revised edn, 1999), pp44-47.

[39] Giles, *Norton before the Garden City,* p24.

[40] (HALS: 65498, f1v) and see Levett, *Studies in Manorial History*, pp140-142.

[41] Levett, *Studies in Manorial History*, p134.

[42] Between 1383 and 1539 only one court was held at Norton each year apart from 1413 and 1539 when there were two. The situation is similar at Hexton where between 1382 and 1397 and again between 1423 and 1445 only one court was held (HALS: DE/B2355/M/1/1/1).

INTRODUCTION

ways, but an increasingly common method was to use two kinds of juries. Inquest juries were most common in the thirteenth century, and involved the swearing in of jurors to determine the facts of the matter in specific cases. There are seven instances of tenants calling for verdicts of this nature in the period from 1248-1268 at Norton. For example, in 1247 (HALS: 65498, f1v) 'Walter son of Robert offered to the lord 10s that he may have an inquest of 24 men of Norton and Newnham concerning obtaining his right to a *ferthlingate* of land', and in 1256 (HALS: 65498, f3) jurors were asked 'concerning an inquisition about two acres of arable land ...'. In 1268 (HALS: 65498, f5v), the jurors presented that William Everard, a persistent offender, had not completed his boonworks services and was amerced. The use of presentment juries spread from Hundred courts into manor courts towards the end of the thirteenth century, and they were used in every court to 'present' a range of cases on behalf of the homage, ie all those who were required to attend the court, rather than just be sworn in to determine a particular case. This proved a very efficient way of dealing with the large numbers of cases coming before the courts.[43] The presentment jurors were there primarily to identify activity which required the court's attention and to present the facts. Slota states that such juries only became common on the St Albans estates in the 1280s.[44] Norton's court books appear to confirm this as the first jurors are listed for the 1289 court (HALS: 65500, f1v) where eight names for Norton and nine for Newnham are given. However, it must be remembered that the court books are copies of the original rolls and that earlier lists may not have been copied. Whether or not this was the case, between 1268 and 1289 there were regular items brought to the court starting with the words 'the jurors present' or 'the jurors say', which suggests that a jury was in place for those years. In 1292, there was an interesting example of their role and the protection provided by the court. There had been a dispute between two parties and the jurors advised that one of the parties (John in the Hale) was making a false complaint. Two years later (HALS: 65502, f1) the guilty party was amerced again, this time because 'he spoke with the jurors after the oath, therefore amerced 2s'. It seems that the man in question had been 'getting at' jurors after the court. In 1308/1309, there are examples of jurors pronouncing on what they believed to be ancient customs of the manor. However, in 1340 the jurors were amerced for not doing their job. On discovering that a widow had demised her dower three years previously without

---

[43] Bailey, *English Manor*, pp173-5.
[44] L A Slota, 'Law, land transfer, and lordship on the estates of St Albans Abbey in the thirteenth and fourteenth centuries', *Law and History Review*, 6:1 (1988), pp119-38.

INTRODUCTION

it being reported to the court, 'all the jurors for the last three years are amerced for concealment'. In 1352, despite the jury confirming that John le Newman held his tenement freely by charter, the court continued to pursue him for the next two years. The lord of the manor himself was in receipt of the court's attention in 1409: 'Next they present that the lord is bound to repair a certain bridge called *Fordbrugge*'.[45] This was mentioned in three successive courts but unfortunately it was not recorded as to whether the lord of the manor acted upon this order. The number of people in the jury in Norton varied from year to year. In many of the early courts there were only six jurors and in 1384 as few as four. From the 1430s, the number settled at 12. At the 1409 View of Frankpledge three of the jurors were elected as chief pledges: those chosen were given the responsibility for collecting the common fine. From 1409 to 1412 different numbers and names of jurors are given for each of the Court and View of Frankpledge. This was because the jurors for the View were representatives of the tithingmen, residents of Norton, whereas the court jurors were the principal customary tenants. However these were one and the same at the 1511 Halimote when it was explained (rather than writing out a separate list of jurors) under the heading that 'All the chief pledges abovewritten (ie those listed under the View of Frankpledge) who are tenants of the lord are chosen and sworn to the Homage of this Court' (HALS: 47296, f1v).

Management of the Estate
The Abbey of St Albans comprised a large and static household of monks, administrators and servants who needed feeding. It therefore looked to its estate for the direct provision of fuel, food, building materials and livestock. It also needed cash to buy luxury goods, pay for services, upkeep its buildings and pay its taxes, so it also needed money from its estate. The Abbey was also a somewhat conservative manager of its estate, mindful to protect the rights, dues and privileges accumulated in the good name of St Alban over centuries. This mind set explains the way in which the Norton court maintained the language and trappings of villeinage well into the fifteenth century, long after it had disappeared on many other estates in the Home Counties and East Anglia.

The ways in which the Abbey managed the manor of Norton over the period covered by the court rolls is impossible to recover without the existence of a good set of manorial account rolls, which are a type of farm account.[46] However, most monastic landlords like St Albans Abbey tended to lease out

---

[45] In the 1409 View of Frankpledge (HALS: 65526, f3).
[46] Bailey, *The English Manor*, pp98-111.

their manors in their entirety before *c.*1200, collecting a fixed annual rent each year: the rent was sometimes a food render, but usually a mixture of grain and cash. Rapid inflation and runaway indebtedness around *c.*1200 forced a change in approach, and St Albans, like many such landlords, moved to exploiting most of their manors directly. In other words, they collected the rents from their tenants, they exploited their 'home farm' (the demesne) themselves, they reared livestock and either sold it on the market or sent it to the Abbey for consumption,[47] and they ran the manor court directly. According to Dyer 'between 1184 and 1214 the greater lords converted their system of management from leasing demesnes by … putting them under the control of officials directly responsible for the profits …. Each manor was put under a local official, a reeve, sergeant or bailiff, who either served as a condition of holding land or was in receipt of rewards in cash or kind'.[48] Honesty and efficiency of the reeve was central to the successful operation of the system. Therefore, the lords required a strong central management team (consisting of stewards, treasurers and auditors) to supervise the local managers.

Even in the absence of a run of manorial accounts, the switch to 'direct exploitation' is evident in the election and activities of manorial officers, which are routinely recorded in the court rolls. Most of these helped to run the manorial demesne, overseen by regular visits from the Abbey's professional officials, for which they either received remission of rent and/or an annual salary. The most important local officer was the reeve, who was effectively the day-to-day farm manager of the manor on behalf of the Abbey, and who was traditionally elected from among the villeins of the manor. The very first item in the Norton court of 1244 mentions William the reeve (his son Walter gave 2s for leave to marry), which indicates that the manor was being directly exploited at this date. The honesty of William was called into question four years later when he contradicted all the villagers over a property dispute. He was amerced 12d. Some villeins were elected year after year, others did the job for one year before a new reeve was elected. It was widely accepted that villeins, whose turn it was to serve as reeve, could pay the lord to be exonerated from the office: if they could afford to pay the fee, and if they had little aptitude for or interest in

---

[47] Norton itself sent poultry and eggs to St Albans (*VCH Hertfordshire*, vol ii, p362 quoting BL: Cotton MS Tiberius E VI ff35-37).

[48] C Dyer, *Making a Living in the Middle Ages. The People of Britain 850-1520* (New Haven and London, 2002), p121.

the post, then this made good sense.[49] If the Abbey's officials, or the villagers themselves, had concerns about the capacity of a villein to perform the role of reeve, then they would take special measures to support him. Sayer the Reeve was appointed at Norton in 1290, with all the villagers 'promising that they will answer for him'.

Locally elected officials

Official	First mention in records	Last mention in records
Reeve	1244	1339
Beadle	1250	1456
Sergeant	1249	1289
Constable (Leet)	1352	1539 and beyond

The reeve had a sergeant and beadle to assist him at Norton, although their exact roles are unknown. On some estates the sergeant performed the same function as the reeve, but the different name signified that he was a salaried rather than an elected position. In 1250, all the villagers went to the great boonday before the accustomed hour without leave of the sergeant, and were attainted by the reeve and the beadle. This would indicate that the sergeant was a paid position at Norton, perhaps part-time, in support of the reeve: in this specific case, he was organising the labour services on the lord's demesne due to be performed by the villeins as part of their rent package. The last mention of a sergeant was in 1289, when the sergeant was accused of unjustly taking a heriot. The last mention of a reeve was in 1339, but the post probably continued for longer until it was made unnecessary when the demesne was leased to a third party and no longer directly exploited by the Abbey itself (see below).

The records show that the beadle was also an elected post, again from the villein tenants of the manor on rotation. In 1440, John Laweman was elected as the lord's beadle and collector of the lord's rent. A year later, John in the Hale was elected and sworn into the post. This shows that the beadle continued to be elected long after the post of reeve was redundant, mainly as a collector of rents and as an administrator to the manorial court. The constable was not an appointment of the manor court, but of the Leet court at the annual View of Frankpledge. The constable was responsible for local law and order, but the early Views were not copied into the court books. The first mention of a

---

[49] In November 1249 William in the Hale gives 2s to the lord, Alexander Ruffus 12d, John son of Henry 2s and Walter son of Alice 12d that they may be exonerated from the office of reeve.

constable was in 1352 when the constable had the duty to deliver John Buschel, a villein, to gaol in St Albans. Thereafter the only references to constables were concerning their election and swearing into office.

These local manorial officials were supervised by, and answerable to, the Abbey's professional and centralised administrators, who themselves are often mentioned in the court rolls.

Officials from St Albans Abbey

Official	First mention in records	Last mention in records[50]
Cellarer	1246	1539
Bailiff	1311	1536
Steward	1434	1534

From 1281-1412, the records regularly give the names of the cellarer, under whose jurisdiction the manor of Norton was placed. Thereafter, this practice was stopped and was not resumed until 1484. All of the cellarers' names and their dates are recorded in Levett (pp163-169) so are not repeated here, apart from the last named in 1539, Lord John Salter, whose name Levett omitted. The cellarer was responsible for feeding the monastic household, and many Benedictine abbeys sub-divided their manors into separate sub-estates for the Abbot, the cellarer and other major obedientaries such as the Sacrist, Prior and Infirmarer.

The steward was usually responsible for a group of manors within a large monastic estate, and would have been a lay member of the Abbey's retinue: usually with a legal background, and a prominent member of the local gentry. He was effectively the Abbey's senior agent on the ground, and was probably the official who held the courts when the cellarer was not present. The first mention of the steward was in 1434 (HALS: 65531, f1) when an heir formally refused to take on his holding in front of both the steward and the cellarer. There are a number of later references in 1532-1534, when formal surrenders were made 'by the hands of the steward' but their names are not given (HALS: 65535, ff2-3). The post of bailiff was regularly mentioned throughout the court books. This was probably a professional member of the Abbey's estate staff, acting as the daily point of contact between a small number of reeves and the steward. Unusually a deputy bailiff was mentioned in 1531 (HALS: 65535, f1), acting in the capacity of recording a deathbed surrender. The concentration of references to bailiffs, sub-bailiffs and stewards in the fifteenth-century courts

---

[50] The office of bailiff and steward continued beyond 1539.

INTRODUCTION

probably reflects the growing professionalization, and bureaucracy, of the Abbey's administration at this time.

During the fourteenth century monastic landlords shifted by degrees back towards the leasing of their estates, and gradually withdrew from direct exploitation of their manorial resources. Some manors were leased in their entirety again, but most manors were subject to a mixed management, in which some elements of the manor were leased to different people, while the lord maintained direct control over aspects such as the manor court and the collection of rents. This 'mixed mode' approach was adopted at Norton. The fact that the manor and Leet courts continued to be held by the Abbey, and their business recorded, throughout the fifteenth century is proof that the Abbey retained direct control of this aspect of manorial administration. Similarly, the beadle continued to be appointed to collect rents throughout this time, and continued to be supervised by the bailiff. The disappearance of references to the office of reeve from the middle of the fourteenth century is strongly suggestive that the demesne of Norton (the lord's arable and pasture lands, manorial complex, dairy, granary etc) had been leased to a third party, or 'farmer'. References to men with the second name *firmarius* (the Latin word for 'farmer') occur in the rolls as early as 1263, but this does not mean that the demesne of Norton was leased. The first significant reference occurs in 1383, when a heriot of two horses was said to be in the custody of 'the farmer'. Again, the survival of manorial accounts for Norton would provide a definitive answer, but, in their absence, it would appear that the demesne of Norton was leased for a cash rent on a fixed term contract in the early 1380s, and possibly earlier. In 1379, it was reported that it was the shepherd's fault that four sheep died in a hailstorm and two were lost. This meant that, at that time, the demesne sheep flock was still run directly on the Abbey's behalf.

In 1394 the court made a general proclamation regarding the requirement to perform services 'for the whole time that John Bradeweye shall be farmer of the said manor'. This was unusual, because the ploughing, mowing and tossing hay services owed as part of the customary rent package of villein tenants were normally commuted for a cash sum rather than made available to the lessee of the demesne. John Bradeweye was probably a local man. In 1391 he and his wife Margery had acquired a tenement at *Halleorchard* from John Boton and re-built it. This was to be the family home for John and his son Walter and his heirs. It appears that John Bradeweye was a villein of Norton, but also a successful businessman. His will is recorded in the court records in 1405, which was a requirement of villeins of the manor, but it reveals a long list of bequests

INTRODUCTION

to the church at Norton, his family and servants, which indicate a wealthy man.[51] In addition, he left money for the church at Baldock as well as 12d for each poor man and woman in Norton and Baldock. John Bradeweye is a good example of the increased social mobility of the later Middle Ages: a villein of Norton who transcended his servile status to become a successful lessee of the demesne of his home manor, Norton, and who extended his business interests into the nearby town of Baldock.

John Bradeweye's story also illustrates the difficulties of sustaining financial success in the depressed agrarian conditions of the fifteenth century. His son, Walter, took over his father's interests in the rectory lands, but financially he was a disaster. Walter got into debt and surrendered all the lands and tenements which had been bequeathed to him by his father, including the family home at *Halleorchard*. His heriot was remitted on account of poverty. The court entry in 1432 (HALS: 65531, f1) was as follows: 'And because the said Walter from the times when he was farmer of the farm of the rectory of Norton was indebted in divers sums of money to the Convent of St Albans ...', which means that he failed to keep up with the required rental payments.

The difficulties in making a success of running the Norton demesne, and the problems facing the tenants themselves during the Great Slump of the mid-fifteenth century, are evident in some incidental references. In 1437 the Abbey entered into an agreement to reduce the charges for heriot for the next 60 years, based on the poverty of the villeins of Norton, and the Abbey relied upon the advice and direction of its farmers in coming to the arrangement '... with the assent and consent of John Poley and Thomas Swalewe, lately farmers there ...'. The survival of a solitary account for the manor in 1488-1489, reproduced in Appendix 1, provides some indication of the structure of the lease. The rents of assize generated over £22 each year, and continued to be collected directly by the Abbey's officials. The demesne was leased mainly for a rent payment in kind, ie the provision of some grain and a much larger quantity of malt for the Abbey. The malt would have been used to make ale, which was a staple of monastic households. The account mentions two further names of farmers, Thomas and Robert Denysshe but we have no other record of them. John Bowles was granted the lease of the manor in 1515 for the unusually long term of 50 years.[52] In 1534, the court records show him acquiring all the empty lands

---

[51] HALS: 65525, f1v. This will is not included amongst the surviving records of the Archdeaconry of St Albans also held at HALS.

[52] Giles, *Norton before the Garden City*, p39. He also held a lease of the neighbouring Manor of Baldock from 1522 (*VCH Hertfordshire*, vol iii, p65).

INTRODUCTION

and pastures in the manor of Norton for the annual rent of 1d per acre. Meanwhile George Hide acquired the rectory and tithes along with John Bradewey's former tenement of *Halleorchard* in 1533.[53] At the Dissolution, the Crown acquired the manor from the Abbey, including the rectory land. Three years later, all were purchased by John Bowles, and so the last farmer of the demesne lands had become the new lord of the manor.

Agriculture
Deborah Giles has deduced from Domesday records that in Norton and Rodenhanger there were ten ploughs for arable produce and two ploughs for meadow, which might have accounted for between 1,170 and 1,560 acres.[54] Of this, the demesne land only amounted to three ploughs, roughly 270-360 acres. There is no medieval survey from which to establish size and the relative proportions of demesne arable, free land, villein land, and pasture within medieval Norton. The court rolls do not provide this type of information.

The absence of manorial accounts and extensive surveys for medieval Norton hinder attempts to reconstruct its landscape and agriculture during the Middle Ages. The court rolls contain a few incidental references to fields, common rights and crops, which enable some preliminary observations to be made. These indicate clearly that its arable fields were mainly open, in the sense that they were divided into small strips, and that individual holdings were scattered rather than held in consolidated blocks. For example, one tenant in 1305 held 'two acres of land ... one acre lies in two parts in the *Southfeld* ... and the other acre lies in two parts in the *North Field*' (HALS: 65503, f4). In the period 1271-1348, there were 16 recorded instances of tenants exchanging small plots of land, normally quarter or half-acre strips. The bounds of each open strip were identified, and delimited from its neighbouring strips, by the use of stone boundary markers, which attract occasional comment from the court when illegally removed.

The medieval fields of Norton were unquestionably open, sub-divided, fields. Whether they were organised into the classic two- or three-field system, with a communal cropping rotation imposed on each field in turn, is another matter entirely. Elizabethan court records from the 1570s make reference to a North, South and Middle Field, implying that a classic three-field system was in operation at that date. If so, it would represent a change from arrangements in

---

[53] *VCH Hertfordshire*, vol ii, p364.
[54] Giles, *Norton before the Garden City*, pp13-15.

the Middle Ages, which were unquestionably more complex. It is significant that in the court rolls the location of individual strips was usually identified by naming the furlong in which they were located, rather than the field, which is characteristic of irregular field systems. References to field names in Norton are very rare – only four separate fields are recorded at different times: Northfield and Southfield (1304-5), Eldefield (five times between 1304 and 1347) and Wiliefield (1311-12 and 1316). This form of referencing is not indicative of the classic two- or three-field system, but it is characteristic of irregular open fields where the furlong, not the field itself, is the principal unit of cropping. Individual furlongs are themselves named on several occasions – for example, Chalkfurlong and Longfurlong.

The impression of an irregular, not regular, field system is strengthened by the fact that hardly any agricultural by-laws are recorded in the court rolls, and descriptions of communal regulations are rare. Regular two-and three-field systems required much close regulation from the manorial court to make them work, and the absence of such regulation at Norton is instructive. Common rights certainly existed over Norton's open fields, but they were mainly common rights to pasture animals over any arable land which was not sown with crops (1454), or over other pasture grounds or meadows, for the half year between 1 August and 2 February (1414). Irregular open-field systems did not impose communal cropping regimes, and were mainly concerned to regulate communal access to pasture, fallows and meadows at restricted times of the year.[55] In the whole of the medieval court roll series there is only one suggestion that some communal cropping regulations existed, when 'William in the Hale has sown half an acre of land with wheat which he ought not to sow except every other year' (1368). Thus Norton appears to conform to the type of irregular open field systems with some partially regulated cropping found in the medieval Chilterns.[56]

The main characteristics of agriculture in Hertfordshire changed little across the Middle Ages, as revealed through B M S Campbell's analysis of demesne agriculture. Across much of the county arable farming was dominated by the production of wheat and oats on a classic three-course rotation: wheat sown in the winter, oats in the spring, with around one third of the arable left fallow each

---

[55] M Bailey, 'The form, function and evolution of irregular field systems in Suffolk, 1300 to 1550', *Agricultural History Review*, 57 (2009), pp15-24.

[56] D Roden, 'The field systems of the Chiltern Hills and their environs', in A R H Baker and R A Butlin, (eds), *Studies of field systems in the British Isles* (Cambridge, 1973), pp325-62.

year. These crops were sown with moderate to low intensity. Norton lay at the northern edge of this farming region, near to the Chiltern region where spring crops such as barley and rye increased in prominence.[57] The court rolls do not mention crops very often, but wheat is prominent when they do. Interestingly, oats are hardly mentioned at all, and the spring crops preferred by the peasants themselves were barley, beans, peas and dredge (an even mixture of barley and oats).

Pastoral farming in medieval Hertfordshire was relatively commercialised, with a focus upon horses rather than oxen as sources of traction, and also upon cows for commercial dairy production: sheep were generally unimportant, although they became more so on the chalk pastures of the Chiltern Hills.[58] The main references to animals relate to heriot payments, which represented the payment of the 'best beast' from the estate of a deceased villein tenant to the lord. The three most common animals were sheep, cows and horses. There were only three records of pigs being chosen for heriot (in 1340, 1343 and 1370). From the earliest courts, the surname Bercarius or Shepherd is mentioned. The Abbey kept a flock of sheep at Norton, as indicated by the failure in 1313/1314 of four tenants to shear the lord's sheep when summoned. Some peasants also kept a large flock of sheep: in 1317/1318, Ralph Boueton was amerced for stocking the pasture beyond his allowance with 64 lambs.[59] The chalk pastures of the Chiltern edge would have provided more scope for sheep rearing than in most other areas of Hertfordshire. From these snippets of information, it appears that Norton lay within an area of moderately intensive arable farming, where wheat and a mixture of spring crops (not just oats) dominated. Its pastoral regime was slightly more intensive, based on some dairying and sheep rearing.

There are hints that some woodland still existed in medieval Norton. In 1331, the curtilage formerly associated with John atte More, the tenant who held by knight's service up to 1306, was granted to Ralph and John Boueton with the

---

[57] B M S Campbell, *English Seigniorial Agriculture 1250-1450* (Cambridge, 2000), pp257, 262-3, 282, 285, 316; M Bailey, 'Introduction', in J Brooker and S Flood, (eds), *Hertfordshire Lay Subsidy Rolls 1307 and 1334*, (HRS, vol xiv, 1998), ppxxiii-xxiv.
[58] Campbell, *Seigniorial Agriculture*, pp106-20, 149.
[59] The Norton wills proved in the St Albans Archdeaconry Court also contain bequests of significant numbers of sheep (HALS: 1AR and 2AR).

INTRODUCTION

intention to 'throw down trees'.[60] This might have been for the clearance of woodland in what had earlier been land held freely. Much later, in the View of Accounts of the Rent Collector in 1488/9, the farmer was paid 6d for the costs of transporting a boar to the Abbot so it seems there was still some woodland in Norton at that time.

The Abbey as lord of the manor also had rights of free fishing and free warren. In 1307, a servant was accused of having 'broken the lord's pond and carried away six pike'. In 1360, five tenants were amerced for not cleansing the pond. The lord's warren appears to have been not just a temptation to villeins for his rabbits: in 1345, three tenants were amerced for poaching larks and other birds in the lord's warren. The only reference to rabbits was in 1313/14, when there were problems with a dog which did 'damage to the rabbits of the lord Abbot'. However, as was often the case, the greatest threat to civil order was from outside the manor as is indicated by the following item dated 1445 (HALS: 65534, f1): the 'Homage presented that the Rector of Letchworth is a common hunter within the lordship of Norton and takes hares etc and makes unlawful ways through the pasture and corn of the lord and his tenants there. Therefore let a writ be made etc'.[61]

Villeins and Villeinage
A villein was a tenant or person legally tied to the lord of the manor. A villein tenant held customary or unfree land in villeinage, owing in return to the lord a range of labour services, produce in kind and various servile incidents. A villein tenant was usually personally unfree as well, a social condition inherited through the male line. Hereditary serfs (*nativi*) owed a range of servile incidents to the lord whether they held land or not. Most obviously, neither villein tenants nor hereditary serfs could leave the manor permanently, or get married, without the lord's express permission. In the following translation the word *nativus* has been translated as villein.

The Abbey of St Albans is traditionally regarded as a conservative and bureaucratic landlord, who possessed a high proportion of villeins and villein land on his manors and who managed them in a heavy-handed manner. The

---

[60] The term knight's service appears only once in Norton's records when in 1350 the death of Master John of Erdeleye is reported. More information can be found in *VCH Hertfordshire* vol ii p362.

[61] A list of rectors appeared in the *Letchworth Parish Magazine* of June 1918 but no name was given between that of Richard att Hoo in 1433 and John Ippyng in 1467 (HALS: DE/X976/18/1).

INTRODUCTION

absence of a manorial survey for Norton means that it is not possible to estimate the relative importance of villeins on the manor, but the court rolls are dominated by references to them and their land. Given that around one half of all rural tenants in England in c.1300 were villeins, it seems likely that the proportion was higher at Norton.

Villein holdings usually came in standardised sizes, and it was forbidden to subdivide or alienate them: these arrangements enabled landlords to keep track of the complex array of labour services attached to them as part of the rent package. Levett has observed that the normal size of villein holding or tenement varied considerably from manor to manor across the St Albans estate. At Winslow the typical holding was a virgate,[62] whereas Codicote seems to have suffered from an excessive subdivision of holdings: in 1332 it was said to have only one half virgate and all other land holdings were smaller.[63] Norton has one record of a full virgate, that held by the Bate family in the 1330-1350 period and later referred to as *Bateslond*. Norton's principal customary tenants were half-virgate holders. Interestingly, attempts to estimate the actual size of such holdings in Norton prove contradictory. A virgate is usually defined as the amount of land tillable by two oxen in a ploughing season, or roughly 30 acres.[64] However, in Norton's court records there are only two instances of quantification of these holdings, both which suggest a different area. In 1336 a tenant was described as holding '16 acres of land that is to say half of half a virgate of land'. Later, in 1347, another was described as holding two quarters of land (ie a half virgate) containing 36 acres of land. Both of these examples suggest that at Norton a virgate was worth 64-72 acres.

Villein holdings at Norton rendered set amounts of labour services, which were a mixture of onerous week works and various seasonal works and boonworks, such as ploughing, haymaking and harvest works.[65] They also rendered heriot, or their best beast, upon the death of the tenant. The incoming tenant also paid a *gersumma*, or entry fine, which also implied swearing an oath of fealty to the

---

[62] Noy, *Winslow Manor Court Books*, 'Introduction', pxvi.
[63] Levett, *Studies in Manorial History*, pp185-6.
[64] A virgate or yardland, sometimes referred to as a quarter of a hide, was about 30 acres. Noy explained that if a holding of 30 acres was made up of separate blocks it might not count as a full virgate (*Winslow Manor Court Books*, pxvi).
[65] In return for these services the tenants were given allowances of food (BL: Cotton MS Tiberius E VI ff35-37).

INTRODUCTION

lord as his villein.⁶⁶ Villein landholders were also liable to tallage, which on the St Albans estate was not an annual cash 'tax' but a 'recognition' payment due upon the election of every new Abbot. These are recorded in the court rolls in 1277 and 1350.⁶⁷ They were also liable to merchet, a payment to marry their sons and daughters; millsuit, a requirement to grind their corn at the lord's mill; leyrwite, a payment for fornication which was a particularly demeaning aspect of serfdom; and they had to obtain their lord's permission to live off the manor for more than a year, which required the payment of chevage. Chevage, leyrwite and merchet were rendered by landless serfs as well as villein tenants. Villeins also had no legal right to inherit under the common law, and so some of their wills are recorded in the Norton court rolls as a form of seigniorial permission to dispose of their goods and chattels as they wished. These wills are a distinctive and important feature of the St Albans manorial courts, because this was not a requirement of villeins on many other English estates, including those of other Benedictine abbeys such as Bury St Edmunds. They provide rare insights into the wealth and piety of late-medieval villeins.

There was, however, a sizeable gap between the legal theory of villeinage and its reality on the ground.⁶⁸ The most obvious difference was the theoretical prohibition on the sale and subdivision of villein land, and the actual arrangements on the manor. In this respect, Norton had much in common with many other places in the Home Counties and East Anglia where an active market in customary land had developed in practice. All villein land in Norton

---

[66] The word '*gersumma*', rather than its more normal translation as an entry fine, has been retained in the translation because it is used throughout the court records to 1460 as a verb as well as a noun, implying more than just a payment, rather the whole process of taking on a customary holding and the implied subjugation to the lord.

[67] In 1350 a new abbot was needed after Michael de Mentmore died in 1349 from the Black Death. The payment in 1277 did not relate to such an appointment and no other reason is given (Abbot John de Hertford died in 1263 and his successor John de Norton did not die until 1290). However extensive rebuilding works were taking place at the abbey, so additional cash was undoubtedly useful. See E Roberts, *The Hill of the Martyr, an Architectural History of St Albans Abbey* (Dunstable, 1993), pp97-107. In both years the tallage was paid by all the St Albans manors.

[68] For a general summary and discussion of the market in customary land, and for the background to the changes over time discussed in this section. See P D A Harvey, ed, *The Peasant Land Market in Medieval England* (Oxford, 1984); and M Bailey, *The Decline of Serfdom in Late Medieval England. From Bondage to Freedom* (Woodbridge, 2014), chapters 2, 13 and 14.

INTRODUCTION

was heritable, so that when a villein died his holdings were automatically transferred to his heir, usually his eldest son. However, there were a growing number of instances where the new tenant was not the heir. The lord permitted these transfers to non-heirs, which were sometimes made after the death of the tenant (*post mortem* transfers) but increasingly during the life of the existing tenant (*inter vivos* transfers), as long as the transfer was recorded and formalised in the manorial court.

This is evidenced by the language used when the land was transferred. Customary land was invariably described throughout the court rolls as being held 'in villeinage ... for the due and accustomed services', and the frequent (and increasing) use of the additional phrase 'at the will of lord' further emphasized that the land could only be transferred to a new tenant within the manorial court (as opposed to the courts of common law, where the title to free land could be defended). The Norton court was careful to use a particular form of wording for these transfers to reiterate this important legal point, in which the tenant surrendered the holding 'into the lord's hands' and subsequently the lord granted the land to the new tenant. The first instance of a 'surrender into the lord's hands' was in 1250 (HALS: 65498, f2) and the new tenant 'gave seisin', accepting all the feudal obligations that accompanied the right to the new holding. The new wording became established for most transfers of holdings from 1263 onwards.

Another important variation from the strict legal theory of villeinage was the way in which the Norton court allowed parcels of villein land to be alienated, or more often to be sub-leased temporarily, to others. From the earliest court records, there are many examples of holdings or part of holdings being leased for a period of years. Again, this reflects the underlying buoyancy of the customary land market, and the persistent demand for land, in this area of the country. This appears to have been a constant area of watchfulness for the Abbey's officials, who were prepared to allow the operation of a land market in customary land, but who also wanted to ensure that no permanent alienations took place without their explicit permission. The early courts contain many references to villein tenants subletting their land without prior permission; the tenants were usually amerced, as a way of providing a retrospective licence, although sometimes the leasing agreement was annulled. In 1272 as many as six tenants were amerced for this practice.

Thus the practice of both selling and subleasing parcels of customary land was permitted, but only with the lord's prior permission, as an explicit pronouncement confirmed in 1315:

INTRODUCTION

'The jurors of Norton and Newnham say that all the villeins of Norton and Newnham with the lord's leave may let, sell and exchange among themselves because they are by custom used and obliged to, and to let their tenements to free men if they shall have the leave of the lord for this and not otherwise.'

Subletting to freemen was a particular concern, because it might lead to a permanent loss of customary land from the Abbey's control. Hence in 1336 the Abbey attempted to impose tighter restrictions on the practice when ordaining

'that no villein henceforth shall alienate or demise to any free man or any stranger any land or tenement nor make any agreement about this with them as long as he can demise the said tenement and land to the lord or to another unfree villein tenant'.

In 1354 a further proclamation was made to the effect that short term leases of one or two years had to be registered with the courts, which must reflect the disruption to the land market in the wake of the Black Death of 1349. When the land market began to pick up again towards the middle of the sixteenth century, the upsurge in subletting is indicated by the practice of starting every court from the 1530s with the following proclamation:

'A proclamation is made that all persons who hold, occupy, or lease any villein lands or tenements of the lord contrary to the customs of the aforesaid manor without estate and licence having been had or obtained from the lord and also all those who in such lands or tenements have rights to claim must come to get licence or estate from the lord for them under penalty of forfeiting the same etc.'

The continued use of the old formula 'held in villeinage' throughout the period of the courts is unusual, because most English landlords dropped this demeaning phrase in the early fifteenth century as part of the wider decay and disappearance of the servile elements of villeinage. It is not easy to track exactly the falling away of the old rent package through the court rolls, but there are occasional hints. Labour services were initially due to the farmer of the manor in the 1380s, but by 1457 it is apparent that they were commuted each year for a cash sum instead: in that year John Blowe was to pay 23s 1d to the farmer of the manor in lieu of the labour services due from his half virgate. Hence the requirement to perform labour services physically on the lord's demesne gradually disappeared, to be replaced by annual cash payments. Clearly the latter were less demeaning. Similarly, the requirement to pay merchet and leyrwite was eventually dropped - the last recorded payment being made in 1357, although it is not certain whether its absence from the court records meant that it was discontinued after that date.[69] Heriot continued throughout, but it was made less burdensome after an agreement between the Abbey and the villein tenants in 1437 to convert it from a render of the best beast (cows and horses could be valued at 10s) to a lower cash render capped at 3s 4d. This represented another erosion of the incidents of villein tenure, such that, by *c.*1460, hardly any of the original servile elements remained on the rent package of villein land.

The changes to the nature of villein tenure were complemented by the emergence of a subtly different form of villein tenure. From the mid-fifteenth century the Abbey could only find tenants for abandoned villein land lying in its hands by altering the form of tenure in a very subtle manner. For example, in 1452 the lord granted to John Albreth senior 26 acres and three roods of land and meadow which had been once held by Sarra de Yerdeley, but which had been lying in the lord's hands for want of a tenant. Albreth held the land not 'in villeinage at the will of the lord for services', but 'by rent service therefrom annually to the lord of fixed rent 3s 4d *per annum* and one pound of cumin and to the office of cellarer annually increase in rent 6s 8d annually *per annum* and suit of Court, fine one capon and fealty'. A year later John Brygger acquired from the lord's hands one cottage 'in villeinage at the will of the lord by rent service therefrom annually to the lord 12d, at the usual terms, fine and heriot when they fall due and common suit of Court'. Both tenants were holding these villein lands heritably 'for rent service', which meant that a new and straight annual cash rent replaced all servile incidents, including labour services although they still owed suit of court, entry fine and heriot. The package of annual cash rent, entry fine, suit of court and heriot were characteristic of copyholds of inheritance in this area in the sixteenth century.

Leyrwite
Leyrwite, the payment levied especially on unmarried villein women for sexual activity, was recorded as early as 1086 in Domesday Book. However it is not until the thirteenth century that it can be found more frequently in manorial records, including in those manors owned by the Abbot of St Albans. Judith Bennett has not only shown that it was a peculiarly English custom but also that it was not levied everywhere: for example, there are no records of leyrwite in

---

[69] Surviving records for Winslow show that the practice continued there until 1377. See Noy, *Winslow Manor Court books* and D Noy, 'Leyrwite, marriage and illegitimacy: Winslow before the Black Death' in *Records of Buckinghamshire* vol 47 part 1 (2007), pp133-51.

INTRODUCTION

those counties along the south coast.[70] In East Anglia it was replaced by the payment of childwite, levied only when an illegitimate child was born: there were 44 cases in Walsham le Willows between 1303 and 1399.[71]

	Norton				Park[72]	Winslow[73]
Decade	Total	Women	Men	Sum total of amercements	Total	Total
1280-1289	1	1	0	6d	1	-
1290-1299	2	1	1	2s 6d	2	-
1300-1309	12	10	2	6s 9d	7	-
1310-1319	10	10	0	5s 0d	3	-
1320-1329	6	6	0	2s 6d	4	2
1330-1339	8	8	0	2s 7d	2	24
1340-1349	16	16	0	6s 2d	0	13
1350-1359	11	6	5	4s 6d	1	2
Totals	**66**	**58**	**8**	**30s 6d**	**20**	**41**

In Norton the records show that 66 people were amerced for leyrwite during the period 1283-1357 (none were so amerced after 1357). The table above shows the number of people per decade and the total value of the amercement collected (the figures for the manors of Park and Winslow are given for comparison). The total amount of money generated in Norton for the Abbot throughout the period was 30s 6d. There were also, however, seven instances where the value of the amercement was not recorded. In addition, there was one occurrence where the amercement was not applied as the woman concerned (Emma Jecob in 1319) was 'poor' and another where the man (John Loveleg in 1352) was amerced but the offence was 'condoned'. The value of this total is still very small compared with the much larger sums generated from heriots and property entry fines.

The value of the amercement in each case was usually 3d, 6d or 12d. These

---

[70] J M Bennett, 'Writing Fornication: Medieval Leyrwite and its Historians', in *Transactions of the Royal Historical Society*, 13, (2003), pp131-162.
[71] R Lock, (ed), *The Court Rolls of Walsham le Willows 1303-50* and *1351-99* (Suffolk Records Society, vols 41 and 45, 1998 and 2002).
[72] These figures are extracted from BL Add MS 40625 and quoted in J M Bennett, 'Writing Fornication', p134. The earliest entry is dated 1237; there are nine cases before 1279 and a further four in the 1370s.
[73] These figures are extracted from Noy, *Winslow Manor Court books* and 'Leyrwite, marriage and illegitimacy'. There are a further four cases from 1360-1377.

INTRODUCTION

values equate easily with payments made for breaking the assize of ale and for neglecting to grind corn at the lord's mill, which were also usually set at 3d to 6d. Only once, in 1299 when Matilda Prodd was amerced, was a pledge of 2s made by her father. Although the court record does not specifically say so, this may have been paid in addition for a licence to marry. The sum of 2s was charged elsewhere in the Norton records for such a licence. In the manor of Park Bennett notes that 'many early fines for fornication were combined with licences to marry'.[74]

There is no evidence in Norton's records to indicate that any pregnancies or illegitimate births resulted from the activities for which leyrwite was levied. There are only two 'bastards' referenced (John Neweman in 1309/10 and Alexander Ward in 1358), neither of whom appear to have any connection with those amerced for leyrwite. Also there is little indication of there being any force involved. Indeed, on seven occasions both male and female parties were named, but the amercement requested was no higher than usual. Often the penalty was pledged by the male perpetrator or a male relative, sometimes named as the father, and in one instance, in April 1283, by a mother for her daughter. At Abbots Langley in 1244 it was levied on a father specifically 'for guarding his daughter badly'.[75] Whereas at Winslow only women were amerced, at Norton both men and women were amerced, suggesting there was not a consistent policy across all St Albans' manors. In Norton, eight out of the 66 amerced were men, some of whom were repeat offenders. In Park four instances of men being amerced were noted before 1350.[76] Only in Cornwall did Bennett find more men than women being amerced.[77]

Other than the fact that leyrwite was only levied on villeins, amercements for leyrwite do not appear to have been restricted to people of a particular level of social status: some offenders held land and buildings, whereas others were poor. It is noticeable that there were some family groups (eg In le Hale, Dipere) for whom it seems to have been almost customary to commit leyrwite. Some were repeat 'offenders' (eg Cecily Dipere, John Loveleg), while others were only mentioned in the Norton manorial records on the one occasion that they were amerced for leyrwite. The fact that an individual had been amerced for leyrwite

---

[74] J M Bennett, 'Writing Fornication', p146.
[75] Manuscript at Sidney Sussex College, Cambridge, quoted by Levett, *Studies in Manorial History,* p235.
[76] BL Add MS 40625 extracted by M Tomkins, 'The Manor of Park in the Fourteenth Century' in *The Peasants' Revolt in Hertfordshire, 1381* (Hatfield, 1981), p66.
[77] J M Bennett, 'Writing Fornication', p 144.

INTRODUCTION

does not seem to have prevented him or her from holding property, marrying or becoming an apparently well-respected member of the manor.

Population trends

Medieval records of Norton do not provide full lists of the people who lived there, and even the manor court records tend to focus upon the activities of the heads of households. However, despite these major drawbacks, it is possible to make some attempts at estimating the level of population at fixed points in the period 1244-1539, and to identify fluctuations around those fixed points.

Most of the population of medieval Norton depended for its livelihood upon agriculture. It did not have its own market (there were nearby markets in Baldock and Hitchin), nor much in the way of craft or industrial activity. Medieval towns tended to have larger populations than rural settlements, although most were still rather small and Hertfordshire was a county of small towns. Nigel Goose has estimated the populations of 22 towns in the county from one of the few reliable fixed points for such calculations, the Lay Subsidy of 1524/5.[78] Ten of the smallest of these towns had populations of less than 400; six were less than 300. So, from this crude baseline, we can probably assume that Norton was unlikely ever to exceed 300 people.

1086: Domesday records show that Norton had 14 villagers, five cottars, a Frenchman, a priest and a slave. In Rodenhanger, there was a virgate holder and a cottar. So, in the whole manor there were 24 heads of household (including the slave). Dyer in his recently published booklet on the history of nearby Caldecote applies a factor of five to this number (two adults and three children) which gives us an estimated population of 120 in Norton in 1086.[79]

1277: the court records include a list of contributors to the tallage of 1277. There were 32 contributors making payments of 6s down to 6d, the variations presumably based on size of holding. A few tenants who acquired tenements and other holdings in the years before the tallage do not appear on the list, but it is impossible to know exactly who was omitted and why (other than freemen, who would not be liable for a servile due). If we make a reasonable guess that around half as many again households did not feature, then there may have been around 50 households in Norton at that time. Using a factor of five per household would give us an estimated population of about 250 in 1277. If this

---

[78] N Goose, 'Urban growth and economic development in early modern Hertfordshire', in T Slater and N Goose (eds), *A County of Small Towns* (Hatfield, 2008), pp101-26.

[79] C Dyer, *Caldecote, Hertfordshire: A History of the Village* (Caldecote, 2010), p8.

INTRODUCTION

is correct, and it probably is the best 'guesstimate', then it represents a doubling of population in the 200 years from Domesday, a large increase but not inconsistent with nationwide population trends. Dyer wrote that by 1300 there were about six million people in England, about three times the total in 1100 and as densely populated as it was in the eighteenth century. 'Many of those who lived between the time of Domesday and 1300 experienced various types of economic growth. If they lived in the countryside they saw the number and size of settlements increase ...'.[80]

1307: the Lay Subsidy for Hertfordshire has been transcribed and published by the Hertfordshire Record Society (HRS).[81] The Subsidy was levied upon the personal property of the lay population. It shows 24 taxpayers for Norton whose payments range from 2s 6½d to 7¼d. In the book's Introduction it is stated that for the whole of Hertfordshire as many as two-thirds of householders may have been missed. This implies that there may have been 72 households in Norton in 1307 if the average for the whole of Hertfordshire were applied to Norton. If we assume five people per household this would result in a population of 360 which is too high an estimate because it would represent more than a 40% increase in population in just 30 years since the 1277 tallage.

Analysis of the court records during the period 1277-1307 shows mainly complete (not partial) transfers or inheritance of land. The courts also give a lot of attention to unauthorised leasing, but these were mainly half and one acre plots with no evidence of splitting of large holdings to accommodate an expansion of tenants in the manor. One instance does stand out: in 1294 the cellarer conveyed two cotlands with unproductive land to two new tenants. It is likely that the population in 1307 was a little higher than in 1277, but somewhere between 250 and 300, rather than the 360 figure calculated above.

1349: the Black Death. In the manor court records there is a remarkably long list of tenants who died in 1349. Analysis of the deaths of those tenants who held the largest land holdings allows us to estimate population figures before and after the plague. Although no 'Extent' exists which records the holdings of each tenant, it is possible to estimate the number of Norton's principal customary tenants, those with holdings of half a virgate (defined above under 'Agriculture'), by analysing each land transfer in the period leading up to the

---

[80] Dyer, *Making a Living in the Middle Ages*, p101.
[81] Brooker and Flood, *Hertfordshire Lay Subsidy Rolls*, p134; ibid, M Bailey, 'Introduction', pxxii.

INTRODUCTION

Black Death. There appear to be fifteen half virgate holders in 1349, seven of whom died that year. Their names are listed below:

Ralph and Agnes Albreth (separate holdings), John Bonde, Richard le Fuller, Walter Sayer, Helen Shepherd and Adam Ward were all half virgate holders who died in the year 1349. The following half virgate holders survived (date of acquisition of holding is shown in brackets): Richard Bate (1341), John Boueton (1343), Agnes Broun (1347), William atte Cherche (1341), Henry Cok (1337), John Dipere (1321), John in the Hale (1347), John and Agnes Oteway (1332).

Therefore, close to a half of the principal customary tenants, the half virgate holders, died in 1349. Levett baldly stated that Norton had lost 35 per cent of its population but there is no explanation of how she came to this view.[82] There were 29 tenants (27 different holdings) who died in autumn 1348 and the full year 1349. If that represented 35 per cent of the total, then it implies there were 83 tenants in the manor at the time. If each tenant was a head of household and each household on average consisted of two adults and three children, Levett's calculations would imply a population of over 400. As stated above, this suggests that Norton was one of the larger villages in Hertfordshire at the time – an unlikely assumption. More reasonably, we might conclude that there were just over 50 tenants, calculating a population of just over 250 before the arrival of the plague, and that it lost about 50 per cent of its population that year.

Numbers of tenant deaths recorded per decade (1244-1460): The manorial records do not give sufficient detail to enable family trees of tenants of Norton to be reconstructed and some heads of household disappear without trace. However, usually when a tenant died and his holding was passed to his heir the court does record that the former tenant had died. The schedule below shows the number of recorded deaths (including implied deaths such as when a tenant was said to inherit the land of his father):

---

[82] Levett, *Studies in Manorial History,* table after p284.

INTRODUCTION

Date	Tenant deaths	Date	Tenant deaths	Date	Tenant deaths
1244-1250	12	1311-1320	24	1381-1390	6
1251-1260	5	1321-1330	22	1391-1400	12
1261-1270	6	1331-1340	22	1401-1410	21
1271-1280	14	1341-1350	47	1411-1430[83]	10
1281-1290	14	1351-1360	15	1431-1440	7
1291-1300	10	1361-1370	13	1441-1450	8
1301-1310	19	1371-1380	10	1451-1460	2

There is no doubt that the 29 deaths from the Black Death show up as an anomaly in these figures, but it is difficult to draw any further firm conclusions. Deaths per decade show a marked increase in the period 1301 to 1340 and this would seem to coincide with national statistics which demonstrate a gradual population decline from the 1290s up until the Black Death, in particular in the years of famine and agricultural crisis in 1315-1322.

However, a slightly different view emerges if we examine the annual record of tenant deaths. Those years when there were more than three tenant deaths per year are shown below.

Date	Tenant deaths	Date	Tenant deaths	Date	Tenant deaths
1271	4	1315	4	1355	6
1273	4	1328	4	1361	5
1290	4	1333	6	1401	4
1295	5	1336	4	1403	5
1307	5	1349	27	1410	4

Although the year 1315 does figure in the above table there is no consecutive series of years which would point to a serious population decline in the village in the period 1290-1348.

Lower numbers of tenant deaths in the decades following the Black Death reflect the massive reduction in overall population, although the spike of 21 deaths in the decade 1401-1410 could well be attributed to further epidemics or

---

[83] Court records from 1416 to 1422 are missing so a 20-year period has been chosen.

INTRODUCTION

unusual food shortages.[84] The reduction in tenant deaths in mid-century may reflect a change in inheritance practice (passing on holdings as death bed or ante-mortem transfers) rather than a real reduction in deaths.

At the beginning of this Introduction, reference was made to archaeological discoveries in Norton which demonstrate that there were parts of the village which were abandoned during the medieval period. There is reference to the 'lost' village of Rodenhanger in the period 1100-1250, which because our records start in 1244 we are not able to corroborate. The Church Field digs provided evidence for an early fourteenth century desertion of a cob-walled building. The deaths per decade indicate slightly higher mortality rates in the early fourteenth century although the annual records do not suggest a step-change reduction in population. A more likely abandonment of settlements occurred following the Black Death in 1349. However, it is worthwhile remarking that throughout the whole of the period 1300-1350 the court records show no evidence of unclaimed holdings (even in 1349 there was only one instance of there being no heir to a tenancy). It is the court records in the century after the Black Death which document a manor in economic decline.

1350-1460: The estimated population of Norton after the Black Death had fallen to around 125, close to the number (120) estimated at Domesday in 1086. There does not appear to be much change in the numbers in Norton across this long period, and certainly no recovery. English population in this period was constrained by either lower fertility and/or high mortality rates, a problem made worse in Norton by some out-migration from the manor.

From 1350 there are regular lists of servile fugitives recorded in the court rolls. Hereditary serfs were not permitted to leave the manor for more than one year without their lord's permission, and the latter was usually granted by the payment of an annual fine for absence (chevage). The Norton courts mainly recorded presentments, and few payments of chevage were actually made. In the court of November 1350 five fugitives were reported and during the reign of Henry VI (1423-1460) 34 different fugitives from 17 families are identified. They reached increasingly diverse locations including: Bedfordshire (Bedford, Dunton, Edworth), Buckinghamshire (Edlesborough), Cambridgeshire (Chesterton, Litlington, St Neots, Willingham), Essex (Colchester), Hampshire

---

[84] 'Debilitating diseases such as tuberculosis and dysentery seem to have been widespread' (D V Stern, *A Hertfordshire Demesne of Westminster Abbey, Profits, Productivity and Weather* (Hatfield, 2000), p37). See also C Dyer, *Standards of Living in the Later Middle Ages* (Cambridge, 1989), pp267-8.

INTRODUCTION

(Southampton), and Hertfordshire (Baldock, Bygrave, Cheshunt, Cottered, Hitchin, Radwell, Shenley, St Albans, Wallington, Weston, Willian). In 1415 William Bate is listed as being a butcher in Baldock. Walter Boton, reported as a fugitive in Hinxworth, is recorded in 1423 as being 'beyond the seas', returning the next year in Colchester. His location then remained unknown before turning up again in Baldock and ending his days in Edworth (Bedfordshire) in 1453. In addition Stephen Flexmere is listed as a bow maker and John Marche as a weaver. Aside from this, there were records of servile fugitives who had had children, had been married and those who had died. We cannot know how comprehensive were these listings, but the court certainly recorded much interesting detail. The last mention of servile fugitives was in 1453, after which they abruptly disappear from the record. Significantly, 1453 is the same year as the last mention of permission to marry being given in Norton (merchet). The Abbey simply gave up tracing and enforcing personal servility at Norton in 1453. The administrative effort in recording and obtaining information about fugitives was hardly worth it, given that few were ever forced to return or paid any chevage to make the tracking worthwhile to the Abbey. Further research is needed to establish whether other manors on the Abbey's estate experienced the same change in 1453, and whether this was part of a deliberate estate-wide policy.[85]

Another, very crude, means of identifying broad population fluctuations is by evaluating the number of times that the court recorded that a tenement had been abandoned or left in disrepair. These are mentioned before the Black Death (the first recorded was in 1301 when John in the Hale was ordered to repair his tenement), but in the immediate period post 1350 these orders became more numerous. In 1359 this reached a peak when no fewer than six tenants were ordered to repair waste in their tenements under pain of a 2s penalty each. The courts continued to report tenants, some of whom had their holdings confiscated; for instance, in 1441 four tenants had their lands and tenements taken as they were 'totally wasted and flattened' (HALS: 65532, f1v). The court tried to counter the contraction in the housing stock of the manor by trying to force new tenants to rebuild dilapidated buildings on their holdings. For instance, in 1442, John Clerke the younger was granted lands and tenements under the condition that he should build a messuage within three years. In total there are about a dozen such references in the period 1244-1539, although some may have been orders to re-build an existing messuage.

---

[85] See Levett, *Studies in Manorial History*, pp235-247 and Noy, *Winslow Manor Court Books*, ppxxiii-xxiv.

INTRODUCTION

1460-1539: a paucity of records. Unfortunately, we have little evidence to help in assessing population levels in the period until 1530 as there are records from only three court meetings which have survived. However, we do have records for the final nine years to 1539.

In these last court meetings there is further evidence of orders by the court for tenants to repair their tenements but no indication that this was an endemic problem. The very first court in 1531 (HALS: 65535, f1) gives juror names at the View of Frankpledge, and there were 15 of them, which in itself was quite a healthy number. Juror numbers at subsequent courts ranged from 10 to 14. Over these last nine years there were only four deaths recorded despite each court on average reporting three or four tenant transfers. In more than half of cases the new tenant was an existing tenant who was expanding his land holding. Norton was becoming a manor of few tenants and they had large land holdings. This trend continues in our remaining Tudor records. That being the case, there was a growing number of sub-tenants who would not be mentioned in the manor court unless being amerced for wrongdoing.

It is difficult to assess the population level at this time, but nationally population was beginning to show decisive signs of upturn from the 1520s. A better understanding of the population of Norton in the sixteenth century requires analysis of parish records which become increasingly available towards the end of the sixteenth century.

Proximity to Baldock

Founded in the early 1140s by the Knights Templar, nearby Baldock was already a thriving town on a major route north out of London before the turn of the thirteenth century. A survey of 1185 reveals that it had 122 tenants, paying money rents rather than feudal services, 31 houses and seven shops.[86] Its growing population had been drawn from surrounding towns and villages, including Norton, no doubt attracted by the growing economic opportunities and entertainments on offer.[87] The *Victoria County History* records that there are references to six inns or public houses in Baldock by the mid sixteenth

---

[86] M Bailey, 'The economy of towns and markets, 1100 to 1500', in Slater and Goose (eds), *A County of Small Towns*, p54, citing M W Beresford, *New Towns of the Middle Ages. Town Plantation in England, Wales and Gascony* (1967), pp452-4.

[87] Between 1307 and 1524/5 the population is estimated to have grown from *c.*400 to *c.*500 inhabitants. See Goose, 'Urban growth and economic development' and Bailey, 'The economy of towns and markets'.

INTRODUCTION

century.[88] It had a regular market and an annual fair. Its townspeople benefited from both personal and commercial freedom, privileges that were not enjoyed by the villein tenants of Norton.

Unlike Hitchin, to the south of Norton, the town of Baldock was only a few hundred yards from the south-east corner of Norton parish. Two riots had taken place there in 1312 so it is hardly surprising that the Abbot of St Albans paid close attention to the dangers of its influence on his villein tenants.[89]

The manor court relentlessly pursued short term leasing of customary land without licence from the lord throughout the period 1244-1539, but residents of Baldock involved in this practice were singled out for special attention. In 1304/1305, three tenants were amerced for unlicensed leasing to people from Baldock. In 1328, no fewer than 13 tenants were named as having leased land to 'certain men from Baldock, therefore amerced'. Afterwards pardoned by the cellarer's grace, they were warned that if any of them were in future convicted of a trespass of this kind, they should give 40d to the lord, 'that is, if he demise to any free man without leave'. Three years later, Alexander Andrew was amerced 6d for demising half an acre of land to John le Kyld of Baldock. Similar distraint orders and amercements were repeated throughout the 1330-1360 period.

Baldock was a common destination for Norton's fugitives - the first, two of them, appeared in the records as early as 1273 (Ralph le Ferim and John Bene) but the numbers increased in the years after the Black Death.

The Abbot was not only concerned with the potential danger from unlicensed leasing of his land by freemen from Baldock and the disappearance of many of his villein tenants to the town. He was also moved to mention in the court about the behaviour of his villein tenants on their regular visits to Baldock's taverns; this was the source of a very specific decree made in Norton's court records in 1338 (HALS: 65513, f4):

> 'The lord has determined and ordained that if any villein tenants of Norton henceforward shall wound any of the villeins their neighbours with knives, swords or sticks or other weapons then he who has done so shall give 20s to the lord and satisfy the party wounded.

---

[88] *VCH Hertfordshire*, vol iii, p66, n6.
[89] These are recorded in the Patent Rolls: *Calendar of the Patent Rolls 6 Edward II*, part I (1894), pp535-41.

INTRODUCTION

Because the lord is given to understand that villein tenants of Norton go commonly to the tavern at Baldock and expend and waste there their goods and chattels to the grave damage of the lord and of those tenants there, the lord has appointed and ordained that in future none may go to the said tavern nor sit there wasting their goods under pain of a heavy amercement.'

The decree continued by ordaining that Norton's tenants should establish a common brewery in Norton and, for good measure, re-iterated that no villein should sell or demise any land or crops of corn to any of Baldock without the leave of the lord.

Surviving medieval documents of Baldock show that by the fifteenth century, some of Norton's tenants also had property in Baldock.[90] Thomas Poley and Walter Bradeway, two of Norton's farmers, were mentioned in Baldock feoffments in 1408-1419. Another feoffment in 1453, mentions Walter Clyfton, William Crane, William Freberne and John Wode, all of whom appear in the Norton court records from 1449-1460. Baldock worthy, John Wilcock, while Master of the Brotherhood of Jesus in Baldock, was accused of encroaching on demesne land in the 1464 court rolls. So, despite the best efforts of the officials at St Albans, it appears that from the early fifteenth century many of Norton's tenants were citizens of Baldock. Family ties with the town were also extensive and Norton inhabitants bequeathed cash, malt and barley to the church there.[91]

Family names of medieval Norton
It was only with the arrival of the Normans that inherited surnames came to be used and then usually only by the nobility. In the thirteenth century people in the Norton court records had quite varied christian names, 48 in total. However use of the names John, Stephen, Walter and William was proportionately very much higher than for example Geoffrey, Margaret, James and Richard. To distinguish, say, one William from another there was a need for further identification which led to the use of patronyms, that is the use of the father's personal or given name. Hence in Norton in 1244 we find John son of Richard and Alexander son of William. Occasionally the mother's name was used and in 1248 we have Alexander son of Emma.

---

[90] See Crellin, *Baldock's Middle Ages*, pp52-77, for translations of several medieval feoffments.
[91] See for example the wills of John Poley, 1436 (HALS: 1AR27r), John Catlowe, 1472 (HALS: 2AR11v), John Wynne, 1479 (HALS: 2AR34v) and William Cornelius, 1498/9 (HALS: 2AR93r).

However, patronyms still left opportunity for confusion and although they continued to be used until 1348 we find that the development of inherited surnames in Norton was well under way. The derivation of surnames can be seen to come from four main sources as follows:

Occupation: William the Reeve, Roger Shepherd, Walter the Muleward, Walter le Haiward, Richard Porcher (derived from the Latin *Porcarius* meaning swineherd), John Maltman, Matthew Thressher, Walter Taillour, William Bedell, Robert Cornemonger, William Bowman, John Coweherd, John Cartere, John le Dryver.[92]

Location: Agnes de la Grene, William at the Church, Stephen de Angulo, Osbert de la Hale, John Appulyerde, Matilda Attewatre, John Attewode, Alice Hyll.

Placename: William de Codicote, Cecily de Cherpenho, Richard de Newenham, Nicholas Bygrave, Hugh Aschwelle.

Nickname: Alexander Ruffus, Richard Redehede, John Cursefote, Robert Holdethypees (probably derived from 'hold thy peace'), Thomas Byg, James Halffhyde, John Loveleg, Alice Swetekin.

The court books record various spellings for Norton's surnames, sometimes even within the same court entry. Initially, many surnames were prefixed with 'de la', 'le', 'de' and 'atte' or 'at the' but by the early fifteenth century these prefixes had disappeared from Norton's records.

Despite a system of surnames it is still not easy to build up a family tree with any certainty as surnames were not always inherited as they are today. Daughters sometimes kept their father's surname when married although mostly the wife is simply recorded by her given name as being 'the wife of ...'. An example of family complexity starts in 1303 when Richard Bate inherited half a virgate of land from his father Osbert Reymond (*sic*). Richard then arranged for this parcel of land to go to his son John when he came of age. It seems unlikely that Richard's under-age son John is the same John Bate who in 1299 married without permission or the John Bate who in 1301 not only married without permission but outside the Liberty of St Albans. The Pledge for Richard Bate's transaction was another John Bate or possibly one of those who married without permission. In 1318 we learn that William, another son of Richard Bate, came after the death of his brother William and took the land which was once Osbert

---

[92] The 1307 Lay Subsidy lists only two Shepherds and a Reeve paying tax (Brooker and Flood (eds), *Lay Subsidy,* p134).

INTRODUCTION

Bate's. It seems that at least Osbert, father of Richard Bate, now carried the surname Bate.

In the manor of Norton where the mobility of its villein tenants was theoretically restricted, surnames do become fixed by the early fourteenth century and are seen to endure into the sixteenth century and beyond.[93] By the early part of the fifteenth century the last mention of three of the family names was as fugitives.

The following table lists some of these families:

First mentioned		Last mentioned	
Osbert de la Hale	1244	John Hale	1511
John Boueton	1244	Margery Boton	1436 fugitive
Agnes de la Grene	1244	Richard Grene	1411
William Bercarius or Shepherd	1244	John Sheparde	1427
Richard Reynold	1245	Thomas & John Reynold	1534
James Albred or Albreth	1245	John Albreth	1539
John Cok	1281	John Cok	1539 & beyond
Geoffrey Geiarde	1289	William & Helen Geiarde	1447 fugitives
Richard Bate	1297	William Bate	1423 fugitive
William Lawman	1395	Nicholas Lawman	1539 & beyond

Place names[94]

In the absence of any maps for medieval Norton, the manorial court records provide abundant evidence for place and street names, and also for their relative locations and adjacencies.[95] This enables us to piece together some aspects of the topography and layout of the parish in the late Middle Ages.

However, the records of the manor court provide place names used by the inhabitants of Norton. We know that there was a bridge called *Ford/Forthe Bridge* because the residents of Norton were complaining to the lord of the manor to undertake repairs. There was meadow land such as *Hallemede* and

---

[93] For a fuller discussion of the development of Hertfordshire surnames see Bailey, 'Introduction', in Brooker and Flood (eds) *Lay Subsidy*, ppxvii-xviii.
[94] A sketch showing some of the key features of medieval Norton and its surrounding parishes is shown on the front endpapers.
[95] The earliest detailed map of Norton c.1700 (HALS: 19336) is shown on the back endpapers.

INTRODUCTION

Longmede. Norton's landscape had numerous springs and ponds but modern water extraction has reduced this to two. However, the records only name *Somers pond* and *Bygraves pond*, both lying close to the Ivel Springs (there was a dispute as to whether *Bygraves pond* was outside the manor). Several properties are in, or close to, *Chirche Lane* (Church Lane beside St Nicholas' church) and therefore likely to be in, or near, the centre of Norton. The records refer to the *King's Highway* which is probably the Icknield Way, the ancient track stretching from East Anglia to Wiltshire that runs along Norton's southern boundary. There were a few named path/tracks such as *Oldbrach Way*, *Pulters Way*, *Stapel Way* and *Mede Way*. Deborah Giles has suggested that the path from the pond at the end of the present day Croft Lane north-east to Stotfold is the ancient Mead Way.

There was no medieval central or local authority responsible for the maintenance of roads. Upkeep of the king's highway was the responsibility of the Leet (Norton's View of Frankpledge), and the costs had to be borne locally. Funds were raised quite frequently through charitable bequests: for example Walter Ronall, in his will of 1471 (HALS: 2AR11v), left two measures of barley towards the *King's Highway*. The grain would be sold and the proceeds from the sale used to fund the cost of materials and labour for the necessary repairs. In 1515/16, Thomas Albreth (HALS: 2AR162v) left 'two loodes of stones to be layde in *Whytyng Lane*' and a further two 'in the strete betwixt my gate and the chirchgate'.

There are numerous examples of tenements being referred to by the name of the tenants. As an example, the court record of 1406 shows that John Boton was fined 6s 8d for committing waste in his tenement called *Botons*. There are several references to *Botons* over the next 125 years. Interestingly, in 1424 two tenements were called *Botons*. One was owned by William Cok senior, the other by William Colwelle and distinguished from the first as 'likewise called *Botons* at the end of the village'. In the Enclosure Award of 1798 there is a reference to Bootings Close, 200 yards on the left up from the church, which possibly relates to *Botons*.[96]

Another example is a tenement called *Bateslond* (Bates land). The court record of 1353 states that a Richard Bate was ordered to repair damage to his tenement called *Bateman*. The records show numerous transactions over the years but in 1430 *Bateslonde* was stated to lie close to another tenement called *Maltemannes*

---

[96] The Act of Parliament is dated 1796 (HALS: DP75/26/1); the map and award were inrolled 27 September 1798 (HALS: QS/E54).

lix

INTRODUCTION

(previously known as *Hathes*). Unfortunately, as with *Botons*, these are the only direct references to *Bateslond*, *Maltemannes* and *Hathes*. More often than not the records only sparsely record place names.

The earliest detailed maps of Norton appear in the 1700s.[97] These indicate the general layout of the manor and a few landmarks still surviving today, such as the Iron Age fort at Wilbury, the Icknield Way, the manor house at Nortonbury, the church of St Nicholas and the source of the Ivel. Wilbury was not mentioned in the records here and Nortonbury not until Elizabethan times.

The 1007 charter and 1086 Domesday survey mention a small manor called Rodenhanger. It is believed this was the abandoned settlement off Green Lane and absorbed into Norton manor after the eleventh century but before the court records began.

In 1335 permission was given for a house to be erected on a curtilage called *Ankerswyk*. Over the next 100 years it had many tenants and appears to be close to the graveyard and to the vicarage. The name lived on into nineteenth century manor court records as Andrews Wicks.[98]

In 1249 the records indicate that a meadow called *Pucsxethurne* had been partially enclosed while in 1458 the lord's meadow was described as *Pokesthorne*. Is this possibly part of what is now known as Norton Common through which the River Pix runs? An alternative view is that there is no relationship and that the name Pix is derived from Middle English *Piche* meaning a fish trap whereas *Puc/Pok* is derived from Puck, ie a goblin.

The court records show that the boundaries with Bygrave appear to be a source of contention, in particular *Mundencroft*, somewhere close to the Ivel Springs. The Norton parish boundaries may not have been the same as the manor and so possibly part of the manor lay in the parish of Bygrave. Medieval field names are not very common in the court rolls, and the references are discussed above. By the later sixteenth century there appear to be three fields in Norton, which is clearly demonstrated in the 1637 Norton Church Terrier.[99] Here the individual acres of glebe lands, assigned to the vicarage of Norton, are described for each of the three fields (the Little Field, Middle Field and Great or White Field). This

---

[97] In addition to those already mentioned *A Topographical Map of Hartford-Shire* by Andrew Dury and John Andrews, 1766 (HRS, 2004) is a very useful source.
[98] HALS: DE/X967/M2, court held in 1862.
[99] HALS: ASA3/1 and DP/75/3/1 with a transcript by H Wilton Hall in DE/X977/7. The transcription was published in the *St Albans Diocesan Gazette* vol 17 no 11 (Nov 1912).

INTRODUCTION

very detailed description gives not only the names the shott or furlong where the individual field strips were held but also the names of the neighbouring landholder, shott or furlong, track, baulk, etc on three neighbouring sides. These names include Runnalow shott, Wisell shott, Duck furlong, Rye furlong, Chosen Hills and Scotchin Hills. By the eighteenth century several maps give clear references to individual field names for example Rye Furlong, Wash Furlong and Miss Furlong on the northern boundary of Norton manor.

On the creation of Letchworth Garden City some place names have survived to be used in the naming of local roads in what was the ancient manor of Norton, for example Northfields, Southfields, Longmead and Hallmead.

The Manor court and Norton post 1539
After the Dissolution Henry VIII granted the manor of Norton to Sir Richard Williams, alias Cromwell, nephew of Thomas Cromwell, and great-great grandfather of Oliver in 1542.[100] A month later Williams sold it to John Bowles of Wallington.

In 1629 the manor was acquired by Richard Cleaver and remained with the Cleaver family until being sold to William Pym in 1680 for the sum of £6,707 10s. The Pyms remained lords of the manor for 223 years until in 1903 their lands, along with those belonging to the vicar, were sold to First Garden City Limited, who became owners of the entire parish and 'lords of the said manor', a title which The Letchworth Garden City Heritage Foundation retains, nominally, to this day. Manorial courts continued to be held until 1916.

During the process of Enclosure from 1796-8 Norton's landscape was changed for ever as new fields were created out of the strips once part of the former open field system. Access to the 70 acre pasture of Norton Common was granted only to the larger land holders, and the road system was modified, based on six new roads with a standard width of 40ft. The whole process cost £2,200, to which everyone had to contribute, the overseers settling up for those too poor to pay.[101]

The individual with the largest landholding at Enclosure was the lord of the manor, Francis Pym, who owned Nortonbury and an additional 530 acres. After Pym, John Pryor of Baldock held 354 acres. Robert Cleere Haselfoote, the

---

[100] The grant, dated 18 February 1542 is recorded on the Pipe Rolls (TNA: Pat33 Hen VIII, pt 6 m16 and a later copy at HALS: Acc 5172).
[101] A copy of the Enclosure award and map of 27 September 1798 can be consulted at HALS (HALS: QS/E54).

INTRODUCTION

rector, owned 10 per cent of the parish, including land that would become Standalone Farm, and received compensation for the loss of tithe the Act incurred. The vicar James Butterfield possessed the vicarage as well as glebe land around Croft Lane. The majority of the remaining land was owned by non-residents, and three plots were allotted to provide an income for Norton's poor.

By 1880, only three farms are marked on the Ordnance Survey map of Norton of that date: Paynes Farm, Standalone Farm and Willbury Farm.[102] Censuses throughout the nineteenth century show that Norton remained an agricultural community with the majority of men listed as agricultural labourers, or with specific roles such as shepherd. Straw was plaited and sold at Hitchin market to fuel the booming hat industry.

A decline in farming towards the end of the nineteenth century led to a lack of rural work. In addition, an increase in Italian hat imports reduced the demand for straw plait, and manufacture in both Bedfordshire and Hertfordshire decreased. These factors caused many residents to move to more industrial areas or emigrate altogether resulting in a steady decline in population.[103]

The twentieth century, however, would mark a turn in fortune for the declining parish. First Garden City Limited was registered in September 1903, with the ambition of bringing Ebenezer Howard's town-country hybrid theory to a reality, addressing the problem of depopulating rural areas and overcrowded towns.[104] Norton became the northern part of the Garden City estate. The site was planned as a whole and Norton was to maintain most of its agricultural lands, with the common also remaining as a 'people's park'. Housing plots were leased with terms to guarantee living and working standards which had previously been lacking. Under the 'lordship' of First Garden City Limited development was swift and just six years after the 1901 census, 1,300 people called Norton their home.

---

[102] Ordnance Survey 6 inches: one mile, surveyed in 1880, sheet VII.
[103] There were 403 inhabitants in the 1841 census but just 169 in 1901.
[104] Ebenezer Howard first published his ideas in *To-morrow! A Peaceful Path to Real Reform* (1898). *Garden Cities of To-morrow* followed in 1902.

INTRODUCTION

Editorial method

The Latin records have been translated into English keeping as closely as possible to the order and format of the original. Where Middle English, Early-Modern English and Old English words have been used in the text they have been shown in *italics*. Where the translation is unusual, the Latin word has been shown alongside in round brackets in italics.

The spelling of Norton place names and field names has been retained as in the original text and italicised. Other place names have been given as written with a modern rendering, if needed, given in square brackets. Christian names have been translated from Latin into the usual English forms, but the spelling of surnames has been retained as in the original (unless otherwise mentioned in the text).

Punctuation and capitalisation have been modernised. Square brackets are used whenever text has been inserted by the editor, followed by a question mark eg [chyrche?] if the insertion is doubtful. Where the translation is uncertain a question mark precedes the doubtful word eg [?chyrche]. Editorial comments shown in the text are in italics eg [*editorial comment*]. Where a gap has been left in the original text, it has been represented thus: [*blank*].

(Round brackets) and ~~deletions~~ used in the original text have been reproduced. If deletions are illegible they have been rendered thus: [~~*illeg*~~].

Bold text indicates lettering used for headings. The use of columns has been reproduced as far as possible as has the use of paragraphs marks which were used extensively in the original text to separate each entry. In the transcript an asterisk * has been used.

Superscript entries in the original have been placed after the name to which they refer eg John Albreth \4d/. All margin notes have been reproduced eg [*l. margin*: villeins].

Money: 12 pennies (12d) = 1 shilling (1s); 20 shillings = 1 pound (£1). All sums given in Roman numerals in the original text have been converted into Arabic.

INTRODUCTION

Abbreviations

BL	British Library
c.	circa
contd.	continued
f	folio
fem	feminine
HALS	Hertfordshire Archives and Local Studies
HHER	Hertfordshire County Council Historic Environment Record
HLF	Heritage Lottery Fund
HRS	Hertfordshire Record Society
illeg.	illegible
l.	left
LGCHF	Letchworth Garden City Heritage Foundation
NCAG	Norton Community Archaeology Group
NHDC	North Hertfordshire District Council
OED	*Oxford English Dictionary*
O/P	Out of print
r.	right
SRS	Suffolk Records Society
TNA	The National Archives (formerly the Public Record Office)
VCH	*Victoria County History*

RECORDS OF THE MANOR OF NORTON IN THE LIBERTY OF ST ALBANS, 1244 - 1539

The first folio of Norton's court book, beginning in 1244 (*HALS 65498, f1*).

HENRY III

[*HALS 65498, f1*] **EXTRACTS FROM THE ROLLS OF HALIMOTES HELD AT THE MANOR OF NORTON IN THE TIME OF KING HENRY, SON OF KING JOHN**

Halimote at Norton after Hokeday the 28th year of the reign of King Henry [*after 12 Apr 1244*]
* Walter son of William the Reeve gives to the lord for licence to marry 2s.
* John son of Agnes de la Grene gives to the lord half a mark for *gersumma*[1] for his father's land and for licence to marry, pledges John Boueton[2] and Osbert de la Hale.

Halimote at Norton on Saturday on the morrow of the Apostles Simon and Jude the 29th year [*29 Oct 1244*]
* Godfrey son of Ailric gives the lord one mark in *gersumma* for the land of his father and that he may have licence to marry so that he may be in the custody of his mother for four years, pledge Osbert de la Hale.
* William Bercarius[3] gives to the lord as *gersumma* 4s for the land of his father.

Halimote at Norton on Friday next before the Feast of St Barnabas the 30th year [*8 Jun 1246*]
* John son of Richard gives to the lord as *gersumma* for the land of his mother one mark and that he may have licence to marry.
* Ralph de la Grene gives 12d for marrying.
* Alexander son of William gives 12d to give his daughter in marriage.

Halimote at Norton on Tuesday next before the Feast of St Lucy in the 30th year of the reign of King Henry [*12 Dec 1245*]
* John Eve gives half a mark as *gersumma* that he may have the land that he

---

[1] *Gersumma* – frequently translated as entry fine, but here the Latin word has been retained throughout. The word is used both as a verb (*gersummare*) and as a noun (*gersumma*). D Noy in *Winslow Manor Court Books* adopts the translation 'paid a *gersum*' when the verb is used. But there are a number of instances in Norton's court books where no monetary sum is directly involved (for instance see alternative uses of the word discussed in footnotes 6 and 8 below).

[2] The surname Boueton is used throughout in this translation although the original may have occasionally been written as Boneton or Boveton.

[3] *Bercarius* meaning shepherd: the records use both words as surnames alternating between the two, sometimes in the same paragraph. This translation shows what was written in the original record.

HENRY III

took from Cecily daughter of William all the days of his life.
* Thomas son of Alfiene 12d, Ralph de la Grene 12d, Bartholomew de la Grene 12d, John Reymund 12d, William at the Church 12d, James Albred 12d, 2s [*sic*], are amerced because they did not plough the land of the lord as they ought to have ploughed it.
* William son of Stynh 2s, Richard Reynold 12d, Osbert Burre 12d are amerced because they did not come to the great boonday as they ought to have come, amerced.

Halimote at Norton on Thursday next after the Feast of the Apostles Peter and Paul in the 31st year [*4 Jul 1247*]
* Stephen de Angulo gives to the lord as *gersumma* for the land of his father 8s.
* James de la Grene gives to the lord for marrying 4s.
* William son of William gives to the lord for marrying 2s.
* Osbert son of John gives to the lord for giving his sister in marriage 6d.

[*HALS 65498, f1v*] Halimote there on Friday next before the Feast of the Apostles Simon and Jude the 31st year [*25 Oct 1247*]
* Walter son of Robert offered to the lord 10s that he may have an inquest of 24 men of Norton and Newnham concerning obtaining his right to a *ferthingate* of land which William son of William holds. Whether the same Walter has the greater right in the aforesaid *ferthingate* of land as he claims it or the same William as he holds it and he finds pledges etc.
* John son of Albred is amerced for his man retained a day from the great boonday 12d.

Halimote at Norton the day of St Leonard the 31st year of the reign of King Henry [*6 Nov 1246*]
* William de Codicote offered to the lord one mark that he may have a verdict of the two villages (*villarum*) of Norton and Newnham concerning obtaining his right whether he has the greater right in half a virgate of land which Alice de la Grene held or James who now holds it. By the pledges of John Eve etc. A day is given at the next Halimote.
* Richard Reynold is amerced for withholding the lord's work by the pledge of John the Bedell 6d.
* Alexander Ruffus is amerced for having married a certain woman without licence 2s.
* The cellarer put James de la Grene in possession of half a virgate of land which Alice de la Grene held to hold to him and his heirs and he gives seven marks as *gersumma* for which he finds as a pledge John son of William etc.

HENRY III

* William son of Thomas is amerced because he did not bring his son before the cellarer to place him in possession of a certain land as an agreement was made before the lord abbot 6d.
* The cellarer put William son of William in possession of one *ferthingate* of land which Richard Cristemasse formerly held so that the same William may have and hold the said land to him and his heirs and it is to be known that William his father shall build a messuage and cultivate the said land and shall grow corn on the same land.
* From James de la Grene a heriot of the value of 6s which the lord abbot took at the last (*extremo*).
* From Osbert in Angulo a heriot of 5s.

Halimote at Norton on Monday next after the Annunciation of the Blessed Mary the 32nd year [*30 Mar 1248*]

* Stephen son of John Buneton gives to the lord 20s as *gersumma* for his father's land.
* From the heriot of John Buneton 4s.
* Osbert son of Thomas gives 3s to the lord as *gersumma* for his father's land.
* Stephen, son of Stephen gives 6d to the lord for marrying a wife.
* Walter son of Walter gives 2s to the lord for marrying a wife. Pledge John Bedell.
* John son of William gives to the lord 12d for giving his sister in marriage.
* Richard son of Richard gives 12d to the lord for obtaining his right to a cotland of land with appurtenances in the village of Norton which Osbert son of Thomas holds, whether the same Richard have greater right to the said land as he claims it, or the same Osbert as he holds it. The villagers (*villata*) say that they do not know another heir of the said land than the said Osbert.

Halimote at Norton on Thursday next before Pentecost the above year [*4 Jun 1248*]

* All the villagers (*Tota villata*) of Norton and of Newnham except William the Reeve, Alexander son of Emma and Stephen Boueton say that it was agreed between William Thomas and Walter son of Robert under the ash tree (*sub fraxino*) in the Court of St Albans that the same William give his daughter with that *ferthlingate* of land which was in contention between them to the said Walter in order that he may [*HALS 65498, f2*] marry her so that the same Walter remain in the wardship of the said William and serve him and obey him and that he find necessaries for him and they say that the same William took him and they kissed to this agreement (*eo pacto osculati sunt*) and that he should remain with him until the age of his daughter should be the time for her

to be married and afterwards the same William rejected the said Walter and failed to keep the agreement with him whereof Walter complains. The cellarer by the decision of the Halimote put Walter in possession of the said *ferthingate* of land with the aforesaid daughter of the said William.
* William the Reeve 12d, Alexander son of Emma 12d, Stephen son of John 12d are amerced because they contradicted all the villagers concerning the verdict.

Halimote at Norton on Monday after the Feast of St James the 32nd year [*27 Jul 1248*]
* Osbert son of Thomas gives 12d to the lord for licence to take a wife, pledge William son of Stephen.
* William the Reeve is amerced half a mark because he purposed (*fuit in consilio*) to marry Alice Saere without licence from the cellarer.
* Ailberne gives 3s to the lord for giving his sister in marriage.
* Walter son of Robert is ordered to answer the daughter of William Thomas about half of a crop (*cruppi*) of land which he recovered to himself of the first year because she is not of full age, two loads of wheat and a load (*summa*) of barley.

Halimote at Norton the day of St Ethel[d]reda the Virgin the 32nd year [*23 Jun 1248*]
* Richard Porcher is amerced 2s because he did not come to reap at harvest, by the pledge of William the Reeve.
* It is ordered that William Everarde and Walter Gerarde be distrained for the want of a man in harvest, who defaulted at every other boonday.
* Stephen son of Osbert amerced 12d because he has not paid in full to his mother her dower, by the pledge of Reymund son of Walter.

Halimote of Norton at Newnham on Friday before the Feast of St Peter in Chains [*Advincula*] the 33rd year [*30 Jul 1249*]
[*r. margin*: in the same roll is contained another Halimote but nothing in it is noteworthy].
* Adam Gerard gives 2s to the lord that he may have permission to tarry at Baldock as long as the lord cellarer shall wish, paying *per annum* six horseshoes at Easter, pledge William de Norton.

Halimote of Norton at Newnham on Friday in the week of Pentecost the 34th year [*20 May 1250*]
* William Sprount surrendered into the lord's hand all his land and the cellarer gave seisin to Albereda sister of the said William of the said land performing

for it the due and accustomed service, and to the same William, as long as he shall live, at All Saints half a quarter of corn. Therefore the said Albereda gives 4s to the lord as *gersumma* and Robert son of Jordan married (*accepit in uxorem*) the said Albereda in the same agreement. Pledge brother John etc.
* Alexander Ruffus 2s, William of the Church 12d, William de Angulo 6d, Stephen de Angulo 12d, John the Palmer 6d, Hugh Heldere 12d amerced because their service with horse and cart was wanting at the granary.

Halimote of Norton at Newnham the day of St Martin the 34th year [*11 Nov 1249*]

* John son of Walter Morebred gives to the lord half a mark as *gersumma* for having his father's land and for licence to marry. Pledge etc.
* [*HALS 65498, f2v*] The wife of William Everard \5s/ the wife of Ralph Smith (*Faber*[4]) \5s/ the wife of Walter Gerard \5s/ are amerced because they sold ale against the Assize. [*l. margin*: brewers]
* The land of John son of Roger is in the hand of the lord with John the heir and his wife are two parts in the hand of the lord and the third part in Hugh Tenor's with the daughter.
* Ralph de la Grene and his companions accused about the meadow of *Pucsxethurne* give to the lord 10s to have peace that their lands may be divided by boundaries by the view of the sergeant and of law-worthy men.
* Osbert Burre gives 4s to the lord.
* William In the Hale gives 2s to the lord, Alexander Ruffus 12d, John son of Henry 2s, Walter son of Alice 12d that they may be exonerated from the office of reeve.

Halimote at Norton on Monday next before the Feast of St Dunstan the 35th year [*15 May 1251*]

* All the villagers of Newnham are amerced 10s for this that they said they were not bound to thresh provender except on the coming of the lord there.
* Eleven men of Norton give 12d to the lord for respite of the plea which is moved between them upon a certain plea of the lord abbot.
* James de la Grene is amerced 12d because he did not brew good ale as he ought.
* John Eve is amerced because he allowed to sell ale which was not good.
* John Bedell is amerced for the same and each of them is a pledge of the other.

---

[4] *Faber*: where the surname *Faber* has been translated as Smith, (*Faber*) is shown after the name. Later, the English word Smith or Smyth appears in the original text.

HENRY III

Halimote of Norton at Newnham in the Vigil of the Blessed Andrew the Apostle the 35th year [*29 Nov 1250*]
* Walter of the Cross is amerced 12d for taking a wife without the lord's licence. Pledge etc.
* All the villagers of Norton are amerced because they went to the great boonday house of the lord before the accustomed hour and without permission of the sergeant for which they are attainted by the reeve and by the beadle.
* Robert, son of William gives 6d to the lord for permission to let two acres of land. Richard son of Ralph gives 6d to the lord for permission to take them until the end of six years and he shall perform the due and customary service.

[*HALS 65499*][5] Halimote of Norton the day of the Holy Cross the 36th year of the reign of King Henry [*14 Sep 1252*]
* Geoffrey son of Geoffrey has given to the lord 5s for seisin of ten acres of land with appurtenances which his father held in the village of Norton.
* The same Geoffrey has given to the lord 12d for having an inquisition of two acres of land in the village of Norton.
* It is to be remembered that two acres which William of Norton has which Geoffrey, son of Geoffrey, claims by hereditary right in the village of Norton are in the lord's hand because they never did *gersumma*[6] in the Halimote. But because the said Geoffrey was bound to the said William in a certain sum of money, the said Geoffrey remitted to the said William the said two acres until the said money should be repaid but the said two acres were never otherwise let and this two of the villagers (*due villate*) say. They say also that the said two acres were never demised to the said William nor his heirs from the said Geoffrey and his heirs, upon their oath.
* William Bedell gave to the lord a mark for permission to *gersumma* his land to the use of his son.

[*HALS 65498, f2v contd*] Halimote at Norton in the Eve of the Blessed James in the 37th year [*24 Jul 1253*]
* William the Reeve has given 12d to the lord for having an inquisition against Stephen de Boueton about a certain ditch between them.

---

[5] This short insert fits into *f2v* but has been given a unique reference by HALS.
[6] The verb *gersummare* seems here to be used to mean the whole process of transfer in the manor court rather than just the payment of a fine or relief. At this court it is used as a past participle and a finite perfect tense verb, both with such a sense.

HENRY III

Halimote at Norton on Wednesday next before the Feast of the Blessed Michael in the 38th year [*23 Sep 1254*]
* Robert son of John has given 3s to the lord for seisin of his land in the village of Norton.
* It is to be remembered that the land which Walter son of Robert held is in the lord's hand.
* John Eve has given 12d to the lord for seven acres of land which he took until the end of four years which he took from Roesia rendering to the same Roesia half a quarter of wheat and half a quarter of oats between the Feast of Michaelmas and Christmas.
* Richard son of Richard has given 2s to the lord for seisin of his land in the village of Norton. Pledge Hugh le Tenur.

[*HALS 65498, f3*] Halimote of Norton on Friday next after the Feast of St Hilary in the 38th year [*16 Jan 1254*]
* Walter Smith (*Faber*) is amerced 6d because he went to another mill rather than his lord's mill.
* It is to be remembered that the land which was John the Palmer's is in the lord's hands.

Court at Norton on Thursday next before the 1st August (*gulam augusti*) the 39th year [*29 Jul 1255*] [*r. margin*: beware for Newnham]
* Walter Foliot has given to the lord 10s for licence to marry the daughter of Thomas Friday and he will give to the said Walter half an acre for the marriage settlement (*maritagium*) and all his land after his death and for this permission he has given to the lord 6d.
* Osbert in Hale has given to the lord half a mark for licence to marry Cristiana, daughter of Godfrey.
* Richard son of Ralph has given to the lord 2s for possession of two acres of land which he took hereditarily from Geoffrey Morebred and from Wymark his wife which land, *viz*, came from her and about which the same Wymark acknowledged before the whole court that henceforth she would never be able to demand any right to the same land for ever and the said Richard has given to Geoffrey and Wymark 10s and a half acre lies in *Pittelesand* and another half acre in *Wamingedane* in *Middelforlonge* and a half acre in *Greweisslade* and a rood between two roads and a rood in *Hordulfesmere*, paying annually 4d and a *bedripp* and a hen at Christmas .
* Walter Gerard, William Everard, Agnes Rolfes, William de Norton amerced because they brewed against the Assize. [*l. margin*: brewers]
* Richard Reinold has let land without the lord's permission so is amerced and

HENRY III

the crop (*vestura*) shall be seized into the lord's hands.
* John Albrid has given to the lord 3s for licence to marry.
* Agnes daughter of Gena gave to the lord half a mark seisin of the land of John her brother in the village of Norton giving annually to the said John half a load of wheat and two bushels of barley and a pair of linen sheets.

[*r. margin against blank space*: for Michaelmas term]

Court at Norton on Monday on the Morrow of St Dunstan in the 40th year [*1256*][7]

* John son of John gives 2s to the lord that he may stay wherever he shall wish until the death of his father and after his father's decease he shall come to the court and shall do for the land what pertains to the said land if he should wish to hold the said land and for making acknowledgment he gives to the lord abbot annually a pound of cumin and meanwhile he is given licence to take a wife whenever and wherever he may wish with free exit and entry.
* The jurors concerning an inquisition about two acres of arable land demised to Richard de Newnham by Edelina, wife of Ailbert, say that one acre was of the lands of Walter her son and that the same Edelina demised to the same Richard two acres of land in the absence of the said Walter her son for one mark to be acquired of the *gersumma*[8] of the said Walter. And that the said Edelina demised to the said Richard in the absence of Walter her son two acres of land. It is decided that the aforesaid Walter retain the aforesaid acre and the said Edelina satisfy the aforesaid Richard about his money.
* Martin son of James was put in possession of all the land which was of Gena, his father's sister, on condition that he should provide for the same Gena all the necessaries according to his ability and he gives to the lord abbot to have possession four marks, so *viz* that if the said Gena should wish to claim her third part thereof she shall do this without impediment or contradiction of the said Martin.
* [*HALS 65498, f3v*] Geoffrey Lambel claims against William de Norton two acres of land which were his father's in Norton whereof he died invested and seised. The same William says that Geoffrey, father of the said Geoffrey was bound to him in a certain sum of money and that for the said sum of money he quitclaimed the said two acres of land to the same William with the lord's permission. And concerning this he put himself on the inquisition. Afterwards came Geoffrey son of Geoffrey in the full court and granted to the same William all his right and claim for the said two acres of land for four

---

[7] An impossible date; none of the three Feasts of St Dunstan fell on a Sunday in 1256.
[8] *Gersumma* here seems to signify inheritance.

HENRY III

quarters of pure wheat to be paid to the same for four years at the Feast of St Michael in the first year and at the beginning of the term and for half a mark paid to the same Geoffrey in hand.
[*l. margin against blank space*: for Michaelmas term]

Court of Norton on Tuesday next before Hokeday the 41ˢᵗ year [*10 Apr 1257*]

Brewers
The wife of Hugh le Tenur	12d	
Walter Gerard	12d	amerced because they have brewed
Thomas Gerard	12d	against the Assize.
Ralph Pike	12d	
William Everard	12d	

* The pledges of Edith to do the services which her husband was accustomed to do, Adam Longus, Richard Sabright etc.
* William the Cowherd married without licence therefore amerced.

[*l. margin against blank space*: for Michaelmas term]

Court of the lord abbot at Norton on Thursday before the Feast of St Luke the Evangelist the 42ⁿᵈ year [*17 Oct 1258*]

* The Lady (*Domina*) Samot 12d, Agnes Rolfes 6d, Matilda wife of William Everard, amerced for breaking the Assize.
* William the Miller, Geoffrey Ponchard in default because they did not come.

Halimote of Norton on Tuesday the morrow of St Martin the aforesaid year [*12 Nov 1258*]⁹

* Roese who was the wife of Richard le Peystur finds her pledge Stephen in le Hale etc that she shall do for her dower the due and customary services which pertain to the said land which she has in name of dower.
* [HALS 65498, f4] From Richard Portario because he took a wife without the lord's licence 12d by the pledge of William de Norton.

Court at Norton on Wednesday next before the Feast of St Clement the aforesaid year [*20 Nov 1258*]

* John son of Henry gives to the lord 2s for licence to marry.

---

⁹ The 'aforesaid year' in this and the following heading appears to signify the calendar year 1258 not the regnal year 42 of Henry III, as the Morrow of St Martin only fell on a Tuesday in 1258, regnally the 43ʳᵈ year (28 Oct 1258 – 27 Oct 1259).

HENRY III

* The same John gives to the lord 2s for having an inquest concerning a third part of the land which the daughter of the said John claims in the name of dower against Richard de Herldon.
* Emma daughter of William gives to the lord 4s for having wardship of her son together with his land until the end of ten years and likewise for heriot.
* Ralph Pike gives 12d to the lord for seisin of one messuage which he took hereditarily from the lord doing the due and customary services so *viz* that when the term of the lord abbot shall pass from the land of William of Norton the said abbot in relation to the tenancy of the said messuage shall support the tenancy of the said Ralph against the said William because that tenement was of the demesne of the said William.
* Richard de Herldon gives to the lord 2s to have a verdict of two villages whether the said Emma ought to have dower of the third part of land or not and puts himself upon Norton and Newnham. Who having been sworn came to say on their oath that the said Emma cannot recover any dower against the said Richard because the husband of the said Emma in the time of his life was not seised and therefore she cannot recover her dower.
* John Eve gives half a mark to the lord for seisin of one *ferthingate* of land which he took hereditarily from William Pollard to himself and his heirs for ever.

Halimote at Norton on Wednesday after the Feast of St Matthew the 43rd year [*24 Sep 1259*] [*r. margin*: beware for Newnham]
* From Stephen de Angulo because he failed of his service in harvest by half a boonday 6d.
* From Walter Gerard because he refused his annual service of six men in harvest for which he was convicted by the inquest [*no amount*].
* Norton presents that Osbert son of Reymund, Richard son of Alrich, John son of William in Angulo and Alan son of William in Angulo are of sufficient age and fit to take land.
* From Felicia wife of Bissopp and her sister for having a decision whether they are their father's heirs or not for agreement[10] (*de fine*) 6d.
* From a certain heriot from Geoffrey White (*Albo*) of Caldecote 6s.
* From John son of Hugh 2s for *gersumma* of the land which was his father's 3s. Also from the same for heriot 12d.

---

[10] Not always followed by a monetary amount, *de fine* has been translated as 'for (or by) agreement' throughout. Later (from 1402) the word '*finis*' followed by a monetary amount was commonly used, and this has been translated as a 'fine'.

HENRY III

Halimote at Norton on Thursday after the Feast of St Margaret the Virgin the 44th year [*22 Jul 1260*]
* Walter Folioth was put in seisin of ten acres of land which were Thomas Friday's, so, nevertheless, that he should do for the said ten acres of land the due and customary services and he gives for having seisin by agreement 5s by the pledge of Richard le Honur.
* Thomas son of Adam takes with the lord's permission ten acres of land which he had bought for the use of his [*sic*] William now deceased to hold from the Feast of St Michael the aforesaid year until the end of 15 years next to come fully completed so that he shall do for the aforesaid ten acres of land the due and customary services and he gives by agreement for having seisin 5s.
* From Steven Boueton because he demised half an acre of land to Ralph son of Walter for a term of seven years without permission of the lord 2s.
* From Ralph son of Walter because he received the same land for a term without permission of the lord.
* Hugh son of John takes with the lord's permission all that land which was John Cursefote's, doing for the said land the due and customary services and he gives by agreement for having seisin 18d by the pledge of Walter the Reeve etc.

[*HALS 65498, f 4v*][11]
For the 45th year.
For the 46th year.
For the 47th year nothing notable.

[*HALS 65498, f5*] **Court held at Norton on Saturday next before the Translation of the Blessed Thomas the Martyr the 48th year [*5 Jul 1264*]**
* Alice daughter of John gives to the lord for *gersumma* of her land and for licence to marry 3s by agreement.

Halimote at Norton on Tuesday next after the Feast of St Martin the 48th year [*13 Nov 1263*]
* Robert le Paumer surrenders into the hand of the lord all the land which he held in Norton and the lord enfeoffs Christiana his sister according to the custom of the court. And the said Christiana shall do for the aforesaid land the due and customary services and she gives for having seisin 2s by the pledge of William the Firmarius and Walter Smith (*Faber*).

---

[11] This page is blank apart from ruled lines and notes as given in the left hand margin.

HENRY III

* Brewers, Agnes wife of Ralph 6d, the wife of Walter Gerard 12d amerced for the Assize of ale.

Halimote at Norton on Tuesday next after the Feast of Holy Trinity the 49th year [*2 Jun 1265*]
* William son and heir of William Thomas has surrendered into the hand of the lord and quitclaimed all his land to the use of William his brother. And he gives for relief and licence to marry half a mark by the pledge of John Bedell and William son of Stephen. [*l. margin*: lacking in the roll – (*defecti in rotl.*)]
* From William son of Stephen for licence to marry Alice who was the wife of William son of Thomas 4s.
* It is to be remembered that Walter son of Walter received from the lord unto him and his heirs all the land which was Ralph Bercarius's and he has licence to marry and he gives for seisin 12d and he will do the customs and services etc by the pledge of John Bedell and Walter le Haiward.

Halimote of Norton on Friday next before the Feast of the Apostles Philip and James the 50th year in the time of the Lord Walter de Wylum cellarer [*30 Apr 1266*]
* Petronilla who was the wife of Walter son of Hugh came and took the land which was of the same Hugh her husband until the coming of age of Walter her son, heir of the said land performing for it all the services etc and her having this farm she gives one mark and if it should happen that the aforesaid heir shall die under age Petronilla shall hold the said land until Stephen her younger son, brother of the aforesaid Walter, who shall be the heir of the aforesaid land, shall come to full age.
* Walter son of Walter Paselewe came and relieved the land of his father and he gives 12d for relief and he gives for increase in rent[12] as much as his father gave 4d at the manor (*ad Manerium*) at Easter and at the Feast of St Michael.
* William Godynow, Osbert son of Reymund and Godfrey Alvered came and surrendered into the lord's hand three small pieces of land and the lord enfeoffed William son of Stephen with the said land and he gives for seisin four capons.

Concerning Michaelmas term.
* Adam Longus for licence to give in marriage Wymark his daughter gives to the lord 2s.

---

[12] This is the first of many entries and margin notes (*incremento redd* or just *increm*). An alternative translation 'rent from increment' is explained in the Glossary.

HENRY III

* William Godynow gives 6d to the lord to have a verdict of 12 about a certain ditch which is between him and William Seeman and it is ordered to have an inspection of that ditch etc and that there be a tour of that ditch with the sergeant etc.

[HALS 65498, f5v] **Halimote at Norton on Wednesday the Octave of the Apostles Peter and Paul the 51st year [*6 Jul 1267*]**
[*l. margin*: nothing noteworthy].

Halimote at Norton on the Morrow of St Hillary the 51st year [*14 Jan 1267*]

* Stephen son of Stephen gives to the lord for licence to marry Joan daughter of Stephen in the Hale 4s.
* William son of Walter gives to the lord for licence to marry a certain woman of *Clahale* [Clothall] 4s.
* William son of Stephen gives to the lord 6d for licence to marry.
* Walter Sigar and Richard Jacob took half a virgate of land which was Walter Ailbern's excepting two acres which Richard de Newnham holds until the end of the next 14 years and they shall do for the said land the due and customary services.

Halimote of Norton on Tuesday next after the Octave of St Michael the 52nd year [*9 Oct 1268*]

* Stephen del Hale has licence to marry Emma daughter of Stephen and gives 3s.
* The jurors represent that William Everard withdrew a certain man at one boonday in harvest therefore he is amerced and it is ordered that he be distrained. Gilbert son of Reymund finds his pledges Ralph atte Grene and John le Bedell that he will build on the lord's land before next Easter and he will pay his expenses (*attractum*)[13] out of his own chattels.
* Thomas Hathewis found a pledge, *viz* Hugh le Dryver, that he will do due service for his tenement etc.

Halimote of Norton on Wednesday next after the Feast of St John before the Lateran Gate the 52nd year [*9 May 1268*]

* All the villagers represent that William Everard ought to find a man at every other boonday and he has withdrawn this for a long time and therefore let him

---

[13] Expenses: Latin *attractum*, haulage or haulage service, the major expense in building a new house.

HENRY III

be distrained for arrears.

Halimote of Norton on the morrow of St Leonard the 53rd year [*7 Nov 1268*]

* John who was the brother of Richard Black came and *gersummavit* the land of his brother and he is thereof seised by doing due service and he gives for seisin 12d, pledge John Cotman.
* From Osbert son of John for giving his daughter in marriage by agreement 12d.
* It is agreed between William Sprount and Albreda his sister that the same William granted to his said sister all that land which should fall to him by inheritance paying therefore annually to the said William two bushels of corn at the Feast of St Michael as long as the aforesaid Albreda shall wish to have and hold the said land.
* Juliana who was the wife of Ralph Blak has granted to John Blak all that part which fell to her in the name of dower so that the same John shall pay annually to the said Juliana one bushel of wheat at the Feast of St Michael. He shall not pay anything at the Feast of St Michael next coming but after that Feast he shall pay the said bushel by pledge of Ralph the Reeve.
* It is ordered that William Everard be distrained for the arrears of his service at harvest and it is presented that the same William ought to find one man at every other boonday and he has withdrawn this, therefore etc.
* Godfrey de la Hirne married without licence, therefore he is amerced 3s. [*l. margin*: Concerning Easter term]

Halimote of Norton on Tuesday next after the Feast of St Luke the Evangelist the 54th year [*21 Oct 1270*]

* William son of Walter has licence to marry Agnes daughter of Stephen del Hale and he gives 12d for licence.
* [*HALS 65498, f6*] Mabel Bofot is seised of the whole tenement which was of Geoffrey her brother's which she has by the gift of the same Geoffrey by the due and customary services and she gives for seisin 6d and it was testified by Lord Reyner, the cellarer, that the said Geoffrey gave the said tenement to Mabel his sister at St Albans by the pledge of John Bedell.
* John son of James and Edith his wife are seised of four acres of land which belonged to Edith's father and lie upon *Druyenhull*, rendering therefore annually to the lord 2s and they give the seisin 2s, pledges Ralph atte Grene and John Reymund.
* Osbert son of John put himself amerced 6d because he did not do his works at harvest as he ought to have done, by pledge of Ralph atte Grene.

HENRY III

* Let William Everard be distrained for the many arrears which are behind at the lord's boondays in harvest.
* William Godeynow has not come, therefore let him be distrained and to the maximum for his ploughing which is behind.

Concerning the same term, on Friday next before the Apostles Simon and Jude [*24 Oct 1270*]
* It is ordered to distrain William Everard for many arrears of one man at the lord's boondays in harvest.
* Walter Gerard shall do one work and for default of one man in autumn which he made, therefore amerced.

Halimote of Norton, on Monday next after the Feast of St John before the Lateran Gate in the 54th year [*12 May 1270*]
* Edith who was the daughter of John son of Henry came and *gersummavit* the land which was her father's and has seisin thereof for the due and customary services and she gives 2s to have seisin by the pledges of Martin Geve [*or Gene*] and Hugh le Dryver.
* Hugh son of Alfred (*Alueredi*) came and *gersummavit* the land which was his father's doing for it the due and customary services and he has seisin thereof. He has licence to marry and gives 3s by the pledge of William son of Stephen.
* William in le Hale came and surrendered into the lord's hands the whole tenement which he held from the lord to the use of John his younger son and the lord put the same John in possession doing for it etc. He shall keep his father as he shall best be able and both for seisin and for heriot of the said William he gives by agreement 18s. Pledge etc.
* John in le Hale gives 12d to have an inquest *viz* concerning how much land belongs to his tenement.
* William Everard is distrained for arrears of service in harvest one man having been withdrawn from every boonday of the lord.
* Walter Everard surrendered into the lord's hand a certain messuage with its croft to the use of John de Norton and the same John has seisin thereof doing the services due and customary for it and the said Walter gives 12d by agreement by the pledge of the said John.

Halimote of Norton on Thursday next after the Feast of St Mark the Evangelist the 55th year [*30 Apr 1271*]
* Inquisition concerning the service of the land which William Everard at one time held and who should be the next heir of the aforesaid William, by John Bedell, John son of Richard, Walter le Neweman, Ralph atte Grene, William

HENRY III

son of Stephen and William atte Chirche, who say upon their oath that William Everard held eight acres of land, one rood less, which Everard his father purchased from the abbot's demesne but whether he has a charter thereof or not they do not know and he pays for it annually 6s 2d. Next they say that the same William held on the other hand half of one croft containing three acres and half of one messuage for 12d yearly and one boonday with ale and another boonday with water. Next the same owes 1d *per annum* for the front of a certain house which abuts on the King's highway (*regiam viam*). And [he owes] suit at the Halimote just as others of the abbot's manor [do] and he owes heriot.

* Edith daughter of John Henry surrendered into the hands of the lord two acres of land and the lord enfeoffed John the Sergeant with the aforesaid land according to the form of the Halimote, paying for it 12d *per annum*.
* Stephen son of Martin gives to the lord 12d by agreement for licence to marry where it shall seem better to do it.
* Thomas Roberd and Adam in the Hale give 6d to the lord for making an exchange of one rood of land.
* Richard son of Hugh the Helder came and relieved the land of his father and gives for having possession of it one capon and another for licence to marry.
* Thomas son of Robert surrendered into the hand of the lord one acre and a half of land and the lord enfeoffed Richard the Reeve of Newnham with it, for performing the due and accustomed services for the aforesaid land. And it is to be known that two roods abut upon *Canmanweye*. Next another rood upon *Ordelesmere* and it abuts upon *Amedich*. Next half an acre lies in *le Dene* and it abuts on *Kokeshavedland*. Next one rood [lies] upon *Longeland*. And he gives 2s for having possession.

[*HALS 65498, f6v*] Halimote of Norton on Thursday next after the Octave of St Martin in the 56th year [*19 Nov 1271*]

* John the son of James *gersummavit* the land of his father and gives to the lord for having entry and for having licence to marry half a mark.
* John Stiward gives to the lord for having licence to marry wherever he shall wish one mark by the pledge of Stephen atte Grene and John Bedell and for *chevage* annually at Christmas two capons (*altilia*).
* William Everard *gersummavit* the land of his father and gives for relief 7s 2d.
* William son of Stephen gives to the lord 12d for licence to give his sister in marriage.

HENRY III

(*HALS 65498, f6v*) The final folio of the courts held in the reign of Henry III.

HENRY III

Halimote of Norton on Wednesday next before the Feast of St Dunstan in the 56th year [*18 May 1272*]

* The jurors present that William son of William Stephen has demised one acre of land to Thomas le Spicer without permission, therefore amerced.
* The same say about Nicholas le Newman because he demised half an acre.
* The same say about William Godinohow because he demised five roods, so etc.
* The same say because William de Hexstanston demised half an acre, so etc.
* The same say that Osbert de la Hale demised one rood, so etc.
* The same say that Thomas Hathewis demised one acre, so etc.
  It is ordered that the same land [*relating to above six bullets*] be taken into the lord's hands and that all the aforesaid be amerced for unlawful leasing.
* Scolastica who was the wife of Robert le Cornemanger came and acknowledged that she holds from the lord abbot by military service and that her heir shall be in the lord's wardship until he shall come to full age.
* From brewers at the View of Frankpledge 6d.
* John del Hale surrendered into the lord's hands one acre of land which lies in *Wysoverhull* and John de Norton is seised thereof by doing etc.
* From the brewers of *Wylie* [Willian] 12d.

Halimote of Norton on Wednesday next before the Feast of St Martin the 57th year [*9 Nov 1272*]

* It is testified concerning the whole Halimote that Roger son of John at some time came into the full Halimote and *gersummavit* the land which was of John son of Henry as next heir for 4s. And afterwards the same Roger withdrew and did not wish to hold the said land nor did he pay the said 4s, but let it lie uncultivated. Afterwards the lord came and took that land into his hand both for work and for other services which were in arrear from the said land. And the lord has seised William son of Reymund of the said land to hold to him and his heirs according to the custom of the Halimote doing for it the due services etc and he has licence to marry.
* From Stephen son of Bartholomew for licence to marry 12d by agreement. From Matilda atte Grene for the same 12d.
* William Everard has not come, therefore let him be distrained.

EDWARD I

[*HALS 65498, f7*] EXTRACTS FROM THE ROLLS OF HALIMOTES IN THE TIME OF KING EDWARD I

Halimote at Norton on Tuesday before the Feast of the Apostles Simon and Jude in the 1st year [*24 Oct 1273*]

* John son of Osbert Burre came and relieved the land which was his father's and he gives for having seisin half a mark. Pledge Saer son of Richard.

Halimote of Norton the day of the Finding of the Holy Cross in the 1st year [*3 May 1273*]

* Stephen the Clerk who was the son of Hugh le Driver came and *gersummavit* the land which was his father's and he has seisin thereof by doing the services thereof due and accustomed and he gives 5s.
* Roysia who was the wife of William Everard came and *gersummavit* the land which was the same William's to the use of William his son and he is seised thereof doing for it the due and accustomed services. And the aforesaid Roysia shall have the said land until the full age of the said William and she gives 8s. And she shall maintain the buildings and all other things and she shall do all the services etc nor shall she commit waste. By the pledge of Walter Amphibal[14], etc.
* Joan who was the wife of Stephen took the land which was her husband's until Agnes, daughter of the same Stephen, shall come to full age, doing the due and accustomed services for it. And the said Joan has licence to marry and she shall maintain the houses and buildings, nor make waste, by the pledge of John del Hale, Walter the Reeve and Walter, son of Walter and she gives for the term 3s.
* Stephen son of Osbert surrenders into the lord's hands all his tenement to the use of William his son and is seised thereof, doing for it the due and accustomed services. And he gives both for seisin and for heriot 4s. And the aforesaid William shall keep Stephen his father and shall find all necessaries for him according to his ability.
* Ralph le Ferim villein of the lord abbot remains at Baldock.
* John Bene, villein of the lord abbot remains there, and it is ordered to distrain their chief pledges because they are disobedient.

---

[14] *Amphibolus*: Latin for a cloak or overall. The remains of the priest St Amphibalus, executed *c.* 304 at St Albans were 'miraculously' discovered in Redbourn in 1178 (*VCH Hertfordshire* vol 4 p416).

EDWARD I

* Walter Hasel, John Cappe and Walter Michel have made agreement[15] for one mark for relief of the land which was of Ralph de Bekeneswell as heirs of the said Ralph and they did fealty before the Halimote.
* From the brewers because they broke the Assize 12d.
* *Wylie* [Willian]. From the brewers of Willian for breaking the Assize of ale 18d.

Halimote at Norton on Thursday next before the Feast of St Denis in the 2nd year [*4 Oct 1274*]

* John son of Stephen Boueton of Norton for *gersumma* of his father's land and for licence to marry gives two marks to the lord. And Margaret, mother of the son John gives to the lord 2s for wardship of the land of the same John for six years and the aforenamed John son of the said Margaret by the plighted faith of the said Margaret finds two pledges to observe this faithfully. And the said Margaret has granted to the same John the produce of one acre for the aforenamed period by an agreement begun between them.

Halimote at Norton on Saturday next after the Feast of St Mark the Evangelist in the 2nd year [*28 Apr 1274*]

* Stephen son of Alice is enfeoffed by the cellarer with one messuage and 12 acres of land which was John Reymund's and he gives to the lord 2s for having entry.
* Richard son of Adam le Kynge gives to the lord 12d because he allowed the daughters of John de Caldecote to leave his house out of the land of the lord abbot without permission of the lord.
* Memorandum concerning the heriot of William Saman *viz* one horse worth 3s.[16]
* Joan, relict of William Saman took the land which was her husband's to hold until William his son and heir should come to full age etc and she gives for the term 12d and he shall pay *gersumma* etc.
* John the Heyward has surrendered etc all the land which he had in Norton and Katherine his daughter is seised thereof, doing etc, and she gives 12d.
* Hugh son of Ailric has a postponement until the Feast of St Michael to build a certain house upon his messuage under penalty etc.

---

[15] *Facire finem* or other variants of the verb appear in the records usually without a monetary amount so have been translated as 'made agreement'.

[16] This and the following three bullets are repeated on *f7v*, the Halimote of the 3rd year, so have been deleted from *f7v* except for the one marked ** as the wording differs.

EDWARD I

[*HALS 65498, f7v*] **Halimote of Norton on Tuesday after the Feast of St Dunstan in the 3ʳᵈ year [*21 May 1275*]**
* Joan relict of William Saman has taken the land which was her husband's to hold until William her son and heir should come up to full age. She gives 12d for having the term and she shall maintain in the meantime the houses etc in as good condition etc by the pledges of William le Neweman and Walter le Hayward. **
* From the brewers of Norton for breaking the Assize of ale 12d. From the brewers of *Wilye* [Willian] for the same 18d.

Halimote of Norton after the Feast of St Michael in the 4ᵗʰ year [*after 29 Sep 1276*]
* John le Bedell surrendered into the hand of the lord half of his land with half of the messuage and John Godinogh is seised thereof, doing the due and accustomed services for it and he gives for seisin 2s.

Halimote of Norton on Monday next after the Octave of Easter in the 4ᵗʰ year [*13 Apr 1276*]
* Walter le Neweman took the land which was Stephen's the son of Stephen except the dower of the said land to hold from the Feast of St Michael next to come until the end of the next seven years but he shall begin now to plough (*warettare*) and he shall maintain the buildings and shall do for it the due and accustomed services. So that the next heir if he shall not wish to have the said land shall answer to the said Walter or his heirs at the end of the said term for all costs, etc.
* John Jacob has taken the land which was John le Paumere's to hold in the aforesaid way.
* Ralph atte Grene has taken John le Balker's land by the agreement of the same John until the end of four years on the abovewritten conditions.
* William son of Walter has taken le Cane's land until the end of seven years upon the abovewritten conditions.
* Stephen son of Bartholomew has taken the land that was of Thomas Hathwis with the consent of the same Thomas, to hold it for seven years upon the abovewritten conditions.
* The land which was Steil's is conveyed to William del Hale to hold it for seven years in the aforesaid manner.
* Thomas Bene is seised of the whole tenement which was Agnes le Camester's, to hold it to him and his heirs according to the custom of the Halimote, doing for it the due and accustomed services.
* Richard Bonde has licence to marry Alice daughter of Hugh.

EDWARD I

* Walter son of John came and *gersummavit* the land which was his father's and was seised therein, performing for it the due and accustomed services, and he gives half a mark.
* From the brewers of both *Wilie* [Willian] and of Norton, four, 6d.

Halimote of Norton on the Feast of St Michael in the 5th year [*29 Sep 1277*]

* From Isabel daughter of James for licence to marry 2s.
* John de Boueton for the same 4s.
* From Godfrey le Neweman that he may not have a wife against his will 4s. Nor any land because a clerk.
* John de Norton took land which was William Smith's (*Faber*), to hold it at farm from this Feast of St Michael until the end of ten years next to come paying for it annually 4s. For shoeing horses of the manor of Norton at two terms of the year, *viz* at Christmas 2s and at Easter 2s.

Tallage:

Margaret de Boueton	3s	Stanfibel	6d
Walter le Newman	2s	Stephen Dame	6d
Bartholomew Reymund	12d	William Reymund	6d
William son of Stephen	12d	Hugh Tater	6d
Nicholas le Neuman	2s	John Iseud	6d
John Aubre	2s	John in le Hale	6d
John Alexander	6d	William in le Hale	18d
Joan Saman	6d	Stephen Ass	3s
Walter Godinhou	6d	Godefrey	6d
Ralph the Reeve	5s	Henry de Neuham	6s
John Burre	6d	Geoffrey le Messer	12d
William Bigge	6d	Martin Osbert	18d
William son of Walter	4s	Adam in le Hale	3s
Saher	4s	Richard Reymund	6d
William of the Church	2s	John Jacob	18d
Stephen son of Ralph	6s	Richard Bonde	6d

[*HALS 65498, f8*] **Halimote of Norton after Easter the 5th year [*after 28 Mar 1277*]**

* William Keghard by the consent of Agnes his wife and Nicholas de Hexston have exchanged alternately half an acre of land.
* The same William and aforesaid Agnes by unanimous assent and will came

EDWARD I

into the full court and surrendered into the lord's hands 4d annual rent issuing from half an acre of land which lies between the croft of John Auber and the croft of Nicholas of Hexston and the same Nicholas is seised thereof, doing the due and accustomed services.

Halimote of Norton after the Feast of St Michael the 6th year [*after 29 Sep 1278*]

* Alan son of William came and *gersummavit* the land of his father, doing for it the due and accustomed services, and gives for seisin half a mark.

Halimote of Norton on Thursday after the Feast of Pentecost the 6th year [*9 Jun 1278*]

* John son of Godfrey *gersummavit* his father's land and gives to the lord for having seisin and for licence to marry 2s.
* Stephen Dame amerced because he married without licence 6d.
* William Gerard is ordered to be distrained because he has not come and because he demised land to Thomas Le Spicer without permission.
* William Bigge demised land to John le Chapman without permission, therefore amerced 6d.

[*r. margin against blank space*: for Michaelmas term the 7th year]

Halimote of Norton on Thursday next after the Octave of Holy Trinity in the 7th year [*8 Jun 1279*]

* Lucy who was the daughter of Albred surrendered all the tenement she had in Norton, so that neither she nor etc whosoever, sworn, etc.
* The land of *Gaffe* [?Gasse] is leased (*tradiditur*) to William in le Hale for six years, doing for it etc.
* Osbert Pusse has surrendered into the hands of the lord all the land he held in Norton and it is decided to distrain John son of Osbert to come and hold that land.
* From Hugh son of Hugh le Coverour because he married without licence of the lord 6d.

Halimote of Norton on the Feast of St Michael in the 8th year [*29 Sep 1280*]

* The lord demised to Ralph the Reeve and John Jacob the tenement which William Godynowe held, to hold it from the Feast of St Michael which is now until the end of six years, doing for it the due and accustomed services.
* The same day the lord demised to Stephen son of Bartholomew for four years the tenement of *Katelote*, doing for it etc.

EDWARD I

Halimote of Norton on Thursday next after the Feast of St Edmund the King the 8th year [*23 Nov 1279*]

* Ralph le Nadelere was arrested to answer to the lord abbot concerning a suit withdrawn for two years at the *alebederepe*.[17] And Ralph came and says that he never made any suit nor ought to make any nor does he wish to put himself upon [the mercy of] a jury, because he is a free man. But the cellarer by virtue of his office held an enquiry and the jurors say that that tenement was accustomed to make that suit, therefore a day is given to him at St Albans at the next court.
* From William atte Chirche because he married his daughter without licence of the lord amerced 6s.
* John Isoude has taken the land which was Osbert Pusse's, doing etc, and gives for having entry together with licence to marry 12d. And he has found pledges that he will maintain it, *viz* John Isoude and John son of Alexander.

[*HALS 65498, f8v*] **Halimote of Norton on Wednesday next before the Feast of Pentecost the 8th year [*5 Jun 1280*]**

* William son of Walter came and *gersummavit* his father's land, doing for it etc, and he gives for having entry together with licence to marry 10s.
* John son of Henry of Brantefeld gives for having an inquisition about one half acre of land and one cottage which Richard le Porcher and his wife held 12d, pledge Richard Partrich of Brantefeld. The inquisition comes and says that John has no right or claim in the aforesaid cottage and land but says it is an escheat of the lord abbot because the mother of the said John whose heir he is was endowed from her father's house with chattels, etc.
* Osbert Reymund, John son of Godefrey and Walter Godeynogh hold a certain tenement which owes to the lord abbot ½d *per annum viz* at Christmas and is three years in arrears; therefore they are all amerced 6d.
* From Robert Leg for licence to marry Mabel de Hexston 6d.
* From William de Boueton 12d and Geoffrey Gegard 6d amerced because they married without the lord's licence.
* The land of John Godynogh has been in the lord's hand for three Halimotes and it is decided by the court that it is the lord's escheat and that the lord may seise whomever he will thereof. And he has enfeoffed John Sayer therein, he doing for it the services and customs, and he gives for seisin 12d.
* Godfrey Neweman has taken all the land of John le Balker which he had in the field of Norton from the Feast of St Michael the 8th year of the reign of King Edward until the end of six years next following fully completed, doing etc.

---

[17] *Alebederepe*: a *bedrip* or boonday with ale provided as refreshment.

EDWARD I

And he gives for having the term 12d.
* John son of Godfrey has exchanged one acre of land with Walter son of John for one rood in a certain field and they give for permission to exchange 12d.
* 12 jurors of Norton present that Margery de Norton is more able to hold her father's land and the same Margery came before the Lord R de Gravele then cellarer and made agreement for one pound of cumin to be paid yearly at the abbot's chamber so that the said Margery be quit of that demand concerning the said land and that she may stay where she will and marry without the permission of anyone and in order to confirm this agreement for the future she has given 20s to the lord abbot.

Halimote of Norton after Easter the 9th year in the time of Brother John le Marynes [*after 13 Apr 1281*]
* William le Neweman came and *gersummavit* the tenement of his father and is thereof seised, and gives for agreement 5s.
* Agnes atte Chirche *gersummavit* the tenement of her father and is thereof seised, doing etc, and has licence to marry, and gives 3s.

Halimote of Norton on the morrow of St Edward in the 9th year – John Marynes cellarer [*1281*][18]
* Walter Aubre because he has married without licence, amerced 12d.
[*l. margin*: villein (*nativus*)][19]
* John Cok surrendered into the lord's hands one messuage and one acre of land.

[*r. margin against blank space*: lacking in the roll]
[*l. margin:* Of the 10th year nothing notable]

Halimote of Norton on Tuesday next before the Feast of the Apostles Philip and James in the 11th year [*2 Apr 1283*]
* Godfrey de Hexston is seised of the tenement which was and ought to have been John Whirle's which tenement on account of the felony of the said John was the lord's escheat so that now if the said John shall come to have the tenement let him pay the value to the said Godfrey and the same Godfrey shall

---

[18] Dating uncertain because there were two St Edwards – King & Confessor and King & Martyr – and the day of the week is not stated. The court was held either on Monday 6th January or Wednesday 19th March 1281.

[19] This is the first of many marginal notes indicating villein status which is written in a different hand. The last of these notes is seen in the record of 1453, which suggests their insertion was some time after that date.

EDWARD I

do the due and accustomed services and he gives for seisin 2s.
* William atte Hale is seised of the tenement which was John Balkar's, performing for it the services and customs, and he gives for seisin 2s.
* Margery Boueton for *leyrewite* of her daughter amerced 6d. [*l. margin*: villein (fem)]
* Christiana Palmere has demised to John Jecob one quarter of land until the end of six years. And the same John shall give to Christiana one bushel of corn and he gives for having the term 12d.
* John son of Bele 6d, John Bene 6d, Katherine Balkere 6d, Emma wife of William atte Leye 6d, Beatrix wife of Walter de Flexemere 6d, [*l. margin*: villeins][20] [*HALS 65500, f1*] Matilda wife of Walter Hogeys 6d all amerced because they have married without the lord's licence.

Term of Michaelmas. Nothing noteworthy.

Halimote of Norton on Tuesday next after the Feast of St Barnabas the Apostle in the 12th year in the time of John Marynes [*13 Jun 1284*]

* Walter in the Hale took one quarter of land with appurtenances which Osbert Goffe [?Gosse] formerly held, performing the customs and services which pertain to the said land.
* John son of Richard surrendered to the lord one quarter of land with appurtenances and the lord seised therein Saer brother of the said John, performing the customs and services which pertain to the said land, and he gives for having entry 3s.
* Saer son of Richard surrendered to the lord one quarter of land in Caldecote and the lord seised thereof John son of Richard, performing the customs and services which pertain to the said land, and he gives for agreement for having entry 3s.
* Margery relict of Stephen because she has married John the Smith (*Faber*) without licence so is amerced. And the same John for having entry to the said Margery gives to the lord 12d.
* Godfrey Neweman has by demise of the lord the wardship of the heir of Stephen and of his land until the same heir [comes] to full age and gives for having wardship 12d.

---

[20] This is the last page of a bound quire. In the bottom right hand corner are written the first few words of the start of the next quire, here being 'Matilda wife of Walter Hogeys'. This system is repeated in all the later quires of the court books.

EDWARD I

Halimote of Norton on Tuesday next after the Feast of St Martin in the 12th year [*14 Nov 1284*]
* Walter Pilcoke surrendered to the lord one cottage and the lord seised thereof Geoffrey Gechard, performing the customs and services which pertain to the said cottage, and he gives for agreement for entry 6d.
* The jurors present that the land of William Everard ought to do works at every other boonday.
* Roger Bercator has licence to marry Juliana in le Hale and gives for licence 18d.

Halimote of Norton on Tuesday after the Feast of Holy Trinity the 13th year [*22 May 1285*]
* The jurors of Norton present that William Thomas has demised to Pagan de Baldock half an acre of land without permission, therefore let it be taken into the lord's hands.
* Next, Nicholas le Neweman has sold one acre of land in an exchange with Nicholas Galwe without licence, therefore let it be taken into the lord's hands.

Halimote of Norton on Tuesday next after the Feast of St Luke the Evangelist in the 13th year [*23 Oct 1285*]
* William Saman came and *gersummavit* his father's land, performing for it the due services and customs, and he gives for *gersumma* and for licence to marry 2s.

Halimote at Norton on Hokeday Tuesday the 14th year [*2 Apr 1286*]
* Ralph son of William came and *gersummavit* the land of his father, performing for it the due and accustomed services, and gives as an agreement for *gersumma* and for licence to marry 10s.

Term of Michaelmas nothing noteworthy.

Halimote of Norton on the eve of St Barnabas the Apostle in the 15th year [*10 Jun 1287*]
* Ellen daughter of William atte Chirche of Norton came and *gersummavit* the messuage and land which Agnes her sister held all her life. And the lord seised her thereof and she gives 4s for having seisin, performing for them the customs and services etc.
* Walter son of Hugh Tatre came and *gersummavit* the messuage of his father with half an acre of land and he gives for *gersumma* 2s.
* Wymark son of Geoffrey Kyng came and *gersummavit* a *ferthlingate* of land

and the messuage of his father and found pledges, Adam in the Hale and Richard Sabrith to maintain the houses in as good a state as he found them and he gives for *gersumma* 12d.
* Walter son of Hugh Tatere has married without licence of the lord, therefore amerced 4s.
* Richard Bonde demised land at farm against the custom of the Halimote so is amerced. Geoffrey Geggeard received the land against the custom of the Halimote etc therefore he is amerced 6d and it is ordered to take the land into the hands of the lord.

[HALS 65500, f1v] Halimote of Norton on the Eve of St Martin the 15th year, time of John de Mar[ines] [10 Nov 1287]
* Katherine daughter of John le Heyward surrendered into the lord's hand one messuage with a *ferthlingate* of land in Norton and the lord seised thereof Richard Parlur and the said Richard will give to the aforesaid Katherine and her heirs two bushels of corn and a bushel of barley and a bushel of beans or peas always on the Feast of St Michael. And the said Richard gives for having entry 2s, pledges Stephen the Clerk and J Jacob.
* Cecily relict of William Water has married without the lord's licence at Sharpenhoe, therefore amerced 2s, pledge Thomas le Grange. [*l. margin*: villein (fem)]

Halimote of Norton on Thursday next after the Feast of Holy Trinity the 16th year [27 May 1288]
* William de Wynselowe came by licence of the lord and has married Ellen atte Chirche of Norton with the tenement which she holds from the lord to hold to him and their heirs, performing the customs and services, and he gives to the lord 6d for entry and for marriage.
* It is ordered to take into the lord's hand the tenement formerly Walter Raymond's unless some one will take it from that hand until etc.

Halimote of Norton the day of the Apostles Simon and Jude in the 16th year in the time of Richard de Hacford [28 Oct 1288]
* Stephen son of Bartholomew surrendered a plot of land next to his tenement and the lord seised thereof Alice daughter of the said Stephen to hold to her and her heirs, performing customs and services for it, and she gives for entry 12d.
* Margaret and Matilda her sister, daughters of Walter Reymond, have taken custody of the tenement of their father for the term of two years, performing customs and services for it etc.

EDWARD I

Halimote of Norton on Wednesday next before the Feast of Holy Trinity in the 17th year – Richard Hakford [*1 Jun 1289*]

* Alice who was the wife of Richard le Bounde comes and claims against the sergeant of the lord that he took unjustly a heriot for the death of her husband because the inheritance descends from her. And because it was found that she was married to her same husband by licence of the lord it was considered that because the man is the head of the woman that the lord should have the said heriot and she take nothing thereof.
* Roger Bercarius came and took with the lord's permission the land which was formerly John le Helder's, to him and his heirs, doing the due services and customs, and he gives for having entry 2s.
* Geoffrey Geiard came and took with the lord's permission the land which was Agnes le Cambester's, doing the due services and customs for it, and he gives for entry 6d.
* Christiana Carlou has demised with the lord's permission to John Clerk one *ferthlingate* of land for four years and gives for the term 12d.
* The jurors present that William Geiard has made a certain exchange with Nicholas le Neweman with the lord's permission, saving the right of any, of a half acre of land which lies between the said Nicholas and Walter Albre against the will of Agnes his wife from whom the land comes and from the true heir and he made her to surrender weeping in the full Halimote and they say that the said Nicholas unjustly holds it because he has not seisin except by the renunciation of the said Agnes.
* Next, upon this matter John Prud came in the time of Lord Luke the cellarer in the 20th year of the reign of King Edward the Saturday next after the Feast of St Matthew the Apostle and sought that an enquiry should be made concerning the same half acre and he had it and that last inquisition said the same that the first had wherefor the lord cellarer ordered the same half acre to be restored to the said John and him to be put in possession of it.

Jurors of Norton:	Richard Reymund	William le Neweman	Ralph son of William
	Walter Sayer	William in the Hale	
	John Alexander	Alan son of William	John in the Hale

Jurors of Newnham:	Walter son of Stephen	Richard Sabright	John Hawys
	Adam in the Hale	John Jacob	John Brid
	John Robin	Ralph Wykyng	Geoffrey Broun

* Thomas son of William Wymark took with the lord's permission for a term of four years the tenement of Martin Ailberne made thereof etc, so that if an heir

EDWARD I

should come within the said term he should pay to the said Thomas the value etc.
* The jurors of Norton [say] that Osbert Reymund is able to hold the land of Thomas Hawys and he has it for a term of six years.
* The jurors of Norton say that Walter Albre is able to hold the tenement of William Shayle and he has it by conveyance of the cellarer for a term of years and he shall have his costs if anyone shall claim and recover it and afterwards he was released.

[*HALS 65501, f1*] [*Half membrane left blank with note in margin*: For Michaelmas term]

Halimote of Norton in Newnham on Thursday after the Feast of St James the 18th year [*27 Jul 1290*]

Jurors:	Ralph the Reeve	John in the Hale	Walter Peronel
	Alan son of Stephen	John Tollere	
	Bate Reymunde	Walter in the Hale	

* William son of Reymund came and *gersummavit* his father's land, doing for it the due and accustomed services, and he gives to the lord as an agreement for *gersumma* 3s. [*r. margin*: beware for Newnham]
* William son of Osbert Gasse [?Gaffe] surrendered into the lord's hand one quarter of land with appurtenances and the lord seised thereof Walter in le Hale, doing the services for it etc, and he gives to the lord for seisin 4s, so that the said William nor anyone in his name could claim any right in the said land for ever.
* Walter son of Godfrey came and *gersummavit* his father's land, doing for it etc, and he gives to the lord as an agreement for *gersumma* 4s. [*r. margin*: villein] [*r. margin*: look out for Newnham]
* The same Walter has licence to marry and he gives 12d.
* Walter son of Reymond came and *gersummavit* his father's land, doing services for it etc, and gives as an agreement for *gersumma* 12d.
* The jurors present that there is no one so able to hold the land of [William] Shail as John Boueton so it is conveyed to the said John by the cellarer for six years.
* John son of Alexander has licence to marry Cristina his daughter to Andrew de Hexston, and he gives for this licence 12d. [*r. margin*: villein]

EDWARD I

Halimote at Norton on the morrow of St Andrew in the 18th year – Hakford [*1 Dec 1289*]
* Walter Pilkoc gives to the lord 6d for holding an enquiry concerning a certain boundary between this Walter and Walter in le Hale.

Jurors:	John Boueton	Richard Reymund	John Alexander
	Alan son of Stephen	Osbert Reymund	William Neweman

* The jurors present that William le Neweman is able to hold the land of Richard Bound and has wardship of the land and of the heir to the full age of the heir, doing for it the due and accustomed services.
* The lord has conveyed the land of William Shail to John de Boueton for the term of six years doing therefore the due and customary services so that if anyone shall claim it within the said term he shall pay his costs to the said John.
* John Boueton has release from the land of the said William Shail for the aforesaid term and he gives for the said release half a mark and he is further released for the time of Richard de Hakford, cellarer.

[*HALS 65501, f1v*] Halimote of Norton on Tuesday next before the Feast of St Margaret the 19th year – Luke Bovindon [*17 Jul 1291*]
* William in the Hale gives to the lord 2s because he married a wife without the licence of the lord and received her into the lord's land, by pledge of John in the Hale. [*l. margin*: villein]
* Walter son of Walter gives to the lord 6d because he married without the licence of the lord, by pledge of John in the Hale.
* Walter de Hardston and Alan son of William give 12d to the lord for making an exchange of four roods of land of which one rood lies in *Longeforlonge* and another in *Dole Rode* and another in *Longmede*.
* John Ysoude an old man surrenders his land into the lord's hand *viz* one messuage with 12 acres of land and John Ysoude his son is seised thereof so that he find lodging for his father and shall support him according to his abilities and he gives 12d.
* The same day all the villagers present Sayer as reeve promising that they will answer for him.

Halimote of Norton on Thursday next after the Feast of St Hilary the 19th year – Luke Bovindon [*18 Jan 1291*]
* Agnes daughter of Stenot surrendered into the lord's hand one messuage with a quarter of land pertaining to the said tenement and the lord seised thereof

EDWARD I

Walter in the Hale, and he will do the due and accustomed services, and he gives for seisin one mark.
* Sara daughter of William de la Hale came and *gersummavit* her father's land and she gives half a mark for seisin.
* Stephen Perunel gives 11s 4d to the lord for licence to marry the said Sara and for entering her and the said land and he shall do the due and customary services, pledges Walter Sayer, John Burr, clerk.

Halimote at Norton on Thursday next after the Ascension of the Lord the 20th year – Luke B[ovindon] [*22 May 1292*]
* Sara daughter of William atte Hale came and *gersummavit* the land which was of William her father and she shall do the due and accustomed services, and gives half a mark.
* Stephen Perunel has licence to marry the said Sara and to enter the said land and he gives 11s 4d to the lord. [*l. margin*: villein]
* Christiana daughter of John le Palmere has demised and let to farm to Ralph de Arlesheye 15 acres of his land from the Feast of St Michael in the 21st year of the reign of King Edward for the term of eight years, so that the said Ralph, he and his heirs, do the due and accustomed services for it until the end of the term, and he gives 4s for having the said term.
* Whereas it has been proved in the time of Lord Richard de Hakford as cellarer in the 17th year of the reign of King Edward by one inquisition and again in the time of Lord Luke de Bovindon as cellarer in the 19th and 20th year of the reign of King Edward by two inquisitions that Agnes wife of William Gerard came unwillingly to a Halimote and was compelled to surrender a half acre of land to the use of Nicholas de Hexston which half acre was conveyed by the lord to John Prud and the said Nicholas owed *per annum* to who ever should hold the same half acre 2d of annual rent. The same Nicholas and John Prud have agreed by the lord's leave to this wording, that Nicholas has remitted the said half acre in so far as it was in him to the said John Prud and the said John has remitted to the said Nicholas the said 2d of annual rent which he was accustomed to receive from the said land forever, by permission of the lord.

Halimote at Norton on Wednesday next after the Feast of Saints Simon and Jude the 20th year [*29 Oct 1292*]
* William Thomas and Ralph son of William by leave of the lord made exchange of a half acre of land in *Wachil* and a rood in *le Crofte* so that William have half an acre and Ralph a rood and they give for permission 6d.
* Whereas a contention was raised between John de Norton and John in le Hale about a certain acre of land lying at *Beriwisehull* because John in le Hale said

that John de Norton never held from him, an inquisition was held as to this. The jurors say upon their oath that the said John de Norton bought the said acre from the said John in le Hale for 10s so it was decided that the said John de Norton hold the land and John in le Hale be amerced for a false complaint.

Halimote of Norton on Tuesday next before the Feast of St Barnabas the Apostle the 21st year – Luke Bo[vindon] [*9 Jun 1293*]

* The jurors present that John son of John of Norton holds one messuage with curtilage of the lord's villeinage which formerly [*HALS 65502, f1*] were of the tenure of John Prud. Next they present that the same John holds one acre of land in villeinage which was John Boueton's and does no service for it.
* Richard le Graunt has committed *leyerwite*, so is amerced 6d. [*r. margin*: villein]

Halimote of Norton the day of Saints Simon and Jude in the 21st year in the time of Luke Bo[vindon] [*28 Oct 1293*]

* William Godynogh because he married without licence is amerced 6d and has licence.
* John, son of Walter Pilkot came and *gersummavit* the land which was his father's and he gives 2s by the pledge of Thomas Ben etc.
* The lord cellarer grants to William, son of John in the Hale, the land which was John Scayl's that he may do the due and customary services, holding to himself and his heirs.
* It is ordered to arrest John Aubray because he removed his goods from the lord's land, that he may come and satisfy the lord. And Walter Aubray and John Prud came and pledged for him that he will henceforth be obedient to the lord in body and goods and nor shall he remove his goods from the lord's land.
* Albreda who was the wife of Ralph, son of William, took from the lord the wardship of the land and of Isabel, daughter and heir of the said Ralph for the term of six years beginning at the Feast of the Purification of the Blessed Mary in the 22nd year of the reign of King Edward to the end of six years, and she will maintain the houses, walls, land and all other things in the state in which they are or better. Pledges John the Clerk, Walter de Harleston and Robert Has and she gives 5s for the term.

Halimote at Norton on Wednesday next after the Feast of Holy Trinity the 22nd year – Luke Bo[vindon] [*16 Jun 1294*]

* John Aubray gives to the lord 2s as an aid, pledge Walter his brother.
* John in the Hale because he spoke with the jurors after the oath, therefore

EDWARD I

amerced 2s.
* The lord cellarer has conveyed to Ralph, son of Osbert and Richard in the Hale two cotlands which are called the *Milnelond* to be divided between them in equal portions, and they will do the due and accustomed services, so that they may hold them to them and their heirs for ever. And it is ordered that because the land is very unproductive for so much service, *viz* weekly for a year, four works and rent, that each of them be quit of his one work per week from the Feast of St Michael to the Feast of St John the Baptist and from that time until the Feast of St Michael they shall do as other cotmen.
* Roger Bercarius has licence to marry Agnes of Hexstonston and he gives 5s. [*r. margin:* villein]
* John Pilkok has licence to marry and gives 12d. [*r. margin*: villein]
[*r. margin against blank space*: Concerning Michaelmas term nothing noteworthy]

[*HALS 65502, f1v*] Halimote at Norton on Thursday after the Feast of St Barnabas the Apostle the 23rd year [*16 Jun 1295*]

* John Reymund took from the lord the land which was Thomas Hawys', [to hold] to him and his heirs, so that he perform the due and accustomed services, and he shall dwell and build here, nor shall he commit waste.
* John Albrid came and *gersummavit* the land which was William Godinoth's, so that he perform the due and accustomed services, and he gives 2s.
* The same John Albrid has licence to marry and gives 6d. [*l. margin:* villein]
* The tenement [of?] Karlowe is taken into the lord's hand.
* Walter de Harleston surrendered into the lord's hand one rood of land against the land of John Boueton and the lord seised thereof Alan son of William and he gives 6d.
* Alan son of William surrendered into the lord's hand a piece of land between Walter de Harleston and Ralph, son of Walter. And the lord seised thereof Walter de Harleston and he gives 6d.
* John Wisot married without licence and has permission and gives for licence 12d. [*l. margin:* villein]
* The sister of John Burre has married without the lord's licence and he [*or she*] gives for licence 6d. [*l. margin:* villein]
* The lord cellarer has conveyed to John son of Osbert Reymund that cotland which was Thomas Hawys', that he may do the due and accustomed services.
* The lord cellarer has granted and conveyed to Robert Hass one quarter of land which was Christine le Palmer's, to hold to him and his heirs, so that he do the due and accustomed services, and he shall be obedient to the lord in all things as long as he shall hold the said land, just like others holding by the same

EDWARD I

tenure. *Viz* in lot and scot, merchet, tallage, and all other services which the said land requires. And if it should happen that the said Robert be found contrarious or to contravene against any part of this agreement[21] it may be lawful for the lord to expel the said Robert from that land and to seize and retain his goods wherever they may be found until the contempt to him shall have been fully made amends for. And he found these sureties that all these services shall be observed, John Burre, John Boueton, and John Prudde. And he gives to the lord for entry 20s by the same pledges.

Halimote at Norton on Monday after the Feast of St Luke the Evangelist in the 23rd year – Luke Bo[vindon] [*24 Oct 1295*]
* John de Hexstanton, called the Dryver, took from the lord that messuage which was Stephen the Clerk's in the village of Norton so that he be in lot and scot, tallage, heriot and all other customs and demands and shall do the due and accustomed services. And he gives to the lord four marks. Pledge John Prudde.

Halimote at Norton the day of St Mark the Evangelist the 24th year [*25 Apr 1296*]
* William le Dipere has licence to marry a daughter of Ralph Reeve and gives to the lord one mark, pledge John Boueton. [*l. margin*: villein]
* Ralph Reymund and Richard in the Hale shall not bring hens for their cotlands with the other cottagers but shall be quit from that service because the hens which they ought to give remain in the manor. And moreover they shall be released from the same each week from Michaelmas to the Feast of St John the Baptist by one work from the Feast of St John the Baptist until Michaelmas they shall do as other cottagers.
* William Thomas is amerced because he demised his land to a certain freeman. Pledge Walter in le Hale.
* John Jacob has licence to marry and gives 6d. Pledge John Prudd. [*l. margin*: villein]
* Osbert Reymund surrendered one messuage into the lord's hand, between Roger Bercarius and the road. And the lord seised thereof Ralph his son and he gives 12d.
* The same Ralph has licence to marry and gives 6d.
* [*HALS 65503, f1*] John in the Hale surrendered into the lord's hand a piece of land just as it lies between Osbert Reymund and William Neweman. And the lord seised thereof Ellen daughter of the said John, so that she may do the due

---

[21] Literally 'against any of the underwritten things' - *contra aliquem subscriptorum*.

EDWARD I

and accustomed services, and she gives 6d.
* The same Ellen has licence to take a husband and she gives 6d so that she may be of the lord's villeins (fem).

[*r. margin against blank space*: For Michaelmas term]
[*r. margin against blank space*: The rolls of the 25th year are wanting]

[HALS 65503, f1v] Halimote of Norton the 26th year – John Stethenache [1297/8]

* The jurors of Norton present that William Saman 3d, William Everard 3d, William Thomas 3d, John de Norton 6d, Walter Fleman, condoned, Richard in the Hale 3d, make default.
* The jurors say that John Saman \villein/ took a wife at Knebworth, and is staying there, so let him be distrained etc.
* William Thomas is amerced because he took a wife without licence of the lord. Afterwards it was discovered that he had licence. [*l. margin*: villein]
* Cecily de Cherpenho is amerced for want of one man at the lord's boonday in harvest.
* John Wisot is amerced 3d because he grinds elsewhere than at the lord's mill.
* Richard Bate gives 4s to the lord for the land which is Godfrey le Newman's to hold for six years so that he shall maintain the house and land in as good a condition as he received them in or in a better and he shall do all the due and accustomed services belonging to the said land. Pledges Walter Sayer and John the Clerk.
* Ellen in the Hale surrendered into the lord's hand a plot of land containing one acre in *Longforlong* just as the fences and ditches of William le Neweman on one side and of Osbert Reymund on the other are marked out. And Walter Seyer surrendered a plot of land containing half an acre in the same place. And John Bate gives to the lord 2s for the said plots of land to hold to him and his heirs for ever by the lord's will. And the said John shall acquit the said Walter of 1d at Christmas.

Halimote at Norton on Friday next after the Feast of Holy Trinity in the 27th year – John Steven [19 Jun 1299]

* The jurors present that William Everard \6d/ and John son of John of Norton \6d/ made default, so are amerced 6d.
* John Bate is amerced 5s because he married without the lord's licence, pledge Bartholomew Reymond. [*l. margin*: villein]
* Matilda Prodd is amerced 2s for *leyrewitt*, pledge John Prodd.
* The relict of Ralph the Reeve gives to the lord 3s 4d for licence to give Isabel his daughter in marriage.

EDWARD I

- Scolastica le Clerkes surrendered into the lord's hand one cottage in Norton. And John, son of Stephen gives 5s to the lord to hold the said cottage to him and his in villeinage.
- John Seman gives 6s 8d to the lord that he may stay outside the manor, so that he come once every year to the View, pledges William Reymond and John the Clerk.
- Walter de Harleston surrendered in to the hand of the lord one curtilage lying between Richard Bate and the said Walter. And Robert Haysh gives to the lord 4s to hold the said curtilage to him and his, doing for it the due and accustomed services.
- John Pope gives to the lord 3s for licence to marry and that he may stay outside the manor. And he will give annually at Christmas two capons, pledges John Boueton and Richard Bate. [*l. margin*: villein]

[*l. margin against blank space*: For Michaelmas term]

[HALS 65503, f2] Halimote of Norton held on Monday after the Feast of St Dunstan in the 28th year – John Ste[venach] [*23 May 1300*]

- The jurors present that William Everard \6d/ and John de Norton \6d/ have made default, therefore they are amerced.
- Next, they say that said William and John ought to have had a man at each boonday in harvest and there were five boondays and so they are in arrears by five man-days.
- Sara the relict of Ralph the Reeve has surrendered into the lord's hand half a virgate of land which he held from the lord. And William le Dipere and Petronilla his wife, daughter of the said Sara made agreement for the said half virgate of land, to hold to them and theirs for ever, performing the due and accustomed services for it. And they will give to the said Sara annually as long as she shall live two quarters of corn, one quarter of barley, one quarter of peas and half a quarter of oats. And the said Sara shall have two rooms next to the door for her whole life so that she shall maintain the said rooms in as good a state or better than when she received them. And that Margaret daughter of the said Sara and Matilda her sister were married with the goods and chattels of the said Sara and her husband and a certain other daughter named Agnes has married a free man without the lord's licence, it is decided that none of the said three daughters can claim, have or demand any right to the said virgate according to the rule and custom of the manor.

EDWARD I

Halimote of Norton held on Tuesday after the Feast of St Hilary held the 28th year – John Stevenach [*19 Jan 1300*]

* Sara relict of Ralph the Reeve gives 3s 4d to the lord for licence to marry Agnes his daughter.
* The jurors present that Maurice Fleman, villein, has married without the lord's licence in Stotfold.
* Matilda Warde amerced for *leyrewit* 12d. [*r. margin*: villein (fem)]
* Rose le Graunt amerced for *leyrewit* 12d, pledge John le Dryver.
* John de Norton \6d/ William Everard \6d/ in default therefore amerced.
* A third part of the land which was of Ralph son of William which Cecily de Cherpenho holds in the name of dower is taken into the lord's hand because the said Cecily is committing waste and is taking away all the stock arising from the said land to Sharpenhoe.
* Richard Bate gives 10s to the lord for the land which is of Isabel daughter of Ralph to hold for eight years doing all due and accustomed services and he shall maintain the houses and land in as good a state as he received them in. Next, he shall maintain the said Isabel in food and clothing during the term.

Halimote of Norton on Friday next before the Feast of St Barnabas the Apostle the 29th year – John Stevenach [*9 Jun 1301*]

* The jurors say that John of Norton and William Everard who owe suit, are in default, so are amerced.
* Item they say that Morice son of Hugh married at Stotfold without the lord's licence, so he is amerced 6d.
* They say that John Bate married without licence of the lord outside the Liberty, therefore amerced 4s. [*r. margin*: villein]
* Next they say that John Nichol married without the lord's licence Matilda daughter of Walter Sayer, therefore amerced half a mark. [*r. margin*: villein]
* And Walter Sayer because he married his daughter without licence of the lord is amerced 4s. [*r. margin*: villein]
* Next they say that Richard Bate has committed waste on the land of Richard Neweman, damage half a mark. And he has a postponement to amend it before the next Halimote under penalty of 10s.
* Next they say that John in the Hale wastes the tenement which he holds. And the same John has found pledges for the repair of the said tenement, *viz* William his son and Richard his son.
* Walter son of Steven le Clerk came and *gersummavit* one cotland which once belonged to John his brother. And Steven Perunel is a pledge that he will do the services due and accustomed. And he will maintain the said cotland with

EDWARD I

its houses and other things in as good a state or better than he received it.
* Amice daughter of Alan *gersummavit* half a virgate of land which was her father's. And she has found pledges that she shall do the services due and accustomed for it *viz* John Boueton and Stephen Perunel and that she shall maintain the said land with its houses in as good state as she received it in. And she has licence to marry. The agreement for *gersumma* is 13s 4d. [*r. margin*: villein (fem)]
* Walter de Harleston gives to the lord 6d for holding an inquisition concerning a certain rood of land which Nicholas le Neweman now holds. The inquisition says that the said Nicholas has no right to the said rood of land and that the said Walter and his ancestors held the said rood of land. Therefore it is decided that the said Walter should hold the said rood of land and the said Nicholas is amerced for unjust detention 6d.

[*HALS 65503, f2v*] Halimote of Norton held on Monday before the Feast of St Lucy the Virgin the 29th year – John Ste[venach] [*12 Dec 1300*]

* The jurors present that William Everard and John of Norton made default, therefore let them be distrained.
* Next, they present that John Prudd has married Matilda his daughter without licence of the lord, therefore amerced 6s 8d. [*l. margin*: villein]
* William le Neweman has married Sarra his daughter without the lord's licence, therefore amerced 12d. [*l. margin*: villein]
* Margaret Bene amerced 3d for *leyrewit*. Ralph Burre amerced 3d because he committed *leyrwit* with the said Margaret. [*l. margin*: villein]
* John son of Stephen the Clerk conveyed to the vicar of Norton all his land to sow for the third sheaf without permission of the lord, therefore let the said land be taken into the lord's hand.
* William Harsch gives 12d to the lord for licence to marry. [*l. margin*: villein]
* Godfrey le Bonde *gersummavit* the land which was his father's and he gives for *gersumma* 5s.

Halimote of Norton the 30th year – John Stevenach [*1301/02*]

* The jurors say that William Everard has made default therefore he is amerced 6d.
* Next they say that Isabel daughter of William Thomas married herself without licence to a certain William of *Piriton* [Pirton] a free man, therefore amerced 6d. [*l. margin*: villein (fem)]
* Next they say that Walter Fleman married without licence therefore amerced 18d. [*l. margin*: villein]
* Next they say that Nicholas le Neweman sold to a certain stranger one acre of

EDWARD I

corn without permission, therefore amerced 12d.
* John in the Hale found pledges *viz* Richard in the Hale and William in the Hale his sons to amend his tenements and repair the houses anew before the next Halimote under penalty of half a mark.

Of Michaelmas term

Jurors: John Prudde   Richard Bate   John in the Hale   John Jecob
         Walter Aubrey   Walter Perunel   William Dipere   Wm Reymond
         Osbert Reymond   John Borre   Robert Hays   John Aubrey

* It is ordered to take into the lord's hand the tenement of William, son of William Everard for default of suit and until it be known that he wishes to pursue it.
* The jurors present that Amice daughter of Alan committed *leyrewit*, therefore amerced 3d.
* Next they present that Walter de Harleston has demised his land to a certain freeman without permission, therefore amerced 3d, pledge Robert Hays.
* Next they present that Stephen Perunell has demised his land to a certain freeman without permission, therefore amerced 3d, pledge Robert Hays.

Halimote of Norton on Monday after the close of Easter the 31st year – John Stevenach [*6 May 1303*]

* The jurors say that Robert le Bercher and Robert Payn made default and because they have entered the lord's fee therefore it is ordered to distrain them to answer.
* The jurors say that Matilda Colines before she married Nicholas le Neweman did not *gersumma* the tenement which the same Nicholas and Matilda held. Therefore for searching the rolls of the time of Brother William de Waltham they give to the lord [*no sum stated*].
* Walter Fleman gives to the lord 2s for one cotland which was William Shayle's and which William in the Hale surrendered into the lord's hand so that he may hold the said cotland to him and his in villeinage by the will of the lord, doing the due and accustomed services for it, he shall give tallage etc.
* John Boueton gives 3d to the lord that he may put Henry his son to letters. [*l. margin*: villein]
* Walter Sayer gives 6d that he may put his son Walter to letters. [*l. margin*: villein]
* Amice daughter of Alan son of William surrendered into the hand of the lord a half yardland of land. And Roger [son of] John Prudde and the said Amice

EDWARD I

give to the lord 13s 4d to hold the said land to him and his by the will of the lord in villeinage without waste, doing the due and accustomed services for it. And for licence to marry at the same time and if they have no heir lawfully begotten of them, [*HALS 65503, f3*] then after the death of the said Roger and Amice the said land with appurtenances shall revert to the heirs of the said Amice, and they give tallage and merchet.

Halimote of Norton the 31st year – John Stevenach [*1302/03*]

* The jurors present that John son of John of Norton and William Everard are in default, therefore let them be distrained.
* Next, the said John and William owe each of them one man at one boonday and withdrew themselves from the said service, therefore let them be distrained.
* Next, they present that Amice, daughter of Alan commits waste in the tenement which she took from the lord and that the houses are lessened in value.
* Next, they present that the land of John in the Hale is lying uncultivated and that the houses are ruinous and lessened in value.
* Next, they present that Isabel, daughter of William Walter has married without the lord's licence, therefore she is amerced 2s.
* Margaret, daughter of Walter Godefray gives 3s to the lord for the land which was her father's, to hold to her and hers for the will of the lord, performing the due and accustomed services for it. And Margery her mother has permission to hold the said land until the said Margaret is of age so that she shall maintain the houses and land in good condition and she shall do all the due and accustomed services until the end of the said term and she gives for the terms 3s.
* John in the Hale surrenders into the lord's hand half a virgate of land. And William in the Hale gives 5s to the lord for holding the said land to him and his, performing the due and accustomed services for it. And he shall give to the said John his father annually so long as he shall live at Michaelmas half a quarter of wheat, half a quarter of beans, half a quarter of barley and half a quarter of peas. And he shall begin the said payment at Michaelmas one year after the next Michaelmas by pledge of Richard in the Hale and Walter Aubrey.

Halimote of Norton the 32nd year – Hugh de Eversdon [*1303/04*]

Jurors:	John Boueton	William le Dipere	John Clerk
	John Prudde	Walter in the Hale	Walter Aubrey

EDWARD I

* The jurors say that William Everard defaults and Laurence de Blayseworth defaults for the tenement which was John of Norton's.
* Next they say that William, son of John Boueton, has married without the lord's licence, therefore amerced half a mark. Pledge J Boueton. [*r. margin*: villein]
* Next they say that William Reymond has married without the lord's licence with Margaret Thomas the lord's villein (fem). Therefore he is amerced 3s. [*r. margin*: villein]
* Next they say that John the Coweherd has married with Margaret Flandon without the lord's licence, therefore amerced 6d. [*r. margin*: villein]
* Next they say that Stephen in the Hale has demised to John the Swone his land without the lord's permission, therefore it is ordered etc.
* Next they say that Walter de Harleston has demised his land without permission to the said John *viz* three half acres of wheat and half an acre of oats, so is amerced 2d.
* Next they say that Walter son of Stephen the Clerk, has closed his last day, therefore it is ordered to seise the said land with the crop into the lord's hand until etc.
* Next they say that William in the Hale has demised half an acre of land sown with Lent seed, therefore amerced 6d. And it is ordered etc.
* Agnes daughter of Stephen the Clerk gives to the lord 3s for one cotland which belonged to Walter son of Stephen, performing for it the due and accustomed services. She shall not make waste. Pledges Walter Loveleg and John Galston.
* Roger Prudde gives 6d to the lord for rectifying metes and bounds between his tenement and the tenements of neighbours and they have a postponement.
* Henry de Erdeleye came and did fealty to the lord for the tenement which he holds from the lord abbot and he acknowledged the services *viz* 40d *per annum*.
* Sarra daughter of Alan surrendered into the lord's hands one rood of land opposite the tenement of Andrew le Helder and Richard Bate gives 12d to the lord for holding the said rood of land to him and his in villeinage for the will of the lord, performing for it the due and accustomed services.

HALS 65503, f3v] **Halimote held there on Tuesday next after the Feast of St Martin in the 32nd year [*17 Nov 1304*]**

Jurors:	John Boueton	John Prudde	Sayer the Reeve
	John Clerk (*clericus*)	William Dipere	Osbert Reymond

EDWARD I

* William Everard was attached to answer the lord for detaining the reaping of one day with one man in autumn. He did not come, therefore John de Boueton and Thomas Granger who pledged the said William are amerced 12d because they have not got the same and it is ordered that he be distrained to answer etc.
* The jurors say that William Everard makes default, therefore amerced 6d.
* Next they say that the said William ought always to do another boonday with one man at harvest on behalf of (*contra*) Laurence de Blayesworth which William has withdrawn himself for ten years past, in each year three man-days, as they fall for the *bederipp* of the village, and the work of one day is worth 1d and is in arrears by 25 days.
* Next they say that the tenement which was John de Norton's is in arrears concerning one man's reaping for seven days in harvest within three years.
* Next they say that Alan the Neweman has married without the lord's licence, therefore amerced 12d. Pledge William Neweman. [*l. margin*: villein]
* Next they say that Alan, son of Stephen, has demised to William the Dipere two acres of land without permission of the lord for a term, therefore amerced. And afterwards the said William came and demanded 17s 9d as debt of the said Alan and he gives 4s to the lord for permission to sow every year one acre of the land which was the said Alan's until he shall have raised the said money, or else if those who hold the tenement which was the said Alan's shall wish to satisfy the same William, they shall compensate the said William 9d for every year.
* Next they say de Harleston demised to John Portarius and Thomas Granger one acre of land without permission of the lord and it is ordered to take this land into the lord's hand, etc. Amerced 3d.
* Next they say that Matilda Colines has demised to Thomas the vicar one acre without permission, therefore amerced 3d.
* Next they say that Amice Aleynes has demised to Thomas Granger her land without permission of the lord, therefore amerced 3d.

Halimote of Norton on Thursday next before the Feast of the Blessed John the Baptist in the 33rd year – Hugh Eversdon [*17 Jun 1305*]

* The jurors say that William Everard \6d/ and Stephen Dame \3d/ default, so are amerced.
* Next they say that Margery Hoghaler has commited *leyrewit* and is a widow, so is amerced 3d. [*l. margin*: villein (fem)]
* Next they say that Agnes Loveleg has married Richard Hawys without the

EDWARD I

lord's licence, so is amerced 12d, pledge [*no name given*]. [*l. margin*: villein (fem)]
* Next they say that William Thomas ought to come to carry hay with two men as others do for a cotland and one *ferthlingate* of land and because he has not come he is amerced and they say that he has been in default of one man annually for a long time past.
* Next they say that Roger Prudde has committed waste on a tenement which he holds, to the damage of etc. And it is ordered to seise the said tenement into the lord's hand until etc.
* William in the Hale surrendered into the lord's hand a plot of land from the curtilage of the same William between his tenement [and the tenement] of Roger Shepherd as it is enclosed and as the metes and bounds show. And Richard in the Hale gives to the lord 2s to hold the said plot to him and his in villeinage at the will of the lord, performing for it the due and accustomed services.
* Ralph le Neweman gives to the lord 12d for licence to marry when he will, pledge William le Neweman. [*l. margin:* villein]
* John Boueton surrenders into the lord's hand one piece of land from the headland of one selion next to the tenements of William Reymond and of Walter Sayer, and it extends in length the same as the enclosure of the curtilage of Alexander the Miller. And William Boueton is seised thereof doing for it the due and customary services.
* William Reymond surrenders into the lord's hand one piece of land from the headland of one selion between the tenement of Alexander the Miller and the aforesaid piece which John Boueton surrendered as above. And William Boueton is seised thereof to hold to him and his in villeinage for the will of the lord and it extends in length the same as the enclosure of the said Alexander the Miller and he gives to the lord for the said two pieces of land 2s by the pledge of John Boueton.
* Roger Prudde and Amice his wife with good assent and unanimous will have surrendered into the hand of the lord one half virgate of land with appurtenances which Alan son of William father of the said Amice once had and held.
* [*HALS 65503, f4*] And Richard Bate gives 40s to the lord for the said half virgate of land with appurtenances just as the said Alan at one time held it, to hold to him and his in villeinage, without any right of the said Roger and Amice or their heirs to reclaim it, doing for it the due and accustomed services and not committing waste, pledges John Boueton, William Dipere, Robert Ays and John Prudde.
* Richard Bate has surrendered into the lord's hand one cottage which is called

EDWARD I

the *Gegges*. And Roger Prudde and Amice his wife are seised thereof, to hold to them and theirs, performing for it the due and accustomed services.
* Richard Bate came and *gersummavit* one half virgate of land which Osbert Reymond his father held, doing for it the due and accustomed services, nor shall he commit waste. And the same Richard surrendered the said half virgate of land into the lord's hands for the use of John son of the said Richard to hold to him and his. And he gives to the lord for *gersumma* for seisin and for permission to hold the said land until the said John come to full age 33s 4d, pledges John Boueton and John Bate.

Halimote of Norton the 33rd year [*1304/05*]

Jurors:	John Boueton	John Prudde	John Borre
	Walter in the Hale	Osbert Bate	Walter Parnele

* The jurors say that Matilda Colines has demised land to a certain John le Swone of Baldock, therefore it is ordered to take the said land into the hand of the lord, 6d.
* Next they say that Walter de Harleston has demised to the same John two and a half acres of land therefore it is ordered to take the said land into the lord's hand, amerced 3d.
* Next they say that Stephen Parnele has demised to the same John one acre of land, so it is ordered to take the said land into the lord's hand, amerced 3d.
* Next they say that Roger Prudde has demised to the same John one acre of land so it is ordered to take the said land into the lord's hand, amerced 3d.
* Next they say that Roger Prudde has demised to a certain William Savyn of Stotfold one and a half acres, so it is ordered etc, amerced 3d.
* Next they say that John Prudde the younger has demised to the same William Savyn two acres of land, so it is ordered etc, amerced 6d.
* Next they say that Richard le Parlour has demised to Walter son of Alexander a freeman one acre without permission, so it is ordered etc, amerced 3d.
* Next they say that William in the Hale has demised to the same Walter one acre of land, so it is ordered, etc. Amerced 3d.
* Next they say that William Thomas has demised to Thomas the Sergeant one and a half acres of land, so it is ordered etc. Amerced 6d.
* Godfrey son of Richard le Bonde gives to the lord 2s for licence to marry Alice daughter of Walter in the Hale. And the same Walter gives to the lord 12d for licence to marry the said Alice, pledge John Boueton.
* Roger Prudde and Amice his wife with one will and assent have surrendered into the lord's hand one plot of land next to the tenement of Alexander the

EDWARD I

Miller extending in length the same as the messuage of the said Alexander extends and the messuage of Roger Molot. And Ralph son of William Neweman gives 12d to the lord for the said plot to hold to him and his in villeinage, doing for it the due and customary services *viz* ½d for release of the rent and service of the said Roger, pledge Walter in the Hale. And he shall build [upon] the said plot.

* It is reported by the jurors that Richard Bate has committed waste upon the tenement of Swetekin to the damage of 4d therefore amerced 4d.
* Saer son of Richard surrendered into the hand of the lord one messuage with a croft which contains three roods of land with two acres of land whereof one acre lies in two parts in the *Southfeld* whereof one half acre lies upon *Chalkforlong* and the other half acre lies in *Whathuldan* and another acre lies in two parts in the *North Field* whereof half an acre lies in *Eldefelde* extending towards the tenement of John Prudde and the other half acre lies upon *Chepforlong* abutting on *Greneweye*. And Margaret daughter of the said Sayer gives 5s to the lord to hold the said land with messuage and croft and for licence to marry when she may wish and she shall pay to the lord a rent with all *bedripps* happening which pertain to the said land with scot and lot and tallage when it falls. And she gives to the lord ½d annually for increase in rent for warranty at the Feast of the Annunciation of the Blessed Mary. [*r. margin*: increase ½d].
* Agnes, daughter of Stephen the Clerk, has surrendered into the lord's hands one cotland which he had after the decease of his father. And John the Palmer and the said Agnes give to the lord 12d for the said cotland with appurtenances to hold for its due and accustomed services, without waste, and for licence to marry at the same time. And if it happen that they should die without an heir, let it revert to the true heirs of the said Agnes, pledge Robert Hays.

Halimote of Norton on Thursday next after the Feast of the Ascension of the Lord in the 34th year – Hugh E[versdon] [*19 May 1306*]

Jurors:	John Borre	Richard Bate	John Prudde
	Walter Sayer	William Thomas	John Isoude
	Robert Hays	Richard in the Hale	

* [*HALS 65503, f4v*] The jurors say that Richard Bate committed waste on the tenement which he holds to 4d damage, so amerced.
* Next they say that the same Richard has allowed one house to fall into ruins

EDWARD I

on the tenement of Ralph son of Walter and it is ordered that he cause it to be rebuilt.
* Next they say that William in the Hale has demised to Laurence de Bleyesworth half an acre of land without the lord's permission, therefore amerced 3d, pledge Richard in the Hale.
* Next they say that John son of Nicholas has demised one acre of land to Thomas the Serjeant without permission therefore amerced 3d and it is ordered to seise it, etc, pledge John Borre.
* Next they say that Matilda Colines has demised three half acres of land to Alexander the Miller without licence so is amerced 3d.
* Next they say that the said Matilda has demised one half acre of land to Walter son of Alexander the Miller without licence, so is amerced 3d.
* Next they say that William in the Hale has demised two acres of land to the said Walter, so is amerced 3d, and it is ordered etc.
* Next they say that Richard le Parlour has demised to the aforesaid Walter, a freeman, half an acre of land without licence so is amerced 3d, and it is ordered etc.
* Roger Prudde and Amice his wife have surrendered into the lord's hand one cottage with its curtilage and other appurtenances just as it has them, between the tenement of Richard Bate and the tenement of Ralph son of Walter. And Alice daughter of Godfrey le Neweman gives to the lord 12d for the said cottage with curtilage and other appurtenances, to hold to her and hers in villeinage by the will of the lord, performing for it the due and accustomed services, and paying an increase in rent of ½d at Michaelmas. [*l. margin*: increase ½d].
* Juliana daughter of Godfrey Hoghaler came and *gersummavit* a *ferthlingate* of land with appurtenances which the said Godfrey held, to hold to her and hers, performing for it the due and accustomed services, nor committing waste, and she gives for *gersumma* 5s.
* Walter Aubrey gives to the lord 3s for licence to marry Matilda his daughter when she will.
* John Boueton gives to the lord for licence to marry when and where he will 5s.

Norton 34th year – Hugh Eversdon [*1305/06*]

Jurors:	John Boueton	John Borre	Walter in the Hale
	John Prudde	Walter Aubrey	William Dipere

* The jurors say that William Everard makes default, amerced.

EDWARD I

* Next they say that Margaret Parlour committed *leyrewit* with John Driver de Hexston, therefore amerced 6d.
* Next they say that Margaret daughter of Sayer commited *leyrewit* with Geoffrey Bercarius, therefore amerced 6d.
* Next they say that Alexander Wisot has married without the lord's licence, so is amerced 12d.
* John Prudde gives to the lord 10s for licence to marry where he shall wish.
* Next they say that Emma daughter of John Prudde has married without the lord's licence and afterwards she came and made agreement with the lord.
* Next they say that Andrew le Helder \2d/ and Matilda Colin ground elsewhere than at the lord's mill, therefore amerced.
* William Thomas came and acknowledged the service which was demanded from him at the last Halimote and ought to do it for the future by the pledge of John Prudd and the said William is amerced for unjust detention, 3d.
* John Bate \3d/ and Richard Bate \6d/ because they ploughed the lord's land badly are amerced.

Norton the 35th year – Hugh Eversdon [*1306/07*]
* The jurors say that William Everard defaults, therefore amerced.
* Next they say that Alice in the Hale has married without the lord's licence so is amerced 6d.
* Matilda relict of John Balston came and *gersummavit* one messuage with one cotland and its appurtenances to the use of Walter son and heir of the said John, to hold to him and his in villeinage for the will of the lord, performing for it the due and accustomed services, nor committing waste. And she gives to the lord for *gersumma* and for permission to keep the said heir and to hold the said messuage and cotland for ten years 2s, the term beginning next Michaelmas.
* [*HALS 65503, f5*] Isabel daughter of Ralph son of William surrendered into the hand of the lord half a virgate of land with appurtenances which the said Ralph her father held in his life. And the lord seised Richard son of Thomas Cok of Newnham and the said Isabel to hold to them and the heirs issuing from them in villeinage, doing the services due and accustomed for it. And if it should happen that the aforesaid Richard and Isabel have no heir between them then after the death of the said Richard and Isabel let it remain wholly to the heirs of the said Isabel. And the said Richard gives to the lord for the said seisin and for licence to marry with Isabel one mark, pledges Richard Bate and John Bate and William Wymark.
* Richard son of Thomas Hawys of Norton comes and seeks a land as his inheritance after the decease of the said Thomas his father, which land John

Bate now holds in the same. And he says that John Bate has no right to hold the same land unless by the demise and the will of the lord. And to know how the said land came out of the hands of the said Thomas into the tenure of the said John an inquisition is held by 12 jurors who say that Thomas at some time long past held the said land which he failed to fallow. And the same land for rents and services unpaid was seised into the lord's hand, and that the lord conveyed the said land many times by his will for rent and services during nearly 30 years in the time of the life of the said Thomas, and the time of the life of a certain John, son and heir of the same Thomas, nor did they seek to obtain the same land. And that the lord after so long a time conveyed the said land to the said John Bate to hold to him and his in villeinage doing for it the due and customary services. The jurors having been asked whether there were survivors of the said Thomas or of John his heir at the time when the same John Bate entered the said land or not say that they have no knowledge thereof and ask for a day and the help of the rolls and they have a day.

Norton Halimote there the 35th year [1306/07]

| Jurors: | Richard Bate | Robert Hays | John Isoude |
| | John Jecob | Walter Parnel | Walter in the Hale |

* Walter Fleman puts himself in the lord's mercy because he reaped the lord's corn badly in harvest, 6d.
* The jurors say that Richard Bate reaped the lord's corn badly in harvest, therefore in the lord's mercy 6d.
* The jurors say that William le Neweman 3d, John Wysot 3d, John Coline 2d, Margery le Hoghaler 2d, Walter de Harleston 2d, Geoffrey Geiard 2d, withdrew from doing suit at the lord's mill, therefore amerced.
* Next, they say that William Everard defaults, therefore let him be distrained.
* Next they say that Richard Bate holds the land which was of Ralph son of William for a term and he has a day to build a new house on the said land before Easter, pledges John Prudde and Walter in the Hale.
* Next they say that Margery le Hoghaler has committed waste on the tenement which she held to 6d damage, pledge Walter Sayer.
* Next they say that John le Dryver bought one messuage with a certain croft adjoining and one acre of land in the field of Norton by charter from a holding of Walter de Aula, doing for it the due and customary services, which charter he surrendered into the lord's hand. And he gives to the lord annually for warranty 1d. And he gives the lord for licence. [*r. margin*: increase 1d]
* Next they say that Margery le Hoghaler has married without the lord's licence.

EDWARD I

And she has leave and she gives to the lord for licence 12d.
* Next they say that John Isoude the younger has committed *leyrewit*, therefore amerced 12d.
* Walter the Miller has taken wardship of the land and heir of Richard le Parlur to hold and maintain without waste for the term of eight years, beginning on the Feast of St Michael last, doing for it the due and accustomed services, so that he shall give to Isabel heir of the said Richard annually during the term a bushel of corn and a bushel of peas at the Feast of St Michael. And he gives to the lord for having the term 5s, pledges Walter Albreth and John Isoude and he will acquit the said land before Katherine de Childewik.
* Juliana daughter of John Jecob gives to the lord 3s for licence to marry when she will, pledge John Jecob.

EDWARD II

[*HALS 65503, f5v*] **EXTRACTS FROM THE ROLLS OF HALIMOTES HELD AT THE MANOR OF NORTON IN THE TIME OF KING EDWARD II**

Halimote of Norton on Monday after the Feast of St Luke the Evangelist in the 1st year – Hugh Eversden [*23 Oct 1307*]

* The jurors say that William Everard makes default: therefore amerced. He is pardoned.
* Next they say that Richard Miller domestic servant of Martin Miller has broken the lord's pond and carried away six pike.
* Next they say that Walter Sparwe married Alice Swetekin without the lord's licence. He comes and gives the lord 12d for obtaining a licence. [*l. margin:* villein]
* Next they say that William le Neweman has married without the lord's licence and afterwards he comes and gives to the lord for obtaining a licence 12d.
* Next they say that Walter in la Hale has come with one horse to the lord's ploughing whereas he ought to come with two horses for two tenements. Therefore because he withdrew for a year, amerced 12d. Pledge Saer the Reeve and William Dipere.
* Next they say that John Boueton and Sayer the Reeve and William Dipere have made a path through the lord's corn, pledge each for the other, amerced 12d.
* Next they say that Richard Bate has not raised a house nor built on the tenement formerly William son of Walter's as he was ordered. Therefore the same Richard is amerced 12d.
* Richard son of Stephen Dame came and *gersummavit* the land which was the said Stephen his father's, to hold to him and his in villeinage, performing for it the due and accustomed services, nor committing waste. Pledges Walter Ward and John Isoude, and he gives to the lord for *gersumma* and for licence to marry 4s by the said pledge.
* John son and heir of John Borre came and *gersummavit* half a virgate of land which the said John Borre his father held, to hold to him and his according to the custom of the manor, performing for it the due and accustomed services, nor committing waste, and he gives the lord for *gersumma* one mark.
* It is reported by the jurors that Walter Loveleg has obstructed a certain way behind his curtilage within his croft and diverted the said way upon the land of the said abbot, therefore the same Walter is amerced 6d, and it is ordered etc.
* John Colin came and *gersummavit* the land which was Nicholas le Neweman's, to hold to him and his, performing for it the due and accustomed

EDWARD II

services, nor committing waste, and he gives to the lord for *gersumma* one mark.
* William son of Godfrey le Neweman gives to the lord 2s for permission to hold the land which was of Alice daughter of the said Godfrey to hold to him and his performing for it the due and accustomed services, nor committing waste.

Norton
* The jurors say that Richard Bate was lacking by one man at haymaking and by one man at the boonday in harvest.
* Next they say that William le Dipere removed one stone which was for a boundary between the lord and the same William, therefore amerced 6d.
* Next they say that William le Dipere and John Standeby removed a stone which was for a boundary (*meta*) between them and the lord's land, therefore amerced 6d.
* Next they say that Richard Bate and Walter Harleston removed a boundary (*metam*) between them and the lord's land, therefore amerced 6d.
* Next they say that Richard Bate and Walter in the Hale removed a boundary between them and the lord's land, therefore amerced 6d.
* Next they say that Alice Hays married Walter in the Hale without the lord's licence, and she gives the lord for permission 12d. [*l. margin:* villein (fem)]
* Next they say that Cecily Sayer has committed *leyrewit* with John Isoude junior, therefore amerced 12d.
* Next they say that John Colin grinds elsewhere than at the lord's mill, therefore amerced 2d.
* Next they say that John Colin has leased the land of John le Swone without the lord's permission therefore it is ordered to seise the said land into the lord's hands [*HALS 65504, f1*] until etc. Afterwards he gives the lord 6d to have permission.
* Next they say that John Colin removed a boundary between him and the lord's land at *Longecroft*, therefore amerced 3d, pledge Roger Shepherd.
* John Balston came after the decease of Walter son and heir of John brother of the said John Balston and *gersummavit* one cotland which was the said Walter's, performing for it the due and accustomed services, nor shall he commit waste, and he gives to the lord for *gersumma* and for licence to marry 2s.
* Walter son and heir of Walter in the Hale came and *gersummavit* half a virgate of land which his father held, to hold to him and his in villeinage, performing for it the due and accustomed services, nor shall he commit waste, and he gives to the lord half a mark.

EDWARD II

* John Colin surrendered into the lord's hand one messuage with appurtenances and one half virgate of land with all appurtenances, just as he held it in the village of Norton. And the lord seised thereof Geoffrey Bercarius, to hold to him and his in villeinage, performing for it the due and accustomed services, nor shall he commit waste. He gives to the lord for possession of the said messuage and aforesaid land 40s.

Norton year 2 – Hugh Eversdon [*1308/1309*]

* Walter son and heir of Walter Sayer came and *gersummavit* all the land with appurtenances which the said Walter his father held in Norton, to hold to him and his, performing for it the due and accustomed services, nor shall he commit waste. And he gives to the lord for *gersumma* and for licence to marry 3s 4d.
* William in the Hale surrendered into the lord's hand one cotland which he held in Norton with appurtenances. And Alexander Wysot gives to the lord 4s for the said cotland to hold to him and his in villeinage, for the will of the lord, performing for it the due and accustomed services, nor shall he commit waste.
* Walter son of William Reymond came and *gersummavit* one cotland which his father held, to hold to him and his in villeinage, performing for it the due and accustomed services, nor shall he commit waste. And he gives to the lord for *gersumma* and for licence to marry 5s.
* The jurors say that John Colin demised to John le Swone two acres of land without the lord's permission, therefore amerced 3d.
* Next they say that Walter son of Alexander is in arrears with the ploughing of three acres of land value 18d, therefore amerced 3d, and it is ordered to raise etc.
* Next they say that Stephen Parnele does not maintain the houses of his tenement and because at the last Halimote he found pledges *viz* John Isoude and Richard in the Hale to amend waste and he did not do it, therefore his pledges are amerced 12d. And it is ordered to distrain the said Stephen to amend the said waste.
* They say that William the Neweman has made waste and he is ordered to amend it and has a day until the next Halimote.
* Next they say that John Boueton has cut down trees around his curtilage to 20d damage therefore amerced etc. Pledges [*blank*].
* Walter in the Hale and Alice his wife surrendered into the lord's hand one plot of land, the land which was of the tenement of Andrew the Helder. And Robert son of Walter of Arlecheseye gives to the lord 12d for the said plot of land which contains in breadth 44 feet at one head and at the other 39 feet and in length nine perches and four feet between the tenement of Richard Parlour

EDWARD II

and the tenement of the aforesaid Walter and Alice, to hold to him and his in villeinage doing for it the due and accustomed services *viz* annually to the lord ½d for release of the rent and service of the said Walter and Alice and he has licence to marry.
* Walter de Harleston surrenders into the hand of the lord one *quartrona* of land with its appurtenances, that is to say one plot of curtilage next to the tenement of Robert Hayss as well as the houses now built, and half of his land just as it lies in the fields. And John Reymond gives to the lord 13s 4d to hold the aforesaid land to him and his in villeinage, performing the services due and accustomed for it. Nor should he commit waste, pledges William Thomas and Richard Bate. And he has licence to marry wherever he shall wish.
* Walter Sayer surrenders into the hand of the lord one plot of land with appurtenances which contains in length 20 feet and in breadth 16 feet. And John Colin and Matilda his wife give to the lord 6d, to hold the aforesaid plot of land just as it lies next to the tenement of Alexander the Miller, to him and his in villeinage, performing the services due and accustomed for it.

Norton year 2 – William Barber [*1308/1309*]

Jurors:	William Dipere	Roger Schepherd	Sayer the Reeve
	John Jacob	Richard in the Hale	Walter Aubrey

* The jurors say in the Hale [*sic*] who holds one tenement by the right of his wife has made waste upon the said tenement to the damage etc. And he finds pledges to amend the said tenement *viz* Roger le Schepeherd and John Jacob amerced 3d.
* The jurors say that Walter the Miller is in arrears with ploughing for the lord for two years past, therefore he and his pledges are amerced 2d *viz* Walter Aubrey and John Isoude. And the said tenement is leased to the said pledges for six years, the term beginning from the Feast of St [*HALS 65504, f1v*] Michael next to come, performing for it the due and accustomed services. And they shall make an agreement about the crop with the heirs of the said Walter and with the lord for arrears of rent and service.
* Next, they say that Richard Bate, who holds the tenement of John his son, has committed waste upon the said tenement, therefore he is amerced, 6d. And it is ordered, etc. And John Jacob and Walter Aubrey and John Boueton and John Bate, who were the pledges of the said Richard for not committing waste, are amerced for the aforesaid trespass, 6d, each man pledging for one another.
* Next they say that Walter de Harleston is in arrears with the ploughing of

EDWARD II

three selions for the Lent season, to damage etc, therefore amerced 6d.
* Walter Sparue gives to the lord 12d for licence to marry where he will, so [*ie provided*] that he does not take his goods [*?or stock*] (*catalla*) out of the lord's Liberty, by the pledge of William Haysh and Richard Bate. [*l. margin*: villein]
* William the Neweman surrendered into the lord's hand one plot of land in his curtilage next to the tenement of John Bate, and it contains in length 40 feet and in width 30 feet. And Alan son of William the Neweman gives 6d to the lord for the said plot, to hold to him and his in villeinage, performing for it the due and accustomed services.
* Walter Sayer gives 6d to the lord that he may have half the crop of an acre of fallow which Walter his father demised to John Balston for 15d which he gave to the said Walter for allowance of the said acre, and this according to the custom of the village. However the jurors say that any heir after the death of his father or mother, after whose death the inheritance falls to him, in such a case shall give and have in the same manner.
* The same Walter son of Walter Sayer gives 6d to the lord for a plot of land which John Colin and Matilda his wife had by permission of the lord from the said Walter Sayer the elder, to hold to him and his in villeinage, performing for it the due and accustomed services.
* Alexander Wisote gives to the lord 6d to enquire whether he ought to exercise common rights with one animal in the pasture of the village for that cotland or messuage containing 12 acres of land which he had by permission of the lord from William in the Hale or not. The jurors say that he cannot exercise common rights in this way, nor ought he by right, therefore it is adjudged etc.
* Because it has been ascertained by a decision of the villagers that a certain way which was formerly made from the King's highway (*regia strata*)[22] to the *Prestescroft* between the curtilage of John le Palmer and the croft of Walter Loveleg is not for the convenience of the village nor of any of the villagers but to the damage of the said John and Walter, therefore John and Walter have permission from the lord to enclose the said way so that no others may come into it. And they give the lord for having permission 18d.

Norton the year 3 William Barber [*1309/1310*]

Jurors:	William Dipere	Roger le Shepherd	John Boueton
	John Jecob	William Thomas	Walter Harleston
	Walter Aubrey	Sayer Reeve	John Tollard

---

[22] References are made to *regia via* and also to *regia strata,* possibly different roads.

EDWARD II

* The jurors say that the tenement of Thomas Bene is in the hands of the lord after the death of the said Thomas who was killed. And hereupon comes a certain John son of Walter de Newnham and lays claim and says that Lucy Abelon was mother of the said John and she was the true tenant of the said tenement, whose heir he is as he says. And he gives to the lord 7d to have an enquiry, pledge Adam, vicar of Newnham. And the jurors say that the said John has no right in the said tenement because although the said Lucy was the true tenant of the said tenement and mother of the same John, the aforesaid John was a bastard and that the said tenement is for the will of the lord. And thereupon comes Matilda, relict of Thomas Bene and is seised of the said tenement with appurtenances to hold for her life without waste, performing for it the due and accustomed services.
* Godfrey le Bonde \2d/, Richard Bate \6d/, and John Bate \2d/ grind elsewhere than at the lord's mill, therefore amerced.
* Roger le Schepherd surrendered into the lord's hands one cotland which was once Richard le Helder's. And Isabel daughter of the said Roger gives the lord half a mark for the said land with appurtenances, to hold it to her and hers without waste, performing for it the due and accustomed services. And she has licence to marry. And the said Roger shall hold the cotland for his life, performing for it etc.
* Alice, relict of John Wisot came and *gersummavit* one cotland, which was the said John Wisot's, to the use of John son and heir of said John, to hold to him and his in villeinage, performing for it the due and accustomed services, nor shall she commit waste. And she gives the lord for *gersumma* and for permission to hold the said land until the majority of the said heir 4s. And the aforesaid John has licence to marry, pledges John Boueton and Alexander Wisot.
* Matilda, relict of Thomas Bene surrenders into the lord's hand all the tenement which the said Thomas held with appurtenances. And John Balston and the said Matilda give to the lord 2s for the said tenement with appurtenances, to hold to them and the heirs begotten between them and to the one of them who survives the longer, and they have licence to marry at the same time. [*l. margin*: villein (fem)]

Norton in the 3rd year in the time of the Prior of Wymondham[23] holding the office of cellarer [*1309/1310*]

* The jurors say that John Godefrey junior has married without the lord's

---

[23] St Albans cellarer, John de Stevenache, may have been appointed Prior of Wymondham as early as 1304 (See *VCH Norfolk,* vol 2, pp336-43).

EDWARD II

licence so is amerced 18d. Pledges John Tollard and John Boueton. [*l. margin*: villein]
* Next they say that Thomas Hays has gone out (*elongavit se*) of the lord's Liberty with his stock, so it is ordered etc. [*l. margin*: villein]
* [*HALS 65505, f1*] Next they say that Matilda daughter of Godfrey has committed *leyrewit*, therefore amerced 3d. Pledge Godfrey le Neweman.
* Next they say that Isabel Thomas has committed *leyrewit*, therefore amerced 6d. Pledge William Thomas.
* Richard Bate gives 6d to the lord for permission to put Henry his son to letters.
* Next they say that Godfrey le Bonde has demised to Richard in the Hale one croft without the lord's permission, therefore amerced 3d.

Halimote of Norton on Wednesday in the Feast of St Hillary in the 4th year in the time of the Prior of Wymondham holding the office of cellarer [*13 Jan 1311*]

Jurors: John Boueton   Geoffrey Bercarius   Roger Bercarius
         Walter Aubrey   William le Dipere   John Jecob

* Richard Bate came after the death of John his son and *gersummavit* all that land with appurtenances whereof the same John was seised, and this to the use of William son of the same Richard, to hold to the same William and his, performing for it the due and accustomed services, nor shall he commit waste, and he gives to the lord for *gersumma*, and for permission to hold the said land until the majority of the said William, 20s. Pledges Richard Cok and Walter Albreth.
* Walter Godefrey came and *gersummavit* the tenement which was Godfrey le Neweman's, to hold to him and his in villeinage, performing for it the due and accustomed services, nor shall he commit waste. And he gives to the lord for *gersumma* and for licence to marry, 10s. Pledges Geoffrey Bercarius and Roger Bercarius.
* The jurors say that John le Swone holds seven acres of land with appurtenances of the fee of Walter de Lynleye and has defaulted. And John le Swone offered to do suit.
* William Thomas because he prevented (*perturbavit*) the lord's heriot after the death of John son of Richard Bate is amerced 4s, pledge John Jecob.
* Richard Bate comes and gives to the lord 10s for heriot of John his son who has died.
* John Balston gives to the lord 6d to put right three half acres of land and

EDWARD II

meadow at *Eldewell* and the jury is ordered to put them right.
* John the Dryvere has surrendered into the hands of the lord one messuage and one croft by the cemetery and *Chirchelane*, with appurtenances. And Thomas son of the said John gives 2s to the lord for the said messuage and croft, to hold to him and his, performing for them the due and accustomed services. And it is in such manner that the said John shall hold the said messuage and croft for the term of his life, pledge the bailiff.

Norton in the 4th year in the time of Thomas de Bovingedon cellarer [*1310/1311*]

Jurors:	John Prudde	Geoffrey Shepherd	Walter Aubrei
	Roger Shepherd	John Boueton	William Dipere
			John Jecob

* The jurors say that John Tollard has given Isabel his daughter in marriage without the lord's licence, therefore amerced 6d. [*r. margin*: villein]
* Next they say that John Boueton has demised to John le Swone one acre of land without the lord's permission therefore amerced 4d.
* Next they say that Walter Harleston has demised to the said John half an acre of land without the lord's permission, therefore amerced 3d.
* Next they say that Christina Parlur has married without the lord's licence, therefore amerced 6d. [*r. margin*: villein (fem)]
* The jurors say that:
  Richard Ame has appropriated of the lord's land to the width of one acre of land, therefore amerced 4d.
  William Hayss has transgressed in the same way, therefore amerced 4d.
  Richard in the Hale and Ralph Bate have transgressed in the same way, therefore amerced 4d.
  Richard Cok and William Thomas have transgressed in the same way to the width of one acre, therefore amerced 4d.
  John the Chaplain and Walter Warde have transgressed in the same way, therefore amerced 6d.
* John son of Walter Gile has permission to [be?] put to letters and gives 12d to the lord, pledge Roger Schepherd. [*r. margin*: villein]
* John Balston and William Haysse give 12d to the lord to put right the boundaries between them next to the church.
* Next they say that a boundary between Walter the Smith (*Faber*) and Walter in the Hale has been removed, therefore they have a day and inspection to put it right.

EDWARD II

[*HALS 65505, f1v*] **Halimote at Norton on Wednesday after the Feast of all Saints the 5th year – Thomas Bo[vingdon]** [*3 Nov 1312*]

Jurors:	Walter Aubrey	John Boueton	John Jecob
	John Prudde	William le Dipere	Roger Bercarius

* Matilda who was the wife of John Colyns came and surrendered all her right which she had in a third part of the tenement of the said John in the name of dower to the use of Geoffrey Bercarius so that the same Geoffrey shall raise at his expense a new house of the length of 20 feet and of the breadth of ten feet on the plot of the said Matilda. And the said Geoffrey shall give to the same Matilda three bushels of wheat and three bushels of peas annually for the life of that Matilda.
* The jurors say that John Bate \2d\ and William Thomas the elder \2d\ have defaulted. Therefore amerced.
* Next they say that Ralph the Cartere has married without the lord's licence. Afterwards he comes and gives 12d to the lord for licence.
* Next they say that Sara daughter of Walter le Hale has married without the lord's licence so amerced 6d.
* Geoffrey Geiard gives to the lord 6d for rectifying the bounds between him and Walter Ward.
* Ralph Carter surrendered into the lord's hand one cottage with appurtenances. And the same Ralph and Isabel his wife give to the lord 12d for the said cottage to hold to them and the heirs begotten of the same, performing for it the due and accustomed services without waste.
* John Isoude surrendered into the lord's hand one plot of land with appurtenances to the use of John Isoude his son to hold to him and his in villeinage, performing for it the due and accustomed services. And he gives to the lord for having entry and for his marriage 18d. And the said plot contains in length 85 feet and in breadth 40 feet.

Norton the 5th year in the time of Thomas de Bovingdon cellarer [*1311/1312*]

* The jurors say that Henry de Erdele is in arrears with the rent of one pound of cumin for a way which he had from John of Norton to the mill, therefore it is ordered etc.
* Next they say that Alan le Neweman grinds elsewhere than at the lord's mill therefore amerced 2d.
* Next they say that Alexander Wysote has married without the lord's licence therefore amerced 12d, pledge Walter Aubrey.

EDWARD II

* Next they say that Geoffrey Geiard married Isabel his daughter without the lord's licence, therefore amerced 12d.
* Next they say that John Boueton has demised to Ralph his son one acre of land without the lord's permission, therefore amerced 12d. And it is ordered to seise the said land into the lord's hand with the crop.
* John the Swineherd (*Porcarius*) has taken from John Boueton one acre of land without the lord's permission, therefore amerced 3d.
* Next they say that Sayer the Reeve has demised to the said John half an acre of land without the lord's permission, therefore amerced 3d.
* Richard the Chapman came and did fealty to the lord for the land which he holds in the *Wiliefeld* and he acknowledged the due and customary services *viz* a rent of 1½d for an acre of land in *Sevene Acres Dene.*
* Richard le Spenser came and did fealty to the lord for the land which he holds in the *Wiliefeld* and he acknowledged that he holds two half-acres of land of which one half acre lies at *Inlondesdiche* next the tenement of Peter the Glover and the other half-acre of land lies at the *Wantes* next the land of John le Mower and the land of the said Richard by the service of 1½d rent *per annum*.
* John son of John Boueton came after the death of William his brother and *gersummavit* one messuage with appurtenances to hold to him and his by the due and accustomed services for it without waste. And he gives to the lord for *gersumma* 3s, pledge John Boueton.
* Robert Hays surrendered into the lord's hand one messuage with a curtilage and other appurtenances as it lies between the tenement of Richard Cok and the tenement of John Reymond. And Isabel daughter of the said Robert gives to the lord 12d for the said messuage with appurtenances, to hold to her and hers without waste by the services due and accustomed for it. And she has licence to marry.
* Walter Warde gives to the lord 6d for having an inquisition for bounding his land between him and Geoffrey Geiard.
* Stephen Parnele recovered against Walter in the Hale one piece of land which the same Walter detained to damage 6d.
* Roger the Swineherd (*Porcarius*) gives to the lord 12d for having the boundary of his land at *Langelondes* rectified.
* Walter in the Hale surrendered into the lord's hand one plot of land between the land of the said Walter and Matilda Ward which contains in length five perches and in breadth 21 feet. And Roger Wilemot and Alice his wife give to the lord 12d for the said plot, to hold to them and theirs in villeinage, performing for it the due and accustomed services.

EDWARD II

[*HALS 65506, f1*] **Norton the 6th year in the time of Thomas de Bovingdon cellarer [*1312/1313*]**

Jurors:	Walter Aubrey	William Dipere	Richard Cok
	John Jecob	Sayer Reeve	Richard in the Hale

* The jurors say that John Burre makes default, therefore amerced 6d.
* Next they say that John Prudde has married Idonia his daughter without the lord's licence. And he has made agreement for 2s, pledge Walter Aubrey.
* Next they say that William atte Chirche has married without the lords licence, and he gives for agreement 2s, pledge Walter Aubrey. [*r. margin*: villein]
* Next they say that Richard Dame has married without the lord's licence and he calls for the record of the roll.
* Next they say that John Isoude has given in marriage Sara his daughter without the lord's licence and he gives to the lord 6d pledge Walter Aubrey.
* Next they say that Roger the Shepherd has given in marriage Sara his daughter without the lord's licence and he gives to the lord 3s. [*r. margin*: villein]
* Next they say that Sara daughter of Walter Sayers has committed *leyrewit*, so amerced 3d, pledge Walter Sayer.
* Next they say that Matilda Swetekyn has committed *leyrewit*, therefore amerced 3d, pledge Walter Swetekyn. [*r. margin*: villein (fem)]
* Next they say that John le Swone who held seven acres of free land in Norton has ended his last day. Therefore the said land is seised into the lord's hand until etc. Afterwards comes Agnes who was the wife of the said John and shows a charter of six acres of which she together with her husband was seised and she did fealty for them and she gives to the lord 12d for acknowledgment. Pledges Laurence Blaseworth and Thomas Sergeaunt. And she shows another charter of one acre which the said John acquired to himself in fee which is seised into the lord's hand until the coming of age of the heir. Afterwards she comes and gives 2s for the said acre until the coming of age of the heir, pledge William Dipere.
* Next they say that Matilda Ward 3d, Alan Neweman 6d, John Prudde 6d grind elsewhere than at the lord's mill. Therefore amerced.
* Richard Bate did not come to reap as he was summoned at harvest, therefore amerced 16d. Pledge John Isoude.
* Laurence de Blaseworth came after the death of Sibyl who was the wife of John de Norton and took wardship of the land and heirs of the said Sibyl until the coming of age of Joan who is 17 years old and of Agnes who is 15 and of Margaret who is 13, saving to the lord abbot the marriages of the said Joan, Agnes and Margaret, doing for it the due and accustomed services, nor shall

EDWARD II

they commit waste. And he gives to the lord for wardship 10s. And he shall maintain the houses and other things belonging to the said land in as good condition as he has received them in. Pledge Thomas Sergeant.

Halimote of Norton on Tuesday next after the Feast of St Barnabas the Apostle in the 6th year – Thomas Bo[vingdon] [*12 Jun 1313*]

| Jurors: | Walter Aubrey | Geoffrey the Shepherd | Richard in the Hale |
| | William Dipere | John Jacob | Roger Bercarius |

* The jurors say that John Burre makes default, therefore amerced, condoned.
* It is reported that John Boueton senior has withheld from the lord's bailiff the heriot for a certain messuage which John Boueton junior used to hold, after the death of the said John, which heriot was one female sheep (*bidens*) worth 20d. And the said John is amerced for the said refusal 6d. And the said sheep is ordered to come, pledge Walter Aubrey.
* Alan son of William le Neweman comes and gives 4s to the lord for *gersumma* of one *ferthlingate* of land which was of William le Neweman, to hold to him and his in villeinage by its due and accustomed services, by the pledge of John Prudd.
* Ralph Boueton came after the death of John Boueton his brother and *gersummavit* one messuage with appurtenances, to hold to him and his in villeinage by its due and accustomed services. And he gives to the lord for *gersumma* and for licence to marry 3s, pledge John Boueton senior.
* The jurors say that Gena Wisot seised Alexander Wisot, a villein of the lord, in one messuage and one piece of land containing one acre of free land by charter. Therefore the said Alexander is ordered to come to give up the charter. Afterwards he came and surrendered the charter and messuage into the lord's hand and was re-seised, performing for it the due and accustomed services. And he gives to the lord for having entry 12d. And he gives to the lord for increase in rent ½d. [*r. margin*: increase ½d]
* Walter son of Alexander the Miller came after the death of his father and did fealty and acknowledged 2s 4d of rent *per annum* and suit at the Great Court of the lord abbot and at the Court of Walter de Lylleleye every three weeks. And he gave security for relief by the pledge of William Dipere and Walter Saleman. Relief 2s 4d.
* Next they say that Gena Wisot seised John son of John Wisot, villein of the lord, in one cottage by charter. Therefore the said John is ordered to come to give up the charter. Afterwards he came and surrendered the charter and land into the lord's hand, and he was re-seised, doing the due and accustomed

services for it. And he shall give to the lord at the Feast of St Michael annually for increase in rent ¼d, pledge Alexander Wisot. [*r. margin*: increase ¼d]
* [*HALS 65506, f1v*] John Bate and Alan le Neweman give to the lord 6d to place and straighten stakes in a certain ditch near their curtilages.
* Alexander le Helder surrendered into the lord's hand one messuage which was at one time of John Alexander between the land of Hugh Grom and of William Seman. And Matilda daughter of the said Andrew gives to the lord 6d for the said messuage, to hold to her and hers. And it is in such a way that the said Andrew shall hold the said messuage for the term of life of this Andrew, with free entry and exit at either door. And after the decease of the said Andrew the said messuage with appurtenances shall remain to the aforesaid Matilda and her heirs forever.

Norton in the 7th year in the time of Thomas de Bovingdon cellarer [*1313/1314*]

Jurors:	Walter Albrethe	Roger Shepherd	Richard in the Hale
	Geoffrey Shepherd	William Thomas	Richard Cok

* Alan le Neweman gives to the lord 6d so that he may hold his tenement between him and John Bate as his father held it, saving a ditch between him and John Bate; which is of the width of two feet and of the length of their curtilages and it shall remain in the possession of the said John according to what is staked by the neighbours.
* The jurors say that Alan le Neweman holds a dog which does damage to the rabbits of the lord abbot therefore amerced 3d.
* Next they say that whereas stakes were placed according to the decision of the jurors chosen for this matter between John Bate and Alan le Neweman the same Alan then refused to assent therefore amerced 6d. And hereupon the same Alan with the lord's permission grants to the said John the ditch where stakes were placed according to what is bounded. Pledge Geoffrey Shepherd.
* Geoffrey the Shepherd surrendered into the lord's hand all that tenement with its appurtenances which was at one time Nicholas le Neweman's. And John Boueton made agreement with the lord for the said tenement to hold to him and his in villeinage, without waste, by the services due and accustomed for it. And the same John Boueton surrendered into the lord's hand all his tenement which he held with all its appurtenances whatsoever. And the said Geoffrey the Shepeherd made agreement with the lord for the said tenement with all its appurtenances, to hold to him and his for the will of the lord without waste,

EDWARD II

performing for it the due and accustomed services. And they give to the lord for the exchange of the said tenements 33s 4d.

Norton in the 7th year in the time of Richard de Tewyng cellarer [1313/1314]

* The jurors say that Joan Alysaundre has married without the lord's licence. And because she is not within the Liberty, therefore it is ordered etc. [*l. margin*: villein (fem)]
* Next they say that John Bate has knocked down one bake house to the damage of his tenement, 3s. Therefore it is ordered etc.
* Isabel, daughter and heir of Richard le Parlour came and *gersummavit* one *ferthlingate* of land which he held on the day on which he died, to hold to her and hers in villeinage, performing for it the due and accustomed services, nor shall she commit waste. And she gives to the lord for *gersumma* 4s.

* Alan le Neweman	3d	Amerced because they did not come to shear the lord's sheep as they were summoned.
Walter in the Hale	3d	
John Bate	3d	
John Balston	3d	

* Alexander son and heir of Andrew le Helder came and *gersummavit* all the tenement which the said Andrew held on the day on which he died, to hold to him and his without waste, performing for it the services due and accustomed. And he gives the lord 10s for *gersumma*, pledge William Thomas.
* Ralph Boueton gives 12d to the lord to have an inquisition of 12 jurors on an agreement between John Boueton, his father and him Ralph, which jurors namely say upon their oath that such agreement between the said John and Ralph was previously agreed (*praelocuta*), that the same Ralph should give to the said John annually for the term of his life three quarters of corn, three quarters of barley, half a quarter of oats and a pair of linen cloths and one acre of straw for the whole tenement of the said John to hold to the same Ralph and his by the lord's permission. Immediately afterwards the said John for his urgent business weighing carefully that it would be more quickly to his advantage otherwise and not content with the said prior agreement, agreed with a certain Geoffrey the Schepherd of Norton that the same Geoffrey should give to the same John a messuage and a half of virgate of land and six marks of silver to have the whole tenement of the said John with appurtenances. And that the said Geoffrey was given possession of the whole tenement of the said John by permission of the cellarer. And that Geoffrey satisfied John with the six marks of silver except 5s which are in arrears. And

having been asked if it be the custom of the village if a father may disinherit a son of what the same son is ready to satisfy the father with as much as any other stranger. And hereupon they have a day, the lord's day next after the Feast of the Translation of St Thomas the Martyr.

[HALS 65507, f1] Halimote of Norton on Thursday next after the Feast of St Edward in the 8th year – Richard de Te[wyng] [*1314/1315*][24]

Jurors:	William le Dipere	Richard in the Hale	Richard Bate
	William Thomas	Roger Bercarius	Alan le Neweman

* The jurors say that the tenement of William Everard owes suit and the same William has closed his last day, therefore the said tenement is seised into the lord's hand until etc.
* Next they say that the tenement of the said William is in arrears by one man for one day in harvest. Therefore etc.
* Next they say that the tenement of Andrew le Helder is in arrears of the ploughing of three selions of Lent season, therefore amerced 4½d.
* Next they say that Walter in the Hale is in arrears of the ploughing of six selions to the damage of the lord 6d. Therefore etc.
* The lord by the decision of the Halimote has leased to Roger the Shepherd the land [of] le Parlour for the term of two years for want of an heir. And if an heir shall come after the said term and shall give *gersumma* let him be admitted. And it is ordered that the houses be viewed. And the said Roger shall do the due and customary services.
* Next they say that Godfrey Bonde \6d/ and John Bate \4d/ grind elsewhere than at the lord's mill, therefore amerced.
* Alexander Wisot has licence to marry and gives the lord 6d.
* The jurors say that Juliana Dame has married without the lord's licence, therefore amerced 6d.
* Next they say that Isabel Alexander has married without the lord's licence, therefore it is ordered that if she be found within the Liberty, she be distrained.
* Ralph Bate gives to the lord 6d to put stakes between him and Roger Schepherd.

---

[24] If Edward the Confessor is meant, with his Feast day on 5th Jan, this court was held on Thursday 9th Jan 1315; if Edward King and Martyr, whose Feast was on 18th March, then it was held on Thursday 20th March 1315 (but as this was Maundy Thursday it seems less likely).

EDWARD II

Halimote of Norton on Thursday next after the Feast of Holy Trinity in the 8th year in the time of J Hurle [*29 May 1315*]

Jurors:	William Dipere	William Thomas	Roger Shepherd
	John Jecob	Richard Cok	Richard in the Hale

* The jurors say that John Burre 3d, William Everard 6d, Henry de Erdele condoned, have defaulted, therefore amerced.
* Next they say that Edith Mulleward \2d\ and John Bate \3d\ grind elsewhere than at the lord's mill, therefore amerced.
* Next they say that Alexander le Helder has married without the lord's licence, therefore amerced 6d, pledge Richard Cok. [*r. margin*: villein]
* The jurors say that Matilda Andrew has married without the lord's licence, therefore amerced 6d. [*r. margin*: villein (fem)]
* William Thomas came and *gersummavit* one cotland which was of William Thomas his father to hold to him and his in villeinage for the will of the lord, doing for it the due and accustomed services, nor shall he commit waste. He gives for *gersumma* 5s.
* John son of Geoffrey Geiard came and *gersummavit* one cotland with appurtenances which was of the said Geoffrey his father, to hold to him and his in villeinage for the will of the lord, doing for it the due and accustomed services, nor shall he commit waste. And he gives to the lord for *gersumma* and for licence to marry 5s and for his father's heriot 12d. [*r. margin*: villein]
* Roger Pilegrym has permission to enter the villein land (*nativam terram*) of the lord and to take Matilda daughter of Andrew le Herde to wife, so [*ie provided*] that he shall not alienate her goods out of the lord's Liberty. And he gives to the lord 2s, pledge of the manner of his entry and for agreement John Boueton.
* The jurors of Norton and Newnham say that all the villeins of Norton and Newnham with the lord's permission may let, sell and exchange among themselves because they are by custom used and obliged to, and to let their tenements to free men if they shall have the permission of the lord for this and not otherwise. And the jurors were:

William Dipere	Richard Cok	John Jecob
William Thomas	Roger Shepherd	Richard in the Hale
Richard Siker	John Jecob	Richard Bate
Adam in the Hale	John atte Crouch	John Isoude

* John Andrew junior of Baldock took from the lord the land with

EDWARD II

appurtenances which was of John le Swon on the day on which he died in the fields of Norton to hold and accept wardship until the coming of age of John son and heir of the said John le Swon, performing for it annually during the term the due and accustomed services. And it is to be known that the said John the heir has now completed the age of 13 years. And he gives for the wardship of the said land 10s.

[HALS 65507, f1v] Halimote at Norton on Wednesday next after the Feast of St Andrew the Apostle in the 9th year J Hurle [3 Dec 1315]

* John son of Simon the Reeve of Munden gives to the lord 2s for having licence to marry Isabel Cartere and to hold the tenement of the said Isabel of which she is possessed to them and the heirs begotten between them. But if they have no heirs between themselves the said tenement with appurtenances shall revert to the true heirs of the said Isabel.
* The vicar of Norton gives 6d to the lord to have stakes rightly placed between him and Walter Whitecok.
* The jurors say that Isabel daughter of Roger le Shepherd has committed *leyrewit* therefore amerced 6d, pledge Roger Shepherd.
* Then they say that Sara daughter of Walter Sayer has committed *leyrewit*, therefore amerced 3d.
* The jurors say that John Bate grinds elsewhere than at the mill of the lord, so amerced 2d.
* Ellen atte Chirche surrendered into the lord's hand a piece of land of the length between her tenement and the King's highway (*regiam stratam*) of 100 feet and of the breadth between her tenement and the highway 20 feet. And William atte Chirche gives to the lord 12d for the said piece of land with appurtenances, to hold to him and his, performing for it the due and accustomed services.
* Margaret relict of Richard Dame came and *gersummavit* the tenement which was of the same Richard, to the use of Reynald son and heir of the said Richard, to hold to him and his in villeinage, performing for it the due and accustomed services, nor shall he commit waste. And he gives for *gersumma* and permission to hold the said tenement with appurtenances without waste until the coming of age of the said Reynald 12d.

Halimote at Norton on Thursday next before the Feast of Holy Trinity in the 9th year – J Hurle [3 Jun 1316]

Jurors:	William Diper	Richard Bate	Roger Shepherd
	Walter Aubrey	Richard in the Hale	Richard Cok

EDWARD II

* The jurors say that Roger Faber has sold one messuage with appurtenances to a certain Walter Warde without the lord's permission. Therefore amerced 6d. And it is ordered to seise the said land into the lord's hand.
* Then they say that the tenement [of] le Parlour for want of the true tenant who went out because of impotence lies without a tenant after the term which Roger le Shepherd had in the same, therefore it is seised into the lord's hand. To hold which the jurors chose Godfrey le Bonde. And the lord transferred the said tenement with appurtenances to the said Godfrey to hold saving the right of anyone.
* The jurors say that Ralph Boueton has married without the lord's licence. And the same Ralph comes and says that he was licensed for three years past and he appeals to the record of the rolls about it.
* John Boueton with the lord's permission demised to Ralph his son his whole tenement with appurtenances to hold for the term of two years and he shall maintain the said tenement in good condition during the said term. And he gives for permission 6d.
* John le Dryver surrendered into the lord's hand two acres of land with appurtenances which he held of the fee formerly of Walter atte Halle in Norton, of which one acre lies between the tenements of William Thomas and of John Prudde, and one half acre lies between the tenements of John Bate and of John Prudde, and one half acre [lies] between the land of Hoghaler and the land of John Albrethe. And Walter son of the said John and Agnes daughter of the same John have made agreement with the lord for the said land with appurtenances, to hold to them or to the one of them who shall live longer and their heirs, performing for it the due and accustomed services, etc.
* Joan daughter of John de Norton came and did fealty to the lord for the tenements which she claims to hold from the lord and she acknowledges the services due and accustomed for them *viz* annual rent 12s 8d and one boonday with one man for one day at harvest and suit at two Halimotes *per annum*.
* Hugh de Bray came and did fealty to the lord for one messuage and 10 acres of land with appurtenances which he claims to hold by the service of 7s 2d rent and one boonday with one man for one day at harvest and one suit at the Halimote *per annum* and for two acres of land on the field of *Wilyen* [Willian] which he claims to hold by the service of 3d rent *per annum*, which messuage and land he had of the gift of John his brother, son and heir of William Everard.
* Walter Smith (*Faber*) surrendered into the lord's hands one messuage with curtilage and other appurtenances just as it is between the tenement of Richard Parlour and the tenement of Walter in the Hale. And Margaret daughter of Walter Warde gives to the lord 3s for the said messuage with appurtenances,

EDWARD II

to hold to her and hers, performing for it the due and accustomed services, nor shall she commit waste.
* Reynald Kyng took from the lord one messuage with curtilage and with a little croft adjacent between the tenement which Ralph the Cartere held on the one side and the tenement of Richard Cok on the other, to hold to him and his heirs, performing annually for the lord abbot the due and accustomed service viz one clove (*unum clavum gareophili*) for all other services except suit at the lord's court.

[*HALS 65507, f2*] **Halimote at Norton on Thursday next after the Exaltation of the Holy Cross in the 10th year – J Hurle [*16 Sep 1316*]**

Jurors:	William Dipere	Richard Cok	Richard in the Hale
	Walter Albreth	Roger Shepherd	William Thomas

* The jurors say that Hugh Everard distrain, John Borre 3d, John Bate 2d make default, therefore amerced.
* They say that Hugh Everard is in arrears with one boonday in harvest, therefore amerced 6d.
* They say that John Bate is in arrears with one boonday and half a boonday in harvest, therefore amerced 6d.
* Next they say that Walter Swetekin grinds elsewhere than at the lord's mill, therefore amerced 2d.
* John Tollard surrendered into the lord's hand all the tenement with appurtenances which he held in Norton. And John son and heir of the said John Tollard gives to the lord 40d for the said tenement with appurtenances, to hold to him and his for the will of the lord, performing for it the due and accustomed services.
* John Borre, chaplain, by the lord's permission demised to Ralph Aubrey all the tenement with all appurtenances which he had in Norton after the death of his father, to hold for the term of 12 years, the term beginning at Michaelmas next coming, rendering for it the due and accustomed services, and to the said John Borre annually 13s 4d at Christmas. And the said John shall maintain the houses of the said tenement and the timber walls at his expense. And the said Ralph or his heirs shall have it roofed and enclosed. Nor shall the same John make any demise or sale of the said tenement without the consent of the said Ralph during the term. And he gives for having the term half a mark. And the same Ralph Aubrey has licence to marry and he gives 40d. And the same Ralph shall perform the suit of the said tenement at the Halimote during the term.

EDWARD II

Halimote at Norton on Thursday next after the Finding of the Holy Cross in the 10th year – Nicholas Flamsted [*5 May 1317*]

Jurors: John Prudde   William Thomas   Walter Aubrey
          Richard Bate   Richard in the Hale   Roger Bercarius

* The jurors say that Alexander the son of Andrew le Helder committed waste on the tenement which he holds to the damage of 12d, therefore it is ordered etc.
* Next they say that Roger Pilegrym wastes the tenement of Matilda his wife to the damage of 12d. Therefore it is ordered to seise the said tenement into the lord's hands.
* Next they say that Christina Parlour has wasted a third part of the tenement which was Richard Parlour's. Therefore by decision of the Halimote it is adjudged that she lose the said dower and Godfrey le Bonde who holds the two parts shall hold and keep the same dower until etc.
* John son and heir of Ralph Bate came and *gersummavit* all the tenement with appurtenances which was of the said Ralph on the day on which he died, to hold to him and his, performing for it the due and accustomed services, nor shall he commit waste. And he gives to the lord for *gersumma* 3s. And he has licence to marry. And he gives for a heriot 12d.
* Emma who was the wife of John Jecob came and *gersummavit* all the tenement with appurtenances which was of the said John Jecob on the day on which he died, to the use of John son and heir of the said John, to hold to her and hers, performing for it the due and accustomed services, nor shall she commit waste. And she gives to the lord for *gersumma* and for leave to hold the said tenement until the coming of age of the said heir, 8s. Pledge Walter Aubrey.
* The jurors say that Alice the daughter of John Prudde has married without the lord's licence. And John Prudde came and made agreement with the lord. And he gives 12d.
* Margery who was the wife of John Tollard the younger *gersummavit* all the tenement with appurtenances which was of the said John on the day on which he died, to the use of Margaret daughter and heir of the said John, to hold to the same Margaret and her heirs, doing for it the due and customary services, nor shall she commit waste. And she gives for heriot 12d and has licence to marry. [*r. margin*: villein (fem)]
* Alexander son of Andrew le Helder by the lord's leave has demised to Richard Cok one half virgate of land with appurtenances which he holds in Norton, to hold for the term of ten years, the term beginning at Michaelmas

EDWARD II

next coming, performing for it the due and accustomed services, nor shall he commit waste, but shall maintain the said tenement in good condition during the term. And he gives to the lord for having the term 4s.

* Richard atte Dane of Codicote and Sara his wife are pleading against Richard Bate in a plea of land, pledges of prosecution John the Bailiff and Hugh Finche. And Richard Bate having been summoned to be at St Albans under the ash tree to answer to the said Richard and Sara on the Saturday next before the Eve of Pentecost on which day the said Richard and Sara appeared in court against the said Richard, who did not come, therefore let the said land be taken into the hand of the lord. And they have Saturday in three weeks on which day Richard Bate seeks to redeem the said land which has been taken into the lord's hand, by William Thomas and Richard Cok. And he has the said day.
* Isabel daughter of Richard le Parlour surrendered into the lord's hand a *ferthlingate* of land with appurtenances which was the said Richard's. And Godfrey le Bond gives to the lord 5s for the said *ferthlingate* of land with appurtenances, to hold to him and his, performing for it the due and accustomed services.
* John Albrethe surrendered into the lord's hand one *ferthelingate* of land with appurtenances as well as (*preter*) all the messuage which he holds.
* [*HALS 65507, f2v*] And Alexander Wysoth gives to the lord 40d for the said *ferthlingate* of land with appurtenances, to hold to him and his, performing for it the due and accustomed services, so that the said John, he and his heirs, shall perform for the said messuage a boonday in harvest and [shall give] a hen with eggs.

Norton in the 11th year – Nicholas Flamsted [*1317/1318*]

Jurors:	Richard in the Hale	Robert Hays	William Thomas
	Roger Bercarius	Richard Cok	Alan Neweman

* The jurors say that Ralph Boueton grinds elsewhere than the lord's mill, therefore amerced 3d.
* Next they say that Ralph Boueton has burdened the pasture beyond his allowance with 64 lambs, to damage 12d, therefore amerced 2s.
* They say that Matilda Boueton married without the lord's licence, therefore amerced 12d. Pledge Ralph Boueton.
* Next they say that Agnes Boueton has committed *leyrewit*, therefore amerced 6d, pledge Ralph Boueton. And the same Ralph pledged the fine (*finem*) for the marriage of the said Agnes.
* Next they say that Alice daughter of John Isoude has committed *leyrewit*,

EDWARD II

therefore amerced 12d, pledge John Isoude. And she has licence to marry.
* Ralph Boueton came and pledged 12d for his father's heriot because he had no animal.
* Ralph Boueton came after the death of John his father and *gersummavit* all the tenement with appurtenances which the said John held on the day on which he died, to hold to him and his, performing for it the due and accustomed services, nor shall he commit waste. And he gives half a mark. Pledges Richard in the Hale and Roger Bercarius.

Halimote of Norton on Friday on the Feast of the Translation of the Blessed Thomas in the 11th year – Nicholas Flamsted [*7 Jul 1318*]

Jurors:	Geoffrey Bercarius	William Thomas	Walter Sayer
	Alan le Neweman	Robert Hays	Richard in the Hale

* The jurors say that the land of William in the Hale is wasted to damage etc and is in arrears with rent and services of the said land. And because Richard in the Hale his brother has sown the said land, the same William has with the lord's leave leased the same land to the said Richard for the term of four years, performing for it the due and accustomed services, so that the said William shall make the delay in houses and croft by doing manual works (*moram faciet in domibus et crofta faciendo opera manualia*).
* Essoins John Andrew guardian of John son and heir of John le Swone. Of suit by Richard Eustach affeeror.
* John the Cornemongere came and did fealty to the lord for one messuage with its appurtenances which he acquired from John the Cornemongere his kinsman, and he acknowledged the services, etc.

Halimote of Norton in the 12th year – Nicholas Flamsted [*1318/1319*]

Jurors:	Geoffrey Bercarius	Richard Borre	Richard in the Hale
	Alan Neweman	William Thomas	Roger Bercarius

* The jurors say that Stephen Parnele and John Bate default, therefore amerced. It is remitted.
* Next they say that Walter atte Hale has not raised again a house on the tenement of *Gaffe* [?Gasse] as he pledged, therefore he finds pledges to restore a house on the said tenement before the next Feast of St Michael, by pledges of William Thomas and Richard Bate.
* Walter in the Hale because he has not come to the lord's work as he was summoned, therefore is amerced 6d.

EDWARD II

* Godfrey le Bonde withdrew himself from two boondays in harvest, therefore amerced 3d. Work 4d.
* It is ordered to attach Ralph Boueton to answer to the lord about the burdening of his pasture.

[HALS 65507, f3] Halimote of Norton on Wednesday before the Feast of St Elphege in the 12th year – Nicholas Flamsted [18 Apr 1319]

Jurors:	Geoffrey Bercarius	Alexander Wisot	Walter son of William
	Alan le Neweman	Walter Aubrey	Roger Bercarius

* The jurors say that Walter Swetekin has demised his land without the leave of the lord to a certain free man. Therefore amerced 2d.
* Next they say that Walter Harleston has demised land without leave of the lord to a certain free man, therefore amerced 2d.
* Juliana Hoghaler with the lord's leave has demised to Roger Bercarius all her tenement with appurtenances to hold for the term of four years, the term beginning at Michaelmas next coming, and he shall perform the due and accustomed services for it, and he gives 12d.
* Walter Aubrey gives to the lord 40d for licence to give his daughter Ellen in marriage, pledge Richard Bate. [r. margin: villein]
* William, son of Richard Bate came after the death of William his brother and *gersummavit* all that tenement with appurtenances which was once Osbert Bate's, to hold to him and his performing for it the due and accustomed services, nor shall he commit waste. And he gives to the lord for *gersumma* 20s. And the same William has licence to marry with Ellen Aubrey. And he gives 40d. [r. margin: villein]
* It is ordered to distrain Robert Norman to show how he entered the lord's fee.
* Godfrey Bonde has leave to put John his son to letters. [r. margin: villein]
* Emma Jacob for *leyrewit* amerced 12d. [r. margin: villein (fem)]

Halimote of Norton on Thursday next before the Feast of St Martin in the 13th year – Nicholas F[lamsted] [8 Nov 1319]

Jurors:	Geoffrey Bercarius	Alexander Wisot	William Thomas
	Alan le Neweman	Walter Reymond	John Balston

* Walter Warde surrendered into the lord's hand all his tenement with appurtenances which he had in Norton. And Alice daughter of the said Walter made agreement with the lord for the said tenement with appurtenances, to hold to her and hers, performing for it the due and accustomed services, nor

EDWARD II

shall she commit waste. Pledges Walter Sayer and Walter Swete. And she has licence to marry. And this is the substance of such acknowledgement, that the said Walter shall hold the said tenement without waste for the term of the life of this Walter, performing for it the due and accustomed services. And when he shall have died the same Walter shall give an heriot.

* The jurors say that Margaret Dame has committed *leyrewit*, therefore amerced 12d. Pledge Walter Loveleg. [*r. margin*: villein (fem)]
* Isabel daughter and heir of John Albrethe came and *gersummavit* one cottage with curtilage and other appurtenances, to hold to her and hers, performing for it the due and accustomed services, nor shall she commit waste. And she gives 6d, pledge Walter Albrethe. And she has licence to marry and gives 6d. [*r. margin*: villein (fem)]
* The jurors say that Walter in the Hale has not repaired his tenement as he was ordered. Afterwards he comes and gives 2s so that he shall not build more largely on his part upon the land of *Gaffe* [?Gasse].
* Next they say that Swetekin Bonde has not repaired the house of one tenement as he was ordered, afterwards he came and said that he will build before Michaelmas next, pledges Richard Bate and Walter in the Hale.

Halimote of Norton on Thursday after the Feast of Translation of the Blessed Thomas the 13th year – Nicholas F[lamsted] [*12 Jul 1319*]

Jurors:	Geoffrey Bercarius	Alexander Wisot	Roger Bercarius
	Alan le Neweman	Walter Aubrey	Walter Reymond

* The jurors say that the tenement of William Everard has made default; therefore let it be distrained.
* Next they say that Robert Saman has married without the lord's licence, therefore amerced 6d. [*r. margin*: villein]
* Next they say that Matilda Colines has committed *leyrewit*, therefore amerced 3d.
* Next they say that Emma Jecob has committed *leyrewit*, therefore amerced. Poor (*pauper*). [*r. margin*: villein (fem)]
* William Hereberd de la Northawe came after the death of John, son of John le Swone, and relieved seven acres of land with appurtenances which he holds from the lord and he acknowledges the due and accustomed services for them *viz* 20d of rent and suit at the Great Court.
* [*HALS 65507, f3v*] Walter in the Hale 2d, Walter Loveleg 2d, Godfrey Bond 2d made default at haymaking, therefore amerced.
* Michael atte Dene and Sara his wife give 12d to the lord to have an inquisition

EDWARD II

about the right which he [*or she*] claims in a land which Richard Bate holds. The jurors say that that woman who had the same land and surrendered it was the right heir.

Halimote of Norton in the 14th year – Richard Stoppesle [*1320/1321*]

* The jurors say that Walter son of Saery the Reeve has married without licence of the lord, therefore amerced 12d.
* Next they say that the tenement of William Everard is in arrears of one boonday in harvest. Therefore it is ordered etc.
* Next they say that Agnes and Margaret daughters of John of Norton are in arrears of one boonday in harvest for all the tenement which was of the said John this year. Therefore amerced 6d.
* William son of William atte Chirche came after the death of Ellen atte Chirche and *gersummavit* all the tenement with appurtenances that was of the said Ellen on the day she died, to hold to him and his, performing for it the due and accustomed services, nor shall he commit waste. And he gives to the lord for *gersumma* 10s.
* Again as before it is ordered to distrain the tenement of William Everard for default.
* Next they say that Godfrey le Bonde is in arrears of one boonday in harvest therefore amerced 6d.
* Next they say that John Geiard is in arrears of one boonday in harvest therefore amerced 6d.
* Next they say that Walter de Harleston is in arrears of one boonday and half a boonday in harvest, therefore amerced 6d.
* Next they say that Ralph Albreth is in arrears of one boonday in harvest, therefore amerced 4d.
* Next they say that Richard Bate has transgressed in the same manner, therefore amerced 6d.
* Walter Swetek for default of three roods of ploughing of fallow in summer amerced 6d.
* Richard atte Dane and Sara his wife brought a case against Richard Bate in a plea of land and they complain of the said Richard that he *deforced*[25] them unjustly of a messuage and half a virgate of land in Norton, and so unjustly because they say that a certain Alan son of William [son] of Stephen had three daughters, namely Amice, Joan and Sara, and that the said Amice and Joan died without heirs and that the said Amice died possessed of the said

---

[25] *Deforce* a Middle English word – to withold property wrongfully from rightful owner.

tenement, whose next heir Sara is as they say. And the said Richard says that he had the said tenement by leave of the lord by the gift of a certain Roger Prudde and of the said Amice his wife who were able to give and sell the said tenement by leave of the lord. And thereof he seeks the record of the roll. And a day is given to them within 15 days of Sunday next at St Albans.

Halimote of Norton on Tuesday on the Feast of St Dunstan in the 14th year [*19 May 1321*]

Jurors:	Geoffrey Bercarius	Walter Aubrey	Richard in the Hale
	Alan le Neweman	Walter Sayer	Roger Bercarius

* The jurors say that the tenement of Everard defaults. And they say further that Perseval has acquired the said tenement. Therefore it is ordered to distrain the said Perseval to show how he entered the said tenement.
* Next they say that Walter Sweteken 2d, Alice Wilemoth 2d, John Cartere 3d, default, therefore amerced.
* Next they say that Godfrey Bonde has demised half an acre of land to a certain free man without the lord's leave therefore amerced 6d.
* Roger son of John Prudde and according to a decision of the Halimote heir of the same John came and *gersummavit* all the tenement which was the said John's on the day he died to hold to him and his without waste, performing for it the due and accustomed services, and he gives one mark.
* William Bate surrendered into the lord's hand one croft enclosed with hedges (*sepibus*) containing one rood of land, just as it lies near the King's highway (*regiam stratam*) and the *Langeforlong*. And John Aubrey made agreement with the lord for the said croft with appurtenances, to hold to him and his, performing for it the due and accustomed services. And he gives half a mark.
* [*HALS 65507, f4*] William son of Richard Bate came after the death of the said Richard his father and *gersummavit* all the tenement with appurtenances which was the said Richard's on the day he died, to hold to him and his, reserving the right of anyone, performing for it the due and accustomed services, nor shall he commit waste. And he gives to the lord 40s for *gersumma*. Pledges Walter Aubrey and Richard in the Hale.
* It is ordered to distrain Richard son of Robert Norman to do fealty for the tenements which were his father's.
* William Thomas has leave to put John his son to letters. And he gives 6d. [*r. margin*: villein]

EDWARD II

Halimote of Norton on Wednesday on the Feast of St Katherine the Virgin in the 15th year Richard Stoppesle [*25 Nov 1321*]

Jurors:	Geoffrey Shepherd	Alexander Wisote	Walter son of William
	John Balston	Richard in the Hale	Walter Sayer

* It is ordered to retain in the lord's hand one messuage with appurtenances which Walter, vicar of the church of Norton, held from the lord in villeinage on the day he died, until etc.
* The jurors present that Perseval Simeon holds the tenement [of] Everard which tenement ought to reap for one day and he did not come, therefore let him be distrained.
* Walter son of Sayer came after the death of Sayer his father and *gersummavit* all the land and tenement which the same Sayer held on the day he died, to hold to him and his in villeinage, performing for it the due and accustomed services. And he gives for agreement 6s 8d. Heriot one horse.
* The bailiff is ordered to cause to be delivered to Albreda Bate a third part of two acres of land which she claims in the name of dower after the death of Richard Bate her husband.
* Juliana le Hoghaler surrendered into the lord's hand one quarter of land which she held of the villeinage of the lord. And William Sayer came and made agreement with the lord for the said land, to hold to him and his in villeinage, performing for it the due and accustomed services. And he gives for agreement 10s. Nor shall he commit waste. And he has licence to marry.
* John Boueton has licence to marry outside the manor. So [*ie provided*] that he come every year to the View of Frankpledge of Norton and to the Halimote there if he should be summoned and needed. And for this he finds a pledge *viz* John Boueton his brother. And he gives to the lord for having licence 3s 4d.
* Petronilla who was the wife of William Dipere surrendered into the hand of the lord one messuage and half an acre a virgate of land with appurtenances. And John son of William Dipere came and made agreement with the lord for the said messuage and said half virgate of land with appurtenances, to hold to him and his in villeinage under this form that the said Petronilla shall hold two cottages within the said messuage and a certain plot of curtilage adjoining just as it is enclosed by hedges and two half acres of land in the *Woweforlong* for term of her life. And the said John shall give annually to the said Petronilla two quarters and six bushels of corn, one quarter of beans and peas as they grow and one quarter and six bushels of better dredge. And after the decease of the said Petronilla the said cottage, plot of curtilage and two half acres of

EDWARD II

land shall revert to the said John and his heirs. And he gives as agreement for having entry and for licence to marry 20s, pledge Walter Sayer and Richard Cok.

Halimote of Norton on Friday after the Feast of St Mark the Evangelist in the 15th year – Richard Stop[pesle] [*30 Apr 1322*]

Jurors:	Geoffrey Bercarius	Richard in the Hale	Alexander Wisot
	Alan le Neweman	Walter Albred	John Balston

* Again as before it is ordered to distrain Persevall Simeon who is tenant of the tenement of Everard because he did not come to reap for one day in harvest.
* The jurors present that Walter Swetkyn has defaulted. Therefore amerced 2d.
* Next they present that the same Walter did not do suit at the lord's mill. Therefore amerced 2d.
* Next they present that Sarra daughter of Saery has married without the lord's licence. Therefore amerced 12d.
* Next they present that Margery daughter of William Thomas has married without the lord's licence. Therefore amerced 3s. [*r. margin*: villein (fem)]
* Next they present that Walter Hasch has married without the lord's licence. Therefore amerced 6d.
* Next they present that Walter le Neweman has married without the lord's licence. Therefore amerced 3d. [*r. margin*: villein]
* Next they present that Cecily Dipere has committed *leyrewit*. Therefore amerced 3d.
* It is reported that all the villagers of Norton except (*preter*) Ralph Boueton have made a private holding (*unum separabile*) in the common pasture of the lord without leave, therefore it is ordered etc.
* [*HALS 65507, f4v*] Margery who was the wife of William the Swineherd (*Porcarius*) came after the death of the said William the Swineherd her husband and relieved the land which she holds from the lord in the name of Thomas son and heir of the same William, and she gives for relief 20d.
* Roger Bercarius came and made agreement with the lord for licence to marry. And he gives 18d. [*l. margin*: villein]
* Alice Wylemot gives the lord 3d to have an inquisition whether she might alienate one cottage with curtilage or no. And the jury say that she has the right to alienate if she should wish to alienate.
* Alexander le Helder and Alice Wylemot his wife came and surrendered into the lord's hand one messuage with curtilage as it lies between the land of John Balston and the land of Walter in the Hale. And Agnes Boueton came and

EDWARD II

made agreement with the lord to hold the said messuage to her and hers, performing for it the due and accustomed services. And she gives to the lord for agreement 12d.

Halimote of Norton on Friday after the Feast of St Luke the Evangelist in the 16th year – William Heron [*22 Oct 1322*]

Jurors:	Geoffrey Bercarius	Walter Sayer junior	Roger Bercarius
	Alexander Wisot	John Balston	Ralph Albry

* Again as before it is ordered to distrain the tenement [of] Everard for the reaping of one day in harvest which is in arrears.
* Walter Reymond entered his son to letters without the lord's leave, afterwards he came and made agreement to obtain leave. And he gives 12d by the pledge of William Bate.
* The jurors present that John Burrei made waste upon his tenement, damage half a mark therefore amerced 6d. And he is ordered to repair etc.
* Next they present that Walter Warde has married without licence of the lord, therefore amerced 12d. [*l. margin*: villein]
* Richard atte Dene and Sarra his wife complain of William Bate concerning a plea of land, pledges of prosecution, Reginald de Frobenhale, Ralph de Thikkeneye. And the said William is summoned against the next Halimote.
* Walter Loveleg came and took from the lord the land of Walter de Harleston which is in the hand of the lord because of the disability of the said Walter, to hold for the term of six years, the term beginning from Michaelmas in the aforesaid year. And he gives for having the term 3s. And the aforesaid Walter Loveleg shall satisfy for the ploughing of the said land ploughed before his time and he shall maintain the said tenement without waste.

Halimote of Norton on Thursday next after the Feast of the Blessed John the Baptist in the 16th year – William Heron [*3 Jun 1323*]

Jurors:	Geoffrey the Shepherd	William Hassh	Roger the Shepherd
	Roger Proudde	William atte Chirche	Richard in the Hale

* Again as before it is ordered to distrain the tenement [of] Everard for the reaping of one day in harvest being in arrears.
* Richard atte Dene and Sarra his wife because they have not prosecuted against William Bate in a plea. Therefore they and their pledges of prosecution are amerced.
* It is ordered to take into the lord's hand one messuage and two selions of

EDWARD II

villein land which William Cok acquired from Isabel Ailbright without the lord's leave.
* The jurors present that Percival Symeon makes default therefore let him be distrained.
* Next they present that John in the Hale has married without the lord's licence therefore amerced. It is remitted because he has made agreement.
* Next they present that Sarra Sayer has married without the lord's licence with William Cok a free man. And she has licence to marry and gives 2s.
* Robert Hassh is dead whose heriot is one cow worth 10s after whose death came John son and heir of the said Robert and *gersummavit* all the land which the said Robert held on the day on which he died, to hold to him and his in villeinage, performing for it the due and accustomed services. And he gives for *gersumma* and for licence to marry 6s 8d. [*l. margin*: villein]
* William Saman is dead, whose heriot is one horse (*afferus*) worth 8s. And Robert son of the said William came and *gersummavit* all the land which the said William held on the day he died, to hold to him and his in villeinage, performing for it the due and accustomed services. And he gives for *gersumma* 2s, pledge Richard Cok.
* The jurors present that Walter Loveleg demised to Thomas Smith (*Faber*) one messuage and one croft for the term of six years without the lord's leave therefore amerced 3d.
* [*HALS 65507, f5*] Next they present that Walter Swetekyn has not done suit at the lord's mill, therefore amerced 2d.
* Stephen Peronell has demised half an acre of villein land to John Andrew of Baldock without the lord's leave therefore it is ordered to take it into the lord's hand and none the less amerced 2d.
* Agnes daughter of Robert de Parys came and *gersummavit* one quarter of land which the same Robert held on the day he died, to hold to her and hers in villeinage, performing for it the due and accustomed services. And she gives for *gersumma* and for licence to marry with William Thomas half a mark, by the pledge of John Robyn.
* Godfrey Bonde surrendered into the lord's hand one half acre and two parts of one rood of land lying at the *Langeforlong* between the land of the vicar of Norton and the land of William Bate. And William Bate came and made agreement with the lord to hold the said land to him and his, performing for it the due and accustomed services. And he gives by agreement for having entry 12d.
* William Bate surrendered into the lord's hand three roods of land whereof half an acre lies at *Langeforlong* and one rood lies at the gore between the land of Roger Prodd and John Hassh. And Godfrey Bonde came and made agreement

EDWARD II

with the lord to hold the said land to him and his, performing for it the due and accustomed services. And he gives by agreement 6d.
* John in the Hale gives to the lord that he may dwell outside the lord's Liberty as long as it shall please the lord 4s. And he shall come hither annually to the View of Frankpledge so that he may follow his tithing. And he shall give to the lord annually at the Feast of St Michael ½d for the land which he has acquired from the Abbot of Waltham in *Arlichesseye* [Arlesey] [*r. margin*: increase in rent ½d]. And for this he finds pledges *viz* Walter in the Hale and Godfrey Bonde. And by the aforesaid agreement the same John has licence to marry. [*r. margin*: villein]
* Roger Pilgrym and Matilda his wife surrendered into the lord's hand one cottage with curtilage between the messuages of William Saman and of Alexander son of Andrew. And the same Alexander and Alice his wife made agreement with the lord to hold the said cottage with curtilage to the same Alexander and Alice and theirs, performing for them the due and accustomed services. And they give as agreement for having entry 12d, pledge Richard Cok.
* Sarra Saman came and made agreement with the lord for obtaining licence to marry, and she gives by agreement 12d. [*r. margin*: villein (fem)]
* Simon Redeheved and Isabel his wife surrendered into the lord's hand one messuage with its appurtenances just as it lies between the *Green Land* and the land of William Saman. And William Cok and Sara his wife made agreement with the lord to hold the said messuage to them and theirs, performing for it the due and accustomed services. And they give by agreement 2s.
* The land which Richard atte Dene and Sarra his wife claim against William Bate was taken into the lord's hand by default of that William and so remains until this day because by the lord's order they have this day at the next Halimote.

Halimote of Norton on Monday before the Feast of the Purification of the Blessed Mary in the 17th year – William Heron [*30 Jan 1324*]

Jurors:	Geoffrey Bercarius	Richard in the Hale	William Wyking
	Alexander Wysot	Walter Reymond	Robert Marschal
	Walter Sayer junior	Geoffrey Sabright	Richard Jacob
	Ralph Aubrey	Nicholas Wymark	Richard Doke

* The jurors of Norton present that William Bate has not come to reap for half a day in harvest, value of work 1d amerced 3d.

EDWARD II

* Next they say that Percival Symyon has not come to reap for one day in harvest therefore let him be distrained to satisfy the lord.
* Next they say that Walter Albreth and William Bate have married without leave of the lord therefore let their tenements be taken into the lord's hand until etc. [*r. margin*: villeins]
* Next they say that Walter in the Hale \3d/, William Bate \3d/, Godfrey Bonde \3d/, Robert Saman \3d/, Agnes Bacon \3d/, Walter Swetekyn \3d/ have not done suit at the lord's mill therefore amerced.
* Next they present that the wife of John Dipere 3d, Sara daughter of Sayes 6d, the wife of Ralph Bacon 6d have brewed and broken the Assize therefore amerced.
* Stephen Perunel surrendered into the lord's hand all his tenement *viz* one messuage and 12 acres of land with appurtenances. And hereupon John Albrith is chosen by the whole Homage to hold the said tenement to him and his, performing for it the due and accustomed services. And he did fealty. And he gives to the lord by agreement and for licence to marry 16d.
* Geoffrey Bercarius for giving Matilda his daughter in marriage gives to the lord 2s. [*r. margin*: villein]
* Walter Albrith for licence to marry gives to the lord 2s. [*r. margin*: villein]
* William Bate finds security to satisfy the lord because he married without licence *viz* Ralph Albrith and Richard Cok.
* Agnes Bate is given licence to marry and she gives for obtaining licence 2s. [*r. margin*: villein (fem)]

[*HALS 65507, f5v*] **Norton Halimote there on Thursday next after the Feast of the Apostles Peter and Paul in the 17th year Robert Saunford [*28 June 1324*]**

Jurors:	Geoffrey Bercarius	Richard Hale	John Balston
	William atte Chirche	Walter Loveleg	Alexander Wyshot

* Ralph Albright \3d/, Richard Cok \3d/, have mainprized William Bate to satisfy the lord because he married without licence. And William has not come, therefore the said Ralph and Richard his pledges are amerced because they have not got him whom they pledged. And it is ordered to take into the lord's hands the land and tenement of the said William until etc. Afterwards he came and made agreement and gives 5s.
* Godfrey Bonde \3d/ and Walter in the Hale \6d/ put themselves in the lord's mercy because they did not come to make the lord's hay.
* The jurors present that Percival Simeon has made default, therefore distrain.

EDWARD II

* Next they present that the same has withdrawn the service of one boonday of one man per day for four years, therefore distrain.
* Richard atte Dane and Sara his wife complain against William Bate in a plea of land, pledges of prosecution Edward atte Hath and Ralph Thikeneye. And it is ordered to summon the said William to be at the next Halimote to answer the same concerning the aforesaid plea.
* Margery le Longe complains against John Martyn concerning a plea of land, pledges of prosecution Nicholas Rodland and James de Elmeham. And the said Margery sues the said John for one messuage, 12 acres and one rood of land which Adam le Longe father of the said Margery acquired from Robert Crok and whereof the said Adam le Long by the lord's leave seised Christine and Margery his daughters to hold for the term of their lives, and to the heirs of the longer liver. And about this the said Margery calls for the rolls of the time of Brother Reyner to warrant. And the aforesaid John comes and says that a certain Agnes, who was the daughter of Christine, sister of the said Margery who now sues, came into the full court and surrendered the said tenements into the lord's hands. And the lord thereof seised John Martyn and Agnes for the term of their lives. And about this he calls for the roll of the time of Brother William le Barbur to warrant. And they have a day at St Albans on the Saturday after the Feast of St James.
* Sara daughter of Saer \3d/, Ralph Boueton \3d/, John Dipere \3d/, Roger Bercarius \3d/ have brewed and sold against the Assize. Therefore amerced.
* William Bonde surrendered into the lord's hand to the use of John Hassh one rood of land lying in *Eldefeld* between the land of William Bate and the land of William atte Chirche. And John Hassh surrendered into the lord's hand to the use of William Bonde one rood of land lying in *Grenedich* between the land of Geoffrey Bercarius and the land of the said John. And they give to the lord for exchange of the said land 6d.

Halimote of Norton on Thursday next after the Feast of St Luke the Evangelist in the 18th year – Robert Saunford [*25 Oct 1324*]

Jurors:	Geoffrey Bercarius	Walter Sayer junior	William atte Cherch
	Alexander Wysotes	Richard Cok	Walter Reymond

* The jurors present that Robert Saman defaults, therefore amerced 2d.
* Next they present that Perseval Simeon has withdrawn himself from the lord's boonday therefore amerced and distrained.
* Next they present that Ellen in the Hale has committed *leyrewit*, so amerced 3d.

EDWARD II

* Next they present that Roger Prudde \3d/, William Bate \3d/, Albreda Bate \3d/ and Walter in the Hale \3d/ have not done suit at the lord's mill, therefore amerced.
* Robert Saman surrendered into the lord's hand one messuage with one *ferthlingate* of land with its appurtenances. And Walter Reymond came and made agreement with the lord to hold the said land to him and his in villeinage, performing for it the due and accustomed services. And for this surrender the aforesaid Walter grants for him and his heirs that the aforesaid Robert may have and hold one house with curtilage and selions of land adjoining for the term of his life and his wife's. And after the decease of the said Robert it shall fully revert to the said Walter and his heirs. And he gives for agreement 5s 8d.
* Roger Prudd surrendered into the lord's hands two roods of land of which one lies between the land of Walter Albright and the land of Nicholas le Neweman and another lies between the land of Walter Albright on either side. And Ralph Boueton surrendered into the lord's hand one piece of land as it lies at *Lombegate* between the land of the lord and the land of the vicar. And the aforesaid Roger and Ralph give to the lord for exchange of the said land 12d.

Halimote of Norton on Thursday next after the Feast of St Barnabas the Apostle in the 18th year – Robert S[aunford] [*13 Jun 1325*]

Jurors:	Geoffrey Bercarius	William Thomas	John Balston
	Richard Cok	William at the Church (*ad Ecclesiam*)	Richard in the Hale

* [*HALS 65508, f1*] The jurors present that Ellen in the Hale married without licence of the lord, therefore amerced 12d. [*r. margin*: villein (fem)]
* Next they present that Alan Neweman has an old ruinous barn, therefore let the aforesaid Alan be put upon oath to rebuild the said house before the next Halimote.
* The jurors present that Roger Prudde \2d/, Swetekyn Bonde \3d/, Walter in the Hale \2d/, Albred Bate \2d/, Alice Maydegod \2d/, Alan Neweman \2d/, Isabel daughter of Roger Bercarius \2d/, William Bate \3d/, Alexander Cok \2d/, John Albred \3d/ have not done suit at the lord's mill, therefore amerced.
* John Isoude is dead whose heriot is one mare worth 4s. And Walter Albrid is charged [with it?]. And John son and heir of the same John came and *gersummavit* all the land and tenement which the said John his father held on the day he died, to hold to him and his in villeinage, performing for it the due and accustomed services. And he gives for agreement 2s.

EDWARD II

* Walter Swetekyn is dead and whose heriot is nothing. And Alice Swetekyn who was wife of the said Walter has made agreement with the lord to hold the land which the aforesaid Walter held until the coming of age of Sarra daughter and heir of the said Walter, nor shall she commit waste. And she gives for agreement 12d.
* Geoffrey Bercarius surrendered into the lord's hand one rood of land as it lies in *Longefurlong* between the land of Walter Sayer and the land of Alexander son of Alexander. And John Hassh surrendered into the lord's hand one rood of land as it lies in the *Wowefurlong* between the land of Geoffrey Bercarius and the land of Walter Reymon. And the lord seised thereof Geoffrey Bercarius and John Hassh to hold to them and theirs by way of exchange, performing for it the due and accustomed services. And they give for agreement 6d.
* Geoffrey Bercarius surrendered into the lord's hands half an acre of land as it lies in the *Malme* between the land of Walter Reymond and the land of Walter Sayer. And Walter Reymond surrendered into the lord's hands one rood of land as it lies at the *Wowefurlong* between the lands of the said Geoffrey on either side. And the lord seised thereof the said Geoffrey and Walter alternately by way of exchange to hold to them and theirs, performing for it the due and accustomed services. And they give for agreement 9d.
* Walter Albrith came and made agreement with the lord for licence to marry Matilda his younger daughter and he gives for agreement 2s. [*r. margin*: villein]

Halimote of Norton on Tuesday next after the Feast of St Nicholas in the 19th year – John Kilsul [*10 Dec 1325*]

Jurors: Geoffrey Bercarius   Alexander Wysot   Walter Sayer the younger
         Alan Neweman   Ralph Boueton   John Balston

* Alan Neweman has a day between this day and Michaelmas to rebuild a certain barn which is ruinous, by the pledge of Roger Prudde and John Jecob.
* John Aubrey puts himself [upon the mercy of the court] because he did not come to harrow the lord's land amerced 2d.
* John Bate made default at seven boondays in harvest which are assessed at 14d, therefore it is decided that he shall pay the arrears to the lord and that he be amerced 2d.
* Richard Bate puts himself [upon the mercy of the court] for a default of half a boonday in harvest worth 1d. Amerced 2d.

EDWARD II

* The jurors present that Persevall Simeon is in arrears for one boonday in harvest and it is worth 2d. Therefore distrain etc.
* The jurors present that Walter in the Hale 2d, Swetekyne Bonde 2d, William Bate 2d, John Albrith 2d, John Reymond, a poor man (*pauper*) have not done suit at the mill of the lord, therefore amerced.
* Next they present that William in the Hale is in arrears of one bushel of grain for bookworks[26] and of the ploughing of three selions. Therefore it is ordered etc.
* Richard atte Dane, Sara his wife, William Bate and Roger Prudde have a day at St Albans on Saturday next after the quindene of St Hilary in a plea of land.
* Because William in the Hale and John Bate senior are unable (*impotentes*) to hold their lands and tenements and could not do the services and customs. Therefore the lord with the consent and election of all the villagers of Norton has leased to Ralph Albrith and Ralph Boueton by equal portions all the land which William in the Hale held. And to John Emmeson all the land which John Bate held, to hold to the said Ralph, Ralph and John for the term of six years, the term beginning at Michaelmas last past, saving the right of anyone and if [*HALS 65508, f1v*] the heirs of the said William in the Hale and John Bate should present their claim within the said term they shall allow to the said Ralph Albrith and Ralph Boueton and John Emmeson all costs and expenses which they have reasonably made by the view of good men, respect being had to the profit which the said Ralph, Ralph and John have received during the term.

Halimote of Norton on Tuesday next after the Feast of the Translation of the Blessed Thomas in the 20th year Robert Saunford [*10 Jun 1326*]

Jurors:	Geoffrey Bercarius	Alexander Wysot	John Balston
	Alan Neweman	William Sayer junior	Roger Bercarius

* The jurors present that Margery Dame, widow, has committed *leyrewit*, therefore amerced and let her land be taken into the lord's hands until etc. Afterwards she made agreement, and gives by agreement 12d.
* The jurors present that Walter Reymond is dead, whose heriot is one cow worth 8d. Afterwards Sarra who was the wife of the said Walter came and *gersummavit* one *ferthlingate* of land and one cotland which the said Walter held on the day he died, to the use of John son and heir of the said Walter, to

---

[26] *Frumenti de Benesad.*

hold in villeinage, doing for it the due and accustomed services. And she gives for *gersumma* 13s 4d.
* William Swetekyn is dead whose heriot is nothing. And it is ordered to take into the lord's hand one cottage which he held from the lord until it shall be known who shall wish to follow.
* The jurors present that Cecily Dipere has committed *leyrewit*, therefore amerced 3d. [*l. margin*: villein (fem)]
* Next they present that Ivetta who was the wife of John Albreth has married a certain free man at *Whelye* [Willian], therefore it is ordered to take into the lord's hands one cottage which she held in the name of dower.
* Richard atte dane and Sarra his wife and William Bate have a day at St Albans to hear their judgment in a plea of land on Monday next after the Feast of the Exaltation of the Holy Cross.
* All the villagers of Norton are charged with the land which William in the Hale and John Bate senior used to hold, which land at the last Halimote in the time of Brother John de Kilsul was leased to Ralph Boueton and Ralph Albryth so that all the villagers shall answer for the services and customs after the Feast of St Michael next to come.
* Margaret daughter of John Jacob made agreement with the lord for licence to marry, and she gives by agreement 6d. [*l. margin*: villein (fem)]
* Matilda Swetekyn came and took from the lord one cottage which William Swetekyn held on the day he died, to hold till the coming of age of Henry son and heir of Walter Swetekyn without waste, reserving the right of anyone. And she gives for having the term 12d.
* Sarra who was the wife of Walter Reymond made agreement with the lord for licence to marry. And she gives by agreement 12d. [*l. margin*: villein (fem)]

Halimote of Norton on Thursday next after the Feast of St Denis in the 20th year – Robert Saunford [*16 Oct 1326*]

Jurors:	Geoffrey Bercarius	John Dipere	William atte Cherch
	Walter Albreth	Walter Sayer	John Balston

* Again as before it is ordered to retain in the lord's hand one cottage which Ivetta Aubrey holds in the name of dower until she shall satisfy the lord for her marriage. [*l. margin*: villein (fem)]
* The jury presents that John Bate who dwells at *Wilmondele* [Wymondley] has married without the lord's licence. Therefore it is ordered to take into the lord's hand all the land which he holds from the lord until etc. [*l. margin*: villein]

EDWARD II

* John Aubrey 2d   John son of William 2d   Richard Cok 2d
  William Bate 2d   Godfrey Bonde 2d   Alexander Andrew 2d
  John Haysh 2d   Ralph Aubrey 2d   William Reymond 2d
  Walter in the Hale 2d   Alan Neweman 2d   Albred Bate 2d
  Did not do suit at the mill, therefore amerced.
* John Aubrey 3d   Ralph Aubrey 2d   Godfrey Bonde 2d
  William atte Cherch 2d   John Dipere 2d   Walter Loveleg 2d
  John son of William 2d   Walter in the Hale 2d   Alexander Andrew 2d
  Roger Prud 2d   William Sayer 2d
  Summoned to do carrying service at St Albans and they did not come, therefore amerced.
* Persevall Simeon is in arrears for one day in the boondays with one man so it is ordered etc.
* The jurors have chosen Alexander Wysot and Richard in the Hale to hold the land which William in the Hale was accustomed to hold and they are seised thereof [*HALS 65509, f1*] by doing the due and accustomed services for it.
* Richard atte Dane and Sara his wife complain against William Bate in a plea of land, pledges of prosecution John de Mundene and William Petipas. And let William Bate be summoned to answer to the same at Norton at the next Halimote.

Number of folios in this book of the Court of Norton written 27.

EDWARD III

[*HALS 65510, f1*] **EXTRACTS FROM THE ROLLS OF HALIMOTES HELD AT THE MANOR OF NORTON IN THE TIME OF KING EDWARD III**

Halimote of Norton on Thursday next after the Feast of St John before the Latin Gate in the 1st year in the time of Robert de Saunford cellarer [*7 May 1327*]

Jurors:	Geoffrey Sabright	John Dipere	Ralph Aubrey
	Walter Aubrey	Walter Sayer junior	Roger Prudde

* Again as before it is ordered to retain in the hands of the lord one cottage which Ivetta Aubrey holds in the name of dower (*dos*)^{27} until she shall give satisfaction for her marriage. Afterwards she came and made agreement. And she gives 12d.
* Again as before it is ordered to retain in the hands of the lord land which John Bate held until he shall give satisfaction for his marriage. Afterwards came and made agreement. And he gives 6d.
* Again as before it is ordered to distrain Percival Simeon because he is in arrears for boonwork in harvest.
* The jurors present that Henry of Erdelee is dead, of whom there is no heriot because he was not resident. And it is ordered to seise into the lord's hand the lands and tenement which the same Henry held on the day he died, until it shall be known who shall will to follow him in it. And that the bailiff should account for the profits.
* Next they present that Percival Simeon owes suit and defaults. Therefore let him be distrained etc.
* Next they present that William in the Hale is dead whose heriot is nothing because he is poor. And it is ordered to seise into the lord's hand the land which the same William held on the day on which he died until etc.
* Next they present that William Haysh is dead whose heriot is one yearling calf, worth 20d.
* Next they present that Richard son of Walter in the Hale is a fugitive with

---

27 *Dos* here is more likely to be dower than dowry, as a wife would not hold her dowry exclusive of her husband but in jointure with him. An interpretation of this entry might be that Yvette has remarried without paying merchet, and her cottage (held for life as dower of her late husband's land) has been seized until she makes composition for her remarriage. This supposes that the custom of the manor allows widows to hold their dower even after remarriage.

EDWARD III

chattels and he has married without licence. Therefore let him be distrained etc.

* John, son and heir of William Haysh came after the death of the said William his father and *gersummavit* all the land which the same William held on the day on which he died, to hold to him and his in villeinage by performing for it the due and accustomed services. And he gives for *gersumma* and for licence to marry 4s.

Halimote of Norton on Thursday next after the Feast of St Denis in the 1st year in the time of Robert de Saunford cellarer [*15 Oct 1327*]

Jurors:	Geoffrey Bercarius	Walter Aubrey	John Balston
	Alexander Wisot	Walter Sayer junior	William atte Chirche

* William Bate came to court against Richard atte Dane and Sarah his wife in a plea of land who had been the plaintiffs and have not come. Therefore it is decided that the aforesaid William go hence without a day. And the aforesaid Richard and Sarah his wife and their pledges are amerced for a non suit 6d.
* The jurors present that Percival Simeon defaults, therefore let him be distrained etc.
* Next they present that Richard son of William in the Hale has married without the lord's licence. Afterwards the said Richard made agreement and gives 12d.
* [*l. margin:* cancelled because relating to Newnham][28] Adam de Newnham, vicar, came and took from the lord a certain garden which is called the *Hallewik* to be held for the term of three years next following, the term beginning at Michaelmas next to come, paying 20s for the said three years of which he has paid in cash one mark
* Simon le White and Mabel his wife claimed against Elias le Palmere one messuage and ten acres of land with appurtenances as the right and inheritance of the said Mabel his wife. And about this he says that a certain Adam le Longe, grandfather of the said Mabel, was seised of the said tenement and land, who gave the said messuage and land to a certain Christina daughter of the said Adam to have and hold to her and her heirs. And from the aforesaid Christina the said tenement descended to a certain Agnes daughter and heir of the said Christina who died without heir of herself.

---

[28] Marginal note applies to this and the next item.

EDWARD III

[*HALS 65510, f1v*] **Halimote there on Wednesday next before the Feast of St George in the 2nd year – Walter Arblaster [*20 Apr 1328*]**

Jurors:	Walter Aubrey	Ralph Boueton	Ralph Aubrey
	Geoffrey le Bercher	Alexander Wisot	Walter Sayer junior

* The jurors say that Saundr Andreu made default at the ploughing of three selions of land of which the work is worth 4d. Therefore amerced 3d.
* John Balston is dead whose heriot is one cow, price 8s. And afterwards came Matilda who was the wife of the said John and *gersummavit* all the land which the same John held on the day on which he died, together with the reversions when they shall fall, to the use of Reynald son and heir of the said John to hold until the majority (*etatem*) of the said Reynald. And he gives for agreement and for licence to marry 6s 8d.
* Walter Loveleg is dead whose heriot is one cow with a calf, price 7s. And Alice who was the wife of the said Walter came and *gersummavit* all the land which the said Walter held on the day when he died to the use of John son and heir of the said Walter to hold until the majority of the said heir. And he gives for agreement and for licence to marry half a mark.
* The jurors say that Isabella daughter of Roger le Schepherd has married without the lord's licence. Therefore amerced 12d.
* The aletasters present that the wife of Robert Percevall \2d/, Richard Cok \2d/, and Roger le Schepherd \2d/ are brewers and sell against the Assize. Therefore amerced.
* The land of Walter de Harleston is in the hand of the lord for want of a tenant. And the jurors have chosen William Sayer to hold the said land.
* Richard atte Dene of Codicote and Sara his wife complain of William Bate of Norton in a plea of land. Pledges of prosecution Robert Legat of Walden and William Haleward of Codicote. And the same [*singular*] is summoned to answer to the same [*plural*] in the same plea. And a day is given to the parties at St Albans on the Saturday on the eve of Pentecost under the ash tree.

Halimote of Norton on Tuesday next after the Feast of St Leonard in the 2nd year – Nicholas Flamsted [*8 Nov 1328*]
* Richard in the Hale has ended his last day whose heriot is one cow, worth 10s, after whose death John, son and heir of the said Richard came and *gersummavit* all the land which the said Richard held, to hold to him and his in villeinage by custom and service. And he did fealty and he gives to the lord for agreement 8s.
* Alan Neweman is dead, whose heriot is one horse worth 3s, after whose death

EDWARD III

came John, son and heir of the said Alan and *gersummavit* all the land which the said Alan held, to have and to hold to him and his in villeinage, doing services and customs for it. And he did fealty and he gives to the lord for agreement 5s. And the same John has licence to marry when he will.
* John Wisoth has married without the lord's licence. The same came and put himself at mercy (*vadit misericordiam*). And he gives to the lord 6d.

Jurors:	Geoffrey Bercar	Alexander Wysoth	William-atte Chirche
	Walter Aubrey	John Dipere	Ralph Aubrey

* The jurors say that Alexander Andreu \2d/, Richard Cok \3d/, John Aubrey \3d/, Agnes Boysscell \2d/, John Wysoth \3d/, all of them have ground elsewhere than at the lord's mill, therefore amerced.
* Cecily Dipere committed *leyrewite* and she came and put herself at mercy (*vadit misericordiam*) and gives 6d.
* The jurors present that John in the Hale and John Boueton are fugitives and removed their goods outside of the lord's fee. He will speak about this on the day of the View (*Visus*).[29]
* Matilda Balston made default at harvest with one man for one day to damage 2d. Therefore amerced 4d.
* Godfrey Bonde made default at a boonday of the lord with two men to damage 4d, therefore amerced 6d.
* The jurors say that the tenement of Walter Harleston has deteriorated in wardship of Walter Loveleg to damage 4s. Therefore it is ordered to levy those 4s to the use of William Sayer to repair the said tenement. The same Walter is dead therefore the executors are amerced for waste 2s.

Halimote of Norton on Tuesday next before the Feast of St Augustine the Bishop in the 3rd year – Nicholas Flamsted [*22 Aug 1329*]

Jurors:	Geoffrey le Bercher	John le Dipere	Ralph Aubrey
	Walter Aubrey	Richard Cok	Alexander Wisot

* Thomas Isoude has married without the lord's licence and removed his goods and chattels outside the Liberty. Therefore it is ordered to attach him to make agreement composition for marriage and for the goods carried away.
* [*HALS 65511, f1*] The jurors present that Hugh le Grom is dead after whose

---

[29] *Visus*: might either mean View of Frankpledge or a visit by the cellarer for a view of the account [an interim hearing of the accounts is usually quarterly; the audit of the account being annual].

EDWARD III

death John son and heir of the said Hugh did fealty. And he gives for relief 2s for one cottage and one rood which he holds from the lord. And he owes suit at the View etc.[30]

* Next they present that Richard Cok held a quarter of a yardland of the tenement of Alexander Andrew beyond the term granted to him lately by the lord, that is to say for two years, therefore amerced 4d.
* Next they present that Walter in the Hale, William Bate, Walter Sayer, Sarra Reymond, John le Dipere, William Sayer, John Reymond, William Thomas, John Hash, John Geiard, John in the Hale, William Reymond and Alexander Andrew have demised lands to certain men of Baldock without the lord's leave therefore they are all amerced. And it is ordered to take all the lands into the lord's hand. And afterwards they are pardoned by the cellarer's grace for the present under this condition that any of them who may be convicted in future of a trespass of this kind shall give 40d to the lord, that is, if he demise to any free man without leave.
* John son of Ralph Bate surrendered into the lord's hand one cotland together with reversion of the dower which Ellen in the Hale holds from the same tenement. And the lord gave possession thereof to Richard Bate to hold to him and his in villeinage by the services due and accustomed for it. And he gives 2s and has licence to marry.
* John Burre of Norton, chaplain, has demised to Ralph Aubrey of the same one messuage and half a yardland of land in Norton to hold from the Feast of St Michael until the end of 12 years next to come fully completed. And the aforesaid Ralph shall do suit for the aforesaid John at the Halimote and other services and customs which pertain to those tenements during the said term. And he gives for having the term 40d.

Halimote of Norton on Tuesday next after the Feast of St Martin in the 3rd year – Nicholas Flamsted [*14 Nov 1329*]

Jurors:	Geoffrey Bercarius	Ralph Aubrey	Alexander Wysot
	Walter Aubrey	William Thomas	Ralph Boueton

* The jurors present that Godfrey Bonde is dead, whose heriot is one young bullock worth half a mark, who held half a yardland of land with appurtenances. And John son of the same is his next heir and of full age. And

---

[30] Hugh le Grom, despite the smallness of his holding, is a free tenant, paying a relief on inheritance, and owing only suit to the View of Frankpledge and not the Halimote Courts.

EDWARD III

the lord gave possession thereof to the said John, to hold to him and his by the services due and accustomed for it. And he gives for having seisin half a mark. And he has licence to marry. And he has done fealty.
* Next they present that Agnes Jacob has committed *leyrewite* so she is amerced 3d.
* They present that

John le Neweman	3d	John Willesson	2d		
Cecily his mother	3d	John Hash	6d	Make default at the	
Alice Bonde	3d	Agnes Hash	2d	suit of the mill and	
Walter in the Hale	3d	Richard in the Hale	3d	grind elsewhere.	
Walter le Neweman	3d	Alice Loveleg	3d	Therefore all are	
Alexander Cok	2d	Alice Swetekyn	2d	amerced.	
William Sayer	3d	John Wisot	2d		

* Adam Ward has entered the lord's unfree land (*nativam terram*) without licence and has married Alice Loveleg. And afterwards he made agreement with the lord for 5s for the said trespass. Pledges Alexander Wysot and John Jacob and they are pledges of the same that he will not commit waste nor alienate goods outside the lord's Liberty.
* Matilda Swetekyn surrendered into the lord's hand one cottage with curtilage adjoining, lying between the tenements of Richard Cok and of John Aubrey. And the lord gave possession thereof to Walter le Neweman to hold to him and his by the services due and accustomed for it, reserving right to anyone. And he gives for agreement 12d. And he did fealty. Pledge William Thomas.

Halimote of Norton on Wednesday next after the Feast of St John before the Latin Gate in the 4th year Nicholas Flamsted [*9 May 1330*]

Jurors:	William atte Cherch	John le Dipere	Ralph Boueton
	Ralph Aubrey	Alexander Wysot	Geoffrey le Shepherd

* The jurors present that Percival Simeon makes default, therefore amerced 6d. And it is ordered to distrain the said Percival to do fealty.
* Walter Neweman gives 12d to the lord to have and to hold that cottage to himself and his heirs which formerly was Ralph le Neweman's whose heir he is, doing for it the due and accustomed services. He shall not commit waste. Pledge John le Neweman. And he has done fealty.
* The jurors present that Alexander Andrew \3d/, Walter Neweman \3d/ and Alice Bonde \6d/ grind elsewhere than at the lord's mill, therefore amerced.
* Thomas son of John le Dryver claims one messuage and two acres of land

EDWARD III

with appurtenances against Sarra de Erdeleye and John her son, pledges of prosecution Richard Cok and John Iseude, therefore it is ordered to summon etc against the Wednesday next after the Feast of Holy Trinity at Norton, on which day the cellarer was absent. And they have a day, the Monday next after the Feast of St Bartholomew.
* [*HALS 65511, f1v*] Olive who was the wife of John le Dryver complains of Sarra of Erdele and John her son in a plea of dower, pledges of prosecution Richard Cok and John Isoude. Therefore it is ordered to summon them etc against the Wednesday after Holy Trinity at Norton.
* John son of Ralph Boueton has leave to go to school and gives 6d, pledge his father.
* Roger son of Ralph Aubrey has leave to go to school and gives 3d.

Court held there on Monday after the Feast of St Bartholomew in the aforesaid year [*27 Aug 1330*]

* Sarra of Erdele and John her son are summoned to answer Thomas son of John le Dryver in a plea of land. And the said Thomas says that Sarra and John have unjustly deforced from him one messuage with one croft with appurtenances next to the cemetery and the *Chirche Lane*. And the said (*dicta*) Sarra[31] in her own person and the said John by his attorney that is to say John Waleys come and say that they therein received ingress and seisin justly by the Lord Hugh, abbot, and that the same Thomas with John his father surrendered the said tenement into the lord's hand to the use of the same [*plural*] in what year they do not know. And they call for the record of the rolls. And afterwards hereupon in the same court they agree with permission in this way, that Thomas recover against the same the said messuage and croft with appurtenances so that then the said Sarra and John may have and enjoy the present crop of the same croft and the said Sarra and John are amerced 6d for unjust detention.
* Olive who was the wife of John le Dryver has recovered against the same Sarra and John her dower from the same lands and tenements by the assent of the said Thomas so that the said Sarra and John may have the crop which is now growing on the dower aforesaid. And so they have agreed with permission. And the said Sarra and John put themselves in mercy, 6d by the said pledge.
* It is ordered to distrain Richard le Spenser to do fealty.
* Sarra and Margaret daughters of Richard Cok have licence to marry and they give 2s.

---

[31] *Dicta:* feminine, so Sarra here is a woman.

EDWARD III

Halimote of Norton on Tuesday next after the Feast of St Katherine the Virgin in the 4th year – Nicholas F[lamsted] [*27 Nov 1330*]

Jurors:	Walter Aubrey	Ralph Aubrey	Ralph Boueton
	Geoffrey Bercarius	John Dipere	Richard Cok

* It is ordered to distrain Percival Simeon to do fealty to the lord and to stop defaulting (*ad sanandum defaltam*).[32]
* It is again ordered to distrain Richard le Spenser of *Wilie* [Willian] to do fealty.
* The jurors present that John son of Emma is dead whose heriot is one horse worth half a mark the tenements are of the inheritance of Agnes his wife. And the tenements of John Bate which were taken into the hands of the lord and leased to John the son of Emma for the term of six years are given back to the same John Bate to hold to him and his for services etc without waste, reserving however to the same Agnes the term in the said tenements until the Feast of Michaelmas next to come.
* Next they present that Sibyl daughter of William in the Hale has married without licence, therefore distrain to make agreement.
* Next they present that Emma daughter of Andrew has married without licence, therefore distrain to make agreement.
* Sarra daughter of John Emmeson has licence to marry and she gives for agreement 2s.

Halimote of Norton on Tuesday next after the Feast of St Mark in the 5th year – Nicholas F[lamsted] [*30 Apr 1331*]

Jurors:	Walter Aubrey	Ralph Aubrey	Ralph de Boueton
	Geoffrey Bercarius	John le Dipere	Alexander Wisot

* It is ordered to distrain the tenants of the land of Percival Symeon to do fealty and to show how they entered into the lord's fee.
* Again it is ordered to distrain Richard le Spenser to do fealty and to show how he has entered into the lord's fee.
* The jurors present that the tenants of the lands of Percival Symeon \distrain/ and Sarra Erdele \sick/ make default, therefore etc.
* Next they present that Matilda Balston has married without the lord's licence to John Hassh, so for an agreement they give 2s. Pledge Ralph Aubrey.

---

[32] *Ad sanandum defaltam* meaning 'to cure [his] default'.

EDWARD III

* [*HALS 65512, f1*] The jury present that Alexander Wisot has married Emma his daughter without licence of the lord. And gives for agreement 2s.
* Next they present that Alexander Andrew has demised half an acre of land to John le Kyld of Baldock without leave, whereas it is forbidden for any tenant to demise to anyone of Baldock any land under penalty of 40d, therefore amerced, and it is ordered to levy for the said penalty 6d. And furthermore it is ordered to seise into the lord's hand the said land together with the crop of the same land. And the beadle shall be charged with the issues.
* Richard son of John Bate has licence to marry. And he gives 2s for agreement.
* Cecily Neweman has licence to marry. And she gives for agreement 2s, pledge [*for both Richard and Cecily, these two entries being bracketed together*] Alexander Wisot.
* Sibyl daughter of William in the Hale has licence to marry. And she gives 6d, pledge John in the Hale.
* Agnes Jacob has licence to marry. And she gives to the lord 6d, pledge Roger Bercarius.
* William son of Geoffrey Bercarius has leave to go to school. And he gives 6d, pledge his father.
* William son of William atte Cherche has leave to go to school. And he gives 6d, pledge his father.
* Ralph Aubrey gives 3d to the lord that bounds and metes may be placed between him and the lord at *Mikelheg*, therefore the jurors and the beadle are ordered to make etc.
* It is ordered to distrain Emma daughter of Andrew to answer to the lord why she has married without the lord's licence.
* The lord has granted to Ralph Boueton and John, son of the same Ralph, a curtilage which was of John atte More with hedges and ditches and all trees growing in the said curtilage so that the said Ralph shall not be charged for waste although he throw down those trees and make his profit of them, to hold the said curtilage with all its appurtenances to the same Ralph and John and the heirs of that John, rendering for it annually 10s at the four usual terms of the year in equal portions. And they give for having entry and with the said trees growing there two marks.

Halimote of Norton on Wednesday next after the Feast of the Epiphany in the 5th year – Nicholas F[lamsted] [*14 Jan 1332*]

Jurors:	Geoffrey Bercarius	John le Dipere	Ralph Albrethe
	Alexander Wysot	John Jacob	William Sayer

- It is ordered to distrain the tenants of the land of Percival Simeon to answer how they have entered the lord's fee, against the next Halimote.
- The jurors present that William Reymond is dead whose heriot is one ploughshare, who held one *ferthinglond* and they do not know who should be the next heir. Therefore it is ordered to seise the said tenement into the lord's hand until etc.
- John Wysot has licence to marry Margaret Tollard. And he gives for agreement 40d.
- The jurors present that John le Kilde of Baldock a free man has acquired from John le Swone seven acres of land, therefore it is ordered to distrain the said John le Kilde to answer how he entered into the lord's fee.
- It is ordered to distrain Richard le Spenser to answer how he entered into the lord's fee and to do fealty.
- It is ordered to distrain Emma, daughter of Andrew, to make agreement why she married without the lord's licence.
- Margaret, daughter of John Tollard gives the lord 12d to have it enquired by a jury what right she has to the tenements which were William Reymond's, pledge John Hash. And it is ascertained by the oath of Walter Albred, Roger Bercarius, Walter Harleston, Alexander Wysot, John Isoude, and William atte Churche[33] that the said Margaret is next and right heir to obtain the said tenements with appurtenances, who came and *gersummavit* the said tenements with appurtenances to hold to her and hers in villeinage by the services due and accustomed for them and she gives for agreement half a mark by the pledge of Alexander Wysot and John Hash.
- Alexander Andrew gives to the lord 6d to have his land again that is to say half an acre which was taken into the hand of the lord because the said Alexander alienated the said land to John Kilde without the lord's leave.

Halimote of Norton on the day of St Dunstan the Bishop in the 6th year – Richard Hederset [*19 May 1332*]

Jurors:	Geoffrey Bercarius	Alexander Wysot	John Hash
	Roger Prudde	John Dipere	William Sayer

- [*HALS 65512, f1v*] It is again ordered to distrain John Kild to answer to the lord how he has entered into the lord's fee that is to say seven acres of land which he has acquired from John le Swon.

---

[33] Atte Churche: this surname is in English from this point; previously it was written as *ad Ecclesiam*.

EDWARD III

* It is again ordered to distrain Richard le Spenser to do fealty etc.
* The jurors present that William de Monden, John le Kyld and Richard Andrew make default. Therefore it is ordered to distrain etc.
* Next they present that William Reymond is dead whose heriot is one ploughshare worth 3d, who held one *ferthinglond*. And Margaret Tollard is his next heir who *gersummavit* the said tenement at the last Halimote.
* John son of John Bate has married without licence of the lord at Stotfold, therefore he is ordered to be attached to answer for it to the lord.
* William son of Walter In the Hale \6d/, Thomas Balston, \forgiven/, Roger Dipere \6d/ and Henry son of Alice Swetekyn \6d/, have leave to go to the clerks' school (*ad scolas clericales*). And they give 18d.
* John le Noreys complains of Walter le Neweman concerning a plea of land that is to say of one cottage with curtilage and of one butt at the headland of one half acre of land with appurtenances in Norton. And afterwards by the lord's leave they agreed this, that the said John should remit and quitclaim to the same Walter and to his, all his right and claim which he had or could have in the said tenements. And the said Walter puts himself in mercy, 3d.
* Walter le Dryver and Agnes his sister surrendered into the lord's hand half an acre of land at *Grondich* between the land of John Bate and of Roger Prudde and it abuts at one headland upon the way leading to *Russheden* and at the other headland upon *Wonfurlong*. And the lord has granted the said land to Ralph de Boueton, to hold to him and his for the services due and accustomed for it, and he gives for agreement 2s.
* Alice Jacob has licence to marry and serve where she will and she gives for agreement 12d.
* Ralph de Boueton surrendered into the lord's hand one cottage with curtilage just as it is enclosed with hedges (*sepibus*) lying between the tenements of Walter the Miller and of John Colyn. And the lord has granted the said tenement with appurtenances to John Maydegode the elder to hold to him and his for the due and accustomed services and he gives 18d.
* John de la Ryver has done fealty and acknowledged that he holds from the lord the third part of one messuage and six acres of land with appurtenances which are of the inheritance of Margery his wife rendering for them annually 4s 2½d rent and he shall do suit at the Halimote and View of Frankpledge with his boondays when it shall belong that is to say suit in common etc.
* And because Richard Andrew entered the lord's fee in the same holding as it is said, it is ordered to distrain the said Richard to answer therefor to the lord and to do fealty etc.
* Walter de Harleston surrendered into the lord's hand one messuage and one *ferthinglond* which he held of the lord without any with-holding. And the lord

EDWARD III

has granted the said lands and tenements with appurtenances to William Saer to hold to him and his by the services due and accustomed for them. And he shall give a heriot both for that tenement and for his own tenement when it shall fall due. And Richard son of the said Walter forgiven and quitclaimed for him and his to the same William Saer and his all the right and claim which he has or can have in the said tenements. And he shall not commit waste. And the said William Saer and his heirs shall pay annually to the same Walter de Harleston and his heirs at the Feast of St Michael one bushel of wheat and one bushel of maslin. And if they do not do so he grants for him and his that the lord's bailiffs shall cause to be levied the said wheat as often as it shall be in arrears for the use of the said Walter and his heirs. And William gives for agreement 5s.

* John Otewey and Agnes his wife complain of John son of Walter Albrede concerning a plea of land, pledge of prosecution Walter de Sopwelle. And he demands one messuage and half a virgate with appurtenances in Norton which ought to have fallen to the same Agnes after the death of Sarra who was the wife of Stephen Parnele her mother whose heir she is and in which lands and tenements the said John Albrede has no entry unless by the said Stephen in the time when the said Sarra was surviving to whom in her life he could not object. And the said John son of Walter Albrede came and did not deny etc. And he grants that the said Agnes should be next heir to obtain the said tenements. Therefore it is decided that the said John Otewey and Agnes his wife should recover etc. And the said John son of Walter Albrede is amerced 3d for unjust detention. And hereupon it was agreed by the lord's leave like this, that the said John son of Walter Albrede has forgiven to the same Agnes all the right and claim in the said land etc. And hereupon came the said John Otewey and Agnes his wife before the cellarer under the ash tree and *gersummaverunt* the said tenements and lands with appurtenances to hold to them and the heirs of that Agnes by the services due and accustomed for them. And they give for agreement half a mark by the pledge of John Albrede. And he shall not commit waste. And they did fealty. And afterwards by the lord's leave the said John Otewey and Agnes his wife demised the said lands and tenements to the same John son of Walter Albrede to hold for the term of six fully complete years next to come, the term beginning at the Feast of Michaelmas next coming. And he shall pay annually to the said John Otewey and Agnes his wife at Norton at the Feast of the Birth of the Lord half a quarter of wheat. And he gives for having the term 12d. And he shall not commit waste. And if the said tenements with appurtenances ought to be further demised at rent (*debeant dimitti ad firmam*) the said John son of Walter Albrede shall be next to hold the said lease by leave of the lord if he

EDWARD III

shall wish, for as much as others will to give.
* Richard atte Dane and Sarra his wife complain of William Bate in a plea of land, pledges of prosecution Hugh Haleward and Ralph de Thikkeneye, therefore it is ordered that they be summoned etc against the next [court] under the ash tree.
* Richard atte Dane and Sarra his wife complain of Albreda Bate concerning the aforesaid plea of land. Pledges of prosecution as above. Therefore it is ordered as above.
* Richard atte Dane and Sarra his wife complain of Walter le Newman concerning a plea of land. Pledges of prosecution as above. Therefore it is ordered as above.

Court held at St Albans under the ash tree on Saturday next after the Feast of the Apostles Peter and Paul [*4 Jul 1332*]

Essoins:
William Bate against Richard atte Dane and Sarra his wife concerning a plea of land, by Thomas, son of John.
Albreda Bate against the same Richard and Sarra concerning the said plea, by Henry Bate.
* [*HALS 65513, f1*] Richard atte Dane and Sarra his wife, plaintiffs, come to court against William Bate and Albreda Bate separately in a plea of land. And the said William and Albreda are essoined above and thus it shall stand over (*remanet*) until the next Halimote.
* Richard atte Dane and Sarra his wife, plaintiffs, come to court against Walter le Neweman in a plea of land and claim against him one cottage with appurtenances in which he has not entry unless by Amice daughter of Alan son of William sister of the said Sarra who had no estate in the said tenement unless in fee tail, that is to say, to her and the lawfully begotten heirs of her body, which certain Amice died without an heir begotten of her whereby the said cottage ought to descend to the said Sarra, sister and heir of the said Amice, etc. And the said Walter unlawfully deforced them thereof, etc. And the said Walter denies it etc and says that he entered the said tenement lawfully by the lord's licence by the said Amice while she was single and had a full estate in the said tenement before the tenure of the said Amice was changed into fee tail as is aforesaid. And concerning this he calls for the record of the rolls of the time of Brother J de Styvenach. And they have a day until the next Halimote.

EDWARD III

Halimote of Norton on Tuesday next after the Feast of St Denis in the 6th year – Richard Heders[et] [*13 Oct 1332*]

Jurors:	Geoffrey Bercarius	Alexander Wisot	William Sayer
	Roger Prudde	John le Dipere	John Hassh

* William de Monden did fealty and acknowledged that he held of the lord one messuage and eight acres of land with appurtenances rendering for them annually to the lord 7s. And as to the other services due from the said tenements the same William has a day to acknowledge them before the next Halimote.
* Richard atte Dane and Sarra his wife because they have not prosecuted against William Bate in a plea of land, therefore he himself and his pledges of prosecution are amerced.
* The same Richard and Sara his wife because they have not prosecuted against Albreda Bate in a plea of land, therefore as above.
* The same Richard and Sara his wife because they have not prosecuted against Walter le Neweman in a plea of land, therefore as above.
* Again it is ordered to attach John son of John Bate to answer why he married without the lord's licence.
* Again it is ordered to distrain John Kyld and Richard le Spenser to answer how they entered the lord's fee and to do fealty.
* William Bate gives 12d to the lord for an enquiry to be held whether any heir who claims his inheritance ought to be allowed to sue for the said inheritance if he has not presented his claim within five Halimotes immediately after the death of his ancestor. And the jurors say that if the said heir know of the death of his ancestor and be of full age, within the realm and out of prison and should not present his claim immediately after the death of his ancestor within the abovesaid period that he ought not to be allowed to claim according to the ancient custom of the manor.
* The jurors present that Reynald Kyng is dead. And the lord has not a heriot because the tenement which he held is of the inheritance of his wife.
* Next they present that Walter Aubrey is dead whose heriot is one cow worth 10s. And Ralph his son is his next heir of full age. And he held one messuage and half a yardland of land with appurtenances. And the said Ralph came and *gersummavit* the said tenement with appurtenances to hold to him and his in villeinage by the services due and accustomed for it. And he gives 20s. Pledge Geoffrey Bercarius. And he shall not commit waste.
* William Bate by the lord's leave has demised to Richard le Cartere and to Thomas Horseman one and a half acres of land lying in *le Malme* at *Levendich*

EDWARD III

to hold for a term of three years. And they give 6d.
* Next the jurors present that John Albred \2d/, John Willesone \2d/, Cecily le Neweman \2d/ and Agnes wife of John Emmeson \2d/, grind elsewhere than at the lord's mill, therefore amerced.
* Next they present that John Reymond married without the lord's licence, so it is ordered to attach etc.
* Cecily and Sarra daughters of Geoffrey Bercarius have licence to marry where they will and they give 4s, pledge their father.
* Richard Cok has licence to marry. And he gives half a mark.
* Agnes daughter of Walter In the Hale has licence to marry. And she gives 12d, pledge her father.

Halimote of Norton on Tuesday after the Feast of the Ascension of the Lord in the 7th year – Richard Hederset [*25 May 1333*]

Jurors:	Geoffrey Bercarius	John le Dipere	John Hash
	Alexander Wisot	William atte Churche	John Jacob

* [*HALS 65513, f1v*] The jurors present that Richard Andreu has entered the lord's fee, therefore he is distrained to do fealty and make acknowledgment etc.
* Next it is ordered to distrain Richard le Spenser for the same, etc.
* Next it is presented that Agnes, daughter of Robert Hash has married without the lord's licence to John Bonde villein of the lord. And afterwards the said John and Agnes made agreement for their marriage. And they give 40d.
* Next they present that Agnes daughter of Stephen the Clerk is dead whose heriot is one cow worth 8s who held one cotland with appurtenances. And Roger her son is her next heir of the age of 16 years, who came and *gersummavit* the said tenement with appurtenances to hold to him and his in villeinage by the services due and accustomed for it. And he gives for agreement 5s. And he has done fealty. And he shall not commit waste. By the pledges of Alexander Wisot and of John Dipere. And Richard le Fuller by the consent of the said heir shall have wardship of the aforesaid land and heir until the full age of the same heir. And he gives for having wardship 20d.
* Next they present that Isabella Hash is dead. And John her son is her next heir, of the age of three years. Who held one cottage with curtilage with appurtenances. And John Ithehale husband of the said Isabella and father of the said heir came and *gersummavit* the said tenement with appurtenances to the use of the said heir, to hold to him and his in villeinage by the services due and accustomed for it. And the said John Ithehale shall have wardship of the

EDWARD III

said tenement and of the heir with appurtenances until the lawful age of the same heir. And he gives 3s.
* John Reymond married without the lord's licence. And afterwards he made agreement and gives 2s.
* Again is it ordered to attach John son of John Bate to answer to the lord why he married without the lord's licence.
* It is ordered to distrain William de Monden to acknowledge by what services he holds his tenement from the lord.
* It is ordered to distrain Richard de Wilye to answer to the lord how he entered the lord's fee and to do fealty and to satisfy for rent being behind.
* The jurors present that a certain toft which formerly was Robert Molot's came into the lord's hand after the death of Reynald Kyng which the said Reynald took from the lord in the time of Brother John de Hurle to hold in villeinage at the will of the lord. Therefore it is ordered to seise the said toft into the lord's hand until etc and that the beadle shall account for the issues.
* Richard Andreu did fealty and acknowledged that he holds from the lord, of the inheritance of Agnes his wife, a third part of one messuage and land which were formerly of John Maist[er] rendering for it annually 4s 4d. And he shall do suit etc. Also, he holds seven acres of land which he acquired from John Kyld rendering for them annually 20d. And he owes heriot and relief when they shall fall due.

Halimote of Norton on Friday next after the Feast of St Michael in the 7th year – Richard H[ederset] [*1 Oct 1333*]

Jurors:	Alexander Wisot	John Dipere	John Hash
	Ralph Albrede	John Jacob	William of the Church (*de Ecclesia*)

* The lord has leased and granted to Walter the Miller a certain toft which was formerly Robert Molot's which came into the hand of the lord after the death of Reynald Kyng who held it for the term of his life, just as it is by metes and bounds, to hold to him and his, rendering for it annually 2s 4d of ancient rent and 1d increase and other due and accustomed services. And he gives for an agreement for having entry half a mark. [*l. margin*: increase 1d]
* The jurors present that Walter Ithehale is dead, who held half a yardland with appurtenances, whose heriot is one cow worth 7s. And Reynald his son is his next heir of the age of 13 years. And Alice who was the wife of the said Walter came and *gersummavit* the said tenement with appurtenances to the use of the said Reynald the heir etc, to hold to the same Reynald and his in

EDWARD III

villeinage by the services due and accustomed for it, so that the aforesaid Alice shall have wardship of the lands and of the heir until the full age of the same heir. And she gives for *gersumma* and for having wardship 13s 4d. And the said Alice afterwards has licence to marry again and she gives 12d.
* Next they present that Margaret who was the wife of Geoffrey Bercarius is dead, whose heriot is one horse worth 7s, who held one messuage with one croft and two acres of land with appurtenances. And Walter Sayer is her next heir, who came and took the said messuage with croft and the said land from the lord, to hold to him and his by the services due and accustomed for them. And he gives 40d. And he shall not commit waste, reserving the right of anyone.
* The jurors present that John Albred and Alice Bonde have married together without licence each the second time. And afterwards they made agreement and give for having licence half a mark.
* Geoffrey Bercarius is dead, whose heriot is one horse worth 10s. And John his son is his next heir, aged 14 years, who came and *gersummavit* all the lands and all the tenements with appurtenances of which the said Geoffrey his father died possessed, to hold to him and his in villeinage by the services due and accustomed for them. And he gives for *gersumma* four pounds. And afterwards Ralph de Boueton came and took from the lord wardship of the lands and tenements of the said Geoffrey together with the body of the said John son and heir of the said Geoffrey to hold for the term of two years next to come. And he gives for having the term 20s. And afterwards the said Ralph made agreement with the lord for the marriage of the said John son of Geoffrey abovesaid and Ellen daughter of the said Ralph so that the aforesaid [*HALS 65513, f2*] John and Ellen have licence to marry together. And he gives for agreement 20s. And it is for the first marriage of the said John and Ellen.
* Ralph Boueton made agreement that John son of the same Ralph and Sara daughter of Geoffrey Bercarius can marry together by the lord's licence. And he gives for agreement 40d. And it is for the first marriage of the said John and Sara.
* Agnes Albred has licence to marry outside the Liberty and gives 5s. And it is for her third marriage and she finds pledges that she will well maintain the lands and tenements which she holds from the lord as dower without waste. And that the goods and chattels must not be removed outside the Liberty by the said Agnes nor hers, by the pledge of Ralph Aubrey and Walter Sayer.
* Again it is ordered to attach John son of John Bate to answer why he married without the lord's licence.
* Still is it ordered to distrain the tenants of the land of William de Monden to do fealty and to acknowledge by what services etc.

EDWARD III

Halimote of Norton on Tuesday in the three weeks of Easter in the 8th year – Richard Hederset [*19 Apr 1334*]

Jurors:	Alexander Wisot	John Jacob	John Hash
	Ralph Albred	Walter Saer	Adam Ward

* John son of John Bate has licence to marry. And he gives 12d, pledge Richard Bate.
* The jurors present that William de Monden makes a default therefore amerced 2d.
* Then they present that Walter Saer is dead who held one messuage and half a yardland of land with appurtenances, whose heriot is one horse worth 6s. And Reynald his son is his next heir of the age of 18 years. Who came and *gersummavit* the said lands and tenement with appurtenances to hold to him and his in villeinage by the services due and accustomed for it. And he has licence to marry for the first time. And he gives half a mark. And he shall not commit waste. And he did fealty, pledges William Sayer and John le Dipere.
* Next they present that William atte Chirche is dead who held one messuage and half a yardland of land with appurtenances, whose heriot is one cow worth 10s and William his son is his next heir of the age ten years. And Idonia who was the wife of the said William came and *gersummavit* the said land and tenement with appurtenances to the use of the said heir, to hold to him and his in villeinage by the services due and accustomed for them. And the said Idonia shall have wardship of the said land and of the heir until the full age of the said heir. And she gives for agreement 10s. And she shall not commit waste.
* Next they present that John Balston married without the lord's licence. And afterwards he made agreement and gives 12d.
* Next they present that Joan daughter of Cecily la Neweman married without licence outside the Liberty therefore it is ordered to attach etc.
* Next they present that Matilda Swetekyn married without licence at Caldecote, so it is ordered to attach etc.
* Next they present that John son of John Boton has licence to marry. And he gives 6d, pledge Adam Ward.
* The aletasters present that the brewers have broken the Assize, so are amerced 11d.
* Idonia who was the wife of William atte Chirche has licence to marry for the second time and she gives 18d.

EDWARD III

Halimote of Norton on Tuesday next after the Feast of St Denis in the 8th year – Nicholas Bewyke [*11 Oct 1334*]

Jurors:	Ralph Aubrey	Alexander Wysot	John Jacob
	John Dipere	John Hash	Adam Ward

* Joan daughter of Cecily le Neweman is attached by the pledges of John le Newman and of the beadle to answer the lord why she married without licence and she did not justify herself nor have the said pledges got her, therefore amerced. And it is ordered to distrain the said Joan against the next etc.
* Matilda Swetekyn is attached by one chest (*cistam*) to answer why she married without licence and she did not justify herself therefore it is ordered to retain it and to take more until etc.
* The jurors present that Ida Prudde has committed *leyrewit*, therefore amerced 2d.
* The aletasters present that the brewers have broken the Assize therefore amerced 14d.
* Matilda daughter of Geoffrey Bercarius has committed *leyrewit* therefore amerced 2d.

[*HALS 65513, f2v*] **Halimote of Norton on Tuesday next after the Feast of St John before the Latin Gate in the 9th year – Nicholas Bewyk [*9 May 1335*]**

Jurors:	Ralph Aubrey	William Sayer	John Hash
	John Albred	John le Neweman	Adam Ward

* John son of Richard le Reve of Munden complains of Walter le Neweman concerning a plea of land, pledge of prosecution John Noreis. And he demands one cottage with appurtenances which was of Isabelle Cartere, formerly his wife, which he ought to hold by joint feoffment etc. And it is ascertained by the record of the rolls of the time of Brother R[ichard] de Hederset, in Easter term in the 6th year of the reign of the King who now is, that the same John who claims had forgiven and quitclaimed all his right, therefore let him take nothing but be amerced.
* John Inthehale made agreement for his first marriage and he gives 18d.
* The jurors present that Alice Swetekyn 2d, John Dipere 2d, John Albred 2d, Henry Boton 2d, John Bonde 2d, Alexander Andreu 2d, grind elsewhere than at the lord's mill therefore amerced.

EDWARD III

* The aletasters present that the brewers have broken the Assize, therefore amerced 12d.
* John Love has licence to marry Ida atte Churche and to have entry to hold that land as long as the said Ida shall live, doing all services and customs of villeinage which pertain to that land. So [*ie provided*] that he does not commit waste nor destruction. And he gives half a mark for having entry and for leave, by the pledge of Ralph Albred and John Iseude, nor shall he remove any goods outside the Liberty of the lord without leave etc by the aforesaid pledge.
* John Iseude has licence to marry a second time and gives 12d. And Richard the son of the same has leave to go to clerks' school (*ad scolas clericales*) by the said agreement.
* Walter Sayer surrendered into the hand of the lord one cottage with hedges (*sepibus*) and ditches and all other appurtenances, which formerly was of Saer the Reeve.[34] And the lord has conveyed the said cottage with appurtenances to Alexander Ward to hold to him and his villeinage by the services due and accustomed for it. And he gives for agreement 2s. And the aforesaid Walter shall acquit the aforesaid Alexander of all services and customs towards the lord for 2d rent *per annum* and one day of *bederip* at harvest for ever.
* John son of Simon le Reve of Munden complains of Walter le Neweman concerning a plea of land, pledge of prosecution etc [*no names*]. And the aforesaid John has not prosecuted, therefore he himself and his pledges are amerced. And the aforesaid Walter may go without a day etc.
* John Jacob and Margaret his wife surrendered into the lord's hand one messuage with adjoining curtilage which Walter Warde formerly held, between the tenement of Richard Parlores and the tenement of Alice Hash, to the use of John Bonde and Agnes his wife. And the lord has conveyed the said tenement with appurtenances to the same John Bonde and Agnes to hold to them and the heirs of that John in villeinage by the services due and accustomed for it. And they give for agreement 5s. And the same John Jacob and his wife give for a heriot now 5s and the said John Bonde and his wife a heriot as often as it shall fall due.
* Reynald Dame is dead who held one messuage and 12 acres of land with appurtenances of which the heriot is one calf worth 3s. And the jurors say that Juliana Dame aunt of the said Reynald is his nearest heir of full age who came and *gersummavit* the said tenement with appurtenances to hold to her and hers by the services due and accustomed for it and she gives for agreement 2s 6d. And hereupon immediately the aforesaid Juliana surrenders into the lord's

---

[34] The English surname 'Reeve' or 'Reve' is used in the Latin text from here rather than the usual *Praepositus* [which hitherto has been translated as Reeve].

EDWARD III

hand all the said tenement without any withholding. And the lord has granted the said tenement to Richard Bate junior, to hold to him and his in villeinage by the services due and accustomed for it. And he gives for agreement 2s. And the cellarer pardons the heriot of the said Juliana.

Halimote of Norton on Tuesday next after the Feast of Michaelmas in the 9th year – Nicholas Bewyk [*3 Oct 1335*]

Jurors: Ralph Boueton   Ralph Albred   John Jacob
           Alexander Wisot William Sayer   Adam Ward

* The jurors present that the tenants of the lands which were Percival Simeon's make default of one *bederip* in harvest to damage 1½d.
* Next they present that the tenants of the lands which were John le Maystre's make default of one *bederip* in harvest to damage 1½d. And it is ordered to distrain all the said tenants to answer about this to the lord, etc.
* Next they present that John Bonde senior \3d/, John Aubrey \3d/, Reynald Balston \3d/ grind elsewhere than at the lord's mill therefore amerced.
* They present that Cecily Dipere committed *leyrewit* so amerced 6d. [*l. margin*: villein (fem)]
* Roger Redhod complains of William Bate, Alexander Wisot and John Wysot concerning a plea of land, pledges of prosecution John Joye and John Wysot. And he says that each of the aforesaid William, Alexander and John unlawfully deforced from him a headland of land at the headlands of three half acres of land in Norton of which William le Couherd his grandfather died seised according to the custom of the manor in villeinage in the time of King Edward grandfather of the king who now is, etc. And the said William, Alexander and John deny etc. And demand a survey (*visus*) of the said land. And it is ordered to deliver to them a survey etc. And hereupon a day is given etc until the next Halimote.
* [*HALS 65513, f3*] Alexander Andreu, Reynald Ithehale and Alice mother of the same Reynald surrender into the lord's hand one plot of land containing two perches in length and two perches in breadth lying between the tenement of John Colyn and the land of John Hash and it abuts upon the King's highway (*regiam viam*). And the lord has granted the said plot of land to John Cok of Holwell and Margery his wife to hold to them and theirs in villeinage by the services due and accustomed for it. And they will give besides the aforesaid services to the lord an increase in rent of 1d at the Feast of St Michael, reserving the right of the aforesaid Reynald who is under age and the right of anyone. And if the said John Cok and Margery his wife and theirs shall build

EDWARD III

there they shall each of them give a heriot as often as it shall fall due. And they give for agreement 4d. [*r. margin*: increase 1d]
* John son of Richard Ithehale surrendered into the hand of the lord one built-upon plot of curtilage which William Ithehale formerly demised to the said Richard his father by the lord's leave which lies between the tenement which was formerly the said William's and the tenement of Roger le Shepherd as the metes and bounds show (*proportant*). And for this surrender the same John has leave to throw down and remove that house now built there with all his goods and chattels there. And the lord has granted to the said John that plot of a certain curtilage which is called *Ankerwyk* as broad and long as the metes and boundaries show, in order that he may build upon that plot the said house, to hold to him and his in villeinage, paying for it to the lord annually an increase in rent of 2d at two terms of the year, that is to say Easter and Michaelmas. And he gives for agreement 12d. And he shall give one heriot both for that plot which is called *Ankerwyk* and for the 12 acres of land which he holds in the common fields which are called *Mullelond* as often as it shall fall due and he shall only give one heriot etc unless he shall acquire more tenements in the future, etc. [*r. margin*: increase 2d]

Halimote of Norton on Tuesday next before the Feast of St Mark the Evangelist in the 10th year – Nicholas B[ewyke] [*16 Apr 1336*]

Jurors:	Ralph Aubrey	Alexander Wysot	Adam Warde
	William Thomas	William Sayer	John Hassch

* Roger Redhod because he has not prosecuted against William Bate, Alexander Wysot and John Wysot in a plea of land, therefore he and his pledges of prosecution, that is to say John Joye and John Wysot are amerced 4d.
* The jurors present that John Aubrey \6d/ and John Gegard \6d/ grind elsewhere than at the lord's mill, therefore amerced.
* Next they present that Alice daughter of Stephen Ithehale, and Ellen Ithehale have committed *leyrewytt*, therefore amerced.
* Next they present that John Hassh is dead who held one cotland of which the heriot is one calf worth 6s. And Thomas Hassh brother of the said John is his next heir of full age who came and *gersummavit* the said tenement with appurtenances to hold to him and his in villeinage by the services due and accustomed for it. And he has licence to marry. And he gives for agreement 3s 4d. And he shall not commit waste.
* Reynald son of William Hassh has licence to marry where he will, and he gives for agreement 12d. And he shall come annually to the View of

EDWARD III

Frankpledge, by the pledge of John Hassh and William Sayer.
* John Reymond has licence to marry, and he gives for agreement 2s.
* The lord has ordained and determined that no villein henceforth shall alienate or demise to any free man or any stranger (*extraneo*) any land or tenement nor make any agreement about this with them as long as he can demise the said tenement and land to the lord or to another unfree villein tenant. And if any unfree tenant shall come against that statute he shall be heavily amerced. And nonetheless he shall give to the lord half a mark.
* Richard Ithehale surrendered into the lord's hand half a virgate of land with appurtenances which William Ithehale formerly held. And the lord conveyed the said half virgate of land with a messuage to Richard le Fuller and Sarra his wife to hold to him and the heirs of this Richard le Fuller in villeinage by the services due and accustomed for it. And they give for an agreement 5s. And he finds pledges that is to say Adam Warde and John Dipere that he shall not commit waste and that he shall be obedient in all things according to what other customary tenants are and shall be. And he shall give tallage, merchet, *gersumma* and heriot as often as they fall due. And he did fealty.
* Roger Prodde demised half an acre of land to John Andreu of Baldock without leave for one crop, therefore amerced 6d.

Halimote of Norton on Tuesday next after the Feast of St Michael in the 10th year – Nicholas Bewyk [*1 Oct 1336*]

Jurors:	Ralph Albred	Ralph Boueton	William Thomas
	Alexander Wysot	John Dipere	John Jacob

* The jurors present that John Hassh, Roger Bercarius, Richard Bate make default. All are sick.
* Next they present that William Bate is dead whose heriot is one horse worth 10s for one tenement and for another tenement one horse worth half a mark, and who held two messuages and two half virgates of land with appurtenances. And Richard his son is his next heir of the age of 14 years on the day of St Martin next to come. And the lord conveyed the said tenements and wardship of the aforesaid heir to Henry Bate, chaplain, uncle of the said heir until Michaelmas next, so that the same Henry perform in the meantime all services and customs which pertain to that land [*HALS 65513, f3v*] and he shall maintain the said heir suitably. And he gives for having the term 10s and shall not commit waste. And then at the Feast of St Michael next ensuing he shall take the said tenements and lands from the lord at rent to the end of six years or to the full age of the said heir by an agreement then to be made with

EDWARD III

the cellarer or he shall pay *gersumma* for the said tenements and lands with all appurtenances to the use of the said heir.
* The jurors present that John Wysot is dead who held one messuage and half a virgate of land of which the heriot is one calf worth half a mark. And Margaret his wife holds the tenement in the name of inheritance.
* Next they present that Walter le Dryver is dead who held a plot of curtilage and three roods of land of which the heriot is nothing. And Agnes sister of the said Walter comes and demands the said land as of the gift of John le Dryver by joint feoffment and thereof she calls for the record of the rolls of the time of John de Hurle, cellarer. And it is reported etc.
* Margaret Tollard who was the wife of John Wysot has licence to marry John atte Hathe of *Stithenache* [Stevenage]. And they give for her marriage and for having entry to the said Margaret 8s by agreement.
* The jurors present that Walter Sayer has demised half an acre of land to Robert de Cadewelle without leave, so he is amerced 6d, and is ordered to take the land into the lord's hand until etc.
* Henry Bate, chaplain, by the lord's leave demised to Walter Beneit of Baldock all that term which he took from the lord of the lands and tenements. which were William Bate's and wardship of Richard son and heir of the said Walter, paying thereof for having the term until Michaelmas next following, 10s, in the name of the said Henry, and he shall perform the services etc. Furthermore the lord has demised to the same Walter after the term of Michaelmas next to come all the aforesaid lands and tenements with all their appurtenances and with reversion of dower when it shall happen and with wardship of the said heir until the end of six years then next ensuing fully to be completed, performing for them the due and accustomed services and not committing waste. And he gives for having the term 30s.
* John Wysot surrendered into the lord's hand one cottage with curtilage which was formerly Ralph Boueton's and he surrendered into the lord's hands 11 acres of land with appurtenances which were of John Wysot his father just as they lie by parcels in the fields of Norton just as the metes and bounds are. And he gives for heriot 3s. And he has leave to serve where he will so [*ie provided*] that he comes annually to the View of Frankpledge and he shall give 2d to his chief pledge. And he shall give annually to the lord for *chevage* at Easter one capon. And he shall give tallage in proportion to his goods as often as it shall happen. And he gives for having leave 3s, by the pledge of Ralph Boueton and Alexander Wysot who bind themselves and theirs to this. And he has licence to marry, and he gives for agreement 6d. And afterwards the lord conveyed the said tenements and lands to Alexander son of Ralph de Boueton to hold to him and his in villeinage by the services due and

accustomed for them. And he gives for agreement 10s, by pledge of his father. And he has leave to go to clerks' school. And he shall give six capons at Easter next following.

Halimote of Norton on Tuesday on the Feast of St John at the Latin Gate in the 11th year [*6 May 1337*]

Jurors:	Ralph Boueton	Alexander Wysot	John Jacob
	Ralph Albred	John Dipere	William Sayer

* The jurors present that Roger Bercarius \2d/, William de Mondene \2d/ make default, therefore amerced.
* Next they present that John Bonde senior \2d/, John Bonde junior \2d/ and Alice Swetekyn \2d/ grind elsewhere than at the lord's mill, so are amerced.
* Next they present that Margaret Tollard has committed *leyrewyt*, so is amerced 6d.
* Sybil atte Churche has got married a second time to a free man without licence. And afterwards he made agreement. And the fine[35] (*finis*) is condoned by the cellarer.
* John Bate by the lord's leave has demised to Richard his son one cotland with appurtenances to hold for a term of 12 years next to come fully completed. And he shall do the services in the meantime. And he gives for agreement 40d.
* The jurors present that Alexander Wysot and John Hassch made an exchange of one half an acre of land which was the said Alexander's at *Wonforlong* for one rood of land which was this John's lying at *Eldebrache*. And afterwards they made agreement for the aforesaid exchange, to hold to them and theirs in villeinage by the services due and accustomed for it. And they give 12s.
* Agnes daughter of Stephen Pernelle has demised by the lord's leave to John Jacob all her lands and tenements in Norton with appurtenances except the reversion of dower which belongs to the aforesaid tenements when it shall fall, for a term of 12 years next to come fully to be completed, the term beginning at Michaelmas next ensuing. And the same John shall maintain the aforesaid tenement without waste for the whole aforesaid term at his own expense. And the aforesaid Agnes shall keep him indemnified in relation to the lord both concerning waste and concerning customs and services which belong to the aforesaid tenement. And he gives for having the term 10s.

---

[35] The first use of the word *finis*, translated as 'fine', used with a verb indicating it was condoned or forgiven. From 1402 it was also used with a monetary amount.

EDWARD III

* John Ronge has licence to marry Margaret Tollard. And they give for agreement half a mark.

[*HALS 65513, f4*] **Halimote of Norton on Tuesday next after the Feast of St Faith the Virgin in the 11th year – Nicholas Bewyke [*7 Oct 1337*]**

Jurors:	William Thomas	John Diper	Adam Warde
	Alexander Wysot	William Sayer	John Jacob

* Richard Cok is dead who held one messuage and half a yardland of land with appurtenances. And Henry his son is his next heir of full age who came and *gersummavit* the said tenement with all its appurtenances to hold to him and his in villeinage by services etc. And he has licence to marry. And he gives for agreement 10s. Nor shall he commit waste.
* The jurors present that Agnes Boueton has demised one cottage with appurtenances to Reynald Balston without leave, so it is ordered etc. And because the said Agnes says in court that she is free while an inquisition says that she is unfree (*nativa*), therefore let the said Agnes be attached and altogether excluded from the said tenement with appurtenances for ever. And afterwards the same Reynald made agreement for the said cottage to hold to him and his in villeinage by the services etc. And he gives for increase in rent for warranty annually ½d at Michaelmas. And he gives for having entry, 40d. [*r. margin*: increase ½d]
* Walter Sayer surrendered into the lord's hand half an acre of land with appurtenances as it lies between the land of William atte Chirche and of Henry Cok and it abuts on the lord's land in *Longehevedlond*. And the lord has granted the said land to Alexander Warde to hold to him and his by the services due and accustomed for it. And he gives for agreement 2s.

Halimote of Norton on Tuesday next after the close of Easter in the 12th year – Nicholas Bewyke [*12 May 1338*]

Jurors:	Stephen Aubrey	John Diper	William Thomas
	Alexander Wysot	William Sayer	Adam Warde

* The jurors present that Petronilla Bonde has committed *leyrewit*, so is amerced 3d.
* The aletasters present that the brewers have broken the Assize, so are amerced 6d.
* [*r.margin*: Decree (*Constitutio*)] The lord has determined and ordained that if any villein tenants (*nativi tenentes*) of Norton henceforward shall wound any

EDWARD III

of the villeins their neighbours (*nativis vicinis*) with knives, swords or sticks or other weapons then he who has done so shall give 20s to the lord and satisfy the party wounded.
* Because the lord is given to understand that villein tenants (*nativi tenentes*) of Norton go commonly to the tavern at Baldock and expend and waste there their goods and chattels to the grave damage of the lord and of those tenants there, the lord has appointed and ordained that in future none may go to the said tavern nor sit there wasting their goods under pain of a heavy amercement. And moreover the lord ordained that the said tenants brew in their own tenements or shall have a common brewery in Norton for selling by the view and regulation of the common tasters and not otherwise. And hereupon John le Dipere is appointed brewer there until the next Halimote. And it is to be known that at each Halimote such brewers should be chosen both by the Homage and by the tasters.
* Next the lord forbids under pain of heavy amercement that no villein may sell to any of Baldock or demise any land or crops of corn without leave of the lord under pain of forfeiture of the said lands and corn to the lord.
* Next the lord forbids that any villeins overburden the common pasture of Norton with foreign sheep (*extraneis*) without the assent and leave of the lord because the sum paid for pasturage (*agistatio*) of such sheep traditionally (*rite*) belongs to the lord.

Halimote of Norton on Tuesday next before the Feast of St Luke the Evangelist in the 12th year – Nicholas Bewyke [*13 Oct 1338*]

Jurors:	John Dipere	William Thomas	Ralph Boton
	William Sayer	Alexander Wysot	John Jecob

* The jurors present that the tenements which formerly were William Bate's are wasted to damage etc, which Walter Bate held for a term of six years. And it is to be known that the said Walter came before the cellarer and surrendered into the lord's hand the whole term which he had in the said lands and tenements. And because the rents and services of the said tenements are in arrears Richard le Fuller comes and acknowledges at this Halimote that he will satisfy the lord for all the arrears of rent and services which are behind from the aforesaid lands and tenements and shall keep the said Walter indemnified in relation to the lord on account of the said arrears. And afterwards he satisfied the cellarer, etc.
* Mabel la Longe in her pure widowhood by the lord's licence demised to Lord Adam Flaon de Newnham one messuage and half a yardland of land with

appurtenances which formerly were of Richard la Longe, father of the said Mabel, in Newnham, to hold to him and his to the end of ten years next to come fully to be completed, performing for them the due and accustomed services, for five marks of silver which the same Lord Adam paid to the same Mabel in hard bargaining (*in arduo negotio*) and at the request of the same Mabel nor shall he commit waste. Fine pending. [*r. margin:* beware for Newnham]

[*HALS 65513, f4v*] Halimote of Norton on Tuesday next after the Feast of St Mark the Evangelist in the 13th year – Nicholas Bewyke [*27 Apr 1339*]

Jurors: Ralph Aubrey   John Shepherd   Adam Warde
         Alexander Wysot   William Thomas   John Ithehale

* The jurors present that Agnes Ithehale \6d\ and Matilda \6d\ daughter of Elizabeth have committed *leyrewyt*, therefore amerced.
* Albreda who was the wife of Richard Bate by the lord's leave demised to John Albred all her dower which belongs to her from the lands and tenements which were formerly Richard her husband's, excepting half an acre of land whereof one rood lies in *Eldefeld* and another rood lies in *Longeforlong* to hold to the same John for the term of the life of that Albreda by service etc. And if the said Albreda should die before Richard son and heir of William Bate shall be of full age then the said John Albred shall hold the said dower with appurtenances until the full age of the said heir by service etc. And he gives for agreement 3s.
* The aletasters present that the brewers have broken the Assize, therefore amerced 11d.
* The lord has conveyed to Adam Warde wardship of Richard son and heir of William Bate and of his lands and tenements to hold in villeinage until the full age of the said heir performing for them the due and accustomed services. And he gives for agreement 3s. Nor shall he commit waste.
* The lord has given leave to Richard le Fuller that he may demise to whom he will of Baldock or elsewhere six acres of his land from the Feast of St Michael next to come until the end of two years then next ensuing by the view of the reeve of the manor. And he gives for having leave 6d.

EDWARD III

Halimote of Norton on Tuesday next after the Feast of St Denis in the 13th year – Thomas Mare [*12 Oct 1339*]

Jurors:	Ralph Aubrey	John Shepeherd	Adam Warde
	Alexander Wysot	John Dypere	William Sayer

* The jurors present that Reynald Balston makes default, therefore amerced 3d.
* John Bonde senior has licence to marry, and gives for agreement 18d.
* The jurors present that John Albred \2d/, John son of Hugh \2d/, John Bonde junior \2d/, and John Bonde senior \2d/, grind elsewhere than at the lord's mill, therefore amerced.
* The aletasters present that the brewers have broken the Assize, therefore amerced 6d.
* Roger Prudde surrendered into the hand of the lord one messuage and a half yardland of land with appurtenances which were formerly his father's. And the lord conveyed all the said lands and tenements to Adam Warde to hold to him and his in villeinage and at the will of the lord by the due and accustomed services. So that then the aforesaid Roger shall hold all the aforesaid lands and tenements in villeinage by services etc for the term of his life, except one house [*or room*] within the said messuage and except four acres of land of the same tenement, of which two acres lie in the field towards Stotfold and the other two acres of land with appurtenances lie in the field towards Baldock, with peaceable coming and going, which house and four acres of land the same Adam shall hold to him and his as is stated. And all the residue of the aforesaid lands and tenements after the decease of the same Roger in the same manner. Nor shall he commit waste. And he gives for agreement 13s 4d. Roger gives as a composition for his heriot 2s.
* Because Walter Sayer is incapable of holding one messuage and a half a virgate of land with appurtenances and has ceased from the accustomed rents and other services which pertain to the said land nor can nor will find any pledges, the lord has leased the said messuage and one *ferthlingate* of land with appurtenances to William Sayer to hold for the term of 12 years next to come fully to be completed, performing for it the services etc, nor shall he commit waste but shall maintain the said tenement in good condition. And he gives for having the term 12d. Next, as to another *ferthlingate* of land which is called *Rageslond* the lord has leased the said land with appurtenances to Alexander Warde to hold for the term of 12 years next to come fully to be completed, performing for it the services, etc. Nor shall he commit waste. And he gives for having the term 12d.

EDWARD III

* John Bonde surrenders into the lord's hand one messuage called *Parlores* tenement. And the lord has conveyed and granted the aforesaid tenement with appurtenances to John atte Hathe to hold to him and his in villeinage and at the will of the lord by services etc. And he gives for agreement 2s. Nor shall he commit waste. And the said John Bonde has granted that he will not sell or alienate anything of the tenement which he now holds to any other than the said John atte Hathe.

Halimote of Norton on Tuesday on the Feast of St Mark the Evangelist the in 14th year – Thomas Mare [*25 Apr 1340*]

Jurors:	John Dipere	William Thomas	Reynald Sayer
	John Jecob	John le Shepherd	John Love

* It is ordered to take into the hand of the lord one acre of land which Henry Cok demised to Alan le Chapman without leave of the lord until etc.
* [*HALS 65513, f5*] The aletasters present that the brewers have broken the Assize. Therefore amerced 3d.
* It is ascertained by examination that Margery Hoghaler \6d/ has demised to William Sayer \6d/ without leave her dower which fell to her after the death of Walter Hoghaler her husband for the last three years. Therefore it is ordered to take into the lord's hands the said tenements with the chattels found in the same until etc. And both of them are amerced. And all the jurors for the last three years are amerced for concealment. And afterwards by the lord's licence it is agreed that the said Margery has demised to the same William the said dower for the whole of her life. And the same William shall do the services etc. So that the same William pay annually to the same Margery two bushels of wheat and two bushels of peas at the Feast of St Michael or to John Dipere the attorney of the same Margery. And if he shall not do it the aforesaid William grants that the lord's bailiff shall cause them to be levied etc. And the said William gives for agreement 6d.
* Alice atte Assh surrendered into the lord's hand one cottage with curtilage as it lies between the tenement of Thomas Ayssh and the tenement of John Bonde junior, with its appurtenances. And the lord conveyed the said tenements with appurtenances to Ralph Thomme and Agnes daughter of Alice to hold to them and theirs in villeinage and at the will of the lord by the services etc. And they give 12d by agreement for the said tenements and for licence to marry.

EDWARD III

Halimote of Norton on Tuesday next after the Feast of St Faith the Virgin in the 14th year – W Wynselowe [*10 Oct 1340*]

Jurors:	John Geoffrey	Ralph Boueton	William Sayer
	Alexander Wysot	John le Dipere	William Thomas

* The jurors present that Walter, vicar of the church of Norton, is dead, who held of the lord one messuage with appurtenances in villeinage, the heriot of which is one pig worth 2s. Therefore it is ordered to take the said tenement with appurtenances into the lord's hand until etc.
* Roger Bercarius is dead who held of the lord two cottages and half an acre of land with appurtenances for which he gave two heriots that is to say one ewe worth 10d and one wether worth 10d. And the jurors say that Isabella daughter of the same is his next heir of full age who came with Walter her husband and *gersummavit* one cottage and half an acre of land with appurtenances which were formerly of the tenements of John Ithehale to hold to them and the heirs of this Isabella in villeinage and at the will of the lord by services etc. And they give for agreement 2s. Nor shall they commit waste. And as to another cottage which formerly was of Richard le Heldere the said Isabella holds it as the gift of the said Roger as appears from the record of the roll of the time of Brother William le Barbour, cellarer in the 3rd year.
* The jurors present that Reynald Saer entered into the dower of Agnes his mother without the leave of the lord, therefore he is amerced 4d. And afterwards the said Agnes by the lord's leave demised to the same Reynald all her aforesaid dower except her dwelling and one croft containing one rood of land to be held for a term of 12 years next ensuing fully to be completed, doing meanwhile the services etc. And the aforesaid Agnes shall reap annually for one day in the lord's wheat harvest in discharge of the services of the said Reynald. And he gives for having the term 12d.
* Agnes Albred by leave of the lord has demised her dower that is to say one third part of one *ferthlingate* of land with appurtenances to John Hasch to hold for term of the life of that Agnes by services etc. And she gives for agreement 12d.
* Agnes Albred by leave of the lord has demised her dower that is to say a third part of half a virgate of land with appurtenances to Ralph Albred to hold for the term of life of that Agnes by services etc. And she gives for agreement 2s.
* The jurors present that Petronilla Bonde has married outside the Liberty without the lord's leave. And John her brother made agreement for the same and gives 12d. [*r. margin*: villein]

EDWARD III

* The aletasters present that the brewers have broken the Assize so are amerced 5d.
* John Colyn came after the decease of his mother Matilda and *gersummavit* one cottage with adjoining curtilage which the said Matilda held by a joint feoffment with John Colyn formerly her husband on the day on which he died to hold to the same John and his in villeinage and at the will of the lord by services etc. And he gives for agreement 6d.
* John son of Adam Warde has leave to go to clerks' school. And he gives for agreement 12d. [*r. margin*: villein]
* William son of Alan le Neweman has licence to marry and to serve and be made an apprentice where he will. And he gives 12d. And he shall come annually to the View of Frankpledge of Norton. And he shall give to the lord one capon as an increment as long as he shall live. [*r. margin*: villein] [*r. margin*: increment one capon]

Halimote of Norton on Wednesday next after the Feast of the Apostles Philip and James in the 15th year – W Wynsel[owe] [*2 May 1341*]

Jurors:	Ralph Boueton	John Dipere	William Thomas
	John Jacob	William Sayer	Adam Warde

* John Prudde is dead who held of the lord one cottage, of which the heriot is one sheep worth 8d. And Margery his wife holds the tenement by joint feoffment.
* Reynald Ithehale is of full age for holding the lands and tenements of Walter Ithehale his father which Alice his mother held until the full age of the same heir that is to say one messuage and half a yardland of land with appurtenances, who comes and says that the said Alice *gersummavit* the said tenements at the time when she took wardship of the same. And the jurors witness this. [*HALS 65513, f5v*] Therefore the same Reynald has seisin thereof. And he has done fealty.
* The jurors present that William atte Cherche is of full age to receive his land that is to say one messuage and one half yardland of land which Idonia atte Cherche his mother held in name of wardship, who [*ie William atte Cherche*] comes and calls for the record of the roll of *gersumma* of the said land etc. And afterwards he has the record by view of the cellarer.
* Reynald Ithehale has licence to marry and gives 2s.
* William atte Cherche has licence to marry and gives 2s.
* The jurors present that Alice Parnele has married without licence and

EDWARD III

afterwards made agreement for the same and gives 12d.
* The aletasters present that the brewers have broken the Assize so are amerced 5d.
* Again it is ordered to retain in the lord's hand one messuage with appurtenances which Walter the vicar of the church of Norton held of the lord on the day he died in villeinage until etc.
* The jurors present that Matilda la Shepherd \6d/, Ellen atte Hale \6d/, Sarra Sayer \6d/, and Sarra la Sewesteresdouter \6d/ have committed *leyrewyt*, so are amerced.
* Matilda la Shepherd has licence to marry and gives 6d.

Halimote of Norton on Thursday on the Feast of St Luke the Evangelist in the 15th year – W Wynsel[owe] [*18 Oct 1341*]

Jurors:	Ralph Boueton	Alexander Wysot	William Sayer
	Ralph Aubrey	John Dipere	Adam Warde

* The jurors present that Richard Fuller has demised to Roger Scharman of Baldock two acres of land in part of the field without leave, therefore amerced 2d.
* Next they present that Alice daughter of Walter Sayer has married without licence and it is reported by the jurors that the said Alice is a vagabond and has been for a long time and has not carried away any goods out of the Liberty, therefore the amercement is forgiven.
* Next they present that John Albred grinds elsewhere than at the lord's mill. Therefore amerced 6d.
* Again it is ordered to retain in the lord's hand one messuage with appurtenances which Walter vicar of the church of Norton held of the lord in villeinage on the day he died, until etc.
* Richard son of William Bate who is of full age came and *gersummavit* all the lands and tenements with appurtenances which his aforesaid father held of the lord in bondage (*in bondagio*) that is to say, two messuages and two half virgates of land with appurtenances in Norton to hold to him and his in villeinage and at the will of the lord by services etc. And he gives 20s. And has licence to marry by the said agreement. Nor shall he commit waste.
* William Thomas lately deceased held of the lord one messuage and one cotland and one *ferthlingate* of land of which the heriot is one cow worth 6s 8d. And John Thomas, chaplain, is his next heir who came and *gersummavit* all the said land with adjoining messuage, to hold to him and his

in villeinage by the services due and accustomed for it. And he gives to the lord for agreement 13s 4d.

Halimote of Norton on Tuesday next before the Feast of St Mark the Evangelist in the 16th year – W Wynselowe [*23 Apr 1342*]

Jurors:	John le Schepherd	John Dipere	Richard Bate
	Ralph Boueton	John Jacob	John Reymond

* John Thomas, chaplain, son and heir of William Thomas surrendered into the hand of the lord one messuage and one cotland and one *ferthlingate* of land with appurtenances and the lord seised thereof Walter Thomas and his heirs to hold to him and his in villeinage by the due and accustomed services for it. And if it should happen that the said Walter die without an heir of his body begotten that then the said messuage and said land shall revert to the heirs of the said John Thomas. And he gives to the lord for agreement and for having licence to marry 13s 4d. And the said John the chaplain made composition for heriot and gave 12d.
* It is ordered to retain in the lord's hand one messuage with appurtenances which Walter, vicar of the church of Norton, held of the lord in villeinage on the day he died until etc.
* [*HALS 65514, f1*] Next they present that John le Dryver has married without licence. And afterwards he came and made agreement and paid 6d.
* Richard Prudde has made an agreement because he has married Sarah the villein of the lord without licence. And he gives for this agreement 6d.
* Next they present that Robert Cadewell of Baldock has acquired one acre of land from Richard Andrew without licence. Therefore it is ordered to seise the said land into the hand of the lord until he shall have done fealty and shall have demonstrated by what right he should enter into the lord's fee.
* Next they present that Alexander Cok has leased to John Andrew of Baldock one acre of land for sowing against the prohibition of the lord. Therefore it is ordered to seise the said land into the hand of the lord until etc.
* The aletasters present that the brewers have broken the Assize, so they are amerced, 10d.
* Helen the daughter of Ralph Aubrey has made agreement because she has married without the lord's licence. And she gives for this agreement 2s. [*r. margin:* villein (fem)]
* Richard in le Hale has the lord's permission to marry Petronilla the daughter of Ralph le Parlour. And they give for the agreement 12d.

EDWARD III

Halimote of Norton on Tuesday next after the Feast of St Edward in the 16th year – W Wynselowe [*15 Oct 1342*][36]

Jurors:	Ralph Aubrey	William Sayer	John Jacob
	John Dypere	Alexander Wysot	John Hassh

* It is further ordered to distrain Robert Cadewell of Baldock to show by what right he is entered into one acre of land which he bought from Richard Andrew, etc.
* The jurors present that Richard Andrew 3d, Reynald Balston 2d, Agnes Clyve [*or Clyne*] [\?*contra:* against/], Sarah of Erdelee 6d make default and so amerced.
* John le Shepeherd, who held of the lord half a virgate of land, is dead, whose heriot is one horse as well as 10s. And Helen his daughter is his next heir of the age of three years. And the lord has given wardship of the said lands together with the wardship of the said heiress until the full age of the said heir to Helen who was the wife of the said John. And the aforesaid Helen gives to the lord for having her term 40s, nor should she commit waste.
* It is ordered to distrain John Groum to show by what right he is entered into the lord's fee. And afterwards he came and showed a charter, etc.
* The jurors present that Matilda le Warde 6d and Cecilia Dyp[er]e 4d have committed *leyrewit*, and so are amerced.
* The aletasters present that the brewers have broken the Assize and so are amerced 3d.
* Adam Warde has permission from the lord to make an exchange with Alexander Andrew of one half acre of land lying above *Lobbegate*, just as it lies between John Bonde and John Hassh. And he gives to the lord for this agreement 6d.
* Alexander Andrew has permission from the lord to make an exchange with Adam Warde of one half acre of land in the *Eldefeld* just as it lies between the land of Richard Bate and the land of Reynald in the Hale. And he gives for this agreement 6d.
* Matilda Balston lately deceased held of the lord one cotland, whose heriot is one cow worth 6s. And her next heir is Reynald Balston her son, who comes and gives to the lord 6s 8d, to hold the said cotland to him and his at the will of the lord by the services due and accustomed for it, saving then the right of anyone, nor shall he commit waste. And he shall be obedient in all things just

---

[36] Dating is uncertain because there were two St Edwards so the October date has been chosen as it fits with the sequence of court dates.

EDWARD III

as the other accustomed tenants of the same tenure.

Halimote of Norton on Tuesday next after the Feast of St John before the Latin Gate in the 17th year – W Wynselowe [*13 May 1343*]

Jurors:	John Diper	John Ysoud	William Sayer
	John Reymond	John Jecob	Reynald Sayer

* The jurors present that Sarra of Yherdelee [\?*eque:* the same/] William of Munden 2d, make default and so are amerced.
* Next they present that Reynald in le Hale lately deceased held of the lord two messuages and two *ferthlingates* of land with appurtenances, whose heriot is one cow worth 5s and one mother sheep worth 12d. And William the brother of the said Reynald is his next heir of the age of 18 years. And Alicia Hasche, mother of the said William, made agreement with the lord for wardship of the land and of the heir, to hold it until the full age of the said heir. And she gives to the lord for having the term 40d.
* [*HALS 65514, f1v*] Ralph Aubrey has permission to marry off Alice his daughter. And he gives for this agreement 2s.
* Ralph Boueton has permission to marry off Petronilla his daughter. And he gives for this agreement 2s.
* Lord Henry Bate has permission to marry off Agnes his sister where and to whom he shall wish. And the agreements are confirmed by the cellarer.
* Henry Cok has leased to Edmund le Frenche three roods of land without permission, therefore is amerced 3d. And afterwards he came and made agreement. And he gives to the lord for this agreement three capons.
* A day is granted to Robert Cadewell until the next Halimote to show by what right he has entered into the lord's fee, etc.
* The aletasters present that the brewers have broken the Assize and so are amerced 5d.
* Lord John Burre the chaplain surrenders into the hand of the lord one messuage and half a virgate of land with appurtenances. And the lord has granted and demised the said messuage and land with all its appurtenances to John of Codicote, chaplain, to hold to him and his at the will of the lord for the services due and accustomed for it, saving the right of anyone then, nor shall he commit waste. And he gives to the lord for the agreement and for heriot 20s. And he has done fealty.
* Lord John of Codicote, chaplain, with the permission of the lord, has demised and confirmed to Lord John Burre, chaplain, for the term of the life of the said same John Burre 13s 4d annual rent to be received and charged annually on

the Feast of the Annunciation of the Blessed Mary for all the lands and tenements in Norton which the same John first had by the grant of the said John Burre with the licence of the lord, binding and charging the lands and tenements aforesaid, with the lord's permission, with distraint by the said John Burre whenever the aforesaid 13s 4d in part or in whole shall happen to be in arrears. And upon this the aforesaid John of Codicote attorns himself concerning the aforesaid 13s 4d in the presence of Brother William of Wynsel[owe] cellarer and of the other tenants.

* John Loveleg has the lord's permission to marry Agnes the daughter of William atte Churche. And he gives for this agreement 2s.
* Agnes the daughter of William atte Churche has permission to marry John Loveleg. And she gives for this agreement 2s.
* Isabella Pernell has permission to marry wherever and whom she shall wish. And she gives for this agreement 12d.
* Ralph Boueton lately deceased held of the lord one messuage called *Halle Orchard* freely and also another messuage and half a virgate of unfree land, for which the same Ralph gave two cows as heriot worth 14s. And John his son is his next heir of full age, who came and paid relief for the said messuage called *Halleorchard*, to hold to him and his for the services etc. And he gives for relief 10s. And also the same John came and *gersummavit* for the said half virgate of land and messuage with all its appurtenances, to hold to him and his in villeinage and at the will of the lord for the services due and accustomed for it, saving then the right of anyone, nor shall he commit waste. And he gives to the lord for this agreement and for entry one mark.

Halimote of Norton on Wednesday next after the Feast of St Lucy the Virgin in the 17th year – W Wynselowe [*17 Dec 1343*]

Jurors:	John Diper	William atte Churche	John Jecob
	Adam Warde	Ralph Aubrey	John Hasshe

* It was ordered at the last Halimote to distrain Robert Cadewell to show by what right etc. It is null and void because he is not a tenant.
* John Bonde the Younger surrenders into the hand of the lord one cottage with appurtenances which lies between the tenement of John Bonde the Elder and the tenement of Ralph Thomas. And the lord transferred the said cottage with all its appurtenances to Laurence Wysot to hold to him and his in villeinage and at the will of the lord for the services due and accustomed for it. And he gives for the agreement and for entry 40d. And he gives for heriot 12d.
* The jurors present that William of Munden and John Mayst[er] owe suit to the

EDWARD III

court of Norton, and because it was held at Newnham therefore it is null and void, etc.
* Next they present that Thomas Balston has made himself an apprentice in Baldock without permission, so he is amerced 3d. And it is ordered to distrain etc. It is confirmed by the cellarer.
* Next they present that Roger Crowe makes default and so he is amerced 3d.
* Margery Tollard lately deceased held of the lord two messuages and two *ferthlingates* of land with all their appurtenances, whose heriot is one draught beast worth 40d and one pig worth 12d. And John her son is next heir of the age of three years as it appears by the jurors. And afterwards John Ronge [*or Rouge*] the husband of the aforesaid Margery came into court and took wardship of the land and of the heir until the full age of the said heir, by the services etc. And he gives to the lord for the agreement to hold for the term and for licence to get married 4s.
* The jurors present that Helen in le Hale has withdrawn herself from the lord's mill and so is amerced 2d.
* The aletasters present that the brewers have broken the Assize and so are amerced 7d.

[HALS 65514, f2] **Halimote of Norton on Tuesday next after the Feast of the Finding of the Holy Cross in the 18th year – W Wynsel[owe] [*4 May 1344*]**

Jurors:	John Dyp[er]e	William atte Church	John Jecob
	John Reymond junior	Richard Bate senior	John Isoude

* Lord Richard Sabryt, rector of the church of Caldecote came and showed his charter of lands and tenements acquired from John atte Bury of Chanton as more fully appears by his charter of feoffment. And he did fealty by Roger le Yhonge of Caldecote because it [*or he*] is of the Fee of the Honour.[37]
* Roger Prudde came in full court and surrendered all the right and claim which he had or might have had in any way whatsoever in the lands and tenements of which Adam le Warde has earlier acquired the reversion after the death of the said Roger, to the use of the said Adam le Warde and his. And it is in such a form that the said Adam and his heirs shall pay annually to the aforesaid Roger for the term of his life three quarters of wheat and one quarter of beans

---

[37] Fee of the Honour. This may refer to the Liberty of St Albans. Caldecote was bought by St Albans Abbey in 1321 and retained until the Dissolution (*VCH Hertfordshire* vol 3 pp217-20).

EDWARD III

and peas of the better crop growing upon the aforesaid land, at three terms of the year, that is to say at the Feast of St Michael one quarter of wheat and one bushel of beans and peas, at the Feast of the Birth of the Lord one quarter of wheat and one bushel of beans and peas, and at the Feast of Easter one quarter of wheat and half a quarter of beans and peas. And also the said Adam and his heirs shall find for the aforesaid Roger the whole tenement with a croft and with all their appurtenances which was once of Walter le Warde.

* Alexander Cok by permission of the lord has leased to Roger Redhod one acre of land for the term of one crop. And he gives for having this term 6d.
* Henry Cok by permission of the lord has leased to the aforesaid Roger Redhod one acre for the term of one crop. And he gives for having this term 3d.
* Alexander Cok has licence to marry. And he gives to the lord for this agreement 12d.
* Laurence Wysot with the lord's permission has married Isabella the daughter of Alice Hasshe. And he gives for this agreement on his behalf and his wife's 2s.
* Sarra of Yherdele, who held of the lord 30 acres of land with appurtenances for the service of 44 days a year with one pound of cumin, is dead, whose heriot is nothing. And Master John of Yherdele is her next heir of full age etc. And because he has not come to receive his land, therefore it is ordered to distrain the said John from day to day until etc.
* The aletasters present that the brewers have broken the Assize and so are amerced 3d.
* The lord has granted to Walter Broun the marriage of Helen formerly the daughter of John le Shepherd, to the use of Geoffrey the son of the said Walter. And when the said Helen shall come to lawful age the said Geoffrey shall hold all the inheritance with lands and tenements and with all other their appurtenances, which were of John le Shepherd, father of the said Helen, on the day on which he died, to hold to him and to the aforesaid Helen and to their heirs in villeinage and at the will of the lord for the services due and accustomed for it. And the said Geoffrey has permission to marry the aforesaid Helen. And he gives for this agreement and for *gersumma* 20s.

Halimote of Norton on Thursday next before the Feast of St Luke the Evangelist in the 18th year – John Bynham [*14 Oct 1344*]

Jurors:	John Diper	Ralph Aubrey	Alexander Wysot
	William Sayer	John Jecob	Richard Bate senior

* The jurors present that the land which Sarra of Yherdele held owes suit [of

EDWARD III

court].
* Next they present that John Aubrey has withdrawn himself from the lord's mill, to the damage of 4d, and so he is amerced 3d, etc.
* Agnes Olyve has married without permission a certain outsider (*extraneus*) and so is amerced. And it is ordered to distrain, etc. And afterwards she made agreement and gives 12d.
* Next they present that Matilda le Warde 6d and Alice Thomas 6d have committed *leyrewit* and so are amerced, 12d.
* The aletasters present that the brewers have broken the Assize and so are amerced 3d.
* Helen le Schepherd has made agreement for a licence to get married. And she gives for this agreement 2s.
* Walter Thomas has made agreement for a licence to get married. And he gives for this agreement 2s.
* John Diper surrenders into the hand of the lord all the tenement and land with all their appurtenances which he has in the village of Norton. And he gives for heriot 40d. And the lord has given and transferred all the tenement and aforesaid land with all their appurtenances to the aforesaid John Dip[er]e and Matilda his wife, to hold to them and to their heirs in villeinage and at the will of the lord for the services, etc nor should they commit waste. They give to the lord for this agreement and for entry 10s.
* Henry Swetekyn came after the death of Walter Swetekyn his father and took from the lord all the tenement and land with all their appurtenances which the said Walter his father held on the day on which he died, to hold to him and his in villeinage and at the will of the lord for the services due and accustomed for it. And he gives for this agreement and for entry half a mark. The same Henry surrendered into the hand of the lord all the aforesaid lands and tenement with all their appurtenances etc. And the lord granted and transferred all the aforesaid lands and tenement with all their appurtenances to Alice Swetekyn the sister of the said Henry, to hold to her and hers in villeinage and at the will [*HALS 65514, f2v*] of the lord by the services due and accustomed for it. And the said Alice gives for this agreement 10s. And she has licence to marry. And the said Henry gives for heriot 40d.
* John Caldewelle has licence to take to wife Alice Thomas. And the fine is condoned by the cellarer.

EDWARD III

Halimote of Norton on Tuesday next after the Feast of St Mark the Evangelist in the 19th year – John Bynham [*26 Apr 1345*]

Jurors:	John Dyp[er]e	Adam Warde	John Cok
	William Wykyng	William Sayer	John Jecob
	William Wymark	Richard Jecob	Ralph Albreth
	John Boueton	Geoffrey Wykyng	Geoffrey Sayer

* Helen in le Hale has licence to marry whensoever and whomsoever she shall wish. And she gives for having this licence 12d.
* Isabella Hasse has licence to marry. And she gives for having this licence 6d.
* The jurors present that William of Munden \afterwards he came/, Walter Nap[er]e \3d/, William Cok \3d/ and Richard Scrag \condoned/ make default and so are amerced.
* John Bate, lately deceased, held of the lord one messuage and one *ferthlingate* of land with the appurtenances of which the heriot is one *jerc'* [?jerkin] worth 12d. And Richard Bate his son is his next heir of full age, who came and paid *gersumma* for the said messuage and land with appurtenances just as fully as his father held them on the day on which he died, to hold to him and his in villeinage and at the will of the lord by the services due and accustomed for them, etc. And he gives to the lord for this agreement and for entry 10s. And he did fealty, etc.
* The jurors present that William in le Hale is of full age to hold two messuages and two quarters of land with the appurtenances which Walter in le Hale his father held, who came and paid *gersumma* for the two messuages and land with appurtenances, to hold to him and his in villeinage and at the will of the lord, by the services due and accustomed for them. And he gives for this agreement and for entry 15s. And he did fealty. And he has licence to marry, etc.
* Alexander Wysot lately deceased held from the heirs of William Fermer freely and intermediately (*per medium*) one messuage and one piece of land containing in full one acre. And upon this Walter son of the same has a day to show his charters etc, until the next Halimote.
* The same Alexander held of the lord one quarterland and one *ferthlingate* of land with appurtenances, of which the heriot is nothing because the messuage formerly of the said holding had been alienated into the hand of William Cok and Isabelle the daughter of Roger Bercarius. And Walter his son is his next heir of full age, who came and paid *gersumma* for the said land with appurtenances together with the reversion of dower when it shall occur, to hold to him and his in villeinage and at the will of the lord by the services due

EDWARD III

and accustomed for it. And he gives to the lord for this agreement and for entry one mark. And he has licence to marry, etc.
* Richard son of John Isoude has licence to marry. And he gives for this agreement 12d.
* John Geiard gives to the lord 6d for licence to marry.
* Alice Olyve committed *leyrewit* and so is amerced 3d.
* Geoffrey Neweman has married without licence and so is amerced 6d. And it is ordered to distrain to make agreement etc.
* The aletasters present that the brewers have broken the Assize and so are amerced 6d.
* Master John of Yherdele came and paid his relief which amounted to 3s 4½d and with one pound of cumin for ten acres of meadow and five acres of free land which Sarra of Yherdele once held. And he has an a day to show his charters and to learn his services, until the next court, etc.
* John Hasse \6d/, Laurence Wysot \4d/ and John Bercarius \2d/ admit poaching larks and other birds in the lord's warren without the lord's permission, etc.
* Robert of Cadewell finds pledges John Dyp[er]e and William Sayer to come to the next Halimote and to show by what right he has entry into the fee of the lord, etc.

Halimote of Norton on Tuesday the Feast of St Luke the Evangelist in the 19th year – John Bynham [*18 Oct 1345*]

Jurors:	Adam Ward	Geoffrey Wykyng	Geoffrey Sabryth
	John Jacob	John Neweman	William Wykyng
	John Cok	John Dypere	Ralph Albreth
	William Sayer	William Wymark	Geoffrey Sayer

* [*HALS 65514, f3*] The jurors present that Walter Nap[er] 3d, William Cok 3d, and Walter the Miller 3d, make default and so they themselves are amerced.
* John Bate lately deceased held of the lord one cottage freely by the rent of 6d a year by the mesne lord (*per medium*) Richard Andreu, whose heriot is nothing, etc.
* The jurors present that John Aubrey has withdrawn himself from the lord's mill, to the damage of half a bushel of mulct, and so he is amerced 6d.
* Next they present that Margery the daughter of Alan Neweman has married without licence and so is amerced 2d. And afterwards she came and made agreement and gives 6d.
* The aletasters present that the brewers have broken the Assize and so are amerced 14d.

EDWARD III

* Further it is ordered to distrain Walter son of Alexander Wysot to show his charters for a tenement that he claims to hold from the lord abbot and this at the next court, etc.
* Alice Olyve came and made agreement because she was married without licence. And she gives 12d.
* Further is it ordered to distrain Robert Cadewell to show by what right he has entry into the fee of the lord, and what he claims to hold from the lord and by what services, etc.
* It is ordered to arrest Robert Bate, John Bonde the elder, John Isoude, Richard Isoude, Reynald Jacob, John William, Walter Reymund the younger, Walter Naper, Thomas Olyve and John Olyve, to answer to the lord at the next Halimote because they have been employed (*deserviunt*) outside the lordship, licence not having been sought nor obtained, nor do they give to the lord any *chevach* [chevage] when they ought to give it, etc.

Halimote of Norton on Tuesday next after the Feast of the Apostles Philip and James in the 20th year – John Bynham [*2 May 1346*]

Jurors:	John Dipere	John Boueton	William atte Churche
	John Jacob	Reynald Sayer	Walter Thomas

* The jurors present that Richard Strag 3d, William Cok 2d and Lord John Burre 3d make default and so are amerced.
* Next they present that William in the Hale 3d and Walter the Muleward 3d have withdrawn themselves from the lord's mill and so are amerced.
* Richard Bate the younger has leased half a virgate of land with appurtenances to John Albreth for the term of two years without permission and so is amerced 3d. And it is ordered to seise the said land into the hand of the lord until etc.
* The jurors present that Margery Parnele has committed *leyrewit* and so is amerced 3d.
* The aletasters present that the brewers have broken the Assize and so are amerced 10d.
* Richard of Clyfford, brother of the vicar of Norton, has made agreement for this that he has married Helen Boueton without the lord's licence. And he gives for this agreement 2s.
* Further, as so many more times, it is ordered to distrain Walter son of Alexander Wysot and Robert Cadewell to show their charters and by what right they have entry into the lord's fee and to do fealty, etc.
* Further it is ordered to distrain Robert Bate, John Isoude, Richard Isoude,

EDWARD III

Reynald Jecob and John William to answer to the lord at the next Halimote for this that they have been employed outside the lordship without licence, nor do they give to the lord any *chevage* when they ought to give it, etc.
* Walter Napere and Thomas Olyve, each of them shall give annually while employed outside the Liberty, one capon for *chevage*, payment beginning on the Feast of the Nativity of St John the Baptist next now coming and afterwards in each year on the Feast of Easter, etc.
* John Olyve has found sureties to be at St Albans on Saturday next before the Feast of St Barnabas the Apostle to make a record of licence to work outside the Liberty, etc.
* The lord has granted and transferred to John Leybourne and Alice his wife one cottage with adjoining curtilage just as it lies between the tenement of the vicar of Norton and the tenement of Alice Swetekyn together with all its appurtenances, to hold to the same and their heirs in villeinage and at the will of the lord by the service 2s a year, without waste. And the fine is condoned by the cellarer. And it shall begin to pay rent from the Feast of St Michael before the date of the court, etc. [*r. margin*: increase in rent 12d]

[HALS 65514, f3v] Halimote there on Tuesday next before the Feast of St Luke the Evangelist in the 20th year – John Bynham [*17 Oct 1346*]

Jurors:	John Dipere	John Cok	William Sayer
	John Jacob	John in le Hale	John Botonn
	William Wikyng	Richard Jacob	Walter Thomas
	Adam Warde	Geoffrey Wikyng	William Saleman

* The jurors present that Master John of Erdele, forgiven, Richard Scrag 3d, and Roger Crowe 3d, owe suit of court and make default and so are amerced.
* Next they present that John Albrethe 6d, John Bonde 3d, Alexander Andreu 3d, Richard Prudde 3d, and William in le Hale 4d, have withdrawn themselves from the lord's mill and so are amerced.
* Walter Newman lately deceased held of the lord two cottages with appurtenances of which the heriot is one brass bowl worth 3d and one chest worth 8d. And John le Neweman sought to be himself admitted to one cottage with appurtenances just as it lies between the tenement of Robert Molote and the tenement of Walter Muleward. And it was shown to the jury that the aforesaid John is the next heir of the aforesaid Walter. The lord granted and transferred the said cottage with appurtenances to the aforesaid John to hold to him and his in villeinage and at the will of the lord by the services due and accustomed for it. And he gives for this agreement 18d. And he has done

EDWARD III

fealty etc.
* Henry Swetekyn gives to the lord 6d to investigate his right to one cottage which Walter le Neweman formerly held. And thereupon the jurors say that the said Henry is the nearest by blood as appears more fully by the record of the roll of the time of Brother Robert Saunford, and he had a record. And afterwards he came and made agreement for the said cottage to hold to him and his in villeinage and at the will [of the lord] by the services due and accustomed for it. And he gives for this agreement 12d.
* The jurors present that Margaret Jacob 3d, Cecilia daughter of Alexander Andreu 3d, Cecilia daughter of Geoffrey le Shepherd 3d, have committed *leyrewit* and so are amerced.
* Reynald Jacob has married without licence and so is amerced 6d. And it is ordered to distrain the said Reynald to make agreement, etc.
* The aletasters present that the brewers have broken the Assize and so are amerced 5d.
* Alexander Andreu surrenders into the hand of the lord 16 acres of land with appurtenances lying in each field of Norton, that is to say a half of half a virgate of land which the said Alexander holds from the lord at will except the messuage with appurtenances without withholding anything. And the lord has granted and transferred the aforesaid 16 acres of land that is to say half of half a virgate of land without withholding anything to John atte Hathe and Sibyl his wife to hold to them and to their heirs from the lord in villeinage and at the will of the lord by the services due and accustomed for them. And he gives to the lord for the agreement 12s. And he has done fealty, etc.
* The lord has granted and transferred to Richard le Fuller a formerly empty plot containing in length 60 feet and in width 50 feet lying between the tenement of John Geiard and the tenement of Isabelle Hogges, to hold to him and his, rendering for it annually 4d at the usual terms in equal portions. And he gives nothing for agreement at entry. And the said Richard is to build competently the said plot with one house within a year. And he shall give heriot when he shall die, etc. [*l. margin*: new rent 4d]
* Again as so many times it is ordered to distrain Walter son of Alexander Wysot and Robert Cadewell to show their charters by what right they are in the lord's fee and to do fealty.
* Again it is ordered to distrain Robert Bate, John Isoude, Richard Isoude and John William to answer to the lord at the next Halimote for this reason that they have been employed outside the lordship without the lord's licence, nor do they give any *chevage* when they ought to give it.
* It is ordered to distrain John Olyve to show a licence to work wherever it shall please him outside the lord's Liberty etc.

EDWARD III

Halimote of Norton on Tuesday next before the Feast of St Elphege the Archbishop in the 21st year – John Bynham [*10 Apr 1347*]

Jurors:	John Diper	Walter Thomas	John Botonn
	William Sayer	John Jacob	Adam Warde

* Reynald Jacob gives to the lord for agreement 2s for licence to marry. And also he gives to the lord yearly one hen (*gallina*) when he withdraws (*trahit*) outside the lordship, that is to say at Christmas, by the pledge of John Reymond.
* Richard Bate 6d and John Geiard 6d put themselves upon the mercy of the court because they have withdrawn themselves from the lord's mill, etc.
* Walter Naper lately deceased held of the lord one cottage and one *ferthlingate* of unfree land and another unfree cottage [held] by him of the right of his wife, of which the heriot is two sheep worth 2s 4d. And Isabella his wife shall hold all the aforesaid as much as is her right.
* The aletasters present that the brewers have broken the Assize and so are amerced 10d.
* Henry Swetekyn surrenders into the hand of the lord one cottage with its curtilage and all other appurtenances just as it lies between the tenement [*HALS 65514, f4*] of John Albrethe and the tenement of Vincent Miles. And the lord has granted and transferred the said cottage and curtilage with all their appurtenances to the aforesaid Vincent Miles to hold to him and his in villeinage and at the will of the lord by the services due and accustomed for them, without waste. And he gives for the agreement 12d. And the said Henry gives for heriot 12d by the pledge of Vincent Miles, etc.

Halimote of Norton on Tuesday next before the Feast of St Luke the Evangelist in the 21st year – John Bynham [*16 Oct 1347*]

Jurors:	John Dypere	Walter Thomas	John Boueton
	Adam Warde	William Sayer	John Hasse

* Agnes the daughter of Alan le Neweman has licence to marry. And she gives for this agreement 2s.
* Margery Hasshe has licence to marry. And she gives for this agreement 3s 4d.
* The jurors present that Alice Swetekyne has committed *leyrewytt* and so is amerced 4d.
* Adam Warde has licence to marry off Matilda his daughter. And he gives for the agreement to have this licence 3s 4d.

EDWARD III

* The aletasters present that the brewers have broken the Assize and so are amerced 6d.
* Richard Scrag and Agnes Olyve his wife surrender into the lord's hand half an acre of land with appurtenances just as it lies upon the *Weufurlong* between the land of Walter Wysot and the land of William Sayer. And the said Agnes, being questioned, agreed. And the lord has granted and transferred the said half acre of land with appurtenances to Thomas Olyve to hold to him and his in villeinage and at the will of the lord by the services due and accustomed for it. And he gives for agreement 18d. And he has done fealty etc.
* Alice Swetekyn surrenders into the hand of the lord all the arable land which she has in the field of Norton which contains 18 acres. And the lord has granted and transferred the said land to John Caldewelle to hold to him and his in villeinage and at the will of the lord by the services due and accustomed for it. And he gives for this agreement 6s 8d. And he has done fealty etc. And the form of the agreement is such that the said Alice and hers shall do for the lord annually four harvest boonworks, and shall also carry to the lord one hen at Christmas and five eggs at Easter for the capital messuage and croft belonging to the aforesaid land. And also the aforesaid Alice and hers shall pay to the aforesaid John annually 4d rent at two usual terms by equal portions. And it shall not be permitted to the aforesaid Alice to sell the said messuage and croft or any part thereof to anyone except the aforementioned John if John himself shall want to give enough for it, etc.
* John Bonde and Henry Cok surrender into the hand of the lord one acre of land of which two roods lie in *Eldefeld*, of which one rood lies between the land formerly of Lord John Burre and the land of John Neweman, and another rood lies between the land of William le Hale and the land of Richard le Fuller, and half an acre lies at *le Mulleweye* between the land of John Reymond and the land of Helen Bercarius. And the lord has granted the aforesaid two roods to John Bonde in the name of an exchange and to Henry Cok half an acre in the name of an exchange, to hold to the same and their heirs in villeinage and at the will of the lord by the services due and accustomed for them. And they give to the lord for the exchange 18d, etc.
* John Ronge [*or Rouge*] is dead, of whom there are two heriots, that is to say one horse worth 3s 4d and one mare worth 5s, who held of the lord two messuages and two quarters of land containing 36 acres of land. And John his son is his next heir of the age of seven years etc. And John Hasshe and Richard Bate the elder have taken from the lord wardship of the lands and tenements and of the said boy until the full age of the said boy, performing the services due and accustomed for them without waste, and they shall maintain between them the said boy in food and in clothing during the aforesaid term.

And they give to the lord for having this term 10s etc.

* John Wymundham, chaplain, surrenders into the hand of the lord one messuage and half a virgate of land with the appurtenances called *Burreslond*. And the lord has granted and transferred the said messuage and land with appurtenances to Agnes the daughter of Walter Broun of Caldecote, to hold to her and hers in villeinage and at the will of the lord by the services due and accustomed for it without waste. And she gives for the agreement 10s. And the said John gives for a heriot 10s. And the said Agnes has licence to marry by the aforesaid agreement, etc.

* John of Hyethe and Agnes Pernele his wife surrender into the hand of the lord half their lands and tenements, that is to say half of one tenement and one half of a virgate of land which were once of Stephen Pernele. And the said Agnes, being questioned, agrees. And the lord has granted and transferred half the said lands and tenements with appurtenances to John in the Hale, Isabelle his wife and Alice their daughter to hold to them and the heirs of the said Alice in villeinage and at the will of the lord by the services due and accustomed for them, without waste. And if the said Alice shall die without an heir lawfully begotten of her, all the aforesaid shall remain to the right heirs of the said John. And they give to the lord for agreement and for entry 10s. And whichever of those aforesaids who shall be tenant shall give heriot when they shall die, and shall make agreement for entry. And the said John and Agnes give for a heriot 3s 4d etc.

Halimote of Norton on Tuesday on the Feast of St John before the Latin Gate in the 22nd year – John Bynham [*6 May 1348*]

| Jurors: | John Dyper | John Bouetoun | Ralph Albreth |
| | John Jacob | Adam Warde | Richard Foller |

* [*HALS 65514, f4v*] The jurors present that Richard Bate the younger has leased to John Alfred half a virgate of land with appurtenances without licence and so is amerced 6d. And it is ordered to seize the said land into the hand of the lord until etc.

* Next they present that John Alfrede 2d, Vincent Miles 2d, John le Vese 2d, have withdrawn themselves from the lord's mill from the Feast of St Michael until Christmas and so are amerced.

* The aletasters present that the brewers have broken the Assize and so are amerced 3d.

* Alice Swetekyn by permission of the lord has leased to Henry Swetekyn her brother half an acre of land with appurtenances to hold to him and his from the

EDWARD III

Feast of St Michael next to come after the date of this court until the end of eight years fully completed. And the said Henry shall perform for the lord the services due and accustomed. And he gives for the agreement for having the term 6d.
* John Reymond has licence to marry. And he gives for agreement 12d.
* John Colyn has licence to marry. And he gives for agreement 12d.

Halimote of Norton on Tuesday next after the Feast of St Luke the Evangelist in the 22nd year – John Bynham [21 Oct 1348]

Jurors:	John Dyper	John Hasse	John Boton
	Adam Warde	William Sayer	Richard le Fuller

* Matilda formerly the wife of John Hawys has licence to marry for a second time. And she gives for this agreement 6s 8d.
* John son of Edmund le Coupere with the lord's permission has leased to John le Neweman one *ferthlingate* of land with appurtenances called *Pernelelond* for the term of 12 years next to come fully completed, the term to start at the Feast of Hokeday next to come after the date of this court. And he gives to the lord for having this term 3s 4d, saving then the right of whoever. And Agnes the wife of the said John, being questioned, agrees, etc.
* The jurors present that William Munden, forgiven, William Yherdele [(*eg*) ?an abbreviation for *egressus est:* he has left], Richard Scrag 3d, Vincent Miles 3d, owe suit of court and make default and so are amerced.
* Alexander Boton is dead, who held of the lord one messuage and one cotland, whose heriot is half one cow worth 4s. And John Boton the elder is his next heir of full age, who came and paid *gersumma* for all the aforesaid lands and tenement with appurtenances to hold to him and his in villeinage and at the will of the lord by the services due and accustomed for them, without waste. And he gives for the agreement 10s. And he has done fealty, etc.
* John in the Hale the younger is of full age to hold one cottage, of which he recalled (*vocat*) the record of agreement previously made. And he has a day to produce the record at the next [court] at St Albans. And thereupon he came and produced the record of agreement previously made in the time of Brother Richard of Hedreset cellarer, etc.
* The jurors present that Cecilia the daughter of Walter Sayer 3d, and Cecilia Schepherd 6d, have committed *leyrewit* and so are amerced.
* John Reymond and Walter Wysot have exchanged two roods of land with appurtenances with the lord's permission, so that the said John shall have for him and his that rood of land just as it lies upon *Mechelecotehale* between the

EDWARD III

land of the lord and the land of Richard Bate the younger. And the said Walter shall receive that rood of land for him and his just as it lies upon the *Eldebrach* between the land of Henry Cok and the land of John Cok. And the aforesaid John and Walter give to the lord for having licence 12d etc.

* Richard Bate made agreement with the lord because he has leased half a virgate of land to John Albrethe without licence. And they give between them in equal portions 2s, etc.
* Roger Albrethe has licence to marry. And he gives for this agreement 12d etc.
* Richard the son of Sarra atte Dene sues Richard Bate the younger in a plea concerning land, pledges for prosecution William Faber and John Hobekyn. And the said Richard was summoned etc who essoined as below. And thereupon the parties aforesaid had a day as above etc.

  Essoins: Richard son of Sarra atte Dene against Richard Bate the younger in a plea concerning land, by John son of John; Richard Bate the younger against Richard son of Sarra atte Dene in a plea concerning land, by Thomas son of John. Assessed.[38]
* Reynald Sayer surrenders into the hand of the lord one *ferthlingate* of land with appurtenances. And the lord has granted and transferred the said *ferthlingate* of land with appurtenances to William Sayer to hold to him and his in villeinage and at the will of the lord by the services due and accustomed for it. And he gives for agreement 10s. And he has done fealty, etc.
* Thomas Hassh is dead, who held of the lord one messuage and one cotland with appurtenances, whose heriot is one mare foal worth 2s. And John his son is his next heir of the age of three years. And Emma Hassh mother of the said John came before the cellarer and received wardship of the lands and tenement together with the heir until the full age of the said heir. And she gives to the lord for agreement [*HALS 65514, f5*] for having the wardship 3s 4d etc.

Halimote of Norton on Tuesday next after the Feast of St Mark the Evangelist in the 23rd year – Adam Wittenham [*28 Apr 1349*]

Jurors:	John Dipere	John Neweman	John Jecob
	Adam Ward	Walter Thomas	Richard le Fuller

* William Munden is dead, who held of the lord one messuage and one croft containing nine acres freely by the service of 7s 3d, and two days *bedrep*

---

[38] This is an example of an entry not normally transcribed into the court books from the roll, but here regarded as important because the absence of the parties caused an adjournment.

EDWARD III

worth 2d, whose heriot is one horse worth 13s 4d.
* Agnes Pernel is dead, who held of the lord half of one messuage and of one *ferthlingate* of land, whose heriot is nothing. And Alice Pernel is her next heir of full age. And John Moreman the husband of the said Alice came and paid *gersumma* for the said tenement with appurtenances to hold to the said Alice and her heirs in villeinage and at the will of the lord by the services due and accustomed for it. And he gives for agreement 3s 4d.
* Alice Swetekyn is dead, who held of the lord one messuage with a croft containing three roods, whose heriot is nothing. And Alice her daughter is her next heir of the age of two years.
* Agnes Olive is dead, who held of the lord one acre of land. And Richard Scragg shall hold the said land for the term of his life by the law of England and the custom of the manor. And he has done fealty, etc.
* The jurors present that John Olive, Richard and Richard son of John Isoud, Walter Reymond, John Gegiard, Thomas Gegiard, Roger Hardleston and Richard Hardleston remain outside the Liberty without licence and so it is ordered to arrest them (*attachiare corpora dictorum*) etc.
* The aletasters present that the brewers have broken the Assize and so are amerced 11d.

Court of Norton on Thursday next after the Feast of the Apostles Peter and Paul in the 23rd year – Adam Wittenham [*2 Jul 1349*]

| Jurors: | John Diper | John Botoun | John Jecob |
| | William Sayer | Roger Albrethe | Walter Thomas |

* John Reymond is dead, who held of the lord one messuage and one quarter of land, whose heriot is one cow worth 3s. And Agnes the daughter of the said John is his next heir of full age, who came and paid *gersumma* for the said tenement and land, to hold to her and hers in villeinage and at the will of the lord by the rod by the services due and accustomed for it. And she gives to the lord for *gersumma* 6s 8d.
* John in le Hale has licence to marry for a second time, with Agnes who was the daughter of John Reymond. And he gives for the agreement 3s 4d. And the said Agnes has licence to marry for the first time by the agreement aforesaid.
* Helen the daughter of John Shepherd is dead, who held of the lord one messuage and half a virgate of land, whose heriot is one cow worth 2s 6d. And Matilda the aunt (*amita*) of the said Helen is her next heir, who came and paid *gersumma* for the said messuage and land, to hold to her and hers in

EDWARD III

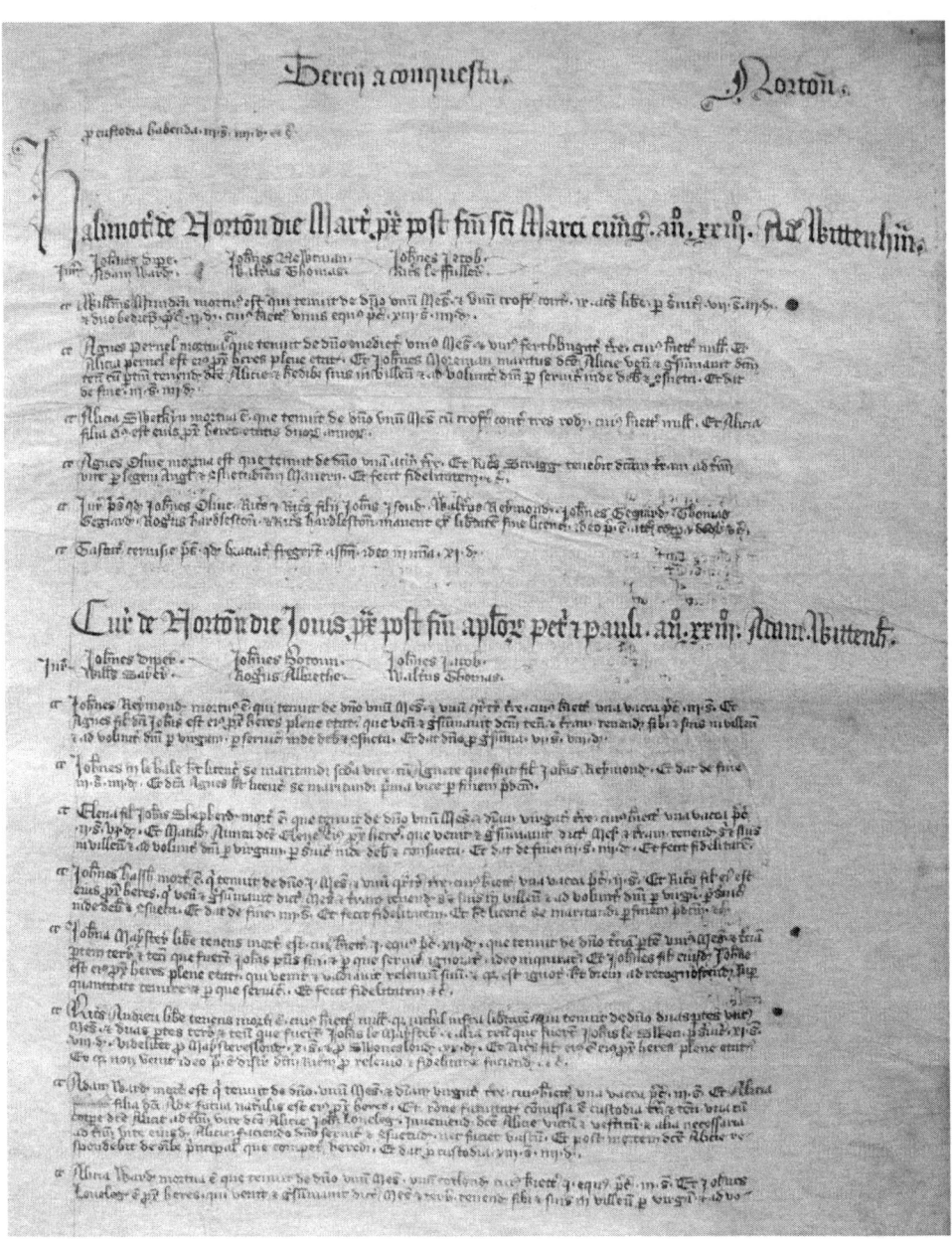

(*HALS 65514, f5*) The first two courts in 1349, the year of the Black Death when 27 tenants died.

EDWARD III

(*HALS 65514, f5v*) The end of the second court in 1349.

EDWARD III

villeinage and at the will of the lord by the rod, by the services due and accustomed for it. And she gives for the agreement 3s 4d. And she has done fealty.
* John Hassh is dead, who held of the lord one messuage and one quarter of land, whose heriot is one cow worth 2s. And Richard his son is his next heir, who came and paid *gersumma* for the said messuage and land, to hold to him and his in villeinage and at the will of the lord by the rod, by the services due and accustomed for it. And he gives to the lord for the agreement 4s. And he has done fealty. And he has licence to marry under the aforesaid agreement, etc.
* Joan Mayster, a free tenant, is dead, whose heriot is one horse worth 12d, who held of the lord the third part of one messuage and the third part of the land and tenement which were of John her father, and by what service it is not known, and so it is being investigated. And John the son of the same Joan is her next heir of full age, who came and paid his relief and because it is not known, he has a day to acknowledge the quantity [*sic*] of tenure and by what services. And he has done fealty etc.
* Richard Andreu, a free tenant, is dead, whose heriot is nothing because nothing [is?] within the Liberty, who held of the lord two parts of one messuage and two parts of the land and tenement which were of John le Mayster and another tenement which was of John le Swon by the service of 11s 8d that is to say for *Maystereslond* 10s and for *Swoneslond* 20d. And Richard his son is his next heir of full age. And because he did not come therefore it is ordered to distrain the said Richard for relief and performing fealty etc.
* Adam Ward is dead, who held of the lord one messuage and half a virgate of land, whose heriot is one cow worth 3s. And Alice the daughter of the said Adam, foolish of nature, is his next heir. And by reason of her foolishness wardship is committed of the land and tenement together with the body of the said Alice for the term of the life of the said Alice, to John Loveleg, to find for the said Alice food and clothing and everything necessary for the lifetime of the same Alice, performing for the lord the services and customs, nor shall he commit waste. And after the death of the said Alice he shall account for all principal things which come together to the heir. And he gives for the wardship 13s 4d.
* Alice Ward is dead, who held of the lord one messuage and one cotland, whose heriot is one horse worth 3s. And John Loveleg is next heir, who came and paid *gersumma* for the said messuage and land, to hold to him and his in villeinage by the rod and at the will [*HALS 65514, f5v*] of the lord, by the services due and accustomed for them. And he gives for the agreement 2s.

EDWARD III

And he has done fealty. And he has licence to marry. And he gives for this agreement 6d.

* John Neweman is dead, who held one messuage and one quarter of land and one cottage, whose heriot is one horse worth 3s 4d and one cow worth 2s. And John the brother of the same is his next heir, who came and paid *gersumma* for the said messuage and land, to hold to him and his in villeinage and at the will of the lord by the rod by the services due and accustomed for it. And he gives for the agreement 2s. And he has done fealty. And he has licence to marry under the aforesaid agreement.
* Walter Wysot is dead, who held of the lord one cotland and one quarter land, whose heriot is nothing. And Laurence, the brother of the same, is next heir, who came and paid *gersumma* for the said land, to hold to him and his in villeinage at the will of the lord by the services due and accustomed for it. And he gives for the agreement 3s 4d. And he has done fealty, etc.
* Ralph Albreth is dead, who held of the lord one messuage and half a virgate of land, whose heriot is one horse worth 6s 8d. And Roger Albreth is next heir of full age, who came and paid *gersumma* for the said messuage and land, to hold to him and his in villeinage at the will of the lord by the services due and accustomed for it. And he gives for the agreement 13s 4d. And he has done fealty. And he has licence to marry under the aforesaid agreement.
* John Veesse is dead, who held of the lord one cottage with one rood of land by the service of 3s a year by charter, whose heriot is one sheep worth 4d. And Margery daughter of the same John, of the age of seven years, is next heir. And because she did not come, so it is ordered to distrain for relief because she holds freely by socage.
* Alexander Andreu is dead, who held of the lord one messuage and one quarter of land, whose heriot is nothing because poor (*pauper*). And Cecilia, daughter of the same, is next heir and did not come, so the aforesaid tenement was granted and handed over to John Hathe, to hold to him and his in villeinage at the will of the lord by the services due and accustomed for it, saving the right of anyone. And he has done fealty. The fine is condoned [by the cellarer].
* Agnes who was the wife of Roger Albreth is dead, who held of the lord one messuage and half a virgate of land, whose heriot is one horse worth 4s. And Geoffrey the brother of the said Agnes is next heir, who came and paid *gersumma* for the said messuage and land, to hold to him and his in villeinage at the will of the lord by the services due and accustomed for it. And he gives for the agreement 20s. And he has done fealty.
* John Cartere is dead, who held of the lord one cottage and two parts of one quarter of land, whose heriot is one cow with calf worth 2s. And Alice the sister of the same John is next heir, who came and surrendered into the hand

EDWARD III

of the lord the aforesaid cottage and land. And the lord granted the said tenement to Richard Bate the elder to hold to him and his in villeinage at the will of the lord by the services due and accustomed for it. And he has done fealty. The fine is condoned.

* John in le Hale is dead, who held of the lord one messuage, one cottage, one cotland, one quarter land, whose heriot is two sheep worth 8d. And John his son is next heir of full age, who comes and gives nothing for *gersumma* because of poverty. And the lord granted the said tenement and land to hold to him and his in villeinage at the will of the lord by the services due and accustomed for it. And he has done fealty, etc.
* Richard le Fuller is dead, who held of the lord two messuages and half a virgate of land, whose heriot is two horses worth 8d. And John the son of the said Richard is next heir, under age. And the lord granted the said tenement to John Albreth besides the messuage next to Elizabeth Hogges, to hold to him and his in villeinage at the will of the lord by the services due and accustomed for it. And the fines are condoned. And if by chance [there is] anyone seeking the said tenement and he shall show what right he may have in it, let him satisfy the aforesaid John regarding outlay and expenses paid out, before he may enter. And he has licence to marry for the third time. And he has done fealty etc.
* Roger Crowe is dead, who held of the lord one messuage and one cotland, whose heriot is one brass bowl worth 8d. And Sarra his sister is next heir, who came and paid *gersumma* for the said messuage and land, to hold to her and hers in villeinage at the will of the lord by the services due and accustomed for them. And she gives for agreement 12d. And she has done fealty. And she has licence to marry under the aforesaid agreement.
* John Isoude is dead, who held of the lord one messuage, one cotland whose heriot is one cow worth 2s. And John his son is next heir and did not come, and so it remained in the hand of the lord. And afterwards the lord granted and transferred the said tenement and land to William atte Church, to hold by services at the will of the lord. The fine was condoned because of poverty.
* John Reymond is dead, who held of the lord one messuage and one quarter land, one cottage and one cotland, whose heriot is one horse worth 6s 6d, one bull calf worth 8d. And Emma his sister is next heir, who came and paid *gersumma* for the said messuage and tenement, to hold to her and hers in villeinage at the will of the lord by the services due and accustomed for them. And she gives for agreement 2s. And she has licence to marry under the aforesaid agreement. And she has done fealty.
* Walter Sayer is dead, who held of the lord one messuage and half a virgate of land, which land remains in the hand of William Sayer and Alexander Ward

EDWARD III

for a term of years with the lord's permission, whose heriot is one sheep worth 4d. And John Sayer his son is next heir, and so, etc.

[HALS 65514, f6] Halimote of Norton on Thursday next after the Feast of St Denis in the 23rd year – Adam Wittenham [*15 Oct 1349*]

Jurors:	William Sayer	Richard Bate junior	John Boueton
	John Jecob	Walter Thomas	William in the Hale

* It is ordered to distrain John Mayster, Richard son of Richard Andreu, Margery daughter of John Veesse, to pay relief and perform fealty.
* John Boueton has licence to marry for a second time. And he gives for having the licence 12d.
* Mabel (*Mabilia*) Neweman has licence to marry for a second time. And she gives for having the licence 2s.
* John Bonde is dead, who held of the lord one messuage and half a virgate of land, whose heriot is one horse worth 18d. And Margery daughter of the said John is next [heir] of the age of eight years. And because of minor age, wardship of land and heir is committed to Rosa Bonde, to hold until the lawful age of the said heir, performing services and customs. And she gives for having wardship and for licence to marry for a second time 2s.
* The jurors present that John Mayster, condoned, and Master John Erdele, condoned, owe suit and make default and so are amerced.
* Matilda Aubrey has licence to marry. And she gives to the lord for having licence 6d.
* Richard atte Lane is dead, who held of the lord one messuage and two cotlands, whose heriot is nothing because of poverty. And Richard his son is next heir, of the age of 14 years. And they remain in the hand of the lord.
* William Cok is dead, who held of the lord one messuage and one rood of land, whose heriot is nothing because of poverty. And Walter his son is next heir, who came and paid *gersumma* for the said messuage and land, to hold to him and his in villeinage at the will of the lord by services and customs. And he gives for agreement 6d. And he gives for licence to marry Cecilia Shepherd 6d. And he has done fealty.
* John Albreth surrenders into the hand of the lord one toft containing one rood lying next to the land called *Whitehickes*. And the lord has granted the said toft to John Albreth and Rosa his wife to hold to the same and their heirs in villeinage at the will of the lord by services and customs. And they give for agreement 6d. And they do fealty.
* Agnes the daughter of William Bate has licence to marry when she shall wish.

EDWARD III

And she gives for having licence 2s 6d.
* Alice Hass gives for licence to marry 2s.

Halimote of Norton on Tuesday next after the Feast of St Elphege in the 24th year – Ralph Whitecherch [*20 Apr 1350*]

Jurors: John atte Crouche   William Wykyng   Geoffrey Sayer
           John Bonde   William Wymark   William Saman

* Sara Crowe surrenders into the hand of the lord one messuage and one *ferthlingate* of land. And the lord has granted [it] to John Love [*or Lone*] and Sara his wife and the heirs between them lawfully begotten, to hold to the said John and Sara his wife and the heirs between them lawfully begotten, by the rod and by court roll, at the will of the lord, by the services due and accustomed. And if it happens that the aforesaid John and Sarah shall beget no heir, then all the messuage with the said *ferthlingate* of land shall fully revert to John the son of Richard Fuller, to hold according to the customs of the manor as above. And he gives for agreement for entry 3s 4d. And he has done fealty.
* Richard son of Richard Andrew of Baldock came to this court after the death of Richard his father and did fealty. And he says that he does not claim the said tenement by hereditary right but by gift [?or sale] from his father.
* The jurors present that John Mayster and Walter Taillour make default and so are amerced [*no amercements added above their names*].
* Walter Melward, who held of the lord one messuage and one acre and a half of land, is dead, of which the heriot is one coat (*tunica*) worth 10d. And Isabella the daughter of the said Walter and John son of Agnes the sister of the said Isabella are the heirs of the said Walter, who came and made agreement with the lord for the said lands, to hold of the lord by the rod and by copy of court roll according to the custom of the manor. And they give for agreement for entry 2s. And they have done fealty.
* Margery the daughter of John le Vese came to this court and paid relief for one cottage and one rood of land which is 2s 4d. And she has done fealty.
* Isabella Meleward has committed *leyrewit* and so it is ordered to distrain against the next court [*ie to force her attendance at the next court*], etc.
* [*HALS 65514, f6v*] Agnes in le Hale has committed *leyrewit* and so is amerced 12d.
* John Loveleg has made agreement with the lord for *leyrewit*. And gives 12d.
* The aletasters present that the brewers have broken the Assize and so are amerced 5d.

EDWARD III

* Agnes Wysot gives to the lord for agreement for licence to marry 2s.
* Master John of Erdeleye who held of the lord one meadow called *Hallemad* and ten acres of pasture and five acres of land lying according to the particulars, by the service of 40d a year and one pound of cumin, [and] held also 16 acres of land by the service of 4½d freely at the usual terms and by suit of court every three weeks and by Knight Service has ended his last day. After his death the lord has seised the aforesaid tenements into his hands because of the minor age of Joan, Amity and Agnes the daughters of William of Erdeleye the brother of the aforesaid John, together with the bodies of the daughters of the aforesaid William. And the lord has granted wardship of the lands and tenements with the marriage of the said daughters to Isabella the mother of the aforesaid daughters until the lawful age of the same. And she gives for agreement for having wardship and marriage 60s. And furthermore she shall perform for the chief lords of the fee during the whole term of minor age of the aforesaid daughters all services just as the aforesaid John in his time was accustomed to do. And it shall not be permitted to the said Isabella to lease the said tenements to anyone without the lord's licence. And if she shall do so, she shall be expelled from the said wardship of lands and tenements. And she has done fealty to perform the services while the aforesaid tenements shall be in her keeping.
* All the villein [*men and women*] tenants give to the lord common tax (*tallage*) in aid [*subsidy*] of the new appointment [*literally: creation*] of a lord abbot, 60s.

Halimote of Norton on Tuesday next after the Feast of St Leonard in the 24th year – Ralph Whitchurch [*9 Nov 1350*]

Jurors:	Adam le Smyth	Reynald Balston	Richard Bate senior
	Geoffrey Broun	Roger Larke	John atte Hathe
	William Cok	William Wymark	John Boton
	Laurence Wysot	John atte Crouche	William Wyking

* The jurors present that Walter Taillour 3d, and Walter Boton 2d, owe suit of court and are in default and so are amerced.
* Walter Boton villein of the lord remains at Stotfold outside the lordship without licence and so it is ordered to arrest him etc.
* Roger Diper villein of the lord remains outside the lordship without licence near Bedford and so it is ordered etc.
* Cecilia Willimot has married without licence and remains at St Albans therefore it is ordered etc.

EDWARD III

* John Isoude and Richard his brother, villeins of the lord, remain outside the lordship at Ely without licence of the lord, therefore it is ordered to arrest them etc.
* Cecilia Sayer daughter of Walter Sayer the younger has licence to marry. And she gives for having the licence 12d.
* The aletasters present that the brewers have broken the Assize and so are amerced 6d.

Halimote of Norton on Tuesday on the Feast of the Finding of the Holy Cross in the 25th year – Ralph Whitchurch [*3 May 1351*]

Jurors: Adam le Smyth   John Boueton   Reynald Balston
          John atte Hathe   Richard Bate senior John Dipere

* John in le Hale surrenders into the hand of the lord one curtilage with appurtenances which is liable for heriot, lying between the tenement of Henry Cok on one side and the tenement of John Willesson on the other. And he gives for heriot 6d. And the lord has granted the said curtilage to Matilda daughter of Robert atte Leye, to hold to her and hers in villeinage by the rod at the will of the lord by services due and accustomed for it. And because the said Matilda is under age, that is to say of the age of two years, wardship is committed to Robert father of the said Matilda, to hold until the full age of the said Matilda by services etc. And he has done fealty. And he gives for the agreement 12d.
* The jurors present that Richard Andrew 2d, Joan the widow of William of Munden 2d, and John Colyn, he came afterwards, make default and so are amerced.
* Cecilia Andrew has married without licence outside the lordship, that is to say at St Albans and so is amerced 3d. And it is ordered to arrest the said Cecilia to make agreement etc.
* [*HALS 65514, f7*] John Loveleg and Agnes in le Hale have committed *leyrewit* and so are amerced 6d.
* John Sayer and Isabella le Meleward have committed *leyrewit* and so are amerced 9d.
* Robert le Hayward has made agreement with the lord that he might marry (*desponsare*) Cecilia Sayer. And he gives 2s.
* The jurors present that John Geiard makes default and so is amerced 3d.
* The aletasters present that the brewers have broken the Assize and so are amerced 6d.
* Geoffrey Broun surrenders into the hand of the lord one messuage and half a

EDWARD III

virgate of land with appurtenances which was once of John Borre the chaplain. And the lord has granted the said messuage and land with their appurtenances to Robert atte Leye, to hold to him and his in villeinage by the rod at the will of the lord by services due and accustomed for it. And he has done fealty. And he gives for agreement 40d.

* Agnes daughter of the late Ralph Albreth has licence to marry. And she gives to the lord for agreement for having this licence 18d.
* The lord has granted to Reynald Balston one messuage and one *ferthlingate* of land with appurtenances called *Moloteslond*, which was of Henry Cok, to hold to him and his in villeinage by the rod at the will of the lord by the services due and accustomed for it. And he has done fealty. The fine is condoned by the cellarer.
* The lord has granted to Reynald Balston one croft formerly of Walter Swetekyn lying between the lane called *Cherche Lane* and the tenement of the said Reynald, to have and to hold to him and his, reserving the right of any, in bondage at the will of the lord by the rod by services due and accustomed for it. And he gives for agreement 18d. And he has done fealty. And if it happens that anyone else shall demand or shall sell a right or claim in the aforesaid croft, and thereupon the aforesaid Reynald shall implead, before he shall accept seisin, it shall be permitted to recover seisin by the consideration of the court, he shall satisfy the same Reynald for all his outlay and expenses paid out for the said croft by the consideration of the Homage of the villagers of Norton. And the said Reynald ought not to be charged for the maintenance or repair of cottages built on the said croft, because they were sold first by the lord.

Halimote of Norton on Thursday next after the Feast of the Conversion of St Paul in the 25th year – Ralph Whitchurch [*1 Feb 1352*]

Jurors: Adam le Smyth   John Boueton   Reynald Balston
          John atte Hathe   Richard Bate senior   John Dipere

* The jurors present that John Jecob 2d, and Walter le Taillour 2d, are in default and so are amerced.
* Next they present that Ralph son of Richard Bate, staying at *Stevenhache* [Stevenage] with Roger Hurleye, and Juliana Tollard staying at Baldock with John Aschewelle, are villeins of the lord and are staying outside the lordship without licence. And so they will be taken etc.
* Next they present that John Buschel is a villein of the lord and all his

EDWARD III

ancestors since the time whose memory to the contrary was not, were villeins of the lord of his manor of Norton, as of right of the church of St Alban, who was present in court and is committed to wardship of the constable of Norton to be taken and delivered to gaol at St Albans, etc.
* The aletasters present that the brewers have broken the Assize and so are amerced 3d.
* Reynald Balston surrenders into the hand of the lord one croft with appurtenances formerly of Walter Swetekyn. And the lord has granted the said croft with its appurtenances to Richard Bate, to hold to him and his in bondage at the will of the lord by the services due and accustomed for it. And he gives for agreement 6s 8d. And he has done fealty etc.
* Again it is ordered to distrain Cecilia Andrewe to make agreement because she has married without the lord's licence.

Court of Norton on Thursday next after the Feast of St Mark the Evangelist in the 26th year – Ralph Whitchurch [*26 Apr 1352*]

| Jurors: | Adam le Smyth | John Boueton | Roger Albreth |
| | John atte Hathe | Richard Bate senior | John Dipere |

* The jurors present that Walter Taillour is in default and so amerced 2d.
* The jurors present that John le Neweman has committed waste upon his tenement. And the said John questioned thereupon says that he holds [*HALS 65514, f7v*] the aforesaid tenement freely by charter. And concerning this he has a day today to produce evidence, etc.
* Roger Albreth has married without licence. And, questioned about this, the said Roger says that he did have licence, and calls for the record of the rolls. And he has a day concerning the record until next Saturday at St Albans.
* Alice atte Cherche has married without licence, and Roger Albreth who has married her came and made agreement with the lord for himself and for the aforesaid Alice. And he gives for the agreement 40d.
* The jurors present that John Loveleg has committed *leyrewyt* and so is amerced. It is condoned.
* Next they present that Roger Albreth has committed *leyrewyt* with Lucy Dipere, so is amerced 6d.
* Next they present that John Isoude staying at Ely, Richard his younger brother staying in the same place, Richard Isoude their brother staying at Weston, Ralph Bate staying at Wymondley with Helen in le Hale, are villeins of the lord and are staying outside the lordship without licence so should be arrested, etc.

EDWARD III

[*l. margin*: villeins and fugitives][39]
* The aletasters present that the brewers have broken the Assize so are amerced 8d.
* Again it is ordered to distrain Cecily Andrewe to make agreement because she has married without the lord's licence.

Court of Norton held on Tuesday on the Feast of St Denis in the 26th year – Ralph Whitech[urch] [*9 Oct 1352*]

Jurors:	Adam Smyth	John atte Hathe	John Dipere
	Walter Thomas	John Boueton	Roger Albrethe

* John Neweman surrenders into the hand of the lord one cottage with a curtilage next to the cottage of Isabelle le Meleward, of which the heriot is 6d in money. And the lord has granted the said cottage with its appurtenances to Geoffrey le Somenour and Juliana his wife, to hold to him and his in unfree tenure for the services due and accustomed for it. And he gives for the agreement 12d. And he has done fealty, etc.
* The jurors present that John Jecob, 2d, and Thomas le Daye, 2d, are in default and so are amerced.
* [*l. margin*: villeins and fugitives] Next they present that Robert Bate staying at Shepreth, John Bate staying at Stotfold, Juliana Tollard staying at Baldock, Thomas Geiard, are villeins of the lord and are staying outside the lordship without licence. Therefore all should be arrested.
* John Loveleg and Agnes Bate have married one another without permission. And they have made agreement for their marryings [*plural*]. And they give for the agreement 2s etc.
* John Neweman had a day until this court to show his charter by which he holds one cottage with appurtenances in Norton upon which he has committed waste as appears in the preceding court, who now comes and shows his charter, etc, and thereupon it is put to him that he is a villein of the lord, and he says that he is not, and concerning this he puts himself upon [the mercy of] the jury. And the jurors have a day about this matter until the next court to make enquiries etc. And meanwhile it is ordered to seize the said cottage into the hand of the lord, etc.
* It is ordered, just as so many times before, to distrain Cecily Andrewe to make

---

[39] This and subsequent marginal notes identifying 'villeins <u>and</u> fugitives' are written in the same hand as the original document, unlike the notes indicating just 'villein' written in a different hand, probably post 1453 – see footnote 19.

EDWARD III

agreement about this, that she has married without the lord's licence. And afterwards she was released etc.

Court of Norton held on Tuesday after the Feast of St Ambrose in the 27th year – Ralph W[hitchurch] [*9 Apr 1353*]

Jurors:	John Jecob	John atte Hathe	John Dipere
	Walter Thomas	John Boueton	Roger Albrethe

* The jurors present that Geoffrey the Tailour makes default so is amerced 2d.
* Next they present that Richard Bate senior has committed waste in the tenement of John Bateman which he holds until the lawful age of the said John, so is amerced 3d. And it is ordered to repair before the next court under penalty of 5s.
* The aletasters present that the brewers have broken the Assize, so are amerced 8d.
* Laurence Wysot surrendered into the lord's hand one cottage with appurtenances next to the tenement of John atte Hathe, of which the heriot is 12d in money. And the lord has granted the said cottage with appurtenances to Simon Cadewellelle [*sic*] to hold to him and his in bondage, by the rod, at the will of the lord by the services due and accustomed for it. And he gives for agreement 18d, and he has done fealty.
* [*HALS 65514, f8*] Again the jurors have a day until the next court to inquire if John le Neweman who holds from the lord one cottage by charter be a villein by blood or free. They say that he is free.

Court of Norton on Thursday next after the Feast of St Faith the Virgin in the 27th year – Ralph W[hitchurch] [*10 Oct 1353*]

Jurors:	William Thomas	John Boueton	Richard Bate junior
	John atte Hathe	John Dipere	Adam le Smythe

* The jurors present that John Hale has withdrawn nine boondays in harvest to the damage of 2s, therefore amerced 40d.
* John Albrethe makes default, so amerced 2d [*text damaged by abrasion*] as above for concealment amerced 12d.
* Isabella Meleward has married without the lord's licence, so it is ordered to distrain her to make agreement etc.
* The jurors present that John Isoude dwelling at Ely, Richard Isoude junior there, Richard Isoude senior at Weston, John Bate at Stotfold, Robert Bate at Shepreth, Juliana Toller at Baldock with John Asshewelle, are villeins and

EDWARD III

dwell outside the lordship, therefore let them be taken etc. [*r. margin*: villeins and fugitives]
* Next they present that Agnes Bate has twice brewed and broken the Assize, therefore amerced 3d.
* John Albrethe has demised half an acre of land to John Broun of Baldock, therefore amerced and it is ordered to take [it] into the lord's hand.
* Reynald Balston has demised one acre of land to Hugh de Aschewelle by leave and he gives for licence to demise the said land for two crops 18d.
* It is ordered to take into the lord's hand one cottage which John le Neweman claims to hold by charter and to account to the lord for the issues thereof etc.
* Robert Hayward \3d/, John Albrethe \2d/, Reynald Balston \2d/ have withdrawn suit at the lord's mill therefore amerced.
* Richard Bate senior was ordered in the preceding court to repair the waste in the tenement of *Bateman* before this day under penalty of 5s and it is not repaired now. Therefore it is decided that he incur the said penalty and that he repair the said waste under penalty of 10s.

Court of Norton on Tuesday next after the Feast of St John before the Latin Gate in the 28th year – John Mote [*13 May 1354*]

Jurors:	Walter Thomas	John Boueton	Richard Bate junior
	John atte Hathe	John Dipere	Adam le Smyth

* The jurors present that Isabella de Erdele 3d, Richard Andrewe 3d, Joan de Monden 2d, John le Kyng 2d, John Jacob 3d, Geoffrey Taburrerre 3d, Alexander Warde 3d, make default, therefore amerced.
* Next they present that William Sayer has committed waste concerning the tenement of Nicholas Sayer his brother, so is amerced 3d. And he is ordered to repair the said waste before the next court under penalty of 3s 4d.
* Richard Bate has committed waste by felling six trees. Damage 12d, so amerced. And it is ordered etc.
* Richard Bate senior was ordered to repair waste committed by him in the tenement called *Bateman* before today and it is not yet repaired, therefore etc. And he is ordered to repair the said waste before the next court under penalty of 10s.
* The aletasters Richard Bate and John atte Hathe present that the brewers have broken the Assize, so are amerced 9d.
* The jurors present that John Isoud and Richard Isoud junior are dwelling at Ely, Richard Isoud senior dwelling at Weston. Therefore let them be taken, etc. [*r. margin*: villeins and fugitives]

EDWARD III

* John Loveleg surrendered into the lord's hand one messuage and half a virgate of land formerly of Roger Proude. And the lord has granted the said messuage and land to Reynald Balston to hold to him and his by rod, saving the right of any, performing for the lord the due and accustomed services, nor shall he commit waste. And he gives for agreement 2s.
* Richard Bate senior surrendered into the lord's hands one messuage and 15 acres of land formerly of Walter Swetekyn and the lord granted the said messuage together with the land to Roger Albrethe to hold to him and his by the rod, performing for the lord the due and accustomed services. And he gives to the lord for agreement 2s.
* [HALS 65514, f8v] Richard Bate senior surrendered into the lord's hands one messuage which Robert the vicar formerly held, and the lord granted the said messuage to the Lord Robert, now vicar of Norton to hold to him and his by the rod, performing for the lord the services due and accustomed for it. And he gives for agreement 2s.
* The jurors present that John Albreth has demised half an acre of land to John Broune of Baldock, and Richard Bate [has demised] another half acre of land to William Parson of the same, which said two acres lie in *le Malme* sown with dredge this year. Therefore it is ordered to take the said land into the lord's hands, and to account to the lord for the issues etc.
* John Loveleg \2d/, Richard Baker \2d/, John Albreth \2d/, William en le Hale \2d/, Roger Frenshe \2d/, John atte Hathe \2d/ and Laurence Wysot \2d/ each of them for two days with one man have made default at the lord's boondays. Therefore amerced.

Court of Norton on Monday in the Feast of the Conception of the Blessed Mary in the 28th year – John Mote [*8 Dec 1354*]

Jurors:	Walter Thomas	John Boueton	Adam Smyth
	John atte Hath	John Diper	William atte Chirch

* William Sayer had been ordered in the preceding court to repair the waste in the tenement of Nicholas his brother before this day under the penalty of 3s 4d, and now it is not repaired so it is decided that he should incur the said penalty. And afterwards the lord has granted to the said William that he may make his profit and will with the said messuage under this condition that he make a new house there etc.
* The lord by his special grace has granted to John Loveleg that he may repair the waste within his tenement before the next court. And unless he shall do so he shall incur a penalty of 10s.

EDWARD III

* It is ordered, just as in other cases, to take into the lord's hand one cottage which John the Neweman claims to hold by charter, and to account to the lord for the profits, etc.
* The jurors present that John Jacob \2d/, Roger Frenssh \2d/, Reynald Sayer \2d/ make default, so are amerced.
* Richard Bate junior is dead, who held of the lord two messuages and one virgate of land, of which the heriot is two horses worth 16s. And because the heir of the said Richard is unable to hold the said land and is under age, the beadle is ordered to account to the lord for the issues etc.
* John Neweman is dead, who held of the lord one messuage and one *ferlingate* of land, of which the heriot is one horse worth 5s and Joan his daughter is his next heir and of the age of ten weeks. And afterwards the lord granted to Christiana, relict of the said John, wardship of the aforesaid lands and heir, to hold until the lawful age of the heir, nor shall she commit waste. And she gives to the lord for having the term 18d.
* Helen Ward is dead who held of the lord one messuage and half a virgate of land, of which the heriot in money is 3s. The lord has granted the said messuage and land to Isabelle Warde as next heir of the aforesaid Helen, to hold to her and hers in villeinage at the will of the lord, rendering for it to the lord and performing all services and customs which are owed for the said tenement. And she gives to the lord for *gersumma* 6s 8d.
* Again a day is given to Richard Bate until the next court to repair the waste in his tenement under penalty of 10s.
* Because in the preceding court the beadle was ordered to take into the lord's hand one half acre of land sown with dredge let by Richard Bate senior to William Parson of Baldock which Richard notwithstanding the aforesaid seisin administered and delivered the aforesaid crop against prohibition etc, therefore amerced 2d. And the said crop is valued by the jury at 10d which it is ordered to raise etc, and nevertheless to answer to the lord for contempt etc.
* Because in the preceding court the beadle was ordered to take into the lord's hand one half acre of land sown with dredge let by John Albreth to John Broune of Baldock, which John Albreth notwithstanding the aforesaid seisin administered and delivered to the said John Broune the aforesaid crop against the aforesaid prohibition, therefore amerced. And the said crop is valued by the jury at 2s which the beadle is ordered to raise from the goods and chattels of John Albreth, etc. Afterwards the lord of his special grace pardons the amercement and 12d so that he pay the other 12d.
* Richard Bate and John en le Hale, aletasters, present that the brewers have broken the Assize, so are amerced 5d.

EDWARD III

* Richard Bate puts himself in mercy because he has withdrawn himself for five days with five men in harvest at the lord's boondays, 10d.
* Isabella Ward came into the court and surrendered into the hands of the lord one messuage and half a virgate of land which were of Helen Ward, of which the heriot in money is 12d. And the lord granted the said messuage and half virgate of land with appurtenances to John Bate, to hold to him and his in villeinage at the will of the lord, rendering for it to the lord and doing all services and customs that are owed for the said tenement. And he gives to the lord for *gersumma* 3s 4d.
* [*l. margin*: New order] The whole Homage is ordered in full court that none of them in future shall demise any house or parcel to one by turn (*sibi in vicem*)[40] for a term of one year or two according to their ancient custom in order that they may claim without the lord's leave but that whoever wishes to let house or land shall seek leave in the court for the term above written without paying any fine (*finem*) to the lord and so the term[s] shall be enrolled and if anyone shall do to the contrary he shall pay 6s 8d to the lord and [*HALS 65515, f1*] otherwise such lands and tenements shall be taken into the lord's hands.

Court of Norton on Tuesday next after the Feast of St Dunstan the Bishop in the 29th year – John Mote [*26 May 1355*]

Jurors: Walter Thomas   John Jecob   Roger Albrethe
John atte Hathe   John Dipere   William atte Churche

* They say that John Colyn 2d, Hugh Travayle 2d, Richard Andrewe 3d, John Kynge 3d, the tenants of the land of Richard Cornemongere of *Wilyon* [Willian] 3d, the tenants of the land of Alice Berthelot of Willian 3d, the tenants of the land of Henry Gardiner of Willian 3d, the tenants of the land of John Hoye of Willian 3d make default, therefore amerced.
* Next they present that Roger Wolere \2d/, John Colyn \2d/, Thomas Cady \2d/ have withdrawn multure from the lord's mill; so are amerced.
* Agnes Loveleg has committed *letherwyt*, therefore amerced 6d.
* John Loveleg is dead who held of the lord two cotlands and one toft with one parcel of land containing in all three roods of land, of which the heriot is one horse, one cow, one young bullock and they are delivered to the manor. And

---

[40] What is being forbidden is probably a lease 'from year to year', in favour of a fixed longer term that must be registered in the court. This suggests that short leases must have been common, and that the copyholders with larger holdings may well have been living off rents rather than cultivating the land themselves.

EDWARD III

the land remains in the lord's hands until it shall be known who is the next heir, etc. It appears below.
* Richard Hasche is dead, who held of the lord two messuages and two *ferthlingates* of land of which the heriot is one cow and the said land remains in the lord's hands, etc.
* Isabella Shepherd is dead, who held of the lord one cotland and one cotland with half an acre of land of which the heriot is two ewe sheep with two lambs and they are delivered to the manor. And the said holding remains in the lord's hands until it be known who is her heir, etc.
* The jury present that John Isowde, Richard Isowde senior, Richard Isowde junior, dwelling at Ely. Robert Bate at Shepreth in county of Bedford, John Hasche and Alice Hasche are villeins of the lord and fugitives and live outside the lordship. Therefore let them be taken etc. [*l. margin*: villeins and fugitives]
* It is ordered to take into the lord's hands the crop of one half-acre of land in *Newehouscroft* sown with dredge let to John Maystre by John Albrethe which half acre was let before the order at the last court held, that is to say of Michaelmas term. Therefore as for penalty and amercement they are forgiven but the beadle is ordered to account to the lord for the issues, etc.
* It is ordered as in other cases to take into the lord's hands one cottage which John the Neweman claims to hold by charter and to account to the lord for the issues, as had been ordered in the last court.
* John atte Hathe and Richard Bate senior, aletasters, present that the brewers have broken the Assize. Therefore amerced 18d.
* John Loveleg is dead, who held of the lord two messuages with two cotlands and one messuage with one half acre of land, of which the heriot is one horse, one cow, a young bullock and they are delivered to the manor. And his next heir is Matilda Loveleg, sister of the said John who being present in court has altogether refused to hold the said messuage and lands by succession, by virtue of which refusal she and her heirs have been wholly deprived by judgement rendered in this court of all title of right or claim in the said messuage and lands. Whereupon the lord gave possession to Agnes in the Hale, formerly wife of the said John to hold to her and hers in villeinage by the services due for them and by law accustomed, nor shall she commit waste. And she gives for agreement and for licence to marry 7s 2d.
* The lord has granted and conveyed to Reynald Balston one messuage and one *quarterlond*, which were formerly of John Tollard, to hold to him and his in villeinage by the services due and accustomed for them. And he gives nothing for agreement because poor.
* The lord has granted and conveyed to Roger le Wheler one messuage and one

EDWARD III

cotland with appurtenances which were formerly of John in the Hale, to hold to him and his in villeinage at the will of the lord by the services due and by law accustomed for them. Fine forgiven. He has done fealty and shall not commit waste, etc, by the pledges of John Dipere and William Sayer.

Court of Norton on Tuesday next after the Feast of St Denis in the 29th year – John Mote [*13 Oct 1355*]

Jurors:	Walter Thomas	John Jecob	Roger Albreth
	John atte Hathe	John Dipere	William atte Chirch

* The jurors present that the tenants of the tenements of William de Munden 3d, John Mayster 3d, Richard Andrew 3d, Walter Taillour 2d, John Gedgerd forgiven, Reynald Sayer forgiven, Hugh Travayle 2d, John Colyne 2d, Simon Taillour 3d, tenants of the land of Richard Cornemongere of *Wilyen* [Willian] 3d, tenants of the land of Alice Bartelott of the same 3d, tenants of the land of John Hoij of the same 3d, tenants of the land of Henry Gardiner 2d, make default, therefore are amerced.
* The jurors present that William Sayer and Alexander Ward took from the lord half a virgate of land for a term of 13 years which term has passed
HALS 65515, f1v] as is testified in full court. Therefore distrain them to make agreement etc.
* A day is given against the next court to John Albreth senior to repair his waste made in his tenement as has been reported by the jurors under penalty of 6s 8d. Pledges John Diper and Roger Albreth.
* The aletasters John atte Hatthe and Richard Bate present that Agnes Bates has brewed and broken the Assize, so is amerced 2d.
* Roger Wheler has made agreement for ten boondays withdrawn by him in harvest for the land formerly of John in the Hale which he now holds. He gives to the lord 2s.
* Walter Ronehale has leave from the lord to throw down two houses of his principal tenement on this condition, that he repair the other houses of his said tenement before the next court under penalty of 6s 8d. Pledge Reynald Balston.
* John Love has a day until the next court to repair the waste which he has caused in his tenement, presented by the jurors, under penalty 6s 8d by the pledge of John Dipere and William Chirch, etc.

EDWARD III

Court of Norton on Tuesday next after the Feast of the Apostles Philip and James in the 30th year – John Mote [*3 May 1356*]

Jurors: Walter Thomas   John Jecob   Roger Albreth
          John atte Hathe   John Diper   William atte Chirche

* Again it is ordered to distrain William Sayer and Alexander Warde to make agreement for half a virgate of land which they had taken formerly from the lord for a term of 13 years and which term has passed, etc.
* John Love because he has not repaired waste as he was ordered at the last court so is amerced 3d and the same man is ordered to repair [it] before the next court under penalty of 6s 8d.
* Jurors present John Maystr \2d/ and Richard Andrewe \2d/ make default so are amerced etc.
* [*l. margin*: villeins and fugitives] John Isoude and Richard Isoude junior and Richard Isoude senior are dwelling at Weston, Robert Bate and Cecily Wilymote at St Albans town, Alice Hasshe at Arlesey and John Hasshe at *Estwyk*, and they are villeins and fugitives. Therefore let them be taken etc.
* Next they present that Christine Neweman has committed *leyrwyt* so is amerced 3d.
* The aletasters present that the brewers have broken the Assize, therefore amerced 13d.
* Again a day is given against the next court to John Albreth to repair the waste caused in his tenement, under penalty of 6s 8d.
* Again a day given before the next court to Walter Ronhale to repair the waste in his tenement, under penalty of 6s 8d.
* The lord has granted and conveyed to Mabel Hasshe the wardship of a messuage and of one *farthing* of land (*unius quadrante terre*) with appurtenances, formerly of Richard Hasshe together with wardship of Robert son and heir of the said Richard, to hold until the lawful age of the said heir in villeinage and at the will of the lord by the services and customs due and accustomed. And she gives to the lord for agreement 2s. And she has done fealty.

Court of Norton on Tuesday next after the Feast of St Faith the Virgin in the 30th year – John Mote [*11 Oct 1356*]

Jurors: Walter Thomas   John Jecob   Roger Albreth
          John atte Hathe   John Dypere   William atte Chirche

EDWARD III

* The jurors present that Joan Monden \2d/, Richard Andrewe \2d/, John Albreth \2d/, Alexander Ward \condoned/, Walter Cok \2d/, Thomas Cady \2d/ make default so are amerced.
* The aletasters present that John Albreth \2d/ and Agnes Bate \2d/ have brewed and broken the Assize so are amerced.
* [*l. margin*: villeins and fugitives] It is ordered to take John Albreth, John Isoude, Richard Isoude junior and Richard Isoude senior dwelling at Weston, Richard Bate and Cecily Wilimot at St Albans, Alice Hasshe at Arlesey, villeins and fugitives of the lord etc.
* Again as so many times it is ordered to distrain William Sayer and Alexander Ward to make agreement for half a virgate of land which they formerly took from the lord for a term of 13 years, which term has passed.
* John Love has incurred the penalty 6s 8d because he has not repaired his waste, as he had been enjoined at the previous court. And he is ordered to repair the said waste before the next court under penalty of 2s.
* A day is given to John Albreth senior to fully repair his waste before the next court under penalty of half a mark.
* A day is given to Walter Ronehale to fully repair the waste in his tenement before the next court under penalty of half a mark.

[*HALS 65516, f1*] Court of Norton on Tuesday next after the Feast of St Augustine in the 31st year – John Mote [*30 May 1357*]

Jurors:	Walter Thomas	John Jecob	Roger Albreth
	John atte Hathe	John Diper	William atte Chirche

* It is ordered to take John Albreth, John Isoud, Richard Isoud junior, Richard Isoud dwelling at Weston, Richard Bate, Cecily Wilymot at St Albans, Alice Assh at Arlesey, Margaret Bond at St Albans and Matilda her sister at Baldock, villeins and fugitives and to take them to St Albans. [*r. margin*: villeins and fugitives]
* The jurors present that Simon Cadewell 2d, John Colyn 2d, Peter Hardewyn 3d, the tenants of the lands of John Andrewe 2d, Richard Andrewe 2d, Hugh Travayle and Parnel his wife 2d, Robert Cadewell 2d make default, so are amerced.
* Next they present that John Bate \3d/, John Boueton \3d/, John atte Hathe \3d/ and Roger Freynssh \3d/ have committed waste in their tenements so are amerced. And it is ordered for each of them to repair the said waste under penalty of 40d.
* Agnes Albreth has committed *letherwitam*, so is amerced 3d.

EDWARD III

* The lord has granted to John Geiard junior a certain piece of land opposite the cemetery built with a certain house made formerly by the lord for a smithy (*fabrica*), to hold to him and his in villeinage by services etc. And he gives to the lord for the said piece of land and house built thereon and for licence to marry 4s 6d and will give annually for rent 12d. [*r. margin*: rent 12d]

Court of Norton, on Tuesday next before the Feast of St Michael in the 31st year – John Mote [*26 Sep 1357*]

Jurors:	Walter Thomas	John Jecob	Roger Albreth
	John atte Hathe	John Dipere	John Boton

* It is ordered to take the villeins and fugitives written above in the previous court etc.
* The jurors present that Walter Taillour \2d\, Hugh Travaill \2d\, Roger Quenhawe \2d\, Richard Andrewe \2d\, Isabella Yherdele \2d\ owe and make default, so are amerced.
* Next they present that Rose wife of John Albreth is a huckstress (*hoccatrix*) and has broken the Assize of ale so is amerced 2d.

Court of Norton on Tuesday next after the Feast of Pentecost in the 32nd year – John Mote [*22 May 1358*]

Jurors:	Walter Thomas	John Jecob	Roger Albreth
	John atte Hath	John Dipere	John Boueton

* A day is given to John Bate to repair his waste before the next court under penalty of 2s. And many others have days etc.
* Walter Thomas has made agreement with the lord to put William and John his sons to letters and he gives to the lord 2s.
* Roger le Frenssh and Emma his wife, she having been questioned, surrendered into the lord's hand one messuage and one *ferlingate* of land of which the heriot in money is half a mark. And the lord has granted the said messuage and land to John Laweman, to hold to him and his in villeinage at the will of the lord by the services due and accustomed for them. And he gives to the lord for agreement 5s. And he has done fealty, etc.
* The jurors present that John Kyng, \2d\, John Albreth \2d\ make default so are amerced.
* Alexander Ward is dead, who held of the lord one cotland, of which the heriot is one brass pot worth 2s. This Alexander was a bastard. Therefore it is ordered to take [it] into the lord's hands and to account for the issues.

EDWARD III

- Next they present that Rose Bonde \2d/ and Adam Smyth \2d/ are regraters therefore amerced.
- William Sayer junior made agreement with the lord for his marriage and for the marriage of [*left blank*] Albreth his wife. And he gives to the lord for agreement 2s.
- It is ordered to distrain Matilda Balston against the next court to satisfy the lord for her marriage, etc.

Court of Norton on Tuesday in the Feast of St Denis, in the 32nd year – John Mote [*9 Oct 1358*]

Jurors:	Walter Thomas	John Jecob	Roger Albreth
	John atte Hath	John Dipere	John Boueton

- [*HALS 65516, f1v*] The jurors present that Richard Andreu \condoned/, Roger Quenehawe \2d/, the tenants of the lands of John Grome \2d/, Isabella de Yherdele \2d/, make default, so are amerced.
- From Richard Bate because he was short of one man for nine days in harvest 3s. From Roger Quenhawe because he was short of one man for one day in harvest 4d. From John Maistre [because he was short of] one man [for one day in harvest] 4d.
- The jurors present that Rose Bonde is a huckstress and has sold ale against the Assize, so amerced 2d.
- A day is given to John Bate to repair his waste before the next court under penalty of 2s. And likewise to many others.
- It is ordered to retain in the lord's hands one cotland formerly of Alexander Ward and to account for the profit thereof.
- It is ordered to distrain Matilda Balston to satisfy the lord for her marriage etc.

Court of Norton on Tuesday on the Eve of the Apostles Philip and James in the 33rd year – John Mote [*30 Apr 1359*]

Jurors:	Walter Thomas	John Jecob	Roger Albreth
	John atte Hathe	John Diper	John Boueton

- Again a day is given to John Bate to repair his waste before the next court, under penalty of 2s. And likewise to many others, etc.
- Margery Bate is dead who held of the lord a third part of two parts of one

EDWARD III

virgate of land in the name of dower.[41] Therefore it is ordered to seise it, etc.
* Walter Cok surrendered into the lord's hands one cottage with curtilage formerly of William Cok, of which the heriot in money is 12d. And the lord has granted the said cottage with curtilage to John Squyer to hold to him and his in villeinage at the will of the lord by the services due and accustomed for it. And he gives for agreement 12d. And he has done fealty, etc.
* Ralph Cok came after the death of Margery Cok his mother and *gersummavit* one cottage formerly of John Cok to hold to him and his in villeinage by rod at the will of the lord by the services due and accustomed for it. And he gives to the lord for *gersumma* 12d.
* The lord has granted to John Smalgrave one cotland, which was formerly of Alexander Ward and which came into the lord's hands by escheat because the said Alexander was a bastard and died without an heir issuing from his body. To hold to him and his in villeinage at the will of the lord by the services due and accustomed for it. And he gives to the lord for agreement 24s. And he has done fealty.
* John Colyn surrendered into the lord's hands one cottage with curtilage, of which the heriot in money is 12d. And the lord has granted the said cottage and curtilage to John le Heir Hayward, to hold to him and his in villeinage at the will of the lord by the services due and accustomed for it. And he gives to the lord for agreement 12d.

Court of Norton on Tuesday next before the Feast of St Denis in the 33rd year – John Mote [*8 Oct 1359*]

| Jurors: | Walter Thomas | John Jecob | Roger Albreth |
| | John atte Hathe | John Dipere | John Boueton |

* Again as on other occasions a day is given to John Bate, Walter Roenhale, Laurence Wysot, John Love, John Albreth and Roger Frensh to repair waste in their tenements under penalty for each of them of 2s.
* Again it is ordered to retain in the lord's hands the third part of two parts of one virgate of land which Margery Bate formerly held in dower and to account for the profits thereof etc.
* The jurors present that Hugh Travaille \2d/ and John Squyer \2d/ make default, therefore they are amerced.

---

[41] Margery must have outlived her mother-in-law, and both had outlived their husbands. Thus her dower is one third of the two-thirds of the family holding which her husband had pending his mother's death.

EDWARD III

- * Ralph Cok has alienated one cottage to John Colyn without leave. Therefore it is ordered to take it into the lord's hands, and to account for the profits thereof, etc.
- * John Messor has abandoned one cottage with curtilage. Therefore it is ordered to take it into the lord's hands and to account for the profits thereof, etc.
- * Walter Roenhale was short of one man at the lord's boondays for two days, so is amerced 3d.

Court of Norton on Tuesday next after the Feast of St Guthlac in the 34th year – John Mote [*14 Apr 1360*]

Jurors:	Walter Thomas	John Jecob	Roger Albreth
	John atte Hathe	John Dipere	John Boueton

- * Again as many times a day is given to John Boueton, Walter Roenhale, Laurence Wysot, John Love and Roger Frenssh to repair waste in their tenements before the next court under penalty for each of them of 2s.
- * The jurors present that John Isoud, Richard Isoud dwelling at Ely, Richard Isoud senior at Weston, John Hassh, [*HALS 65517, f1*] Margaret daughter of Rose Bonde at St Albans, Cecily Andreu there, villeins and fugitives are dwelling outside the lordship. Therefore it is ordered to take them and bring them to St Albans etc. [*r. margin*: villeins and fugitives]
- * Reynald Sayer is dead who held of the lord one messuage and one *quartrona* of land, of which the heriot is one young bullock, worth 5s. And John his son is his next heir aged six years. And afterwards Matilda Sayer mother of the said John came and took the said land from the lord with wardship of the said heir. To hold until the full age of the said John in villeinage, at the will of the lord by the services due and accustomed for them. And she gives for agreement 12d.
- * The lord has granted to John Umfrey one cottage with curtilage which John Hayward abandoned to hold to him and his in villeinage at the will of the lord by the due and accustomed services and customs. And he gives nothing for the agreement because poor.
- * Ralph Cok surrendered into the lord's hands one cottage with curtilage formerly of John Sprot, of which the heriot in money is 20d. And the lord has granted the said cottage and curtilage to John Colyn, to hold to him and his in villeinage at the will of the lord by the services due and accustomed for it. And he gives to the lord for agreement 20d.
- * Geoffrey Taborer and Juliana his wife, she having been questioned,

EDWARD III

surrendered into the lord's hands one cottage with curtilage lying between the tenements of Thomas Kady on either side and it extends from the King's highway (*regia via*) to the field called *Longefurlong*, of which [*plural*] the heriot in money is 12d. And the lord has granted and conveyed the said cottage and curtilage with all their appurtenances to John Geiard, Katherine his wife and Agnes their daughter, to hold to them and the heirs of the said Agnes in villeinage at the will of the lord by the services due and accustomed for them. And they give to the lord for an agreement 18d, etc.

* The lord has granted to Thomas Olyve a third part of two parts of one virgate of land which Margaret Bate formerly held in dower, to hold to him until the full age of William Isoud heir of the said land, in villeinage at the will of the lord by the services due and accustomed for it. And the fine is forgiven.
* The jurors present that John Jecob has married without the lord's licence Alice Bate, villein of the lord. And afterwards they came and made agreement. And they give 40d to the lord.
* Next they present that Adam Smyth \2d/, Olive Isoud \2d/, John Dipere \2d/, Robert Hayward \2d/, have brewed and broken the Assize, therefore amerced. And Rose Bond is a huckstress and has sold ale against the Assize. Therefore amerced 2d.

Court of Norton on Tuesday next after the Feast of St Matthew the Apostle in the 34th year – John Mote [*22 Sep 1360*]

Jurors:	Walter Thomas	John Gecob	Roger Albreth
	John atte Hathe	John Dipere	John Boueton

* Again as many times a day is given to John Bate, Laurence Wysot and Roger Frenssh to repair waste caused in their tenements before the next court under penalty for each of them of 2s.
* A day is given to Walter Roenhale to repair his waste before the next court under penalty of loss of his tenement, etc.
* It is ordered to take John Isoud, Richard Isoud, dwelling at Ely, Richard Isoud senior at Weston, Alice daughter of Thomas atte Nasshe at Arlesey, John Hasshe, Margaret Bonde at St Albans, Cecily Andreu there, villeins and fugitives, and to bring them to St Albans, etc. [*r. margin*: villeins and fugitives]
* The jurors present that John Colyn \2d/, Hugh Travayll \2d/, Walter Taillour \2d/, Roger Quenehawe \2d/, make default therefore they are amerced.
* John son of John Boueton has licence to marry. And he gives 2s for agreement.
* The jurors present that John Bate \2d/, John Albreth \2d/, Richard Bate \2d/,

EDWARD III

John Boueton junior \2d/, and John Smalgrave \2d/ have not cleansed the pond etc.

Court of Norton on Tuesday next after the Feast of St Ambrose in the 35th year – John Mote [*6 Apr 1361*]

Jurors:	Walter Thomas	John Gecob	Roger Albreth
	John atte Hathe	John Dipere	John Boueton

* Matilda daughter of Rose Bonde gives 12d to the lord as an agreement for licence to marry.
* John Albreth gives 6d to the lord for an agreement for leave to put Adam his son to letters.
* Next they present that Adam Smyth \2d/, and John Dipere \3d/ have brewed and broken the Assize, therefore amerced.
* Again as many times a day is given to John Bate, Laurence Wysot and Roger Frenshe to repair their wastes before the next court under penalty for each of them of 2s.
* Again as many times a day is given to Walter Roenhale to repair his waste before the next court under penalty of losing his tenement etc.
* [*HALS 65517, f1v*] [*l. margin*: villeins and fugitives] It is ordered to take John Isoude, Richard Isoude staying at Ely, Richard Isoude senior at Weston, Alice daughter of Thomas atte Nasshe at Arlesey, John Hasshe, Margaret Bonde at St Albans, Cecily Andrewe there, villeins and fugitives, etc.

Court of Norton on Tuesday next after the Feast of St Denis in the 35th year – John Mote [*12 Oct 1361*]

Jurors:	John Diper	John Boueton	Walter Thomas
	John Gecob	Reynald Balston	William atte Chirche

* The jurors present that Roger Quenehawe makes default of common suit, so amerced 2d.
* Matilda the wife of Adam Smyth is dead who held of the lord one messuage and half a virgate of land formerly of John Shepherd, of which the heriot is one horse worth 10s. And John her son is of the age of 14 years and is her next heir. And because the same John is incapable and of minor age wardship of the land and of the heir is committed to John Boueton, and the fine is forgiven.
* Henry Cok is dead who held of the lord one messuage and one croft containing half an acre, of which the heriot is one horse. The same held one

EDWARD III

toft and one *ferlingate* of land, of which the heriot in money is 4s. And John his son is his next heir aged 15 years. And because the same John is of minor age wardship of the land and tenement and of the aforesaid heir is committed to Walter Hayward and Alice his wife, to hold to them until the lawful age of the said heir, in villeinage at the will of the lord by the due and accustomed services. And they give to the lord by agreement two small hens (*pulcinos*), etc.

* Thomas Olyve is dead, who held of the lord one messuage and one croft containing in the whole one acre and three roods and he held also one toft with a croft containing one acre and he held half an acre lying upon *Woweforlong*, of which the heriot is two plates. And Thomas his son of the age of eight years is his next heir. Therefore it is ordered to take [it] into the lord's hand until etc.
* John Colyn is dead, who held of the lord one cottage of which the heriot is one brass pot worth 40d. And Cecily his daughter of the age of four years is his next heir. Therefore it is ordered to take [it] into the lord's hand until etc.
* John Maistre is dead, who held of the lord one messuage with a garden containing half an acre lying next to the tenement formerly of William de Munden, and one croft lying at the *Hoomulle* containing three acres and two acres of meadow lying at *Hoomullemore* and one acre of land lying at *Blakenhurst* between the land of the vicar of Norton and the land of Henry Cok, and one acre of land lying at *Wyserhull* between the land of Laurence Wysot and land of Henry Cok, and half an acre of land lying there between the land formerly of John Basily on either side, and one rood and a half lying upon *Ikenyldesshot* between the land of John Basily on either side, of which the heriot is one horse worth 3s. And the aforesaid John died without an heir therefore it is ordered to seise it as an escheat, etc.
* The lord has granted to John atte Hathe one *ferlingate* of land called *Parlourslond* formerly of Henry Cok, to hold to him and his, reserving the right of any, in villeinage at the will of the lord by the due and accustomed services. And the fine is forgiven by the cellarer.
* Again as many times a day is given to John Bate, Laurence Wysot, Roger Frensshe and Walter Roenhale to repair their waste before the next court under penalty for each of them of 2s.
* [*l. margin*: villeins and fugitives] It is ordered to take John Isoud, Richard Isoud staying at Ely, Richard Isoud senior at Weston, Alice daughter of Thomas atte Nassche at *Alrichessey* [Arlesey], John Hassh, Margaret Bond, Cecily Andrewe, villeins and fugitives, and take them to St Albans, etc.

EDWARD III

Court of Norton on Tuesday next after the Feast of St Mark in the 36th year – John Mote [*26 Apr 1362*]

Jurors: John Diper   Walter Thomas   John Boueton
          William Sayer   John Jecob   Reynald Balston

* The jurors present that Isabella Yherdele \2d/, Margery Basely \forgiven/, Clemence Dipere \2d/, John atte Hathe \3d/, make default therefore amerced.
* Matilda Sayer who was the wife of Reynald Sayer is dead, who held of the lord one messuage and one *ferlingate* of land until the lawful age of John son of the said Reynald which John is likewise dead. And William Sayer, her uncle, is her next heir. And the said William of full age being present in the court altogether refused to hold the said messuage and land. Therefore it is ordered to take into the lord's hands the said messuage and land and to account for the profits, etc.

Court of Norton on Tuesday on the Feast of St Nicholas in the 36th year – John Mote [*6 Dec 1362*]

Jurors: John Dipere   Walter Thomas   John Jecob
          William Sayer   John Boueton   Reynald Balston

* They present that Walter Taillour \2d/, and Simon Cadewell \2d/ default, therefore amerced.
* [*HALS 65518, f1*] Nicholas Lacheford and Amice his wife, kinswoman and one of the heirs of John Yherdele, that is to say the daughter of a certain William, brother of the said John, and Agnes sister of the said Amice, kinswoman and another of the heirs of the said John have a day before the next court to perform their fealty and to acknowledge etc.
* It is ordered to retain in the lord's hand one messuage and one *ferlingate* of land whereof Reynald Sayer died seised, of which messuage and land William Sayer is next heir and he has in full court completely refused to hold them, and to account for the issues.
* Again it is ordered to retain in the lord's hands one cottage formerly of John Colyn until etc. And one messuage with appurtenances formerly of John Maistre whereof the said John Maistre died seised without heir, as an escheat, and to account for the issue.
* It is ordered to take John Isoud, Richard Isoud staying at Ely, Richard Isoud senior at Weston, Alice daughter of Thomas atte Nasshe at *Alrichessay* [Arlesey], John Hasshe, Margaret Bonde, Cecily Andreu, villeins and fugitives.

EDWARD III

Court of Norton on Tuesday next before the Feast of St Barnabas the Apostle in the 37th year – John Mote [*6 Jun 1363*]

Jurors:	John Dipere	Walter Thomas	John Boueton
	William Sayer	John Jecob	Reynald Balston

* Again it is ordered to retain in the lord's hand one messuage and one *ferlingate* of land whereof Reynald Sayer died seised, of which messuage and land William Sayer is next heir and he has in full court completely refused to hold them, and to account for the profits etc.
* Again as many times it is ordered to retain in the lord's hands one cottage formerly of John Colyn until etc, and one messuage with appurtenances formerly of John Maistre, whereof the same John died [seised] without an heir, and to account for the profits.
* [*r. margin*: villeins and fugitives] It is ordered to take John Isoud, Richard Isoud staying at Ely, Richard Isoud senior at Weston, Alice daughter of Thomas atte Nasshe at *Alrichessay* [Arlesey], John Hassh, Margaret Bonde and Cecily Andrewe, villeins and fugitives.
* The jurors present that Walter Sayer \2d/ has brewed and broken the Assize, so is amerced. Agnes Bate \2d/ and Rose Bond \2d/ are regraters.
* Nicholas Lacheford and Amice his wife, kinswoman and one of the heirs of John Yherdele, that is to say a daughter of a certain William, brother of the said John and Agnes sister of the said Amice, kinswoman and another of the heirs of the said John have a day until the next court to do their fealty and to acknowledge etc.
* Robert Larke surrendered into the lord's hands one cottage with curtilage formerly John Carter's, situated next to the vicarage, of which the heriot in money is 12d. And the lord granted the said cottage and curtilage with appurtenances to Walter Breynton, chaplain, to hold to him for the term of his life, in villeinage however at the will of the lord by the due and accustomed services. And he gives for agreement 18d.

Court of Norton on Tuesday next before the Feast of St Michael in the 37th year – John Mote [*26 Sep 1363*]

Jurors:	John Dipere	Walter Thomas	John Boueton
	William Sayer	John Jecob	Reynald Balston

* Again as many times it is ordered to retain in the hands of the lord one cottage formerly of John Colyn until etc, and one messuage with appurtenances formerly of John Maistre, after whose death the aforesaid messuage with

EDWARD III

appurtenances fell into the hands of the lord as an escheat, and to account for the profits etc.
* Nicholas Lacheford and Amice his wife, a kinswoman and one of the heirs of John Yherdele that is to say a daughter of a certain William the brother of the aforesaid John, and Agnes the sister of the aforesaid Amice a kinswoman and the other heir of the said John, have come and done fealty and acknowledged to hold from the lord one meadow called *Hallemed* containing ten acres, and five acres of land adjoining, freely by the service of 40d *per annum* and one pound of cumin for the lease of the cook. And suit of court every three weeks. And 16 acres of land freely by the service of 4½d.
* The jurors present that Roger Quenehawe made default, so is amerced 2d.
* Next they present that William Sayer has brewed and broken the Assize, so amerced 2d.
* The lord has granted to John Smyth one messuage and one *ferlingate* of land formerly of Reynald Sayer, of which messuage and land William Sayer is next heir and he has altogether refused in full court to hold the said messuage and land, to hold to him and his in villeinage at the will of the lord by the services due and accustomed. And he has done fealty. And the fine is forgiven. And the substance is such that if anyone else shall come seeking to have the right, and wishes to claim the said messuage and land with appurtenances, that he shall satisfy John for all his costs and expenses laid out around the said messuage and land with appurtenances by a decision of the whole Homage before he have entry into the same etc.

[HALS 65518, f1v] Court held there on Tuesday in the Feast of St Barnabas the Apostle in the 38th year – John Mote [*11 Jun 1364*]

Jurors: John Dipere, William Sayer, Walter Thomas, John Boueton, William atte Chirche

* The jurors present that Agnes Bate \2d/, and Rose Bond \2d/ are regraters and have broken the Assize of ale, therefore amerced.
* [*l. margin*: villeins and fugitives] It is ordered to take John Isoud, Richard Isoud staying at Ely, Richard Isoud senior at Weston, Alice daughter of Thomas atte Nasshe at *Alrichhessay* [Arlesey], John Hassh, Margaret Bond, Cecily Andreu, villeins and fugitives, etc.
* Again as many times, it is ordered to retain in the lord's hands one cottage formerly John Colyn's until etc. And one messuage with appurtenances whereof John Maistre died seised and which came into the lord's hands as forfeited and to account for the issues.

EDWARD III

* John Jecob is dead who held of the lord one messuage and half a virgate of land and one cotland of which the heriot is one horse and it is given to the heir. And his next heir is John his son of full age who came and *gersummavit* the said messuage and land with appurtenances, to hold to him and his in villeinage at the will of the lord by the due and accustomed services. And the fine is forgiven.
* Simon Cadewell surrendered into the lord's hand one cottage with curtilage situated between the tenement of John atte Hathe and the tenement of Laurence Wysot, of which the heriot in money is 12d. And the lord granted the said cottage and curtilage with appurtenances to John atte Hale, to hold to him and his in villeinage at the will of the lord by the due and accustomed services. And the fine is forgiven.

Court of Norton, on Tuesday next after the Feast of St Hilary in the 38th year – John Mote [*14 Jan 1365*]

Jurors:	John Dipere	Walter Thomas	William atte Chirch
	William Sayer	John Boueton	John Smyth

* [*l. margin*: villeins and fugitives] It is ordered to take John Isoud, Richard Isoud staying at Ely, Richard Isoud senior at Weston, Alice daughter of Thomas atte Nasshe at *Alrichessay* [Arlesey], John Hassh, Margaret Bond, Cecily Andreu, villeins and fugitives.
* Again just as many more times it is ordered to retain in the lord's hands one cottage formerly of John Colyn until etc. And one messuage with appurtenances whereof John Maistre died seised, and that fell into the lord's hands as forfeited, and to account for the profits.
* The jurors present that William Vynter \forgiven/, the tenants of the land of Yherdele \2d/, default, so are amerced.
* John Geiard is dead, who held of the lord one cotland, of which the heriot is one cow worth 8s. And John Geiard his son of full age is his next heir. And it is ordered to take [it] into the lord's hands until etc.
* John Boueton gives to the lord for licence to marry Ellen his daughter, 18d.

Court of Norton on Tuesday in the Eve of St George in the 39th year – John Mote [*22 Apr 1365*]

Jurors:	William Sayer	John Dipere	William atte Chirche
	John Boueton	Walter Thomas	Roger Albreth

EDWARD III

* The jurors present that William Vynter \forgiven/, Roger Quenehawe \2d/, William Dyke \forgiven/, Agnes Yherdele \forgiven/, John Bate \2d/, Elizabeth Mulleward \forgiven/, are in default.
* [*l. margin*: villeins and fugitives] It is ordered to take John Isoude, Richard Isoud staying at Ely, Richard Isoud senior at Weston, Alice daughter of Thomas atte Nasshe at *Alrichessey* [Arlesey], John Hassh, Margaret Bond and Cecily Andreu villeins and fugitives.
* John atte Hath surrendered into the lord's hand one messuage and one *ferlingate* of land called *Bondeslond*, of which the heriot in money is 6d. And the lord has granted the said messuage and land to John atte Wode and Margaret his wife, to hold to them and theirs in villeinage at the will of the lord by the due and accustomed services. And they give to the lord for agreement 6d.
* Reynald Balston gives to the lord as agreement for the marriage of Emma his daughter 18d.

Court of Norton on Friday next after the Feast of the Epiphany of the Lord in the 39th year – John Mote [*9 Jan 1366*]

Jurors: John Boueton   Walter Thomas   Roger Albreth
          John Dipere   William atte Chirche   John Smyth

* It is ordered to take John Isoud and Richard Isoud dwelling at Ely, Richard Isoud senior at Weston, Alice daughter of Thomas atte Nasshe at *Alrichesey* [Arlesey], John Hasshe, Margaret Bond and Cecilia Andreu, villeins and fugitives, and to bring them etc.
* The jurors present that William Dike \forgiven/, William Vinter \2d/, Roger Quenehawe \2d/, Nicholas Yerdele \2d/, Robert Yerdele Wright \2d/, John Bate and Walter Taillour \2d/ default, so are amerced.
* [*HALS 65518, f2*] Sarra Jecob made agreement with the lord for licence to marry. And she gives 6d.
* John Bate surrendered into the lord's hands one messuage and half a virgate of land formerly of Roger Prudde, of which the heriot is nothing because poor. And the lord has granted the said messuage and land with appurtenances to Walter atte Watre, to hold to him and his in villeinage at the will of the lord for the due and accustomed services. And the fine is forgiven.
* Walter Thomas surrendered into the lord's hand one cotland formerly of Isabella Hoges, and it shall remain in the lord's hands. And the beadle is ordered to account for the issues.
* The lord has granted to Walter Thomas one cotland formerly of Walter

EDWARD III

Reymound which Roger Frensh and Emma his wife lately held by right of the said Emma and they afterwards waived it, to hold to him and his in villeinage at the will of the lord by the due and accustomed services. And the substance is such that if anyone shall come and shall will to claim the said cotland, that he shall repay the same Walter for all the costs and expenses laid out around the said cotland before he may have seisin in the same. The fine is forgiven.

Court of Norton on Tuesday next after the Feast of St James the Apostle in the 40th year – John Mote [*28 Jul 1366*]

Jurors:	John Boueton	Walter Thomas	Roger Albreth
	John Diper	William atte Chirche	John Smyth

* William Sayer is dead who held of the lord two messuages and two half virgates of land with appurtenances, of which the heriots are two horses of which one is granted to the heir. After whose death William son of the same William being of full age is his next heir, who came and *gersummavit* the said messuage and land with appurtenances, to hold to him and his in villeinage at the will of the lord by the due and accustomed services. And he gives to the lord for *gersumma* and for heriot 26s 8d.
* [*r. margin*: villeins and fugitives] It is ordered as many times to take John Isoud, Richard Isoud dwelling at Ely, Richard Isoud senior at Weston, John Hassh, Margaret Bonde and Cecily Andreu villeins and fugitives.
* It is ordered to retain in the lord's hands one cotland, formerly of Isabelle Hoges, vacant. And to account for the profits.
* John Smyth complains of Walter Thomas in a plea of land in which he complains that he has disseised him of one acre of land lying in the *Malmes* between the land of William Sayer and the land of Lawrence Wysot which acre of land is parcel of one *ferlingate* of land which the same John acquired of Roger Frenshe and unlawfully retains etc to the damage etc. And the aforesaid Walter denies the force and injury. And he says that the said acre is parcel of one cotland which cotland he had by the lord's grant. And this he wishes to verify by a jury. And the aforesaid John likewise. Wherefore an inquest is charged therewith which says that a half acre of land lying next the land of Lawrence Wysot is parcel of the said *ferlingate* of land and ought to pertain to it by right and as to the other half acre of land which lies next the land of William Sayer they say that the said half acre of land is parcel of the said cotland and has belonged to it from the time which is no longer in memory. Therefore it is decided that the same John recover seisin of the said half acre of land lying next to the land of Lawrence Wysott. And the said

EDWARD III

Walter is amerced 2d for unjust detention. And as to the other half acre of land he is amerced 2d for a false plaint.
* Walter Taillour surrendered into the lord's hands one messuage and one croft of land adjoining containing one rood and lying at the *Grene* next to the land of John Smyth formerly of Roger Frenshe, of which the heriot in money is 9d. And the lord has granted the said messuage and croft with appurtenances to Thomas Plomere, to hold to him and his in villeinage at the will of the lord by the due and accustomed services. And he gives to the lord for agreement 9d. And he has done fealty.

Court of Norton on Tuesday next after the Feast of St Lucy the Virgin in the 40th year – John Mote [*15 Dec 1366*]

Jurors:	John Boueton	Walter Thomas	Roger Albreth
	John Dipere	William atte Chirche	John Smyth

* The jurors present that William Vintere \2d/, William Dyke\ 2d/, Robert Wright \2d/, Richard Yerdele \2d/, Roger Quenehawe \2d/, Geoffrey Adam \2d/, Clemence Dipere \2d/, default, so are amerced.
* [*r. margin*: villeins and fugitives] It is ordered as many times to take John Isoude, Richard Isoud dwelling at Ely, Richard Isoud senior at Weston, John Hassh and Cecily Andrewe villeins and fugitives, etc.
* Again it is ordered to retain in the lord's hands one cotland formerly of Isabella Hoges, vacant, etc. and to answer for the issues.

Court of Norton on Tuesday in the Feast of St Matthew the Apostle in the 41st year – John Mote [*21 Sep 1367*]

Jurors:	John Boueton	Walter Thomas	Roger Albreth
	John Dipere	William atte Chirche	John Smyth

* [*r. margin*: villeins and fugitives] It is ordered as many times to take John Isoud and Richard Isoud dwelling at Ely, Richard Isoud senior at Weston, [HALS 65518, f2v] John Hasshe, Margaret Bonde and Cecily Andreu villeins and fugitives etc.
* The jurors present that William Vinter \2d/, William Dyke \2d/, Roger Quenehawe \2d/, Robert Wright \2d/, Nicholas Yerdele \2d/, Clemence Dipere \2d/, John atte Hath \forgiven/, John atte Wode \2d/, default, therefore amerced.
* John the son and heir of Adam Smyth being of full age came and *gersummavit* one messuage and half a virgate of land with appurtenances called *Sheperdes*

EDWARD III

to hold to him and his in villeinage at the will of the lord by the due and accustomed services. And he gives to the lord for *gersumma* 3s 4d.
* John the son of Adam Smyth surrendered into the hands of the lord one messuage and half a virgate of land called *Sheperdes* of which the heriot in money is 3s 4d. And the lord has granted the said messuage and land with appurtenances to John Boueton, to hold to him and his in villeinage at the will of the lord by the services and customs due and accustomed. And he gives to the lord for agreement 3s 4d. And he did fealty etc.

Court of Norton, on Thursday in Easter Week in the 42nd year – John Mote [*13 Apr 1368*]

| Jurors: | John Boueton | Walter Thomas | Roger Albreth |
| | John Diper | William atte Chirche | John Smyth |

* The jurors present that William Vynter \afterwards he came/, William Dyke \2d/, the tenants of the lands formerly of Robert Cadewell \2d/, Geoffrey Mulleward \2d/ and Isabella his wife owe suit and default so are amerced
* [*l. margin*: villeins and fugitives] It is ordered as many times to take John Isoud, Richard Isoud dwelling at Ely, Richard Isoud senior at Weston, John Hassh, Margaret Bonde and Cecily Andreu, villeins and fugitives and lead them etc.
* Agnes daughter of Richard Bate junior gives to the lord for agreement for licence to marry, 12d.
* The jurors present that Reynald Balston has sown one rood of land of one *ferlingate* of land formerly of Henry Cok, vacant, with dredge and it lies next to *Stapelwey*, without leave of the lord. Therefore seise it into the lord's hands and answer for the issues.
* Next they present that William in the Hale has sown half an acre of land with wheat which he ought not to sow except every other year without leave of the lord. Therefore it is ordered to take it into the lord's hands and to account for the profits.

Court of Norton, on Monday next before the Feast of St Lucy, Virgin, in the 42nd year – John Mote [*11 Dec 1368*]

| Jurors: | John Boueton | Walter Thomas | Roger Albreth |
| | John Dipere | William atte Chirche | John Smyth |

* [*l. margin*: villeins and fugitives] It is ordered as many times to take John Isoud, Richard Isoud dwelling at Ely, Richard Isoud senior at Weston, John

EDWARD III

Hasshe, Margaret Bond, Cecily Andreu, and John Albreth villeins and fugitives etc and to lead them etc.

* The jurors present that William Vinte \2d/, William Dyke \2d/, Roger Quenehawe \2d/, Nicholas Yerdele \2d/, Robert Wright 3d, owe suit, make default, so are amerced.
* Richard Bate is dead, who held of the lord one cotland, of which the heriot is nothing and it is ordered to seise [it] into the lord's hands and to answer for the issues.
* The jurors present that Reynald Balston has felled four *elmes* [elms] in his tenement and sold them without leave of the lord, to damage 2d which it is ordered to levy.

Court of Norton on Thursday in the week of Pentecost in the 43rd year – John Mote [*24 May 1369*]

Jurors:	John Boueton	John Smyth	Robert Hayward
	John Dipere	William atte Chirche	Walter Thomas

* [*l. margin*: villeins and fugitives] It is ordered as many times to take John Isoud, Richard Isoud dwelling at Ely, Richard Isoud senior at Weston, John Hasshe, Cecily Andreu, and John Albreth villeins and fugitives etc.
* The jurors present that William Vyntere \2d/ and William Dyke \2d/ owe suit and make default, therefore amerced.
* Next they present that William in the Hale and John atte Hathe have not ground at the lord's mill to the damage of the miller etc.

[HALS 65518, *f3*] Court of Norton on Tuesday next before the Feast of St Michael in the 43rd year – John Mote [*25 Sep 1369*]

Jurors:	John Boueton	John Smyth	Walter Thomas
	John Dipere	William atte Chirche	

* [*l. margin*: villeins and fugitives] It is ordered as many times to take John Isoud, Richard Isoud dwelling at Ely, Richard Isoud senior at Weston, John Hassh, Cecily Andreu, and John Albreth villeins and fugitives etc.
* The jurors present that Robert Wright and Agnes his wife \2d/, Nicholas Yerdele and Amice his wife \2d/, Geoffrey Adam \2d/ default, therefore amerced.

EDWARD III

Court of Norton on Tuesday next before the Feast of St Peter which is called in Chains in the 44th year – John Mote [*30 Jul 1370*]
Jurors: John Boueton, John Dipere, John Smyth, William atte Chirche, Walter Thomas
* [*r. margin*: villeins and fugitives] It is ordered as many times to take John Isoud, Richard Isoud dwelling at Ely, Richard Isoud senior at Weston, John Hassh, Cecily Andreu, and John Albreth villeins and fugitives, and to bring them etc.
* Walter Roenhale and Agnes his wife, she having been questioned (*examinata*) surrendered into the lord's hand one toft with curtilage between the tenement of John in the Hale and the tenement of Laurence Wisot, of which the heriot in money is 6d. And the lord granted the said toft and curtilage with appurtenances to John in the Hale and Joan his wife to hold to him and his in villeinage at the will of the lord for the due and accustomed services. And they give the lord for agreement 6d.
* The jurors present that William Vintere \2d/, William Dyke \2d/, Clemence Dipere \2d/, default, therefore amerced.

Court of Norton on Tuesday next before the Feast of St Lucy the Virgin in the 44th year – John Mote [*10 Dec 1370*]

Jurors:	John Boueton	William atte Chirche	Roger Albreth
	John Smyth	Walter Thomas	William atte Hale

* Isabella Milleward is dead who held of the lord a moiety of one cottage and of one acre of land adjoining and a moiety of one rood called *Malotes* of which the heriot is one pig and it is sold for 4s. And John atte Wode a kinsman of the said Isabella is her next heir who came and *gersummavit* the said moiety with appurtenances to hold to him and his in villeinage at the will of the lord for the due and accustomed services. And he gives to the lord for agreement 2s.
* [*r. margin*: villeins and fugitives] It is ordered as many times to take John Isoud, Richard Isoud dwelling at Ely, Richard Isoud senior at Weston, John Hasshe, Cecily Andreu and John Albreth, villeins and fugitives etc.
* The jurors present that Walter Hayward has cut down two elms in his tenement and has sold them without leave of the lord, therefore amerced 2d.
* John atte Wode by leave of the lord has demised to Geoffrey Adam one cottage, one acre adjoining and one rood of land called *Malotes* formerly of Walter Mullewardes to hold unto him for the term of the life of the said

EDWARD III

Geoffrey in villeinage at the will of the lord for the due and accustomed services. And he gives for having the term 2s.

Court of Norton on Tuesday next before the Feast of St Peter which is called in Chains in the 45th year – John Mote [*29 Jul 1371*]

Jurors:	John Boueton	William atte Chirche	Roger Albreth
	John Smyth	Walter Thomas	William atte Hale

* [*r. margin*: villeins and fugitives] It is ordered as many times to take John Isoud, Richard Isoud dwelling at Ely, Richard Isoud senior at Weston, John Hasshe, Cecily Andreu and John Albreth, villeins and fugitives etc.
* The jurors present that William Vintere \2d/, William Dyke \2d/, owe suit and make default, so are amerced.
* John Fuller of full age came after the death of Richard Fuller his father and *gersummavit* one cottage with appurtenances situated between the tenement of Laurence Wysot and the tenement formerly of John Geiard, to hold to him and his in villeinage at the will of the lord by the due and accustomed services. And he gives to the lord for *gersumma* 6d.
* John Fuller surrendered into the hands of the lord one cottage with appurtenances situated between the tenement of Laurence Wysot and the tenement formerly of John Geiard, of which the heriot in money is 12d. And the lord has granted the said cottage with appurtenances to Richard Hobkyn to hold to him and his in villeinage at the will of the lord by the due and accustomed services. And he gives to the lord for agreement 12d.
* Matilda Dipere surrendered into the hands of the lord one messuage and half a virgate of land which messuage and land she formerly had of the gift of John Dipere her husband, of which the heriot is forgiven on account of poverty. And the lord has granted the said messuage and land with appurtenances to John Dipere to hold to him and his in villeinage at the will of the lord by the due and accustomed services. And the fine is forgiven.

[HALS 65518, f3v] Court held on Tuesday before the Feast of St Michael the 45th year – John Mote [*23 Sep 1371*]

Jurors:	John Boueton	William atte Chirche	Roger Albreth
	John Smyth	Walter Thomas	William in the Hale

* It is ordered as many times to take John Isoud, Richard Isoud dwelling at Ely, Richard Isoud senior at Weston, John Hassh, Cecily Andreu and John Albreth, villeins and fugitives etc.

EDWARD III

Court of Norton on Tuesday next after the Feast of St James the Apostle in the 46th year – John Mote [*27 Jul 1372*]

Jurors:	John Boueton	William atte Chirche	Roger Albreth
	John Smyth	Walter Thomas	William in the Hale

* [*l. margin*: villeins and fugitives] It is ordered as many times to take John Isoud, Richard Isoud dwelling at Ely, Richard Isoud senior at Weston, John Hassh, Cecily Andreu and John Albreth, villeins and fugitives and to bring them etc.
* The jurors present that Clemence Dipere \2d/, William Le Vintere \2d/, Nicholas Yerdele \2d/, Robert Wright \2d/ owe suit and default therefore etc.

Court of Norton on Monday next after the Feast of St Lucy the Virgin in the 46th year – John Mote [*20 Dec 1372*]

Jurors:	John Boueton	William atte Chirche	Roger Albreth
	John Smyth	Walter Thomas	William in the Hale

* The jurors present that William Dyke \2d/, Nicholas Yerdele 2d and Amice his wife[42] \2d/, Robert Wright and Agnes his wife \2d/, Thomas Palmere \2d/, owe suit and default so are amerced.
* They present that all the tenants have not ground at the lord's mill. Therefore they are commanded that henceforth they grind at the lord's mill under penalty of 20s.
* [*l. margin*: villeins and fugitives] It is ordered as many times to take John Isoud, Richard Isoud dwelling at Ely, Richard Isoud senior at Weston, John Hassh, Cecily Andreu and John Albreth, villeins and fugitives, and bring them to St Albans etc.

Court of Norton on Tuesday on the morrow of St James the Apostle in the 47th year – John Mote [*26 Jul 1373*]

Jurors:	John Boueton	William atte Chirche	Roger Albreth
	John Smyth	Walter Thomas	William in the Hale

* [*l. margin*: villeins and fugitives] It is ordered as many times to take John Isoud dwelling at Ely, Richard Isoud senior at Weston, John Hasshe, Cecily

---

[42] Husbands and wives together being fined for non attendance at the court. Possibly because their property is held in jointure. 'Joint feoffments' are also referred to.

EDWARD III

Andreu and John Albreth, villeins and fugitives, and bring them etc.
* They present that Nicholas Yerdele and Amice his wife \2d/, Robert Wright and Agnes his wife \2d/, William Vyntere \2d/, Clemence Dypere \2d/, Thomas Plomere \2d/, default therefore amerced.
* The jurors present that Thomas Plomere has cut down ten trees in his tenement without the lord's leave, to the lord's damage 2s, which it is ordered to levy etc.

Court of Norton on Tuesday in the Eve of St Matthew the Apostle in the 47th year – John Mote [*20 Sep 1373*]

Jurors:	John Boueton	Walter Thomas	William Sayer
	John Smyth	Roger Albreth	William atte Chirche

* The jurors present that William Vinytere \2d/, Robert Yerdele \2d/, Nicholas Yerdele \2d/, Clemence Dipere \2d/ make default, therefore amerced.
* Robert Hayward gives to the lord for agreement for the marriage of Agnes his daughter 12d.
* The lord has granted to John Freberne one cottage with curtilage which Walter late the vicar of Norton waived and it is situated between the vicarage and the croft of Roger Albreth, to hold to him and his in villeinage at the will of the lord by the due and accustomed services. And he gives the lord for agreement 12d.

Court of Norton on Tuesday in the Feast of St Leo the Pope in the 48th year – Robert Chestan [*27 Jun 1374*]

Jurors:	John Boueton	Walter Thomas	William Sayer
	William atte Chirche	John Smyth	Robert Hayward

* The jurors present that William Vynitere \2d/, Nicholas Yerdele \2d/, Robert Yerdele \2d/, Sarra Kadwell \2d/, William Dyke \2d/, default therefore amerced.
* [*HALS 65518, f4*] Thomas Plomere surrendered into the hands of the lord one cottage with adjacent land, one rood formerly of William Cok and one messuage and one *quartrona* of land formerly of John Hasshe, of which the heriot in money is 6s 8d. And the lord has granted the said cottage, messuage and land with appurtenances to Robert Lark, to hold to him and his in villeinage at the will of the lord by the due and accustomed services. And he gives to the lord for agreement 12d.

EDWARD III

* The lord has granted to John in the Hale one toft, one croft containing one acre and three roods of land formerly of Stephen Peverel, to hold to him and his in villeinage at the will of the lord by the due and accustomed services. And he gives to the lord for agreement 12d.
* The lord has granted to John Fuller one cottage with appurtenances situated between the tenement of Laurence Wysott and the tenement formerly of John Geiard which Robert Hobbekyn held and lately waived, to hold to him and his in villeinage at the will of the lord by the due and accustomed services. And he gives to the lord for agreement 2s.

Court of Norton on Tuesday next before the Feast of St Thomas the Apostle in the 48th year – Robert Chestan [*19 Dec 1374*]

Jurors:	William atte Chirche	William Sayer	Robert Hayward
	Walter Thomas	William in the Hale	Reynald Balston

* The jurors present that William Vyntere \2d/, Nicholas Yerdele \2d/, Robert Wright, Henry Fox \2d/, default so are amerced.
* Next they present that Richard Isoud is dwelling at Ely, William Bate at *Pekesden* [Pegsdon], John Bate in the court of the Lord the King, John Isoud at Weston therefore it is ordered to take them etc. [*r. margin*: villeins and fugitives]
* Thomas Olyve of full age came after the death of Thomas Olyve his father and *gersummavit* one toft and two crofts with half an acre lying by parcels whereof one croft is called *Olyves* and the other croft is called *Pernel*, to hold to him and his in villeinage at the will of the lord by the due and accustomed services. And he gives the lord for *gersumma* 3s 4d. And he has done fealty, etc.
* John Boueton surrendered into the hands of the lord one messuage and half a virgate of land formerly of Geoffrey Shepherd, of which the heriot in money is 20d. And the lord has granted the said messuage and land with appurtenances to John Boueton to hold to him for the term of his life so that after decease of the same John the said messuage and land with appurtenances shall for ever wholly remain to John the younger son of the same John, to hold to him and his in villeinage at the will of the lord by the due and accustomed services. And he gives to the lord for agreement 20d.

EDWARD III

Court of Norton on Monday on the Eve of the Apostles Philip and James in the 49th year – Robert Chestan [*30 Apr 1375*]

Jurors: William atte Chirche   William Sayer   Robert Hayward
         Walter Thomas   William in the Hale   Roger Albreth

* [*r. margin*: villeins and fugitives] It is ordered as many times to take Richard Isoud dwelling at Ely, William Bate at *Pekesden* [Pegsdon], John Bate in the court of the Lord the King, John Isoud at Weston, villeins and fugitives, etc.
* The jurors present that Henry Fox \2d/ and John Fuller \2d/ default, so are amerced.
* The lord has granted to William Vintere leave to place his fold on his land within the lordship and to drive his sheep to his fold so that he shall not pasture all his sheep in the fields within the said lordship. And the fine is forgiven.
* John Smyth is dead who held of the lord two messuages and two *quartron[as]* of land, of which the heriot is two horses worth 32s. And William his son, aged 14 years, is his next heir. And because the same William is under age, the lord has granted wardship of the land and of the heir to Christina the mother of the aforesaid William, to hold to her until the lawful age of the said William, in villeinage at the will of the lord by the due and accustomed services. And the fine is forgiven. And she has found pledges that she will not remove the mortuaries (*principalia*)[43] of the heir nor any testamentary legacies (*per testamentum legata*) by the pledge of John Boueton and William Sayer.

Court of Norton on Tuesday before the Feast of St Nicholas the Bishop the 49th year – Robert Chestan [*4 Dec 1375*]

Jurors: William atte Chirche   William Sayer   Robert Hayward
         Walter Thomas   William in the Hale   Roger Albreth

* [*r. margin*: villeins and fugitives] It is ordered as many times to take John \Richard/ Isoud dwelling at Ely, John Bate dwelling in the Court of the King, John Isoud at Weston, John Hasshe, villeins and fugitives, etc.
* William Dyke is dead who held freely of the lord 15 acres of land and

---

[43] These are the main household goods and farming equipment appurtenant to individual holdings; the goods which a tenant took over on entering a tenement and which it was his obligation to leave behind on his death or when he surrendered a holding.

EDWARD III

meadow. And William his son, aged ten years, is his next heir. Therefore it is ordered to seise the said land reserving the rights of anyone, until the lawful age of the said heir, etc.
* The jurors present that Amice Yerdele \2d/, Agnes Yerdele \2d/ and John Geiard \2d/ make default, so are amerced.
* The jurors present that Reynald Balston has let to John Moredon of Baldock one and a half acres of land lying in *le Malmes* without the lord's leave. Therefore let it be taken into the lord's hands, etc.
* Next they present that the same Reynald has let to Hugh Dunne one acre of land without the lord's leave. Therefore it is ordered as above.
* [*HALS 65518, f4v*] Next they present that Laurence Wysot has let to Alice Parson two acres of land without the lord's leave. Therefore it is ordered to seise [it] etc and to account for the issues.
* Robert Shepherd has surrendered into the lord's hands one cottage with croft adjoining containing one acre, formerly of William Cok, of which the heriot in money is 12d. And the lord has granted the said cottage and land with appurtenances to Walter Wilcok, to hold to him and his in villeinage at the will of the lord by the due and accustomed services. And he gives to the lord for agreement 12d.
* William Bate gives to the lord for agreement for licence to marry 12d.
* Margaret, who was the wife of Simon Cadewell surrendered one third part of one cottage which belonged to her after the death of the same Simon in the name of dower. And the lord has granted the said third part of the same cottage to John in the Hale, to hold to him and his in villeinage at the will of the lord by services etc. And the fine is forgiven.
* William atte Chirche surrendered into the lord's hands one cotland formerly of John in the Hale and it remains in the lord's hands, so it is ordered to account for the issues.

Court of Norton on Thursday next before the Feast of St Margaret the Virgin in the 50th year – Robert Chestan [*17 Jul 1376*]

Jurors:	John Boueton	William Sayer	William in the Hale
	Walter Thomas	William atte Chirche	Roger Albreth

* The jurors present that William Vyntere \2d/, and Christina Smyth \2d/, make default. Therefore amerced.
* Thomas Olyve has let to Roger Wheler three acres of land without the lord's leave. Therefore it is ordered to take [them] into the lord's hands and to account for the issues.

EDWARD III

* John Freberne surrendered into the lord's hands one cottage situated between the vicarage and the tenement formerly of Walter Swetkynne, of which the heriot in money is 6d. And the lord has granted the said cottage to Walter Wilcok, chaplain, to hold to him and his in villeinage at the will of the lord by the due and accustomed services. And he gives to the lord for agreement 6d.
* Walter Wilcok surrendered into the lord's hands one cottage with land adjoining containing in all one rood next to the tenement late of John Smyth, of which the heriot in money is 12d. And the lord has granted the said cottage and land with appurtenances to John Freberne, to hold to him and his in villeinage at the will of the lord by the due and accustomed services. And he gives to the lord for agreement 6d.
* Robert Lark has committed waste in his tenement formerly of John Hasshe and he is ordered to repair the said waste before the next court under penalty of 20s.
* [*l. margin*: villeins and fugitives] It is ordered as many times to take Richard Isoud at Ely, John Bate dwelling in the Court of the Lord the King, John Isoud at Weston, John Hassh, villeins and fugitives, etc.

Court of Norton on Monday next before the Feast of St Michael in the 50th year – Robert Chestan [*22 Sep 1376*]

Jurors:	John Boueton	William Sayer	William in the Hale
	Walter Thomas	William atte Chirche	Roger Albreth

* [*l. margin*: villeins and fugitives] It is ordered as many times to take Richard Isoud at Ely, John Bate dwelling in the Court of the Lord the King, John Isoud at Weston, John Hassh, villeins and fugitives, etc.
* The jurors present that William Vyntere \2d/, William Dyke \2d/, Stephen Leye \2d/, William Lorkyn \2d/, Geoffrey Adam \2d/, Henry Fox \2d/, John Fuller \2d/, Thomas Olyve \2d/ make default so are amerced.
* The lord has granted to William Bate one messuage and one *quartrona* of land, formerly of John Hassh, to hold to him and his in villeinage at the will of the lord by the due and accustomed services. And the fine is forgiven.

Court of Norton on Tuesday next after the Feast of St Ambrose in the 51st year – Robert Chestan [*7 Apr 1377*]

Jurors:	William atte Chirche	William Sayer	Roger Albreth
	John Boueton	William in the Hale	

EDWARD III

* The jurors present that William Vyntere owes suit and defaults, so is amerced 2d.
* Next they present that John Geiard has committed waste in his tenement so he is ordered to repair the said waste before the next court under penalty of losing [it].
* Thomas Olyve surrendered into the lord's hands one toft with croft adjoining formerly of Thomas Dryver containing one and a half acres of land, and one toft and one croft [HALS 65518, f5] and a half acre of land formerly of Walter son of John Dryver, of which the heriot in money is 20d. And the lord has granted the said toft and land with appurtenances to John Freberne, to hold to him and his in villeinage at the will of the lord by the due and accustomed services. And he gives to the lord for agreement 20d.
* The lord has granted to John Smyth one cottage and a moiety of half a virgate which John atte Wode recently surrendered into the lord's hands, to hold to him and his in villeinage at the will of the lord by the due and accustomed services. And the fine is forgiven.
* Matilda and Agnes daughters of Walter Thomas have licence to marry. And the fine is forgiven.
* It is ordered as many times to take Richard Isoud at Ely, John Bate dwelling in the Court of the Lord the King, John Isoud at Weston, and John Hasshe, villeins and fugitives, and to bring them etc.
* The lord has granted to John Smyth leave to remove one house from the tenement late of Walter Roenhale and to rebuild the said house in his tenement formerly of John atte Wode from the Feast of St Michael next to come for one year following and the said house is valued at 10s and unless he shall have rebuilt the said house within the said term in the said tenement he shall pay to the lord the aforesaid 10s, etc.
* The lord has granted to John Geiard a moiety of half a virgate of land formerly of William Neweman to hold to him and his in villeinage at the will of the lord by the due and accustomed services and the fine forgiven.

The number of folios written in this book of the Court of Norton contains 24.
[*The following pages are written in a different hand*]

RICHARD II

(*HALS DE/B2355/M/1/1/1*) The first of a series of folios in a new hand bound in the Hexton court book.

RICHARD II

[*HALS DE/B2355/M/1/1/1, f1*] **EXTRACTS FROM THE ROLLS OF HALIMOTES HELD AT THE MANOR OF NORTON IN THE TIME OF KING RICHARD II**

Court held there on Tuesday next after the Feast of St James the Apostle in the 1st year of the reign of King Richard II in the time of Brother Robert Chestan as cellarer [*28 Jul 1377*]

* [*l. margin in the same hand:* villeins] It is ordered just as many more times, to seize Richard Isoude at Ely, John Bate and John Isoud at Weston, John Hasshe at Holme, villeins and fugitives.

[Jurors:]	William atte Cherche	William Sayer	Roger Albreth
	John Boueton	William in the Hale	

* The jurors present that Nicholas Hayward 2d, John Geiard the miller 2d, are in default and so amerced.
* John Bouenton and William in the Hale are pledges for Laurence Wysod, that he shall repair the waste he committed in the tenement formerly of Thomas Hasshe before the next court under penalty of half a mark.
* A day is given to John Smyth to build one house of the new tenement called *Parlours* before the Feast of Easter, by the pledge of John Bradewey, under the penalty of 20s.
* A day is given to John Dipere to repair the waste committed in his tenement, and so it is ordered to repair it before the next court under the penalty of 3s 4d.
* The lord has granted to John Wright and Margery his wife one cottage one acre and three roods of land formerly of Walter Milleward, to hold to them, until the lawful age of John the son and heir of John atte Wode, in villeinage at the will [of the lord] for the services etc. The lord also has granted to the same the principal sum which amounts to 7s, to hold to them until the lawful age of the said heir. So, that is to say, that the aforesaid John and Margery agree to cause to be paid the principal or its equivalent value when the heir shall come of age.
* John Fuller surrenders into the hand [of the lord] one cottage situated next to the tenement late of John Love [*or Lone*], of which the heriot in money is 12d. And the lord has granted the said cottage with its appurtenances to John Smyth, to hold to him and his in villeinage at the will of the lord for the services etc. And he gives for the agreement 12d.
* Richard Wyther puts himself [upon the mercy of the court] for trespass in the lord's corn four times.

RICHARD II

The Court held there on Monday next before the Feast of St George in the 2nd year of the reign of King Richard II in the time of Brother Robert Chestan as cellarer [*18 Apr 1379*] [*HALS DE/B2355/M/1/1/1, f1v*]

Jurors: John Bouenton   William atte Cherche   William in the Hale
         William Sayer   John Gecob

* The jurors present that William Vinttere \2d/, John Geiard the younger \condoned/, William Dike \2d/, made default and so are amerced.
* Next they present that John Geiard the miller has alienated to John Geiard one cottage with two acres of land with appurtenances without the lord's permission and so it is ordered to seise into the hand of the lord and account to the lord for the income etc.
* Next they present that Cristina Smyth has committed waste on her holding to 12d worth of damage.
* Next they present that John in the Hale, shepherd, by his fault four sheep died because he did not guard them well in a certain icy rainstorm and also by his fault he lost two sheep, to 10s 8d worth of damage.
* Next they present that John Isoud at Weston, Richard Isoud at Ely, John Batte stay outside the lordship so it is ordered to seize them etc, and to bring them etc.
* [*l. margin:* villeins and fugitives] Next they present that John Geiard is staying with John Flexmere, Richard Geiard with Henry Frowyk, Agnes Bate at Chicksands, villeins and fugitives and to bring them etc. And Christina Smyth.
* The lord has granted to John Hassh one toft and half of one half virgate once of William Saman, to hold to him and his in villeinage at the will of the lord by services etc. And he gives to the lord for this agreement 2s.
* Christina Smyth finds as pledges John Bradwey and John Bouenton, that she will well and faithfully pay all her rent and perform services etc issuing from her tenement and from one *ferlingate* of land once of Reynald Sayer likewise, etc.

Court held there on Tuesday next before the Feast of St Ambrose in the 3rd year of the reign of King Richard II in the time of Brother Robert Chestan as cellarer [*3 Apr 1380*]

Jurors : John Bouenton   William Sayer   Roger Albrith
          William atte Chirche William in the Hale   Robert Hayward

RICHARD II

* The jurors present that William Vinytere \2d/, William Dike \2d/, Stephen ~~leyh~~ Leygh \2d/, William Lorkyn \2d/, make default and so are amerced etc.
* Next they present that John Malet makes default and so is amerced etc.
* Reynald Balton surrenders into the hand of the lord one ~~messuage~~ cottage and one cotland [*HALS DE/B2355/M/1/1/1, f2*] with the appurtenances formerly of Thomas Bene, of which the heriot in money is 12d. And the lord has granted the said cottage and cotland with their appurtenances to Nicholas atte Watre, to hold to him and his in villeinage at the will of the lord for services. And he gives to the lord for this agreement 12d etc.
* John Geiard surrenders into the hand of the lord one cottage, one garden with one croft adjoining, and two acres of land of which one acre lies upon *Cefforlong* and one acre lies upon *Gildrytthesdane*, of which the heriot in money is 12d. And the lord has granted the said cottage, garden, croft and land with their appurtenances to John Geiard the younger, to hold to him and his in villeinage at the will of the lord for services etc. And he gives to the lord for this agreement 12d.
* [*l. margin:* villeins and fugitives] It is ordered just as other times, to seize John Isoude staying at Weston, Richard Isoude at Ely, John Bate, William Geiard staying at Boreham with John Flaxmer, Richard Geiard with Henry Frowyk and Agnes Bate at Chicksands, villeins and fugitives.

The Court held there on Tuesday the Feast of St George in the 4th year of the reign of King Richard II in the time of Brother Robert Chestan as cellarer [*23 Apr 1381*]

Jurors:	John Bouenton	William Sayer	Roger Albrith
	William atte Chirche	William in the Hale	Robert Hayward

* [*l. margin:* villeins and fugitives] It is ordered just as so many more times to seize John Isoude staying at Weston, Richard Isoude at Ely, John Bate, William Geiard staying at Boreham with John Flaxmer, Richard Geiard with Henry Frowyk and Agnes Bate at Chicksands, both villeins and fugitives, etc.
* Walter the Vicar is convicted for his recognizance against Smyth so the same Walter owes to the same William and unlawfully keeps 20d for one lamb and two calves sold to the same William [*sic*] and so is amerced so he is ordered to pay.
* John in the Hale puts himself [upon the mercy of the court] for a licence to agree with John Cok in a plea of trespass.
* William atte Chirch the younger is convicted in full court against Roger Albreth for his recognizance in a plea, that he owes him 12d and withholds it

RICHARD II

unlawfully, for one lamb promised to him by an agreement made between them, so he is amerced and it is ordered to levy it.
* The jurors present that William Vynt[er] \2d/, William Dyke \2d/, owe suit and make default and so they are amerced etc.
* Next they present that John in the Hale has committed waste in the tenement formerly of Stephen Parnel, by digging one ditch upon which elms used to grow, and is therefore amerced etc.
* [DE/B2355/M/1/1/1, f2v] Next they present that John Wryghte and Margaret his wife have leased one cottage with two crofts of land containing one acre and three roods of land to William atte Chirche the younger without the lord's permission, and so it is ordered to seise [it] into the hand of the lord and to account for the income.
* John in the Hale is convicted by the inquisition against Reynald Balston in a plea concerning a broken covenant, to 6d damage of that Reynald, so amerced, etc.
* Reynald Balston is convicted by the inquisition against John in the Hale in a plea concerning a broken covenant to 4d damage of that John, and so is amerced, etc.
* John Wright and Margaret his wife by the lord's licence have leased to William atte Chirche the younger one cottage with two crofts of land containing one acre and three roods, to hold to him until the lawful age of John the son and heir of John atte Wode in villeinage at the will of the lord for services etc. And he gives to the lord for agreement 12d.

Court held there on Tuesday next after the Feast of St Leo the Pope in the 5th year of the reign of King Richard II in the time of Brother Robert Chestan as cellarer [2 Jul 1381]

[r. margin: another court of the 5th year follows][44]

Jurors:	John Bouenton	William Sayer	Roger Albreth
	William atte Chirch	William in the Hale	John Gecob

* [l. margin in the same hand: villeins] It is ordered, just as many more times, to seize John Isoud staying at Weston, Richard Isoud at Ely, John Bate [and] William Geiard staying at Boreham, Richard Geiard with Henry Frowyk and Agnes Bate at Chicksands and William Bate at Huntingdon outside the lordship, etc, therefore to seize them, etc.

---

[44] On f3v below (HALS: DE/B2355/M/1/1/1).

RICHARD II

* The jurors present that William Vyntere \2d/, William Dike \2d/, owe suit of court and make default, so they are amerced.
* Next they present that Laurence Wysot has leased to John Tece one acre and one rood and it is sown with dredge without the lord's permission, so it is ordered ~~to charge~~ to seise it into the lord's hand and to account to the lord for the income.
* Laurence Wysot is convicted by the inquest against William atte Chirche in a plea of detinue of chattels, 2s 6d which it is ordered to levy.
* Next Laurence is convicted by the inquest against William Smyth in a plea of trespass to 10d damage so is amerced and it is ordered to levy it.
* John in the Hale is amerced for a false plea against John Bouenton in a plea of trespass etc.
* John Bouenton the elder surrenders into the lord's hand half an acre of land lying at [HALS DE/B2355/M/1/1/1, f3] Grendyche between the land of Walter Day and the land formerly of Richard Bate. And the lord has granted the said land with its appurtenances to John Freb[ar]ne, to hold to him and to his in villeinage at the will of the lord for services. And [he gives] to the lord for the agreement 8d.

Court held there on Tuesday next before the Feast of St Ambrose in the 6th year of the reign of King Richard II in the time of Brother Robert Chestan as cellarer [*31 Mar 1383*]

Jurors:	John Bouenton	William in the Hale	John Gecob
	William Sayer	Roger Albreth	Walter Cok

* [*l. margin in the same hand:* villeins] It is ordered [as] many more times to seize John Isoud staying at Weston, Richard Isoud at Ely, John Bate, William Geiard staying at Boreham, Richard Geiard staying with Henry Frowyk, Agnes Bate at Chicksands, William Bate [at] Huntingdon, outside the lordship, therefore etc, therefore it is ordered to seize them.
* Next they present that William Dik defaults and so is amerced etc.
* Next they present that William atte Chirche has died, who held from the lord one messuage and half a virgate of land and one toft and one cotland formerly of John Isoude, of which the heriot is two horses worth 30s, and they are in the custody of the farmer (*firmarius*). And William his son of full age is his next heir, who came and paid *gersumma* for one messuage and half a virgate of land with their appurtenances, to hold to him and his in villeinage at the will of the lord for services. And he gives to the lord for *gersumma* 2s. And the toft and cotland formerly of John Isoud remains in the custody of the hand of

RICHARD II

the lord for want of a tenant, therefore it is ordered to account for the income, etc.
* Next they present that Robert Hayward has died, who held from the lord one messuage and half a virgate of land formerly [*sic*] with appurtenances, of which the heriot is one brass pot worth 12d. And John his son of the age of 13 years is his next heir. And because of the junior age of the said John the said messuage and land remains in the hand of the lord and so it is ordered to account for the income.

Court held there on Tuesday next before the Feast of St George in the 7th year of the reign of King Richard II in the time of Brother Robert Chestan as cellarer [*19 Apr 1384*]

Jurors:	John Bouenton	William in the Hale	John Gecob
	William Sayer	Roger Albreth	Walter Cok

* The jurors present that William Dik \2d\, William Vyntere \2d\, default and so are amerced etc.
* Next they present that William in the Hale has appropriated to himself from the soil of the lord one baulk in the nature of a boundary at *Banforlong* and is therefore amerced etc.
* [*HALS DE/B2355/M/1/1/1, f3v*] Next, they present that John Bouenton has committed waste upon his tenement and so it is ordered to repair the said waste before the next court under the penalty of 12d.
* John Bouenton surrenders into the hand of the lord one cotland called *Maydingodes*. And the lord has granted the said cotland with its appurtenances to Walter the Vicar of Norton, to hold to him and his in villeinage at the will of the lord for services, etc. And he gives to the lord for this agreement 2s.
* [*l. margin in the same hand:* villeins] It is ordered just as so many times, to arrest John Isoud staying at Weston, Richard Isoud at Ely, John Bate, William Geiard at Boreham, Richard Geiard staying with Henry Frowyk and William Bate at Huntingdon, villeins and fugitives, etc.
* John in the Hale and Agnes his wife, the daughter of Roger Albreth, give to the lord for agreement about their marriage 12d. [*l. margin:* villeins]
* The lord has granted to Thomas the household servant of Walter the Vicar of Norton one curtilage called *Ankerwyk* lying next to the graveyard, to hold to him and his in villeinage at the will of the lord for services, etc. And he gives to the lord for this agreement 4d.

RICHARD II

Court held held [*sic*] there on Tuesday next before the Feast of St Michael the Archangel in the 5th year of the reign of King Richard II in the time of Brother Robert Chestan as cellarer [*24 Sep 1381*]

Jurors:	John Bouenton	William atte Chirche	Roger Albreth
	William in the Hale	William Sayer	Robert Hayward

* It is ordered just as so many times to arrest John Isoud staying at Weston, Richard Isoud at Ely, John Bate, William Geiard at Boreham with John Flexmere, Richard Geiard with Henry Frowyk and Agnes Bate at Chicksands outside the lordship.
* The jurors present that William Vyntere \condoned/, William Dike \2d/, are in default and so amerced etc.
* John Geiard sues Thomas Burgate in a plea of trespass. And the said Thomas is attached by the pledge of John Brad\wey/ because he does not have anyone as a pledge and so is amerced. And it is ordered to seize (*attachiare*)[45] him in readiness for the next court.
* Nicholas Hayward sues Thomas Burgate in a plea of trespass concerning a pledge to prosecute etc. And the said Thomas is attached by the pledge of the bailiff and because he did not have anyone as pledge therefore he is amerced etc. And it is [ordered] to attach him in readiness for the next court.
* William Thomas sues Thomas Burgate in a plea of trespass. And the said Thomas is attached by the pledge of the bailiff and because he did not have anyone as pledge therefore he is amerced. And it is ordered that he be attached in readiness for the next court.
* John Bouenton is convicted by the inquisition against Daye in a plea of debt to 39s worth of damage so etc, which it is ordered to be levied etc.
* [*HALS 65519, f1*] Walter Wilcok, chaplain, surrenders into the hands of the lord one cottage with curtilage situated next to the vicarage (*juxta vicariam*), of which the heriot in money is 12d. And the lord has granted the said cottage and curtilage with its appurtenances to the said Walter to hold to him and his for the term of his life so that after the decease of the same Walter the said cottage and curtilage shall come to Thomas Wilcok, to hold to him and his in villeinage at the will of the lord for services etc. And they give to the lord for agreement 12d.

---

[45] *Attachiare* can mean to arrest or to seize goods, to force payment or attendance, ie distraint, and it is not clear which sense is meant here.

RICHARD II

Court held there on Tuesday next before the Feast of St Petronilla the Virgin, in the 8th year of the reign of King Richard II in the time of Brother Robert Chestan cellarer [*3 May 1385*]

Jurors: John Bouenton   William in the Hale   Walter [*no surname*]
           William Sayer   Roger Albreth

* The jurors present that William Dik \2d/, Stephen Leyr \2d/ and Amice his wife are in default, therefore amerced, etc.
* Next they present that William atte Cherche is dead, who held from the lord one messuage and half a virgate of land with appurtenances, [of which the heriot is] one cow worth 6s 8d. And John his son, of the age of four years is his next heir. And on account of his minority the lord has granted wardship of the said ~~heir~~ messuage lands and heir to William Clerk, to hold to him and his until the lawful age of the said heir, in villeinage at the will of the lord for services, etc. And he gives to the lord for having the term 12d.
* Next they present that John Geiard junior is dead who held from the lord three cotlands, one *quartrona* of land and one cotland of land and one cottage and two acres of land, of which [the heriots are] two cows, one horse and one sheep (*multo*). And William, his son, of the age of nine years is his next heir, therefore it is ordered to take it into the lord's hands and to account to the lord for the issues.
* Next they present that John Bouenton has committed waste in his tenement, so he is ordered to repair the said waste under penalty of 6d.
* Next they present that John Smyth has committed waste in his tenement by felling trees to the damage of 6d.
* The lord has granted to John in the Hale one messuage and half a virgate of land with appurtenances which John Draper afterwards abandoned [*waiviavit*], to hold unto him and his in villeinage at the will of the lord for services. And the fine is forgiven.
* Mortuaries (*Principalia*) of William Geiard *viz* one plough with coulter and ploughshare worth 2s, one brass pot and one plate worth 5s, one cart worth 18d, one bushel bound with iron worth 12d, one axe worth 4d, one *sedecod*[46] worth 3d, one harrow worth 4d, one threshing sledge (*tribula*) worth 2d, one mattock worth 6d, which remain in the custody of John Cokke.
* Mortuaries (*Principalia*) of John atte Chirche, *viz* one plough with all apparatus worth 4s 4d, one horse worth 8s, [*HALS 65519, f1v*] one brass pot and one plate worth 5s, one chest worth 5s, one barrel worth 3s 4d, 50 bushels

---

[46] A seedbag: cod is an Old English word for a bag (*OED*).

RICHARD II

worth 12d, one cart worth 3s, one saddle, one *hane*[47] and one pair of traces, worth 12d, one *sedecod* worth 2d, which remain in custody. Next one cask (*tina*) worth 4d.

Court held there on Monday next before the [Feast of the] Apostles Philip and James in the 9th year of the reign of King Richard II in the time of Robert Chestan cellarer [*30 Apr 1386*]

Jurors:	John Bouenton	William in the Hale
	William Sayer	Roger Albreth

* The jurors present that William Vyntere \2d/, William Lorkyn \2d/, William Dike \2d/, default, so are amerced etc.
* It is ordered just as many times, to seize John Bate dwelling at Huntingdon, Isoude at Weston, Andrew in the Hale at Huntingdon, William Geiard at Boreham, Richard Geiard at St Albans, villeins and fugitives etc and to bring etc.
* Next they present that Walter Daye who held from the lord one messuage and half a virgate of land is dead without heir, whose heriot [is] one horse worth 6s 8d. So it is ordered ~~to take them~~ to seise into the hands of the lord and to account for the issues.
* Next they present that John Bouenton has not repaired his waste as he was ordered to do at the last court, so it is ordered to levy 6d from the goods and chattels of the same John for the lord's use.
* Next they present that John Smyth \2d/ has committed waste in his tenement so he is ordered to repair the said waste by the next court under penalty of 3s 4d.
* The lord has granted to William Colwell one cotland with appurtenances formerly of Alexander Wysot and which Laurence Wysot once held and afterwards abandoned, to hold to him and his in villeinage at the will of the lord for services etc. And he gives to the lord for agreement 3s 4d.
* The lord has granted to John Frebarn one messuage and one croft of land containing half an acre situated between the tenements of John Smyth and of John Isoude which formerly Laurence Wysot once held and afterwards abandoned, to hold to him and his in villeinage at the will of the lord for services etc. And the fine is forgiven.
* The lord has granted to John Cok one messuage and one *quartrona* of land

---

[47] Written in the original as *hane*: from the context a misspelling of the English word hame.

RICHARD II

with appurtenances which John Geiard formerly held, to hold to him and his in villeinage at the will of the lord for services etc. And to the lord as agreement 2d is forgiven.
* The lord has granted to John Maltman one cottage, two acres of land and one cotland called *Wardeslond* which John Geiard held, whereof one acre lies at *Gildrischdene* and the other acre lies at *Cefforlong*, to hold to him and his until the lawful age of William Geiard the heir of the given lands. And he gives to the lord for the agreement 6d.
* [*HALS 65520, f1*] The lord has granted to John Scot one cottage with appurtenances which John Geiard formerly held, to hold unto him until the lawful age of William son and heir of the said John Geiard, in villeinage at the will of the lord, rendering for it for it [*sic*] annually to the lord for all services 2s, nor shall he commit waste, by the pledge of John Bradeweye.
* The lord has granted to Roger Albreth one cottage and one croft of land containing one rood which John Albreth formerly held, to hold to him and his in villeinage at the will of the lord, rendering for it annually to the lord for all services 13d.
* Matthew Tresth complains of Henry Tanner in a plea of debt, pledge of prosecution John Scot, therefore it is ordered to summon the said Henry against the next court to answer to the aforesaid Matthew in the aforesaid plea.
* Laurence Wysot is convicted by an inquest against John Maltman in a plea of debt of 3s 9d which it is ordered to levy for the use of the said John and the said Laurence is amerced for unlawful detention.
* Laurence Wysot complains of John Maltman in a plea of debt, pledge of prosecution William Sayer, therefore it is ordered to summon the said John to be here at the next court to answer to the aforesaid Laurence in the aforesaid plea.
* The same Laurence complains of the same John in a plea of trespass, by the aforesaid pledge, therefore it is ordered to attach the said John against the next court.

Court held there on Tuesday next after the Feast of St Tiburtius in the 10th year of the reign of King Richard II in the time of Brother Robert Chestan cellarer [14 Aug 1386]

Jurors:	John Bouenton	William in the Hale	John Gecob
	William Sayer	Roger Albreth	John Cok

* Laurence Wysot puts himself [upon the mercy of the court] for leave to agree with William Durnall in a plea of trespass.

RICHARD II

* [*l. margin*: villeins] It is ordered as many times to take John Bate dwelling at Huntingdon, John Isoude at Weston, Andrew in the Hale at Huntingdon, William Geiard at Boreham, Richard Geiard at St Albans, villeins and fugitives.
* Next they present that John Bouenton has committed waste in his tenement, so he is amerced etc. And he is ordered to repair the said waste before the next court under penalty of 3s 4d.
* Next they present that John Bouenton the younger has committed waste in his tenement, so he is amerced. And he is ordered to repair the said waste before the next court under penalty of 12d.
* Next they present that Nicholas Hayward has committed waste in his tenement, so he is amerced. And he is ordered to [*HALS 65520, f1v*] repair the said waste before the next court under penalty of half a mark.
* It was ordered at the last court to attach Henry Tannere to answer to Matthew Tressher in a plea of debt, which Henry is attached for three sheep worth 3s, therefore it is ordered to retain them and it is ordered just as other times to attach him against the next court.
* William Colwell is convicted, by an inquest, against John in the Hale in a plea of trespass to the damage of 8d, so etc.
* The same William is convicted by an inquest against John Hassh in a plea of trespass to the damage of 2d, so is amerced.
* John Maltman is convicted by an inquest against Laurence Wysot in a plea of debt to 2s 6d damage so is amerced, which it is ordered to levy, etc.

Court held there on Tuesday next before the Feast of St Ambrose in the 11th year of the reign of King Richard II in the time of Brother Robert Chestan cellarer [*31 Mar 1388*]

Jurors:	John Bouenton	William in the Hale	John Gecob
	William Sayer	Roger Albreth	John Cok

* The jurors present that William Wynter \2d/, William Dike \2d/ and Stephen Leye default, so they are amerced.
* Next they present that John Bouenton has committed waste in his tenement, so he is amerced. And he is ordered to repair the said waste before the next court under penalty of half a mark.
* Matthew Thressher is amerced because he has not prosecuted his plaint against Henry Tannere by the pledge of John Cook.

RICHARD II

Court held there on Tuesday next after the Feast of the Finding of the Holy Cross in the 11th year of the reign of King Richard II in the time of Brother Robert Chestan cellarer [5 May 1388]

Jurors:	John Bouenton	William in the Hale	John Gecob
	William Sayer	Roger Albreth	John Cok

* [*l. margin:* villeins] It is ordered as many times to take John Bate [dwelling] at Huntingdon, William Bate at *Newenton*, John Isoude at Weston, Richard Geiard at St Albans, and Richard Isoude at Ely, villeins and fugitives, etc, and to bring them etc.
* Next they present that William Vynter \2d/, William Lorkyn \2d/, Stephen Leye \2d/ and William Dike \2d/ default, so they are amerced.
* [*HALS 65521, f1*] Next that Agnes atte Hath has ended her last day without an heir, who held from the lord one cottage and one *quartrona* of land formerly of John Willesson, of which the heriot is one sheep worth 12d, so it is ordered to seise it into the hand of the lord and render account for the income.
* The testament of Agnes atte Hath is proved before Brother Robert Chestan the cellarer of the Monastery of St Albans in these words 'In the name of God Amen, etc'. The executor of the same testament is William Bowman and he is to have the administration of it.
* The lord has granted to John Maltman one messuage and one *quartrona* of land with appurtenances formerly of Agnes atte Hath, which certain messuage and land were seised into the hand of the lord because it was revealed by an inquisition that Agnes atte Hath died without an heir to it, to hold to him and his in villeinage at the will of the lord by services etc, the term to start from the Feast of St Michael next to come after the date of these present writings. And the fine is forgiven.
* John Maltman puts himself [upon the mercy of the court] for permission to make an out of court settlement with John in the Hale in a plea of trespass, so is amerced, etc.
* John in the Hale puts himself [upon the mercy of the court] for permission to make an out of court settlement with John Maltman in a plea of trespass, so is amerced, etc.

RICHARD II

Court held there on Tuesday the Feast of St Ambrose in the 14th year of the reign of King Richard II in the time of Brother Robert Chestan as cellarer [*4 Apr 1391*]

Jurors:	John Bouenton	Roger Albreth	John Botun the younger
	William Sayer	John Gecob	William Colwell
	William in the Hale	John Cok	

* The jurors present that William Vyntere \condoned/ and Stephen Leye \condoned/ default so they are amerced.
* Next they present that Thomas Willcok has sold one toft with curtilage called *Ankerys* to Nicholas Hayward and that Nicholas aforesaid has sold the said toft with curtilage to John Bette the chaplain, so it is ordered to seise it into the hand of the lord and to render account for the income.
* Next they present that William Hale has committed waste upon his tenement by cutting down two elms causing 2s 6d damage to the lord, which it is ordered to charge him and he is amerced etc.
* Next they present that the same William aforesaid has sold the two elms outside the lordship after which they have been seized by the bailiff and so he is amerced etc.
* Next they present that John Gecob has committed waste upon his tenement by cutting down six elms without the lord's permission, causing 5s damage to the lord, which it is ordered to levy and he is amerced etc.
* John atte Hale surrenders into the hand of the lord one cottage with curtilage situated between the tenement of John atte Hathe and the tenement of Laurence Wysot, of which the heriot in money [*sum not entered*] [*HALS 65521, f1v*] And the lord has granted the said cottage, curtilage, toft and curtilage with appurtenances to the said John in the Hale and Isabel his wife to hold to them and theirs in villeinage at the will of the lord by services etc. And they give to the lord for agreement [*sum not entered*].
* John Botonn senior surrendered into the lord's hands one hearth called *Halleorchard* lying between the tenement of William atte Chirche on the one hand and the tenement formerly John Smyth's on the other. And the lord has granted the said hearth with appurtenances to John Bradewey and Margery his wife, to hold to them and ~~theirs~~ the heirs of that John in villeinage at the will of the lord ~~by services~~ rendering thence thence [*sic*] annually to the lord as rent during the whole lives of John and Margery themselves 6s 8d for all services. And after the decease of the said John and Margery performing all other services.

RICHARD II

Court held there on Tuesday the Feast of St George in the 15th year of the reign of Richard II in the time of Brother Robert Chestan cellarer [*23 Apr 1392*]

* John Assh is convicted by the inquest against John in the Hale in a plea of trespass to 6d damage of the said John which it is ordered to levy and he is amerced.
* The jurors present that William Lorkyn defaults so he is amerced.
* Next they present that Roger Albreth is dead who held from the lord two messuages, half a virgate of land and one *quartrona* of land formerly Ralph Albreth's, of which the heriot is one horse and one cow. And Walter Albreth, his son, of full age, is his next heir, who came and *gersummavit* the said messuage and land with appurtenances, to hold to him and his in villeinage at the will of the lord by services etc. And the fine is forgiven.
* The testament of Roger Albreth is proved before Brother Robert Chestan, commissary, in these words, 'In the name of God Amen, etc'. And the administration of the goods of the said deceased is committed to Walter his son and to Alice his wife, his executors, and they shall have administration thereof.
* Walter Wilcok, chaplain, surrenders into the lord's hands one cottage with curtilage situated between the vicarage and the tenement of Roger Albreth of which the heriot in money, 6d, is forgiven. And the lord has granted the said cottage and curtilage to John Martyn, chaplain, to hold to him and his in villeinage at the will of the lord by services etc. And he gives to the lord 20d for agreement.
* Walter Wilcok the chaplain surrenders into the hand of the lord one cotland containing 12 acres of land formerly of John Boton. And the lord has granted the said cotland with appurtenances to John Martyn the chaplain, one toft with its curtilage called *Ankeryswyk* formerly of William atte Cherche, to hold to him and his in villeinage at the will of the lord, rendering for it annually to the lord 2d for all services except suit of court. And he gives to the lord for agreement 12d.
* [*HALS 65522, f1*] The lord has granted to John Martyn, chaplain, one toft with curtilage called *Ankery Wyk* formerly of William atte Chirche, to hold to him and his in villeinage at the will of the lord, rendering for it annually to the lord 2d for all services except suit of court. And he gives to the lord for agreement 8d.
* John Frebarne and Margery his wife, she having been questioned, surrender into the lord's hands one messuage and one croft of land containing in the whole half an acre of land formerly Roger Shepherd's, of which the heriot is

RICHARD II

6d. And the lord has granted the said messuage and land with appurtenances to Thomas Frere, to hold to him and his in villeinage at the will of the lord by services etc. And the fine is forgiven.

* The lord has granted to Thomas Frere one messuage and one *quartrona* of land formerly of Richard Assh to hold to him and his in villeinage at the will of the lord by services etc, and he gives to the lord for agreement 12d.

Court held there on Tuesday next before the Feast of St George in the 16th year of the reign of Richard II in the time of Brother Robert Chestan cellarer [*22 Apr 1393*]

Jurors:	William Bouenton	Walter Albreth	John Boton junior
	William Sayere	John Gecob	William Colwell
	John in the Hale	John Cok	

* The jurors present that William Colwell has committed waste in his tenement by permitting his houses to become ruinous, therefore amerced. He is ordered to amend the said waste before the next court under penalty of 3s 4d.
* John Boton senior surrenders into the lord's hand one acre of land lying in *Longe Croft* between the land of the lord and the land of Walter Albreth and one headland abuts upon above (*super super*) the croft of John in the Hale and another headland upon *Grenewey*. And the lord has granted the said land with appurtenances to Walter Bradewey, to hold to him and his in villeinage at the will of the lord by services etc. And the fine is forgiven.
* John Bradewey and Margery his wife, she having been questioned, surrender one hearth (*astrum*) called *Halleorchard* newly built [which] they lately acquired from John Boton senior situated between the tenement of William atte Chirche on the one side and the tenement of John Smyth on the other, of which the heriot is forgiven. And the lord by his special grace has granted the said hearth with appurtenances to the said John and Margery his wife, to hold to them for the term of their lives in villeinage [*HALS 65522, f1v*] at the will of the lord rendering for it annually to the lord during all their lives 3s 4d for all services except suit of court. And after their decease, the said hearth with appurtenances shall remain to Walter son of the said John and to Alice his wife, to hold unto them for the term of their lives by the abovesaid service. And [after] the death of the aforesaid Walter and Alice the aforesaid hearth with appurtenances shall remain to the rightful heirs of the aforesaid Walter and Alice by the service of 10s a year, to hold to them under the form and condition abovesaid. And the fine is forgiven.

RICHARD II

Court held there on Tuesday next before the Feast of Philip and James in the 17th year of the reign of Richard II in the time of Brother Robert Chestan cellarer [*28 Apr 1394*]

Jurors:	William Bouenton	Walter Albrethe	John Boton junior
	William Sayere	John Jecob	William Colwell
	John in the Hale	John Cok	

* John Assh is convicted by his acknowledgement of a debt to Walter Bradewey to his damage 4s 2d which it is ordered to levy and he is amerced.
* The jurors present that William Vynter made ~~waste~~ default, so he is amerced.
* Next they present that William Colwell has not repaired the waste made in his tenement as contained (*sicut habuit*) in the orders at the last court under penalty of 3s 4d, therefore let him incur the said penalty. And he is ordered to repair the said waste before the next court under penalty of 6s 8d.
* Next they present that John Jecob has committed waste in his tenement by allowing his houses to become ruinous, so he is amerced. And he is ordered to amend the said waste before the next court under penalty of 3s 4d.
* Next they present that the said John has committed waste by cutting down two elms to the lord's damage 2s 4d, which it is ordered to levy and he is amerced.
* William Geiard, brother of Agnes Geiard, of full age, comes after the death of the said Agnes and *gersummavit* one cottage with curtilage, to hold to him and his in villeinage at the will of the lord by services etc. And the fine is forgiven.
* William son and heir of John Geiard, of full age, comes after the death of the said John and *gersummavit* two cottages and two acres of land with appurtenances, to hold to him and his in villeinage at the will of the lord by services etc. And he gives to the lord 3s 4d for agreement and he has done fealty.
* John atte Wode, kinsman and heir of Isabel Milleward, of full age (*fidelicet*), son [*HALS 65522, f2*] of John atte Wode son of Agnes atte Wode sister of the said Isabel came and *gersummavit* one cottage with curtilage and two acres of land to hold to him and his in villeinage at the will of the lord by services etc. And he gives to the lord for agreement 6d.
* The lord has granted to Thomas Frere one messuage and one *quartrona* of land formerly of John atte Hath, to hold to him and his in villeinage at the will of the lord by services etc. And he gives to the lord for agreement 2s. And he has done fealty.
* The lord has granted to Thomas Salman one messuage and half a virgate of land formerly of Robert Hayward, to hold to him and his in villeinage at the

RICHARD II

will of the lord by services etc. And the fine is forgiven.
* The lord has granted to William Laweman one messuage and one *quartrona* of land formerly John Smyth's, to hold to him and his in villeinage at the will of the lord by services etc. And the fine is forgiven.
* The lord at the instance and petition of his tenants of the manor of Norton has granted to the same tenants to each of them holding half a virgate of land that he, for the whole time that John Bradeweye shall be farmer of the said manor, shall pay annually for his works in money 16s namely for works called *smalewerkes* and for ploughings of nine selions of land annually at the Feasts of the Nativity of the Lord, the Annunciation of the blessed Virgin Mary, the Nativity of St John the Baptist and Michaelmas in equal portions 9s 4d and for works of mowing and tossing hay annually at the Feast of the Nativity of St John the Baptist 8d. And for harvest works annually on the Feast of St James the Apostle 6s. Every tenant of half a virgate of land shall also pay annually at the Feast of All Saints for one bushel of grain for boonworks 6d.[48] And whoever shall hold more shall pay more and who shall hold less shall pay less according to the quantity of his holding, nothing being taken from the lord. And further, the lord has granted to the same tenants and to each of them that they for the whole time aforesaid should be charged [*burdened*] with ploughings for one week of ploughing. And the same tenants and each of them have agreed that if any of them should fail in any payment of the said money at any term of payment of the same that he who thus should fail in payment should do alone those works for which they should owe money according to the form of the grant aforesaid for all that year.

Court held there on Tuesday next before the Feast of St George in the 18th year of the reign of Richard II in the time of Brother Robert Chestan cellarer [*20 Apr 1395*]

Jurors:	John Boton senior	John Hassh	John Boton junior
	William Sayer	Walter Albreth	William Colwell
	John in the Hale	John Cok	

* John Hassh is convicted by his acknowledgement against William Daye in a plea of debt [*HALS 65522, f2v*] to the damage of the said William of 11½d which it was ordered to levy and he is amerced etc.
* John Boton is convicted by his acknowledgment against William Daye in a plea of debt to the damage of the said William of 6d which it was ordered to

---

[48] *Frumenti de Beuside* may alternatively read *Frumenti de Benside*.

RICHARD II

levy and he is amerced etc.
* Next it is presented that Stephen Leye has made default so he is amerced.
* John Cok surrenders into the lord's hand one toft and one cotland formerly Stephen Clerk's, whose heriot is forgiven. And the lord has granted the said toft and cotland with appurtenances to John Maysent and Margery his wife, to hold to them and theirs in villeinage at the will of the lord by services etc. And the aforesaid John Maysent has found one pledge that he would well and faithfully maintain the said toft and cotland without waste *viz* the aforesaid John Cok. And the fine is forgiven.
* John Hassh surrenders into the lord's hand all his estate and term which he has in one messuage and half a virgate of land formerly William atte Hale's. And the lord has granted the said estate and term, messuage of term with appurtenances to Nicholas Taillour, to hold to him and his in villeinage at the will of the lord by services etc. And the fine is forgiven. And he has done fealty.
* Thomas Frere surrenders into the lord's hand one messuage and half an acre of land formerly of Laurence Wysot, of which the heriot is forgiven. And the lord has granted the said messuage and land with appurtenances to John atte Brugge, to hold to him and his in villeinage at the will of the lord by services etc. And the fine is forgiven. And he has done fealty.
* Thomas Salman is convicted by his acknowledgement against Walter Badewey [*sic*] in a plea of debt to the damage of the said Walter 13s, which it is ordered to levy, and he is amerced etc.
* The lord has granted to William Colwell one *quartrona* of land with appurtenances formerly Alexander Wysot's, to hold to him and his in villeinage at the will of the lord by services etc. And And [*sic*] he gives to the lord for agreement six chickens etc.
* William Lawman surrenders one messuage and one *quartrona* of land formerly of John Laweman senior[49] whose heriot is forgiven, and the lord has granted the said messuage and land with appurtenances to John Laweman, to hold to him and his in villeinage at the will of the lord by services etc. And the fine is forgiven.
* The lord has granted to William Geiard one hearth and one cotland formerly of Alexander Warde, to hold to him and his in villeinage at the will of the lord by services etc. And the fine is forgiven.
* The lord has granted to John Bradeweye and Margery his wife one croft of land called *Hale Croft* containing eight acres and one rood of land lying

---

[49] John Lawman senior's will was proved in the St Albans Archdeaconry court in 1420 (HALS: 1AR6v). The Norton court records for the period 1416-23 are missing.

RICHARD II

between the land of William [*HALS 65522, f3*] atte Cherche on one side and land of John Laweman on the other and one headland abutts upon *Hallewyke* and another headland upon a headland called *Londhedlond* to hold to them for the term of their life in villeinage at the will of the lord, rendering for it annually to the lord 3s 4d for all services except suit of court. And after the decease of the aforesaid John and Margery his wife the aforesaid croft of land with appurtenances shall remain wholly to Walter Bradeweye and Alice his wife, to hold to them for the term of their life in villeinage at the will of the lord, rendering for it annually to the lord 3s 4d for all services except suit of court. And the fine is forgiven.

Court held there on April 11th in the 19th year of the reign of Richard II in the time of Brother Robert Botheby cellarer [*11 Apr 1396*]

Jurors:	John Boton senior	Walter Albreth	John Boton junior
	William Sayere	John Hassh	William Colwell
	John in the Hale	John Cok	

* The jurors present that William Vynter \forgiven/, Stephen Leye \2d/ and William Leye \2d/ default so etc.
* Next they present that John Gecob is dead, who held from the lord one messuage and half a virgate of land once of John Jecob his father, and one cottage and one cotland formerly Roger Prudde's, of which the heriots are two horses worth 20s. And John Jecob his son of full age is his next heir who came and *gersummavit* the said messuage, cottage and land with appurtenances. And he gives to the lord for agreement 10s. And he has done fealty.
* Next they present that John Boton \the elder/ has committed waste in his tenement by permitting his houses to be ruinous. He is to amend the said waste before the next court under penalty of 6s 8d.
* John Martyn, chaplain, surrenders into the hand of the lord one cottage with curtilage situated between the vicarage and the tenement of Roger Albreth, formerly of Walter Wilcok, chaplain, one cotland containing 12 acres of land formerly of John Boton and one toft with curtilage called *Ankerswyk*, formerly of Walter atte Cherche of which the heriots are two horses worth 26s 8d. And the lord has granted the said cottage with curtilage, the said cotland and the said toft with curtilage called *Ankerwyk* to Justine Martyn, to hold to her and hers in villeinage at the will of the lord by services etc, and by rendering thence annually to the lord for the said toft with curtilage called *Ankereswyk* 2d for all services except suit of court. And she gives to the lord for

RICHARD II

agreement 3s 4d.

* The lord has granted to John Laweman one messuage and half a virgate of land formerly of Walter Daye to hold to him and his in villeinage at the will of the lord by services etc with the free rent of the same messuage pertaining to the office of bursar during the term of four [years?] after the date of the court next to come only (*dumtaxat*)[50] excepted. And after the end of four years rendering all services, rents, [*HALS 65522, f3v*] and customs etc. And the purpose is such that the aforesaid John shall according to his ability well build and maintain a certain barn being in the said messuage. And the fine is forgiven.

Court held there on Tuesday in the Feast of the Apostles Philip and James in the 20th year of the reign of Richard II in the time of Robert Botheby cellarer [*1 May 1397*]

Jurors:	John Boton senior	Walter Albreth	John Boton junior
	William Sayere	John Hassh	William Colwell
	John in the Hale	John Cok	

* John Cok is convicted by his acknowledgement against William Geiard in a plea of debt to 3s damage of the said William, which it is ordered to levy and he is amerced.
* The jurors present that William Vyntere \2d/ and Stephen Leye \2d/ have made default so they are amerced.
* Next they present that John Boton senior has not repaired his waste committed upon his tenement just as contained in the orders at the last court under penalty of 6s 8d, therefore he shall incur the said penalty and is ordered to amend before the next court under penalty of 13s 10d.
* Next they present that Nicholas atte Water has committed waste in his tenement by allowing his houses to be ruinous, so he is amerced, etc. And he is ordered to amend the said waste before the next court under [penalty of] 6s 8d.
* Next they present that John Laweman has committed waste in his tenement formerly Ralph Daye's, so he is amerced. And he is ordered to amend the said waste before the next Feast of St Michael which shall be in the year after the Feast of St Michael after the date of this court next to come, under penalty of four pounds, and upon this he has found pledges *viz* William Laweman and William Colwell.

---

[50] *Dumtaxat* means literally at least or at most.

RICHARD II

* Next they present that William Geiard has planted willows on the lord's land, so he is amerced. And he is ordered to amend etc.
* Next they present that John Smyth is dead without heir, who held from the lord one cottage and one *quartrona* of land, formerly of John atte Wode and one cottage with appurtenances formerly of John Fuller, of which the heriots are two sheep worth 2s. And it is to seise the said cottages and land with appurtenances into the lord's hand until etc and to account for the income. And thereupon the lord has granted the said cottages and land with appurtenances to Beatrice Smyth, wife of the said John, to hold to her and hers in villeinage at the will of the lord by services, etc. And the form is this that if any heir should come and claim the said cottages and land he shall satisfy Beatrice for all the expenses and outlay spent upon the said cottages and land before he shall have entry to the same by the view and consideration of the whole Homage. And she gives to the lord for agreement six chickens.
* [*HALS 65522, f4*] Justine Martyn surrenders into the hands of the lord one cottage with curtilage situated between the vicarage and the tenement of Roger Albreth which formerly was Walter Wilkok's, chaplain, of which 2s heriot in money is forgiven. And the lord has granted the said cottage and curtilage with appurtenances to Thomas Love and Alice his wife to hold to them and theirs in villeinage at the will of the lord by services etc. And he gives to the lord for agreement 2s.
* The testament of John Smyth was proved before Brother Robert Botheby, commissary for this matter, of which the tenor follows in these words, 'In the name of God amen etc'. And administration of the goods of the said deceased was granted to Beatrice his wife and she shall have the administration thereof etc.
* John atte Wode surrenders into the hands of the lord one messuage and two acres of land formerly of Walter Milleward situated between the tenement formerly John Wilkyn's and the tenement of John Tallard, the heriot of which is 3s 4d in money. And the lord has granted the said messuage and land with appurtenances to Joan Lyle to hold to her for the term of her life only, and after the decease of the said Joan the said messuage and land with appurtenances shall remain to Walter Bradeweye her son, to hold to him and his in villeinage at the will of the lord by services etc. And he gives to the lord for agreement 6s 8d.

RICHARD II

Court held there on Tuesday next after the Feast of Easter in the 21st year of the reign of Richard II in the time of Brother Robert Botheby cellarer [*9 Apr 1398*]

Jurors:	John Boton senior	John Hassh	William Colwell
	John in the Hale	John Cok	William Sayere
	Walter Albreth	John Boton	

* William Sayere junior is convicted by his acknowledgment against John Hale in a plea of debt to the injury of the said John of 9d which it is ordered to levy etc.
* John Hassh is convicted by his acknowledgment against Walter Albreth in a plea of debt to the injury of the said Walter of one quarter and two bushels of barley which it is ordered [to levy] and he is amerced.
* The jurors present that William Wynter \2d\ and Simon Leye \2d\ make default so they are amerced.
* Next they present that John Boton senior has committed waste in his tenement by allowing houses to become ruinous, so he is amerced. And he is ordered to repair the said waste before the next court under penalty of losing the aforesaid tenement.
* Next they present that John Hassh has committed waste in his tenement by allowing his houses to become ruinous, so he is amerced. And he is ordered to repair the said waste before the next court under penalty of 6s 8d.
* [*HALS 65522, f4v*] Walter Bradewey and Alice his wife, she having been questioned, have surrendered into the hands of the lord one messuage and one acre and a half of land formerly of John atte Wode situated between the tenement formerly John Wylkyn's and the tenement of John Tallard, of which the heriot in money is 3s 4d. And the lord has granted the said messuage and land with appurtenances to William Colwell and Joan his wife to hold to them and to the heirs of that William in villeinage at the will of the lord by services etc. And he gives to the lord for agreement 3s 4d.
* John atte Wode surrenders into the hands of the lord half an acre formerly of Walter Milleward, lying between the croft of John Botonn junior and the land formerly of Richard Haston. And the lord has granted the said land with appurtenances to Walter Bradewey to hold to him and his in villeinage at the will of the lord, rendering for it yearly to the lord 2d for all services except suit of court. And the fine is forgiven.
* The lord has granted to Walter Bradewey two butts of land formerly of John Warde lying between land of William Geiard and the croft called *Swetkynnes*,

RICHARD II

to hold to him and his in villeinage at the will of the lord, rendering for them yearly to the lord 4d for all services except suit of court.

Court held there on Wednesday next after the Feast of St Ambrose, in the 22nd year of the reign of Richard II in the time of Brother William Heyworth cellarer [*9 Apr 1399*]

Jurors:	William Laweman	John Hassh	William Colwell
	Walter Albreth	John Cok	William Sayere
	John in the Hale	John Boton junior	

* The jurors present that William Wyntere \2d/, the tenants \2d/ of Jakemanes Puncard make default so they are amerced.
* Next they present that John Hassh has not repaired his waste committed in his tenement by allowing his houses to become ruinous, as contained in the orders at the last court under penalty of 6s 8d, therefore he should incur the aforesaid penalty. And he is ordered to repair the said waste before Michaelmas under penalty of 13s 4d.
* Next they present that Nicholas atte Water has not repaired his waste committed in his tenement by allowing his houses to become ruinous as contained in the orders at the last court under penalty of 6s 8d, therefore he should incur the aforesaid penalty. And he is ordered to repair the said waste before Michaelmas under penalty of 13s 4d.
* Next they present that John Laweman has not repaired his waste committed in the tenement [*HALS 65522, f5*] formerly Ralph Daye's as in the orders at the court held at Norton in the 20th year of Richard II under penalty of four pounds, so he should incur the aforesaid penalty and he is ordered to repair the said waste etc and furthermore it is ordered to seise into the lord's hands all the lands and tenements which the same John holds of the lord until etc.
* Reserving the right of anyone, the lord has granted to Henry Ronhale one messuage and half a virgate of land which John Jacob lately abandoned to hold to him and his in villeinage at the will of the lord by services etc. And it is like this, that if any heir should come and wish to claim the said messuage and land, that he shall satisfy the same Henry for all his costs and expenses laid out around the said messuage and land before he shall have entry to the same by the view and discretion of the whole Homage. And he gives to the lord for agreement two capons.
* It is ordered to take into the lord's hands all the lands and tenements which John Boton held of the lord for the waste that has been made in the same, until etc.

HENRY IV

NORTON IN THE TIME OF KING HENRY IV

[*HALS 65522, f5v*] **Court held on Tuesday before the Feast of the Apostles Philip and James in the 1st year of the reign of King Henry IV in the time of Brother William Heyworth cellarer [*27 Apr 1400*]**

Jurors:	William Laweman	John Hasshe	William Sayere
	Walter Albreth	John Cok	William Colwell
	John in the Hale	John Boton junior	

* It is ordered to take Andrew in the Hale at *St Neodum* [St Neots] and William Bate at *Radeswell* [Radwell], villeins and fugitives etc and to bring them to St Albans etc. [*l. margin*: villeins]
* The jurors present that William Vyntere \2d/, Thomas Polley \2d/, William Gravele \2d/, Master John Cook \2d/, John Smyth \remitted/ and William Fermer \4d/ default so they are amerced.
* Again John Hassh is ordered to have repaired the waste he has committed in his tenements by the next court under penalty 13s 4d.
* Again Nicholas atte Water is ordered to have repaired the waste he has committed in his tenements by the next court under penalty 13s 4d.
* Next they present that William Wyntere has unjustly received and impounded divers beasts of divers tenants of Norton in *Mundescroft* so he is amerced.
* John Laweman is elected as the lord's beadle and collector of the lord's rent and is sworn.
* Matilda Hayward surrendered into the lord's hands one toft with curtilage formerly of John in the Hale, heriot three chickens (*pulcini*), and the lord has granted the said toft and curtilage with its appurtenances to Richard Frere to hold to him and his in villeinage at the will of the lord by the services etc. And he gives to the lord for agreement three chickens.
* Justina Martyn surrendered into the hands of the lord 12 acres of land lying in the field of Norton in divers parcels which were formerly of John Martyn, chaplain, and the lord has granted the said land with appurtenances to John Frebarne to hold to him and his in villeinage at the will of the lord by services etc. And he gives to the lord for agreement two capons.

HENRY IV

Court held on Wednesday after Easter week in the 2nd year of the reign of King Henry IV in the time of Brother William Heyworth cellarer [*13 Apr 1401*]

[Jurors:] William Laweman   John Cok   William Sayere
         Walter Albreth   John Boton
         John in the Hale   William Colwell

* [*HALS 65523, f1*] John Dipere puts himself [upon the mercy of the court] for leave to agree with William Geiard in a plea of debt to 2s 3d damage of the said William which it is ordered to levy and he is amerced.
* John Laweman is convicted, by his acknowledgment, against John atte Chirche in a plea of debt to 2s damage of the said John, which it is ordered to levy and he is amerced.
* The jurors present that William Vynter \2d/, Thomas Poley \2d/, Richard Easton \2d/, Margaret Guele \2d/, John, kinsman of the rector of *Wylye* [Willian] \2d/ for the tenement lately of Robert Cornmongere make default so they are amerced, etc.
* Next they present that Thomas Salmon is dead who held from the lord one messuage and half a yardland of which the heriot is one horse value 12s. And Mabel wife of Thomas Frere is his next heir, so it is ordered to take [it] into the lord's hands until etc.
* Next they present that John Hassh has ended his last day, who held from the lord one cottage and one cotland, whose heriot [is] one sheep, value 16d. And Amice his daughter aged [*blank*] years is his next heir so it is ordered to take [them] into the lord's hands until etc.
* Next they present that John Colwell has committed waste in his tenement by allowing his house to be ruinous therefore amerced. And it is ordered to repair the said waste before the next court under penalty of 2s.
* Next they present that Beatrice Salmon has committed waste in her tenement by allowing her house to be ruinous therefore amerced. And it is ordered to repair the said waste before the next court under penalty of 2s.
* Next they present that Richard Frere has ended his last day, who held from the lord one toft with curtilage formerly John in the Hale's, whose heriot [is] one sheep with a lamb worth 16d. And John Frere the elder, his brother, of full age is his next heir. And it is ordered to take [it] into the hands of the lord until etc.
* The will of Thomas Salmon was proved before Brother William Heyworth, cellarer, commissary in this case of which the substance follows in these words 'In the name of God Amen'. And administration of the goods of the

HENRY IV

said deceased [is] granted to Felicia his wife and to John in the Hale his executors and they have administration in the form of law etc.
* John in the Hale is elected to the office of beadle and is sworn.
* Again it is ordered to take into the lord's hands one toft and all the land formerly of Walter Sayere because John Laweman has committed waste in the same and to answer to the lord for the issues.
* John Laweman complains of John atte Chirche in a plea of debt, pledge of prosecution, the bailiff, [*HALS 65523, f1v*] and in which it is pleaded that he owes to him and unjustly detains 3s 4d for two sheep killed by the said John, damage 20d. And the aforesaid John, present in court, denies the force and injury etc and says that he is not guilty and demands that it be inquired into; and the said John likewise. And they have a day until the next court.
* The lord granted to William Taillour one messuage and half a yardland of land formerly of John Boton, reserving the right of anyone, to hold to him and his in villeinage at the will of the lord by services etc, the free rent of the said tenement being excepted for a term of three years when levied. And after the term of three years all services, rents etc to be rendered. And the fine is condoned.

Court held there on Tuesday in the Feast of St Ambrose in the 3rd year of the reign of King Henry IV in the time of Brother John Blebury cellarer [*4 Apr 1402*]

Jurors:	William Laweman	John Cok	William Sayere
	Walter Albreth	John Boton junior	
	John in the Hale	William Colwell	

* [*l. margin:* villeins and fugitives] Again it is ordered as many times to take John Isoude at Weston, William Bate at Baldock, Andrew Hale at Willingham, William Boton at Wallington and William Bacon, villeins and fugitives etc and to bring them to St Albans etc.
* The jurors present that William Vynter \2d/, Thomas Taillour \2d/ [and] the tenants of Robert Cornemongere \2d/ make default, therefore they are amerced.
* Next they present that Beatrice Salman committed waste in her tenement by allowing her house to be ruinous. And she is ordered to repair the said waste before the next court under penalty of 6s 8d.
* John Laweman, because he has not prosecuted his plaint against John atte Chirche in a plea of debt so he is amerced.
* Next they present that Agnes Hassh has committed waste in her tenement by

HENRY IV

allowing her house to be ruinous so she is amerced. And she is ordered to repair the said waste before the next court under penalty 6s 8d.
* The lord has granted to Agnes Hassh one cottage and one cotland which Amice Hassh daughter of John Hassh lately gave up to hold to her and hers in villeinage at the will of the lord by services etc. And the fine is two capons.
* John Frere brother and heir of John Frere of full age came and *gersummavit* [*HALS 65524, f1*] one toft with curtilage formerly of John in the Hale. To hold to him and his in villeinage at the will of the lord for services etc. Fine two capons.
* It is ordered to levy from William Saiere 6d for one peck of corn, one peck draget and three pecks of oats for the use of John in the Hale which he recovered against him in the court.
* The lord granted to Simon in the Hale one messuage and half a virgate of land formerly of Thomas Salman which messuage and land Thomas Frere and Mabel his wife is next heiress of the said Thomas *viz* sister of the said Thomas Salman lately gave up, to hold to him and his in villeinage at the will of the lord by services etc. Fine two capons.
* Beatrice Salman surrendered into the hand of Lord Walter Bradewey the third part of one messuage and half a virgate of land which belongs to her by the gift of Thomas Salman lately her husband. And the lord has granted the said third part to Simon in the Hale to hold to him and his in villeinage at the will of the lord for services etc. Fine two capons.
* The lord has released to John in the Hale and Isabel his wife a certain annual rent of 18½d which they used to pay for one croft of land called [*blank*] for the term of their life so that after the decease of the aforesaid John and Isabel his wife [and] their heirs may have and hold the said croft of land with appurtenances, doing and rendering all due and accustomed services.
* The first proclamation made according to the custom of the manor concerning vacant lands and tenements being in the lord's hands, that the heirs of the aforesaid land and tenements shall come and lay their claims to the aforesaid lands and tenements before the third court to be held, under penalty of eviction from the aforesaid lands and tenements.

Court held there on Tuesday before the Feast of St George in the 4th year of the reign of Henry IV in the time of Brother John Blebury cellarer [*17 Apr 1403*]

Jurors:	William Laweman	John Cok	William Sayere
	Walter Albreth	John Boton junior	
	John in the Hale	William Colwell	

HENRY IV

* [*l. margin*: villeins] Again it is ordered as many times to take John Isoude at Weston, William Bate [*HALS 65524, flv*] in Baldock, Andrew Hale at Willingham, William Boton at Wallington and William Bacon are villeins and fugitives etc and to bring them to St Albans.
* The jury present that William Vynter \2d/, Thomas Badewelle \2d/, John Saunford \2d/ default, so they are amerced.
* Next they present that Justina Martyn has ended her last day, who held from the lord one toft called *Ankerswyk*, of which the heriot is nothing because she had nothing within the lordship and Margaret her daughter, wife of Hugh Smyth is her next heir. And it is ordered to siese into the lord's hands until etc.
* Next they present that William Taillour has committed waste in the tenement of Beatrice Salman by allowing her house to be ruinous, therefore amerced, etc. And he is ordered to repair before the next court under penalty of half a mark.
* [*l. margin*: villeins] John atte Cherche, son and heir of William Atte Chirche of full age came into the court and *gersummavit* one messuage and half a virgate of land formerly of William atte Cherche to hold to him and his in villeinage at the will of the lord for services etc. And he gives to the lord for an agreement for licence to marry 12d.
* The lord has granted to William Colwell one toft and one *quartrona* of land formerly of John Tollard to hold to him and his in villeinage at the will of the lord for services etc. Fine six chickens.
* The lord has granted to John in the Hale the younger one *quartrona* of land formerly of John Reymond, to hold to him and his in villeinage at the will of the lord for services etc. Fine six chickens.
* The lord has granted to Henry Ronhale one cotland, formerly of Reynald Bolston, to hold to him and his in villeinage at the will of the lord for services etc six chickens.
* A second proclamation was made according to the custom of the manor concerning vacant lands and tenements being in the hands of the lord, that the heirs of the aforesaid land and tenements may come and make their claims to the aforesaid lands and tenements before the third court to be held, under penalty of eviction from the said lands and tenements.
* The lord has granted to John atte Hatthe and Joan his wife one toft and one cotland formerly of Richard Bate senior, to hold to him and his in villeinage at the will of the lord for services etc. And the fine is six chickens.

HENRY IV

[*HALS 65525, f1*] **Court held there on Tuesday after the close of Easter in the 5th year of the reign of Henry IV in the time of Brother John Blebury cellarer [*29 Apr 1404*]**

Jurors:	William Laweman	John Cok	John Sayere
	Walter Albreth	John Boton junior	
	John in the Hale	William Colwell	

* [*l. margin:* villeins and fugitives] Again it is ordered as many times to take John Isoude at Weston, William Bate at Baldock, Andrew Hale at Willingham, William Boton at Wallington, villeins and fugitives etc and to bring them to St Albans and Margery Bacon at Wallington.
* The jurors present that William Vynter \2d/, Agnes Yerdele \2d/, Thomas Caldewelle \2d/, Richard Daye \2d/, William Geiard make default, so they are amerced.
* The lord has granted to William Colwell junior one hearth and one cotland called *Sandes*, to hold to him and his in villeinage at the will of the lord for services etc. Fine two capons.

Court held there on Tuesday after the Feast of St George in the 6th year of the reign of Henry IV in the time of Brother John Blebury cellarer [*28 Apr 1405*]

Jurors:	William Laweman	John Cok	Henry Roonhale
	Walter Albreth	John Boton junior	John Sayere
	John in the Hale	William Colwell	

* Again it is ordered, as so many times, to take John Isoude at Weston, William Bate at Baldock, Andrew Hale at Willingham, William Boton at Wallington, villeins and fugitives and to bring them to St Albans etc.
* William Taillour and Beatrice his wife, she having been questioned, have surrendered into the lord's hands one messuage and half a virgate of land formerly of John Boton, of which the heriot in money is 3s 4d. And the lord has granted the said messuage and land with appurtenances to William Cok senior, to hold to him and his in villeinage at the will of the lord for services etc. Fine 3s 4d.
* William Taillour and Beatrice his wife, she having been questioned, have surrendered into the hands [*HALS 65525, f1v*] of the lord one cottage formerly of John Fuller, of which the heriot is three chickens. And the lord has granted the said cottage with appurtenances to John Cook, to hold to him and his etc.

HENRY IV

And the fine is three chickens.

* William Sayer has surrendered into the lord's hand one messuage and half a virgate of land formerly of William his father and one toft and one *quartrona* of land formerly of Richard Haston, no heriot. And the lord has granted the said messuage, toft and land with appurtenances to the said William and Agnes his wife, to hold to them for the term of their life in villeinage at the will of the lord for services etc, and after the decease of the aforesaid William and Agnes the said messuage and toft and land with appurtenances shall remain to John Boton junior, to hold to him and his etc. And he gives to the lord both for a fine and for having the term 3s 4d and six capons.
* The lord has granted to William Colwell one *quartrona* of land formerly of John Neweman, to hold to him and his in villeinage at the will of the lord for services etc. Fine 3s 4d.
* The jurors present that William Vyntere \2d/, Agnes Yerdele \2d/ make default, so they are amerced.
* The testament of John Bradewey is proved before Brother John Blebury, cellarer and commissary for this case of which the content follows in these words: 'In the name of God, amen, I John Bradewey of Norton, on Friday next before the Feast of the Annunciation of the blessed Mary in the year of the Lord 1403 make my testament in this manner. First I leave my soul to God, the Blessed Mary and All the Saints and my body to be buried in the cemetery of the church of St Nicholas of Norton.[51] I leave to the high altar 3s 4d. I leave to the porch (*porticui*) of the church of Norton 60s. I leave to the fabric of the church of Baldock 6s 8d. I leave to my grandson John 40s to support him at school (*inveniendum ad scolas*) while it shall last. I leave to Margery daughter of Walter my son 100s for her marriage. I leave to John Helder 6s 8d and an upper garment (*epitogium*). I leave to Malcot servant of the same, 6s 8d. I leave to each poor man and woman in the town of Baldock and Norton 12d. I leave all the residue of all my goods not bequeathed to Walter my son and ordain and appoint the said Walter my son and Hugh [*blank*] my faithful executors to dispose of them for my soul and for all my benefactors as shall seem most expedient to them. It is done here on the day and year abovesaid.'

---

[51] 'Next' prefixes each clause in the Testament given on this and on the following pages but has been omitted in the translation.

HENRY IV

Court held there on Tuesday next after the close of Easter, in the 7th year of the reign of King Henry in the time of Brother John Blebury cellarer [*18 May 1406*]

Jurors: William Lawman   John Cok   Henry Roonale
Walter Albreth   John Boton junior   John Boton senior
John in the Hale   William Colwell

* The jurors present that John Saunford \2d/, Richard atte Dene \2d/, Joan Smyth \2d/, Thomas [*HALS 65526, f1*] Caldewall \2d/, Simon Smyth of *Wylion* [Willian] \2d/, William Geiard \2d/, William Vynter \2d/ and Hugh Smyth \2d/ owe suit of court and make default, therefore amerced.
* [*l. margin:* villeins and fugitives] Next they present that William Geiard at Bygrave, John Geiarde at St Albans and his issue, William Bate at Baldock and Agnes his daughter there, John Isoude at Weston, John his son there, farmer (*firmarius*) of John Cornevaile, knight, and his issue, Andrew Hale and Richard Geiard at Bygrave and John Jacob and where he dwells is not known therefore let it be inquired, they are villeins and fugitives, therefore it is ordered to take and bring them to St Albans.
* [*l. margin*: villeins] Next they present that John Boton at *Wylion* [Willian] is a villein of the lord and has put Walter his son to learning without leave of the lord, therefore it is ordered to distrain the aforesaid John to make agreement with the lord for the aforesaid trespass before the next court.
* Next they present that William Taillour \20s/ has committed waste in his tenement called *Wodeslond*, so he is amerced, and it is ordered to take [it] into the lord's hands.
* Next they present that William Taillour has alienated the said tenement with appurtenances to John Boton senior without leave of the lord, so it is ordered to seise [it] etc.
* Next they present that John Boton \6s8d/ has committed waste in his tenement called *Botons*, so is amerced, and is ordered to amend before the next court under penalty of 20s.
* Next they present that Nicholas atte Water is allowing the houses to be ruinous in his tenement formerly of Reynald Balston, so he is ordered to amend [them] before the next court under a penalty of 3s 4d.
* Next they present that Thomas Frere cut down timber in his tenement called *Megys*. Therefore it is ordered to take possession.
* Thomas Stafford \2d/ is convicted against William Taillour concerning a plea of trespass, damages assessed at 12d, therefore amerced. It is ordered to levy.
* William Laweman complains of John Lorkyn concerning a plea of debt.

HENRY IV

Pledges of prosecution Walter Albright and John Hale. And the bailiff and bedell are ordered to attach John against the next court.

* The testament of William Sayer of Norton was proved before Brother John Blebury cellarer and commissary for this purpose of which the tenor follows in these words: 'In the name of God, amen, I William Sayer of Norton on the day of St Katherine 1405 make my testament in this manner. Firstly I commend my soul to Almighty God, the blessed Mary and All the Saints and my body to be buried in the cemetery of the church of St Nicholas of Norton. I leave to the high altar of the said church 2s. I leave to the repairs of the said church 6s 8d. I leave to the convent of St Albans 2s. [I leave] to the altar of the Blessed Mary 2s. [*HALS 65526, f1v*] I leave to the altar of St Thomas 2s. I leave to the light of St Nicholas 12d. I leave to the parish clerk 6d. I leave the residue of all my goods to my executors to pay my debts and to do all these things. I constitute my executors John Hale junior and William Laweman giving special and general power to them to hold and to dispose of my goods as may seem best to profit my soul (*expedire*), on the abovesaid day and year.'

Court held there on Tuesday next after the close of Easter in the 8th year of the reign of Henry IV in the time of Brother John Blebury cellarer [*26 Apr 1407*]

Jurors:	William Laweman	John Cok	William Colwell
	Walter Albreth	John Boton senior	Henry Roonale
	John in the Hale	John Boton junior	

* The jurors present that John Vynter \2d/, Walter Bradewey \2d/, Thomas Poley \2d/, Thomas Caldewell of *Wylion* [Willian] \2d/, John Schepherd \2d/, Richard atte Dene \2d/, William the miller \1d/, William Geiard the miller \1d/, William Geiard of Bygrave \1d/, Hugh Smyth of Baldock \2d/ and John de Hathe of Wallington owe suit and make default, therefore they are amerced etc.
* [*l. margin*: villeins] Next they present that William Geiard at Bygrave, John Geiard at St Albans. And it is ordered to enquire concerning his issues before the next court. William Bate at Baldock, Agnes his daughter at Hitchin, John Isoude at Weston, John his son farmer there, John Cornevaile. And it is ordered to inquire concerning the issues of the same before the next court. Andrew Hale at Chesterton in the county of Cambridge, Richard Geiard at Bygrave, William Boton at *Cokereth* [Cottered], Alice Boton at Baldock

HENRY IV

espoused to William son of Thomas Webbe without licence of the lord[52] and Alice in the Hale at Baldock are villeins and fugitives. Therefore it is ordered to take and bring them to St Albans, etc.
* Next they present that John Boton has not yet repaired the waste done in his tenement as ordered at the last court under penalty of 20s. Therefore he incurs the penalty, and he is ordered to amend [it] before the next court, under penalty of losing [it] etc.
* John Cok puts himself [upon the mercy of the court] for leave to agree for a trespass in his garden by cutting down apple bearing trees, so he is amerced etc.
* William Colwell is convicted by his own acknowledgment of a plea of trespass against Richard Dewebury, damage assessed at 3s 2d. So ordered to levy it and he is amerced.
* William Laweman has not prosecuted his plaint against John Lorkyn in a plea of debt so he is amerced.
* It is ordered to enquire before the next court concerning a half acre of land which Walter Bradewey holds [*HALS 65526, f2*] in *le Longecroft* whether he holds it by copy or by charter.
* It is ordered to retain in the lord's hands one tenement called *Megis* lately in the tenure of Thomas Frere and to answer to the lord for the issues until etc.
* It is ordered to retain in the lord's hands one tenement called *Wodeslond* lately in the tenure of William Taillour and to answer to the lord for the issues until etc.
* Again it is ordered to distrain John Boton to make agreement with the lord because he has put his son to learning without the lord's leave etc before the next court under the penalty which hangs over (*incumbit*) etc.

Court held there on Tuesday after the end of Easter in the 9th year of the reign of Henry IV in the time of John Blebury cellarer [*15 May 1408*]

Jurors:	William Laweman	John Cok	William Colwell
	Walter Albreth	John Boton senior	Henry Roonale
	John in the Hale	John Boton junior	

* The jurors present that Thomas Caldewell \2d/, Richard atte Dene \2d/,

---

[52] This phrase precedes Alice Boton's name (*sponsata Willelmo filio Thome Webbe sine licencia domini*), but appears to relate to her rather than to William Boton, and also makes better sense thus.

HENRY IV

William Vynter \2d/, Thomas Poley \2d/, William Geiard \2d/, William Geiard [*sic*] \2d/, William Neweman \2d/, William de Bygrave \2d/, and Hugh Smyth of Baldock \2d/, owe suit and make default, therefore they are amerced, etc. [*l. margin*: villeins]

* Next they present that William Geiard at Bygrave, John Geiard and his issue at St Albans, William Bate at Baldock, Agnes his daughter at Hitchin, John Isoude at Weston, John his son farmer of John Cornevaile and his issue there, Andrew Hale at Chesterton in the county of Cambridge, Richard Geiard at Bygrave, William Boton, John Jacob, Alice Assh at Shenley, Margery Boton at *Codreth* [Cottered] espoused to William son of Thomas Webbe without the lord's licence, Alice Boton and Alice in the Hale at Baldock are villeins and fugitives so it is ordered to take and bring them to St Albans, etc.
* Next they present that William Geiard the miller has committed waste in his tenement by cutting down trees to the damage of the lord, 18d, which is ordered to be levied.
* Again it is ordered to retain in the hand of the lord one tenement called *Megys* late in the tenure of Thomas Frere and one tenement called *Wodeslond* late in the tenure of Thomas Taillour and to answer to the lord for the issues until etc.
* [*HALS 65526, f2v*] John atte Hathe surrendered into the lord's hands the copy of one toft and of one cotland formerly of Richard Bate the elder. And it shall remain in the lord's hand etc.

View of Frankpledge held there on Tuesday after the Feast of the close of Easter in the 10th year of the reign of Henry IV in the time of Brothers John Blebury and Simon Wyndesore as cellarers [*7 May 1409*]

[Jurors:]	Walter Laweman	John Laweman	William Colwell
	Walter Albreth	Henry Roonale	John atte Cherche
	John Cok	John Boton junior	William Cok
	John Sampforthe		

* John atte Cherche, William Cok and John Sampforthe are elected to the office of chief pledges and took the oath etc.
* The chief pledges having been sworn present that they give by fixed agreement (*de certo fine*) this day 13s 4d.[53]
* Next they present that Joan Smyth owes suit (*adventum*) and makes default, so

---

[53] The first reference to the common fine, an annual 'voluntary' payment to the lord of the manor by all the suitors; *de certo fine* means 'concerning a certain agreement'.

HENRY IV

etc, but remitted because she is infirm.
* Next they present that John Hikes is outside the tithing and renders himself, therefore he is amerced etc.
* Next they present that Walter Bradeway is outside the tithing and renders himself, therefore amerced etc.
* Next they present that one ewe sheep came as a stray at the Feast of the Purification of the Blessed Mary and is dead and her skin remains in the custody of John atte Hale, value 3d.
* Next they present that John, domestic servant of Walter Bradewey \2d/, is outside the tithing and the said Walter 2d, answers for him, therefore they are amerced etc.
* Next they present that William Geiard, miller, has taken excessive toll, therefore he is amerced.
* Next they present that John Sampforthe is a common brewer and has broken the Assize, so he is amerced.
* Next they present that William Geiard \1d/ and John atte Cherche have ditches that have not been cleaned out to the nuisance of passers by next to the cemetery there, so they are amerced etc.
* Next they present that John Freberne has manure on the King's highway (*regia via*) to the nuisance of passers by, therefore he is amerced etc.
* Next they present that Nicholas Hayward \1d/, and William Geiard have ditches not cleansed [HALS 65526, f3] to the injury of passers by at *Blakryshelane*, therefore they are amerced.
* Next they present that the lord is bound to repair a certain bridge called *Fordbrugge*.
* Walter son of John Boton is put into a tithing and takes the oath etc.
* William Laweman and John Laweman are chosen to the office of constable and took the oath.

Court held the same day and year as written above etc

Jurors:	William Laweman	John Cok	Henry Roonale
	Walter Albreth	John Boton junior	John atte Cherche
	John in the Hale	William Colwell	William Cok

* The jurors present that William Vynter \2d/, William Geiard \2d/, Richard atte Dene \2d/, Thomas Cadewell of *Wyleon* [Willian] \2d/, Joan Smyth \remitted/, John Schepherd \2d/ and William Cadewell \2d/ owe suit and make default, so they are amerced etc.
* [*l. margin*: villeins] Next they present that William Geiard at Bygrave, John

HENRY IV

Geiard and his issue at St Albans, William Bate at Baldock, Agnes his daughter at Hitchin, John Isoude at Weston, John son of the same and his issue there, Andrew Hale at Chesterton in County Cambridge, Richard Geiard at Bygrave, William Boton, John Jacob, Alice Asshe at Shenley, Margery Boton at *Codreth* [Cottered] married to William son of Thomas Webbe without the lord's licence, Alice Boton and Alice in the Hale at Baldock, William son of John Boton and Joan Boton at Cheshunt are villeins and fugitives therefore etc.

* Next they present that John Boton is dead who held from the lord one messuage and half a virgate of land, whose heriot is one horse [worth] 6s 8d. And they say that William his son is his next heir and of the age of 17 years. It is ordered to take it into the lord's hands until etc.
* Afterwards the lord granted the said messuage and land with appurtenances to John Colwell, saving the right of anyone, to hold to him and his in villeinage at the will of the lord for the services due for it. And the condition is such that if anyone shall come and make his claim to the aforesaid messuage and land that he shall satisfy the aforesaid John for all his outlay and expenditure done around the aforesaid messuage and land by the discretion of the advice of the lord. And he gives to the lord for agreement 6s 8d, it is condoned. And he did fealty etc.
* Next they present that John in the Hale is dead who held from the lord one toft and one croft containing one acre of land and three roods of land formerly of Stephen Pernel, one cottage with curtilage formerly of Simon Cadewell situated between the tenement of John atte Hathe and the tenement of Laurence Wysot and one toft with curtilage situated between the tenement of John in the Hale and the tenement of Laurence Wysot of which the heriot is one little water pot (*urciolus*), one plate and one acre worth etc. [*HALS 65526, f3v*] And they say that Andrew in the Hale, his son, is his next heir and of full age who is outside the lordship, therefore it is ordered to take it into the lord's hands until etc.
* Next they present that John atte Cherche \2d/, Thomas Frere \2d/ and John Cok \2d/ have committed waste in their tenements, therefore they are amerced etc. And it is ordered to amend before the next court under penalty of forfeiture.
* Again it is ordered to retain in the lord's hand one tenement called *Miggys*, one tenement called *Wodlondes* and one toft and one cotland formerly of Richard Batte, and to answer to the lord for the issues until etc.
* Nicholas Taillour surrendered into the lord's hands all the estate and term which he has in one messuage and half a virgate of land formerly of John Hasshe, of which the heriot is one horse worth 5s. And the lord has granted

HENRY IV

the said messuage and land with appurtenances to John Laweman junior to hold to him and his in villeinage at the will of the lord for services etc. And he gives to the lord for agreement three capons and he has done fealty.
* William Colwell surrendered into the lord's hand one *quartrona* of land called *Balstones*, and it is ordered to retain it and answer to the lord for the issues until etc.
* Thomas Frere surrendered into the lord's hand one *quartrona* of land so it is ordered to account for the issues until etc.

View of Frankpledge held on Tuesday after the close of Easter in the 11th year of the reign of Henry IV in the time of Brothers Simon Wyndesore and John Blebury as cellarers [*22 Apr 1410*]

Jurors:	William Laweman	John Laweman	William Cok
	Walter Albreth	Henry Roonale	John Samphorthe
	John Cok	William Colwell	

* The chief pledges of the jury present that they are giving for the fixed ancient agreement to this day 13s 4d.
* Next they present that John Samphorthe owes suit (*adventum*) and makes default, therefore he is amerced.
* Next they present that Walter Bradewey \2d/, William his servant \2d/, John, servant of the vicar 2d, are outside the tithings. Therefore they are amerced.
* Next they present that Matilda atte Chirche justly raised the hue on the vicar of Norton (*vicariam de Norton*).
* [*HALS 65526, f4*] Next they present that the lord is bound to repair a bridge called *Fordbrigge*, therefore he is ordered to repair it etc.
* Walter Albreth junior is put in the tithing and has taken the oath etc.

Court held there the day and year above mentioned etc

Jurors:	William Laweman	John Cok	William Cok
	Walter Albreth	William Colwell	
	John in the Hale	Henry Roonale	

* [*l. margin*: villeins] Next they present that William Geiard at Bygrave, John Geiard and his issue at *Sanctum* [St Albans], William Bate, Agnes late the wife of William Baker married to John Webbe at Baldock, William Boton at *Edysburgh* [Edlesborough], Agnes Bate at Hitchin, John Isoude at Weston, John his son and his family in the same place, Andrew Hale at Chesterton, Richard Geiard at Bygrave, William Boton, John Jacob, Alice Asshe at

223

HENRY IV

Shenley, Margaret Boton at *Codereth* [Cottered] married to William Webbe, Alice Boton, Alice in the Hale at Baldock, William Boton and Joan Boton at Cheshunt are villeins and fugitives therefore it is ordered that they be taken etc.
* Next they present that William Vynter \2d/, William senior \2d/, Richard atte Dene \2d/, Thomas Cadewell \2d/, William Cadewell \2d/, William Dageney \2d/ and Hugh Smyth \2d/ owe suit and make default, so they are amerced etc.
* Next they present that John atte Cherche is dead, who held from the lord one messuage and half a virgate of land, a virgate of land of which the heriot is one horse, value 10s. And Alice his daughter aged half a year is his next heir and because of the minority of the said heir wardship of the said messuage and land with appurtenances is committed to William Lyntok vicar of the church of Norton, to hold to him and his in villeinage at the will of the lord until the lawful age of the said heir, by services etc. And he gives to the lord for agreement 12d.
* Next they present that the vicar has a ruinous messuage therefore he is ordered to amend it before the next court under penalty of 40s.
* Next they present that William Colwell has committed waste in his tenement lately of John Boton, so he is amerced, and he is ordered to amend it before the next court under penalty of 40s.
* Next they present that William Colwell has committed waste in his tenement late of John atte Cherche, so he is amerced. And it is ordered to amend it before the next court under penalty of 20s.
* Next they present that Richard Dewebury has committed waste in the tenement late of John Cok, so he is [*HALS 65526, f4v*] amerced. And he is ordered to amend before the next court under penalty of 6s 8d.
* The testament of John atte Cher[c]he was proved before Brother John Blebury commissary for this purpose in the year of the Lord 1410, of which the tenor follows in these words: 'In the name of God, amen. Firstly I leave my soul to God and my body to be buried in the cemetery of Norton. I leave 12d to the high altar of the same church 12d. I leave to the repairing of the said church four bushels of barley, to the parish clerk two pecks of barley. I leave the residue of all my goods to my executors to pay my debts having appointed these as my executors, Lord William Lyntok, vicar of the church of Norton and Thomas Colwell giving to the same special and general power to hold and dispose of my goods as may seem most expedient in the peril of soul and thereof they have the administration in form of law etc.'
* The testament of John Boton was proved before John Blebury, commissary for this purpose in the year of the Lord 1410 of which the tenor follows in these words: 'In the name of God, amen. Firstly I leave my soul to God and my

body to be buried in the cemetery of Norton. I leave four bushels of barley to the high altar of the same church. I leave four bushels of barley to the repairs of the said church. I leave one bushel of barley to the light of St Mary. I leave one bushel of barley to the light of St Nicholas. I leave 4d to the parish clerk. I leave the residue of all my goods to my executors to pay my debts. And to have all these things done I appoint these as my executors, Richard Dewebury and Joan my wife, giving them general and special power of my goods to hold and dispose as may seem best in the peril of [my] soul [and thereof they have the administration in form of law].'

* Next they present that John Boton, junior, is dead who held from the lord two messuages and half a virgate of land and one *quartrona* of land, whose heriot is two horses worth 20s. And they say that Margery his daughter of a quarter of a year is his next heir. And because of the minority of the said heir the [aforementioned] messuage and land remain in the hand of the lord until etc.
* Next they present that John Frere junior is dead who held from the lord one toft with curtilage, of which the heriot is one horse value 13s 4d. [And they say] John his brother is his next heir and of full age. And they shall remain in the hand of the lord, etc. And it is ordered to answer for the issues until etc.
* It is ordered to retain in the lord's hand one messuage and half a virgate of land late of John Boton senior, one cottage and two tofts with appurtenances late of John in the Hale, one tenement called *Meggis*, one tenement called *Wodelondes*, one toft and one cotland, formerly Richard Bate's, one *quartrona* of land called *Balstones* and one *quarter* of land lately Thomas Frere and to answer to the lord for the issues until etc.
* [*HALS 65526, f5*] The testament of John Boton was proved before Brother John Blebury, commissary for this purpose in the year of the Lord 1409, of which the tenor follows in these words: 'Firstly I leave my soul to God etc. Next I leave to the high altar half a quarter of barley. I leave to the repairing of the church half a quarter of barley. I leave to the light of the blessed Mary one bushel of barley. I leave to the light of St Nicholas one bushel of barley. I leave to the parish clerk 4d. I leave the residue of all my goods to my executors Richard Dewebury and Joan my wife to pay my debts giving to the same power over my goods that they may dispose of them for my soul as may seem to best speed it. And thereof they have administration.'

HENRY IV

View of Frankpledge held there on Tuesday next after the close of Easter, in the 12th year of the reign of King Henry IV in the time of Brother John Blebury as cellarer [*12 May 1411*]

Jurors:	William Laweman	Henry Roonale	William Cok
	Walter Albreth	William Colwell	John Samphorthe
	John Cok	John Laweman	

* The chief pledges of the jury present that they give for the ancient firm agreement to this day 13s 4d.
* Next they present that Walter Bradewey \2d/, William his servant \2d/, Hugh Wodeward \2d/, Thomas Broune \2d/, John Henyngham \2d/, Richard Grene servant of Richard Dewebury and John Boughton \2d/ servant of the vicar are outside the tithings.
* Next they present that John Samporthe chief pledge makes default. Therefore he is amerced.
* Next they present that Agnes Wodeward has made an assault on Matilda in the Hale, therefore she etc.
* Next they present that William Geiard is a miller and has taken excessive multure, therefore he is amerced.
* Next they present that John Benet has abandoned divers goods and cattle to the value of 13s 4d and they remain in the custody of the farmer.
* Next they present that the lord is bound to repair the bridge called *Forthebrigge* therefore etc.

Court held there the day and year abovesaid

Jurors:	William Laweman	John in the Hale	John Cok
	Walter Albreth	Henry Roonale	William Cok
			William Colwelle

* [*HALS 65526, f5v*] The jurors present that William Wynter \2d/, Thomas Pole \2d/, Hugh Smyth \2d/, William Geiard the younger \2d/, Richard atte Dene \2d/, Thomas Cadewell \3d/, William Dageney \3d/ owe suit etc.
* [*l. margin*: villeins and fugitives] Next they present that William Geiard at Bygrave, John Geiard at St Albans, William Bate, Agnes Webbe at Baldock, William Boton at Edlesborough, Agnes Bate, Hitchin, John Isoude at Weston and John his son, Andrew Hale at Chesterton, Richard Geiard at Bygrave, William Boton, John Jacobbe, Alice Asshe at Shenley, Margery Boton at *Codereth* [Cottered], Alice Boton, Alice in the Hale at Baldock, William Boton and John Boton at Cheshunt, are villeins and fugitives so it is ordered to

HENRY IV

take them etc.
* Next they present that the vicar has never remedied the waste committed in the messuage late of John atte Cherche as contained in the orders at the last court, under penalty of 3s 4d so he incurs the penalty.
* Next they present that William Colwell has never remedied the waste committed in the messuage late of John atte Cherche and of John Boton as contained in the orders at the last court under penalty of 100s so he incurs the penalty.
* Next they present that Richard Dewebury holds one cottage late of John Cok without an estate and he has not remedied the waste committed therein just as contained in the orders at the last court under penalty of 6s 8d so he incurs the penalty etc.
* It is ordered to take into the lord's hands one messuage and one cotland called *Hassh* which William Dageney and Joan Hassh his wife sold to William Frebarne without the lord's permission, and to answer to the lord for the issues, etc.
* Again it is ordered to retain in the lord's hands two messuages, half a virgate of land and one *quartrona* of land late of John Boton the younger, one toft with curtilage late of John Frere the younger, one messuage and half a virgate of land late of John Boton the elder, one cottage and two tofts late of John in the Hale, one toft called *Meggis*, one tenement called *Wodelondes*, one toft and one cotland once of Richard Batte, one *quartrona* of land called *Balstones* and one *quartrona* of land late of Thomas Frere, and to answer to the lord for the issues until etc.

View of Frankpledge held there on Tuesday next after the close of Easter in the 13th year of the reign of King Henry IV in the time of Brother John Blebury as cellarer [*3 May 1412*]

William Laweman	Henry Roonale	William Cok
Walter Albreth	William Colwell	John Samphorthe
John Coke	John Laweman	John in the Hale

[*The following is written in a different hand*]
[*HALS 65527, f1*] They present that they give to the lord by ancient sure agreement to this day 13s 4d.
* Next they present that John Samphorth and John Colwell owe suit and make default, therefore they are amerced.
* Next they present that Walter Bradwey and John Honygome are outside the tithing, so they are amerced.

HENRY IV

* Next they present that Nicholas Heyward has a ditch not cleansed at *Bakerslane*, therefore it is ordered to amend before the next court, under a penalty of 6d.
* William Jyryshe and Hugh Wodeward are put in tithing and take the oath etc.
* Walter Albreth and William Cok are elected to the office of constable and took the oath, etc.

Halimote held the day and year above written in the 13th year

Jurors: Wm Laweman   John in the Hale   John Cok   Wm Colwell
       Walter Albreth   Henry Ronehale   Wm Cok

* The Homage present that William Wyntere, Thomas Pole, Hugh Smyth, William Gegeard senior, Richard at Dene, Thomas Cadewell, William Cadewell and John Samphorth owe suit and make default, so they are amerced.[54]
* [*l. margin*: villeins] They present that William Gegeard at Bygrave, John Gegeard at St Albans, William Bate, Agnes Webbe at Baldock, William Boton at Edlesborough, Agnes Bate at Hitchin, John Isoude at Weston and John his son, Andrew Hale at Chesterton, Richard Gegeard at Bygrave, William Boton, John Jacobbe, Alice Assh at Shenley, Margery Boton at *Codreth* [Cottered], Alice Boton, Alice Inthehale at Baldock, William Boton with the Prince and John Boton at Cheshunt are villeins and fugitives therefore amerced.

[*l. margin with bracket to next three paragraphs*: villeins]
* Next they present that Alice Beton has got married without licence of the lord to John Sampson, tanner of Baldock, therefore a writ (*iō b̄re*).
* They present that Joan Assh has married without licence of the lord to William Dagney, cordwainer/tanner/tawyer (*allutar*) of Baldock, therefore a writ.
* Next they present that William Gegeard put his son John to letters without leave of the lord, therefore it is ordered to distrain him to satisfy the lord for the said trespass.
* Next they present that Matilda Hale has committed waste in the tenement which she holds as dower, therefore it is ordered to repair before the next court on pain of losing it.
* Next they present that the vicar has committed waste in the tenement lately of John at Cherche and William Colwell in the tenement lately of the aforesaid John, so he is amerced and is ordered to repair it on pain of losing it.

---

[54] The amount payable is not placed over the names as in previous entries.

HENRY IV

* Next they present that Thomas Love has committed waste in his tenement therefore he is amerced and it is ordered to repair it under penalty of 3s 4d.
* Next they present that Richard Dawebury holds one cottage late of John Cok without estate, therefore it is ordered to take into the hands of the lord and to answer to the lord for the issues until etc.
* It is ordered to retain in the lord's hand one messuage and one cotland called *Hash* which William Dageney and Joan Hash his wife alienated to William Freberne, two messuages, half a virgate of land and one *quartrona* of land late of John Boton junior, one toft with curtilage late of John Frere junior, one messuage and half a virgate of land late of John Boton senior, one cottage and two tofts late of John Inthehale, one toft called *Megges*, one tenement called *Wodelondes*, one toft and one cotland formerly of Richard Bate, one *quartrona* of land called *Balstones*, and one *quartrona* of land late of Thomas Frere and to answer to the lord for the issues until etc.
* The lord granted to John Freberne one toft and land adjoining containing in all two acres of land late of John Inthehale shepherd to hold to him and his in villeinage at the will of the lord for services etc and he gives to the lord for agreement 12d. And he did fealty. [*The following is in a different hand*]

HENRY V

(*HALS 65528, f1*) The first of only a few folios of records in the time of Henry V.

HENRY V

NORTON IN THE TIME OF KING HENRY V

[*HALS 65528, f1*] **Halimote held there on Tuesday next after the Feast of St Michael in the 1ˢᵗ year of the reign of King Henry V [*3 Oct 1413*]**

Jurors:	William Lawman	John Inthehale	William Collewelle
	Walter Albreth	Henry Ronale	John Lawman
	John Cok	William Cok	

* Next the jurors present that William Geiarde at Bygrave, John Geiarde at St Albans, William Bate, Agnes Webbe at Baldock, William Boton at Edlesborough, Agnes Bate at Hitchin, John Isowde at Weston and John his son, Andrew Hale at Chesterton, Richard Geiarde at Bygrave, William Boton, John Jacob, Alice Assh at Shenley, Margery Boton at *Codreth* [Cottered], Alice Boton, Alice Inthehale at Baldock, William Boton with the Lord the King, John Boton at Cheshunt are villeins and fugitives, therefore it is ordered to take them etc. [*l. margin:* villeins]
* William Geiard has leave to put John his son to letters and gives 12d for agreement. [*l. margin*: villein]

Halimote held there on Tuesday next after the Feast of the Finding of the Holy Cross in the 1ˢᵗ year of the reign of King Henry V [*9 May 1413*]

Jurors:	William Lawman	Henry Ronale	William Colwelle
	Walter Albreth	John Cok	John Laweman
	John Inthehale	William Cok	

* Next they present that William Geiarde at Bygrave, John Geiarde at St Albans, William Bate, Agnes Webbe at Baldock, William Boton at Edlesborough, Agnes Bate at Hitchin, John Isowde at Weston and John his son, Andrew Hale at Chesterton, Richard ~~Bygrave~~ Geiarde at Bygrave, William Boton, John Jacob, Alice Assh at Shenley, Margery Boton at *Cokreth* [Cottered], Alice Boton, Alice Inthehale at Baldock, William Boton with the Lord the King, John Boton at Cheshunt are villeins and fugitives, therefore etc. [*l. margin:* villeins]
* It is ordered to distrain William Geiarde to satisfy the lord because he put John his son to letters without the lord's leave, therefore it is ordered to distrain him to satisfy the lord for the trespass.
* Next they present that John Healder is dead who held of the lord one cottage with curtilage of which the heriot is one brass pot worth 16d. And the said

HENRY V

cottage and curtilage shall remain in the hands of the lord until etc. Therefore it is ordered to seise it etc.
* Next they present that Matilda Hale has not repaired the waste committed in her tenement therefore it is ordered to seise it. [*l. margin:* villein (fem)]
* William Lyncok, the vicar, surrenders into the lord's hand all the estate and term which he has in one messuage and half a virgate of land late of John at Chyrche. And the lord has granted the said messuage and land with appurtenances to Thomas Tyler to hold to him and his until the lawful age of Alice, daughter and heir of the said John atte Chyrche for services etc. And the condition is such that when the said Alice shall come to full age that she shall satisfy the said Thomas Tyler for his costs laid out upon the said cottage.
* It is ascertained by the rolls of the court that one messuage and one cotland have been seised into the lord's hand because William Dageneye and Joan Hassh his wife [have granted] the said messuage and land with appurtenances to William Freberne without leave of the lord. And afterwards the lord granted the said messuage and land with appurtenances to the said William Freberne, to hold to him and his in villeinage at the will of the lord by services etc. And he gives for agreement two capons, etc.

Halimote held there on the day and Feast of the Apostles Philip and James in the 2nd year of the reign of King Henry V [*1 May 1414*]

Jurors:	William Laweman	Henry Ronale	William Cok
	Walter Albreth	William Colwelle	John Inthehale
	John Cok	John Lawman	

* The jurors present that Richard Geiarde and John Geiarde at St Albans, William Geiarde at Bygrave, Walter Boton at *Henxtworth* [Hinxworth], William Boton at Luton, William Bate, Agnes Webbe at Baldock, Agnes Bate at Hitchin, John Isowde at Weston and John his son, Andrew Hale at Chesterton, William Boton, John Jacob, Alice Assh at Shenley, Marjory Botone at *Codreth* [Cottered], Alice Boton, Alice Inthehale at Baldock, William Boton with the Lord the King, Joan Boton at Cheshunt are villeins and fugitives etc. [*l. margin:* villeins]
* [*HALS 65528, f1v*] Next they present that Matilda Attewatre is dead who held of the lord, and what she held from the lord is not known, whose heriot is one sheep worth 16d. And Walter her son is her next heir. And the aforesaid land shall remain in the hand of Nicholas Attewatre lately her husband, to hold to him by the law of England because between them they had children. And it is to be enquired what he holds before the next court.

HENRY V

* Next they say that Walter Bradweye has ploughed one meadow called *Erdelesbuttes* in which they had common pasture from the time of the Feast of St Peter which is called in Chains until the Feast of the Purification of the Blessed Mary from the time of which there is no longer memory. So it is ordered to put it right before the next court under penalty of 6s 8d, for the next court etc.

Halimote held there on the 16th day of April in the 3rd year of the reign of Henry V [*16 Apr 1415*]

Jurors:	William Laweman	Henry Ronale	William Cok
	Walter Albreth	William Collewelle	John Inthehale
	John Cok	John Lawman	

* The jurors present that Thomas Love is dead who held of the lord one cottage formerly of John Dryvere, and it is ordered to take it into the lord's hands until etc.
* Next they say that William Geiarde at Bygrave, John his son at St Albans, William Bate, butcher (*carnifex*) at Baldock and his children, Agnes Bate with two other sons and one daughter together with their issue at Weston. And the Homage is ordered to make enquiry concerning all their children before the next court. Richard Geiard at St Albans, William Boton at Luton, Walter Boton at *Henxteworth* [Hinxworth] with Joan Lardyner, Margery Boton wife of William Webbe at *Codreth* [Cottered], Joan Boton at Cheshunt and the issue of Andrew at Hale at Chesterton, Joan Assh wife of Nicholas Daye of Shenley near *Newmarkeyate* are villeins and fugitives therefore etc.
* William Geiarde has leave to stay outside the lordship wherever he shall wish. And he gives to the lord annually for *chevage* 12d, first term of payment at the Feast of St Michael the Archangel next to come after one whole year. [*l. margin:* villein]
* To this court comes John Colwelle and seeks that the lord will grant to him of his special grace one messuage and half a virgate to himself before granted as appears in the court in the 10th year of the reign of Henry IV lately of John Boton which land and tenement have come into the lord's hands because he has never repaired the waste committed in the said messuage as he was ordered to at divers courts in divers years of the same King. And the lord of his special grace has granted to the said John the said messuage and land with appurtenances, to hold to him and his in villeinage at the will of the lord by services etc. And the condition is such that if any heir shall come and make his claim to the aforesaid messuage and land with appurtenances, that he shall

HENRY V

satisfy the said John Colwelle for all expenditure and expense made around the said messuage at the discretion of the lord's counsel. And he gives for agreement 3s 4d and he has done fealty.
* Thomas Frere surrenders into the lord's hands one messuage and one *quartrona* of land formerly of Richard Assh of which the heriot is one capon. And the lord has granted the said messuage and land to the said Thomas and Mabel his wife, to hold to them and the heirs of the said Thomas in villeinage at the will of the lord by services etc. And they give to the lord for agreement one capon.
* The lord has granted to William Cok junior one messuage and one *ferlingate* of land formerly of John Wyllemessone and lately of Thomas Frere called *Heches*, to hold to him and his in villeinage at the will of the lord by the services due and by law accustomed. And he gives for agreement 12d. And the condition is such that the said William shall be quit of paying the fixed rent *viz* 22¾d annually from the Feast of St Michael next after the date of this court until the end of three years next following fully completed. And also the said William shall maintain all the houses belonging to the said tenement as for carpentry, roofing, plastering, taking from the cellarer sufficient timber by the cellarer's delivery and he has done fealty.
* [*l. margin:* villein] It is ascertained by an inquiry of the court that John Geiard villein of the lord dwelling at St Albans has married without the lord's licence so is amerced 12d. And it is ordered to attach the said John to make agreement for his marriage. And afterwards the said John came and satisfied the lord for his marriage. And he gives for agreement 6s 8d.
* [*l. margin:* villein] John Geiarde son of William Geiarde villein of the lord dwelling at St Albans has leave to remain without the lordship and he gives for his *chevage* annually at the Feast of Easter 20d.

Halimote held there on the 12th day of May in the 4th year of the reign of King Henry V [*12 May 1416*]

[*The remaining court records in the reign of King Henry V 1416-1422 are missing.*]

HENRY VI

NORTON IN THE TIME OF KING HENRY VI

[*HALS 65529, f1*] **Halimote held there on Tuesday next after the Feast of St Mark the 1st year of the reign of King Henry VI [*27 Apr 1423*]**

Jurors:	John Hale senior	William Cok junior	Simon Hale
	William Laweman	Walter Albreth	John Hale junior
	Walter Albreth senior	John Lawman	
	William Cok senior	John Colwelle	

* The jurors present that Robert Geiarde, John Geiarde, William Bate, Margery Boton at Baldock, John Gerarde son of William Gerarde at St Albans, William Boton unknown where, Thomas Isowde and Gilbert Isowde sons formerly of John Isowde senior and their issue at Weston, John Isowde at *Clotale* [Clothall], Walter Boton beyond the seas (*ultra partes marinas*), Margery Boton wife of William Webbe at *Codreth* [Cottered], Joan Assh at Ditton, John Geiarde son of William Geiarde [in] London are villeins and fugitives, therefore it is ordered to take them etc.
* The lord has granted to William Cok junior one toft and half a virgate of land formerly of Osbert Bate and afterwards of Richard Bate, one toft and half a virgate formerly of Adam Stevenessones lately of the said Richard Bate called *Bateslond*, to hold to him and his from Michaelmas next to come after the date of this court until the end of five years next ensuing, paying for them to the lord annually the whole fixed rent and for all labour services due to the manor 26s 8d and suit of court, etc. The fine is forgiven. And he did fealty.
* It is again ordered to distrain the tenant of the land of William Wyntere to do fealty to the lord before the next court, etc.
* Walter Bradwey surrenders into the lord's hands for himself and his heirs all right and claim which he has, had or in any manner may have in the future, of and in one messuage with curtilage situated upon one hearth built anew called *Halleorcharde* formerly of John Bradweye his father just as it lies between the tenement formerly of William atte Chyrche on the one side and the land of John Lawman on the other and one headland (*caput*) abutts on *Hallewyke* and the other on the headland (*forera*) called *Longhedelonde*. Next he surrenders all his right into the hands of the lord for himself and for his heirs which he had in one croft of land called *Hallecrofte* containing seven acres and in one rood of land lying between the land formerly of the said William atte Chyrche and the land formerly of the said John Lawman so that neither the same Walter nor any of his future heirs might demand any right or claim to the

HENRY VI

aforesaid messuage and lands with appurtenances, but from every action of law about it should be wholly excluded, etc.

Halimote held there on Tuesday next before the Feast of St Dunstan the Bishop in the 2nd year of the reign of King Henry VI [*16 May 1424*]

Jurors:	John Hale senior	John Colwelle	John Laweman
	Walter Albreth senior	John Hale junior	Walter Albreth junior
	William Cok senior	Simon Hale	
	William Laweman	William Cok junior	

* The jurors say that John Geiarde at St Albans, Margery Boton at *Codrethe* [Cottered], William Boton, where unknown, Thomas Isowde and Gilbert Isowde formerly the sons of John Isowde senior and their issue at Weston, John Isowde at *Clotale* [Clothall], Walter Boton about Colchester, Margery Boton wife of William Webbe at *Codreth* [Cottered], Robert Geiarde son of William Geiarde senior at Baldock with John Marche, weaver (*webbe*), John Geiarde son of William Geiarde, London, and Joan Assh at Ditton, are villeins and fugitives therefore etc.
* The jurors say that John Poley has committed waste upon the tenement formerly of Joan Assh by allowing houses to fall. And he is ordered to amend it before the next court under penalty of 6s 8d, etc.
* Next they say that William Cok senior has committed waste upon the tenement called *Botons* by allowing houses to fall. And he is ordered to amend it before the next court under penalty of 6s 8d etc.
* Next they say that William Colwelle has allowed his tenement, likewise called *Botons* at the end of the village, to be ruinous, and he is ordered to amend it before the next court under penalty of 6s 8d.
* Next they say that John Poley has allowed his tenement to be ruinous, the tenement which he holds until the full age of the heir of John Lawman. And he is ordered to amend it before the next court under penalty of 6s 8d, etc.
* Again it is ordered to distrain the tenant of the land late of William Wynter to perform fealty to the lord at the next court etc.
* Walter Bradwey surrenders into the lord's hands one acre of land lying in *Longerefe* between demesne land and land of Walter Albryth, two *buttes* of land formerly John Warde's lying between land late of William Geiarde and a croft called *Swetekynnes*. And the lord has granted the said lands with appurtenances to William Freberne and Margery his wife, to hold to them and the heirs of that William in villeinage at the will of the lord by services etc.

HENRY VI

And he gives for agreement [*blank*].

* The lord has granted to William Freberne three tofts lying together with one pyghtle adjoining of which tofts one is called *Meggesdame* and another called *Shayles* and the third called *Geiardes* to hold to him and his from the date of this court until the end of 21 years rendering for them annually to the lord 20d and suit of Halimote for all services. Fine forgiven.
* William Colwelle lying on his deathbed has surrendered into the lord's hands one messuage, one acre and a half of land formerly of John Attewode situated between the tenement of Joan Wylkyn and the tenement formerly of John Tollarde of which the heriot is one sheep worth 12d. And the lord has granted the said messuage and land with appurtenances to John Colwelle and Alice his wife, to hold to them and theirs in villeinage at the will of the lord by services etc. And they give for agreement 3s 4d. And they did fealty.

[HALS 65529, f1v] Halimote held there on Tuesday in the Feast of the Apostles Philip and James in the 3rd year of the reign of King Henry VI [*1 May 1425*]

Jurors:	John Hale senior	John Colwelle	Simon Hale
	Walter Albreth senior	John Hale junior	Richard Attedener
	William Cokke senior	John Lawman	Simon Smyth
	William Laweman	Walter Albreth junior	

* The jurors present that John Geiarde at St Albans, Margery Boton at *Coderethe* [Cottered], William Boton, unknown where, Thomas Isowde and Gilbert Isowde formerly sons of John Isoude senior and their issue at Weston, John Isowde at *Clotale* [Clothall], Walter Boton about Colchester, Margery Boton wife of William Webbe at *Codereth* [Cottered], Robert Geiarde son of William Geiarde senior at Baldock with John Marche, weaver, John Geiarde son of William Geiarde, London, and Joan Hatthe at Ditton, are villeins and fugitives etc.
* It is again ordered to distrain the tenant of the land late of William Vynter to do fealty to the lord at the next court etc.
* It is ordered to distrain the tenant of the land late of Joan Huntyngdon of *Willyen* [Willian] to do fealty to the lord for the lands and tenements lately of the said Joan at the next court etc.
* It is again ordered to John Poley and to John Colwelle to have their ruinous and destroyed tenements mended because of failure to repair under the penalty which shall continue (*sub pena qua incumbit*), etc.

HENRY VI

Halimote held there on Tuesday in the Feast of St George the Martyr in the 4th year of the reign of King Henry VI [*23 Apr 1426*]

Jurors:	John Hale senior	John Colwelle	Walter Albreth
	Walter Albreth senior	John Hale junior	Simon Smyth
	William Cok senior	John Lawman	
	William Laweman	Simon Lawman	

* The jurors present that John Geiarde at St Albans, Margery Boton at Bedford and she is married to William Webbe, Thomas Isowde, Gilbert Isowde, John Isowde, sons formerly of John Isowde senior and their issue at Weston, John Geiarde son of William Geiarde at *Yerdele* [Ardeley], Margery Boton at Baldock with John Edward, are villeins and fugitives, therefore it is ordered to take them etc.
* It is ordered to warn John Berney and William Cok junior to repair their ruinous tenements before the next court under the penalty which shall continue etc.
* Again it is ordered to John Poleye and John Colwelle to repair their ruinous tenements before the next court etc on pain of losing them.
* Again it is ordered to distrain the tenant of the lands late of William Vyntere and the tenant of the lands late of Joan Huntyngdon in *Willyen* [Willian] to make recognizance to the lord for doing fealty to the lord at the next court etc.

Halimote held there on Tuesday next after the close of Easter in the 5th year of the reign of King Henry VI [*20 May 1427*]

Jurors:	John Hale senior	John Colwelle	Walter Albreth junior
	Walter Albreth senior	John Hale junior	Simon Smyth
	William Cok senior	John Lawman	William Freberne
	William Lawman	Simon Hale	William Geiarde

* The jurors present that Margery Boton at *Codereth* [Cottered] and she is married to William Webbe, John Geiarde at St Albans, Thomas Isowde at Weston, Gilbert Isowde in the same place, John Isowde, son formerly of John Isowde senior, there, Walter Boton, where unknown, Robert Geiarde son of William Geiarde at Weston, John Geiarde son of William Geiarde at *Yerdele* [Ardeley], Margery Boton at Baldock, are villeins and fugitives, therefore it is ordered to take them etc.
* Next they say that John Colwelle has not yet repaired his ruinous tenement called *Botons* as he was ordered under penalty of losing it. And afterwards the same John comes and puts himself in the lord's grace binding himself to have

HENRY VI

repairs well and competently made in the said tenement called *Botons* so that that tenement shall be sufficient for the dwelling of any man according to the manner and custom of the village and that the said tenement shall be prepared and repaired for this before the Feast of the Nativity of St John the Baptist which shall be in the year 1427 under penalty of 40s to be levied from his goods for the lord's use if he shall not do it. Moreover the same John shall appoint and have a tenant in the said tenement before the Feast of St John aforesaid under the aforesaid penalty etc.

* Next they say that Matilda, daughter and heiress of John Cok is of full age to receive her inheritance *viz* one cottage with curtilage formerly of the said John which Matilda came and *gersummavit* the said cottage with curtilage and appurtenances, to hold to her and hers in villeinage at the will of the lord by the services due and accustomed for them. And she did fealty.
* [*HALS 65530, f1*] The jurors say that John Berney allowed one cottage with curtilage formerly of John Geiarde to be in the lord's hand. And he withdrew himself voluntarily therefrom. And the lord has granted the said cottage with curtilage to Robert Holdethypes and Dionisia his wife, to hold to them and theirs in villeinage at the will of the lord for the term of their lives and the life of the longer liver of them, by the services due and accustomed for them. Fine two capons. Etc.
* The lord has granted to John Burgeyn one cottage with curtilage formerly of John Sheparde, to hold to him and his in villeinage at the will of the lord by the services due for them and by law accustomed, under this condition that the said John shall pay or cause to be paid to the cellarer of St Albans at the Feast of St John the Baptist next to come 6s 8d and at the Feast of Easter then next following 6s 8d. And unless he shall do so the said surrender shall be held null, etc.
* The lord has granted to Thomas Rassh and Matilda his wife one toft called *Dyperes* with one croft of land lying below the said toft on the north side containing by estimation half an acre of land, to hold to them and theirs from Michaelmas next to come after the date of the present writing until the end of 40 years next ensuing, ~~6s 8d~~ rendering annually to the lord 12d and suit of court for all services etc. Fine 12d, etc.
* The lord has granted to William Freberne two tofts [and] two cotlands, whereof one is called *Meggesdame* and the other is called *Shayles,* to hold to him and his from Michaelmas next to come after the date of this court until the end of 40 years next ensuing, rendering for them to the lord ~~12d~~ 10s and suit of court for all services. Fine 12d.
* William Lawman pledged for William Cok junior that he repair his ruined tenement before the Feast of St Michael next to come under penalty of 40s.

HENRY VI

And unless he shall do this the said William Lawman has granted that [the 40s] should be levied from his own goods for the use of the lord.

* It is again ordered to distrain the tenant of the land late of William Wyntere *viz* Lord Philip Thorneburye, knight, and the tenant of the lands late of Joan Huntyngdon of *Wyllyen* [Willian] *viz* Nicholas Bygrave, to make their acknowledgement and fealty to the lord for their lands and tenements at the next court etc.
* The lord has granted to Walter Hale 27 acres of land lying by parcels in the fields of Norton late of Walter Bradeweye, to hold to him from Michaelmas next to come after the date of this court until the end of six years, rendering for them annually to the lord for each in the first two years of the aforesaid six years 6s 8d and all the fixed rent, and after the said two years rendering annually to the lord 10s and all the fixed rent due for them. Fine forgiven.

Halimote held there on Tuesday next after the Feast of St George the Martyr in the 6th year of the reign of King Henry VI [*27 Apr 1428*]

Jurors:	John Hale senior	John Colwelle	Walter Albreth junior
	Walter Albreth	John Hale junior	Simon Smyth
	William Cok senior	John Lawman	William Freberne
	William Lawman	Simon Hale	William Geiarde

* The jurors present that Margery Boton at *Coderethe* [Cottered] is married to William Webbe, John Geiarde at St Albans, Thomas Isowde at Weston, Gilbert Isowde, John Isowde, formerly sons of John Isowde senior, Robert Geiarde son of William Geiarde, there, John Geiarde son of William at *Yerdele* [Ardeley], Margery Boton at Baldock, Walter Boton, unknown where, are villeins and fugitives, so etc.
* Next they say that Henry Ronale is dead[55] who held of the lord one messuage and half a virgate of land formerly of John Jacob, of which the heriot is one horse worth 16s. And they say that Richard Ronale his son is his next heir and of full age, who came and *gersummavit* the said messuage and land with appurtenances, to hold to him and his in villeinage at the will of the lord by services etc. And he gives for agreement 20d.
* William Cok junior surrenders into the lord's hands one messuage and one cotland formerly called *Hathes* now called *Maltmannes*, of which the heriot in money is 40d. And the lord has granted the said messuage and land with appurtenances to John Valley, to hold to him and his in villeinage at the will

---

[55] Henry Ronale's will was proved in 1427/8 at St Albans (HALS: 1AR14v).

HENRY VI

of the lord by services etc. Fine 2s.
* Again it is ordered to distrain the tenant of the land formerly of William Vyntere *viz* Lord Philip Thornebury knight and the tenant of the land late of Joan Huntyngdon of *Wyllyen* [Willian] *viz* Nicholas Bygrave to make their acknowledgement and fealty to the lord for their lands and tenements at the next court etc.

Halimote held there on Tuesday next after the Feast of St Elphege in the 7th year of the reign of King Henry VI [*26 Apr 1429*]

* The jury present that William Cok junior, London, and his issue, Margery Boton at Bedford is married to William Webbe, and Margery Boton daughter of John Boton there, John Geiarde at St Albans, Thomas Isowde at Weston, Gilbert Isowde, John Isowde formerly son of John Isowde senior, there, Robert Geiarde son of William Geiarde there, John Geiarde son of William Geiarde at *Yerdele* [Ardeley], Margery Boton at Baldock, Walter Boton, unknown where, are villeins and fugitives therefore etc.
* The lord has granted to Thomas Rassh one hearth and one cotland which Henry Ronale lately held called *Wardeswyke* to hold to him for the term of 20 years next to come and fully completed after the date of this court, rendering annually to the lord 5s 4d and suit of court etc. Fine one capon etc.
* William Cok junior surrenders into the lord's hand one messuage and one *quartrona* of land with appurtenances formerly of Richard Cok and lately of [*HALS 65530, f1v*] John Cok, of which the heriot in money is 20d. And the lord has granted the said messuage and land with appurtenances to William Falley, to hold to him and his in villeinage at the will of the lord by services etc. Fine 12d.
* It is ordered to distrain the tenant of the lands formerly of William Wynter and the tenant of the land formerly of Joan Huntyngdon of *Wyllyen* [Willian] to make their acknowledgement to the lord by the next court etc.

Halimote held there on Tuesday next after the Feast of the Ascension of the Lord in the 8th year of the reign of Henry VI [*25 May 1430*]

Jurors:	John Hale senior	John Colwelle	Walter Albreth junior
	Walter Albreth senior	John Hale junior	Simon Smyth
	William Cok senior	John Lawman	William Freberne
	William Lawman	Simon Hale	Richard Ronale

* The jurors present that William Cok junior within the parish of *Hakeney* [Hackney] near London, Margery Boton at Bedford, and she is married to

HENRY VI

William Webbe, Margery Boton daughter of John Boton with the said William, John Geiarde at St Albans, Thomas Isowde at Weston, Gilbert Isowde, John Isowde formerly son of John Isowde senior there, John Geiarde son of William Geiarde at *Yerdele* [Ardeley], Walter Boton, unknown where, William Geiarde and Thomas his son at Bygrave, John Geiarde and William Geiarde sons of William Geiarde senior at Baldock are villeins and fugitives, therefore it is ordered to take them etc.

* It is ordered to take into the hands of the lord one cottage with curtilage formerly of John Geiarde and late of John Berney and afterwards of Robert Holethypes because the said Robert Holethypes has committed a certain felony for which he withdrew himself. And afterwards the lord granted the said cottage with curtilage to Dionisia Bybat daughter of Richard Bybat and Thomas her son to hold to them and theirs in villeinage at the will of the lord by services etc. Fine 6s 8d.
* It is ordered to take into the lord's hand one toft formerly of Hugh Smyth because he ceased paying rent *per annum*. And account to the lord for the issues etc.
* The lord granted to William Cok butcher (*bocher*) senior three selions of land, parcel of one virgate of land called *Bateslonde* which virgate of land is in the lord's hand of which the said three selions lie next to the tenement of the said William abutting with one head on the land of the said William towards the east and south and with another head on the tenement called *Maltemannes* which John Valley now holds, to hold to him for the term of 40 years next to come, at the will of the lord, paying for it 3d annually and suit of court for all services etc. Fine forgiven.
* It is ordered to distrain tenant of lands late of William Vyntere and tenant of lands late of Joan Huntyngdon to make fealty to the lord before the next court etc.

Halimote held there on Tuesday next before the Feast of St George in the 9th year of the reign of King Henry VI [*17 Apr 1431*]

Jurors:	John Hale senior	John Colwelle	Walter Albreth junior
	Walter Albreth senior	John Hale junior	Simon Smyth
	William Cok	John Lawman	William Freberne
	William Lawman	Simon Lawman	Richard Ronale

* The jurors present that Margery Boton at Bedford and she is married to a certain William Webbe, Margery Boton daughter of John Boton, with the said William there, John Geiarde at St Albans, Thomas Isowde at Weston, Gilbert

HENRY VI

Isowde, John Isowde formerly son of John Isowde senior there, John Geiarde son of William Geiarde at *Yerdele* [Ardeley], Walter Boton, of whom it will be enquired, William Geiarde and Thomas Geiarde his son at Bygrave, John Geiarde and William Geiarde formerly sons of William Geiarde senior at Baldock are villeins and fugitives. Therefore etc.

* To this court came Richard Bygrave and acknowledged that he holds of the lord one messuage built upon, formerly of Cecily Norman as appears by the outside [of the roll?] by the service of 20d rent a year and suit of court and he did fealty.
* It is ordered to distrain tenants of lands late of William Vynter and now of Lord Philip Thorneburye to do fealty to the lord for the lands and tenement now of the said lord before the next court, etc.

Halimote held there on Tuesday next after the Feast of the Finding of the Holy Cross in the 10th year of the reign of King Henry VI [*6 May 1432*]

Jurors:	Walter Albreth Senior	John Hale junior	William Freberne
	William Cok	John Lawman	Richard Renale
	William Lawman	Simon Hale	
	John Colwelle	Walter Albreth junior	

* The jurors present that Margery Boton at Bedford, and she is married to a certain William Webbe, Margery Boton daughter of John [*HALS 65531, f1*] Boton with the said William there, John Geiarde at St Albans, Thomas Isowde at Weston, Gilbert Isowde and John Isowde late sons of John Isowde senior there, John Geiarde son of William Geiarde at *Yerdele* [Ardeley], Walter Boton, of him it should be enquired, William Geiarde and Thomas his son at Bygrave, John Geiarde and William Geiarde son of William Geiarde senior at Baldock are villeins and fugitives therefore etc.
* Next they say that Hugh Smyth is dead who held from the lord one croft of land called *Ankerwyke*. And it is ordered to take it into the lord's hands until etc.
* Next they say that Simon Hale, John Colwelle and Walter Lawman have ruinous houses so they are amerced. And it is ordered to repair them before the next court under penalty of 6s 8d, etc.
* Walter Bradwey surrenders into the lord's hands one messuage built anew formerly of John Bradweye in Norton which is called *Halleorchyerde* and which is situated between the tenement formerly of Walter atte Chyrche on the one side and the tenement formerly of John Smyth on the other, of which the

heriot is remitted on account of poverty. And because the said Walter from the times when he was farmer of the farm of the rectory of Norton was indebted in divers sums of money to the Convent of St Albans by his own will and for a certain corrody granted to him for the term of his life within the monastery of St Albans he made the said surrender to the use of the lord and Convent which certain messuage with appurtenances was assigned to the said Convent for their rectory, etc.

Halimote held there on Tuesday next after the Feast of the Ascension of the Lord in the 11th year of the reign of King Henry VI [*26 May 1433*]

Jurors: William Cok   John Lawman   Richard Ronale
         Walter Lawman   Simon Hale   John Albreth
         John Colwelle   Walter Albreth junior Walter Hale
         John Hale junior   William Freberne

* The jurors present that Margery Boton at Bedford, and she is married to a certain William Webbe, Margery Boton daughter of John Boton with the said William there, John Geiarde at St Albans, Thomas Isowde at Weston, Gilbert Isowde late son of John Isowde senior there, William Geiarde, John and Thomas sons of the same William at Bygrave, John Geiarde and William Geiarde sons of William Geiarde senior at Baldock are villeins and fugitives therefore etc.
* The jurors say that William Falley is dead[56] who held from the lord a messuage and a cotland formerly of Matilda Balston, of which the heriot is one horse worth 5s. And they say that John his son is his next heir and of full age, who in full court has refused to hold the said messuage and lands with appurtenances. And hereupon the lord has granted the said messuage and land with one pightle lying below the said messuage now called *Balstonys Grove* to John Nele, to hold to him and his in villeinage at the will of the lord by the services due and accustomed for them. And he gives to the lord for agreement 6s 8d. And he has done fealty.
* Again it is ordered to retain in the lord's hand one croft of land called *Ankereswyke* late of Hugh Smyth of Baldock etc.
* Again it is ordered to distrain Lord Philip Thornebury to do fealty to the lord for the land and tenement late of William Vynter before the next court etc.

---

[56] William Vally's will was proved in 1432 at St Albans (HALS: 1AR19v).

HENRY VI

Halimote held there on Tuesday next after the Feast of the Ascension of the Lord in the 12th year of the reign of King Henry VI [*11 May 1434*]

* The jury present that Margery Boton at Bedford, and she is married to a certain William Webbe, Margery Boton daughter of John Boton with the said William, John Geiarde late of London is now dead but his issue there, Thomas Isoude and John Isowde at Weston, Gilbert Isowde son of the late John Isowde senior there and their issues there, John Geiard son of the late William Geiarde senior at Baldock, William Geiarde son of the said William senior at London with Stephen Flexmere are villeins and fugitives. Therefore etc.
* Next they say that John Hale senior is dead,[57] who held from the lord one messuage and a half virgate of land formerly of John Dypere, one toft and one *ferlingate* of land formerly of John Reymonde, of which the heriots are two horses of the value of 40s. And they say that John Hale, son of the said John senior, is his heir and is of full age, who is present at the court before the cellarer and the steward and who voluntarily refused to hold and have the said messuage, toft and land with appurtenances. And therefore the lord has granted the said messuage, toft and land with appurtenances to Walter Hale, brother of the said John Hale junior, to hold to him and his in villeinage at the will of the lord by services etc. And he gives for agreement 6s 8d and he did fealty.
* Next they say that Matilda Lawman late the wife of William Lawman senior is dead,[58] who held from the lord one messuage, one *ferlingate* of land formerly of William Sayer and afterwards of Walter Thomas, one toft called cotland formerly of William Thomas and afterwards of Walter Thomas, of which the heriots are two horses and one cow value 50s. And they say that John Lawman son of the said William and Matilda is next heir and of full age who came and *gersummavit* the said messuage, toft and land with appurtenances, to hold to him and his in villeinage at the will of the lord by services etc. And he gives for agreement 6s 8d. And he did fealty.
* Next they say that William Geiarde has alienated to Thomas Rowley one messuage with curtilage and with two acres of land without leave of the lord. So it is ordered to take the said messuage and curtilage with appurtenances into the lord's hands, etc.
* [*HALS 65531, f1v*] Again it is ordered to take into the lord's hands one croft of

---

[57] John Hale senior's will was proved in 1433 at St Albans (HALS: 1AR22v). His son Walter was appointed sole executor.
[58] Matilda Lawman's will was proved in 1433 at St Albans (HALS: 1AR22r) along with her late husband's will. The manor court records do not record his death.

land called *Ankereswyke* late of Hugh Smyth of Baldock, and to account to the lord for the issues before the next court. Afterwards it is decided by the court that the said Hugh Smyth died thereof seised and no heir has come to lay claim to the said croft therefore let proclamation be made that the next heir should come and make his claim before the third court on pain of losing it. And now is the first proclamation.

* Mabel Frere in her pure widowhood surrenders into the lord's hand one messuage and one *quartrona* of land formerly of Richard Assh, of which the heriot is one capon. And the lord has granted the said messuage and land with appurtenances to William Frace, to hold to him and his in villeinage at the will of the lord by services etc. Fine one capon, and he did fealty.

Halimote held there on Tuesday next after the Feast of the Finding of the Holy Cross in the 13th year of the reign of King Henry VI [*10 May 1435*]

Jurors:	William Cok	Simon Hale	John Albrethe
	John Colwelle	Walter Albreth junior	Walter Hale
	John Hale	William Freberne	John Burgeyne
	John Lawman	Richard Ronale	Thomas Rassh

* The jurors present that Margery Boton at Bedford, she is married there to William Webbe, the issue of John Geiarde now defunct, London, John Geiarde son of the late William Geiarde has manumission, William Geiarde son of the said late aforesaid William at *Sarum* [Salisbury], Thomas Isowde, John Isowde and Gilbert Isowde at Weston and their issues there, are villeins and fugitives, therefore it is ordered to take them, etc.
* And they say that John Burgeyne, lying on his deathbed,[59] surrendered into the lord's hands one cottage with curtilage formerly of John Hale, shepherd, of which the heriot is one young bull (*boviculus*). And the lord granted the said cottage with curtilage to Marion late the wife of the said John Burgeyne, to hold to her and hers in villeinage at the will of the lord etc, reserving right to whomsoever. And meanwhile she shall not commit waste. And she gives to the lord for agreement 3s 4d, and she did fealty.
* It was ascertained in the preceding court as the jurors presented that William Geiarde alienated to Thomas Rowleye one messuage with curtilage and two acres of land without leave of the lord for which reason the bailiff was ordered in the same court to take the said land and tenements [*sic*] into the lord's hand.

---

[59] John Burgun's will was proved in 1434 at St Albans (HALS: 1AR23v).

HENRY VI

And they were seised. And the said William comes into this court and puts himself into the lord's grace to have again the said lands and tenements. And the lord granted the same [*plural*] to him of his grace. And he gives to the lord one capon for agreement and he has done fealty.

* It is ordered to distrain John Stanneforde for the lands and tenement of Robert Cornemonger in *Willyen* [Willian] lately of Richard atte Dane, for fealty and homage to be done to the lord before the next court etc.
* A second proclamation was made that the next heir of Hugh Smyth of Baldock deceased should come and make his claim to the land and tenements late of the said Hugh called *Ankereswyke* before the third court on pain of losing them, and now this is the second proclamation etc.

Halimote held there on Tuesday next after the Feast of St George the Martyr in the 14th year of the reign of King Henry VI [*24 Apr 1436*]

Jurors:	William Cok	Simon Hale	John Albreth
	John Colwelle	Walter Albreth junior	Walter Hale
	John Hale	William Freberne	Thomas Rassh
	John Lawman	Richard Rounale	Walter Lawman

* The jurors present that Margery Boton wife of William Webbe at Bedford, the issue of John Geiarde defunct, London, John Geiarde son of the late William Geiarde has manumission, William son of the same William at *Sarum* [Salisbury], Thomas Isowde, John Isowde and Gilbert Isowde at Weston and their issue there are villeins and fugitives, therefore it is ordered to take them etc.
* To this court came Nicholas Bygrave and acknowledged that he holds from the lord freely by charter one tenement with appurtenances in *Willyen* [Willian] formerly of Joan Norman by the service of 20d *per annum*. And he did fealty.
* John Stanford came and acknowledged that he holds from the lord one tenement with appurtenances in *Wyllyen* [Willian] formerly of Robert Cornemonger and lately of Richard atte Dene by the service of 6d a year. And he did fealty.
* A third proclamation was made according to the custom of the manor that the next heir of Hugh Smyth should come and make his claim to the land and tenements lately of the said Hugh before the third court under penalty of losing them. And because there is no heir who wants to claim them therefore it is ordered to take the aforesaid lands and tenements into the lord's hands and account to the lord for the issues until etc.

HENRY VI

* The jurors say that John Hale, Simon Hale and John Colwelle have allowed their houses to fall. Therefore the said John Hale is amerced. And it is ordered to seise into the lord's hands the houses and tenements of the said Simon and John Colwell, and to account to the lord for the issues until etc.

[*HALS 65532, f1*] **Halimote held there on Tuesday next after the Feast of the Saints Tiburtius and Valerianus in the 15th year of the reign of King Henry VI [*18 Apr 1437*]**

Jurors:	William Cok	Simon Hale	John Albreth
	John Colwelle	Walter Albreth junior	Walter Hale
	John Hale	William Freberne	Thomas Rassh
	John Lawman	Richard Ronale	Simon Smyth

* The jurors present that William Geiarde at London with Stephen Flexmere, *bowyere* [bowmaker], Thomas Isowde, Gilbert Isowde and their issue at Weston, and John Isowde deceased has male issue there, they are villeins and fugitives. Therefore it is ordered to take them.

* Next they say that John Valey alienated his tenement which was once of William Geiarde, to John Sadeler without leave, therefore it is ordered to seise [it] etc.

* Again it is ordered to retain in the lord's hands the land and tenements of John Hale, Simon Hale and John Colwelle because they are very ruinous, and to account to the lord for the issues before the next court etc.

* Next they say that John Poley is dead,[60] who held from the lord one cotland, formerly of John Assh, of which the heriot is one horse. And they say that Thomas Poley junior is his next heir and he is of full age, who came and *gersummavit* the said messuage and one cotland with appurtenances, to hold to him and his in villeinage at the will of the lord by the services due and accustomed for them etc. And he gives to the lord as *gersumma* 20d.

* William Lawman comes and seeks to be admitted to one messuage and one *quartrona* of land formerly of John Lawman senior and to one messuage and a half virgate of land formerly of Walter Daye which John Lawman father of the said William held on the day he died. And he is admitted by the lord, to hold to him and his in villeinage at the will of the lord by services etc. And he gives to the lord for agreement 6s 8d. And he did fealty.

---

[60] John Poley's will was proved at St Albans in 1436 (HALS: 1AR27r). This will also recorded interests in land and tenements in Baldock, Bygrave and Willian, in addition to many bequests.

HENRY VI

* The lord at the instance and supplication of his poor tenants of his manor of Norton, with the assent and consent of John Poley and Thomas Swalewe, lately farmers there, of his special grace has remitted, released and pardoned to his tenants their customary heriot which he was accustomed to have from the lands, tenements, cottages, hearths and tofts of the said tenants after the death of each of them and after each alienation of such lands tenements cottages hearths or tofts by the said tenants every single time it happened from the date of this court until the end of 60 years next ensuing and fully completed. This being understood nevertheless that whereas the aforesaid tenants or any of them after their deaths or the deaths of any of them or each alienation by them or any of them made, they were accustomed or one of them was accustomed to give for heriot or for his kind of heriot from each kind of messuage and virgate of land, from every cottage and virgate of land, from every hearth and virgate of land, from each toft and virgate of land and from each messuage, cottage, hearth or toft and half virgate of land and from any messuage, cottage, hearth and *quartrona* of land, and from each messuage, cottage, hearth or toft and quarter of land, and from any messuage, cottage, hearth or toft by itself their best animal or best moveable chattel according to the custom of the said manor to their grave distress and insupportable charge the lord of his special grace grants for himself and his successors that the tenants and their heirs shall give for the said heriot for the term of 60 years after the death of each and after any alienation from each messuage, cottage, hearth or toft and virgate of land 3s 4d in money and from each messuage, cottage, hearth and toft and half virgate of land 20d and from every messuage, cottage, hearth, toft and *ferlingate* of land 20d and from every messuage, cottage, hearth or toft and quarter of land 12d, and from each messuage, cottage, hearth or toft by itself and with one acre or three acres of land on condition that the said tenants and each of them shall well and sufficiently repair and maintain and keep them sufficiently repaired and also make diligent search for other tenants to the lord to possess, hold and rebuild vacant tenements to the profit and convenience of the lord and shall apply continual diligence about this. If anyone shall do otherwise this grant or release shall be without force and effect.

HENRY VI

Halimote held there on Tuesday before the Feast of the Apostles Philip and James in the 16th year of the reign of Henry VI [*29 Apr 1438*]

Jurors:	William Cok	Simon Hale	John Albreth
	John Colwelle	Walter Albreth	John Hale
	William Colwelle	William Freberne	Walter Hale
	John Lawman	Richard Ronale	Thomas Rassh

* The jurors present that William Geiarde, London with Stephen Flexmere, bowmaker, Thomas Isowde and Gilbert Isowde and their issues at Weston. And that John Isowde deceased has male issue there, are villeins and fugitives therefore it is ordered to take them, etc.
* Next they say that Walter Albreth senior is dead,[61] who held from the lord two messuages, half a virgate and one *quartrona* of land late of Roger Albreth his father, of which the heriots are two sheep worth 20d a head. And they say that John Albreth son of the said Walter is his next heir and he is of full age, who came and *gersummavit* the said messuage and lands with appurtenances, to hold to him and his villeinage at the will of the lord by services etc. Fine 6s 8d.
* It is ordered to retain in the hands of the lord one tenement which Dionisia wife of Robert Holdethypees alienated to John Sadeler without leave of the lord, etc.
* John Hale senior, Walter Hale and John Colwelle are ordered to cause their ruinous tenements to be repaired before the next court under penalty of losing them.

[*HALS 65532, f1v*] Halimote held there on Tuesday next after the Feast of St Mark the Evangelist in the 17th year of Henry VI [*28 Apr 1439*]

Jurors:	John Laweman	Simon Hale	John Albreth
	John Colwelle	Walter Albreth	John Hale
	William Laweman	William Freberne	Walter Hale
	William Cok	Richard Ronale	Thomas Rasshe

* The jurors present that William Geiarde with Stephen Flexmere [in] London,

---

[61] Walter Albrey senior made his will on 4 March 1436/7. It was proved shortly after 7 August 1437 at St Albans (HALS: 1AR29r), his son John being named as executor. Although the surname Albrey is written in the will register, the family name appears to be interchangeable with Albreth: perhaps there y = thorn (th).

HENRY VI

Thomas Isowde senior and Gilbert Isowde and their issues at Weston, and the issue of John Isowde deceased there, are villeins and fugitives, therefore it is ordered to take them etc.

* The lord has granted to John Albreth 15 acres and three roods of land and meadow formerly of Sarra of Yerdeley as appears by the extent which William Dyke lately held whereof are ten acres of meadow called the *Hallemede* to hold unto the aforenamed John from Michaelmas next to come until the end and term of seven years next to come and fully completed, by the service of rent annually therefrom to the lord for fixed rent of the aforesaid meadow 3s 4d and one pound of cumin. And to the office of cellarer annually for increase in rent 6s 8d for all services except suit of court. Fine is remitted, and he did fealty.
* The lord has granted to Thomas Geiarde one messuage formerly of Geofrey Geiarde afterwards of John Geiarde and Emma Geiarde and lately of Robert Holdethypes to hold to the aforenamed Thomas and his heirs in villeinage at the will of the lord by service of rent annually therefrom to the lord for fixed rent 4d. And to the office of cellarer annually for increase in rent 8d for all services except suit of court. The fine is forgiven, and he has done fealty.
* John Hale senior is ordered to have repaired his ruined tenements before the next court under penalty of 6s 8d. Walter Hale for like under the same penalty. Walter Albreth junior under penalty of 3s 4d before the Feast of All Saints next, etc.
* It is ordered to take into the lord's hand all the land and tenements of Dionisia Hale and William Lawman because they are totally flattened. And to account to the lord for the issues.

Halimote held there on Tuesday after the Sunday in Whites [*ie the first Sunday after Easter*] in the 18th year of the reign of King Henry VI [*17 May 1440*]

Jurors:	John Albreth	William Cok	Walter Hale
	John Colwelle	Simon Hale	John Hale
	John Lawman	Walter Albreth	Thomas Rassh
	William Lawman	William Freberne	Richard Rowenhale

* The jurors present that William Geiarde London with Stephen Flexmere, Thomas Isowde senior and Gilbert Isowde with their issue at Weston and the issue of John Isowde deceased are villeins and fugitives, therefore it is ordered to take them.

HENRY VI

* John Hale senior, Walter Hale, Simon Hale and William Lawman are ordered to repair their wasted and ruinous tenements before the next Feast of All Saints, each of them under the penalty of 6s 8d etc.
* Cecily daughter of Walter Albreth gives to the lord 12d for licence to marry etc.

Halimote held there in the Feast of St Mark the Evangelist the 19th year of the reign of King Henry VI [*25 Apr 1441*]

Jurors:	John Albreth	Walter Hale	John Nele
	John Collewelle	John Hale	
	John Laweman	Thomas Rassh	
	William Cok	Richard Rowenhale	

* The jurors present that Walter Hale at Baldock, William Geiarde London with Stephen Flexmere, Agnes daughter of John Hale at Edworth with John Mustele, John son of Walter Hale at *Lytlelyngton* [Litlington], Cecily Albreth married to Roger Saburgh, Thomas Isowde senior, Gilbert Isowde with their issue and the issue of John Isowde deceased at Weston are villeins and fugitives therefore it is ordered to take them etc.
* William Geiarde surrenders into the hands of the lord by the hands of John Moredon by leave of the lord one messuage with curtilage and two acres of land, of which the heriot is one sheep worth 18d. And the lord has granted the said messuage and curtilage and land with appurtenances to Helene Geiarde wife of the said William, to hold to her at the will of the lord for the term of her life only by the services due etc. And after the death of the said Helen the said messuage curtilage and with appurtenances shall remain to John son of the said William, to hold to him and his etc. Fine one capon and she did fealty.
* It is ordered to take into the lord's hands all the lands and tenements which Simon Hale, John Hale senior, William Lawman and Walter Hale hold from the lord by the rod because they are totally wasted and flattened, and to account to the lord for the issues before the next court etc.
* It is ordered to distrain Thomas Cadwelle to be at the next court to show how he entered the fee of the lord *viz* into the lands and tenements late of Thomas Cadwelle his father etc.

HENRY VI

[*HALS 65533, f1*] **Halimote held there on Tuesday next after the Feast of St George the Martyr in the 20th year of the reign of King Henry VI [24 Apr 1442]**

Jurors:	William Freberne	John Inthehale	John Albreth
	John Colwelle	Richard Rowenhale	William Lawman
	John Lawman	John Nele	William Frace
	William Cok	Walter Albreth	

* It is ordered to distrain Thomas Yonge to do homage to the lord and fealty at the next court.
* It is ordered to distrain Thomas Cadwelle to be at the next court to show how he entered the lord's fee, etc.
* Again it is ordered to retain in the lord's hands all the lands and tenements which Simon Inthehale, John Inthehale senior, Walter Inthehale and William Lawman senior hold from the lord by the rod because they are totally wasted and flattened.
* Walter Inthehale at Baldock, William Geiarde, London with Stephen Flexmere, Agnes daughter of John Inthehale at Edworth with John Mustele, John son of Walter Inthehale at *Lytleyngton* [Litlington], Cecilia Albreth married to Roger Saburgh, Thomas Isowde senior, Gilbert Isowde with their issue and the issue of John Isowde deceased at Weston, are villeins and fugitives. Therefore it is ordered to take them etc.
* John Clerke occupies and tends [?half an acre] of land in *le Lytlemalm* and half an acre of land on the *Eldewelhylle* without leave of the lord and without estate etc. And they are parcel of a *quartrona* of land called *Odeslonde*, therefore it is ordered to seise [it] etc.
* Marion Burgon alienated to John Lawman one cottage without leave of the lord so it is ordered to seise [it] etc.
* The Homage present that Philip Thorneburye knight has encroached with the water of his pond called *Someresponde* upon the land of the lord in Mundencroft in width by estimation 20 feet, and they say that willows growing on the bank of the said pond are within the lordship and the parish of Norton.
* And they say that the parish of Bygrave make their processional way on

HENRY VI

rogation days[62] within and through the said croft called *Mundencroft* within the parish of Norton, etc, therefore counsel must be had with the lord.

* They say further that the lord of this manor or his farmer commoned with his draught horses (*averiis*) and animals in the meadow of Philip Thornebury called *Russhmede viz* from the Feast of St Peter in Chains until the Feast of the Purification of the Blessed Mary the Virgin etc.

* Because Simon ithe Hale has not repaired the waste committed in one messuage and a half virgate of land formerly of John Burre just as he was ordered at many earlier courts and because he is able to hold the said lands and tenements therefore it is decided and the lord has granted the said lands and tenements to John Clerke the younger, to hold to him and his in villeinage at the will of the lord by the due services etc, under this condition that he build the aforesaid messuage within three years from the Feast of St Michael next ensuing. Fine forgiven. And he has done fealty.

* Because Walter Inthehale has not repaired the waste committed in one messuage and half a virgate of land formerly of John Reymonde and of John Dyper as he was ordered at many earlier courts, therefore the lord has granted the said messuage and lands with appurtenances to John Clerke senior, to hold to him and his in villeinage at the will of the lord by services etc, on condition that the same John Clerke build the said messuage within three years from the Feast of St Michael next ensuing. Fine forgiven, and he has done fealty.

Halimote held there on Wednesday next before the Feast of St Matthew the Apostle in the 21st year of the reign of King Henry VI [*19 Sep 1442*]

Jurors:	John Lawman	Richard Rouenhale	William Frace
	William Cok	John Albreth	John Colwelle
	John Inthehale	Walter Albreth	John Clerke
	William Freberne	William Lawman	Thomas Geiarde

* The jurors present concerning villeins and fugitives as appears within [the roll] in the court of Easter term etc.

---

[62] A common feature of Rogation days was the ceremony of 'beating the bounds', in which a procession of parishioners, led by the incumbent, churchwarden, and choirboys, would proceed around the boundary of their parish and pray for its protection in the forthcoming year.

HENRY VI

Halimote held there on Tuesday in the eve of the Apostles Philip and James in the 21st year in the reign of King Henry VI [*30 Apr 1443*]

Jurors:	John Albreth	Walter Albreth	John Clerke
	John Lawman	William Lawman	William Freberne
	William Cok	Richard Rowenhale	Walter Lawman
	John Neele	John Hale	Thomas Rasshe

* The jurors present that William Geiarde, late in London with Stephen Flexmere, now at Southampton, Agnes daughter of John Hale [*HALS 65533, f1v*] married to Roger Paternoster at Edworth without licence, Walter Inthehale there, Cecily Albreth having been allowed to marry Roger Saburgh of Letchworth, Gilbert Isowde, John Williams and Agnes daughter of the same Roger, William and John sons of Thomas Isowde deceased and John Isowde son of John Isowde deceased at Weston. And Joan daughter of the said Thomas Isowde deceased married without licence to Thomas son of Thomas Cooke of *Wyllyen* [Willian] are villeins and fugitives, therefore etc.
* Next they present that Philip Thorneburye, knight, has encroached for himself from the lord's land into the croft called *Mundencrofte* with his pond called *Somersponde* in width by estimation 20 feet, and the said pond is within the lordship and parish of Bygrave, therefore etc.
* Again it is ordered to retain in the lord's hands all the lands and tenements of Simon Inthehale, John Inthehale senior because they are totally wasted and flattened, and to account to the lord for the issues until etc.
* Because William Lawman has not repaired the waste made in one messuage and one *quartrona* of land formerly of John Lawman senior as contained in the orders of the four immediately preceding courts, therefore the lord has taken the said messuage and lands into his hands. And he has granted them with appurtenanes to John Nele to hold to him and his in villeinage at the will of the lord by services etc. Fine forgiven and he did fealty.
* The lord has granted to John Blowe one messuage and half a virgate formerly of Walter Inthehale and late of Robert Taylour which John Lawman senior refused to hold from the lord by services etc. To hold to the said John Blowe, to him and his in villeinage at the will of the lord by services etc. Fine forgiven etc.
* Marion Burgon in her pure widowhood surrenders into the hands of the lord one cottage lying next to *Parloureslonde* formerly of Margery Jecob, of which the heriot in money is 6d. And the lord has granted the said cottage with appurtenances to John Lawman junior, to hold to him and his in villeinage at the will of the lord by services etc, under such a condition however that the

HENRY VI

said John should pay or cause to be paid to the said Marion or her certain attorney on the Monday next before the Feast of St Dunstan next to come 6s 8d of English money without further delay, or the present surrender and grant of the same shall be held for nothing, provided also that Marion shall have her easement of a room situated on the left side of the hall of the said cottage with free entry and exit for the whole life of the said Marion without hinderance from John, fine 3s 4d, he did fealty.
* The lord granted to Walter Clyfton one messuage formerly of Geoffrey Geiarde and lately of Robert Holdethypees which fell to the lord by way of escheat on account of a felony committed by Thomas Geiarde late tenant of the said messuage whereof he was indicted, to hold to the said Walter and his in villeinage at the will of the lord by services etc, rendering for it annually 12d and suit of court for all services. Fine 40d, and he did fealty.

Halimote held there on Tuesday next after the Feast of the Finding of the Holy Cross in the 22nd year of the reign of King Henry VI [5 May 1444]

Jurors:	William Freberne	John Colwelle	John Nele
	John Albreth	William Frace	John Lawman Sr
	William Cok	John Clerke	John Lawman Jr
	William Albreth	Thomas Rassh	John Hale

* [*l. margin*: villeins] The jurors present that William Geiarde late of London with Stephen Flexmere now at Southampton, Agnes daughter of John Hale, wife of Roger Paternoster of Edworth married to him without licence, Walter Inthehale there, Cecily Albreth licenced to marry Roger Saburgh of Letchworth, Gilbert Isowde, John Williams and Agnes daughter of the same Roger, John and William, sons of Thomas Isowde deceased and John Isowde son of John Isowde deceased at Weston, and Joan daughter of the said Thomas Isowde married without licence etc, are villeins and fugitives therefore etc.
* [*l. margin*: villein (fem)] Margery daughter of John Albreth gives to the lord for licence to marry the first time 12d.
* And they say that John Clerke has his tenement ruinous and wasted. And he is ordered to repair [it] before Michaelmas next under penalty of losing it etc.
* The lord has granted to William Colwelle one messuage and half a virgate of land formerly of William Sayer and of Walter Sayer, deceased, and half a virgate of land formerly of Walter Harleston and of John son of William, deceased, and late of John Hale junior which came and were taken into the lord's hands on account of waste as appears by divers preceding courts, to

HENRY VI

hold to the aforenamed William and his in villeinage at the will of the lord by services etc. Fine forgiven etc.

Halimote held on Tuesday next before the Feast of St George the Martyr in the 23rd year of the reign of King Henry VI [*20 Apr 1445*]

Jurors:
William Freberne	William Cok	John Lawman Sr
Walter Albreth	William Frace	John Lawman Jr
John Neele	John Albreth	Richard Rowenhale
Thomas Bradwey	John Colwelle	John Blowe

* The jurors present that Walter Hale dwelling at Edworth, John Hale and John his son there, Agnes daughter of the said John Hale wife of Roger Paternoster there, John son of Walter Hale at *Lytlelyngton* [Litlington] in the county of Cambridge, William Geiarde late of London now in Southampton, Gilbert Isowde, John Williams and Agnes daughter of the same Gilbert, William Isowde son of Thomas Isowde, deceased, John Isowde son of John Isowde, deceased, at Weston, and Joan daughter of Thomas Isowde at *Wyllyen* [Willian] married to Thomas Cooke there, are villeins and fugitives therefore it is ordered to take them etc.
* Next they present that the tenement of John Clerke is totally wasted and ruinous and that the said John is not able to maintain [it]. [*HALS 65534, f1*] Therefore it is ordered to take the said tenement with appurtenances into the lord's hands and provide it with another sufficient tenant.
* Next they present that Thomas Poley is dead, who held from the lord freely by charter five half acres of land of the holding formerly of Sarra de Yerdele. Therefore it is ordered to distrain the tenants of the land aforesaid to be at the next court to make relief and fealty to the lord etc and to show how they entered the lord's fee, etc.
* The jurors present that Simon Smyth is dead, who held from the lord two tenements in *Wyllyen* [Willian] by what services they do not know. Therefore it is ordered to distrain the tenants of the aforesaid lands and tenements of the said Simon that they may be at the next court to show how they entered the lord's fee etc and to make to the lord relief and fealty etc.
* It is ordered to distrain John Yonge to be at the next court to show how he entered the lord's fee *viz* into one croft called *Mundene Crofte* and in divers other lands in the village of Norton and to make relief and fealty to the lord etc.
* Joan lately wife of John Laweman complains against John Nele in a plea of dower and declares that she will sue her aforesaid plaint in the form and nature

HENRY VI

of a Writ of Dower, of which she has nothing. Pledges of prosecution John Laweman and William Freberne. Therefore the beadle is ordered to summon the said John Nele or his bailiff to be at the court of the Lord John, abbot of St Albans at St Albans beneath the ash tree within the abbey held according to the custom of the manor on the Tuesday in the week of Pentecost to answer the said Joan in the said plea etc.

* Next the Homage present that the rector of Letchworth is a common hunter within the lordship of Norton and takes hares etc and makes unlawful ways through the pasture and corn of the lord and his tenants there. Therefore let a writ be made etc.

Halimote held there on Tuesday the morrow of St Mark the Evangelist in the 24th year of the reign of King Henry VI [26 Apr 1446]

* John Colwelle complains against John Bryddeshale in a plea of debt (*super dd*) 4s 6d. The beadle is ordered to attach the said John Brydeshale or his bailiff. And the beadle responds that he attached [him] by one sheep. And the aforesaid John Brydeshale having been commanded has not appeared. And the beadle is ordered as at other times to attach the same John etc so that he be at St Albans at the court under the ash tree on Monday in the week of Pentecost next to come to be held to answer to the said John Colwell in the said plea, etc.
* All the tenants are ordered to grind at the lord's mill under penalty of 3s 4d each etc.

Halimote held there on Tuesday next before the Feast of St George the Martyr in the 25th year of the reign of King Henry VI [18 Apr 1447]

Jurors:	Thomas Bradewey	John Colwelle	John Nele
	John Albreth	John Lawman Senior	Richard Rowenhale
	William Cokke	John Lawman Junior	John Blowe
	Walter Albreth	William Freberne	William Frace

* It is ordered to distrain Thomas Yonge for the lands late of William Vyntere and the tenants of the land late of Simon Smyth of *Welwen* [Willian] to be at the next court to show how they entered the fee of the lord and to make to the lord relief and fealty, etc.
* The jurors present that Walter Inthehale and John his son, John Hale, John his son, Beatrice and Margery, daughters of the same John and Agnes daughter of

HENRY VI

the same, wife of Roger Paternoster at Edworth, William Geiarde at Baldock, Gilbert Isowde, John Williams and Agnes, daughter of the same at Weston, John son of John Isowde at London, Joan daughter of Thomas Isowde, wife of Thomas Cooke of *Wyllyen* [Willian], are villeins and fugitives therefore etc.

* William Isowde son of Thomas Isowde at St Albans with John Grove, *smyth*. And he gives annually for *chevage* 2d.
* Helen Geiarde in her pure widowhood surrenders into the hands of the beadle by leave of the lord one cottage late of William Geiarde, of which the heriot in money is 10d. And the lord has granted the said cottage with appurtenances to Walter Hale, to hold to him and his in villeinage at the will of the lord by services etc. Fine 3s 4d, and he did fealty.
* Walter Hale surrenders into the hands of the lord one cottage late of William Geiarde, of which the heriot in money is 10d. And the lord has granted the said cottage with appurtenances to Walter Hale, to hold to him and his in villeinage at the will of the lord by services, etc. Fine 3s 4d and he did fealty.
* John Neele surrenders into the lord's hands one messuage and one cotland formerly of Matilda Balston and before of Thomas Reve, of which the heriot in money is 10d. And the lord has granted the said messuage and cotland with appurtenances to Henry Nele, to hold to him and his in villeinage at the will of the lord by services etc. Fine 20d. And he did fealty.

Halimote held there on the 16th day of April, in the 26th year of the reign of King Henry VI [*16 Apr 1448*]

Concerning villeins and fugitives it appears plainly in the court held here last year etc and all other things well.

[*HALS 65534, f1v*] Halimote held there on Monday after the Feast of the Finding of the Holy Cross in the 27th year of the reign of King Henry VI [*5 May 1449*]

Jurors:	Thomas Bradweye	John Lawman	John Neele
	John Albreth	Richard Rowenhale	John Fysh
	Walter Albreth	Walter Lawman	Henry Nele
	John Colwelle	William Frace	

* It is ordered to distrain John Yonge to be here at the next court to show how he entered the lord's fee and to do homage and fealty to the lord etc.
* It is ordered to take into the lord's hands all the lands and tenements of John Blowe and Walter Lawman because they felled the timber of the said tenements and totally wasted the said tenements, etc, therefore etc.

HENRY VI

* John Smyth is ordered to be at the next court to show his charters concerning one cottage late of John Lawman, parcel of the land called the *Halle Londe* formerly of John Newman, etc.
* It is ordered to take into the lord's hands one cottage late of William Geiarde now of Walter Clyfton because it is totally wasted, etc.
* The jurors present that John Stangforde, William Crane and Richard Redehede have ploughed up the land of the lord and his tenants etc, to enlarge their lands etc, and it is ordered to amend before the next court under penalty for each of them 4d, etc.
* William Cok is dead[63] who held of the lord one messuage and one croft and half an acre of land formerly of Hugh Grome and afterwards of Clement Dypere, one toft and half a virgate of land formerly of John, son of Nicholas Newman, and afterwards of Ralph Boton and half of one toft and half a virgate of land formerly of Richard Cok, of which the heriots in money are 5s. And they say that Thomas his son is his next heir thereof and of full age who came and *gersummavit* the said tenements with appurtenances, to hold to him and his in villeinage at the will of the lord by services etc. Fine 3s 4d and he did fealty.

Halimote held there on Tuesday next after Sunday in Whites in the 28th year of the reign of King Henry VI [*26 May 1450*]

Jurors:	Thomas Bradweye	John Lawman	John Neele
	John Albreth	Richard Rowenhale	Thomas Cok
	Walter Albreth	William Lawman	John Blowe
	John Colwelle	William Frace	

* The jurors present that John Hale at Edworth, John his son and their issue there, Beatrice daughter of the same married without licence to Sutton of Dunton, Agnes daughter of the same married without licence to John Paternoster of Edworth, Margery daughter of the same with John Mustele there, Walter Hale with that John Mustele there, and John Hale son of the same with the same John there are villeins and fugitives. Therefore it is ordered to take them etc.
* The jurors say that William Freberne is dead, who held from the lord one toft with croft adjoining containing one and a half acres formerly of Thomas Dryver and one toft and one croft and half an acre of land formerly of Walter, son of John Dryver, of which the heriots in money are 20d. And they say that

---

[63] William Cok senior's will was proved in 1449 at St Albans (HALS: 1AR57r).

HENRY VI

William his son is his next heir and of full age who came and *gersummavit* the said toft curtilage and land with appurtenances, to hold to him and his in villeinage at the will of the lord by services etc. Fine 20d and he did fealty.

* It is ordered to retain in the hands of the lord all the lands and tenements of John Blowe because they are totally wasted etc and account to the lord for the issues until it be provided with a tenant etc.
* Again it is ordered to distrain John Smyth to show how he holds one cottage lately of John Lawman parcel of the holding called *le Hallelond* formerly of John Newman etc.
* Again it is ordered to retain in the lord's hand one messuage with a curtilage late of William Geiarde because Walter Clyfton tenant thereof allowed it to be wasted and totally ruinous. And now to this court comes Thomas Huckulle and Agnes his wife and took from the lord the said messuage and curtilage with appurtenances to hold to them and theirs in villeinage at the will of the lord by the service of a rent annually to the lord of 12d a year and suit of court, for all services etc. Fine for having entry 12d and they did fealty.
* Again it is ordered to retain in the hands of the lord one messuage, half a virgate and one *quartrona* of land formerly of William Sayer late of John Hale junior and afterwards of Walter Lawman because they are totally wasted. And the said Walter is not capable to repair and maintain the said tenements etc. And now to this court came Thomas Bradweye and took from the lord the said tenements with appurtenances to hold to him and his in villeinage at the will of the lord by service of rent thereof annually to the lord all the fixed rent and common suit of court, and annual farm rent (*firmacio*) of the manor 21s per year for all services etc. Fine 2s 6d. And he has done fealty.
* The jurors present that Henry Nele is dead[64] who held from the lord one messuage and one cotland formerly of Matilda Balston lately of William Duche, of which the heriot in money is 10d. And they say that Alice daughter of the said Henry is his next heir thereof and of the age of three years and because of the minority of the said Alice and the said tenement is also ruinous and there is no one of the blood of the said Alice able to maintain or repair the aforesaid tenement, the lord has granted the said tenement with appurtenances to John son of Walter Albreth and Margaret his wife to hold to them and theirs in villeinage at the will of the lord by services etc. And if the aforenamed Alice when she shall come to lawful age or any other shall come in future and claim or demand the said tenements with appurtenances and recover them, the lord wills that the said Alice and also he who thus shall recover the aforesaid tenements shall satisfy the said John and Margaret, their heirs and assigns

---

[64] Henry Neel's will was proved in 1449 at St Albans (HALS: 1AR58r).

before they might have entry. Fine 10d and they did fealty.
* [*HALS 65534, f2*] Next they say that William Cok is dead, who held from the lord a moiety of half a virgate of land formerly of John Wyllesson called *Hathes* otherwise called *Maltmannes* and lately John Valley, held one toft and one cotland formerly of Agnes daughter of Stephen Clerke and lately John Cok, held for a term of 40 years three selions of land, parcel of a virgate of land called *Bateslonde* lying next the tenement of the said William abutting with one head upon the land of the same William towards the east and another head upon the tenement called *Maltmannes* towards the south, of which the heriots in money are 10d. And they say that Thomas Cok his son is his next heir thereof and of full age who came and *gersummavit* the said tenement with appurtenances, to hold to him and his in villeinage at the will of the lord by services etc and by annual rent service of the aforesaid virgate of land for the said three selions 3d *per annum*. Fine 20d and he did fealty.
* Walter Albreth gives to the lord for agreement to marry Matilda his daughter to John Shelforde 12d, etc.

Halimote held there on Tuesday after the Feast of the Annunciation of the Lady in the 29th year of the reign of King Henry VI [*30 Mar 1451*]

Jurors:	John Albreth	William Lawman	John Blowe
	Walter Albreth	William Frace	Thomas Bradwey
	John Lawman	John Nele	John Fysshe
	Richard Rowenhale	Thomas Cok	John Albreth junior

* The jurors present that it appears more fully in earlier courts concerning villeins and fugitives etc, therefore let them be taken etc.
* The beadle is ordered to distrain John Yonge and Richard Harre to be at the next court to show how they entered the lord's fee, and to do homage and fealty to the lord etc.
* Again it is ordered to distrain John Fyssh before the next court to show how he holds one cottage late of John Lawman, parcel of the land called the *Hallelonde* late of John Newman etc. Afterwards he showed a charter and is exonerated. And he accounts to the lord for 6d *per annum* etc.

HENRY VI

Halimote held there on Monday before the Feast of St George the Martyr in the 30th year of the reign of King Henry VI [*17 Apr 1452*]

Jurors:	John Albreth senior	William Lawman	John Fyssh
	John Colwelle	William Grace[65]	John Albreth junior
	Walter Albreth	John Neele	William Freberne
	Richard Rowenhale	John Blowe	Walter Lawman

* The jurors present concerning villeins and fugitives as appears more fully in earlier courts etc.
* Thomas Bradwey caused waste and distress by felling and carrying away the timber of a vacant and in hand tenement called *Bates* without the lord's leave to the lord's damage 6s 8d which it is ordered to levy etc. And he shall be amerced for the aforesaid trespass at the lord's will.
* Next they say that William Cok villein of the lord is dead who held of the lord one messuage, one acre and one rood of land formerly of Walter Attewatre called *Heywarde* just as it is situated and lies between the messuage formerly of Roger Albreth and one plot of land (*placeam*) formerly of Alexander Cooke and the said acre abuts on the way called *Mylleweye* at one end (*caput*) and at the other end on the *Gorehegge*, of which the heriot in money is 12d. And they say that Thomas Cok his son is his next heir thereof and of full age who came and *gersummavit* the said messuage and land with appurtenances, to hold to him and his in villeinage at the will of the lord by rent service therefrom annually to the lord, 2s 4d, fine and heriot when they fall due and suit of court. Fine one capon etc.
* It is ordered to distrain the tenants of the lands of John Yonge and Richard Harre to be at the next court to show how they entered the lord's fee and to do homage to the lord etc.
* The lord granted to John Albreth senior, 26 acres and three roods of land and meadow formerly of Sarra de Yerdeley whereof ten acres are of the meadow called *Hallemede*, to hold to him and his etc by rent service therefrom annually to the lord of fixed rent 3s 4d *per annum* and one pound of cumin and to the office of cellarer annually increase in rent 6s 8d annually *per annum* and suit of court, fine one capon and he did fealty.

---

[65] This appears to be the same person as William Frace who was regularly listed as a juror around this time.

HENRY VI

Halimote held there on Tuesday next before the Feast of St George the Martyr in the 31st year of the reign of King Henry VI [*17 Apr 1453*]

Jurors: Thomas Bradweye   John Albreth junior   William Lawman
         John Albreth senior John Neele   John Colwelle
         Walter Albreth   William Frace   John Blowe
         John Lawman   Richard Rowenhale   Thomas Cok

* The jurors present that John Hale and John his son at Edworth, Walter Hale there, John son of the same, where they do not know, Gilbert Isowde and the issue of the same, and John Isoude at Weston are villeins and fugitives, therefore it is ordered to take them etc.
* They present that the willows by *Bygraveponde* are totally within the parish and lordship of Norton and say that Philip Thorneburye, knight, and others, his tenants and parishioners of Bygrave, make unlawful ways there. And the said Philip claims [*HALS 65534, f2v*] the bank there with the said willows belongs to his lordship of Bygrave and is within the aforesaid parish of Bygrave in disherison of the lord etc and to the prejudice of the parishioners of Norton aforesaid because they say that the said bank with the willows are, and from the time of which there is no memory have been within the lordship and parish of Norton, therefore the said Philip and the tenants and parishioners of Bygrave aforesaid are amerced for the said trespass 3s 4d. And it is further to be consulted (*consulendum est*) with the lord and his counsel, etc.
* William Freberne surrenders into the lord's hands one toft with croft adjoining containing two acres formerly Thomas Dryvere's and one toft, one croft and half an acre of land formerly of Walter son of John Dryvere, of which the heriots in money are 20d. And the lord has granted the said tofts, crofts and land to Thomas Hukhylle and Agnes his wife to hold to them and theirs in villeinage at the will of the lord by services etc. Fine 20d and they did fealty etc.
* John Albreth senior gives to the lord for licence to marry Joan his daughter this first time 8d. [*l. margin*: villein]

HENRY VI

Halimote held there on Tuesday the morrow of St John before the Latin Gate, in the 32nd year of the reign of King Henry VI [7 May 1454]

Jurors: Thomas Bradweye   John Laweman   Richard Rowenhale
         John Albreth senior   John Albreth junior   William Frace
         John Colwelle   Thomas Cok   John Neele
         William Albreth   William Lawman   John Blowe

* The lord has granted to Thomas Huchylle and John Lawman one toft called *Ankereswyke* to hold to them and theirs in villeinage at the will of the lord by services etc rendering for it annually to the lord 2d, fine and heriot when they fall due and common suit of court. Fine one capon. And they did fealty
* The lord has granted to John Brygger one cottage with appurtenances formerly of Thomas Love to hold to him and his in villeinage at the will of the lord by rent service therefrom annually to the lord 12d, at the usual terms, fine and heriot when they fall due and common suit of court. Fine one capon. And he did fealty.
* The jurors present that five acres of land formerly of Sarra de *Yerdele* called *Yerdelebuttes* and ten acres of meadow formerly of the said Sarra are common of the tenants of Norton *viz* the said land except in the time in which it is sown and the said meadow except from the Feast of the Purification of the Blessed Mary the Virgin at which times they are always in severalty otherwise not etc.

Halimote held there on Friday next before the Feast of St George the Martyr in the 33rd year of the reign of King Henry VI [18 Apr 1455]

Jurors: Thomas Bradweye   John Lawman   Richard Rowenhale
         John Albreth senior   John Albreth junior   William Frace
         John Colwelle   Thomas Cok   John Neele
         William Albreth   William Laweman   John Blowe

* The jurors present that Philip Thornebury, knight, encroached upon the soil of the lord and of his tenants, in *Mundencrofte*, by estimation 24 feet in length and seven feet in width, and ditched the aforesail soil in order to enlarge his land there and his pond called *Somerespond*. They say further that upon the aforesaid soil they make illegal ways etc. Therefore let a writ be made etc.
* The lord has granted to Thomas Hukhylle and Agnes his wife one toft and one *quartrona* of land called *Wodes* to hold to them and theirs in villeinage at the

HENRY VI

will of the lord by rent service annually to the lord 4d *per annum*, fine and heriot when they fall due for all services except suit of court. Fine one capon. And they did fealty.
* It is ordered to distrain Richard Hurre to do fealty to the lord for the lands and tenements which he holds from the lord in *Wylye* [Willian] before the next court etc and to show how he entered the fee of the lord etc.

Halimote held there on Tuesday next before the Feast of St George the Martyr in the 34th year of the reign of King Henry VI [20 Apr 1456]

Jurors:	Thomas Bradwey	John Albreth junior	Richard Rowenhale
	John Albreth senior	Thomas Cok	William Frace
	Walter Albreth	William Lawman	John Neele
	John Lawman	John Calwelle	John Blowe

* The jurors present that Philip Thorneburye less than lawfully has broken the lord's soil upon the holding called *Mundens* which John Roo holds from the lord because the same Philip has altered the course of water by making one ditch in the wrong course (*in inrectum cursum*) there and also the processional way etc. And he is ordered to amend etc under penalty of 40s.
* It is ordered to distrain Richard Hurre and the tenants of the land and tenements called *Munden* which John Roo holds that they may be at the next court to show how they entered the fee and to make relief and fealty etc.
* [*HALS 65534, f3*] The Homage present that Nicholas Bygrave is dead, who held from the lord freely by charter in *Wyllyen* [Willian] one messuage and 180 acres of land by estimation called *Bygraves*. Therefore the beadle is ordered to distrain the tenants of the said lands and tenements to be at the next court to give relief and fealty to the lord and to show how they entered the lord's fee etc.

Halimote held there on Wednesday next after the Feast of St Mark the Evangelist in the 35th year of the reign of King Henry VI [27 Apr 1457]
* John Blowe surrenders into the lord's hands one messuage and half a virgate and one *quartrona* of land formerly of Walter Hale of which the heriots in money are 5s. And the lord has granted the said messuage and lands with appurtenances to Robert Bayly and Elizabeth his wife, to hold to them and theirs in villeinage at the will of the lord by the service of all the fixed rent and suit of court etc and to the farmer of the manor for works therefor due 23s 1d.

HENRY VI

Fine 5s and he did fealty.

* It is ordered to distrain the tenant of the land lately of John Roo called *Mundens*, Richard Hurre of *Wyllyen* [Willian], and the tenants of the lands and tenements late of William Hurre there to be at the next court to give relief and fealty to the lord and to show how they entered the lord's fee etc.

Halimote held there on the 11th day of April in the 36th year of the reign of King Henry VI [*11 Apr 1458*]

Jurors:	Thomas Bradweye	John Nele	John Collewell
	John Albreth senior	William Frace	Thomas Cok
	Walter Albreth	John Shelford	John Albreth
	William Lawman	Richard Rowenale	Robert Bayly

* It is ordered to distrain the tenants of the land late of Philip Thornebury, the tenants of the land called *Mundens* and the tenants of the land and tenements of Richard Bygrave and of Richard Hurre late of *Willyen* [Willian] to be at the next court to show how they entered the lord's fee and to give relief and fealty to the lord.
* At this court the lord pardons Thomas Bradewey, John Albreth senior, Walter Albreth, John Lawman, John Nele, William Frace, Richard Rownale, John Collewell, Thomas Cok and John Albreth junior, *viz* to each of them a penalty of 3s 4d incurred to the lord for encroachments made by them in the lord's meadow at *Pokesthorne* and in the long field, 60 perches, and for unlawful ways made through the lord's severalty, on condition however that they amend the aforesaid encroachments before the next court failing which each of them shall satisfy to the lord the said penalty.

Halimote held there on Tuesday next before the Feast of St George the Martyr the 37th year of the reign of King Henry VI [*17 Apr 1459*]⁶⁶

Jurors:	Thomas Bradwey	Thomas Laweman	John Shelford
	John Albreth senior	John Nele	Richard Rowenhale
	Walter Albreth	William Frace	John Colwelle
	Thomas Cok	John Albreth junior	John Laweman

* The Homage present that Robert Bayly has committed waste in his tenement

---

[66] A new hand begins here, according to Levett the same as in 1412 (Levett, *Studies in Manorial History*, p85)

HENRY VI

which he recently purchased from John Blowe by allowing the aforesaid tenement to be ruinous and wasted. And also they say that the same John does not wish to pay to the lord the rent due for it and the accustomed services for it, wherefore the lord has taken the said tenement with its appurtenances into his hands. And being in his possession he has granted out of his hands the aforesaid tenement with its appurtenances to Thomas Albreth, to hold to him and his in villeinage at the will of the lord by the services due for it etc. And the lord wills that if the said Robert or any other should come afterwards and recover the said tenement against the said Thomas that then the said Thomas or he who thus shall recover the said tenement shall satisfy the same Thomas his heirs and assigns for all his expenses laid out about the said tenement before he may have entry to the same. Fine 3s 4d. And he did fealty etc.

* [HALS 65534, f3v] It is ordered to distrain the tenants of the lands late of Philip Thornebury, the tenants of land and tenements late of John Yonge and formerly of the said Philip, the tenants of the lands and tenements called *Mundens* and the tenants of lands and tenements late of Nicholas Bygrave and of Richard Hurre in *Wyllyen* [Willian] that they may be at the next court to show how they entered into the lord's fee and to make relief and fealty to the lord etc.

Halimote held there on the Feast of St George the Martyr in the 38th year of the reign of King Henry VI [*23 Apr 1460*]

Jurors:	John Albreth senior	William Frace	Thomas Albreth
	Walter Albreth senior	Thomas Cok	Richard Colwell
	John Laweman	Richard Rowenhale	Thomas Poley
	John Neell	Thomas Hukhyll junior	John Shelford

* The Homage present concerning villeins dwelling outside the lordship as appears in earlier courts etc.
* Next they present that John Fysshe alienated to Walter Laweman two acres and one cottage late of William Geiard without the lord's leave. Therefore it is ordered to seise the said cottage and land into the lord's hands and to account to the lord for the issues etc until etc.
* Next they present that John Colwell is dead,[67] who held from the lord one messuage, one and a half acres of land, formerly of John at Wode and late of William Colwell his father, one toft and one *quartrona* of land formerly of Alexander Wysot late of the said William, and one messuage and a half

---

[67] John Colwell's will was proved in 1459 at St Albans (HALS: 1AR97v).

HENRY VI

virgate of land formerly of John Boton, of which the heriots in money are 3s 4d. And they say that Richard Colwell his son is his next heir thereof and of full age, who came and *gersummavit* the said lands and tenements with appurtenances, to hold to him and his in villeinage at the will of the lord by the services due for them etc. Fine 3s 4d, and he has done fealty.

* The lord granted to John Chalton one toft called *Haleswyke* with one croft adjoining containing by estimation two acres of land, to hold to him his heirs and assigns in villeinage at the will of the lord by services, rendering for it annually to the lord 2s *per annum* at the usual terms, fine and heriot when they fall due and common suit of court, provided that the said John his heirs and assigns upon the premises shall make and build anew upon the said toft a dwelling within seven years next to come from the date of this court under penalty of forfeiture of the toft and croft aforesaid, fine remitted. And he did fealty etc.
* It is ordered to distrain the tenants of the lands called *Mundens* late of Philip Thornbury, the tenants of the lands late of that Philip called *Yonges*, and the tenants of lands late of Nicholas Bygrave in *Wyllyen* [Willian] that they may be at the next court to show how they entered into the lord's fee and to do homage, relief and fealty to the lord.

[*Note in a different hand*] The number of folios in this book containing writings of the court of Norton [is] eight.

EDWARD IV

NORTON [SURVIVING COURT ROLLS FOR THE PERIOD 1461–1539]

[*HALS 40706, f1v*][68] **View of Frankpledge held there on Tuesday next before the Feast of Pentecost in the 4th year of the reign of King Edward IV [*15 May 1464*]**

Chief pledges:	Thomas Hukhyll the elder	John Albreth the younger	Richard Colwell
	John Albreth the elder		Thomas Albreth
	Walter Albreth	Thomas Cok	John Rasshe
	John Laweman	William Frace	Thomas Hukhyll
	John Neel	Richard Rownhale	the younger

* The jurors present that they give to the Lord King for a certain agreement [or fine] on this day by custom 13s 4d \for 6s 8d/.[69]
* *Wylyen* [Willian]: Next they present that John Jordan \2d/ Thomas Cadevell \2d/ and John Staunford \2d/ of the hamlet of Willian ought to attend and are in default therefore etc.
* Next they present that John Jordan \2d/ and Christina Bygrave \2d/ brewers have broken the Assize of ale.
* Thomas Rowenhale, Thomas Chyrysten are put into tithings and swear oaths.

Now concerning the Court: **Halimote held there on the aforesaid day and year**

* **Essoins**: none today
* The Homage presents that John Wylcock, 2d, Thomas Poley, 2d, and Thomas Bradwey owe suit of court and default.
* John Chalton, 3d, because he does not prosecute his suit against Thomas Hukhyll the elder concerning a plea of detinue of chattels and so is amerced.
* It is ordered to distrain John Deynes for the lands and tenements called *Blakesley*, the Fraternity of the Holy Trinity in Baldock, for the lands and tenements called *Maistereslond*, John Pulter, for the lands and tenements late of Nicholas Bygrave in *Wylyen* [Willian], John Appulyerde for one meadow called *Moremede* late of Philip Thornebury Knight, that they should be at the

---

[68] This Norton court is preceded by Codicote's View of Frankpledge and Halimote on the morrow of St Mark the Evangelist in the 4th year of Edward IV [*26 April 1464*].

[69] Perhaps the superscript entry means that only 6s 8d was paid with the remainder forgiven as in the later court of 1484.

EDWARD IV

next court to show in what way they have entered into the lord's fee etc and to perform relief and fealty to the lord, etc.

* Next they present that John Wylcok has encroached upon the demesne land with a dead hedge of six perches length and so is under the penalty of 6s 8d. And it is ordered that he make amends before the next court under the penalty of 10s or he shall be seized by writ, etc.
* Next they present that John Fyshe surrenders into the hand of the lord one toft and two acres of land formerly of William Geiard situated between the tenement of Thomas Rashe on the south side and the land of the lord on the north side *Bakkereslane* and the land of the lord, of which the heriot this time in money is 10d. And the lord has granted the said toft and land with appurtenances to John Neel and Richard Rowenhale, churchwardens of the parish of Norton to hold to them for services, to be sold and the money raised to be spent for the benefit of the new belltower of the aforesaid church to be newly built. For these agreements 10d, and it is given by the lord to the aforesaid works. And they do fealty.

[*Radwell's Halimote follows on the same day*]

RICHARD III

[*HALS 40709, f2*]⁷⁰ **NORTON: View of Frankpledge with Court held there on Tuesday the 3rd day of May in the 2nd year of Richard III in the time of Lord John Rothebury as cellarer [*3 May 1484*]**

Chief Pledges: [All sworn]

John Laweman	Thomas Brygge	John Brygger
Walter Albreth	William Knott	Thomas Warde
Thomas Albreth	Nicholas Hervy	Walter Lawman
John Albreth	John Hukhill the elder	

Common Fine: The jurors present that they are giving to the Lord King as a common fine up to this day 13s 4d, of which they have paid 6s 8d and the residue by the grace of the lord is forgiven this time.

Default: Next they present that John Ronale, Thomas Rouser, Thomas Huckyll the younger and John Shelford, ought to attend the aforesaid court and make default and so are amerced etc.

[*Note at bottom of membrane*: More follows on the other roll]

---

⁷⁰ Norton's court is preceded by Newnham's View of Frankpledge Wednesday 4th May.

HENRY VIII

[*HALS 47296 f1v*]⁷¹ **NORTON:** View of Frankpledge with Court held there on Tuesday the 20th May the 3rd year of the reign of King Henry VIII in the time of Lord Thomas Paytwyn as cellarer [*20 May 1511*]⁷²

Chief Pledges: Sworn

John Renold	John Aubery	Thomas Phipp
John Huckull	Thomas Hervy	Thomas Carver
Thomas Coke	William Purcell	John Nele
Thomas Laurence	John Awbery the younger	John Rawnall

Common Fine: The jurors present that they give to the Lord the King for common agreement to this day 13s 4d whereof 6s 4d[*sic*] has been paid and for the residue they submit themselves to the lord amerced.

Defaulters: The land of John Aplierd, gentleman, Richard Huckull, William Wyn, Agnes Whyth, owe attendance and suit of court and have made default so they are amerced.

Assaults:
* The jurors present that the vicar of Norton has assaulted Margaret Renold with a stick and has drawn blood, so the same vicar is amerced, 8d.
* Next they present that Thomas Emson has assaulted Thomas Faunt with a stick, so the same T Emson is amerced.
* Next they present that the vicar \8d/ has assaulted Joan Burcher so the same vicar is amerced etc.

Nuisances: Next they present that John Burcher has a *hegrow* which has branches overhanging the King's highway [*regiam viam*] to the nuisance of the people of the Lord the King, so he is amerced. And he is ordered to remedy it before the next court under pain of 4d.

Constables: Thomas Coke, Thomas Laurence, are elected to the office of constable and have taken their oaths about it.

Affeerors: John Renold, John Albury senior, who advise an amercement of at least 2d from gentlemen as pay.

---

⁷¹ Norton's court follows Hexton's court of Monday 19th May. HALS: 47295-47310 were in this order in the 17th century when numbered '*Rot: i*' etc. Each membrane is signed J Maynard or John Maynard.

⁷² The month is damaged in the heading so it could be March or May but the only Tuesday falling on the 20th in 1511 is in May.

HENRY VIII

NORTON: Halimote held there on the above day and year

Essoins: Master John Wrygh clerk, John Hale, Nicholas Laweman
Proclamation: A proclamation is made that all persons who hold, occupy or lease any lands or tenements of the lord's bondmen without licence against the custom of the manor and also all those who in such lands or tenements have right to claim, shall attend for licence or estate according to the custom of the manor under pain of eviction and forfeiture of the same etc.
Default
* All the chief pledges abovewritten who are tenants of the lord are chosen and sworn to the Homage of this court, who present that the land of John Aplyerd, Richard Huckull, William Wyn, James Wylson, owe suit of court and have made default so they are amerced.
* The jurors present that Thomas Phipp is dead[73] and that Thomas Phipp his son is his next heir and is of full age.
* Next they present that John Renold has surrendered into the lord's hands one messuage with appurtenances called *Andrewes* and *Wysettes* to the use of Thomas Empson.
* Next they present that Thomas Cok has surrendered into the lord's hands one cottage with appurtenances called *Rascoykes* to the use of Robert Key.
* William Faunt in full court surrenders nine and a half acres of land whereof five acres called *Magodysland* of *vacant lond* of which one acre lies next to *Pulterswey* near land of the vicar of Norton and another acre lies upon *Wolver*[lond] between lands of Richard Hukkull and Nicholas Hervy on either side and two acres lie upon *Mysfurlong* and *Refurlong* and five acres lie next to *le Bedwyff* near land of Thomas Phipp and three acres of *vacantlandes* on *Ouercotnale* and *Nethercotnale* lie next to land of Thomas Albreth on one side and land of Thomas Brigger on the other side and one acre at *Grauelpittes* and half an acre lying at *Litelcotnale*. And the lord has granted the aforesaid lands to Thomas Pratt to hold unto him and his of the lord in villeinage at the will of the lord by the services due and accustomed for them, making agreement and he has done fealty.
* William Faunt in full court surrenders one toft and one *farthingland* of land called *Wodes* two acres of vacant land whereof two half acres lie in *le Malme*, three roods lie next to the common baulk and abut upon a headland of Walter Albreth towards the west and one rood lies in *Langfurlong* which certain two acres of land Joan the widow of Henry Wylcokes now holds for which the tenant of the aforesaid tenure is bound to render 2d ancient rent. And the lord

---

[73] Thomas Fyppe's will was proved in 1510 at St Albans (HALS: 2AR143r).

HENRY VIII

grants the aforesaid toft and land except those things previously excepted, to Thomas Pratte to hold unto him at the will of the lord by the services thence due and accustomed. [?Fine and heriot forgiven]. And he has done fealty.

[*HALS 65535, f1*][74] **NORTON: View of Frankpledge with Court held there on Tuesday 23rd day of May in the 23rd year of the reign of King Henry VIII in the time of Lord Robert Blakeney as cellarer [*23 May 1531*]**

Homage: Sworn for the King and for the lord

Thomas Fypp	Robert Pechytt	Thomas Ronall
John Byrg	William Passell	Nicholas Laman
Thomas Laurens	Robert Hyll	Robert Bygrave
John Albreth the elder	Thomas Cok	Robert Chaterton
Symon Mosse	John Ronall	John Laman

Common Fine: The jurors aforesaid present that they are giving to the King for a common agreement to this day a fixed sum of 6s 8d paid in court to the bailiff.
Tithingmen: Thomas Andrew, William Garrow and John Fypp are sworn for the Lord the King.
Tipplers: Next they present that John Albreth the elder \2d/ and Antony Fantylcastyll \2d/ are common tipplers and sell beer with measures that are not stamped so each of them is amerced as appears over their names.
Constables: William Rocheford and Thomas Ronall are elected to the office of constable and are sworn.
Penalties: A day is given for all the inhabitants to adequately repair the *stokes* by the next Feast of St John the Baptist under pain of forfeiting to the lord 6s 8d. And the same day to making the village archery targets[75] under pain of 6s 8d.
Order:
* Next it is agreed that no outsider dwelling outside this lordship shall exercise common rights in the commons of this manor before the next Feast of St Michael the Archangel under pain of forfeiting 6s 8d for each of them acting against this rule.
* Next they present that the *comyn* baulk called *Shipcothedge* and now in

---

[74] This series of rolls, which are exclusively Norton, were severely damaged and required conservation prior to translation. Many parts are illegible. The translation is shown in chronological order but the membranes are stitched in reverse order.

[75] 1515 Statute 6 Henry VIII c2: 'that buttes be made in everie citie towne and place ... and the inhabitants and dwellers in everye of them to exercise themself with long bowes in shotinge at the same'.

HENRY VIII

dispute between John Cok of Radwell and William Iver, that it always was and was accustomed to be like a *comyn* baulk and that neither the aforesaid John Cok nor William Iver have any right or title to the said baulk.

The lord's Court: Halimote held there on the aforesaid day and year, whereof see the essoins and defaults.

Proclamation: The same proclamation is made as at previous courts.

* Next they present that John Byrg in full court did surrender into the hands of the lord one messuage called *Salvyers* and *Hastynges* with its appurtenances to the use of William Rocheford and his heirs according etc.
* Next they present that John Smyth of Baldock, having been ill for the past two years and longer, who now lies on his deathbed, has surrendered into the hands of the lord by the hands of John Albreth, the deputy bailiff there, three acres of arable land, part of one virgate of land called *Bates* as appears in the 22nd year of Henry VII to the use of Joan Heyworth the widow of William Heyworth, daughter of the aforesaid John Smyth and her heirs with this intention, to perform the last will of the same John Smyth.

End of this court.

[*HALS 65535, f2*] **NORTON: View of Frankpledge with Court held there on Tuesday next before the Feast of the Finding of the Holy Cross in the 24th year of the reign of King Henry VIII in the time of Lord Robert Blakeney as cellarer [*30 Apr 1532*]**

Homage: Jurors

Thomas Fyp	John Albreth the	Thomas Cokke	Thomas Rannall
Simon Mosse	elder	Nicholas Lawman	Robert Pychett
John Berger	Robert Bygrave	John Rannall	William Racheford
John Lawman	William Passell		

Common Fine: The aforesaid jurors say upon their oath that they are giving to the Lord the King as a common fine up to this day as a fixed sum according to ancient custom 13s 4d of which they have paid 6s 8d.

Constable: Robert Pychett is elected to the office of constable in place of William Rocheford and is sworn.

Bakers: Next they present that Antony Fancastell \2d/ and John Albreth \2d/ are bakers of human bread and brewers of ale and have broken the Assize so they are amerced as appears above their names etc.

HENRY VIII

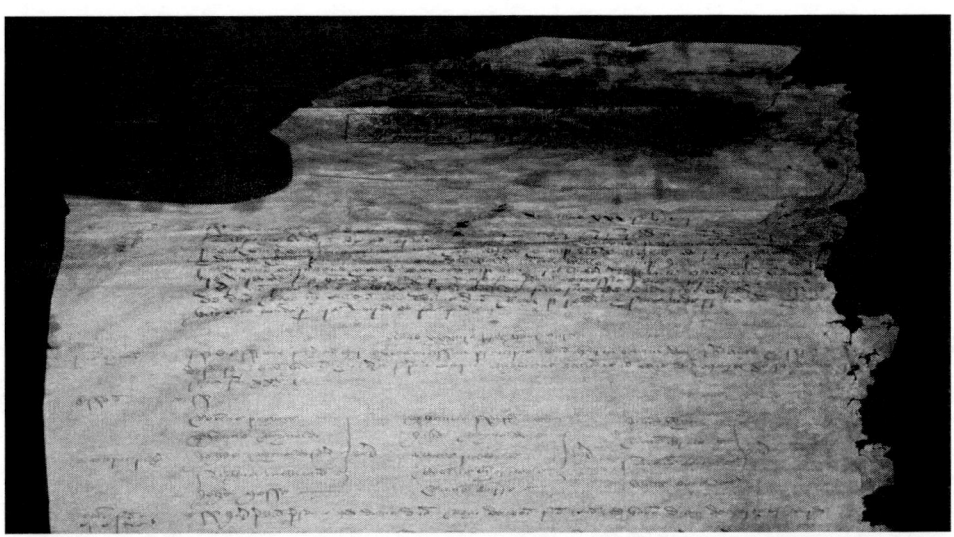

Examples of *HALS 65535*, a roll of Norton records which required conservation before translation work could begin. The courts run from 1531 until 1541.

HENRY VIII

Miller: Next they present that William Wyn \2d/ is a miller and has taken tolls excessively so etc.
Nuisance: Next they present that William Kympton must make up the common way at *Gor Gapp* [which] is very noisome and decaying because of this William's failure, so he is ordered to have it mended before the Feast of St Michael the Archangel next to come under penalty of 3s 4d then forfeiture etc.
Put in Tithings: John Mosse is sworn into the tithing of the Lord the King etc.
Affeerors: Robert Pychett and William Rocheford.

Halimote held there on the abovewritten day and year of which see the essoins and defaults in the papers

Essoins: None.
Proclamation: A proclamation is made that all persons who hold, occupy, or lease any bondman lands or tenements of the lord contrary to the customs of the aforesaid manor without estate and licence having been had or obtained from the lord and also all those who in such lands or tenements have rights to claim must come to get licence or estate from the lord for them under penalty of forfeiting the same etc.

* All the abovewritten who are the lord's tenants are elected, charged and sworn onto the Homage of this court for the lord, who present that Thomas Reynar keeps the houses that he has in his wife Christina's right very ruinous and decaying, so he is ordered to have them repaired before the next court under penalty of forfeiting the same etc, as well as one barn.
* And likewise they present that the aforesaid Thomas has another house called *Frasys* likewise in decay so he is ordered to repair it before the next court under penalty of forfeiture etc.
* Next with the consent and advice of the lord and with the consent of the whole Homage of the aforesaid court it is ordered and provided that in the absence of the bailiff of the aforesaid manor and not otherwise, Thomas Fypp and John Albreth jointly or separately with two or more tenants called by either of them may have authority and power to take all surrenders of all tenants of the aforesaid manor lying on their deathbeds, and also to present such surrenders at the lord's court just as the aforesaid bailiff may take and present such surrenders, etc. And they have taken an oath in full court to faithfully perform this, etc.
* Next they present that William Gatys has sold one acre and a half of land of which one acre lies upon *Chalfurlong* and abuts upon the demesne land called

HENRY VIII

the *Eighteen acres*, and half an acre of it lies in the *Mawme* and abuts upon a headland of Thomas Fypp on the south side, to the use and behoof of Robert Pechet his heirs and assigns etc.

More concerning the 23rd year of Henry VIII on the back.

* [*HALS 65535, f2v*] Next they present that William Wyn holds one mill which was demesne land in the time of Lord Thomas Ramryche etc.
* Next they present that Henry Punt and Joan his wife by virtue of the testament and last will of John Smyth after the day of the court, she having been questioned alone, have surrendered into the lord's hands by the hands of the Hundred three acres of arable land, part of one virgate of land called *Baty* as is more fully contained in a copy of the court roll of the 22nd year of Henry VII, to the use of Robert Pychett his heirs and assigns.
* At this court William Gatys surrendered into the hands of the lord by the hands of the steward of the aforesaid court three half acres of land of which one acre lies upon *Chalfurlong* and abuts upon the demesne land called the *Eighteen Acres* and half an acre of it lies in the *Mawme* and abuts upon a headland of Thomas Fypp on the south side, to the use and behoof of Robert Pychett his heirs and assigns. And the lord has granted the aforesaid land with appurtenances to the aforenamed Robert Pychett to hold unto him and his, of the lord in villeinage, at the will of the lord according to the custom of the aforesaid manor, for the rents and services formerly due and accustomed for it, for which the tenant in the time of Thomas Raynold paid ½d a year, the fine when it falls due and suit of the lord's court. The common fine this time is condoned for [*blank*] and he has done fealty and is admitted tenant thereof, etc.

Void because enrolled in the 25th year of Henry VIII following [*see HALS 65535 f8v below*]

* After the day of the aforesaid court, that is to say on the 4th day of October in the aforesaid year of the aforesaid King, Henry Punte and Joan his wife came before John Newporte of the Hundred and out of court, she having been questioned alone by the aforesaid Hundred, by virtue of a certain surrender of John Smyth late of Baldock just as more fully appears in the 26th year of Henry VIII with this intention, to perform and fulfil the testament and last will of the same John, surrendered into the hands of the lord by the hands of the said Hundred, three acres of arable land, part of one virgate of land called *Bate* as in a copy of the 22nd year of Henry VII more fully appears, to the use and behoof of Robert Pychett his heirs and assigns. And the lord has granted the

HENRY VIII

aforesaid land with appurtenances to the aforenamed Robert Pychett, to hold unto him and his, of the lord in villeinage, at the will of the lord according to the custom of the aforesaid manor for the rents and services formerly due and accustomed for it, the fine when it shall fall due and suit of the lord's court. The common fine on this occasion is condoned for [*blank*]. And he has done fealty and is admitted tenant thereof, etc.

The end of this court.

[*HALS 65535, f3*] **View of Frankpledge with Court held there on Tuesday that is to say the 13th day of May in the 25th year of the reign of King Henry VIII in the time of Lord Thomas Whetehamstede as cellarer [*13 May 1533*]**

Homage: Jurors

Thomas Fypp	Thomas Cocke	Nicholas Lawman
Robert Pychett	John Raynolde	John Lawman
John Albery	Thomas Raynolde	John Mosse
Robert Bygrave	William Lycheworth	Robert Hyll

Common Fine: The aforesaid jurors present that they are giving to the Lord the King as a common fine to this day as a fixed sum according to ancient custom 13s 4d of which they have paid in full court 6s 8d.
Constable: John Ronnall and Nicholas Lawman are elected to the office of constable and sworn etc.
Put in Tithings:
* Edward Fypp, Robert Andrewe, Richard Burre, Thomas Rocheford and William Lawrence are sworn into the tithing of the Lord the King etc.
* Next they present that Thomas Becketh is of the age of 12 years and upwards and is not sworn into the tithing of the Lord the King so the bailiff is ordered to summons him so that he be at the next court held there to be sworn etc.

Tipplers and Brewers: Next they present that Antony Famekylcastell \4d/ and John Albrey \2d/ are common beersellers and brewers and have broken the Assize of ale and when selling victuals take excessive profit, so they are amerced just as appears above their names etc.
Penalties imposed:
* Next they present that Antony Fanckylcastell does not brew his ale according to the Assize of the price of malt so he is ordered that he does not do so under penalty of 40d.
* Next they present that Thomas Raynard has one ditch lying between the

HENRY VIII

dwellinghouse of Thomas Cockes and the dwellinghouse of the aforesaid Thomas Raynard and it is very noisome not scoured to the nuisance of the lord's tenants, so he has a postponement to scour the aforesaid ditch before the Feast of St John the Baptist next to come under penalty of 20d.

* Next they present that John Ronnold has encroached with a certain boundary upon the land of Thomas Fypp and likewise with the same boundary has encroached upon the land of Thomas Byg containing by estimation ten perches or more or less, so he is ordered to have the said boundary removed before the Feast of the Purification of the Blessed Mary the Virgin next to come under penalty of 20d etc.

Put in Tithings: Next they present that William Huggyn is of the age of 12 years and more and has not been sworn into the tithing of the Lord the King so the bailiff there is ordered to summons him so that he be at the next court held there to be sworn etc.

The lord's Court: Halimote held there on the abovewritten day and year whereof see the essoins and defaults in the papers

Proclamation: A proclamation is made that all persons who hold, occupy, or lease any bondman lands or tenements of the lord contrary to the customs of the aforesaid manor without estate and licence having been had or obtained from the lord and also all those who in such lands or tenements have rights to claim must come to get licence or estate from the lord for them under penalty of forfeiting the same etc.

* All the chief pledges abovewritten being tenants of the lord are elected, charged and sworn onto the Homage of this court for the lord.
* Who present that Thomas Raynard and Christina his wife have alienated two acres of land with appurtenances to the use of Robert Pechytt his heirs and assigns etc.
* Next they present that Simon Mosse is dead[76] since the last court who lying on his deathbed surrendered into the hands of the lord, by the hands of John Albrey and Thomas Fyppe two tenants chosen by the whole Homage and sworn, one toft and one croft with appurtenances to the use and behoof of John Mosse the younger his heirs and assigns etc.
* Next they present that William Kympton has his tenement ruinous and decaying for want of repairs so he has a postponement to repair the aforesaid tenement before the Feast of St Peter which is called in Chains, under penalty

---

[76] Simon Mosse's will was proved in 1532/3 at St Albans (HALS: 2AR220v).

HENRY VIII

of 40d.
* Next they present that John Langeley has been dead for 12 years past (at a guess) who at the time of his death held under the lord by bondman tenure divers lands with appurtenances. And they say that Margaret and Elizabeth the daughters of the aforesaid John are his next heirs (the aforesaid Margaret is of the age of 16 years by estimation and the aforesaid Elizabeth is of the age of 12 years) of all those lands of which the aforesaid John died seised etc.
* Next they present that Thomas Raynard had a postponement and a penalty at the last court to repair all his houses as well as one barn that are very ruinous and decaying for want of repairs which certain houses he has and holds by right of Christina his wife, before this court under penalty of forfeiting the same, and he has not repaired them. And the aforesaid Thomas Raynard had the same postponement and penalty to repair another house called *Frosys* and he has not repaired it.
* And the aforesaid Thomas Raynard has the same penalty as above to repair all the aforesaid houses before the next court under the aforesaid penalty etc.
* At this court it is reported both by the Homage and by scrutiny of the court rolls of the aforesaid manor that John Langeley has been dead for 12 years now past and longer, who at the time of his death held of the lord by bondman tenure three acres of arable of which one acre lies in *Chalfurlong* and another acre thereof lies in *Foxhole* and another acre thereof lies on a furlong called *Ouerwey* just as appears by copies of the court rolls of the 11th year of King Henry VIII. And furthermore they say that Margaret and Elizabeth daughters of the aforesaid John are the next heirs of the said John, and that the aforesaid Margaret is now of the age of 16 years and that the aforesaid Elizabeth is now of the age of 12 years, and by reason of the minority of age of the said Margaret and Elizabeth the lord has granted wardship of the same Margaret and Elizabeth together with the aforesaid lands to Henry Ponte and Joan his wife the mother of the said Margaret and Elizabeth until the said Margaret and Elizabeth shall arrive at their full age, to hold to them and their assigns of the lord by the rod and the will of the lord according to the custom of the aforesaid manor for the rents and services formerly due and accustomed for them, so that after the minority of age of the said Margaret and Elizabeth the lord will grant the aforesaid lands with appurtenances to the aforesaid Margaret and Elizabeth to hold to them and theirs of the lord by the rents and services aforesaid etc. The fine both this time for having such wardship and for entry of the aforesaid Margaret and Elizabeth into the premises is condoned when they shall arrive at their full ages.

More on the back.

HENRY VIII

* [*HALS 65535, f3v*] At this court John Albreth surrendered into the hands of the lord by the hands of the steward of the aforesaid court four acres of arable land of which one acre lies in the *Mysfurlong* one headland thereof abuts upon *Ryve Furlong*, another acre thereof lies in *Sheff Furlong* abutting upon *Ned* [*illeg*] another acre thereof lies in *Estfurlong* one headland of which abuts upon *Grendyche* and another acre thereof lies at *Debedens Shott* abutting upon *Cotnald* to the use and behoof of Richard Bowles gentleman his heirs and assigns. And the lord has granted the aforesaid lands with appurtenances to the aforenamed Richard to hold unto him and his, of the lord at the will of the lord according to the custom of the aforesaid manor for the rents and services formerly due for them and accustomed. The fine this time is condoned for [*blank*] and he has done fealty and is admitted tenant thereof etc.
* At this court it is both reported by the Homage and by scrutiny of the court rolls of the aforesaid manor that for two years and more last past William Rocheford has unlawfully held and occupied one messuage half a virgate of land and half of a half of a virgate of land once of William Sayer, late of John Hale and Walter Lawman, without estate and licence of the lord, against the custom of the aforesaid manor until the day of the present court in deception of the lord and his court aforesaid, that it is the full custom that he shall forfeit all the aforesaid premises according to the aforesaid custom, so the aforesaid William after many proclamations often called in the court of the aforesaid manor by the Hundred to have an estate and licence to the aforesaid messuage and other premises, has cared little (*minime curavit*) so it is ordered by the court that he be for ever completely excluded according to the aforesaid custom. And after such possession by the bailiff here certified how the aforesaid William had occupied the aforesaid messuage and other premises with appurtenances against the noted custom as is aforesaid, improvidently and unlawfully, did not seek copies of court rolls of the aforesaid manor as he ought, the lord by his great favour has graciously released and granted the aforesaid messuage and other premises with appurtenances by the same lord, to hold the aforesaid messuage and other premises with appurtenances unto the aforenamed William unto him and his, of the lord in villeinage at the will of the lord according to the custom of the aforesaid manor for the rents and services formerly due and accustomed for them, the fine when it shall fall due and suit of the lord's court. The common fine this time is condoned for [*blank*]. And he has done fealty and is admitted tenant thereof.
* At this court it is certified by Thomas Fypp and John Albreth the chief tenants there sworn and elected by the whole Homage to take surrenders of all the tenants of the lord of the said manor lying on their deathbeds in the absence of the bailiff there, that Simon Mosse lying on his deathbed surrendered into the

hands of the lord by the hands of the said Thomas Fypp and John Albreth in the presence of Thomas Ryse, clerk, vicar of Norton and John Ronnold, tenants of the lord there this being witnessed one toft with adjoining croft containing two acres and a half once of Thomas Dryver, and one toft and half an acre of land once of Walter son of John Dryver and likewise surrendered two acres of land, part of one toft and one *quartrona* of land called *Reedes* as appears in the 1st year of Henry VII whereof two half acres lie in the *Malme*, three roods thereof lie next to the *comyn* baulk and abut upon a headland late of Walter Albreth towards the west and one rood lies in *Leyfurlong*, to the use and behoof of John Mosse the younger his heirs and assigns, of which the heriot on this occasion is condoned for [*blank*]. And the lord has granted the aforesaid toft, croft and land with all and singular their appurtenances to the aforesaid John Mosse to hold unto him and his of the lord in villeinage at the will of the lord according to the custom of the aforesaid manor for the rents and services formerly due and accustomed for them. The fine and heriot when they fall and suit of the lord's court common fine this time are condoned for [*blank*] and he has done fealty and is admitted tenant thereof etc.

* At this court Henry Ponte and Joan his wife, she being questioned alone by the steward of the aforesaid court, by virtue of a certain surrender of John Smyth late of Baldock just as more fully appears in the 21st year of Henry VIII with this intention to perform and fulfil the testament and last will of the same John Smyth, have surrendered into the hands of the lord by the hands of the said steward three acres of arable land, part of one virgate of land called *Bates* as appears more fully in a copy of the 22nd year of Henry VII, to the use and behoof of Robert Pychett his heirs and assigns. And the lord has granted the aforesaid lands with appurtenances to the aforenamed Robert Pychett to hold unto him and his of the lord in villeinage at the will of the lord according to the custom of the aforesaid manor for the rents and services formerly due and accustomed for them. The fine when it shall fall and suit of the lord's court common fine this time are condoned for 18d and he has done fealty and is admitted tenant thereof etc.
* At this court it is both reported by the Homage and by scrutiny of the court rolls of the aforesaid manor that for seven years and longer now gone by, John Ronale the younger has unlawfully held and occupied 17 acres of land, part of 43 acres of land of *Acremelond* as appears in the 16th year of Edward IV without estate and licence of the lord against the custom of the aforesaid manor until the day of the present court in deception of the lord and his aforesaid court, that it is the full custom that all the aforesaid 17 acres be forfeit according to the aforesaid custom, moreover the aforenamed John, after many frequent proclamations made in the aforesaid manorial court for such

HENRY VIII

estate and licence to the same land to be obtained, cared little, so it is ordered by the court that those 17 acres of land be forfeit and for the lord's bailiff there to seize them into the hands of the lord, excluding all who claim rights in them completely and forever according to the aforesaid custom. And after such possession by the bailiff here certified how the aforesaid John had occupied the aforesaid 17 acres of land against the noted custom as is aforesaid, improvidently and unlawfully, did not seek copies of court rolls of the aforesaid manor as he ought, the lord by his great favour has graciously released and granted the aforesaid 17 acres of land by the same lord, to hold the aforesaid 17 acres of land unto the aforenamed John unto him and his, of the lord in villeinage at the will of the lord according to the custom of the aforesaid manor for the rents and services formerly due and accustomed for them, the fine when it shall fall due and suit of the lord's court. The common fine this time is condoned for [blank]. And he has done fealty and is admitted tenant thereof.

Affeerors: Thomas Fypp, John Albreth, sworn.

The end of this court.

[HALS 65535, f4] **NORTON: View of Frankpledge with Court held there on Tuesday next after the Feast of St Philip and James the Apostles in the 26th year of the reign of King Henry VIII in the time of Lord Thomas Whethamsted as cellarer [5 May 1534]**

Essoins: [blank]
Chief Pledges: Sworn

Thomas Phyp	Thomas Reynold	Nicholas Lawman
John Albreth	John Reynold the elder	John Lawman
Robert Pechett	William Rocheford	Robert Hyll
Thomas Cock	John Mosse	Robert Bygrave

Common Fine: The jurors present that they are giving to the Lord the King as a common fine there up to this day a fixed sum of 6s 8d.
Bakers and Brewers: Next they present that Antony Fankylcastell \4d/ and John Albreth \1d/ are common bakers of bread and brewers of ale so they are amerced, that is to say, each of them as appears above their name etc.
Stray: Next they present that John Bowles esquire has one sheep, white in colour, which has been straying into the precinct of this View for the past year and a day and is worth 12d.

HENRY VIII

Constable: Thomas Mosse is elected to the office of constable in the place of Thomas Reynold, charged and sworn, etc.

Nuisance: Next they present that Thomas Fypp, John Mosse and Thomas Reynold have a ditch that is not scoured lying in a certain alley called *Towerslane*, very noisome, causing a nuisance to the pledge, so etc. And they are ordered to amend it before the Feast of St Michael the Archangel under penalty of 12d for each of them.

The lord's Court: held there on the abovewritten day and year

Proclamation: A proclamation is made that all persons who hold, occupy, or lease any bondman lands or tenements of the lord contrary to the customs of the aforesaid manor without estate and licence having been had or obtained from the lord and also all those who in such lands or tenements have rights to claim must come to get licence or estate from the lord for them under penalty of forfeiting the same etc.

* John Albreth in full court surrendered into the hands of the lord by the hands of the steward of the aforesaid court one messuage and one cotland once of Matilda Balson as appears in a certain copy [of court roll] of the 18th year of Henry VII, which messuage and cotland the said John Albreth has and holds for the term of his life then to the use and behoof of Richard Bowles, gentleman, under the following condition, that is to say that if the said John Albreth his heirs or assigns shall pay or cause to be paid to a certain John Bowles esquire his executors or assigns on the Feast of the Nativity of St John the Baptist next to come after the same court 30s sterling that then this present surrender shall be void and of no force, otherwise it shall stand in all its force and effect.

* At this court John Laweman surrendered into the hands of the lord by the hands of the steward of the aforesaid court four [?*erasure*] half of land and one butt, of which one half acre lies in *Chalfurlong* another half an acre thereof lies [in] *Mylfurlong* another half acre thereof lies in *Longedene* and another half acre thereof lies in *Goreshotte* and the aforesaid butt lies above *Gorehyed* in *Goreshott* aforesaid to the use and behoof of Thomas Ronale and Antony Ronale son of the said Thomas and the heirs of this Antony. And the lord has granted the aforesaid four half acres and butt of land with appurtenances to Thomas Ronale and Antony and the heirs of this Antony, of the lord at the will of the lord according to the custom of the aforesaid manor, for the rents and services formerly due and accustomed for them. The fine of the aforesaid Thomas on this occasion is condoned for [*blank*] and he has done fealty etc.

HENRY VIII

* At this court Thomas Ronale and Christina his wife, she having been questioned alone by the steward, surrendered into the hand of the lord by the hands of the steward two acres of land, half an acre of which lies in *Oldbrache*, another above *Depdene*, and another half [*illeg*] to the use of Robert Pechette and his heirs [*illeg*]. And the lord has granted the aforesaid [*illeg*] with appurtenances to the aforesaid Robert to hold to him and his of the lord in villeinage [*illeg*] according to the custom of the said manor by rents and services [*illeg*] fealty and is admitted [*illeg*].
[*Note at bottom of roll in a different hand*:   concerns Richard Bowles, Hertfordshire and Bedfordshire].
* [*HALS 65535, f4v*] At this court the lord has granted out of his hands, for diverse causes and considerations motivating him, to John Bowles esquire all and singular the empty lands and pastures lying and being in the fields of Norton aforesaid with all and singular the appurtenances of the same which certain lands and pastures at present are held of the lord by copy or copies of court rolls of the aforesaid manor, not [*illeg*] in the tenure and occupation of anyone at farm for a term of years [*illeg*], to hold all the aforesaid lands and pastures with all and singular their appurtenances to the aforesaid John his heirs and assigns of the lord by the rod at the will of the lord according to the custom of the aforesaid manor, rendering for them annually to the lord and his successors at the usual terms for each acre thereof 1d and suit to the lord's court and he gives [*illeg*] for having his [*illeg*] thereof it is condoned for [*blank*] and he has done fealty and is admitted tenant thereof.

[*HALS 65535, f5*] **NORTON: View of Frankpledge with Court held there on Tuesday next after the Feast of St George the Martyr in the 27th year of the reign of King Henry VIII in the time of Lord Thomas Whethamsted as cellarer [*27 Apr 1535*]**

Essoins: [*blank*]
Chief Pledges: Sworn
John Fypp	William Passell	Thomas Ronale
John Albreth	John Ronale the elder	Nicholas Lawman
Thomas Cock	John Ronale the younger	Robert Bygrave
William Rocheford	John Lawman	John Mosse

Common Fine: The jurors present that they are giving to the Lord the King as a common fine up to this day 6s 8d.
Constable: Robert Bygrave is elected to the aforesaid office, charged and sworn, etc.

HENRY VIII

Tipplers and Brewers: Next they present that Antony Fankylcastell \2d/ and Thomas Rowsse \2d/ are brewers and retailers of ale and have broken the Assize of ale and when selling victuals take excessive profit, so they are amerced, that is to say, each of them as appears over their names etc.

Nuisance: Next they present that John Ronale and Emma his wife are ill governed to the nuisance of their neighbours so they have a postponement to be removed from this village before the Feast of St Michael the Archangel under penalty of 20s.

Miller: Next they present that William Wyne is a common miller and takes excessive tolls for it, so he is amerced 2d.

Court of the lord: there held on the day and year abovewritten

Proclamation: A proclamation is made that all persons who hold, occupy, or lease any bondman lands or tenements of the lord contrary to the customs of the aforesaid manor without estate and licence having been had or obtained from the lord and also all those who in such lands or tenements have rights to claim must come to get licence or estate from the lord for them under penalty of forfeiting the same etc.

* At this court the Homage presents that Thomas Cock[77] since the last court surrendered into the hands of the lord by the hands of John Albreth a tenant of the lord there in the presence of Thomas Ronale, John Mosse and John Lawman, one messuage in which the aforesaid Thomas now lives and all the land belonging to the same messuage, to the use and behoof of the aforesaid Thomas and Joan his wife for the term of their life and the life of the longer liver and after their decease all the premises with appurtenances shall remain wholly to the use and behoof of Nicholas Cock the son of the aforesaid Thomas and Joan and of Margery his wife and their heirs lawfully begotten of the bodies of the same Nicholas and Margery, [but] if it should happen that the said Nicholas and Margery shall die without heirs lawfully begotten of their bodies, then all the premises with their appurtenances shall remain wholly to the right heirs of the aforesaid Thomas Cock.

* At this court the Homage presents that Anna the wife of John Isard is dead since the last court and that John Isard has an estate for the term of his life both in one messuage and one *quartrona* of land formerly of John Lawman and likewise in nine acres of land called *Vacontlond* of which three acres lie at

---

[77] This is the first of three similar entries in this court relating to the affairs of Thomas Cock and what eventually becomes a deathbed surrender. His will was proved in 1535 at St Albans (HALS: 2AR233v).

HENRY VIII

Dedewyff and four acres lie at *Lytlecotnale* and half an acre lies [at] *Dylrodys* and half an acre lies upon *Wyddergrene* and another acre. And likewise in one toft and half a virgate of land once of John Burre and late of Simon [?Hale] of which the heriot on this occasion is condoned for [*blank*]. And furthermore they say that William Cammock is a kinsman and next heir of the aforesaid Anne in the reversion to the premises when it shall fall after the death of the aforesaid John Isard which certain William came and sought of the lord to be admitted to the reversion of the aforesaid messuage and other premises with appurtenances. And the lord has granted the reversion of the premises with appurtenances when it shall fall to the aforesaid William, to hold unto him his heirs and assigns of the lord by the rod at the will of the lord according to the custom of the aforesaid manor for the rents and services formerly due and accustomed for it. The fine on this occasion is condoned for [*illeg*], and he did fealty etc.

* At this court the Homage presents that Thomas Cock since the last court surrendered into the hands of the lord by the hands of John Albreth a tenant of the lord there in the presence of Thomas Ronale, John Mosse and John Lawman, one messuage and half a virgate of land called *Botons*, to the use and behoof of the aforesaid Thomas and Joan his wife for the term of their life and the life of the longer liver, and after the death of the aforesaid [*Thomas and Joan*] to the use and behoof of Nicholas Cock and Margery his wife and their heirs lawfully begotten of their [bodies] and if the said Nicholas and Margery [happen to die without] heirs of their bodies lawfully begotten then the aforesaid messuage ... [*Note at foot of page:* more of the same court on the other side] [*HALS 65535, f5v*] it shall remain to the right heirs of the aforesaid Thomas Cock, of which the heriot on this occasion [*illeg*] aforesaid messuage [*illeg*] aforesaid Thomas Cock and Joan his wife [*illeg*] his assigns for the term of [*illeg*] for the rents and services formerly [due and accustomed] for it [*illeg*] after the death of the aforesaid Thomas Cock and Joan his wife the lord has granted [*illeg*] and land with appurtenances to the aforesaid Nicholas and Margery, to hold unto him and his heirs [*illeg*] lawfully begotten for the aforesaid rents and services [*illeg*] Margery shall die without heirs of their bodies lawfully begotten [*illeg*] of the land with appurtenances shall remain wholly to the right heirs of the aforesaid Thomas Cock [*illeg*]. The fine both of the aforesaid Thomas Cock and Joan and of the aforesaid Nicholas and Margery [*illeg*] for [*blank*] and they have done fealty etc.

* The Homage presents that Thomas Cock is dead since the last court [*illeg*] on his deathbed surrendered into the hands of the lord by the hands of John Albreth one of the customary [tenants] of the aforesaid manor chosen and sworn to take surrenders of all customary [tenants of the manor] aforesaid

lying on their deathbeds in the absence of the bailiff there and not otherwise, one toft [*illeg*] virgate of land called *Botons*. And the lord has granted the aforesaid toft and land with appurtenances [to Joan] the widow of the aforesaid Thomas Cock, to hold unto her and her assigns for the term of her life [*illeg*] and services formerly due and accustomed for it. And after the death of the aforesaid Joan [*illeg*] the aforesaid toft and land with appurtenances to Nicholas Cock and Margery his wife, to hold to them and the heirs between them lawfully begotten for the aforesaid rents and services etc and if the aforesaid Nicholas and Margery shall die without heirs between them lawfully begotten then the aforesaid toft and land with appurtenances shall wholly remain to the right heirs of the aforesaid Thomas Cock. The fines both of the aforesaid Joan and of the aforesaid Nicholas and Margery on this occasion are condoned for 3s 4d. And they have done fealty etc.

The end of this court.

[*HALS 65535, f6*] **NORTON: View of Frankpledge with Court held there on Tuesday 16th May in the 28th year of the reign of King Henry VIII in the time of Lord Thomas Whethamsted as cellarer [*16 May 1536*]**

Essoins: None
Chief Pledges: Sworn

Robert Pechett	Nicholas Lawman	Richard Burre
Thomas Fypp	John Mosse	William Cammock
William Rocheford	John Ronale the elder	John Burger
John Albreth	John Ronale the younger	
Thomas Ronale	Robert Bygrave	

Common Fine: The aforesaid jurors present that they are giving to the Lord the King as a common fine there to this day as a fixed sum 6s 8d.
Constables: Thomas Ronale is elected to the aforesaid office in the place of John Mosse, charged and sworn. And Robert Bygrave is charged and sworn to the aforesaid office as before etc.
Brewer: Next they present that Antony Fankylcastell is a common brewer of ale and has broken the Assize thereof so he is amerced 2d.
Miller: Next they present that William Wynne is a common miller and has taken tolls excessively, so he is amerced 2d.

Court of the lord: held there on the day and year abovewritten etc.

Proclamation: A proclamation is made that all persons who hold, occupy, or lease any bondman lands or tenements of the lord contrary to the customs of the

HENRY VIII

aforesaid manor without estate and licence having been had or obtained from the lord and also all those who in such lands or tenements have rights to claim must come to get licence or estate from the lord for them under penalty of forfeiting the same etc.

* Thomas Phypp son of John Phypp in full court surrendered into the hands by the hands of John Newporte of the Hundred and for a certain sum of money to him in hand paid by Thomas Phypp the elder has remitted and released all his right estate title claim interest and demand of and in one messuage and half a virgate of land to the aforenamed Thomas Phypp the elder and his heirs for ever etc. And he gives for having the enrolment thereof 12d.
* Next they present that Thomas Reynard by right of his wife Christiana holds one tenement once *Fraysses* which certain tenement he holds for the term of the life of the said Christiana and it is very ruinous for want of repairs so he has a postponement to repair the said tenement before the next court under penalty of 40d.
* William Kympton surrendered in full court into the hands of the lord by the hands of John Newporte of the Hundred 28 acres of land called *Vacontlondes*, rendering for it as formerly to the lord 6s 8d. The fine this time is condoned. And the aforesaid William likewise surrendered into the hands of the lord by the hand of the said Hundred vacant lands containing by estimation 30 acres of land as more fully appears in the court roll of the 11th year of the aforesaid King by the rents and services due and accustomed for it. The fine this time is condoned.
* And the aforesaid William likewise surrendered into the hands of the lord by the hands of the said Hundred one messuage and half a virgate of land and one *quartrona* of land with the said messuage and half [virgate] always excepted, once of Walter Hale just as appears in the 35th year of Henry [*illeg*] and use of Nicholas Lawman and his heirs of which the heriot this time is condoned.
* The lord has granted the aforesaid messuage and land with appurtenances to the aforenamed Nicholas, to hold unto him and his heirs of the lord by the rod at the will of the lord according to the custom of the manor for the rents and services formerly due and accustomed for it. The fine this time is condoned and he has done fealty and is admitted tenant thereof etc.
* John Lawman in full court surrendered into the hands of the lord by the hands of John Newporte one toft and one cotland, one *quartrona* of land containing by estimation [*illeg*] called *Tollers* which Walter Lawman [*illeg*] first held to the use of [*illeg*] Ronale and his heirs, of which the heriot on this occasion is condoned. [*illeg*] toft and land with appurtenances to the aforesaid Thomas Ronale to hold unto him and his heirs [*illeg*] of the lord by the rod at the will

of the lord according to the custom of the aforesaid manor services rendering to the lord 3s 4d. The fine this time is condoned for [*illeg*]. And he has done fealty.

[*HALS 65535, f6v*] **28th year of the reign of King Henry VIII**

Ryce the vicar: After the day of the preceding court, that is to say on the 17th day of the said month in the aforesaid year of the aforesaid King, Robert Chaterton out of court did surrender in to the hand of the lord by the hand of the aforesaid cellarer one cottage with appurtenances late of Thomas Love and one pyghtle enclosed with hedges and ditches lying next to the said cottage on the west side to the use and behoof of Thomas Ryse vicar of Norton aforesaid and his heirs. And the lord has granted the aforesaid cottage and pyghtle with appurtenances to the said Thomas Ryse to hold to him and his heirs of the lord by the rod at the will of the lord according to the custom of the aforesaid manor by the rents and services formerly due and accustomed for them. The fine on this occasion is forgiven for [*blank*] and he has done fealty and is admitted tenant thereof.

* At this court the Homage presents that Thomas Cock is dead since the last court, who on his deathbed surrendered into the hands of the lord by the hands of John Albreth one of the customary tenants of the aforesaid manor having been chosen and sworn to take surrenders of all the customary tenants of the aforesaid manor, lying on his deathbed, in the absence of the bailiff there and not otherwise, four acres of land of *Vacontlondes* of which two acres lie in *Whetyldale*, half an acre lies upon *Oldwelhyll* and three halves lie in one piece at *Pourtesole* [*or Pourtehole*]. And the lord has granted the aforesaid four acres of land with appurtenances to Joan the widow of the aforesaid Thomas Cock, to hold unto her and her heirs of the lord in villeinage at the will of the lord according to the custom of the aforesaid manor for rendering the ancient rent of 8d to the lord. The fine on this occasion is 8d. And she has done fealty etc.

Release: At this court John Isard for 20s sterling to him in hand paid by William Cammock, surrendered remitted and released and wholly for him and his assigns for ever quitclaimed to the aforenamed William, being in his full and peaceful possession and seisin, and to his heirs and assigns for ever, all his right or estate title claim interest and demand which he the aforenamed John for the term of his life ever had, has or in any way in the future might have, of and in one messuage and one *quartrona* of land once of John Laweman and of and in nine acres of land called *Vacontlondes* and of and in one toft and half a virgate of land once of John Burre and late of Simon Hale with their appurtenances just

HENRY VIII

as appears in the rolls of the court of the 27th year of the aforesaid King, that is to say so that neither he the aforenamed John Isard nor anyone else in his name might henceforth claim demand or sell any right estate title claim interest and demand of and in the aforesaid messuage and other premises with appurtenances nor in any part of the same or in any way in the future but from every action of law estate title claim interest and demand thereof and of any part thereof shall forever be completely excluded and shut out by these presents. The fine for this enrolment is 12d.

[HALS 65535, f7] **NORTON**: **View of Frankpledge with Court held there on Tuesday 12th June in the 29th year of the reign of King Henry VIII in the time of the Lord Robert Catton by divine permission abbot of the exempt monastery of St Alban** [*12 Jun 1537*]

Essoins: None
Chief Pledges: Sworn

Robert Pechett	Thomas Ronale	John Ronale the younger
Thomas Fypp	Nicholas Lawman	Robert Bygrave
William Rocheford	John Mosse	William Cammock
John Albreth	John Ronale the elder	Richard Burre

Common Fine: The aforesaid jurors present that they are giving to the Lord the King as a common fine there up to this day a fixed sum of 6s 8d.
Tipplers of Ale: Next they present that Antony Fankylcastell and John Albreth are common tipplers of ale and when selling victuals take too much profit so they are amerced, that is to say each of them 2d.
Miller: Next they present that William Wyne is a common miller and takes tolls excessively so he is amerced 2d.
Assault: Next they present that Richard Plomer made an assault upon the wife of John Ronale so he is amerced 2d.
Constable: John Ronale the elder is elected to the aforesaid office in the place of Thomas Ronale, and Robert Bygrave and he is charged and sworn to the aforesaid office as before.

Court of the lord: held there on the abovewritten day and year.

Proclamation: A proclamation is made that all persons who hold, occupy or lease any bondman lands of tenements against the custom of the aforesaid manor without estate and licence from the lord having been had or obtained, and

also all those who in such land or tenements have rights to claim shall come to get a licence or estate from the lord under penalty of forfeiting the same etc.
Defaults:
* The Homage presents that Thomas Monyngham, James Halffhyde and Thomas [*illeg*] Robert Reynard owe suit to the aforesaid court and have made default so they are amerced that is to say each of them 2d.
* William Purcelle in full court surrendered into the hands of the lord by the hands of John Newporte of the Hundred nine acres of land called *Vacontlond* of which one acre lies at *Lobgate* abutting upon *Lyndyche*, another acre lies in *Foxeholez* abutting upon *Mylwey*, two acres lie at *Waterdenfylde* abutting upon *Pulterswey*, one acre in *Depdeneshotte* abutting upon the demesne land, three roods lie nearby (*prope per*) *Depdenebalk* abutting upon *Oldbrachewey*, half an acre upon *Grenedyche* abutting upon *Medewey*, half an acre lying upon *Holwell* abutting in *le Towne Mede*, one acre at *Chefurlong* abutting upon *Medewey*, half an acre at *Chefurlonge* abutting upon *Medewey*, three roods upon the stone abutting upon *Shyrebalk*, and the lord has granted the aforesaid nine acres of land with appurtenances to Robert Hyll, to hold unto him and his heirs in villeinage at the will of the lord for the rents and services formerly due and accustomed for them and he gives to the lord as a fine [*illeg*] and he has done fealty etc.

Affeerors: Robert Pechett, Thomas Fypp.

[*HALS 65535, f8*] **NORTON: View of Frankpledge with Court held there on Tuesday that is to say the 21st day of May in the 30th year of the reign of Henry VIII by the grace of God of England and France King, defender of the faith, Lord of Ireland and on earth supreme head of the Church of England, in the time of Lord Richard the abbot of the exempt monastery of St Alban [*21 May 1538*]**

Essoins: [*blank*]
Chief Pledges: Sworn

Robert Pechette	Robert Hylle	Nicholas Cock
Thomas Ronale the elder	William Rocheford	John Wygges
Thomas Fypp	Nicholas Lawman	John Ronale the younger
John Mosse	John Burges	Robert Burre
John Ronale	Robert Bygrave	

Common Fine: The aforesaid jurors present that they are giving to the Lord the King as a common fine up to this day a fixed sum of 6s 8d.

HENRY VIII

Constables: Robert Hylle is elected, charged and sworn to the aforesaid office in the place of Robert Bygrave, and John Ronale is charged and sworn to the aforesaid office as before etc.

Tippler: Next they present that Antony Fankylcastell is a common tippler of ale and sells with measures that are not approved so he is amerced 2d.

Miller: Next they present that William Wyne is a common miller and takes excessive tolls so he is amerced 2d.

Tithings: Next they present that Thomas Marysshe is of the age of 12 years and has not been sworn, so he is ordered to be at the next View to be sworn under penalty of 6d.

Stray: Next they present that John Bowles esquire has one mother sheep, black in colour, which has come within the precinct of this View as a stray for the past year and a day and it is worth 8d.

Penalties Imposed: All inhabitants of the aforesaid village are ordered to practise sufficiently at the targets in order to maintain their archery skills[78] before the Feast of St John the Baptist next to come, under penalty of 6s 8d.

Nuisance: Next they present that Thomas Monyngham of Luton has one ditch not scoured lying opposite *Mundyns Close* very noisome causing a nuisance etc, so he is ordered to scour it before the Feast of St John the Baptist under penalty 20d.

Court of the lord: held there on the abovewritten day and year.

Proclamation: A proclamation is made that all persons who hold, occupy, or lease any bondman lands or tenements of the lord contrary to the customs of the aforesaid manor without estate and licence having been had or obtained from the lord and also all those who in such lands or tenements have rights to claim must come to get licence or estate from the lord for them under penalty of forfeiting the same etc.

Pains: Next the Homage presents that Thomas Reynard holds by right of his wife Christiana one tenement called *Bayles* and it is very ruinous for want of repairs, that is to say in timbers and in roofing, so he is ordered to have the said tenement adequately repaired before the next general court under penalty of forfeiting the same etc.

Affeerors: Robert Pechette, Thomas Ronale the elder.

---

[78] *Quod facient sufficient[er] per metar[um] ad manutenend[um] artem sagittand[i]*: grammatically messy, with targets in genitive plural case after '*per*', but the intended meaning is probably 'to practise enough at the targets in order to maintain their archery skills'.

HENRY VIII

[*HALS 65535, f8v*] **NORTON:** A Court held there on Saturday the 19th day of April in the [30th] year of the reign of King Henry VIII [by the grace of God] King of England and France, defender of the faith, and on earth Supreme Head of the Church of England in the time of Lord John Salter[79] as cellarer [*19 Apr 1539*]

Essoins: None
Homage: Sworn

Thomas Phypp	Nicholas Cockes	Thomas Reynard
Robert Pechette	William Cammock	John Ronale
Thomas Ronale	William Rocheford	
Nicholas Lawman	John Cock	

The Homage presents that Robert Hyll holds one tenement of new construction with half an acre of land adjoining the same, once part of the holding of Walter Hale as appears in the 1st year of the aforesaid King Henry, and likewise he holds nine acres of land called *Vacontlond* just as appears in a copy of the 29th year of the aforesaid King, and furthermore the Homage presents that the aforesaid Robert on the 1st day of December in the 30th year of the aforesaid King at Norton aforesaid did commit a felony and immediately fled the country. So by the custom of the aforesaid manor he has forfeited the said tenement and lands with appurtenances into the hands of the lord, and afterwards the lord granted the aforesaid tenement and lands with appurtenances to Alice the wife of the aforesaid Robert, to hold unto her for the term of her life, of the lord, in villeinage, at the will of the lord, for the rents and services formerly due and accustomed for it, and after the death of the said Alice the lord has granted the aforesaid tenement and lands with appurtenances to Richard Hylle the son of the aforesaid Robert and Alice, to hold unto him and his heirs of the lord in villeinage at the will of the lord for the services aforesaid etc. The fine on this occasion for having her entry into the premises after such a forfeiture is condoned. And she has done fealty etc
Affeerors: none

---

[79] Levett ends her list of St Albans' cellarers with Robert Blakeney (Levett, *Studies in Manorial History*, p169). However these two courts of 1539 show Lord John Salter. The abbey surrendered to Henry VIII in December 1539.

HENRY VIII

[*HALS 65535, f9*] **NORTON:** View of Frankpledge with Court held there on Tuesday next after the Feast of the Finding of the Holy Cross in the 31st year of the reign of Henry VIII, by the grace of God King of England and France, defender of the faith, Lord of Ireland and on earth Supreme Head of the Church of England in the time of Lord John Salter as cellarer [*16 Sep 1539*]

Essoins: [*blank space*]
Chief Pledges:

Robert Pechette	Thomas Ronale	Richard Burre
Thomas Phyp	Nicholas Lawman	William Cock
John Mosse	Nicholas Cockes	James Phypp
John Ronale the elder	John Burges	John Wygges
John Ronale the younger	Robert Bygrave	Sworn

Common Fine: The jurors present that they are giving to the Lord the King as a common fine up to this day a fixed sum of 6s 8d.
Sworn into Tithings: Thomas Norrys, Thomas Wygges and John Wyllyams are sworn into tithings of the Lord the King.[80]
Constable: Nicholas Lawman and Richard Burre are elected, charged and sworn to the aforesaid office
Miller: Next they present that William Wyne \2d/ is the common miller and has taken tolls excessively.
Brewers: Next they present that Antony Fankylcastell and John Lord are common brewers and have broken the Assize thereof so they are amerced, that is to say, each of them 2d.

The lord's Court: held there on the abovewritten day and year.

Proclamation: A proclamation is made that all persons who hold, occupy or lease any bondman lands or tenements or have or obtain by estate and licence of the lord contrary to the custom of the aforesaid manor, and also all those who in such lands or tenements have a right to be claimed, shall come to receive their estate or licence from the lord according to the custom of the aforesaid manor under penalty of forfeiture.
Pains Imposed:
* Next they present that William Rocheford has one tenement called a *Halhouse* very ruinous and decayed by failure to repair, that is to say in the timber and

---

[80] Tithings has been crossed out but then 'stet' written over it.

HENRY VIII

roofing, so he is ordered to have the said tenement repaired before the Feast of All Saints under penalty of 6s 8d.

* Next they present that Thomas Reynard holds by right of his wife Christiana one tenement for the term of the life of the said Christiana very ruinous and decayed in one chamber at the eastern end of the said tenement so he is ordered to have the said tenement repaired before the Feast of All Saints under penalty of 6s 8d. [*marginal note in different, legal hand. Cross symbol followed by 'Reynard'*]
* Next they present that Thomas Pratte has one barn very ruinous and decayed by failure to repair so he is ordered to repair it before the Feast of All Saints under penalty of 6s 8d.
* John Albreth in full court surrendered into the hands of the lord by the hands of John Newporte of the Hundred one acre and a half of land and meadow of which the said acre lies at *Stanyhyll* and the said half acre behind one close called *Kyndales* and the said meadow called *Collesmede* and the lord has granted the aforesaid land and meadow with appurtenances to Richard Bowles, gentleman, to hold unto him and his heirs of the lord by the rod at the will of the lord by the rent payable by the former tenant of the holding of the aforesaid John Albreth, 1½d and the fine is condoned and he has done fealty and is admitted tenant.
* Thomas Bygg in full court has surrendered into the hands of the lord by the hands of John Newporte of the Hundred two messuages and half a virgate of land and a *quartrona* of land once of John Albret and afterwards of Walter Albreth and late of Simon Mosse together with a croft excepted [from this surrender?] called *Swetkyns* now in the tenure of Thomas Bryges, part of the aforesaid *quartrona* of land and likewise he has surrendered a hearth and 16 acres of land belonging to the same hearth called *Bonnys*. And likewise he has surrendered one toft and one cotland of land called *Geggys*... abutting upon *Wardysgrene*, of which the heriot this time [is] ... worth 5s 8d. And the lord has granted the aforesaid messuages lands hearth and toft and other premises with their appurtenances except what was previously excepted to the aforesaid Thomas Bygg to hold unto him for the term of his life of the lord by the rod at the will of the lord by the rents formerly due and accustomed and after the death of the aforesaid Thomas Bygg the said messuages hearth and toft and other premises shall remain fully to William North and his wife the daughter of the aforesaid Thomas Bygg, to hold to him and his heirs of the lord by the rod at the will of the lord by the rents and services. The fine this time both of the same Thomas Bygg and of the aforesaid William North and of his wife Alice is condoned for 6s 8d and they have done fealty.

HENRY VIII

More of the same on the other side.

[HALS 65535, f9v] **Continuation of the year** [damaged]

* T Phypp pays for heryates for lands late of Thomas Phypp his father.
* Thomas Phypp in full court did surrender into the hands of the lord by the hands of John Newporte of the Hundred one messuage and half a virgate of land late of Margaret Phipp widow, mother of the said Thomas, of which the heriot on this occasion is condoned for [illeg] and the fine is 3s 4d.
* And the aforesaid Thomas Phypp likewise surrendered into the hand of the lord one cottage of new construction and half a virgate of land called *Beges* in an *odum* called *Wat* [damaged] of which the heriot on this occasion is condoned for 2s. And the fine is 12d.
* And the aforesaid Thomas Phypp likewise surrendered one toft and one *quartrona* of land called *Harpennes* as appears in the 10th year of King Henry VII of which the heriot on this occasion is condoned. And the fine is 12d.
* And the aforesaid Thomas Phypp likewise surrendered into the hands of the lord one acre of land and pasture called *Fullers Parcell*, 18 acres of land of *Acremellond* as appears in the 16th year of King Edward III of which the fine is condoned for 12d. And the lord has granted the aforesaid messuage, cottage, toft and land and other premises with their appurtenances to the aforesaid Thomas Phypp and Elizabeth his wife to hold unto them for the term of their lives and the life of the longer liver, of the lord at the will of the lord by the rents and services formerly due and accustomed for them, so that after the deaths of the aforesaid Thomas Phypp and Elizabeth his wife the aforesaid messuage cottage toft and land and other premises with their appurtenances shall remain wholly unto Edward Phypp, son of the aforesaid Thomas Phypp and Elizabeth, to hold unto him and his heirs of the lord at the will of the lord by the rents and services aforesaid etc. The fine and heriot of both the aforesaid Thomas and Elizabeth and of the aforesaid Edward are itemized above. And they did fealty etc.
* John Albreth son of Walter Albreth in full court for a certain sum of money paid to him in hand by John Cock, surrendered into the hands of the lord by the hands of John Newporte of the Hundred and gave up and released and wholly for him and his heirs for ever quitclaimed to the aforesaid John Cock, being now in his full and peaceable possession and seisin and to his heirs and assigns for ever all his right estate title interest and claim that the aforesaid John Albreth ever had or in any way he or they [ie his heirs] could ever have of and in 20 acres and three roods of land and meadow once of Sara de Yerdeley and late of Henry Albreth, of which ten acres are called *Holmede*

HENRY VIII

just as more fully appears in the court roll of the 7th year of the aforesaid King, namely so that neither he the aforesaid John Albreth nor his heirs nor anyone else by them for them or in their names might henceforth claim, seek or sell any right, estate, title, claim, interest and claim whatsoever of or in the aforesaid 20 acres and three roods of land and meadow with appurtenances nor in any part of them, but shall from all action of law, estate, title, claim, interest and claim be completely and for ever excluded by these presents. The fine for making this enrolment is condoned for 12d.

Appendix 1 – Norton Account (1488/89)

[*British Library Add. Roll 33509*] **NORTON: View of John Symondes, rent collector and bailiff with permission of the lord abbot of the exempt monastery of St Albans, from the Feast of St Michael the Archangel in the 4th year of Henry VII to the same feast in the following year, the 5th of the same King, that is for one whole year [*29 Sep 1488 to 28 Sep 1489*]**

Arrears	Account of money received from Rents of Assize [*fixed rents*] and works of the tenants there for one whole year from the Feast of St Michael in the 4th year aforesaid. Part of £88 8s 3d being the arrears of Robert Denyssh, collector there for the same 4th year as fully appears at the foot of his account over and above £66 4s 7¼d. The residue of the said £88 8s 3d is charged on Thomas Denysshe who stands surety for the said Robert in the account for the King's 6th year now as in the same will fully appear. Total as appears	£22 3s 7¾d
Rents of Assize	Summary of the money by the same account received from rents of assize and works of the tenants there for the time of the accounts as particularly appears by the revenue given above and remains towards the account… Total as appears	£22 3s 7¾d
Receipts for grain	Money over the account owed on the price of 4 quarters of grain received from Thomas Denyssh as part of 24 quarters of grain bought from the said Thomas for the use of the said abbot. The price of a quarter with carriage is 5s as fully appears in the account of the said Thomas Denyssh for the 6th year. Thus is owed to him on the said account for 24 quarters of grain received for the use of the abbot from the aforesaid Thomas on his oath and except the 20 quarters he delivered to the abbot's granary as witnessed by the account of the abbot's	20s

APPENDIX I

	granarius.	
	Summary of the money as above owed on the price of 29 quarters of malt received from the aforesaid Thomas Denyssh as part of 129 quarters of malt bought from the same Thomas for the use of the said abbot at the price per quarter with carriage of 3s 4d as will appear in the said Thomas' account for the 6th year. Thus is owed to him on the said account for the aforesaid 129 quarters of malt for the abbot by the oath of the aforesaid Thomas Denyssh except for the 100 already delivered to the abbot's granary as is shown on the account of the abbot's granarius. Total: 116s 8d Sum total received with arrears: £50 3s 11½d	£4 16s 8d
Allowance for clothes	Money allowed to him for his clothes for this year and next year, each year 6s 8d, of which nothing has been delivered to him out of the lord's wardrobe as testified by the account of the abbot's wardrobe keeper. Total as appears	13s 4d
Allowance for carriage	Summary of the money in the said account allowed for the carriage of 20 quarters of grain, part of the 24 quarters bought from Thomas Denyssh, for each quarter carried from Norton to the monastery and delivered for the use of the abbot 8d.	13s 4d
	Summary of the money allowed for the carriage of 80 quarters of malt bought from Thomas Denyssh and carried from Norton to the said monastery and delivered there for the use of the said abbot, for each quarter so carried 5d.	33s 4d
	Summary of the money allowed for the carriage of 20 quarters of grain \13s 4d/ and 20 quarters of malt \8s 4d/ bought from John Wilcokkys, for each quarter of grain carried as above 8d and malt 5d in total:	21s 8d
	Summary of the money allowed for the carriage of	6d

APPENDIX I

one boar bought from Thomas Denyssh and carried to the said monastery and delivered for the use of the abbot.
Total: 68s 10d
Total of all the aforesaid allowances: £4 2s 2d.

And therefore is owed: £46 21½d [*£46 1s 9½d*]. Out of which has been paid to the lord abbot on Christmas Eve 5th year of the King [*24 Dec 1489*] by the archdeacon £8; and also by the reeve 40s; at the Feast of All Saints in the same year [*1 Nov 1489*] by Robert Botry £6; and in the week then following by the chaplain of the lord abbot £4 13s 4d.

Therefore towards the account remains £20 13s 4d. And the money paid to John Wodeward, supervisor (*superius*) of all the abbot's manors for repairs to the manor houses there this year on the oath of the said supervisor 30s. And the allowance for costs and expenses for travelling to Hatfield on the order of the lord for the purchase of grain 2s. Therefore is owed £23 16s 5½d.

Appendix 2 - Charter of Æthelred (1007)

This charter is the earliest surviving written document which mentions Norton and confirms its ownership by St Albans Abbey. The document was written in Latin with boundary details given in Anglo-Saxon. It makes reference to the earlier (eighth century) donation of Norton, Rodenhanger and Oxhey to St Albans Abbey by King Offa. However the absence of any surviving pre-1007 documents confirming this calls into question the truth of the claim.

It was printed from the original by A S Napier and W H Stevenson in *The Crawford Collection of early charters and documents now in the Bodleian Library* (Oxford, 1895) as number XI on pages 24 to 27. A slightly different version, from a French copy of the manuscript, was printed by H Pierquin in *Recueil général des chartes anglo-saxonnes: les Saxons en Angleterre (604-1061)* (Paris, 1912), which is useful for correcting holes and worn patches in the original. There is also a version in Matthew Paris's *Chronica Majora* (published by H R Luard in *Matthæi Parisiensis, Monachi Sancti Albani, Chronica Majora*, vol. VI: *additamenta* (1882), pages 24-7), which was probably copied directly from the original manuscript.

The following translation of the entry for Norton, Rodenhanger and Oxhey with Batchworth was made by Keith Fitzpatrick-Matthews, whose permission to publish is gratefully acknowledged.

'Endorsement: This is the three land deeds for Norton, Rodenhanger and Oxhey with Batchworth, which Archbishop Ælfric and his brother Abbot Leofric[81] bought and King Æthelred [donated] to St Albans for God Almighty as a perpetual inheritance.

Through God and Our Lord Jesus Christ, reigning for ever: insofar as the merits of the blessed martyrs are to be celebrated everywhere throughout the whole world with divine praises and the prayers of those who shed their blood for the name of Christ are to be cherished with all earnestness, nevertheless, the glorious victory of the blessed martyr Alban, who himself underwent martyrdom for Christ, is especially to be honoured by the people of the English settled in the confines of the Britains.

---

[81] Both Ælfric and his brother Leofric were abbots of St Albans although there is some confusion about their dates. According to E B Fryde et al, *Handbook of British Chronology*, Ælfric was Archbishop of Canterbury from 995 to 1005.

APPENDIX II

Therefore I, Æthelred, king of the whole of Britain by the grace of Almighty God, concede the ownership of three lands to the Monastery of the aforementioned martyr for ever, so that on the fearful Day of the Great Judgement I may deserve to stand heir to the heavenly kingdom through the protective intercessions of the saints. Of these, two lie together – that is at Norton and one hide at Rodenhanger – and the third is situated on its own, which is generally known by the name of Oxhey.

Offa, King of the Mercians, formerly possessed it with royal jurisdiction and granted it to the aforementioned monastery, free under eternal law, for the love of so great a martyr who rests in it. But it was violently taken away after his death through the power of certain wicked people and for a long time was unjustly severed from that place, until eventually it was possessed by Ealdorman Leofsige, who was exiled, banished from his homeland, expelled through his own offence. My faithful Archbishop Ælfric and Abbot Leofric, his brother, giving the price, bought that same portion and granted it to me so that I might restore to God what had been God's and obtained it through asking with most humble devotion.

So, after the death of the Archbishop named above, through the intercession of his brother, I ordered this charter of my donation and its renewal to be written, in which I ordain – as much by my own authority as by God's – that no superior or inferior person of whatever rank might presume to take away this share from the holy martyr, no matter what the pretence, whether in my time or that of my successors; but this statute of renewal be permanent and forever, and may all efforts to the contrary be annulled. And let the possession of the aforementioned freely donated lands be in perpetuity – which things are remembered as much by the King of the Mercians as by the Shrine of St Alban – which he enriched with all those possessions he had introduced with all devotion, with three exceptions: contributions for military campaigns, the restoration of bridges and of fortresses; may all the rest belonging to it, fields, pastures, meadows, woods and the rest remain free. So if anyone there shall presume to violate these decrees, may he lack the blessing of Almighty God and all the saints, and of me and all of the Christians; and may he be damned and enter an eternal curse; unless he shall rightly have atoned more quickly for what he had offended against God and his holy martyr Alban.

These are the boundaries going round the holding of those same (places):
* These are the land boundaries of Norton: first from *Radwell Head* to *Wilbury*; from *Wilbury* along *Stotfold Dyke*; then along *Stotfold* boundary

APPENDIX II

until it comes to the boundary stump; then into the stream; along the stream until it comes back to *Radwell Head*.

* These are the land boundaries of the hide at Rodenhanger: first at the *Broad Water* from the *Smooth mound* to the street; along the street until it comes to *...y...an clearing*; from the *clearing* until it comes to *Frobury post*; from the *post* to *...thingham gap*; from the *gap* to *Eadwine's boundary*; then straight on after the *boundary* up to *Withy Height*; then back to the *Smooth mound*.

* These are the land boundaries of Oxhey and Batchworth: first from Watford into *Pudworth*; from *Pudworth* into *Mapledore gap*; from the *gap* to the east *nook* to the *noble boundary*; from the *boundary* to the *Crucifix*; from the *Crucifix* to the *small oak*; from the *oak* to the *boundary thorn*; from the *thorn* to the *hollow*; from the *hollow* to the *birch clearing*; from the *clearing* into *Cuthhelming tree*; from the *tree* onto the *stile*; from the *style* to *R...ding spring*; from the *spring* to the *Colne Bridge*.

This generous charter was written in the year of the Lord's Incarnation 1007, fifth indication, with the knowledge of these witnesses, of whom, these are the names:

I, Æthelred, king of the English, for the love of God and the holy martyr Alban, renew this donation with congratulating heart and I order to entrust the renewal with this pen; I, Ælfheah, Archbishop of the church of Canterbury, have imposed my sign of the Holy Cross upon this royal donation; I, Queen Ælfgifu, have consented with devoted spirit; I, Wulfstan, Archbishop of the church of York, have agreed to this charter; I, Æthelstan, son of the king, with my younger brothers, have applaudingly agreed; I, Æthelwold, the current Bishop of the church of Winchester, have given my assent; I, Ordbryht, bishop of the South Saxons, have confirmed; I, Bishop Æthelwulf, have co-signed; I, Bishop Lyfing, have consolidated; I, Bishop Godwine, have co-sealed; I, Bishop Ælfhun, have confirmed; I, Ælfgar, with the rest of my co-bishops, have concluded; I, Abbot Ælfweard; I, Abbot Ælfsige; I, Abbot Wulfgar; I, Abbot Ælfsige; I, Abbot Ælsige; I, Abbot Germanus; I, Abbot Ælfhere; I, Abbot Brihtwold; I, Abbot Ælfmær; I, Abbot Eadnoth; I, Abbot Godeman; I, Ealdorman Ælfric; I, Ealdorman Leofwine; I, Eadric the thegn; I, Ælfgar the thegn; I, Æthelmær the thegn; I, Athelwold the thegn; I, Leofwine the thegn; I, Godric the thegn; I, Æthelwine the thegn; I, Byrhtsige the thegn; I, Ulfkytel the thegn; I, Æthelric the thegn; I, Ælfgar the thegn; I, Oswig the thegn; I, Leofwine the thegn; I, Ælfwig the thegn; I, Æthelwine the thegn; I, Athelwold the thegn.'

Glossary

abbot: The head or superior of an abbey. The Abbot of St Albans was the lord of the manor of Norton until the Abbey's dissolution under Henry VIII. Abbots attended the House of Lords, as do bishops today.

acre: The area of land that one man could plough with oxen in one day. Its extent was laid down by statute in the reigns of Edward I, Edward III, Henry VIII and most recently Victoria, when it was fixed at 4,840 square yards (approx 4,047 square metres).

affeeror: A person appointed to determine the value of fines and amercements (qv), typically charged with adjusting a generally prescribed penalty according to the particular circumstances of an offender and his or her offence.

aid: A payment to the lord to help defray extraordinary expenses.

albederepe: a bedrip or boon day (qv) with ale provided as refreshment.

alienate (one's holding): Transfer, give up, or lose the possession of property.

amerce: Pronounced 'amerss'. To punish or fine with an amercement (qv).

amercement: A financial penalty made at the discretion of a manorial court.

appurtenance: A lesser right or property belonging with a greater, and passing in ownership with it.

assize: An ordinance governing weights and measures. The Assize of Ale refers to its quality, or to the quantity of ale in a cask and its price.

attaint: (verb) Either to accuse, or to prove an accusation.

attorney: Any person, not necessarily legally qualified, appointed to act on someone's behalf: their agent.

bailiff: The agent of the lord of the manor, probably salaried, who managed the estate and collected rents, etc. His duties were similar to those of the reeve (qv) and he was also elected at the Halimote.

baulk: Pronounced 'bawk'. A ridge left unploughed between furrows within an open arable field. *See also* headland.

beadle: The beadle seems to have carried out different duties in different jurisdictions. In the case of Norton, he appears to have been an under-bailiff and collector of monies due to the lord.

Beaker ware: Late Neolithic, early Bronze Age earthenware pottery of a bell shape often decorated with toothed stamps.

bedrip (various spellings): *See also* boon day and albederepe.

benesad (benside, beuside): In the context of *frumenti de benesad*, it means grain for boonworks.

GLOSSARY

biconical: A style of early Bronze age pot found widely in north western Europe with a deep, largely plain, outwardly flared body. The sides and lid then make a sharp, inward change of direction as if two cones had been placed one on top of the other base to base.

bondage: A form of slavery: bondsmen and women (*cf* villeins) were not free to leave the manor.

boon day, boon works, great boonday, bedrip: A service that tenants had to perform for the lord at certain times of year, eg harvest. Those doing this service were often provided with food and ale by the lord.

bursar: Treasurer or paymaster.

bushel (of barley etc): A dry measure of volume, which varied from place to place and from time to time, and sometimes according to the commodity being measured. An Act of Henry VII made it equal to eight gallons of wheat, but an imperial bushel is now equivalent to 80 pounds (36.4 litres) of distilled water.

butt (at the headland): A butt could have several meanings: it might be a ridge formed between two parallel furrows; or a measure for a parcel of land; or an irregularly shaped piece of land separated from other holdings; or a parcel of land on the edge of a field; or the boundary of the manor.

cellarer: Originally, the duties of a monastic cellarer were to look after the storage and distribution of its provisions; manors were assigned to him from which these provisions were derived. At St Albans, the cellarer became the most important estate official and often acted as the abbot's deputy.[82]

chaplain: A priest employed to chant (sing) prayers for the souls of the departed.

charter: A written document which proves the validity of rights, land holdings, or agreements between a lord and his tenants. In Norton's records it is only used in connection with holdings claimed to be held freely.

chevage: Annual payment made by a villein for permission to live outside the manor.

clerk: A man in holy orders, a priest.

commissary: Someone given a special task, eg to act as executor to a will.

commit waste: To allow or cause property to fall into disrepair.

common agreement: *See* fixed ancient agreement.

common baulk: This may be either the baulk (qv) abutting on the common, or the baulk between two holdings, and shared between them.

---

[82] Levett, *Studies in Manorial History*, pp109-111.

GLOSSARY

common rights: The legal rights to use the manor's common land, eg to graze animals, collect fuel etc.
condone: To permit an action retrospectively without penalty, eg marrying without leave of the lord.
constable: An officer of the parish, or in Norton's case, the manor, appointed to keep the peace and perform certain duties. From the time of Henry IV, at least, Norton had two constables.
corrody: A form of pension, or grant, especially one given in the form of provisions, by religious houses, such as the Abbey of St Albans.
cotland: A piece of arable land, about five acres in extent; a smallholding held on customary tenure.
cotman or cottar: An unfree smallholder of a cotland.
coulter: Pronounced 'koal-ter'. The iron blade fixed at the front of a plough that makes a vertical cut in the soil.
court baron: A manorial court which enforced the customs of the manor. It was the property of the lord and a private jurisdiction. The main business of the court included surrenders and transfers of land, admitting new tenants and the agricultural management of commons and wastes. Disputes between tenants could be resolved there (J Richardson, *The Local Historian's Encyclopedia* (Barnet, 2nd edn. 1986)). In Norton it was known by its alternative name of Halimote (qv).
court leet: A manorial court usually held less than twice a year. It dealt with petty offences, such as breaking of the various assizes (of ale, or weights and measures), causing damage to property or creating a nuisance (such as leaving a ditch uncleared). It was a court of record and a public jurisdiction presided over by the lord or his representative (Richardson, *Encyclopedia*). In Norton it was known as the View of Frankpledge (qv), at which tenants were held responsible jointly for their behaviour.
croft: A piece of enclosed land that may be used for either crops or pasture, often adjacent to a dwelling.
cumin: The most widely used spice in the medieval period. In England, it cost about 2d per pound. It was sometimes used as payment for taxes or rents.
curtilage: A piece of ground attached to a house, or the whole plot, including the house and other buildings.

daub: *See* wattle and daub.
***de Angulo*:** Latin phrase used as an identifying 'surname' for someone who lives on an odd corner of land.
dead hedge: Hedge made of interwoven poles or woody cuttings stuck into the ground.

GLOSSARY

deforce: To dispossess someone of their rightful property. Always in the Norton documents used in conjunction with the word 'unjustly' or 'unlawfully'.

demesne land: The land held and worked by the lord of the manor for himself (now termed 'in hand').

demise: To transfer property, whether by lease, will or otherwise, from one person to another.

detinue: The unlawful withholding or detention of personal property.

disherison: Disinheritance; the act of disinheriting.

distrain: The temporary confiscation of land and/or goods to enforce a court's decision or recover a debt.

dower: The portion of an estate that a widow is allowed to hold for her life after her husband's death.

dredge, draget (peck): A mixture of grains, especially oats and barley, sown together.

enfeoff: To put someone into a fief (qv).

escheat: The reversion of a property to the lord of the manor on the grounds that there is no legal heir under the terms of the original grant.

essoin: (noun) An excuse put forward for not appearing at the court, or else the tenant making it. (verb) To offer an excuse for not appearing at the court.

extent: The valuation put on a piece of land or other property, often used to assess the amount of tax owing; a survey.

farm: A fixed yearly amount payable as rent or tax.

farmer: In the context of Norton, the farmer was someone who managed the demesne lands, contracted to collect the taxes, fines etc for the lord, and paid a fixed sum to the lord for the privilege. He would then keep the balance.

fealty (do fealty): The loyalty due to a feudal lord by his tenants. To 'do fealty' is to make a public profession of this loyalty, an oath of fidelity.

fee (lord's fee): The lord's fee was the estate he held on condition of loyalty to his own superior (*see also* fief).

fee tail: An estate where inheritance was restricted to a particular line of (usually male) heirs.

feoffment: Pronounced 'feffment'. The grant of ownership of a freehold property.

ferlingate (ferthingland, ferth(e)lingate, ferthingate): Pronounced 'ferlinggat'. This form does not appear in *OED*. A *ferling* was a quarter of either a virgate (qv) or a hide (qv).

GLOSSARY

fief, feoff: An inheritance held from a superior in return for homage (qv) and other services.

fine: A payment made to the lord in settlement, to show that a transaction in the manor court was 'finished' (*cf* the French word 'fin' – 'end'); also a money payment to the lord to obtain a specific concession. (Bailey, *The English Manor*, p243)

fixed ancient agreement, ancient sure agreement: An agreement that is so long-established that its origins are beyond the memory of man. Alternatively called 'common agreement'.

frankpledge: The system by which every member of a tithing (qv) was answerable for the conduct of all the other members – they would bring criminals to justice and report on criminal activities.

freeman: Someone who is free of all feudal duties, and may come and go as he chooses. A freeman was entitled to use the royal courts.

gersumm: Originally, a gersum was a valuable item or a costly gift (*OED*), but it came to mean a payment to the lord of the manor made on entry to a property. It is as often used as a verb, for the process of entering the property, as it is as a noun. The fact that it was originally a valuable item was a surety for the good faith of the tenant.

glebe: Land belonging to a church, the income from which was used to support a priest.

gore: This is a wedge-shaped strip of land at the side of an irregularly shaped field.

Grooved ware: A pottery style of the British Neolithic period – a flat bottomed pot with straight sides sloping outwards and grooved decoration around the top. Many have been found at henge (qv) sites.

halimote: Etymologically, this is the meeting (mote) of the hall (or manor). The court, or halimote, primarily administered the customs of the manor with regard to tenure, including changes in ownership of the manor's lands, and the manorial officials, such as the reeve or bailiff were elected. *See* court baron.

hame: One half of a horse collar.

headland: A strip of land next to the boundary, left unploughed as a convenient place to turn the plough at the end of the furrow.

hearth: As it occurs in the phrase 'messuage, cottage, hearth or toft', a hearth must differ from the others in some way. Perhaps it was the only building containing a fireplace.

GLOSSARY

henge: A circular or oval-shaped flat area enclosed by a boundary earth work, usually a ditch with an external bank with one or two entrances cut through it. Its original purpose and function is not yet fully understood by archaeologists but is generally thought to be a ceremonial or ritual meeting place.

heriot: Originally, this was the war equipment (weapons, armour, etc) given back to the lord on a tenant's death. This was later changed to the tenant's best live animal or possession, and in Norton, by the time of Henry III, it was generally commuted to a money payment. A death duty.

hide: An uncertain area of land, around 120 acres (approx 48.6 hectares). The unit was used for tax purposes.

Hokeday: The second Tuesday after Easter Sunday: this was an important term-day, on which rents were paid, Hokeday and Michaelmas dividing the year into its summer and winter halves. In 1257, a court was held on the Tuesday before this, ie the Tuesday immediately after Easter Monday.

homage: The public, and formal, acknowledgment of allegiance made by a tenant to his lord. 'The Homage' means the whole body of tenants taken together.

huckstress: A female hawker, pedlar.

hundred: An administrative division of the shire, the unit of local government between the county and the vill (qv). Its derivation is obscure, but may be connected with the number of hides (qv) or the number of families originally in the division.

Impressed ware: Highly decorated pottery of the later Neolithic period in use from the third to the early second millennium BC. Its surface was decorated with impressions made with fingers, sticks or other tools.

increase in rent: The Latin word *incrementum* means simply 'increase' or, rather obviously, 'increment', but is this an increase in the rent to be paid? If so, the amounts mentioned are insignificant (as little as ¼d or ½d). In his book on the manorial rolls of Walsham le Willows[83], Ray Lock explains that after discussion with Professor Christopher Dyer of Leicester University, he concluded that the 'increase' is a small addition to the amount of land held by the tenant, newly acquired in whatever way, and the extra rent is for that land. However, in Norton, most of the references are to land that was, or had previously been, held freely, and this would imply that the lord was now claiming ownership, and therefore rent, for the first time.

incumbent: the holder of an ecclesiastical office; the parish priest.

---

[83] R Lock, *The Court Rolls of Walsham le Willows 1351-99* (SRS vol 45, 2002), pvii.

GLOSSARY

inquisition: An official inquiry into the facts of a matter. Also the group of people who carry out the inquiry.

King's highway: A major road connecting towns or villages, not leading simply to another part of the same village.

knight service: A form of tenure which provided the funds to pay for a knight, including his military equipment. *See also* military service.

La Tène: Named after an archaeological site in Switzerland discovered in the nineteenth century, archaeologists now use this term for describing the artefacts belonging to late Iron Age Celtic culture in pre-Roman Britain. Metal objects found at La Tène are characterized by stylized faces and entwined plant ornament.

letters (put to letters): To put someone to letters was to have them taught to read and write, usually with the intention of their becoming a priest.

leyrwite: Pronounced 'lair-wit'. A fine paid to the manorial lord when a villein woman fornicated. (Bailey, *The English Manor*, p244)

Liberty (of St Albans): An area where jurisdiction was held by the local lord, in this case the Abbot of St Albans: the King's rights were devolved to the Abbot.

lithics: Artefacts made of stone, primarily worked stone for use as tools.

load: A unit of measure or weight which can vary by locality and substance, for example wheat is usually 40 bushels (qv) (*OED*).

lot and scot: 'Lot' was a local tax. 'Scot' was a tax levied according to the payer's ability to pay.

malm: A soft chalky rock. By extension, it is a light loamy soil formed by the decomposing rock, and by further extension, it became the name of a field where this was the predominant type of soil.

manumission: Formal grant of freedom to a villein and his descendants.

mark: A unit of currency worth two thirds of a pound, ie 13s 4d.

maslin: Pronounced 'mazzlin'. A mixture of grains, or of grains and pulses.

merchet: Pronounced 'mertchet'. A fine paid by villein tenants to the lord for permission to marry off a daughter.

mesne lord: Pronounced 'meen'. A mesne lord is one who holds his fief from a superior, and has vassals himself.

messuage: Pronounced 'mess-wij'. Originally a piece of land that was intended to have a dwelling built on it, together with any outbuildings. Later it became such a building and its adjacent land.

metes and bounds: Formal boundary markers.

GLOSSARY

military service: The duty of a vassal to serve as a soldier as and when the lord demanded. If the vassal was a woman, or too young or too old or too frail to serve, the service could be commuted to a money payment. *See also* knight service.
moiety: A half.
mortuary: Payment due to the local parish priest from the estate of a dead man.
mulct: Payment in kind to the miller for grinding corn (a proportion of the ground corn).

nativus: A man born as a serf, a villein (qv).
neonate: A newborn child.

owe suit (of court): To have a duty to attend the court.

pains: Penalties, punishments.
peck: A measure of volume equivalent to a quarter of a bushel (qv), which varied by place and in time, and sometimes according to the commodity being measured. In 1824 it was fixed at two imperial gallons (approx 9.1 litres).
perch: A measure of length used for calculating the size of a plot of land. Originally it could vary from place to place, but is now fixed at 5½ yards (approximately 5.03 metres).
pightel, pyghtle: A small parcel of land, of no definite extent.
pledge: (noun) A person who gives surety for another; or, a member of the frank-pledge (qv). (verb) To give a surety for someone else or for an action. The phrase 'chief pledge' is used in the rolls as a synonym for 'juror'.
ploughshare: The large pointed blade of the plough.
processional way: On Rogation Days, parishioners perambulated the boundaries of the parish so that those boundaries were remembered. The route taken was the 'processional way'.
provender: Food, in particular dry food, for horses or cattle.
pyghtle: *See* 'pightel'.

quarter (a quarter of corn): A dry measure of capacity, varying in amount over time and from commodity to commodity. Now fixed at eight bushels (approx 291 litres).
quarter (of land): A measure of area, varying between 50 and 250 acres (approx 20.2 and 101 hectares).
quartrona (of land): Probably a quarter of a virgate or of a hide.
querne stone: millstone for grinding corn.
quindene (of St Hilary): The fifteenth day after a festival or saint's day.

GLOSSARY

quire: Four sheets of paper or parchment folded to form eight leaves.

quitclaim: To renounce a claim to land.

recognizance: A bond or obligation agreed in court by which a person undertakes to perform some act or observe some condition.

reeve: The local official responsible for day-to-day management of the manor, elected by the manorial tenants at the Halimote. Similar to the bailiff (qv).

regrater: A trader who bought goods to sell at a higher price into the same market. By cornering the market in a particular commodity, regraters could make large profits at the expense of their fellows. This was considered unfair, and so subject to amercement.

release: To relinquish a claim (to land, etc) or to treat an obligation as having been carried out.

relict: The widow of a deceased man. Literally the one 'left behind'.

relief: Payment made to the lord by the heir of a tenant on taking up possession of the vacant estate.

rent: A periodic payment for the use of land.

repair waste: To bring a property back up to its proper state after it had been allowed to fall into disrepair or to cultivate land that had become overgrown or derelict.

rod (by the rod): A symbol of the lord's authority – held at the will of the lord.

Rogation (Days): In the calendar of the Western Church, four days are traditionally set apart for solemn processions to invoke God's mercy. The faithful typically observed the Rogation Days by fasting in preparation to celebrate the Ascension and farmers often had their crops blessed by the incumbent at this time, which always occurs during the spring in the Northern Hemisphere. A common feature of Rogation Days was the ceremony of 'beating the bounds', in which a procession of parishioners, led by the incumbent, would proceed around the boundary of their parish and pray for its protection in the forthcoming year. This was also known as 'Gang-day'.

rood (of land): An area measuring a quarter of an acre (or 40 square perches), in metric terms 1011.75 square metres, but which may have varied from this depending on the locality.

sedecod: Seedbag (*cod* is an Old English word for a bag).

seisin: Pronounced 'seezin'. Literally 'possession'. As seisin was granted at a court, it was a legally binding grant of possession, and so protected from seizure.

GLOSSARY

selion: A piece of land of indeterminate size between two furrows formed by the ploughing. Also called a 'narrow-land'.

sergeant: An officer whose duty is to enforce the judgements of a tribunal or the commands of a person in authority; one who is charged with the arrest of offenders or the summoning of persons to appear before the court. In status similar to a bailiff.

severalty (the lord's): Land held privately and enclosed, and so not in common for the use of the whole manor.

smalewerkes: 'Small works' – tasks of minor importance.

socage: Tenure which was exchanged for certain goods or services which were not military in nature. Socage tenure passed automatically from one generation to the next.

steward: a senior estate administrator to whom the bailiffs (qv) reported. He usually had a legal background, and was a prominent member of the local gentry. He probably held the courts when the cellarer was not present.

suit (doing suit at the lord's mill): 'Suit of court' was attendance by a tenant at the lord's court. To do suit at the lord's mill was the obligation to use the lord's mill and no-one else's. This was required of villeins.

tallage: An arbitrary tax, originally levied by the crown, but by extension at a later date imposed by any superior on his unfree tenants (qv).

tenants (customary tenants): Customary tenants were those liable or subject to customs or dues of various kinds. Later the same phrase was used simply to mean 'tenants according to the customs of the particular manor'.

tenement: Literally a 'holding'. In theory all the land of England belonged to the king, and he then granted holdings to his vassals, who in turn granted holdings – tenements – to their tenants.

terrier: A detailed record of land holdings.

tippler: A retailer of alcoholic beverages.

tithing (outside the tithing): In the Saxon period a group of ten householders who stood security for each other; by the medieval period each male over the age of 12 (or 16, depending on local custom) was obliged to be in a tithing for the purposes of the frankpledge (qv). Anyone found not to be in a tithing was amerced. (*See*, for example, the records of the court held on 7 May 1409.)

toft: A homestead, a site on which a house may be built.

traces (pair of): Straps connecting the collar of a draught animal to a crossbar (the swingletree) that allows free movement for the animal's shoulders.

unfree (tenure): *See* villeinage.

GLOSSARY

vacant land: Land without a tenant.

vicar: The priest carrying out religious duties at the parish church. In Norton he was appointed by the Abbot.

vicarage: The property tenanted by the vicar.

view (of frankpledge): A system by which members of a community were responsible for the behaviour of one another, monitored by the annual View. *See* court leet (qv).

vill: the local unit of civil administration (Bailey, *The English Manor*, p246).

villein: A peasant attached to a manor or entirely subject to a lord. Translation of the Latin *nativus*.

villeinage: A type of tenure whose obligations and terms were determined and enforced in the manor court; also called bondage or unfree tenure.

virgate: A land measure that varied in extent from place to place, and from time to time. In many cases it was about 30 acres (approx 12.1 hectares) – a quarter of a hide.

wardship: The guardianship and custody of a minor until they come of age.

warettare: To plough land and let it lie fallow for a period of time before sowing.

waste (commit waste): To damage. Tenants accused of 'committing waste' have either allowed their property to fall into disrepair, or have deliberately caused damage to it (in at least one case by chopping down trees without permission).

wattle and daub: a woven lattice of wooden strips (the wattle) covered with a sticky combination (the daub) usually of wet soil, clay, animal dung and straw, used for making the walls of a building.

wether: An adult male sheep, especially a castrated ram.

yardland: A land measure, typically of about 30 acres. As quartrona (qv) and virgate (qv).

The Hertfordshire Record Society

The Hertfordshire Record Society exists to make Hertfordshire's historical records of all kinds more readily available to the general reader. Since 1985 a regular series of texts has been published.

ALAN THOMSON, Chairman
HEATHER FALVEY, Hon Secretary
IAN FISHER, Hon Treasurer
SUSAN FLOOD, Hon General Editor

Membership enquiries and orders for previous publications to the Hon Treasurer, 2 Fairview Cottages, Amwell Hill, Great Amwell, nr Ware, SG12 9RA.

Annual Subscription (2013-2014) £17.50

Previous publications:

I *Tudor Churchwardens' Accounts.* Edited by Anthony Palmer (1985) O/P

II *Early Stuart Household Accounts.* Edited by Lionel M Munby (1986) O/P

III *'A Professional Hertfordshire Tramp' John Edwin Cussans, Historian of Hertfordshire.* Edited by Audrey Deacon and Peter Walne (1987) O/P

IV *The Salisbury-Balfour Correspondence, 1869-1892.* Edited by Robin Harcourt Williams (1988) O/P

V *The Parish Register & Tithing Book of Thomas Hassall of Amwell* [Registers, 1599-1657; Tithing Book, 1633-35]. Edited by Stephen G Doree (1989) Price £6.00

VI *Cheshunt College: The Early Years.* Edited by Edwin Welch (1990) O/P

VII *St Albans Quarter Sessions Rolls, 1784-1820.* Edited by David Dean (1991) O/P

VIII *The Accounts of Thomas Green, 1742-1790.* Edited by Gillian Sheldrick (1992) O/P

HERTFORDSHIRE RECORD SOCIETY

IX   *St Albans Wills, 1471-1500.* Edited by Susan Flood (1993) O/P

X   *Early Churchwardens' Accounts of Bishops Stortford, 1431-1538.* Edited by Stephen G Doree (1994) Price £6.00

XI   *Religion in Hertfordshire, 1847-1851.* Edited by Judith Burg (1995) Price £6.00

XII   *Muster Books for North & East Hertfordshire, 1580-1605.* Edited by Ann J King (1996) Price £6.00

XIII   *Lifestyle & Culture in Hertford: Wills and Inventories, 1660-1725.* Edited by Beverly Adams (1997) Price £6.00

XIV   *Hertfordshire Lay Subsidy Rolls, 1307 and 1334.* Edited by Janice Brooker and Susan Flood, with an Introduction by Dr Mark Bailey (1998) Price £6.00

XV   *'Observations of Weather': The Weather Diary of Sir John Wittewronge of Rothamsted, 1684-1689.* Edited by Margaret Harcourt Williams and John Stevenson (1999) Price £19.00 (members £15.00)

XVI   *Survey* of *the Royal Manor of Hitchin, c1676.* Edited by Bridget Howlett (2000) Price £6.00

XVII   *Garden-Making and the Freeman family A Memoir of Hamels, 1713-1733.* Edited by Anne Rowe (2001) Price £18.50 (members £15.00)

XVIII   *Two Nineteenth Century Hertfordshire Diaries, 1822-1849.* Edited by Judith Knight and Susan Flood (2002) Price £19.50 (members £15.00)

XIX   *"This little commonwealth": Layston parish memorandum book, 1607-c1650 & 1704-c1747.* Edited by Heather Falvey and Steve Hindle (2003) Price £21.00 (members £15.00)

XX   *Julian Grenfell, soldier and poet: letters and diaries, 1910-1915.* Edited by Kate Thompson (2004) Price £20.00 (members £15.00)

XXI   *The Hellard Almshouses and other Stevenage Charities, 1482-2005.* Edited by Margaret Ashby (2005) Price £21.00 (members £15.00)

XXII   *A Victorian Teenager's Diary: the Diary of Lady Adela Capel of Cassiobury, 1841-1842.* Edited by Marian Strachan (2006) Price paperback £9.99

HERTFORDSHIRE RECORD SOCIETY

XXIII *The Impact of the First Civil War on Hertfordshire, 1642-1647.* Edited by Alan Thomson (2007) Price £22.00 (members £17.50)

XXIV *The Diary of Benjamin Woodcock Master of the Barnet Union Workhouse, 1836-1838.* Edited by Gillian Gear (2008) Price £22.00 (members £17.50)

XXV *Datchworth Tithe Accounts, 1711-1747.* Edited by Jane Walker (2009) Price £22.00 (members £17.50)

XXVI *John Carrington's Diary*, I, *1798-1804.* Edited by Susan Flood (not yet published)

XXVII *Humphry Repton's Red Books of Panshanger and Tewin Water, 1799-1800.* With an Introduction by Twigs Way (2011) Price £30.00 (members £17.50)

XXVIII *The Receipt Book of Baroness Elizabeth Dimsdale, c1800.* Edited and with an Introduction by Heather Falvey. Price £22.00 (members £17.50)

XXX *Weston School Logbooks, 1876-1914.* Transcribed by Joan Amis, Margaret Bowyer and Janet Gunn; edited and with an Introduction by Margaret Ashby. Price £22.00 (members £17.50)

Maps:

The County of Hertford From Actual Survey by A Bryant In the Years 1820 and 1821 (2003; reprinted 2012) Price £8.50 (members £5.00)

A Topographical Map of Hartford-Shire by Andrew Dury and John Andrews, 1766 (2004) Price £9.50 (members £8.50)

For more information visit www.hrsociety.org.uk

Bibliography

Printed Primary Sources
Brooker, J and Flood, S (eds), *Hertfordshire Lay Subsidy Rolls, 1307 and 1334* (HRS, vol xiv, 1998)
Calendar of the Patent Rolls 6 Edward II, Part I (London, 1894)
Dury, Andrew, and Andrews, John, *A Topographical Map of Hartford-Shire* (1766, reprinted HRS, 2004)
Karn, N and Smith, D M (eds), *English Episcopal Acta, Ely 1109-1197* (Oxford, 2005)
Lock, R (ed), *The Court Rolls of Walsham le Willows 1303-50* and *1351-99* (Suffolk Records Society, vols 41 and 45, 1998 and 2002)
Morris, J, (ed and trans), *Domesday Book 12: Hertfordshire* (Chichester, 1976)
'Norton Church Terrier 1637', *St Albans Diocesan Gazette*, vol 17 no 11 (Nov 1912), pp228-30
Noy, D (ed), *Winslow Manor Court books 1327-1377* and *1423-1460* (Buckinghamshire Record Society, vol 35, 2011)
Post Office Directory Hertfordshire (1859)
Riley, H T (ed), *Annales Monasterii S Albani* (2 vols, 1870-71)
Riley, H T (ed), *Gesta Abbatum Monasterii S Albani* (3 vols, 1867-69)
Riley, H T (ed), *Registra Quorundam Abbatum Monasterii S Albani* (2 vols, 1872-73)

Secondary Sources
Bailey, M, 'Introduction', in J Brooker and S Flood, (eds), *Hertfordshire Lay Subsidy Rolls 1307 and 1334*, (HRS, vol xiv, 1998)
Bailey, M, *The English Manor, c.1200-c.1500* (Manchester, 2002)
Bailey, M, 'The economy of towns and markets, 1100 to 1500', in T Slater and N Goose (eds), *A County of Small Towns* (Hatfield, 2008), pp46-66
Bailey, M, 'The form, function and evolution of irregular field systems in Suffolk, 1300 to 1550', *Agricultural History Review*, 57 (2009), pp15-24
Bailey, M, *The Decline of Serfdom in Late Medieval England. From Bondage to Freedom* (Woodbridge, 2014)
Bennett, J M, 'Writing Fornication: Medieval Leyrwite and its Historians', in *Transactions of the Royal Historical Society*, 13, (2003), pp131-162.
Beresford, G, *Caldecote: The Development and Desertion of a Hertfordshire Village* (London, 2009)
Beresford, M W, *New Towns of the Middle Ages. Town Plantation in England, Wales and Gascony* (1967)

BIBLIOGRAPHY

Campbell, B M S, *English Seigniorial Agriculture 1250-1450* (Cambridge, 2000)
Crellin, V, *Baldock's Middle Ages* (Baldock, 1995)
Dyer, C, *Caldecote, Hertfordshire: A History of the Village* (Caldecote, 2010)
Dyer, C, *Making a Living in the Middle Ages. The People of Britain 850-1520* (New Haven and London, 2002)
Dyer, C, *Standards of Living in the Later Middle Ages* (Cambridge, 1989)
Fitzpatrick-Matthews, K and T, *The Archaeology of Letchworth Garden City* (North Hertfordshire Museums Service, 2009)
Fryde, E B, Greenway, D E, Porter, S, and Roy, I (eds), *Handbook of British Chronology* (Cambridge, 1996)
Giles, D, *Norton before the Garden City* (Baldock, 2003)
Goose, N, 'Urban growth and economic development in early modern Hertfordshire', in T Slater and N Goose (eds), *A County of Small Towns* (Hatfield, 2008), pp101-26
Gover, J E B, *The Place-Names of Hertfordshire* (Cambridge, 1938, reprinted 1970)
Harvey, P D A, *Manorial Records* (revised edn, 1999)
Harvey, P D A, (ed), *The Peasant Land Market in Medieval England* (Oxford, 1984)
Howard, E, *To-morrow! A Peaceful Path to Real Reform* (1898)
Howard, E, *Garden Cities of To-morrow* (1902)
Levett, A E, *Studies in Manorial History* (Oxford, 1938)
Martin, C T, *The Record Interpreter: A Collection of Latin Words and Names used in English Historical Manuscripts and Records* (2nd edn, 1910)
Matthews, K J, and Burleigh, G R, 'A Saxon and early medieval settlement at Green Lane, Letchworth', *Hertfordshire's Past*, 26 (Spring 1989), pp27-32
Moss-Eccardt, J, and others, 'Archaeological Excavations in the Letchworth area', *Proceedings of the Cambridge Antiquaries Society*, LXXVII (1988)
Noy, D, 'Leyrwite, marriage and illegitimacy: Winslow before the Black Death' in *Records of Buckinghamshire* vol 47 part 1 (2007)
Page, W, (ed), *Victoria County History, Hertfordshire* (4 vols, 1902-14)
Razi, Z, and Smith, R, *Medieval Society and the Manor Court* (Oxford, 1996)
Richardson, J, *The Local Historian's Encyclopedia* (Barnet, 2nd edn, 1986)
Roberts, E, *The Hill of the Martyr, an Architectural History of St Albans Abbey* (Dunstable, 1993)
Roden, D, 'The field systems of the Chiltern Hills and their environs', in A R H Baker and R A Butlin (eds), *Studies of field systems in the British Isles* (Cambridge, 1973), pp325-62

BIBLIOGRAPHY

Slota, L A, 'Law, land transfer, and lordship on the estates of St Albans Abbey in the thirteenth and fourteenth centuries', *Law and History Review*, 6:1 (1988), pp119-38

Stern, D V, *A Hertfordshire Demesne of Westminster Abbey, Profits, Productivity and Weather* (Hatfield, 2000)

Tomkins, M, 'The Manor of Park in the Fourteenth Century' in *The Peasants' Revolt in Hertfordshire, 1381* (Hatfield, 1981), pp55-81

Williamson, T, *The Origins of Hertfordshire* (Hatfield, 2010)

Index of Persons

Many surnames were prefixed with 'de la', 'le', 'de' and 'atte' but these prefixes have not been shown in the index. Likewise suffixes such as 'the elder' or 'the younger' are not shown.

Some references are limited to the first name only. In those cases, where a title is also given eg Thomas the vicar, it is indexed with Thomas as the surname, viz 'Thomas, vicar'. Sometimes a name such as Alexander, son of William (with no surname) is given, so it has been indexed as 'William, Alex, son of'. Where only one first name has been given with no other information it is not indexed.

Where the surname is not given, but a relationship is shown eg Agnes, wife of Roger Albreth, it is indexed as 'Albreth, Agn, wife of Rog', whereas Agnes Albreth is simply shown as 'Albreth, Agn'.

Occasionally, a title is given but no first or surname eg Prior of Wymondham, and this is indexed in the subject index, under 'Manorial officials, prior', rather than in the index of persons.

The following abbreviations have been used:
Agn, Agnes; Alex, Alexander; Ali, Alice; And, Andrew; Bart, Bartholomew; bro, brother; daur, daughter; Edw, Edward; Eliz, Elizabeth; Fred, Frederick; Geof, Geoffrey; Hen, Henry; Isa, Isabel(la); Jas, James; Jos, Joseph; Kath, Katherine; Mar, Martin; Marg, Margaret; Margy, Margery; Mati, Matilda; Matt, Matthew; Nic, Nicholas; Ral, Ralph; Ric, Richard; Rob, Robert; Rog, Roger; Si, Simon (Symon); sis, sister; Ste, Stephen (Steven); Thos, Thomas; Walt, Walter; Wm, William.

Abelon
Lucy, 56
Adam
Geof, 176-8, 184
Thos, son of, 11
vicar of Newenham, 56, 90
Ælfgar
Bishop, 306
thegn, 306
Ælfgifu
Queen, 306
Ælfheah
Archbishop, 306
Ælfhere
Abbot, 306
Ælfhun
Bishop, 306
Ælfmær
Abbot, 306
Ælfric
Archbishop, 304, 304n, 305
Ealdorman, 306
Ælfsige
Abbot, 306
Ælfweard
Abbot, 306
Ælfwig
thegn, 306
Ælsige
Abbot, 306
Æthelmær
thegn, 306
Æthelred
King, 304-6
Æthelric
thegn, 306
Æthelstan
son of the King, 306
Æthelwine
thegn, 306
Æthelwold
Bishop, 306
Æthelwulf
Bishop, 306

INDEX OF PERSONS

Ailbern(e) (Ailbert)
  Edelina, wife of, 8
  Mar, 29
  Walt, 8, 13
Ailric
  Godfrey, son of, 1
  Hugh, son of, 20
Alan
  Amice, daur of, 39-41, 75, 101
  Joan, daur of, 75
  Sar(r)a, daur of, 42, 75
Albreth (Ailbright, Albery, Albre(y),
  Albred(e), Albret(he), Albrid, Albright,
  Albrith, Alb(u)ry, Albryth, Auber(y),
  Aubray, Aubre(i), Aubrey, Awebery)
  Adam, son of John, 166
  Agn, *l*, 105, 119, 160
  Agn, daur of John, 68
  Agn, daur of Ral, 149
  Agn, wife of Rog, 143
  Ali, daur of Ral, 124
  Ali, wife of Rog, 200
  Cecilia (Cecily), 252-3, 255-6
  Cecily, daur of Walt, 252
  Ellen, 73
  Geof, bro of Agn, wife of Rog, 143
  Helen, daur of Ral, 122
  Hen, 299
  Isa, 80
  Isa, daur of John, 74
  Ivetta, 87, 89, 89n
  Ivetta, wife of John, 87
  Jas, *lviii*, 2,
  Joan, daur of John, 264
  John, *xlv, lviii*, 2, 8, 22-3, 33-4, 40, 68,
    71, 74, 76, 82, 84-8, 92, 94, 109-10,
    103, 105, 107, 116-17, 121, 128, 130-2,
    134, 138, 144-5, 152-5, 157-61, 163,
    165-6, 176-80, 196, 244, 246-8, 250-4,
    256-68, 270, 272-3, 275-6, 280-1,
    283-90, 292-3, 298-300
  John, son of Walt, 100
  Lucy, daur of, 23
  Marg, wife of John, 261
  Margy, daur of John, 256
  Mati, 145
  Mati, daur of Walt, 47, 85, 262
  Ral, *l*, 69, 75, 79, 81-2, 86-9, 91-7,
    104-10, 113, 116-17, 119, 121-5, 127,
    129-30, 136, 143, 149, 200
  Ral, son of Walt, 102
  Rob, 189
  Rog, 138-9, 143, 150-2, 154, 156, 158-66,
    171-5, 177-80, 182-4, 187-200, 205,
    207, 250, 263
  Rog, son of Ral, 95
  Rosa (Rose), son of John, 145, 161
  Ste, 114
  Thos, *lix*, 268, 270, 272, 274
  Walt, 25, 29-30, 33, 40-2, 47, 50, 54-5,
    57-9, 61-3, 67-8, 69-70, 73-4, 76, 78,
    82, 84-5, 87, 89-93, 96, 98, 100, 102,
    200-3, 205-6, 208-13, 215, 217-21, 223,
    226-8, 231-3, 235-44, 246-8, 250, 250n,
    251-4, 257-64, 266-8, 270, 272, 274,
    284, 298-9
  Walt, bro of John, 34
  Walt, son of John, 68
  Wm, 256, 265
Alexander (Alysaundre)
  Alex, son of, 85
  Ali, wife of, 81
  Isa, 65
  Joan, 64
  John, 22, 29, 31, 63
  John, son of, 24, 30
  Walt, son of, 45, 53
Aleynes
  Amice, 43
Alice
  Ste, son of, 20
  Walt, son of, *xxxiiin*, 5
Alfiene
  Thos, son of, 2
Alfred(e)
  Hugh, son of, 15
  John, 136
Alvered
  Godfrey, 12
Ame
  Ric, 58
Amphibal
  Walt, 19, 19n
Andrew(e) (Andreu)
  Agn, wife of Ric, 104
  Alex, *lv*, 88, 92-4, 97-8, 107, 109, 123,

INDEX OF PERSONS

32-3, 143
  Alex, son of, 81
  Cecilia (Cecily), 148, 150-1, 164-79
  Cecilia, daur of Alex, 133, 143
  Emma, daur of, 96-8
  John, 66, 72, 80, 111, 122, 160
  Mati, 66
  Ric, 99, 103-4, 122-3, 130, 142, 145-6, 148, 153, 156, 158-62
  Ric, son of Ric, 145-6
  Rob, 280
  Saundr, 91
  Thos, 275

Angulo
  Alan, son of Wm, 10
  John, son of Wm, 10
  Osbert, 3
  Ste, *lvii*, 2, 5, 10
  Wm, 5, 10

Appulyerde (Aplierd, Aplyerd)
  John, *lvii*, 270, 273-4

Arblaster
  Walt, 91

Arlesheye (Arlecheshey)
  Ral, 32
  Rob, son of Walt, 53
  Walt, 53

Aschwelle (Asshewelle)
  Hugh, *lvii*, 153
  John, 149, 152

Assh(e) (Ass) (*see also* Nasshe)
  Agn, daur of Ali, 118
  Ali, 118, 160, 220, 222-3, 226, 228, 231-2
  Joan, 228, 233, 235-6
  John, 200, 202, 248
  Ric, 201, 234, 246
  Ste, 22

Athelwold
  theyn, 306

Attedener (*see* Dene)
Attewode (*see* Wode)
Attewatre (*see* Water)
Aubrey (Auber(y), Aubray, Aubre(i), Awebery) (*see* Albreth)
Aula (*see* Halle)
Ays (Ayssh) (*see* Hays)

Bacon
  Agn, 82
  Margy, 215
  Ral, 82
  Wm, 212, 214

Badewelle
  Thos, 214

Badewey (*see* Bradewey)

Bailiff
  John, 71

Baker
  Agn, wife of Wm, 223
  Ric, 154
  Wm, 223

Baldock
  Pagan, 27

Balker(e) (Balkars)
  John, 21, 24, 26
  Kath, 26

Bal(s)ton (Bolston)
  Emma, 172
  John, 48, 52, 55-8, 64, 73, 77-9, 82, 84-7, 90-1, 106
  John, bro of John, 52
  Mati, 92, 96, 123, 162, 244, 259, 261, 286
  Mati, wife of John, 48, 91
  Reynald, 109, 114, 117, 123, 147-50, 153-4, 157-8, 166, 168-9, 172, 175-6, 181, 183, 189-90, 214, 217
  Reynald, son of John, 91
  Thos, 99, 126
  Walt, son of John, 48, 52

Barber (Barb(o)ur)
  Wm, 54-5, 83, 119

Bartelott
  Ali, 158

Bartholomew
  Ste, son of, 18, 21, 23, 28

Basily (Basely)
  John, 167
  Marg, 168

Bate(s) (Batte, Bette)
  Agn, 82, 151, 153, 158, 160, 169-70, 188-91, 193, 223, 226, 228, 231-3
  Agn, daur of Ric, 175
  Agn, daur of Wm, 145, 217-8, 220, 222
  Agn, sis of Hen, 124
  Albreda, 84, 101-2

INDEX OF PERSONS

Albreda, wife of Ric, 77, 116
Ali, 165
  Hen, 101, 111-12, 124
  Hen, son of Ric, 57
  John, *lvii*, 36, 38, 45, 48-9, 54-6, 59,
    63-70, 72, 85-7, 89, 96-7, 99, 102,
    104-6, 113, 129-30, 151-2, 156, 160-3,
    165-7, 172, 181-2, 184-5, 187-93, 195,
    197-8
  John, son of John, 99, 102, 105-6
  John, son of Ral, 93
  John, son of Ric, 45, 54, 57
  Marg, 165
  Margy, 162-3, 163n
  Osbert, *lvii, lviii*, 45, 73, 235
  Ral, 49, 58, 65, 70, 93, 150
  Ral, son of Ric, 149
  Ric, *l, lvii, lviii, lix*, 36-8, 40, 42, 44-9,
    51-2, 54-7, 61, 65-7, 70-7, 85, 93, 106,
    109, 111, 116, 122-3, 126-7, 129, 131,
    134-6, 138, 144-5, 147-50, 152-8, 160,
    162, 165, 175-6, 191, 214, 220, 222,
    225, 227, 235
  Ric, son of John, 97, 113
  Ric, son of Wm, 111, 116, 121
  Rob, 131, 133, 151-2, 157, 159
  Walt, 115
  Wm, *liii, lviii*, 73, 76, 79-84, 86-91, 93,
    101-2, 109-12, 115-16, 121, 145, 181-4,
    190-2, 198, 210, 212, 214-15, 217-18,
    220, 222-3, 226, 228, 231-3, 235
  Wm, son of Ric, *lvii*, 57
Bateman
  John, 152
Bayly
  Eliz, wife of Rob, 266
  Rob, 266-8
Becketh
  Thos, 280
Bedel(l)
  John, 2-3, 5, 12, 13-16, 21
  Wm, *lvii*, 6
Bekeneswell
  Ral, 20
Bele
  John, son of, 26
Ben(e)
  John, *lv*, 19, 26

  Marg, 39
  Mati, relict of Thos, 56
  Thos, 21, 56, 189
Benet (Beneit)
  John, 226
  Ric, son of Walt, 112
  Walt, 112
Bercar(ius) (Bercator, Bercher) (*see*
  Shepherd)
Berger (*see* Burger)
Berney
  John, 238-9, 242
Berthelot (Bartelott)
  Ali, 156
Beton
  Ali, 228
Bette
  John, 199
Bewyke
  Nic, 107, 109-11, 114-16
Bigge (Byg(g))
  Thos, *lvii*, 281, 298
  Wm, 22-3
Bissopp
  Felicia, wife of, 10
Black (Blak)
  John, 14
  John, bro of Ric, 14
  Juliana, wife of Ric, 14
  Ric, 14
Blakeney
  Rob, 275-6, 296, 296n
Blaseworth (Blayesworth, Bleyesworth)
  Laurence, 42-3, 47, 61
Blebury
  John, 212-3, 215-20, 223-7
Blowe
  John, *xliv*, 255, 257-66, 268
Bofot
  Geof, bro of Mabel, 14
  Mabel, 14
Bond(e) (Bound(e))
  Agn, wife of John, 103, 108
  Ali, 94, 105
  Ali, wife of Godfrey, 45
  Ali, wife of Ric, 21, 29
  Geof, 65, 74
  Godfrey, 39, 45, 56-7, 68, 70-1, 73, 75-6,

327

INDEX OF PERSONS

    80-2, 88, 92-3
    Godfrey, son of Ric, 45
    John, *l*, 103, 107-9, 113, 117-18, 123, 125, 131-2, 135, 145-6
    John, son of Godfrey, 73, 93
    Marg, 160, 165-76
    Marg, daur of Rose, 164
    Margy, daur of John, 145
    Mati, daur of Rose, 166
    Mati, sis of Marg, 160
    Petronilla, 114, 119
    Ric, 21-2, 28-9, 31, 45
    Rosa (Rose), 145, 162, 164-6, 169-70
    Swetekin (Swetekyn(e)), 74, 83-4, 86
    Wm, 83
Borre (*see* Burr)
Botheby
    Rob, 205-8
Botry
    Rob, 303
Boughton (Boton(e), Botonn, Bot(o)un, Boue(n)ton, Bouetoun, Boveton, Buneton)
    Agn, 71, 78, 114
    Alex, 137
    Alex, son of Ral, 112
    Alex, son of Ste, 3
    Ali, 218, 219n, 220, 222, 224, 226, 228, 231-2
    Ellen, daur of John, 171
    Ellen, daur of Ral, 105
    Emma, wife of Ste, 3
    Helen, 107, 131
    Hen, son of John, 40
    J, 42
    Joan, 222, 232-4
    Joan, wife of John, 225
    John, *xxxv, xxxix, l, lviii, lix*, 1, 1n, 3, 22, 30-1, 33-5, 37, 39-40, 42-5, 47, 51, 53-60, 62-4, 66, 68, 72, 77, 80, 92, 106, 129, 131-2, 134, 136-7, 139, 145, 147-54, 160-6, 168-84, 187-203, 205-6, 208-13, 215-22, 224-9, 231, 233, 241, 244, 269
    John, son of John, 60, 106, 165, 181
    John, son of Ral, 95, 97, 105, 125
    John, son of Ste, 20
    Marg, 22, 224

    Marg, wife of Ste, 20
    Margy, *lviii*, 26, 220, 222, 226, 228, 231-3, 235-8, 240-7
    Margy, daur of John, 225
    Mati, 71
    Petronilla, daur of Ral, 124
    Ral, *xxxix*, 62, 64, 68, 71-3, 78, 83-7, 91, 93-7, 99, 105, 109, 111-13, 115, 119-22, 124-5, 260
    Ral, son of John, 60
    Ste, 3, 6, 20
    Ste, son of John, 3
    Walt, *liii*, 147, 232-3, 235-8, 240-4
    Walt, son of John, 217, 221
    Wm, 24, 44, 201-2, 212, 214-15, 218, 219n, 220, 222-4, 226, 228, 231-3, 235-7
    Wm, son of John, 42, 60, 222
Bovindon (Boving(e)don)
    Luke, 29, 31-3, 35
    Thos, 58-9, 61-3
Bowles
    John, *xxxvi, xxxvii, lxi*, 285, 287, 295
    Ric, 283, 286-7, 298
Bowman
    Wm, *lvii*, 198
Boysscell (*see* Buschel)
Bradewey(e) (Badewey, Bradwey(e))
    Ali, wife of Walt, 201, 205
    John, *xxxv, xxxvi, xxxvii*, 187-8, 193, 196, 199, 201, 203-4, 216, 235, 243
    John, grandson of John, 216
    Margy, wife of John, *xxxv*, 199, 201, 204
    Margy, daur of Walt, son of John, 216
    Thos, 257-67, 270
    Walt, *lvi*, 201-2, 204-5, 207-8, 213, 218-9, 221, 223, 226-7, 233, 235-6, 240, 243
    Walt, son of John, *xxxv, xxxvi*, 201, 216
    Wm, servant of Walt, 226
Brantefeld
    Hen, 24
    John, son of Hen, 24
Bray
    Hugh, 68
Breynton
    Walt, 169
Brid
    John, 29

INDEX OF PERSONS

Brihtwold
  Abbot, 306
Broun(e)
  Agn, daur of Walt, *l*, 136
  Geof, 29, 127, 147-8
  Geof, son of Walt, 127
  John, 153-5
  Thos, 226
  Walt, 127, 136
Bryddeshale
  John, 258
Bryg (Brigger, Brugge, Bryges, Brygge(r), Byrg)
  John, *xlv*, 204, 265, 272, 275-6
  Thos, 272, 274, 298
Burger (Berger, Burges)
  John, 276, 290, 294, 297
Burgate
  Thos, 193
Burgeyn(e) (Burgon, Burgun)
  John, 239, 246, 246n
  Marion, 253, 255
  Marion, wife of John, 246
Burr(e) (Borre, Burrei, Bury)
  John, 22, 32, 34-5, 40, 45-7, 51, 61-2, 66, 69, 79, 93, 124, 126, 131, 135, 149, 254, 289, 292
  John, son of John, 51
  John, son of Osbert, 19
  Osbert, 2, 5, 19
  Ral, 39
  Ric, 72, 280, 290, 293, 297
  Rob, 294
Buschel (Boysscel)
  Agn, 92
  John, *xxxiv*, 149
Bybat
  Dionisia, 242
  Thos, son of Dionisia, 242
Byg(g) (*see* Bigge)
Bygrave
  Christina, 270
  Nic, *lvii*, 240-1, 247, 266, 268-70,
  Ric, 243, 267
  Rob, 275-6, 280, 285, 287, 290, 293-5, 297
  Wm, 220

Bynham
  John, 127, 129-32, 134, 136-7
Byrhtsige
  thegn, 306

Cadewell(e) (Cadevell, Cadewellelle, Cadwelle, Caldewall, Caldewell(e), Calwelle, Kadwell)
  John, 128, 135, 266
  Marg, wife of Si, 183
  Rob, 112, 122-5, 130-1, 133, 160, 175
  Sarra, 180
  Si, 152, 160, 168, 171, 183, 222
  Thos, 215, 217-19, 221, 224, 226, 228, 252-3, 270
  Wm, 221, 224, 228
Cady (Kady)
  Thos, 156, 160, 165
Caldecote
  John, 20
Cambester (Camester)
  Agn, 21, 29
Cammock
  Wm, 289-90, 292-3, 296
Cane
  [land of], 21
Cappe
  John, 20
Carlou
  Christiana, 29
Carter(e)
  Ali, sis of John, 143
  Isa, 67, 107
  Isa, wife of Ral, 59
  John, *lvii*, 76, 143, 169
  Ral, 59, 69
  Ric, 102
Carver
  Thos, 273
Catlowe
  John, *lvin*
Catton
  Rob, 293
Chalton
  John, 269-70
Chaplain
  John, 58

INDEX OF PERSONS

Chapman
  Alan, 118
  John, 23
  Ric, 60
Chaterton
  Rob, 275, 292
Cherpenho
  Cecily, *lvii*, 36, 38
Chestan
  Rob, 180-4, 187-203
Childewik
  Kath, 50
Church(e) (Cherch(e), Chirch(e), Chyrche)
  Agn, 25
  Agn, daur of Wm, 27, 125
  Ali, 150
  Ali, daur of John, 224
  Ellen, 28, 67, 75
  Ellen, daur of Wm, 27
  Ida, 108
  Idonia, wife of Wm, 106
  Idonia, 120
  John, 194, 211-12, 214, 220-2, 224,
    227-8, 232, 235, 243
  John, son of Wm, 194
  Mati, 223
  Sybil, 113
  Walt, 205
  Wm, *l*, *lvii*, 2, 5, 16, 22, 24, 27, 61, 67,
    75, 79, 82-4, 87-8, 90, 92, 94, 97-8,
    103-4, 106, 114, 120, 125-6, 131, 144,
    156, 159-60, 166, 170-84, 187-91,
    193-4, 199-201, 214
  Wm, son of Wm, 75, 97, 106, 191
Chyrysten
  Thos, 270
Clerk(e) (Clerk(e)s)
  Agn, daur of Ste, 42, 46, 103, 262
  John, *liii*, 29, 42-3, 33, 36, 37, 253-4,
    256-7
  John, bro of Walt, son of Ste, 38
  John, son of Ste, 39
  Rog, son of Agn, 103
  Scolastica, 37
  Ste, 19, 28, 35, 38-9, 42, 46, 103, 204,
    262
  Walt, son of Ste, 38, 42
  Wm, 154, 158, 189-90, 194

Clyfford
  Ric, 131
Clyfton
  Walt, *lvi*, 256, 260-1
Clyve (*or* Clyne)
  Agn, 123
Codicote
  John, 124-5
  Wm, *lvii*, 2
Cock(e) (Cockes, Cok(e), Cokke, Cook(e))
  Alex, 84, 94, 122, 127, 263
  Hen, *l*, 114, 118, 124, 127, 135, 138,
    148-9, 166-7, 175
  Hen, son of Ric, 114
  Isa, wife of Ric, son of Thos, 48
  Joan, wife of Thos, 259, 288-90, 292
  John, *lviii*, 25, 109, 129-30, 132, 138,
    163,189, 194-9, 201-6, 208-13, 215,
    217-24, 226-9, 231-3, 239, 241, 262,
    276, 296, 299
  John, son of Hen, 167
  Marg, daur of Ric, 95
  Margy, 163
  Margy, wife of John, 109
  Margy, wife of Nic, 288-90
  Mati, daur of John, 239
  Nic, 288-90, 294, 296-7
  Ral, 163-4
  Ric, 57-8, 60-1, 63, 66-7, 69-71, 78, 80-4,
    88, 91-6, 103, 114, 241, 260
  Ric, son of Thos, 48
  Sara, wife of Wm, 81
  Sarra, daur of Ric, 95
  Thos, 48, 255, 257, 259-60, 262-8, 270,
    273-6, 280-1, 285, 287-8, 288n, 289-90,
    292
  Walt, 160, 163, 191-2
  Walt, son of Wm, 145
  Wm, *lix*, 80-1, 129-31, 145, 147, 163,
    180, 183, 215, 220-1, 223, 226-8,
    231-44, 246-8, 250-4, 256-8, 260,
    260n, 262-3, 297
Colin(e) (Colines, Colyn(e), Colyns)
  Cecily, daur of John, 167
  John, 49, 51-5, 59, 99, 109, 120, 137, 148,
    156, 158, 160, 163-5, 167-71
  Mati, 40, 43, 45, 47-8, 74
  Mati, wife of John, 54-5, 59, 120

330

INDEX OF PERSONS

Colwell(e) (Collewell(e))
Ali, wife of John, 237
Joan, wife of Wm, 208
John, 211, 222, 227, 233-8, 240-4, 246-8, 250-4, 256-60, 263-5, 267-8, 268n
Ric, 268-70
Thos, 224
Walt, 206
Wm, *lix*, 195, 197, 199, 201-6, 208-13, 214-21, 223-4, 226-8, 231-3, 236-7, 250, 256, 268
Cook(e) (*see* Cock(e))
Cornelius
Wm, *lvin*
Cornemonger(e) (Corne(r)manger)
John, 72
Rob, *lvii*, 18, 211, 247
Ric, 156, 158
Scholastica, wife of Rob, 18
Cornevaile
John, 217-8, 220
Cotman
John, 14
Coupere
Edmund, 137
John, son of Edmund, 137
Coverour
Hugh, 23
Hugh, son of Hugh, 23
Cow(e)herd (Couherd)
John, *lvii*, 42
Wm, 9, 109
Crane
Wm, *lvi*, 260
Cristemasse
Ric, 3
Crok
Rob, 83
Cromwell
Thomas, *lxi*
Cross
Walt, 6
Crouch(e)
John, 66, 146-7
Crowe
Rog, 126, 132, 144
Sara, 146
Sarra, sis of Rog, 144

Cursefote
John, *lvii*, 11

Dageneye (Dag(e)ney)
Wm, 224, 226-9, 232
Dame
Juliana, 65, 108
Marg, relict of Ric, 67
Margy, 86
Reynald, 108
Reynald, son of Ric, 67
Ric, 61, 67
Ric, son of Ste, 51
Ste, 22-3, 43, 51
Dawebury (Dewebury)
Ric, 219, 224-7, 229
Day(e)
Ral, 206, 209
Ric, 215
Thos, 151
Walt, 191, 195, 206, 248
Wm, 203
Dene (Attedener, Dane, Deynes)
John, 270
Mic, 74
Ric, 71, 75, 79, 81, 83, 86-8, 90-1, 101-2, 217-19, 221, 224, 226, 228, 237, 247
Ric, son of Sarra, 138
Sara, wife of Mic, 74
Sara(h) (Sarra), wife of Ric, 71, 75, 79, 81, 83, 86-8, 90-1, 101-2
Sarra, 138
Denyssh
Rob, *xxxvi*, 301
Thos, *xxxvi*, 301-3
Dewebury (*see* Dawebury)
Dik(e) (Dyke)
Wm, 172, 174-80, 182-4, 188-95, 197-8, 251
Wm, son of Wm, 183
Diper(e) (Dyper(e))
Cecilia, 123
Cecily, *xlvii*, 78, 87, 92, 109
Clemence, 168, 174, 177, 179-80
Clement, 260
John, *l*, 82-3, 87-9, 92-4, 96-8, 102-4, 106-7, 111, 113-15, 117-31, 134, 136-9, 148-54, 156, 158-66, 168-72, 173-8,

INDEX OF PERSONS

    187, 211, 245, 254
John, son of Wm, 77
Lucy, 150
Mati, 178
Mati, wife of John, 128
Petronilla, wife of Wm, 37, 77
Rog, 99, 147
Wm, 35, 37, 40, 42-4, 47, 51-2, 54-5, 57-9, 61-2, 65-7, 69, 77

Doke
Ric, 81

Draper
John, 194

Driver (Dryver(e))
Agn, sis of Walt, 99, 112
Hugh, 13, 15, 19
John, *lvii*, 38, 48-9, 57, 68, 94-5, 112, 122, 185, 233, 264, 284
Olive, wife of John, 95
Thos, 185, 260, 264, 284
Thos, son of John, 57, 94-5
Walt, 99, 112, 260, 264
Walt, son of John, 185, 264, 284

Duche
Wm, 261

Dunne
Hugh, 183

Durnall
Wm, 196

Eadnoth
Abbot, 306

Eadric
thegn, 306

Easton
Ric, 211

Edward
John, 238

Elizabeth
Mati, daur of, 116

Elmeham
James, 83

Emma
Alex, son of, *lvi*, 4
John, son of, 96

Empson (Emmeson, Emson)
Agn, wife of John, 103
John, 86, 96, 103

Sarra, daur of John, 96
Thos, 273-4

Erdeleye (Eredele, Erdelee, Erdele, Yerdele(y), Yherdele(e))
Agn, 172, 183, 215-6
Agn, daur of Wm, 147
Agn, sis of Amice (Lacheford), 168-70
Amice, 183
Amice, wife of Nic, 176, 179-80
Amity, daur of Wm, 147
Hen, 42, 59, 66, 89
Isa, 153, 161-2, 168
Isa, mother of Joan, 147
Joan, daur of Wm, 147
John, 127, 130, 132, 145, 147, 168-70
John, son of Sarra, 95
Nic, 172, 176, 179-81
Ric, 174
Rob, 180
Sarah, 123
Sar(r)a, *xlv*, 95, 95n, 96, 124, 126-7, 130, 251, 257, 263, 265, 299
Wm, 137, 147

Eustach
Ric, 72

Eve
John, 1-2, 5, 7, 10

Everard(e)
Hugh, 69
John, son of Wm, 68
Mati, wife of Wm, 9
Roysia, wife of Wm, 19
Walt, 15
Wm, *xxx*, 4-5, 7, 9, 13-16, 18-19, 27, 36-43, 47-9, 51, 65-6, 68, 74-5
Wm, son of Wm, 19, 40

Eversdon
Hugh, 41, 43, 46-8, 51, 53, 69

Faber (*see* Smyth)
Falley (*see* Valley)
Famekylcastel (Fancastel, Fan(c)kylcastell, Fantylcastyll)
Anthony, 275-6, 280, 285, 288, 290, 293, 295, 297

Faunt
Thos, 273
Wm, 274

INDEX OF PERSONS

Fermer (Ferim, Firmarius)
Ral, *lv*, 19
Wm, 11, 129, 210
Finch
Hugh, 71
Flamste(a)d
Nic, 70-4, 91-4, 96-7
Flandon
Marg, 42
Flaon
Adam, 115
Fleman
Maurice, 38
Walt, 36, 39-40, 49
Flex(e)mere (Flaxmer, Flax(e)mere)
Beatrice, wife of Walt, 26
John, 188-9, 193
Ste, *liii*, 245, 248, 250-3, 255-6
Walt, 26
Foliot(h)
Walt, 7, 11
Foller (*see* Fuller)
Fox
Hen, 181-2, 184
Frace (*see also* Grace)
Wm, 246, 253-4, 256-60, 262-3, 263n, 264-8, 270
Frebarn(e) (Freberne)
John, 180, 184-5, 191, 195, 200, 210, 221, 229
Margy, wife of John, 200
Margy, wife of Wm, 236
Wm, *lvi*, 227, 229, 232, 236, 238-44, 246-8, 250-1, 253-4, 256-8, 260-1, 263-4
Frenche (Frensh(e), Frenssh(e), Freynssh)
Edmund, 124
Emma, wife of Rog, 161, 173
Rog, 154-5, 160-1, 163-5, 166-7, 173
Frere
John, 213, 225, 229
John, bro of John, 225
Mabel, 246
Mabel, wife of Thos, 211, 213, 234
Ric, 210-1
Thos, 201-2, 204, 211, 213, 217, 219, 220, 222-3, 225, 227, 229, 234

Friday
Thos, 7, 11
Frobenhale
Reg, 79
Frowyk
Hen, 188-93
Fuller (Foller)
John, 178, 181-2, 184, 187, 207, 215
John, son of Ric, 144, 146
Ric, *l,* 103, 111, 115-16, 121, 133, 135-8, 144, 146, 178
Sarra, wife of Ric, 111
Fypp(e) (Fyp, Phipp, Phyp(p))
Edw, 280, 299
Eliz, wife of Thos, 299
Jas, 297
John, 275, 287, 291
Marg, 299
Thos, 273-4, 274n, 275-6, 278-81, 283-5, 286, 290-1, 293-4, 296-7, 299
Fysh(e) (Fysshe)
John, 259, 262-3, 268, 271

Gaffe (Gasse, Goffe, Gosse)
Osbert, 26, 30
Wm, son of Osbert, 30
[land of], 23
Gallow (Galwe)
Nic, 27
Wm, 275
Galston
John, 42
Gardiner
Hen, 156, 158
Gatys
Wm, 278-9
Gecob (*see* Jacob)
Gena (*see also* Geve)
Agn, daur of, 8
John, son of, 8
Geoffrey
Geof, son of, 6
Gerard(e) (Gechard, Gedgerd, Geg(ge)ard, Ge(g)iard)
Adam, 4
Agn, 29, 165, 202
Agn, wife of Wm, 32
Emma, 251

INDEX OF PERSONS

Geof, *lviii*, 24, 27, 28-9, 49, 59-60, 66, 251, 256
Helen(e), *lviii*, 252, 259
Isa, daur of Geof, 60
John, 66, 75, 93, 110, 130, 133-4, 139, 148, 158, 161, 165, 171, 178, 181, 183, 185, 187-9, 193-4, 196, 202, 217-18, 220-1, 223, 226, 228, 231-2, 234-47
John, son of Geof, 66
John, son of Wm, 233, 252
Kat, wife of John, 165
Ric, 188-93, 195, 197-8, 217-18, 220, 222-3, 226, 228, 231-3
Rob, 235-8, 240-1
Thos, 9, 139, 151, 251, 254, 256
Thos, son of Wm, 242-4
Walt, 5, 7, 9-10, 12, 15
Wm, *lviii*, 23, 29, 32, 189-97, 202, 204, 206-8, 211, 215, 217-18, 220, 222-1, 223, 226, 228, 231-3, 235-6, 238, 240-8, 250-3, 255-7, 259-61, 268, 271

Germanus
Abbot, 306

Geve (*or* Gene)
Mar, 15

Gile
John, son of Walt, 58
Walt, 58

Glover (the)
Peter, 60

God(e)frey (Godefray, Geof)
John, 119
John, son of, 23-5
Marg, daur of Walt, 41
Margy, mother of Marg, 41
Mati, daur of, 57
Walt, 41, 56-7
Walt, son of, 30

Godeman
Abbot, 306

Godinohow (Godeynogh, Godeynow, Godinoth, Godinhou, Godynogh, Godynow(e))
John, 21, 24
Walt, 22, 24
Wm, 12-13, 15, 18, 23, 34, 33

Godric
Thegn, 306

Godwine
Bishop, 306

Grace (*see also* Frace)
Wm, 263

Grange(r)
Thos, 28, 43

Graunt
Ric, 33
Rose, 38

Gravele
R, 25
Wm, 210

Grene
Agn, *lvii, lviii*, 1
Ali, 2,
Bart, 2
Jas, 2, 3, 5
John, son of Agn, 1
Mati, 18
Ral, 1-2, 5, 13-15, 21
Ric, *lviii*, 226
Ste, 16

Grom(e) (Groum)
Hugh, 63, 92-3, 93n, 260
John, 123, 162
John, son of Hugh, 93

Grove
John, 259

Guele
Marg, 211

Hacford (Hakford)
Ric, 28-9, 31-2

Hale(s) (I(n)thehale)
Adam, 16, 22, 28-9, 66
Agn, 116, 146, 148, 157
Agn, daur of John, 252-3, 255, 257
Agn, daur of Ste, 14
Agn, daur of Walt, 103
Agn, wife of John, 192
Ali, 48, 219-20, 222, 224, 226, 228, 231-2
Ali, daur of John, 136
Ali, daur of Ste, 110
Ali, mother of Reynald, 109
Ali, wife of Walt, 53, 104, 120
And, 195, 197, 210, 212, 214-15, 217-18, 220, 222-3, 226, 228, 231-3

INDEX OF PERSONS

Beatrice, daur of John, 258, 260
Cristiana, wife of Osbert, 7
Dionisia, 251
Ellen, 36, 83-4, 93, 110, 121, 126
Ellen, daur of John, 36
Emma, wife of Stephen, 13
Helen, 129, 150
Isa, wife of John, 199, 136, 213
Joan, daur of Ste, 13
Joan, wife of John, 177
John, *xxx, xxxiii, lviii*, 15, 18-19, 22,
   29-31, 33-6, 38, 40-1, 80-1, 92-3, 97,
   103, 107, 116, 119, 132, 136-7, 139,
   144, 148, 152, 155, 158, 171, 177, 181,
   183, 188-92, 194, 197-203, 205-6,
   208-15, 217-19, 221-2, 225-9, 231-8,
   240-5, 245n, 246-8, 250-8, 260-1, 264,
   274, 283
John, son of John, 103, 144, 264
John, son of Ric, 91, 110
John, son of Walt, 252, 257
John, son of Wm, 15
Juliana, 27
Margy, daur of John, 258
Mati, 226, 228, 232
Osbert, *lviii*, 1, 7, 18
Reynald, 109, 120, 123-4
Reynard, son of Walt, 104
Ric, 35-6, 40-1, 44-7, 53-4, 57-8, 61-3,
   65-7, 69-72, 76-9, 81-2, 84, 88, 91, 94,
   110-11, 122, 253
Ric, son of John, 38
Ric, son of Walt, 89
Ric, son of Wm, 90
Sara, daur of Walt, 59
Sibyl, daur of Wm, 96-7
Si, 213, 235-8, 241, 243-4, 246-8, 250-5,
   289, 292
Ste, 9, 13-14, 42, 110
[tenement of], 54
Walt, 26, 30-2, 35, 42, 45-7, 49, 51-3,
   58-60, 64-5, 68, 72, 74, 78, 81-2, 84,
   86, 88-9, 93-4, 99, 103-4, 120, 129,
   132, 240, 244-8, 250-60, 264, 266, 291,
   296
Walt, son of Walt, 52
Wm, *xxxiiin, xxxviii*, 5, 14-15, 21-3, 26,
   29, 31-2, 40-2, 44-5, 47, 53, 55, 72,
   86-90, 96-7, 110-11, 129, 131-2, 135,
   145, 154, 175-9, 181-4, 187-99, 204
Wm, bro of Reynald, 124
Wm, son of John, 33, 38
Wm, son of Walt, 99

Haleward
Hugh, 101
Wm, 91

Halffhyde
Jas, *lvii*, 294

Halle (Aula) (*see also* Hale)
Walt, 49

Hardewyn
Peter, 160

Har(d)leston (Hardston)
Ric, 139
Ric, son of Walt, 100
Rog, 139
[unnamed], 43
Walt, 31, 33-4, 37, 39-40, 42, 45, 49, 52,
   54-5, 58, 73, 75, 79, 91-2, 98-100, 256

Harre (*see* Hurre)

Hasel
Walt, 20

Hash (Harsch, Hasch(e), Has(s), Hasse
Hassh(e))
Agn, 94, 212-13
Ali, 127, 157, 159-60, 146
Alicia, 108, 124
Amice, 213
Amice, daur of John, 211
Eliz, 103
Emma, 138
Isa, 103, 129,
Joan, 227, 229, 232
John, 80, 83, 85, 93-4, 96, 98, 102-4,
   106-7, 109-11, 113, 119, 123, 125, 130,
   134-5, 137, 142, 157, 159, 164-80,
   184-5, 187, 188, 197, 203-6, 208-11,
   213, 222
John, son of Isa, 103
John, son of Thos, 138
John, son of Rob, 80
Mabel, 159
Margy, 134
Reynald, son of Wm, 110
Ric, 157, 159
Ric, son of John, 142

INDEX OF PERSONS

Rob, 33-5, 80, 103, 159
Thos, 110, 138, 187
Walt, 78
Wm, 39, 79, 110-11
Haston
Ric, 208, 216
Hath(e) (Hatt(h)e)
Agn, 198
Edw, 83
Joan, 237
Joan, wife of John, 214
John, 112, 118, 133, 143, 147-54, 156-68, 171-2, 174, 176, 199, 202, 214, 218, 220, 222
Sibyl, wife of John, 133
Hathewis (Hathwis, Hawys)
John, 29, 137
John, son of Thos, 49
Mati, wife of John, 137
Ric, son of Thos, 48
Thos, 13, 18, 21, 30, 34, 48-9
Hays (Ays, Ayssh, Haysh, Hayss)
Ali, 52
Isa, daur of Rob, 60
John, 88
John, son of Wm, 90
Rob, 37, 40, 44, 46, 49, 54, 60, 71-2
Thos, 56, 118
Wm, 55, 58, 89-90
Hayward (Haiward, Heyward, Heyworth Hyeward) (*see also* Messer)
Agn, daur of Rob, 180
Ali, wife of Walt, 167
Joan, 276
John, 20, 28, 163-4
John, son of Rob, 192
Kath, daur of John, 20, 28
Mati, 210
Nic, 187, 193, 197, 199, 221, 228
Rob, 148, 153, 165, 176, 180-2, 188-9, 192-3, 202
Walt, *lvii*, 12, 21, 167, 177
Wm, 209-11, 276
Hederset (Hedreset)
Ric, 98, 102-4, 106-7, 137
Helder(e) (Healder, Heldron)
Alex, 63, 66, 78
Alex, son of And, 64, 70

And, 42, 48, 53, 63-5, 70
Hugh, 5, 16
John, 29, 216, 231
Mati, daur of And, 63
Ric, 56, 119
Ric, son of Hugh, 16
Henry
Edith, daur of John, 16
John, 16
John, son of, *xxxiiin*, 5, 9-10, 15, 18
Henyngham (Honygome)
John, 226-7
Herde
And, 66
Mati, daur of And, 66
Hereberd de la Northawe
Wm, 74
Herldon
Ric, 10
Heron
Wm, 79, 81
Hertford
John, *xliin*
Herv(e)y
Bishop of Ely, *xvi, xvin*
Nic, 272, 274
Thos, 273
Hexstonton (Hexston, Hexstanton)
Agn, 34
And, 30
Cristina, daur of And, 30
Godfrey, 25
John, 35
Mabel, 24
Nic, 23, 32
Wm, 18
Heyward (*see* Hayward)
Hikes
John, 221
Hirne
Godfrey, 14
Hob(e)kyn (Hobbekyn)
John, 138
Ric, 178
Rob, 181
Hog(g)es (Hogeys)
Eliz, 144
Isa, 133, 172-3

INDEX OF PERSONS

Mati, wife of Walt, 26, 26n
Walt, 26, 26n
Hoghaler
  Godfrey, 47
  Juliana, 73, 77
  Juliana, daur of Godfrey, 47
  [land of], 68
  Margy, 43, 49, 118
  Walt, 118
Holdthype(e)s (Holethypes)
  Dionisia, wife of Rob, 239
  Rob, 239, 242, 250-1, 256
Hoo
  Richard, *xln*
Honur
  Ric, 11
Honygome
  John, 227
Horseman
  Thos, 102
Hoye (Hoij)
  John, 156, 158
Huckyll (Huchylle, Huckull(e), Hukhill
  Hukhyll(e), Hukkull)
  Agn, wife of Thos, 261, 264-5
  John, 272-3
  Ric, 273-4
  Thos, 261, 264-5, 268, 270, 272
Hugh
  Abbot, 95
  John, son of, 10, 117
  Morice, son of, 38
  Ste, son of, 12
  Walt, son of, 12
Huggyn
  Wm, 281
Huntyngdon
  Joan, 237-8, 240-2
Hurle (Hurleye)
  J(ohn), 66-7, 69, 104, 112
  Rog, 149
Hurre (Harre)
  Ric, 262-3, 266-8
  Wm, 267
Hyethe
  John, 136
Hyll(e)
  Ali, wife of Rob, *lvii*, 296

  Ric, 296
  Rob, 275, 280, 285, 294-6

Ippyng
  John, xln
Isoud(e) (Isard, Iseud(e), Isowde, Ysoud(e))
  Agn, daur of Gilbert, 257
  Ali, daur of John, 71
  Anna, wife of John, 288
  Gilbert, 235-8, 240-8, 250-3, 255-7, 259, 264
  Joan, daur of Thos, 255-7
  John, 22, 24, 31, 46, 49-54, 59, 61, 66, 71-2, 84, 95, 98, 108, 122, 124, 126, 130-1, 139, 144, 148, 150, 152-3, 157, 159-60, 166-79, 181-2, 184-5, 187-95, 197-8, 212, 214-15, 217-18, 220, 222-3, 226, 228, 231-2, 235-8, 240-8, 250-3, 255-7, 259, 264, 288-9, 292-3
  John, son of John, 84, 144, 217-18, 220, 222-3, 226, 228, 231-2, 259
  Olive, 165
  Ric, 131, 133, 139, 150, 152-3, 157, 159-60, 164-79, 181-2, 184-5, 187-93, 198
  Ric, bro of John, 148, 150
  Ric, son of John, 108, 130
  Ric, son of Ric, 139
  Sara, daur of John, 61
  Thos, 92, 235-8, 240-8, 250-3, 255-7, 259
  Wm, 165, 250-3, 255-7, 259
Ithehale (*see* Hale)
Iver
  Wm, 276

James
  Isa, daur of, 22
  John, son of, 14, 16
  Mar, son of, 8
Jacob(be) (Jecob, Gecob)
  Agn, 94, 97
  Ali, 99
  Emma, *xlvi*, 73-4
  Emma, wife of John, 70
  J, 28
  John, 21-3, 26, 29, 35, 40, 49-50, 54-5, 57-9, 61-2, 66, 70, 85, 87, 94, 97, 103-4, 106-9, 111, 113-15, 118, 120, 122-7,

INDEX OF PERSONS

 129-32, 134, 136, 138-9, 145, 149,
 151-3, 155-6, 158-66, 168-9, 171, 188,
 190-2, 196-9, 201-2, 205, 209, 217,
 220, 222-3, 226, 228, 231-2, 240
John, son of John, 171
Juliana, daur of John, 50
Marg, 133
Marg, daur of John, 87
Marg, wife of John, 108
Margy, 255
Reynald, 131-4
Ric, 13, 81, 129, 132
Sarra, 172

John
Agn, wife of, 96
Ali, daur of, 11
Edith, wife of, 14
Edith, daur of, 15
Hugh, son of, 11
John, son of, 8
Osbert, son of, 2, 14
Rob, son of, 7
Rog, son of, 18
Ste, son of, 4
Thos, son of, 101
Walt, son of, 22, 25

Jordan
John, 270
Rob, son of, 5

Joye
John, 109-10

Jyryshe
Wm, 228

Kadwell (*see* Cadewell)
Kady (*see* Cady)
Karlowe
[tenement of], 34
Keghard
Agn, wife of Wm, 22
Wm, 22
Key
Rob, 274
Kild(e) (Kydd, Kyld(e))
John, *lv*, 97-9, 102, 104
Kilsul
John, 85, 87

Knott
Wm, 272
Kydd (*see* Kild(e))
Kympton
Wm, 278, 281, 291
Kyng(e)
Adam, 20
Geof, 27
John, 153, 156, 161
Reynald, 69, 102, 104
Ric, son of Adam, 20
Wymark, son of Geof, 27

Lacheford
Amice, wife of Nic, 168-70
Nic, 168-70
Laman (*see* Law(e)man)
Lambel
Geof, 8
Lane
Ric, 145
Ric, son of Ric, 145
Langeley
Eliz, daur of John, 282
John, 282
Marg, daur of John, 282
Lardyner
Joan, 233
Lark(e)
Rob, 169, 180, 184
Rog, 147
Laurence (Laurens, Lawrence)
Thos, 273, 275
Wm, 280
Law(e)man (Laman)
Joan, widow of John, 257
John, *xxxiii*, 161, 204, 204n, 205-6,
 209-12, 220-1, 223, 226-7, 231-3,
 235-8, 240-8, 250-62, 264-8, 270, 272,
 275-6, 280, 285-8, 291-2
Margy, wife of John, 205
Mati, 245, 245n
Nic, *lviii*, 274-6, 280, 285, 287, 290-1,
 293-4, 296-7
Si, 238, 242
Thos, 267
Walt, 220, 243-4, 247, 259, 261, 263,
 268, 272, 283, 291

INDEX OF PERSONS

    Wm, *lviii*, 203-4, 206, 209-13, 215,
      217-19, 221, 223, 226-8, 231-3, 235-43,
      248, 250-5, 260, 262-7
Leg (Legat)
    Rob, 24, 91
Leofric
    Abbot, 304, 304n, 305
Leofsige
    Ealdorman, 305
Leofwine
    Ealdorman, 306
    thegn, 306
Leybourne
    Ali, wife of John, 132
    John, 132
Leye (Leygh, Leyr)
    Amice, wife of Ste, 194
    Emma, wife of Wm, 26
    Mati, daur of Rob, 148
    Rob, 148-9
    Si, 208
    Ste, 184, 189, 194, 197-9, 204-6
    Wm, 26, 205
Longe
    Adam, 83, 90
    Agn, daur of Christina, 83, 90
    Christina, daur of Adam, 83, 90
    Mabel, 115
    Margy, 83
    Ric, 116
Longus
    Adam, 9, 12
    Wymark, daur of Adam, 12
Lord,
    John, 297
Lorkyn
    John, 217, 219
    Wm, 184, 189, 195, 198, 200
Love (*or* Lone)
    Ali, wife of Thos, 207
    John, 108, 118, 146, 158-60, 163-4, 187
    Sara, wife of John, 146
    Thos, 207, 229, 233, 265, 292
Loveleg
    Agn, 44, 156
    Ali, 94
    Ali, wife of Walt, 91
    John, *xxxiii*, *lvii*, 125, 142, 146, 148,

      150-1, 154, 156-7
    John, son of Walt, 91
    Mati, 157
    Walt, 42, 51, 55, 74, 79, 80, 82, 88, 91-2
Lycheworth
    Wm, 280
Lyfing
    Bishop, 306
Lyle,
    Joan, 207
Lynleye (Lylleleye)
    Walt, 57, 62
Lyncok (Lyntok)
    Wm, 224, 232

Maister (Maistre, Mayster, Maystr(e))
    Joan, 142
    John, 104, 109, 125, 145-6, 157-9, 162,
      167-71
    John, father of Joan, 142
    John, son of Joan, 142
Malet
    John, 189
Maltman
    John, *lvii*, 196-8
Marche
    John, *liii*, 236-7
Mare (*see* More)
Marines (Marynes)
    John, 25-6, 28
Marschal
    Rob, 81
Martin (Martnes, Martyn)
    John, 83, 200, 205, 210
    Justina, 205, 207, 210, 214
    Ste, son of, 16
Marysshe
    Thos, 295
Maydegod(e)
    Ali, 84
    John, 99
Maynard
    John, 273n
Maysent,
    John, 204
    Margy, wife of John, 204
Mel(e)ward (*see* Muleward)

INDEX OF PERSONS

Mentmore
Michael, *xliin*
Messer (Messor) (*see also* Hayward)
Geof, 22
John, 164
Michel
Walt, 20
Miles
Vincent, 134, 136-7
Miller
Alex, 44, 46-7, 54, 62
Mar, 51
Ric, 51
Walt, 50, 54, 99, 104, 130
Walt, son of Alex, 47, 62
Wm, 9, 218
Mill(e)ward (*see* Muleward)
Molot(e)
Rob, 104, 132
Rog, 46
Monden(e) (*see* Munden)
Monyngham
Thos, 294-5
More (Mare)
John, *xxxix*, 97
Thos, 117-18
Morebred
Geof, 7
John, son of Walt, 5
Walt, 5
Wymark, wife of Geof, 7
Moredon
John, 183, 252
Moreman
John, 139
Mosse
John, 278, 280-1, 284-8, 290, 293-4, 297
Si, 275-6, 281, 281n, 283, 298
Thos, 286
Mote
John, *xxv, xxvii*, 153-4, 156, 158-66, 168-80
Mower
John, 60
Muleward (Mel(e)ward, Mill(e)ward, Mulleward(es))
Agnes, sis of Isa, 146
Edith, 66

Eliz, 172, 177
Geof, 175
Isa, 146, 148, 151-2, 202
Isa, daur of Walt, 146
Isa, wife of Geof, 175
John, son of Agn, 146
Walt, *lvii*, 131-2, 146, 177, 187, 207-8
Munden(e) (Monden(e))
Joan, 153, 160
Joan, widow of Wm, 148
John, 88
Wm, 99, 102, 104-6, 113, 124-5, 129, 137-8, 148, 158, 167
Mustele
John, 252, 260
Margy, wife of John, 260

Nadelere
Ral, 24
Naper(e)
Isa, wife of Walt, 134
Walt, 129-32, 134
Nasshe (*see also* Assh(e))
Ali, daur of Thos, 165-72
Thos, 165-72
Nele (Neel(e), Neell)
Ali, daur of Hen, 261
Hen, 259, 261, 261n
John, 244, 252-3, 255-60, 262-8, 270-1, 273
New(e)man(n) (Neuham, Neuman)
Agn, daur of Alan, 134
Agn, wife of John, 137
Alan, 59, 61, 63-5, 71-4, 76, 78, 84-6, 88, 91-2, 120, 130, 134
Alan, son of Wm, 55, 62
Ali, daur of Godfrey, 47, 52
Cecily, 97, 103, 106-7
Cecily, mother of John, 94
Christine, 159
Christiana, relict of John, 155
Geof, 130
Godfrey, 22, 24, 26, 36, 47, 52, 57
Hen, 22
Joan, daur of Cecily, 106-7
Joan, daur of John, 155
John, *xxxi, xlvii*, 94, 107, 130, 132, 135, 137-8, 143, 150-3, 155, 157, 216, 260-2

340

INDEX OF PERSONS

John, bro of John, 143
John, son of Alan, 92
Mabel, 145
Margy, daur of Alan, 130
Nic, 18, 22, 27, 29, 39-40, 51, 63, 84, 260
Ral, 44, 94
Ral, son of Wm, 46
Ric, 38
Sarra, daur of Wm, 39
Walt, 15, 21-2, 78, 94, 99, 101-2, 107-8, 132-3
Wm, 21, 25, 29, 31, 36, 39, 43, 44, 46, 49, 51, 53, 55, 62, 185, 220
Wm, son of Alan, 120
Wm, son of Godfrey, 52
New(e)nham
Adam, 90
John, son of Walt, 56
Ric, *lvii*, 8, 13
Walt, 56
Newporte
John, 279, 291, 294, 298-9
Nichol(as)
John, 38
John, son of, 47
Mati, wife of John, 38
Noreys (Noreis, Norrys)
John, 99, 107
Thos, 297
Norman
Cecily, 243
Joan, 247
Ric, son of Rob, 76
Rob, 73, 76
North
wife of Wm, 298
Wm, 298
Norton
Agn, daur of John, 61, 75
Joan, daur of John, 61, 68
John, *xliin*, 15, 18, 22, 33, 36-9, 41-3, 59, 61, 68, 75
John, son of John, 33, 41
Marg, daur of John, 61, 75
Margy, 25
Sibyl, wife of John, 61
Wm, 4, 6-9, 10

Offa
King, *xv*, 304-5
Olive (Olyve)
Agn, 128, 135, 139
Ali, 130-1
John, 131-3
Thos, 131-2, 135, 165, 167, 181, 183-5
Thos, son of Thos, 167
Ordbryht
Bishop, 306
Osbert
Mar, 22
John, son of, 23
Ste, son of, 4, 19
Oswig
thegn, 306
Oteway (Otewey)
Agn, wife of John, *l*, 100
John, *l*, 100

Palmer(e) (Paumer(e))
Agn, wife of John, 46
Christiana, 26
Christiana, daur of John, 32
Christiana, sis of Rob, 11
Christine, 34
Elias, 90
John, 5, 7, 21, 32, 46, 55
Rob, 11
Thos, 179
Pa(r)lour (Parlores, Parlur)
Christina, 58, 70
Isa, daur of Ric, 50, 64, 71
[land, tenement of], 65, 68
Marg, 48
Petronilla, daur of Ral, 122
Ral, 122
Ric, 28, 45, 47, 50, 53, 64, 68, 70-1, 108
Parnel(e) (Pernel(e), Pernelle, Peronell, Perunel(l))
Agn, 136, 139
Agn, daur of Ste, 113
Ali, 120, 139
Isa, 125
Margy, 131
Sara, wife of Ste, 32
Sarra, wife of Ste, 100
Ste, 32, 38-40, 45, 53, 60, 72, 80, 82, 100,

INDEX OF PERSONS

    113, 136, 190, 222
    Walt, 30, 40, 45, 49
Parson
    Ali, 183
    Wm, 154-5
Partrich
    Ric, 24
Parys
    Agn, daur of Rob, 80
    Rob, 80
Paselewe
    Walt, 12
    Walt, son of Walt, 12
Passell
    Wm, 275-6, 287
Paternoster
    Agn, wife of John, 260
    Agn, wife of Rog, 256, 258
    John, 260
    Rog, 255-7, 259-60
Payn
    Rob, 40
Paytwyn
    Thos, 273
Pechett(e) (Pechytt, Petchet, Pychett)
    Rob, 275-6, 278-81, 284-5, 287, 290, 293-7
Percevall
    Rob, 91
Petipas
    Wm, 88
Peverel
    Ste, 181
Peystur
    Ric, 9
    Roese, wife of Ric, 9
Phyp(p) (Phipp) (*see* Fypp)
Pike
    Ral, 9-10
Pilcoke (Pilkoc, Pilkok, Pilkot)
    John, 34
    John, son of Walt, 33
    Walt, 27, 31, 33
Pilgrim (Pil(e)grym)
    Mati, wife of Rog, 70, 81
    Rog, 66, 70, 81
Piriton
    Isa, daur of Wm, 39

    Wm, 39
Plomer(e) (Plomore)
    Rob, 293
    Thos, 174, 180
Pole(y) (Poly, Poleye, Polley)
    John, *xxxvi, lvin*, 236-8, 248, 248n, 249
    Thos, *lvi*, 210-11, 218, 220, 226, 228, 248, 257, 268, 270
Pollard
    Wm, 10
Ponchard
    Geof, 9
Ponte (Punt(e))
    Hen, 279, 282, 284
    Joan, wife of Hen, 279, 282, 284
Pope
    John, 37
Porcher
    Ric, *lvii*, 4, 24
Portario (Portarius)
    John, 43
    Ric, 9
Pratt(e)
    Thos, 274-5, 298
Prud(d) (Prodd, Proud(d)e, Prudd(l)e)
    Ali, daur of John, 70
    Amice, wife of Rog, 44-5, 47
    Amice, wife of Rog, son of John, 40-1
    Emma, daur of John, 48
    Ida, 107
    Idonia, daur of John, 61
    John, 29, 32-3, 35-6, 39-42, 44-9, 58-9, 61-2, 68, 70, 76, 120
    Margy, wife of John, 120
    Mati, *xlvii*, 36
    Mati, daur of John, 39
    Ric, 122, 132
    Rog, 42, 44-5, 47, 76, 79-80, 84-5, 88-9, 98-9, 102, 111, 117, 126, 154, 172, 205
    Rog, son of John, 40-1
    Sarah, wife of Ric, 122
Pulter
    John, 270
Purcell(e)
    Wm, 273, 294
Pusse
    Osbert, 23-4

INDEX OF PERSONS

Quen(e)hawe
Rog, 161-2, 165-6, 170, 172, 174, 176

Racheford (see Rocheford)
Ralph
Agn, wife of, 12
Albreda, wife of, 33
Isa, daur of, 33, 38
Ric, son of, 6-7, 10
Saer, son of, 19, 26, 46
Ste, son of, 22
Ramryche
Thos, 279
Rassh(e) (Rashe)
John, 270
Mati, wife of Thos, 239
Thos, 239, 241, 246-8, 250-2, 256, 271
Redehede (Redeheved, Redhod)
Isa, wife of Si, 81
Ric, *lvii*, 260
Rog, 109-10, 127
Si, 81
Reeve (Reve)
Agn, daur of Sara, relict of Ral, 37-8
John, son of Ric, 107
John, son of Si, 67, 108
Marg, daur of Sara, relict of Ral, 37
Mati, daur of Sara, relict of Ral, 37
Ral, 14, 22-3, 30, 35, 37-8
Ric, 16, 107
Saer(y), 31, 42, 51, 54-5, 60-1, 75, 108, 108n
Sara, relict of Ral, 37-8
Sayer, *xxxiii*, 55, 61
Si, 67, 108
Thos, 259
Walt, 11, 19
Walt, son of Wm, *xxxii*, 1
Walt, son of Saery, 75
Wm, *xxxii, lvii*, 1, 3-4, 6
Re(y)nold (Raynold(e), Reinold, Ronnold)
John, *lviii*, 273, 280, 285
Marg, 273
Ric, *lviii*, 2, 7
Thos, *lviii*, 279-80, 285-6
Reymond(e) (Raymond, Reymon, Reymound, Reymund(e))
Agn, daur of John, 139

Bart, 22, 36
Bate, 30
Emma, sis of John, 86
Gilbert, son of, 13
John, 2, 14, 20, 54, 60, 86, 93, 103-4, 111, 122, 124, 126, 134-5, 137, 139, 144, 214, 245, 254
John, son of Osbert, 34
John, son of Walt, 86
Marg, daur of Walt, 28
Mati, daur of Walt, 28
Osbert, *lvii*, 24, 30-1, 34-6, 40, 43, 45
Osbert, son of, 10, 12
Ral, 35
Ral, son of Osbert, 34
Ric, 22, 29, 31
Sarra, 93
Sarra, wife of Walt, 86-7
Walt, 28, 73-4, 79, 81, 83-7, 131, 139, 172
Walt, son of, 30
Walt, son of Wm, 53
Wm, 22, 37, 40, 42, 45, 53, 88, 93, 98-9
Wm, son of, 18, 30
Reynar(d) (Raynard, Reyner)
Christi(a)na, wife of Thos, 278, 281-2, 291, 295, 298
Rob, 294
Thos, 278, 280-2, 291, 295-6, 298
Reyner
Lord, 14
Richard
Abbot, 294
John, son of, *lvi*, 1, 15, 26
Ric, son of, 3, 7
Saer, son of, 19, 26, 46
Roberd
Thos, 16
Robert
Thos, son of, 16
vicar, 154
Walt, son of, *xxx*, 2-4, 7
Robin (Robyn)
John, 29, 80
Rocheford (Racheford)
Thos, 280
Wm, 275-6, 278, 283, 285, 287, 290, 293-4, 296-7

343

INDEX OF PERSONS

Rodland
  Nic, 83
Roger
  John, son of, 5
Rolfes
  Agn, 7, 9
Roo
  John, 266-7
Ron(e)hale (Rannall, Rawnall, Renale, Roenhale, Ronale, Ron(n)all, Roonale, Rouenhale, Rounale, Rowen(h)ale, Rownhale)
  Agn, wife of Walt, 177
  Anthony, 286
  Christina, wife of Thos, 287
  Emma, wife of John, 288
  Hen, 209, 214-15, 217-21, 223, 226-8, 231-3, 240, 240n, 241
  John, 272-3, 275-6, 280-1, 284, 287-8, 290, 293-7
  Ric, 240-4, 246-8, 250-3, 254, 257-60, 262-8, 270-1
  Thos, 270, 275-6, 286-8, 290-1, 293-5, 296-7
  Walt, *lix*, 158-60, 163-7, 177, 185
  wife of John, 293
Rothbury
  John, 272
Rouge (Ronge)
  John, 114, 135, 126
  John, son of John, 135
Rouser
  Thos, 272
Rowley(e)
  Thos, 245-6
Rowsse
  Thos, 288
Ruffus
  Alex, *xxxiiin, lvii*, 2, 5
Ryce (Ryse)
  Thos, 284, 292
Ryver
  John, 99
  Margy, wife of John, 99

Saburgh (Sabright, Sabrith, Sabryt(h))
  Agn, daur of Rog, 255-6
  Geof, 81, 89, 130
  Ric, 9, 28-9, 126
  Rog, 252-3, 255-6
Sadeler
  John, 248, 250
Saer(e) (Saery) (*see* Sayer(e))
Salmon (Sal(e)man, Saman, Se(e)man)
  Beatrice, 211-14
  Felicia, wife of Thos, 212
  Joan, 22
  Joan, relict of Wm, 20-1
  John, 36-7
  Rob, 74, 80, 82-4
  Sarra, 81
  Thos, 202, 204, 211-13
  Walt, 62
  Wm, 13, 20-1, 27, 36, 45, 47, 61, 63, 80-1, 132, 146, 188
  Wm, son of Wm, 20-1
Salter
  John, *xxxiv*, 296, 296n, 297
Samot
  Lady, 9
Samphorth(e) (Sampforthe, Samporthe)
  John, 220-1, 223, 227-8
Sampson
  John, 228
Saunford
  John, 214, 217
  Rob, 82-4, 86-7, 89-90, 133
Savyn
  Wm, 45
Sayer(e) (Saer(e), Saery, Saiere, Saye(r)s, Seyer)
  Agn, mother of Reynald, 119
  Agn, wife of Wm, 216
  Ali, 4
  Ali, daur of Walt, 121
  Cecilia, 148
  Cecilia, daur of Walt, 137
  Cecily, 52
  Geof, 129-30, 146
  John, 24, 145, 148, 215
  John, son of Reynald, 164, 168
  Marg, 48
  Marg, daur of, 46
  Mati, 164, 168
  Nic, 153-4
  Reynald, 118-19, 124, 131, 138, 155, 158,

INDEX OF PERSONS

    164, 168-70, 188
Reynald, son of Walt, 106
Sar(r)a, 78, 80, 82-3, 121
Sara, daur of Walt, 61, 67
Walt, *l*, 29, 32, 36, 38, 40, 44, 46, 49,
    53-5, 61, 67, 72, 74, 76-9, 81, 83, 85,
    87, 89-91, 93, 105-6, 108, 112, 114,
    117, 121, 137, 144, 148, 169, 194, 212,
    256
Walt, son of Walt, 40, 53
Wm, 77, 86, 88, 91-4, 97-8, 100, 102,
    106-7, 109-11, 113-15, 117-21, 123-4,
    127, 129-30, 132, 134-5, 137-9, 144-5,
    153-4, 158-60, 162, 168-71, 173, 180-4,
    187-93, 195-9, 201-3, 205-6, 208-13,
    216, 218, 245, 256, 261, 283
Wm, father of Wm, 216
Scharman
    Rog, 121
Scot
    John, 196
Scrag(g) (Strag)
    Ric, 129, 131-2, 135, 137, 139
Sergea(u)nt (Serjeant)
    John, 16
    Thos, 62
Sewesteresdouter
    Sarra, 121
Shayle(s) (Scayl, Shail)
    John, 33
    Wm, 30-1, 40
Shelford(e)
    John, 262, 267-8, 272
Shep(e)herd (Bercar(ius), Bercator,
    Bercher, Burcher, Schep(h)erd, Sheparde,
    Shepherde, Shephers)
    Cecila, 137, 145
    Cecilia, daur of Geof, 133
    Cecily, daur of Geof, 103
    Geof, 48, 53, 57-9, 62-4, 72-4, 76-9, 81-7,
    90-4, 96-8, 102-3, 105, 107, 133, 181
    Godfrey, 57
    Helen, *l*, 128, 135
    Helen, daur of John, 123, 127, 139
    Isa, 157
    Isa, daur of Rog, 56, 67, 84, 91, 119, 129
    Joan, 273
    John, *lviii*, 116-18, 122-3, 127, 139, 166,

    218, 221, 239, 273
John, son of Geof, 105
Marg, wife of Geof, 105
Mati, 121
Mati, daur of Geof, 82, 107
Mati, daur of John, 139
Ral, 12
Rob, 40, 183
Rog, *lvii*, 27, 29, 34-5, 44, 52, 54-9, 61-3,
    65-74, 76, 78-9, 83-4, 86, 91, 97-8,
    110-11, 113, 119, 129, 200
Sara, daur of Geof, 105
Sara, daur of Rog, 61
Sarra, 103
Wal, 119
Wm, *lviii*, 1, 1n
Wm, son of Geof, 97
Sigar
    Walt, 13
Siker
    Ric, 66
Simeon (Symeon, Symyon)
    Percival (Perseval(l)), 77-8, 80, 82-3, 86,
    88-90, 94, 96, 98, 109
Smalgrave
    John, 163, 166
Smith (Faber, Smyth(e))
    Adam, 147-54, 162, 165-6, 174
    Beatrice, 207
    Christina, 183, 188
    Christina, wife of John, 182
    Hugh, 214, 217-18, 220, 224, 226, 228,
    242-4, 246-7
    Joan, 217, 220-1
    John, 26, 170-82, 184-5, 187, 194-5, 199,
    201, 203, 207, 210, 243, 260-1, 276,
    279, 284
    John, son of Mati, 166
    Marg, wife of Hugh, 214
    Margy, wife of John, 26
    Mati, wife of Adam, 166
    Ral, 5, 5n
    Rog, 68
    Si, 217, 237-8, 240-2, 248, 257-8
    Thos, 80
    Walt, 7, 11, 58, 68
    Wm, 22, 138, 189, 191
    Wm, son of John, 182

INDEX OF PERSONS

Somenour
 Geof, 151
 Juliana, wife of Geof, 151
Sopwelle
 Walt, 100
Sparwe (Sparue)
 Walt, 51, 55
Spenser
 Ric, 60, 95-6, 98-9, 102-3
Spicer
 Thos, 18, 23
Sprot
 John, 164
Sprount
 Alb(e)reda, sis of Wm, 4, 14
 Wm, 4, 14
Squyer
 John, 163
Stafford
 Thos, 217
Standeby
 John, 52
Sta(u)nford (Stangforde, Stanneforde)
 John, 247, 260, 270
Steil
 [land of], 21
Stenot
 Agn, daur of, 31
Stephen
 Agn, daur of, 19
 Alan, son of, 30-1, 43
 Ali, daur of, 28
 Joan, wife of, 19
 John, son of, 37
 Ste, son of, 3, 13, 21
 Walt, son of, 29
 Wm, 18
 Wm, son of, 4, 12-13, 15-16, 19, 22
 Wm, son of Wm, 18
Stethenache (Steven, Stevenach(e), Styvenach)
 John, 36-41, 56n, 101
Stevenessones
 Adam, 245
Stiward
 John, 16
Stoppesle
 Ric, 75, 77-8

Strag (*see* Scrag)
Stynh
 Wm, son of, 2
Swalewe
 Thos, *xxxvi*, 249
Swetek(yn) (Swete(kin), Swetekyne, Swetkyn(ne))
 Ali, *lvii*, 51, 85, 94, 99, 107, 113, 128, 132, 134-6, 139
 Ali, daur of Ali, 139
 Hen, 128, 133-4, 136-7
 Hen, son of Walt, 87
 Hen, son of Ali, 99
 Mati, 61, 87, 94, 106-7
 Sarra, daur of Walt, 85
 [tenement of], 46
 Walt, 61, 69, 73-6, 78, 80, 82, 85, 87, 128, 149-50, 154, 184
 Wm, 87
Swineherd
 John, 60
 Margy, wife of Wm, 78
 Rog, 60
 Thos, 78
 Wm, 78
Swon(e)
 Agn, wife of John, 61
 John, 42, 45, 52-3, 57-8, 61, 67, 72, 74, 98, 142
 John, son of John, 67, 72, 74
Symondes
 John, 301

Taborer (Taburrerre)
 Geof, 153, 164
 Juliana, wife of Geof, 164
Taillour (Taylour)
 Beatrice, 215
 Geof, 152
 Nic, 204, 222
 Rob, 255
 Si, 158
 Thos, 212, 220
 Walt, *lvii*, 146-7, 149, 161, 165, 168, 172
 Wm, 212, 214-15, 217, 219
Tallard (*see* Toller)
Tanner(e)
 Hen, 196-7

INDEX OF PERSONS

Tater(e) (Tatre)
  Hugh, 22, 27-8
  Walt, son of Hugh, 28
Tece
  John, 191
Tenor (Tenur)
  Hugh, 5, 7, 9
Tewyng
  Ric, 64-5
Thik(k)eneye
  Ral, 79, 83, 101
Thomas (Thomme)
  Agn, daur of Walt, 185
  Ali, 128
  Isa, 57
  John, 121-2
  John, son of Walt, 161
  John, son of Wm, 76
  Marg, 42
  Margy, daur of Wm, 78
  Mati, daur of Walt, 185
  Osbert, son of, 3, 4
  Ral, 118, 125
  vicar, 43
  Walt, 122, 128, 132, 134, 138-9, 145,
    151-4, 156, 158-66, 168-85, 245
  Wm, 3-4, 12, 27, 32, 35-6, 39, 44-6, 48,
    54-5, 57-9, 63-6, 68-73, 76, 78, 80, 84,
    93-4, 110-11, 114-16, 118-22, 152, 193,
    245
  Wm, son of, 3, 12
  Wm, son of Walt, 161
  Wm, son of Wm, 12
Thornebury(e)
  Philip, 240-1, 243-4, 253-5, 264-6,
    267-70
Thressher (Tresh, Tressher)
  Matt, *lvii*, 196-7
Toller(e) (Tallard, Tollard(e))
  Isa, daur of John, 58
  John, 30, 55-6, 58-9, 69-70, 98, 157,
    207-8, 214, 237
  John, son of John, 69
  John, son of Margy, 126
  Juliana, 149, 151-2
  Marg, 70, 98-9, 112-14
  Marg, daur of John, 70, 98
  Margy, 126

  Margy, wife of John, 70
Travayle (Travaill(e), Travayll),
  Hugh, 156, 158, 160-1, 163, 165
  Parnel, wife of Hugh, 160
Tressher (Tresth)
  Matt, 196-7
Tyler
  Ali, daur of Thos, 232
  Thos, 232

Ulfkytel
  thegn, 306
Umfrey,
  John, 164

Valley (Valey, Falley)
  John, 240, 242, 244, 248, 262
  Wm, 241, 244, 244n
Veesse (Vese)
  John, 136, 143, 145-6
  Margy, daur of John, 143, 145-6
Vinte(r) (Vintere, Vinttere, Vynitere, Vynt,
  Vynter(e), Wynter(e))
  John, 218
  Wm, 171-2, 174-85, 188-93, 195, 197-9,
    202, 205-6, 208-12, 214-17, 220-1, 224,
    226, 228, 235-8, 240-4, 258

Waleys
  John, 95
Wallingford
  Wm, *xxv*
Walter
  Isa, daur of Wm, 41
  Petronilla, wife of, 12
  Ral, son of, 11, 34, 47
  Reymond, son of, 4
  vicar, 77, 121-2, 189, 192
  Walt, son of, 3, 12, 19, 31
  Wm, 41
  Wm, son of, 13, 21-2, 24, 51
Waltham
  Wm, 40
Ward(e)
  Adam, *l*, 94, 106-7, 109-11, 114, 116-17,
    120-1, 123, 125-6, 129-30, 132, 134,
    136-8, 142
  Alex, *xlvii*, 108, 114, 117, 144, 153,

INDEX OF PERSONS

158-63, 204
Ali, 142
Ali, daur of Adam, 142
Ali, daur of Walt, 73
Helen, 155-6
Isa, 155-6
John, 208, 236
John, son of Adam, 120
Marg, daur of Walt, 68
Mati, 38, 60-1, 123, 128
Mati, daur of Adam, 134
Thos, 272
Walt, 51, 58-60, 68, 73, 79, 108, 127
Water (Attewatre, Watre)
  Cecily, relict of Wm, 28
  Mati, *lvii*, 232
  Nic, 189, 206, 209-10, 217, 232
  Walt, 172, 263
  Walt, son of Mati, 232
  Wm, 28
Webbe
  Agn, 226, 228, 231-2
  Agn, wife of John, 223
  John, 223,
  Thos, 219, 219n, 220, 222
  Wm, 224, 233, 235-8, 240-7
  Wm, son of Thos, 219-20, 222
Wheler (Wolere)
  Rog, 157-8, 183
Whetehamstede (Whethamsted),
  Thos, 280, 285, 287, 290
Whirle
  John, 25
White (Whyth)
  Agn, 273
  Geof, 10
  Mabel, wife of Si, 90
  Si, 90
Whit(e)church (Whitecherch)
  Ral, 146-52
Whitecok
  Walt, 67
Whyth (*see* White)
Wikyng (Wyking, Wykyng))
  Geof, 129-30, 132
  Ral, 29
  Wm, 81, 129-30, 132, 146-7

Wilco(c)k (Wilcokkys, Willcok,
  Wylcok(es))
  Hen, 274
  Joan, widow of Hen, 274
  John, *lvi*, 270-1, 302
  Thos, 193, 199
  Walt, 183-4, 193, 200, 205, 207
Wilemot(h) (Wil(l)imot, Wilymot(e),
  Wylemot)
  Ali, 76, 78
  Ali, wife of Rog, 60
  Cecilia, 147
  Cecily, 159-60
  Rog, 60
Willesone (Willesson)
  Alex, son of, 1
  Jas, 274
  John, 94, 103, 148, 198, 262
William(s) (Wyllyams)
  Agn, daur of John, 259
  Alan, son of, 23, 29, 31, 34, 44, 75
  Alex, son of, *lvi*, 1
  Ali, wife of, 12
  Cecily, daur of, 2
  Emma, daur of, 10
  John, 131-3, 255-7, 259, 297
  John, son of, 2-3, 88
  Ral, son of, 27, 29, 32-3, 38, 48-9
  Ric, *lxi*
  Rob, son of, 6
  Walt, son of, 73, 77
  Wm, son of, 2
Wilye
  Ric, 104
Wisot(e) (Wisoth, Wyshot, Wysod,
  Wysot(h), Wysote(s), Wysoth, Wysott)
  Agn, 147
  Alex, 48, 53, 55-6, 59, 62-3, 65, 71, 73-4,
    77-9, 81-3, 85-6, 88, 90-4, 96-8, 102-4,
    107, 109-17, 119, 121, 123, 127, 129,
    131, 133, 195, 204, 268
  Ali, relict of John, 56
  Emma, daur of Alex, 97
  Gena (Gina), 62
  Isa, wife of Laurence, 127
  John, 34, 36, 49, 56, 62, 92, 94, 98,
    109-10, 112
  John, son of John, 56, 62

INDEX OF PERSONS

Laurence, 125, 127, 130, 143, 147, 152, 154, 163-7, 171, 173, 177-8, 181, 183, 187, 191, 195-7, 199, 204, 222
Marg, wife of John, 112
Walt, 129, 131, 133, 135, 137-8, 143
Wittenham
Adam, 138-9, 145
Wode (Attewode)
Agn, 202
John, *lvi, lvii*, 172, 174, 177, 185, 187, 190, 202, 207-8, 237, 268
John, son of John, 187, 190
Marg, wife of John, 172
Wodeward
Agn, 226
Hugh, 226, 228
John, 303
Wolere
Rog, 156
Wright (Wrygh(te))
Agn, wife of Rob, 176, 179-80
John, 187, 190
Marg, wife of John, 190
Margy, wife of John, 187
Rob, 174, 176, 179-81
Rob Yerdele, 172
Wulfgar
Abbot, 306
Wulfstan
Archbishop, 306
Wygges
John, 294, 297
Thos, 297
Wylkyn
Joan, 237
John, 207-8
Wyllemessone
John, 234
Wylum
Walt, 12
Wymark
Nic, 81
Thos, son of Wm, 29
Wm, 29, 48, 129-30, 147
Wymundham
John, 136
Wyn(e) (Wynne)
John, *lvin*

Wm, 273, 278-9, 288, 290, 293, 295, 297
Wyndesore
Si, 220, 223
Wyns(e)lowe
Wm, 28, 119-26
Wynter (*see* Vinte(r))
Wyther
Ric, 187

Y(h)erdele (*see* Erdeleye)
Y(h)onge
John, 257, 259, 262-3, 268
Rog, 126
Thos, 253, 258
Ysoud (*see* Isoud)

INDEX OF PLACES

Locations within the Manor

All locations within the manor are shown in italics in the translation.

Acremel(l)ond, 284, 299
Amedich, 16
Andrewes, 274
Andrews Wick, *lx*
Ankereswyk(e) (Ankerswyk, Ankerwy(e), Ankery Wyk, Ankerys, Ankeryswyk), *lx*, 110, 192, 199, 200, 205, 214, 243-4, 246-7, 265

Bakerslane (Bakkereslane), 228, 271
Baldock Road, *xiv*
Balstones, 223, 225, 227, 229
Balstonys Grove, 244
Banforlong, 192
Bate(s) (Bateman, Bateslond(e), Baty), *xli, lx, lix*, 153, 235, 242, 262-3, 276, 279, 284
Bayles, 295
Bedwyff, 274
Beges, 299
Beriwisehull, 32
Blackhorse Road, *xii, xiii, xv, xvi*
Blakenhurst, 167
Blakesley, 270
Blakryshelane, 221
Bondeslond, 172
Bonnys, 298
Bootings Close, *lix*
Botons, *lix, lx*, 217, 236, 238-9, 289-90
Boundary stump, 306
Burreslond, 136
Bygraveponde, *lix*, 264
Bygraves, 266

Cade Close, *xviii*
Canmanweye, 16
Cashio Lane, *xviii*
Cefforlong, 189, 196
Chalfurlong (Chalkforlong, Chefurlong(e), Chepforlong), *xxxviii*, 46, 278-9, 282, 286, 294
Cherche Lane (Chirche Lane), *xv, xviii, lix*, 57, 95, 149
Chosen Hills, *lxi*

Church Field, *xvi, xvii, xviii, xix, xx, lii*
Collesmede, 298
Cotnald, 283
Crofte, 32
Croft Lane, *xviii, lix, lxii*
Debedens Shott (Depdeneshotte), 283, 294
Dedewyff, 289
Dene, 16
Depdene, 287
Depdenebalk, 294
Dole Rode, 31
Druyenhull, 14
Duckfurlong, *lxi*
Dylrodys, 289
Dyperes, 239

Eastern Way, *xviii*
Eighteen Acres, 279
Eldebrach(e), 113, 138
Eldefeld(e), *xxxviii*, 46, 83, 116, 123, 135
Eldewelhylle (Eldewell), 57, 253
Erdelesbuttes, 233
Estfurlong, 283

field of Willian, 68
field towards Baldock, 117
field towards Stotfold, 117
Fordbrigge (Fordbrugge, Forthebrigge), *xxxi, lviii*, 221, 223, 226
Foxeholez (Foxhole), 282, 294
Frasys (Fraysses, Frosys), 278, 282, 291
Fullers Parcell, 299

Gaffe [?Gasse], 23, 72, 74
Gegges (Geggys), 45, 298
Geiardes, 237
Gildrischdene (Gildrytthesdane), 189, 196
Glebe Road, *xviii*
Gorehegge (Gorehyed), 263, 286
Goreshott(e), 286
Gor gapp, 278
Grange playing fields, *xviii*
Grauelpittes, 274

INDEX OF PLACES

Great Field, *lx*
Green land (Grene), 81, 174
Green Lane, *xvi, xvin*
Gren(e)dyche (Grenedich, Grondich), 83, 99, 191, 283, 294
Grenewey(e), 46, 201
Greweisslade, 7

Hale Croft (Hallecrofte), 204, 235
Haleswyke (Hallewik, Hallewyke), 90, 205, 235, 269
Halhouse, 297
Hallelonde, 260, 261, 262
Hallemad (Hallemed(e), Holmede), *lviii, lxi*, 147, 170, 251, 263, 299
Halle Orchard (Halleorcharde, Halleorchyerde), *xxix, xxxv, xxxvi, xxxvii*, 125, 199, 201, 235, 243
Harpennes, 299
Hash (Hassh, Hathes, Heches), *lx*, 227, 229, 234, 240, 262
Hastynges, 276
Heywarde, 263
Holwell, 294
Hoomulle, 167
Hoomullemore, 167
Hordulfesmere, 7

Icknield Way, *xii, xiii, xviii, lix, lx*
Ikenyldesshot, 167
Inlondesdiche, 60
Ivel, *xiii, xv, xvii, lix, lx*

Katelote, 23
King's highway, *xxviii, lix*, 16, 55, 67, 76, 109, 165, 221, 273
Kokeshavedland, 16
Kristiansand Way, *xii, xiii, xv*
Kyndales, 298

Langeforlong (Langfurlong, Leyfurlong, Longeforlong(e), Longefurlong, Longforlong), 31, 36, 76, 80, 85, 116, 165, 274, 284
Langelondes (Longeland), 16, 60
Levendich, 102
Litelcotnale (Lytlecotnale), 274, 289
Little Field, *lx*
Lobbegate (Lobgate, Lombegate), 84, 123, 294

Londhedlond (Longehevedlond, Longhedelonde), 114, 205, 235
Longe croft, 52, 201, 219
Longdene, 286
Longerefe, 236
Long field, 267
Longfurlong, *xxxviii*
Longmede, *lix, lxi*, 31
Lyndyche, 294
Lytlemalm, 253

Magodysland, 274
Maistereslond (Maystereslond), 142, 270
Malme(s) (Mawme), 85, 102, 154, 173, 183, 274, 279, 284
Malotes, 177
Malt(e)mannes, *lx*, 240, 242, 262
Maydingodes, 192
Mechelecotehale, 137
Medeway, *lix*, 294
Megges (Meggis, Megis, Megys, Miggys), 217, 219, 220, 222, 225, 227, 229
Meggesdame, 237, 239
Middle Field, *xxxvii, lx*
Middelforlonge (Mylfurlong, Mysfurlong), 7, 274, 283, 286
Mikelheg, 97
Milnelond, 34
Miss Furlong, *lxi*
Moloteslond, 149
Moremede, 270
Mullelond, 110
Mulleweye, 135
Munden(s), 266-9
Mundencroft(e) (Mundene Crofte, Mundescroft), *lx*, 210, 253-5, 257, 265
Mundyns Close, 295
Mylleweye (Mylwey), 263, 294

Ned [*illeg*], 283
Nethercotnale, 274
Newehouscroft, 157
North Field, *xxxvii, xxviii, lxi*, 46
Nortonbury, *xii, xvii, xviin, xviii, xx, xxix, lx, lxi*
Norton Common, *xviii, lx, lxi*
Norton Hall, *lxii*
Norton Road, *xii, xiii, xviii, xx*

351

INDEX OF PLACES

Odeslonde, 253
Oldbrache (Oldbrachewey), *lix*, 287, 294
Oldwelhyll, 292
Olyves, 181
Ordelesmere, 16
Ouercotnale, 274
Ouerway, 282

Parlores (Parloureslonde, Parlours, Parlourslond), 118, 167, 187, 255
Paynes Farm, *lxii*
Pernel (Pernelelond), 137, 181
Pittelesand, 7
Pix, *lx*
Pokesthorne (Pucsxethurne), *lx*, 5, 267
Pourtehole (Pourtesole), 292
Prestescroft, 55
Pulterswey, *lix*, 274, 294

Radwell Head, 305-6
Rageslond, 117
Rascoykes, 274
Reedes, 284
Refurlong, 274
River Ivel (*see* Ivel)
River Pix (*see* Pix)
Rodenhanger, *xii, xiii, xvi, xxxvii, xlviii, lii, lx*, 304-6
Runnalow shott, *lxi*
Russheden, 99
Russhmede, 254
Ryve Furlong, *lxi*, 283

St Nicholas church, *xvi, xvii, xviii, lix, lx*, 216, 218, 224-5
Salvyers, 276
Sandes, 215
Sevene Acres Dene, 60
Scotchin Hills, *lxi*
Shayles, 237, 239
Shefford Lane, *xx*
Sheff Furlong, 283
Sheperdes, 174-5
Shipcothedge, 275
Shyrebalk, 294
Somerespond(e) (Somersponde), *lix*, 253, 255, 265
Southfeld, *xxxvii, xxxviii, lxi*, 46
Standalone Farm, *xviii, lxii*

Stanyhyll, 298
Stapelwey, *lix,* 175
Stapleton's Field, *xii, xiii, xiv, xviii*
Stotfold boundary, 305
Stotfold Dyke, *xviii*, 305
Swetekin (Swetekynnes, Swetkynnes, Swetkyns), 46, 208, 236, 298
Swoneslond, 142

Tollers, 291
Towerslane, 286
Towne Mede, 294

Wachil, 32
Wamingedane, 7
Wantes, 60
Wardeslond, 196
Wardeswyke, 241
Wardysgrene, 298
Wash Furlong, *lxi*
Wat [*damaged*], 299
Waterdenfylde, 294
Weufurlong (*see* Wonforlong)
Whathuldan, 46
Whetyldale, 292
White Field, *lx*
Whitehickes, 145
Whytyng Lane, *lix*
Wilbury (Hill), *xiii, xv, lx*, 305
Wilbury Farm, *lxii*
Wiliefeld (*see also* field of Willian), *xxxviii*, 60
Wisell shott, *lxi*
Wodelondes (Wodes, Wodeslond, Wodlondes), 217, 219-20, 222, 225, 227, 229, 265, 274
Wolver[lond], 274
Wonforlong (Weufurlong, Wonfurlong), 99, 113, 135
Works Road, *xii*
Woweforlong (Wowefurlong), 77, 85, 167
Wyddergrene, 289
Wyserhull (Wysoverhull), 18, 167
Wysettes, 274

Yerdelebuttes, 265
Yonges, 269

INDEX OF PLACES

Places outside the manor

Places outside the manor of Norton have been transcribed as their modern spelling except where the location is unsure; variations in spelling in the original text are shown in italics and in brackets. This list does not include place names/locations which form part of names cited in the index of persons, such as Sarra de Erdeleye or Cecily de Cherpenho. Places are in Hertfordshire unless otherwise stated.

Abbots Langley, *xxii, xlvii*
Ardeley *(Y(h)erdele)*, 171, 238, 240-3
Arlesey, Beds (*Alrichessay, Alrichessey, Arleches(s)eye, Arlicheseye*), 81, 159-60, 165-72
Aston Abbots, Bucks, *xxviii*

Baldock (*Baldok(e)*), *xiii, xv, xvii, xxviiin, xxxvi, xxxviin, xlviii, liii, liv, lv, lvi, lvin, lxi*, 4, 19, 45, 66, 80, 93, 97-8, 111-12, 115-17, 121-3, 126, 146, 149, 151-5, 160, 183, 212, 214-20, 222-4, 226, 228, 231-3, 235-8, 240-7, 248n, 252-3, 259, 270, 276, 279, 284
Barnet, *xxii, xxv, xxvin*
Batchworth, 304, 306
Beaulieu, Hants, *xxviii*
Bedford, Beds (*Bedeford(e)*), *lii*, 147, 238, 241-7
Belvoir, Lincs, *xxviii*
Boreham (*Borham*), 189-93, 195, 197
Bramfield, *xxii, xxiin, xxiii, xxvi, xxviii*
Bury St Edmunds, Suff, *xlii*
Bygrave (*Bigrave*), *liii, lx*, 217-18, 220-3, 226, 228, 231-3, 242-4, 248, 253, 255, 264

Caldecote, *xix, xixn, xlviii, xlviiin*, 10, 26, 106, 126, 136
Canterbury, Kent, *xvi*, 304, 306
Cashio, *xxii, xxvin, xxviii*
Chanton, 126
Cheshunt (*Chesthunte*), *liii*, 222, 224, 226, 228, 231-3
Chesterton, Cambs (*Chestertone, Chysterton*), *lii*, 218, 220, 222-3, 226, 228, 231-3
Chicksands, Beds (*Chiksond(e)*), 188-91, 193

Chiltern Hills, *xxxviii, xxxviiin, xxxix*
Clothall (*Clahale, Clotale*), 13, 235-7
Codicote, *xxii, xxviii, xli*, 71, 91, 270n
Colchester, Essex, *lii*, 236-7
Cottered (*Codereth, Codreth(e), Cokereth*), *liii*, 218, 220, 222, 224, 226, 228, 231-3, 235-8, 240
Croxley, *xxii, xxv, xxvin*

Ditton, Kent (*Dytton*), 235-7
Dunton, Beds, *lii*, 260

Edlesborough, Bucks (*Edesburgh, Edysburgh*), *lii*, 223, 226, 228, 231
Edworth, Beds (*Eddeworth*), *lii*, 252-3, 255-7, 259-60, 264
Ely, Cambs, *xvi, xvin*, 148, 150, 152-3, 157, 164-79, 181-2, 184-5, 187-93, 198
Estwyk (either Astwick, Beds, or Eastwick), 159

Grandborough, Warks, *xxviii*

Hackney, Middx (*Hakeney*), 241
Hexton, *xxin, xxii, xxiin, xxiii, xxiv, xxv, xxvi, xxvin, xxviii, xxixn*, 186, 273n
Hinxworth (*Henxt(e)worth*), *liii*, 232-3
Hitchin (*Huchyn, Hycchen, Hychyn*), *xv, xxvii, xlviii, liii, lv, lxii*, 218, 220, 222-3, 226, 228, 231-2
Holme, Hunts, 187
Holwell (*Holewelle*), 109
Huntingdon, Hunts (*Huntyngdon*), 190-2, 195, 197-8

Knebworth, 36

Letchworth (*Lec(c)heworth*), *xl, xln*, 255-6, 258

INDEX OF PLACES

Letchworth Garden City, *xiii, xiiin, xv, xvin, lxi*
Litlington, Cambs (*Lytle(l)yngton*), *lii*, 252-3, 257
Little Horwood, Bucks, *xxviii*
London, *xxvii*, 235-7, 241, 245-8, 250-3, 255-7, 259
Luton, Beds (*Luyton*), 232-3, 295

Munden (*Mundene*), 67, 107-8

Newenton (possible misspelling of Newnham), 198
Newmarkeyate (near Shenley), 233
Newnham (*Newenham*), *xxviii, xxx, xliv*, 2-7, 10, 29-30, 48, 56, 66, 90, 115-16, 126, 272n
Northaw, *xxv, xxviii*

Oxhey, 304-6

Park, *xxii, xxv, xxvin, xlvi, xlvii, xlviin*
Pegsdon, Beds (*Pekesden*), 181-2

Radwell (*Radeswell*), *xiii, xxviii, liii*, 210, 271, 276
Redbourn, 19n

St Albans (*Sanctum*), *xiii, xv, xvi, xxi, xxii, xxv, xxvi, xxviii, xxviiin, xxix, xxx, xxxn, xxxi, xxxii, xxxiin, xxxiv, xxxvi, xxxvin, xxxixn, xl, xli, xlii, xliin, xlv, xlvii, liii, lv, lvi, lviii*, 3, 14, 19n, 24, 71, 76, 83, 86-8, 91, 101, 126n, 132, 137, 147-8, 150, 159-60, 164-7, 179, 195, 197-8, 204n, 210, 212, 214-15, 217-20, 222-3, 226, 228, 231-40, 240n, 241-244, 244n-246n, 248n, 250n, 258-59, 260n-261n, 268n, 274n, 281n, 288n, 293, 294, 296n, 301, 304, 304n
St Neots, Cambs (*St Neodum*), *lii*, 210
St Paul's Walden, *xxviii*
Salisbury, Wilts (*Sarum*), 246-7
Sharpenhoe, Beds (*Cherpenho, Sarpenhoe*), 28, 38
Shenley (*Shenle, Shenley(e)*), *liii*, 220, 222, 224, 226, 228, 231-3

Shepreth, Cambs (*Schepereth(e), Scheprethe*), 151-2, 157
Southampton, Hants, *liii*, 255-7
Stevenage (*Stevenhache, Stithenache*), 112, 149
Stotfold, Beds, *lix*, 38, 45, 99, 117, 147, 151-2, 305

Tynemouth, N'humb, *xxviii*
Tyttenhanger, *xxin, xxii, xxiin, xxv*

Wallington (*Walyngton*), *liii, lxi*, 212, 214-5, 218
Walsham le Willows, Suff, *xlvi, xlvin*
Weston, *liii*, 150, 152-3, 159-60, 164-79, 181-2, 184-5, 187-93, 195, 197-8, 212, 214-15, 217-18, 220, 222-3, 226, 228, 231-3, 235-8, 240-48, 250-3, 255-7, 259, 264
Willian (*Welwen, Whelye, Wilie, Willyen, Wilye(n), Wilyon, Wyleon Wylie, Wylion, Wyllyen, Wylye(n)*), *liii*, 18, 20-2, 68, 87, 96, 156, 158, 211, 217-18, 221, 237-8, 240-1, 247, 248n, 255, 257-9, 266-70
Willingham, Cambs (*Willyngham, Wyllyngham*), *lii*, 212, 214-15
Winchester, Hants, 306
Winslow, Bucks, *xxvin, xxviii, xxviiin, xli, xlin, xlvn, xlvi, xlvin, xlvii, liiin*
Wymondham, Norf, *xxviii*, 56-7
Wymondley (*Wilmondele, Wylmondele*), 87, 150

York, Yorks, 306

Index of Subjects

Account, view of, *xxi, xxxvi, xl*, 92n, 301-3
Agriculture (*see also* Crops)
  common baulk, 274-5
  common rights, *xxxvi, xxxvii*, 55, 71, 72, 78, 115, 182, 233, 254, 265, 275
  enclosure of meadow, 5
  encroachment, 31, 42, 52, 55, 58-60, 97, 192, 206, 233, 253-5, 260, 264, 271, 275, 281
  farm equipment, 4, 5, 98-9, 194, 194n, 195, 195n
  farming irregularities, *xxxix, xl*, 39, 42, 49, 57, 155, 175, 233
  field system, *xxxvii, xxxviii, lx*
  money payments substituted for services/heriots, *xxxv, xliv, xlv*, 203, 249
  unproductive/vacant land, xlix, 34, 173, 175, 213-14, 263, 274, 287, 291
Animals, types of (*see also* Hunting)
  animals, livestock (unspecified), 55, 126, 210
  boar, *xl*, 303
  cows, bulls, bullocks, calves, oxen, *xxxix, xli, xlv*, 80, 86, 89, 91, 93, 102-4, 106, 108, 110, 112, 121, 123-5, 137, 139, 142-4, 157, 164, 171, 189, 194, 200, 226, 245-6
  dogs, *xl*, 63
  hares, rabbits, *xl*, 63, 258
  horses, mares, foals, *xxxv, xxxix, xlv*, 5, 20, 22, 51, 77, 80, 84, 91, 96, 105-6, 111, 123, 135, 138-9, 142-5, 155-7, 166-7, 171, 173, 182, 191, 194-5, 200, 205, 211, 222, 224-5, 240, 244-5, 248, 254
  pigs, *xxxix*, 119, 126, 177
  sheep, ewes, lambs, wethers, *xxxv, xxxix, xxxixn*, 62, 64, 71, 115, 119, 120, 124, 134, 143-5, 157, 182, 188-9, 194, 197-8, 207, 211-12, 221, 232, 237, 250, 252, 258, 285, 295
Apprentice (*see* Occupations)
Archery, 275, 295, 295n
Archaeology
  cursus, *xii, xiii, xiv*
  enclosures, *xii, xiv, xv, xvii*

  geophysical surveys, *xiii, xx*
  henge, *xii, xiii, xxiv, xv*
  pottery, *xiii, xiv, xv, xvii, xviii, xix*
  ridge and furrow, *xvii, xviii, xx*
Assize of ale/bread, broken (*see* Crime)

Bastardy, 56, 161,163
Birds, poultry
  capons, chickens, hens, eggs, *xxxiin, xlv*, 7, 12, 16, 35, 37, 71, 112-13, 120, 124, 132, 134-5, 167, 204, 207, 209-10, 213-16, 223, 232, 234, 239, 241-2, 252, 263, 265-6
  larks and other birds, *xl*, 130
Black Death, *xliin, xliv, xlix, l, li, lii, liii, lv*, 140n
Brewing (*see also* Assize of ale)
  brewers of Willian, 18, 20, 21, 22
  order regarding a common brewery, 115
Buildings, instructions to build (*see also* Church *and* Milling)
  bake house, 64
  barn, 84-5, 206
  granary, 5, 301-2
  instructions to build, 3, 13, 13n, 20, 34, 46-7, 49, 59, 109, 110, 133, 158, 161, 185, 187, 234, 254, 269
  mill, *xvi, xvii, xviiin, xx, xlii, xlvii*, 279
  newly built, 54, 201, 235, 243
  not built as ordered, 51, 72, 74
  smithy, 161

Charter of Æthelred, 1007, *xiii, xiiin, xv, xvi, lx*, 304-6
Charters (*see also* Free tenure)
  held, 49, 143, 247
  questioned whether held, *xxxi*, 16, 129-31, 133, 150-3, 155, 157, 219, 257, 260, 266
  showed, 61, 123, 126, 262
  surrendered, 62
Chevage, *xlii, lii, liii*, 4, 8, 16, 37, 81, 112, 131-4, 233-4, 259
Children (*see* Wardship)
Christmas, 7, 16, 22, 24, 36-7, 69, 100, 127, 134-6, 303

355

INDEX OF SUBJECTS

Church and clergy (*see also* Manorial officials)
belltower, 271
beneficiary in will/testament, 216, 218, 224-5
boundaries next to, 58
chaplain, 69, 93, 111-12, 121-2, 124, 136, 149, 169, 184, 193, 199-200, 205, 207, 210, 303,
churchwarden, 271
rector, *lxii*, 126, 211, 258
rectory farm, 244
vicar, 39, 43, 56, 67, 77, 80, 84, 90, 119, 121-2, 131-2, 154, 167, 180, 189, 192, 223-4, 226-8, 232, 273-4, 284, 292
vicarage, *lx, lxii*, 169, 180, 184, 193, 200, 205, 207
Clothing, 19n, 129, 146, 216, 302
Court books, *xxi, xxii, xxiii, xxiv, xxv, xxvi, xxvin, xxix, xxx, xxxiii, xxxiv, lvii*
Court rolls, *xxi, xxiii, xxv, xxvi, xxvin, xxvii, xxx, xxxi, xxxii, xxxiv, xxxv, xxxvii, xxxviii, xxxix, xli, xlii, xliii, xliv, lii, lvi, lx*
Court procedure
ash tree, St Albans court, *xxix*, 3, 24, 71, 76, 83, 86-7, 91, 100-1, 132, 137, 150, 258,
common fine, fixed agreement, *xxvi, xxxi*, 220, 220n, 223, 226-7, 270, 270n, 272-3, 275, 279-80, 285, 287, 290, 293-4, 297
common fine excused, 276, 280, 283-5
concealment, 118, 152
contempt, 4, 63, 155
fines or amercements for non-attendance, *passim*
pledge not to remove goods, 33, 105, 108
pledges amerced, 43, 53, 54, 82, 90, 102, 108, 226
presented to wrong Court, 125
record of rolls, 40, 49, 61, 67-8, 76, 83, 95, 101, 107, 112, 119-20, 133, 137, 146, 150, 232, 243, 279, 282-5, 287, 291, 293, 299
suit at Great Court, 62, 74
suit every three weeks, 62, 147, 170

Courts (*see also* View of Frankpledge)
baron, *xxix*
hundred, *xxviii, xxx*, 279, 283, 291, 294, 298-9
leet, *xxviii, xxix, xxx, xxxiii, xxxv, lix*
Crime and nuisance
assault, *xxvi, xxviii*, 226, 273, 293
assize of ale, broken, *xlvii*, 5, 7, 9, 12, 18, 20-2, 82-3, 91, 106-8, 114, 116-18, 120-4, 126-8, 130-1, 133-6, 139, 146-8, 150-3, 155, 157-62, 165-6, 169, 170, 221, 270, 275-6, 280, 285, 288, 290, 293, 295, 297
assize of bread, broken, 276, 285
bridge not repaired, *xxxi*, 221, 223, 226
ditch offences, 190, 221, 228, 265-6, 280, 286, 295
felony, 25, 130, 150, 210, 223, 242, 256, 296
highway obstructed, 221, 273, 27
neighbours in Baldock, wounding, 114
regraters, 162, 169-70
removed goods, 33, 92
St Albans goal, 150
stray sheep, 285, 295
tenants ill-governed, 288
trespass, unlawful ways, *xl*, 51, 187, 258, 264
Crops
barley, *xxxix, lvi, lix*, 4, 8, 28, 37, 41, 64, 208, 224-5
beans and peas, *xxxix*, 28, 37, 41, 50, 59, 77, 86, 86n, 118, 126, 203, 203n
corn, *xl, xlii, xlvii, lvi*, 3, 5, 14, 26, 28, 37, 40, 49-51, 64, 77, 115, 187, 213, 258
draget, dredge, *xxxix*, 77, 154-5, 157, 175, 191, 213
grain, 86, 203, 301-3
hay, 44, 203
malt, *xxxvi, lvi*, 302
maslin, 100
oats, *xxxviii, xxxix*, 7, 37, 42, 64, 213
rye, *xxxix*
straw, 64
unspecified, 115
wheat, *xxxviii, xxxix*, 4, 7-9, 14, 41-2, 59, 100, 119, 126-7, 175

INDEX OF SUBJECTS

Customs of the manor
 brewery, 115
 common rights, *xxxvi, xxxvii*, 55, 71, 72, 78, 115, 182, 233, 254, 265, 275
 inheritance claims (time limit), 102
 leasing orders and proclamations, 66, 97, 102, 111, 156, 274, 278, 281, 286, 288, 290, 293, 295, 297
 money payments, 203, 249
 tavern in Baldock, *lv*, 115
Custumal, *xxin*

Desmesne (*see* Land and tenements)
Disputes and pleas
 broken covenant, 254
 debt, plea of, 43, 54, 189, 191, 193, 196-7, 202-4, 206, 208, 211-13, 217, 219, 257, 270
 dower, plea of, 4, 10, 95, 257
 land, plea of, 2-3, 6, 8, 10, 15, 24, 29, 32, 39, 49, 56, 64, 71, 75, 75n, 79, 81, 83, 86-8, 90-1, 94-5, 98-102, 107-10, 133, 138, 173-4
 trespass, plea of, 189, 191, 193, 193n, 196-8, 200, 217, 219
Domesday book, *xiii, xvi, xvin, xvii, xxxvii, xlv, xlviii, xlix, lii, lx*

Easter (except when mentioned in court dates)
 must build before, 13, 49, 187
 payment date, 4, 12, 22, 101, 112-13, 127, 132, 135, 234, 239
Education
 go to clerks' school, 99, 108, 113, 120
 put to letters, to school, 40, 57, 58, 73, 76, 79, 95, 97, 161, 166, 216-17, 219, 228, 231
Enclosure Act 1796 and Awards 1798-9, *lix, lixn, lxi, lxin*
Escheat, forfeiture, 24, 25, 163, 167-8, 170, 256
Essoins, 72, 101, 138, 270, 274, 276, 278, 281, 285, 287, 290, 293-4, 296-7
Extent, *xlix*, 251

Farm equipment (*see under* Agriculture)
Fee of the Honour, 126, 126n

Fee tail, 101
Fish, pond, *xx, xl, lx*, 51, 166, 253, 255, 264-5
Free tenure (*see also* Charters)
 claims held freely, 24, 114, 130, 150, 152, 170, 247
 free rent, 206, 212
 free tenant died, 61, 125, 129-30, 138, 142-3, 147, 182, 257
Fugitives, *xxviii, lii, liii, lv, lviii*, 19-20, 36, 89, 92, 139, 147, 149, 151, 151n, 153, 157, 159-61, 164-8, 170-82, 184-5, 187-93, 195, 197-8, 210, 212, 214-15, 217, 219-20, 222, 224, 226, 228, 231-3, 235-8, 240-8, 250-60, 262-4, 268

Heriots
 animals, *xxxv, xxxix, xli*, 20, 62, 77, 80, 84, 86, 89, 91, 93, 96, 102-6, 108, 110-12, 119-21, 123-6, 134-5, 137-9, 142-5, 155-7, 164, 166-7, 171, 173, 177, 182, 191, 194-5, 198, 200, 205, 207, 210-11, 215, 222, 224-5, 232, 237, 240, 244-6, 248, 250, 252,
 clothing, 129, 146
 condoned, forgiven, *xxxvi*, 85, 87, 89, 102, 109, 112, 127, 129, 130, 139, 142-3, 145, 172, 176, 178, 200-1, 204, 207, 214, 216, 244, 275, 284, 289, 291, 298-9
 farm equipment, 98-9
 household goods, 132, 144, 161, 167, 192, 222, 231
 land, 29
 money, *xlv*, 3, 10, 15, 19, 57, 66, 70, 108, 112, 117, 122, 124-5, 128, 134, 136, 148, 151-2, 155-6, 161, 163-5, 167, 169, 171, 173-5, 177-8, 180-1, 183-5, 187, 189, 193, 200, 207-8, 215, 240-1, 255, 259-64, 266, 269, 271
 pledge, 72
 poultry, 210, 215, 234, 246
 prevented, withheld, 57, 62
 unspecified, 299
Homage, *xxx, xxxi, xl*, 82, 115, 149, 156, 170, 207, 209, 228, 233, 253, 258, 266-8, 270, 274-6, 278, 280-4, 288-9, 292, 294-6
Household goods, 8, 64, 132, 144, 161,

INDEX OF SUBJECTS

167, 182n, 192, 194, 222, 231
Hunting, fishing, warren (*see also* Animals), *xl*, 51, 130, 258

Inquisition, Inquest, *xxx*, 2, 6, 8, 10, 15, 24, 29, 32-3, 39, 49, 60, 64, 74, 78, 114, 173, 190-1, 193, 196-8, 200

Juries, jurors
  presentment juries, *xxx*
  spoke with jurors, *xxx*, 33

Knights service, *xxxix*, *xln*, 147

Land and tenements
  abandoned holding, 164, 194-5, 209
  arrangements for former tenants, 8, 15, 19, 31, 37-8, 48, 50, 63, 77, 100, 118, 255
  arrears of rent, 24, 54, 59, 64, 72, 115
  at farm, let to farm, farm rent, *xxxi*, 22, 28, 32, 261, 287
  committed waste, ruinous, *lix*, 38, 41, 44, 46, 49, 53-4, 70, 72, 74, 79, 84-5, 92, 115, 150-5, 158-67, 184-5, 187-8, 190, 192, 194-5, 197, 199, 201-2, 205-6, 208-12, 214, 217, 219, 222, 224, 227-9, 232-3, 236-8, 243, 248, 250-7, 259-61, 267, 278, 281-2, 291, 295, 297-8
  demesne, grants of land from, 16, 279
  demised to free man, 35, 39-40, 47, 73, 76
  demised to man from Baldock, 45, 93, 97, 111-12, 116, 121-3, 153-5, 183
  enclosed plots, closes, 44, 76-7, 99, 108, 292, 295, 298
  exchange of holdings, *xliv*, 16, 22, 25, 27, 29, 31-2, 34, 44, 64, 83-5, 113, 123, 135, 137, 184
  garden, 90
  holdings in Willian, 247, 257-8, 266, 269
  increase in rent, 12, 12n, 46-7, 49, 62-3, 81, 104, 109-10, 114, 132-3, 251, 263
  joint holding, 97, 107, 112, 120, 128, 145, 179n, 199, 216
  leasing orders and proclamations, *xliii*, *xliv*, *xlix*, *lv*, 66, 97, 102, 111, 156, 156n, 274, 278, 281, 286, 288, 290, 293, 295, 297

  quitclaims, 8, 12, 99-100, 107, 292, 299
  rents of assize, 301
  show how entered lord's fee, 40, 73, 96, 98, 102-3, 122-4, 130-1, 133, 252-3, 257-9, 262-3, 266-9, 271
  tofts, 104, 145, 156, 166-7, 177, 181, 185, 188, 191, 199-200, 204-5, 210-12, 214, 216, 220, 222, 225, 227, 229, 235, 237, 239, 242, 245, 249, 260-2, 264-5, 268-9, 271, 274, 281, 284, 289-92, 298-9
  unoccupied, without heirs, 28, 41, 65, 157, 168-71, 229, 246-7

Leasing (*see under* Land and tenements)
Leyrwite
  couple, *xlvii*, 39, 148, 150
  man, *xlvi*, *xlvii*, 33, 49, 146, 150
  woman, *xlv*, *xlvi*, *xlvii*, 26, 36, 38-40, 43, 48, 52, 57, 61, 67, 71, 73-4, 78, 83, 86-7, 92, 94, 107, 109-10, 113-14, 116, 121, 123, 128, 130, 133-4, 137, 146, 156, 159-60

Liberty (of St Albans), *xxvii*, *lvii*, 38, 55, 57, 64-6, 81, 92, 94, 105-6, 108, 119, 121, 126n, 132-3, 139, 142

Manorial officials (excluding those named)
  abbot, *xiii*, *xvi*, *xxviii*, *xxix*, *xxxiv*, *xl*, *xlii*, *xliin*, *xlv*, *xlvi*, *lv*, 3, 5, 8-10, 16, 18-20, 23-5, 42, 51, 61-3, 69, 81, 131, 147, 293-4, 301, 302, 303, 304, 304n
  affeerors, 72, 273, 278, 285, 294-6
  ale tasters, 91, 106-8, 114, 116-19, 121-4, 126-8, 130-1, 133-6, 139, 146, 148, 150-3, 155-60
  bailiff, *xxix*, *xxxii*, *xxxiv*, *xxxivn*, *xxxv*, 58, 62, 71, 77, 89, 100, 118, 193, 199, 212, 218, 246, 258, 275, 278, 280-1, 283, 285, 290, 292, 301
  beadle, *xxxiii*, *xxxv*, 6, 97, 104, 107, 155, 157, 172, 210, 212, 218, 258-9, 262, 266
  bursar, 206
  cellarer, *xxv*, *xxvi*, *xxvii*, *xxix*, *xxxiv*, *xlv*, *xlix*, *lv*, 2-4, 20, 24-5, 29-30, 33-4, 64, 92n, 93, 95, 100, 109, 112-13, 115, 120, 124, 126, 128, 132, 138, 143, 149, 167, 234, 239, 245, 251, 263, 292, 296n
  chief pledge, 19, 112, 220, 223, 226, 270,

358

INDEX OF SUBJECTS

272-4, 281, 285, 287, 290, 293-4, 297
constable, *xxxiii*, *xxxiv*, 150, 221, 228, 273, 275-6, 280, 286-7, 290, 293, 295, 297
deputy bailiff, 276
farmer, *xxxv*, *xxxvi*, *xxxvii*, *xl*, *xliv*, *lvi*, 191, 203, 217-18, 220, 226, 244, 249, 254, 266
granarius, 302
prior, 56-7, 56n
reeve, *xxix*, *xxxii*, *xxxiii*, *xxxiiin*, *xxxiv*, *xxxv*, *lvii*, 5-6, 31, 108n, 116, 303
rent collector, *xl*, 301
sergeant, *xxxii*, *xxxiii*, 5-6, 13, 29
steward, *xxvii*, *xxxii*, *xxxiv*, *xxxivn*, 245, 279, 283-4, 286-7
supervisor, 303
taker of deathbed surrenders, 278, 281, 283, 289, 292
wardrobe keeper, 302

Manumission, 246-7

Marriage
man licensed, 1-3, 5, 7-9, 12-16, 18, 20, 21, 23-4, 27-8, 30, 32, 34-5, 39, 41, 44-8, 51-7, 59, 62, 65-7, 69-70, 73, 77-8, 80-2, 87, 90-4, 97-8, 103, 105-8, 110-13, 117-18, 120-2, 125-30, 134, 136, 138-9, 142-5, 147, 161-2, 165, 171, 183, 192, 214
outside manor, where he/she will, 16, 37, 47, 55, 77, 99, 103, 105, 110, 112, 120, 124-5, 129
shall not be against will, 22
to a freeman, 37, 39, 80, 94, 113
to a vagabond, 121
without licence, 2, 4, 6, 9, 14, 23-4, 26, 28, 31, 33-4, 36, 38-9, 42-3, 48-9, 51-2, 56, 58-61, 64-6, 68, 70-1, 74-5, 78-82, 84, 87, 89-92, 94, 96-9, 102-7, 113, 119-22, 128, 130-1, 133, 147-8, 150-2, 162, 165, 228, 234, 255-6, 260
woman licensed, 1-4, 11-12, 14, 16, 18, 22-3, 25, 36-9, 46, 50, 56, 60, 70, 72, 74, 80-2, 85, 87, 95-7, 99, 103, 105-6, 112-13, 121, 124-5, 128-9, 134, 136, 144-9, 157, 166, 172, 175, 180, 185, 252, 256, 262, 264

Merchet, *xlii*, *xliv*, *liii*, 35, 41, 111

Mesne lord, 130
Michaelmas (except when mentioned in court dates)
action required by, 20, 72, 74, 85, 185, 206, 209, 239, 254, 256, 278, 286, 288
date for start of lease, 11, 21-4, 32, 48, 50, 54, 69-70, 73, 79, 86, 90, 93, 96, 100, 111-12, 116, 137, 157, 198, 235, 239-40, 251
miscellaneous, 34-5, 87, 136, 203, 275
payment date, 7, 9, 12, 14, 28, 41, 47, 63, 81, 100, 109-10, 114, 118, 127, 132, 233-4, 301

Military service, 18

Mill
excessive tolls, 226, 278, 288, 290, 293, 295, 297
grinds elsewhere, 7, 36, 48-9, 52, 56, 59, 61, 65-7, 69, 71, 78, 80, 82, 84, 86, 88, 92, 94, 103, 107, 109-10, 113, 117, 121, 126, 128, 130-2, 134, 136, 153, 156, 176, 179, 258
miller, 176, 187-8, 218, 220-1, 226, 278-9, 288, 290, 293, 295, 297

Monastery, *xxvii*, *xxviii*, 198, 244, 293-4, 301-3, 305

Occupations (*see also* Manorial officials; *for* miller *see* Mill)
apprentice, 120, 126
attorney, 95, 118, 256
bow maker, 248
butcher, 233, 242
clerk, 22, 32, 218, 224-5, 274, 283
commissary, 200, 207, 211, 216, 218, 224-5
cook, 170
huckstress, 161-2, 165
servant, 51, 192, 216, 221, 223, 226
shepherd, *xxxv*, *xxxix*, *lvii*, *lviin*, *lxii*, 1n, 229, 246
smith, 5n, 259
weaver, 236, 237

Peasants' revolt, *xxvii*, *xlvii*
Proclamations (*see* Customs of the manor)

359

INDEX OF SUBJECTS

Relief, 6n, 12, 16, 20, 62, 78, 93, 93n, 104, 125, 130, 142-3, 145-6, 257-8, 266-9, 271
Roads, paths, ways, xix, xx, lix, lxi, 7, 16, 35, 51, 55, 55n, 67, 76, 99, 109, 165, 221, 253, 258, 263-7, 273, 278
Rogation days, 254, 254n

Services
  bedripp, haymaking, reaping, 7, 24, 24n, 43, 46, 49, 61, 74, 77-9, 81-2, 108-9, 119, 138
  boonworks, xxx, xxxiii, xli, 2, 4, 6, 10, 13, 14-16, 27, 36-7, 41, 43, 48, 52, 65, 68-9, 71, 73, 75, 83, 85-6, 88-9, 92, 99, 135, 152, 154, 156, 158, 164, 203
  carrying to St Albans, 88
  gives services outside manor, 131-3
  granary, 5, 301-2
  harrow, 85
  hen, eggs, 35, 71, 135
  ploughing, 2, 15, 21, 48, 51, 53-4, 65, 75, 79, 86, 91, 203
  pond, 166
  small works (*smalewerkes*), 203
  thresh provender, 5
Spices
  clove, 69
  cumin, *xlv*, 8, 25, 59, 127, 130, 147, 170, 251, 263
Stocks, repair of, 275

Taxation
  aid, 33, 147
  tallage, *xlii, xliin, xlviii, xlix*, 22, 35, 40-1, 46, 111-12, 147
Tenants (*see* Land and tenements)
Tenure (*see* Free tenure; Land and tenements)
Terrier, *lx, lxn*
Testaments (*see* Wills)
Tithing, *xxvi, xxxi*, 81, 221-3, 226-8, 270, 275, 278, 280-1, 295, 297, 297n
Trees (*for* ash tree, *see* Court procedure)
  boundary, 306
  cut, felled, *xl*, 53, 97, 153, 176-7, 180, 190, 194, 199, 202, 217, 219-20, 259, 263
  willows planted, 207

View of Frankpledge (*see also* Courts)
  meetings, *xxvi, xxvin, xxix, xxxi, xxxin, xxxiii, liv, lix*, 18, 220, 223, 226-7, 270, 272-3, 275-6, 280, 285, 287, 290, 293-4, 297
  must come to, 37, 77, 81, 92, 92n, 93, 93n, 99, 110, 112, 120, 295
Villeins (*see* Chevage; Leyrwite; Merchet; Services)

Wardship
  agreement ignored, 4-5
  committed waste, 92, 152, 224, 236
  established, 1, 10, 12, 18, 20, 21, 26, 31, 33, 41, 50, 56-7, 61, 67, 70, 85, 87, 91, 103-6, 111-12, 116, 123-4, 126, 135, 138, 142, 144-5, 147-8, 150, 155, 159, 164, 166-7, 182, 187, 190, 192, 194, 196, 222, 225, 261, 282
Weather (icy rainstorm), 188
Wills, testaments
  deathbed surrenders, 237, 246, 276, 278, 281, 283, 288n, 289, 292
  St Albans wills, *xxxixn, lvin, lix*, 204n, 240n, 244-6n, 248n, 250n, 260n, 261n, 268n, 274n, 281n, 288n
  text of wills, *xxvi, xxvin, xxxv, xxxvin, xlii*, 198, 200, 207, 211, 216, 218, 224-5
Women
  accused of assault, 226
  claimed/inherited tenement, 4, 11, 14, 28, 32, 37, 41-2, 46-7, 56, 60-1, 63-4, 68, 75, 78, 80, 96, 108, 112, 118, 128, 134, 136, 139, 143-4, 146, 148, 155, 157, 168, 183, 187, 205, 207, 212-13, 224-5, 239, 246, 252, 261, 276, 281
  committed waste, 188, 211-12, 228
  consent of wife to transfer, 7, 22, 29, 32, 135-7, 161, 164, 177, 200-1, 208, 215, 279, 283, 287
  dower, *xxx*, 4, 8-10, 14, 21, 38, 59, 70, 77, 87, 89, 89n, 93, 95, 99, 104-5, 112-13, 116, 118-9, 129, 163, 163n, 165, 183, 213, 228, 257-8
  services, must do, 9, 14, 119
  will, testament, 198

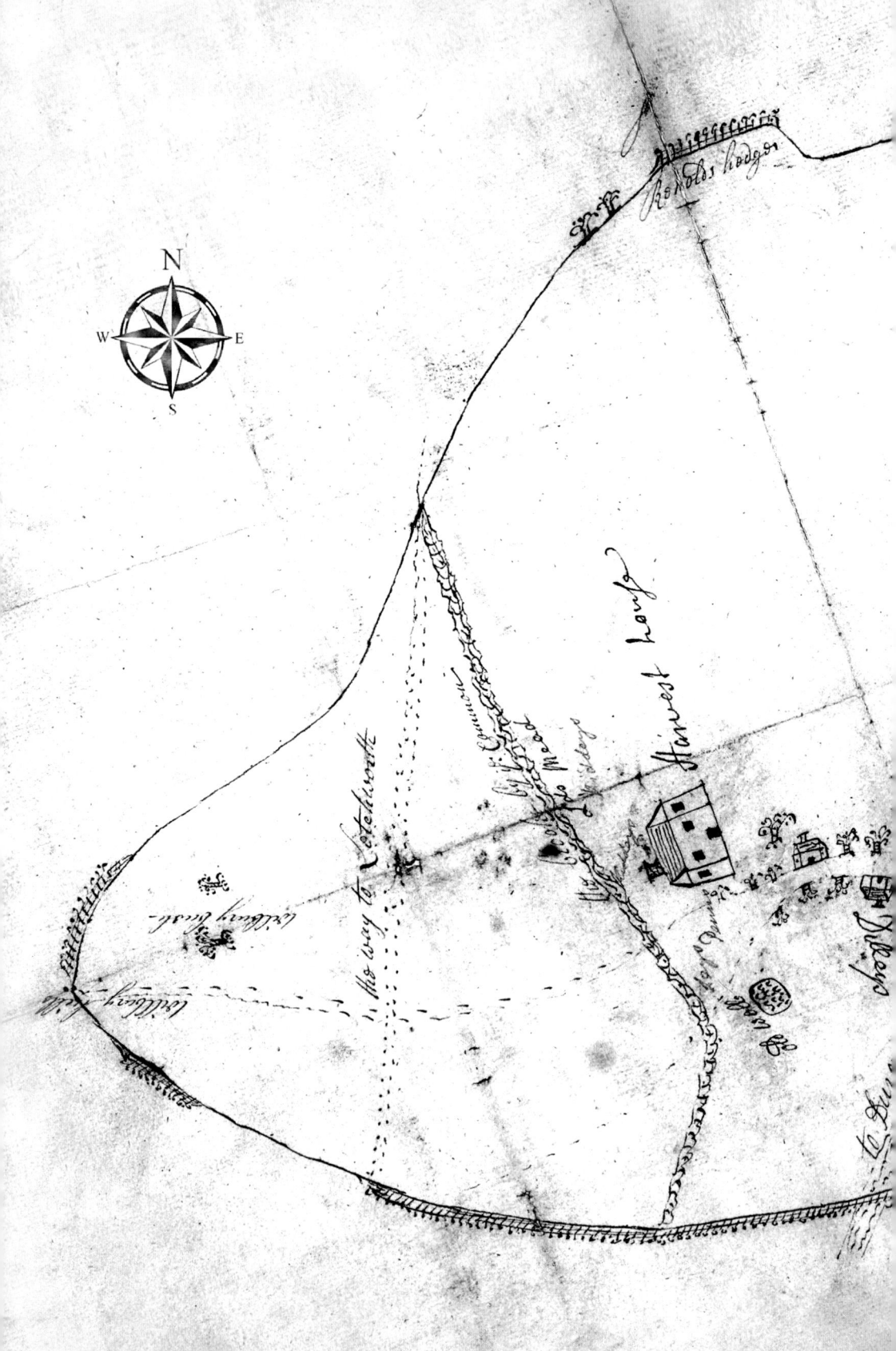